DATE DUE

MAR 1 0 2003		
FEB 2 4 2005		

The Idea of Love

CONCEPTS IN WESTERN THOUGHT SERIES

GENERAL EDITOR: MORTIMER J. ADLER

INSTITUTE FOR PHILOSOPHICAL RESEARCH

The Idea of Love

by
Robert G. Hazo

FREDERICK A. PRAEGER, *Publishers*
New York • Washington • London

FREDERICK A. PRAEGER, PUBLISHERS
111 Fourth Avenue, New York, N.Y. 10003, U.S.A.
77–79 Charlotte Street, London W.1, England

Published in the United States of America in 1967
by Frederick A. Praeger, Inc., Publishers

Library of Congress Catalog Card Number: 67–22290

Printed in the United States of America

This book is dedicated, with love,
to my entire family, especially to my aunt and guardian,
Katherine Helen Abdou, R.I.P.,
and to my brother, Samuel John Hazo

Persons Engaged in the Work of
the Institute for Philosophical Research
1961–1967

RESEARCH STAFF
SENIOR FELLOWS

Mortimer J. Adler

Otto A. Bird

William J. Gorman

Robert G. Hazo

V. J. McGill

A. L. H. Rubin

Charles Van Doren

RESEARCH ASSOCIATES

Betty Beck Bennett

Ann Quinn Burns

Paul Cornelius

Katherine Farnsworth

Ross Firestone

Edgar V. Meyer

Harvey Meyers

Charles T. Sullivan

Gerald Temaner

Jeffrey Weiss

ADMINISTRATIVE AND CLERICAL STAFF

Marlys A. Buswell

Helen M. Kresich

Theresa A. Panek

Denise Ryan

Carter Nelson Sullivan

Frances S. Ward

Celia Wittenber

BOARD OF DIRECTORS
INSTITUTE FOR PHILOSOPHICAL RESEARCH

Mortimer J. Adler

Mortimer Fleishhacker, Jr.,
　Chairman

Robert P. Gwinn

Prentis C. Hale

Daggett Harvey

Louis Kelso

Harold F. Linder

Arthur L. H. Rubin

Hermon D. Smith

Leonard Spacek

Acknowledgments

This work, as the title page indicates, is the product of the Institute for Philosophical Research. The research on which it is based was conducted by the staff, and the formulations advanced, as well as the conclusions arrived at, represent a great deal of consultation and collaboration. However, since the task of presenting these results in book form was assigned to me, I must bear final responsibility for the contents of the work, as well as for its faults.

It is impossible in this place to mention everyone who, directly or indirectly, took some interest in this study, but I want particularly to express my gratitude to all those who participated in the formative and continuing conversations about the work as a whole. I want to thank the Institute's director for the opportunity to write the book. I am especially grateful to one whose interest, enthusiasm, and intellectual generosity—from beginning to end—were of the greatest possible help: Arthur L. H. Rubin.

ROBERT G. HAZO

Chicago, 1967

Foreword

The Idea of Love is one of a series of studies of basic ideas undertaken by the Institute for Philosophical Research. The Institute was established in 1952 with the avowed purpose of taking stock of Western thought on subjects that have been of continuing philosophical interest from the advent of philosophy in ancient Greece to the present day. In pursuing this task, it hoped to clarify the recorded discussion of such basic ideas as freedom, justice, happiness, love, progress, equality, and law. It aims to transform what, in every case, at first appears to be a chaos of differing opinions into an orderly set of clearly defined points of agreement and disagreement that give rise to real issues and make possible the kind of rational debate that constitutes genuine controversy.

What we are given to start with in each case is a diversity of opinions the pattern of which is seldom clear. To put order into that diversity and to render it intelligible require a creative effort to construct the controversies that are implicit in it. Only by an explicit formulation of the pattern of agreements and disagreements, together with the reasons for the latter, can we delineate the issues and indicate how they have been or might be disputed. Too often reasons have not been given for positions that have been persistently advanced. In consequence, important issues have not been disputed in a way that carries the controversy forward and brings it nearer to a resolution.

The Institute has proceeded on the assumption that the issues in the field of any basic philosophical idea concern matters about which objective truth is ascertainable. The future resolution of these issues depends upon more sustained and more rational efforts to deal with them than the history of Western thought has so far exhibited; and the initiation of such efforts depends in turn upon a clear and precise understanding of the issues.

Providing this has been the sole aim of the Institute's work from the beginning.

To accomplish its aim, the Institute has developed certain procedures and a distinctive method of work. Its approach to the study of the recorded discussion of basic philosophical ideas is essentially dialectical. The materials being studied—the major documents in the literature of any philosophical subject—are historical in the sense that each has a date and place in the history of thought about that subject; but the Institute's study of these materials is *nonhistorical* in aim. It deliberately abstracts from their historical context and pattern. It views them as if they were all contemporary—as if the documents represented the voices of participants confronting one another in actual discussion. The Institute's approach is also *nonphilosophical* in the sense that it does not undertake to develop or defend a theory of the idea under consideration. The only truth with which the Institute is directly concerned is truth concerning the body of thought about a particular subject, not truth about the subject thought about. The Institute, therefore, refrains from taking part in the discussion that it attempts to clarify. It makes a sustained effort to be impartial in its treatment of all points of view and to deal with them in an objective and neutral manner. It strives to function as a detached bystander or impartial observer, not as a critic or judge assessing the merits of conflicting claims and awarding a verdict.

It should be clear why an intellectual enterprise thus designed and directed is facilitated by a collaborative effort under institutional auspices; it would be almost impossible for a single person working alone to accomplish effectively. On any basic idea, the volume of literature to be examined and interpreted is tremendous, even if only the most significant and representative documents are selected for study. In the process of interpretation and in the attempt to treat all points of view with impartiality, the desired neutrality is more likely to be achieved by many individuals working together than by the most determined effort of a single individual. Collaboration and consultation tend to offset the idiosyncrasies of individual temperaments and intellectual biases. The advantage of teamwork is not only the pooling of diverse abilities but also the correction of blind spots and the checking of prejudices.

The first product of the collaborative effort of the Institute's staff was a two-volume study, *The Idea of Freedom,* Volume I of which was published in 1958, and Volume II in 1961. That study exemplified the Institute's dialectical method in the treatment of a basic idea; and its results provided a good measure of what can be achieved by the application of that method. The present study, *The Idea of Love,* represents an adaptation of the same method to the treatment of another basic idea. Like *The Idea of Freedom,* it is a product of the collaborative efforts of the Institute's staff. While the task of writing this book was undertaken by one member of the staff, Mr. Robert Hazo, a team formed from other members of the staff helped in the examination and interpretation of the literature under consideration; the formulations proposed by Mr. Hazo were checked and criticized by his colleagues; and the manuscript was revised in accordance with suggestions made by them. The names of the collaborators specifically engaged in the production of the present volume, together with the names of other members of the Institute's staff and the members of its Board of Directors, will be found on page vi.

Of all the ideas so far subjected to dialectical analysis by the Institute, the idea of love proved to be the most difficult—more difficult than the idea of freedom, and much more difficult than the ideas of progress, justice, and happiness. One measure of its difficulty is the wide variety of meanings of the term as it is used in the literature of the subject, ranging from the identification of love with sexual desire, at one extreme, to the conception of love, at the other extreme, as purely disinterested benevolence—a supernatural mode of love made possible by Divine help. Another indication of the difficulty is the thinness of the thread of common meaning that runs through all these uses of the term. Still another is the set of related terms—tendency, judgment, desire, benevolence, friendship, sexuality—that must be dealt with in order to clarify the discussion of human love.

Mr. Hazo has, in my judgment, brought order and clarity into this discussion by discovering the underlying distinctions that animate different approaches to love, and by applying these distinctions with unfailing precision. His opening chapter gives the reader the basic lexicon of analytical terms needed for understanding diverse theories of love. Once the reader understands the distinction between acquisitive and benevolent desire, and the subordinate distinction between self-interested and disinterested benevolence, he is prepared for the series of questions to which different theories of love give opposite or at least divergent answers. These are set forth in the first part of Chapter 2, and are followed by questions that involve the relation of judgment—esteem and valuation—to tendency or desire. Mr. Hazo reserves the five or more special issues about the properties of love for the end of this chapter, and then devotes his third chapter to clarifying the controversy about supernatural human love—a controversy that has occupied a central place in Christian theology, from its beginnings to the present day.

With the exception of this third chapter, in which the three or four major positions in the controversy about supernatural human love are documented by reference to the relevant literature, Mr. Hazo has wisely separated his documentation of the controversy about natural human love,

set forth *in extenso* in Part II of this book, from his dialectical clarification
of that controversy in Chapters 1, 2, and 4 of Part I. This enables the
reader to see the pattern of the discussion in its broad outlines before he
immerses himself in its variegated details. The reader should, in my
judgment, be equally grateful to Mr. Hazo for the perspicuity and precision of the pattern and for the insight and sympathy with which he has
applied it to the interpretation of the capital passages in the extensive
literature on love. The careful reader will, I think, agree with me that
Mr. Hazo's analysis of the idea and his clarification of the discussion make
possible the writing of a better book on the subject than any now available
—a book that will systematically attempt to answer all the questions set
forth at the end of Chapter 4.

There is one point of similarity between the idea of love and the idea of
freedom, to which I would like to call attention. In the dialectical clarification of these two ideas, the distinction and the relation between the self
and the other are pivotal. The dominance of the self is common to all
forms of freedom; subjection to the other characterizes all deprivations of
freedom. In the case of love, the fundamental difference between the
egoistic and the altruistic modes of love—involving the distinctions between
acquisitive and benevolent desire and between self-interested and disinterested benevolence—stems from exclusive concern with the self, from exclusive concern with the other, or from some admixture of both concerns. In
contrast to freedom and love, justice places primary emphasis on the welfare or good of the other; and happiness, on the well-being or perfection of
the self. The discovery of such points of similarity and difference between
ideas, especially ideas that are architectonic in man's thinking about his life
and its values, is one of the valuable by-products of the Institute's effort in
the field of these ideas.

The Institute for Philosophical Research was established on grants from
the Ford Foundation and the Old Dominion Foundation. When the Ford
Foundation grant expired in 1956, the Old Dominion Foundation continued to support the Institute's work and was subsequently joined by other
benefactors. I wish to express the Institute's gratitude to the sources of
financial support that made it possible for it to complete its work on the
idea of freedom after the expiration of the Ford grant, and beyond that to
produce not only the present work on the idea of love but also studies of
the idea of justice, the idea of progress, and the idea of happiness. These
four studies are now being published simultaneously. Other studies, one
on the idea of equality and one on language and thought, are currently
being undertaken and should be ready for publication in the near future.

In the period since 1962, the following foundations have made substantial contributions to the Institute: the Old Dominion Foundation, the

Houghton Foundation, the General Service Foundation, the Liberal Arts Foundation, the Olive Bridge Foundation, and the Paul Jones Foundation. These acknowledgments would not be complete without an expression of special gratitude for the friendship and support of three men in particular —Paul Mellon and Ernest Brooks, Jr., of the Old Dominion Foundation, and Arthur Houghton, Jr., of the Houghton Foundation.

Mortimer J. Adler

Chicago
May, 1966

Contents

xv

The Idea of Love

General Introduction

The Nature and Limits
of the Inquiry

A. The Literature About Love

The initial survey of the literature of almost any basic idea reveals considerable and often bewildering diversity in conception and emphasis. Such diversity is pronounced in the case of love. The variety in style, method, and media is no less remarkable. Poems, plays, songs, psalms, novels, biological and medical treatises, anthropological dissertations, psychological studies, philosophical and theological analyses, erotica, exhortative tracts, cultural surveys, polemical works, practical manuals, and case histories all present themselves as relevant to the understanding of love. Clearly, the application of the dialectical method to the whole literature would not only be inappropriate but impossible. Before a dialectical analysis may be attempted, this diversity must be reduced.

Such a reduction is not a distortion since we do not claim to be attempting a comprehensive treatment of all aspects of the subject. The effect is rather to delineate that part of the literature to which the application of our method can be profitable. Accordingly, we have set for ourselves the task of examining that part of the whole literature that can be called expository and analytical, and that is, directly or indirectly, concerned with analysis as controlled by definition.

3

Limiting ourselves to expository literature removes a great deal, for it
constitutes but a small fraction of all the writing on the subject. Love is the
most frequent and central theme in all imaginative literature. Compared
with the treatment of the subject in stories, drama, verse, and song, the
amount of didactic, discursive analysis in prose is slight.

Even within the realm of nonimaginative literature, there is undeniably
much more concern with the practical aspects of the subject than with the
theoretical. Books of rules, of all kinds, filled with prescriptions and
proscriptions about the proper practices and rituals of love point to the
principal contemporary interest in the subject and are not without numerous parallels in the past. Such literature dwarfs the literature of systematic
analysis that we have found principally in three fields: philosophy, psychology, and theology.[1]

B. The Range of Love

The expository literature, however slight a part of the total literature on
love, reveals, even on cursory perusal, a very great range of reference.
Perhaps every human action has been called—in one way or another—an
act of love. The range of the idea encompasses the nonhuman also. Taking
the works we have examined in this book as a whole, we find that love has
been attributed to everything in the universe either as loving or as being
loved—or both.

Stones are said to love the center of the earth. The upward motion of
fire is called a function of its love. The attraction of iron filings to a magnet
is described as the effect of love. Careful observation has resulted in tracts
written on the love life of amoebae, paramecia, snails, and ants. The mating
of certain spiders is preceded by movements called love dances. Dogs, cats,
horses, camels, and elephants are said to love their masters as well as each
other. Men talk of their love for women, a woman, other men, children,
themselves, humanity, money, art, domesticity, principles, a cause, an
occupation, adventure, security, ideas, a country, life, loving itself, a

[1] Arthur Schopenhauer remarks that "one ought . . . to be surprised that a thing
which plays throughout so important a part in human life has hitherto practically
been disregarded by philosophers altogether, and lies before us as raw material." (*The
Metaphysics of the Love of the Sexes*, p. 338.) Commenting on the lack of modern
interest in the question of what love is, Theodor Reik says, "I assert that the last
serious book which penetrated this secret domain was *De l'amour* by Stendhal. It was
written one hundred and thirty-five years ago—which is a long time when you
consider the psychological import of the subject. Since then nothing of real value,
revealing the origin and nature of love, has been brought home from the numerous
voyages of discovery undertaken." (*A Psychologist Looks at Love*, Ch. I, Sect. 3, p.
11.) In the same vein, José Ortega y Gasset remarks, "For many years much has been
said about love affairs and little about love." (*On Love*, "Features of Love," p. 10.)

beefsteak, or wine. According to one view, the propagation of plants, the procreation of animal species, as well as the perpetual and perfect movement of heavenly bodies are all inspired by love. In learned treatises, angels and devils are often differentiated by the quality of their love. God is said to be Love.[2]

Confronted with this immense range, we decided to focus our analysis on that part of the literature about man. Though we shall be obliged to consider nonhuman love, our principal concern is human love. We deal with subhuman and superhuman love only when a conception of human love cannot be understood fully without so doing. Human beings are said to love, not only themselves and other men, but also subhuman beings and superhuman beings. With regard to the object of love, however, our primary concern is also with man. Though we are obliged, here and there, to consider human love for subhuman and superhuman objects, we do so only insofar as such consideration casts light on human love for human beings.

This concentration on love among human beings is not an arbitrary limitation. As we are concerned with what all the authors say about love, we found it necessary to focus on a love relationship about which they all had something to say. All authors concerned with the question of what love is discuss love among human beings. Some discuss this love relationship exclusively, some primarily, and some parenthetically or incidentally. But no other aspect of the subject commands universal attention.

Limiting the subject in this way does not imply a theory of love, nor does it involve any assumption about the relative importance of interpersonal love. It merely allows us to control better our analysis of love by concentrat-

[2] Modern writers in psychology who have a perspective on this range have noted it. Sigmund Freud observes the "casual and undifferentiated way in which the word 'love' is employed by language." (*Civilization and Its Discontents*, Ch. IV, p. 49.) After remarking on the amplification of the word "love," C. G. Jung comments, "Thus we find ourselves in the unprofitable situation of beginning a discussion about a matter and a concept of absolutely unlimited extent and indefiniteness." (*Contributions to Analytical Psychology*, p. 207.) Reik speaks directly to the point. "Love is one of the most overworked words in our vocabulary. There is hardly a field of human activity in which the word is not worked to death. It is not restricted to expressing an emotion between the sexes, but also expresses the emotion between members of a family. It signifies the feeling for your neighbor, for your friend, and even for your foe, for the whole of mankind, for the home, social or racial group, nation, for all that is beautiful and good, and for God Himself. It is almost incredible that it can be equal to its many tasks. . . . Its diversity of meaning, its adaptability and its capability of quick change are astonishing. It is used to describe the infatuation of a boy and girl, and at the same time the noblest and most spiritualized aims of men. The word is used in psychology and philosophy, in religion, ethics and education, in social fields of all kinds. It is indispensable wherever men live together. But time tells on it and it shows all the signs of the wear and tear to which it has been subjected." (*A Psychologist Looks at Love*, Ch. I, Sect. 3, pp. 9–10.)

ing on conceptions that refer to phenomena familiar to all and which, in addition, most people have in mind when they discuss love.

Excluded from primary consideration are: God's love for His creatures; man's love for God; love for truth, beauty, and justice, *i.e.*, the relation between man as lover and abstract ideas or ideals as objects of love; love for country, *i.e.*, the relation between man as lover and a nonpersonal though personified community of men; love for self that involves no other human being; love for animals; and love for things, be they consumable goods, useful instruments, or works of art. What remains is love among human beings, of the same sex or of the opposite sex, of equal or unequal age, character, etc.

C. The Plan of the Book

Even within the sphere of love among human beings, many subordinate differentiations are made. In fact, the authors seldom deal with interpersonal love generically, preferring, rather, to consider the different types or forms of it that they can observe and describe. The writing is punctuated with phrases such as sexual love, paternal love, filial love, courtly love, passionate love, unrequited love, unconditional love, etc. Contraries, such as spiritual *vs.* carnal love, conjugal *vs.* romantic love, mature *vs.* adolescent love, heterosexual *vs.* homosexual love, and love as therapy *vs.* love as disease, occur frequently in the literature. Occasionally, certain loves are said to exclude things such as pity, malevolence, familiarity, sacrifice, etc.

Many of these qualifications, distinctions, and exclusions occur within theories in which the authors do not bother to offer a statement of a general conception of love. (In fact, few authors define love, and even fewer treat it as a separate subject of inquiry, often discussing it in treatises devoted to other subjects.) Where an author mentions and discusses only types of interpersonal love, we try to discover what these types have in common. We assume that a proponent of a theory of love can be expected to provide identical answers to the questions: What is love among human beings? and What do the types of love among human beings mentioned have in common? If the answer to these two questions is not the same, the author is discussing more than one subject.

In addition to the above-mentioned difficulty, there are other problems. Some authors try to encompass the whole panorama of phenomena that has been called the sphere of love in a comprehensive theory, while others are concerned with but one relationship in which they have a special interest. In addition, some authors begin with God as the focal point for their thinking on love; others begin with basic biological needs; still others take feminine beauty as their point of departure. Some authors affirm that immortality is the aim of love, while others say it is the progress of the human race. Some say that the purpose of love is the enjoyment of physical pleasure, while others say it is the key to spiritual happiness.

To resolve the difficulties of analysis and handle the differences in conception, we attempt, in each case, to isolate the basic notion or notions that are common to all the interpersonal loves of which an author treats. We are, first of all, concerned with discovering which notion or notions he says or implies *must* be present in his conception of any such loves; and second, which notions *may*, in addition, be present to distinguish his conceptions of different types of such love. In other words, we are concerned, primarily, with determining what any given author's *core* conception of love among human beings is, and only secondarily shall we deal with the additional characteristics, traits, or properties he may employ to distinguish the various loves with which he is concerned.

Those notions, one or more of which we find to be necessarily part of any author's conception of human love, we have chosen to call critical. All of them were derived from a careful study of the literature. As we shall see when we get to the actual classification of theories, conceptions of love range from the simple to the complex according as they involve only one critical notion, or two or more. The names we have assigned to these notions are the critical terms of our analytical vocabulary. An explanation of what each critical term signifies is made in the first chapter of Part I.

In Chapter 2 of Part I, we proceed directly to set forth whatever controversies about love among human beings we have been able to find and formulate in the literature on natural love. Before discussing the issues that constitute the controversies, we suggest the most general description of the idea of love compatible with all the conceptions of it we have found. The formulations of the issues are ours in the sense that we have phrased questions to which we maintain that the authors, in the course of expounding their different theories, give conflicting answers. In setting forth these issues about natural love, little documentation of the positions and arguments attributed to the various authors is given. Because of the amount of the material and the consequent difficulty of presenting it in the course of discussing issues, we decided to put it in Part II, where the authors' theories of natural love are set forth in full. Each theory is set forth in one place.

In Chapter 3 of Part I, we pass from considerations of purely natural love among human beings to considerations of human love conceived by certain writers as subject to supernatural conditions. According to revealed religion, there is a love that would not exist were it not for God's help. In Chapter 3, then, we deal with what are, for the most part, theological treatments of love, *i.e.*, theories in which God's love for man is seen as having a transforming effect on man's love for God and for his fellowmen. Human love, thus influenced, we call "supernatural" to indicate that its existence presupposes a power that lies beyond what its theorists conceive as man's natural endowments.

The theological discussions with which Chapter 3 deals would lead us far afield if we were to examine them in all aspects. Accordingly, we attempt to set forth the principal positions in the controversy about the nature of supernatural human love in the Christian tradition. Focusing again on man, we deal with God's love only insofar as it helps us to an understanding of the difference, according to theologians, between the natural and supernatural forms of human love and the difference in conceptions of the latter. Because we set forth only representative and not comprehensive documentation for the principal positions taken in this controversy, it is possible to present that documentation within Chapter 3.

Finally, in Chapter 4, the last chapter of Part I, we set forth certain formal criteria for a theory of love. In so doing we make no claim as to what love is and is not. These criteria are general questions that the writers of coherent theories must face, though they may give very different answers to them.

Part II is concerned wholly with the presentation of the documentation for the theories of natural love. In the first chapter of this part, Chapter 5, we explain how we propose to set forth and classify the various theories and what this classification is intended to show. Chapters 6 through 9 contain our presentation of the authors' theories, analyzed by the critical notions and classified according to the principles explained in Chapter 5. Though comprehensiveness is attainable only in principle, an effort has been made to include every significant variety of theory about love discoverable in the systematic literature on that subject, and to keep repetition to a minimum.

Our purpose throughout this book is to find what it is that unites—and divides—the thinkers of the past and present who have written of human love. These writers, separated by time, nationality, language, tradition, and personality, have dealt with love each in his own way. The variety of views is impressive, but the "anarchy of systems" is also embarrassing. It is our hope that a dialectical analysis of the diverse theories of human love will provide some understanding of what unifying threads relate them to one another, what differences separate them from one another, and what agreements and disagreements exist among them.

I

Human Love:
The Discussion

I

The Critical Notions
and Terms

Love is generally understood to be a tendency of some sort. Most authors think of it as an appetite or impulse toward action, as an inclination toward some form of good to be possessed or accomplished. By referring to it as a feeling, emotion, or desire, they imply that love is not an act of thought or an attitude of mind. Though the kinds of tendency these authors call love are often different, they all agree that love is tendential.

This view is not unanimous. There are a few authors for whom love is essentially a matter of cognition and a few for whom it is partially so. For these writers, a judgment about the worth of an object—admiring, respecting, or valuing it—is a component in love. They deny that love is located in the tendential sphere of human behavior alone, and insist that it belongs, also, in greater or lesser degree, to the sphere of judgment.

The division between the sphere or order of tendency and the sphere or order of judgment is the most basic in the literature about love. It gives us the two most general headings for our analysis. All the critical notions and terms we shall use in dealing with theories of love fall under one or the other of these two headings.

Tendency in general is to be distinguished from particular tendencies or

11

desires. Among the latter, the most significant analytical distinction is that between acquisitive and benevolent desire. Each of these types of desire, in turn, takes a number of subordinate forms, which must be differentiated. In addition, there are two special types of desire—sexual desire and the desire for union—which often are said to be either part of love or the whole of it.

In the sphere of judgment, the basic distinction is that between esteem and valuation. Esteem, in turn, takes different forms, manifesting itself as admiration, on the one hand, or as resepct, on the other.

We shall use the phrase "theory of love" to refer to the whole account that an author gives of the subject. We shall use the phrase "conception of love" to refer to his answer to the question—What is love? It is our contention that every author who attempts to say what human love is employs at least one of the above notions in expounding its nature. We find theories in which love is equated with tendency in general, conceived as nothing but benevolence, or identified as acquisitive desire. We also find theories in which love is conceived as a complex—a mixture of benevolent and acquisitive tendencies, a combination of benevolence and sexual desire or the desire for union, or some form of desire combined with admiration or respect.

When we say that we have found these basic notions in the literature on love, we do not mean that we have found a common notional vocabulary there. On the contrary, each author, as might be expected, has a vocabulary largely his own. Any two who make the same distinction—as between a man's judging that something is *good in itself* and his judging that something is *good for him*—generally do not express that distinction in the same words. This holds true for all the other basic distinctions that we shall employ, such as that between acquisitive and benevolent desire, or between disinterested and self-interested benevolence. It also applies to the naming of such notions as sexual desire or the desire for union.

For this reason, we have found it necessary to designate our own set of terms for the basic notions employed by the authors in their accounts of the nature of love. Thus we employ the term "esteem" to signify a man's judgment that someone is *good in himself*, apart from any desires he may have for that person; and the term "valuation" to signify a man's judgment that someone is *good for him* or is a fitting recipient of a *good from him*. "Esteem" and "valuation" are the pair of terms we have chosen to convey the same distinction between these two modes of judgment, even though the authors do not express it in these words.

All our other critical terms function in the same way, to help clarify a discussion in which a relatively small number of fundamental notions constantly recur, their recurrence often concealed or obscured by the confusing variety of expressions used by different authors. How theories of love differ and what they have in common is far from clear on the surface of the literature. We hope we can make it clearer by our use of a small set of critical terms representing the range of notions used in the whole literature.

Short of inventing an entirely new set of terms, the confusion caused by the variety of language cannot be avoided entirely. Some of the terms we use here are also used by the authors, often in different senses. The term "desire," which we have taken as a simple synonym for tendency, inclination, wish, or want, some authors have used to designate a certain kind of tendency, *i.e.*, one that springs from deficiency. The term "sexual," which we have employed in the narrowest possible sense, sometimes has been used to refer to a whole set of inclinations, many of which are not obviously physical. The reader, therefore, will want to keep in mind the distinction between our use of the words we shall discuss in this chapter and the use of the same words by the authors.

There is another problem that arises in this literature. The vocabulary used by the authors to identify and discuss love is exceedingly rich and complex. It contains some terms that are generally used to refer to some aspect of love and others that are not generally so used. Authors write of tenderness, of passionate longing, of affection, liking, compassion, etc. It is one thing to understand what an author means by these terms and another to see whether or not he includes these terms in his language of love and what they signify in his theory. Since we are here concerned with what others say about love and not with our own theory of the subject, we cannot simply assume that what an author calls sympathy, for instance, is part of what he understands love to be.

Language must be our guide here. Certain words in Western languages are traditionally related to the subject under discussion. Though the consistency of that usage is under examination in this book, we must assume that, when an author uses these common expressions, he is referring to the subject under consideration. Whatever ancillary terms he relates to the basic word for love in his mother tongue can be assumed also to be referring to some aspect of the subject. Ancillary terms not so related by the author himself must be presumed to be excluded from his language of love. To proceed otherwise would be to risk superimposing on an author a theory that extends far beyond what he would be willing to call love. The author himself must indicate how far his theory of the subject extends.

Our concern in this chapter is not with the theories themselves but with the exposition of the meaning of the critical terms employed to examine them. We shall deal first with the terms that fall in the sphere of tendency and then with the terms that fall in the sphere of judgment.

In the sphere of tendency, we shall try to give precision to our use of the following terms: (1) tendency in general; (2) acquisitive desire in two forms: (a) simple acquisitive desire and (b) mixed acquisitive desire; (3) benevolent desire in two forms: (a) self-interested benevolence and (b) disinterested benevolence. In addition, we shall distinguish several subordinate forms of self-interested benevolence. We shall then describe our use of (4) sexual desire and (5) the desire for union, distinguishing the two different forms taken by the latter. In the sphere of judgment, we shall do the same for (1) esteem and (2) valuation, and for the two forms of esteem: (a) admiration and (b) respect. Not counting the subordinate forms of esteem, acquisitive desire, benevolent desire, and the desire for union, this will give us seven critical terms with which to work.

The critical notions signified by these terms are flexible in their applicability to theories of love. An author may conceive love as tendency in general and employ the notions of acquisitive and benevolent desire to distinguish kinds of love. Another author may conceive love as acquisitive desire only, and use the notions of sexual desire and the desire for union to distinguish kinds of love. Still another author may describe the core of love as benevolence and use the notions of sexual desire, the desire for union, esteem, and valuation to distinguish the various kinds of love or to signify their properties.

The reason for this flexibility is that the critical notions are not logically coordinate, nor are most of them mutually exclusive. Thus an author may say that love is tendency in general, and also claim that all tendency is acquisitive—that every man acts ultimately only for his own good. This author is saying that tendency in general and acquisitive desire are identical. He may even add the notion of desire for union, claiming that all tendency is not only acquisitive but that it also always aims at union. A different author may use these notions in another way. He may say that love is tendency in general but claim that all tendency is divided into acquisitive and benevolent desire. He may add that the desire for union takes a benevolent form. Though all authors who advance theories of love share a minimal common understanding of what the critical notions mean, they apply these notions to the phenomena in different ways, use them in their analyses on different levels of generality, and form their conceptions through many different combinations of them.

Apart from any existential application that authors may make of the tendential notions, they are related structurally to each other. Tendency in general logically divides into acquisitive desire and benevolent desire. Sexual desire is a form of acquisitive desire. The desire for union is a form either of acquisitive or benevolent desire.

A. Tendency

All five of the following critical terms stand for notions that refer to inclinations toward movement. It should be noted, however, that many of the authors who conceive love in the sphere of tendency do not mean that love exists only when desire is unfulfilled and promptly ceases to exist after desire has been satisfied. Some do mean just this. But, for others, love is tendential in the sense that there is a prevailing disposition to act in a certain way, even though the desire to act in that way is recurrent rather than continuous. For these authors, in other words, desire may be actual or latent. In some theories, for example, the essence of love is said to be benevolence. Yet the authors of these theories affirm that love is present not only when the lover actually desires to do something for his beloved but also at other times. The benevolent person's love is said to be continuous, though the desires that produce action on his part are not.

1. *Tendency in general*

We usually attribute purposeful tendency to living things. When we speak of human or animal desires, we frequently have in mind inclinations or impulses that are preceded by an awareness of something that calls for an action on our part and are followed by that action. Tendency thus mediates between the awareness of something to be done and the doing of it: It is occasioned by the one and leads to the other. But there is another sense of tendency in which it refers to a need or want that is inherent in the very nature of a living thing, as, for example, a gregarious animal's need for association with its kind.

According to the views of some, such natural needs exist apart from conscious perception of objects or aims. In gregarious animals, the natural tendency to associate is said to preexist the awareness of occasions or opportunities for carrying out the herding impulse. According to this analysis, the fact that plants lack cognitive powers does not preclude their having natural tendencies. A plant's natural need for sunshine is understood as similar to a gregarious animal's natural need for the presence of the herd: In both there is a natural inclination that aims in a certain direction without any conscious awareness of that aim.

While conscious desire can be attributed only to conscious living things whose cognitive powers enable them to apprehend things as desirable, natural tendency, thus understood, can be attributed not only to *all* living things, whether conscious or not, but also to every and any thing that has a natural inclination to move in a certain direction or react in a certain way. What a modern physicist calls the latent, as contrasted with the kinetic, energy of a heavy body, which, being supported, only *tends to fall* but *does not actually do so*, the ancients referred to as a natural tendency on the part of such bodies. It was in this sense that they attributed natural "appetite" to inorganic bodies. As they saw it, the natural tendency of a heavy body to fall was like the natural tendency toward self-preservation in all living organisms.

Tendency thus understood as covering every natural inclination as well as all conscious desires and impulses is tendency in its broadest sense—a sense in which the term has cosmic significance and applies to the inclinations of the sun and stars and galaxies as well as to the movements of the smallest particles, the chemical elements, all plants, animals, and men. Writers who think of love as a cosmic principle conceive of it as tendency in this broadest or most general sense.

Within the restricted sphere of human relationships, tendency in its most general sense covers every human inclination that moves or impels one human being to act in a certain way toward others. Such tendencies may take the form of conscious desires, emotional impulses, or deliberate choices; they may also be nothing more than instinctive needs or unconscious yearnings. Tendency in general thus includes every and any inclination, predisposition, or desire that one human being may have toward others—anything from the frenzied madness of a transient infatuation to the permanence of an affection that defies mortality. Taken in this generic way, the term "tendency" covers wants, needs, wishes, impulses, or aversions that may be carnal or spiritual, innate or acquired, instinctive or deliberate, conscious or unconscious, perverse or sublime, selfish or altruistic, emotional or intellectual.

Tendency in general, as distinct from specific types of desire, is one of our critical terms, because we have to deal with theories of love in which every form or manifestation of human inclination is regarded as a form or manifestation of love. The authors of such theories usually go on to treat the different kinds of human love. When they do so, other of the critical notions then come into play; for no treatment of the kinds of love is possible without going beyond tendency in general to modes of tendency such as acquisitive desire, benevolent desire, sexual desire, or the desire for union. The authors need not employ all of them, since an affirmation that love is tendency in general is consistent with a denial that there can be a tendency such as, say, benevolent desire.

Though most of the authors say that love is tendential, few of them equate love with tendency in general. For the most part, we find theories in which love is understood as this or that specific desire, or some combination of desires or inclinations. When an author approaches love in this way and denies, directly or by implication, that certain other desires have anything to do with it, he is clearly rejecting the notion of tendency in general as relevant to the question of what love is. Thus, an author who claims that love and sexual desire are wholly separate could not also claim that the broadest identification of love is tendency in general, since sexual desire is a tendency.

All desires on the part of human beings, be they deliberate, unconscious, or instinctive, can be understood in terms of the end or goal to which they point, the directions in which they tend, or the particular goods toward which they aim. They also can be more generally distinguished by the notions of giving and getting—two of the most familiar ways of describing human motives. Broadly speaking, our definitions of acquisitive and benevolent desire are based upon these notions and the distinction between self and other that they imply. The two types of desire are distinguished, not by what is sought but by for whom it is sought. The controlling aim of acquisitive desire is to get what the self wants or needs. The controlling aim of benevolent desire is to give to another what he may want or need.

Though the most general distinction between the two types of desire is made in terms of getting and giving, simply identifying acquisitive desire with getting and benevolent desire with giving is not a sufficient explanation of either. Additional qualifications can be, and often are, placed on both inclinations. Sometimes both getting and giving are said to be present in a complex or bivalent tendency. Though acquisitive and benevolent desires are mutually exclusive in the sense that it is impossible for both getting and giving to be dominant motives in a given desire, many authors combine the two motives by making one a means to the other, or by making one concomitant with and subsidiary to the other.[1] Variations on how one gets or gives are also brought into play. These complications require a more elaborate discussion of the two desires, or rather of the forms that each takes. The different specifications placed on acquisitive and benevolent desire are reflected in these subordinate forms. The broad distinction between the two desires—whether getting or giving is the primary aim—nevertheless remains a valid one throughout this discussion and the simplest way of differentiating the two inclinations.

---

[1] Several authors suggest that it is possible to desire in such a way that the lover is simultaneously and equally concerned with his own good and that of his beloved. In such cases, the desire can be said to be acquisitive or benevolent, not by the proportion of the acquisitive motive to the benevolent one but by how these motives are related. In other words, as long as giving is not ordered to getting as a means to an end, the desire is a benevolent one, even though the motive to get may be as strong as the one to give. The minimal requirement for benevolence is that one gives to another for his own sake.

One further point concerning acquisitive and benevolent desire must be made. It is the distinction between an instinctive inclination, or innate tendency, as contrasted with a deliberate desire. No author denies that acquisitive desire can take either form. It can express itself as physical impulse and unconscious urge, or as conscious desire. Benevolent desire is, for the most part, conceived of as an impulse of which man is not only always aware, but as something that he intends consciously. The subordinate forms—particularly mixed acquisitive desire, self-interested benevolence, and disinterested benevolence—are forms of both acquisitive and benevolent desire expressed on the level of consciousness or intention. Such subordinate forms are generally said to presuppose, at least, some awareness of the aims of one's own desires.

The conscious aim of a desire, of course, may not be its basic or real aim. An author may claim that real benevolence is humanly impossible, that all such desires are illusions depending on ignorance or self-deception and that they derive from acquisitive roots. Whenever such a claim is made, it will be duly noted in the presentation of a theory. Whether real or apparent, however, benevolent desire is still present as a psychic phenomenon whenever someone seeks to enhance the welfare of another, at least primarily for the other person's own sake.

2. *Acquisitive desire*

Whatever form it may take, acquisitive desire always has a good for the self as its characteristic aim; ultimately, the one desiring wants to get. Such an inclination arises from a deficiency in the self and points toward the fulfillment of that deficiency through the acquisition, consumption, or achievement of whatever is sought. When the aim is fulfilled and the good is realized, the desire is satisfied. For the purpose of defining acquisitive desire it makes no difference whether satisfaction or pleasure is the aim of the desire, as the hedonists maintain, or whether such satisfaction is merely a concomitant of the particular good sought, as others claim. In either case, the distinguishing characteristic of acquisitive desire is that it is an inclination aiming primarily and finally at a change in the self; whatever it points to is only a means of accomplishing that change, as when we seek food in order to eat it.

As human beings need or want each other in a variety of ways and for a variety of reasons, acquisitive desire is rarely, if ever, absent from a human relationship. Acquisitiveness may be merely one of a number of inclinations which enter into the relationship, or it may be the dominant or sole motive. As long as such a desire lasts, and in the respects in which it occurs, it implies an indifference to someone else's welfare, except as a means to the enhancement of one's own. The presence of acquisitiveness in a human relationship does not necessarily imply a continual or all-encompassing indifference to another's welfare; those whom we use one minute we may die for the next. On the other hand, when, despite opportunities to be benevolent, the only inclination toward another remains acquisitive, a general indifference to the other person's welfare for his own sake is clearly evinced. Associations based on expediency or convenience are of this nature, lasting only as long as those involved prove useful to each other.

To intend to use food is necessarily to intend to destroy it, but to intend to use a person is not invariably understood as involving an intention to harm him. The fulfillment of an acquisitive desire, it is contended, need not involve injury to the person to whom it is directed. This is presumed to be clear in commonplace instances, as when a child asks to have an inaccessible toy, or when an old man asks to be helped in climbing a flight of stairs. Governor and governed, employer and employee, teacher and student, salesperson and customer, even man and wife may have no other motive but to use each other to mutual advantage. Even one who uses his acquaintances for social or business advancement may intend them no injury in manipulating them to his own end. It is even possible that in being used by another a person is given a sense of purpose that he lacked and wanted. Although such a result cannot be a part of the controlling aim of acquisitive desire—and still have it remain acquisitive—the fulfillment of such a desire can perhaps have good effects on another.

Acquisitive desire, on the other hand, does not preclude the intention of harming whoever is the means of its fulfillment. The person who is the object of a desire for revenge obviously is intended injury. A man who uses someone else to achieve a position to which the other person also aspires is willing to block the other person for the sake of his own advancement. A thief seeks to deprive others of what is rightfully theirs. Competing generals, candidates for office, and athletes triumph only at the expense of frustrating the desires of their opponents. Indeed, any intention to gain that necessitates someone else's loss goes beyond the innocuous use of another.

There are two basic forms of acquisitive desire: simple and mixed. In its simple form, the only aim of the desire is the welfare of the self. But, since getting what one wants often necessitates an expedient interest in the good of another, acquisitive desire also may take an indirect and mixed form. The desirer does seek the good of another, but only insofar as that good is a means to his own good. Both forms of the desire are acquisitive, because in each the dominant or primary aim is to get rather than to give.

a. *Simple acquisitive desire*

Getting without giving—simple acquisitive desire—is most frequently directed toward things and not people. A man's interest in food, drink, or money is normally a direct interest in them as means to an end. They are, for the most part, openly valued for the uses to which they can be put, and treated accordingly. They gratify us, not we, them.

Simple acquisitive desire is by no means entirely limited to things. The direct use of one human being by another occurs as a matter of course in all human relationships. There are times when we want and get something from associates without having to give anything in order to get it. Their acquiescence to our desire sometimes does not even imply a tacit understanding that we would or will reciprocate.

Much rarer are relationships—unless they are transitory—in which all the desires of one person toward others take the simple form of acquisitive desire. People, unlike things, have desires and often expect compensation or reciprocity as a condition of fulfilling the needs or wants of another. When it characterizes a whole relationship, therefore, acquisitive desire more often takes its mixed rather than its simple form.

Although infrequent, relationships wholly dominated by simple acquisitive desire may occur. Some historians represent absolute monarchs as having been able to require others to indulge their whims without having been required to give them anything to dispose them to do so. A student may be interested in a teacher only as a vehicle for information or knowledge that he wants, and not be required to give the teacher anything in order to get it. Extortionists and blackmailers, by definition, want to get what they can, and have been known to succeed without giving anything but empty promises. Rape is undoubtedly the most dramatic, the most extreme, and the clearest expression of a simple acquisitive desire. Even the relatively mild cases in which people maneuver, pressure, or shame others into doing things they would not otherwise choose to do are expressions of this desire, since nothing is given in order to get.

b. *Mixed acquisitive desire*

As with all acquisitive desire, this form has getting as its final aim. It is called mixed because it involves giving in order to realize that aim. The mixed form of acquisitive desire is distinguished from benevolent desire in that the giving involved is never a final, primary, or controlling aim. Its acquisitive character necessitates wanting the good for another always and only as a means to one's own good.

Bribery would seem to be a clear instance of the mixed form of acquisitive desire. A service is requested of another and money or some benefit is offered as an enticement; giving to the other person is intended only as a tactical means for getting. Similarly, if a man bestows favors or benefits on a woman only because he hopes they will enable or dispose her to satisfy his wants, his desire is acquisitive. In fact, the instances when something is given solely to incline the recipient to a desired action or acquiescence seem to be legion in everyday life. The salesperson's smile is a commonplace instance. Presumably, such instances range from daily business transactions in which payments are made for articles and services to the negotiations that go on at high levels of international diplomacy.

Giving as a means need not precede getting, in the order of time. In the case of bribery, one normally has to give before one gets. Often, however, our desires are fulfilled by others on the tacit understanding or explicit promise that we will do something for them right after we get what we want or on another occasion. When the giving occurs is of little moment; the important point is that it is done for the sake of getting.

The giving that is part of the mixed form of acquisitive desire is not always directed to inspiring action on the part of others. A man driven to expiate guilt feelings may give a great deal to others only because his doing so provides him with some solace, some amelioration of his pangs of conscience. Although he gives only in order to get, the realization of his aim does not require any action on the part of those who receive his benefits.

The recipient of tactical beneficence may be fully aware of the real motivation behind the giving. In the past, slaveowners often fed, clothed, and housed their charges well because the slaves would not otherwise be able to perform useful services, or at least not so well. In such cases, neither the slaves nor their owners were likely to be under any illusion as to why this was being done. Many voluntary arrangements, commercial or otherwise, are made strictly on the basis of giving in order to get, without any pretense of other motives by the parties involved.

The literature suggests that, in other circumstances, the effectiveness of giving in order to get may require the pretense of benevolence. A man who flatters his superior for the sake of advancement probably would not succeed if his superior were aware of his real and hidden motive. Similarly, professions of benevolent intentions coupled with some actual beneficence often are necessary for realizing ambitions that are, in themselves, in no way benevolent. In other words, *apparent* benevolence is often the condition of possibility for the fulfillment of acquisitive desire.

Beneficence, therefore, can spring from more than one motive. Though they are different inclinations, mixed acquisitive desire and benevolent desire can have identical effects. If a philanthropist gives a large amount of money to an institution of higher learning, the desire behind his action might be acquisitive or benevolent. If his real aim is to provide students with more scholarships, faculty with increased salaries, or both with expanded facilities to thereby enhance their welfare, his desire is benevolent. If he makes his donation only because he wishes to increase his stature in the community or only because he would suffer a mild social ostracism if he did not, his desire is acquisitive, since he is giving only in order to get.

3. *Benevolent desire*

If aiding, protecting, or improving other persons can be the controlling aim of a human desire, that desire has the character of what we call benevolence. Some authors deny that such an inclination is humanly possible. All actions on behalf of others, all caring about others are, they say, ultimately for the sake of, and directly or indirectly referable to, the interest of the self. Mixed acquisitive desire is, for them, the ruling notion. Benevolent desire is the notion appropriate to the thought of authors who claim that there is a kind of desire that can be described as an inclination to give rather than to get. Seeking the good of another for his own sake is its hallmark in all of its forms.

Maternal affection is often held up as the prototype of benevolence; the mother's inclination is described as a willingness to do anything, even sacrifice her life, for the sake of the offspring. Those who are habitually considerate in their everyday encounters with others have benevolence or kindliness ascribed to them. Benevolent motives are also attributed to those, sometimes called humanitarians, whose lives appear to be dedicated to aiding their fellowmen. A willingness to contribute to the welfare of humanity is the final standard by which nations as well as individuals have been judged. There is no lack of those who claim to be guided by considerations of another's good in their dealings with that person. On a more general level, national and international organizations exist by the score whose announced purposes are to minimize or eliminate a variety of human miseries. Political programs are often proclaimed to be in the interest of all mankind.

For the most part, the recipients of human beneficence are other human beings.[2] Good for the recipient may be the only aim of benevolent desire,

[2] Benevolent desire is directed occasionally to things or animals. An old man who spent a happy childhood in a certain house might well wish that dwelling cared for and preserved, even though he has long since ceased to live in it or even to see it. Animals may be kept alive and cared for long past the point where they are useful because of their owners' benevolence. The instances when dogs or cats have been the recipients of legacies to insure that they will not be abused may have been inspired by a comparable motive.

or his good may be sought in conjunction with a good for the self—for the one who desires benevolently. When only the good of another is sought, the desire takes the form of disinterested benevolence. When, in addition to the good of another, a secondary and concomitant good for the self is sought, the desire takes the form of self-interested benevolence. The good of another, therefore, may not be the exclusive aim of benevolent desire, but it must at least be its controlling aim.

a. *Self-interested benevolence*

All benevolent desires that do not aim *exclusively* at the good of another are self-interested. Such desires have a complex motive, pointing simultaneously at a good for another as well as a concurrent or reflexive good for the self. If a desire is to be deemed benevolent, its principal aim must be giving—the inclination to act for the sake of someone else's good. In the view of a number of authors, the presence and primacy of an inclination to give does not preclude the anticipation of getting. As long as the inclination to acquire is genuinely subsidiary to the inclination to give, the desire is not an acquisitive but rather a benevolent one.

Acquisitive and benevolent desire cannot be attributed to the same person in the same respect at the same time; as primary or controlling aims of a desire, getting and giving are mutually exclusive. We have already seen that getting and giving are both present in mixed acquisitive desire, with the latter subordinated to the former. What distinguishes that desire from self-interested benevolence is the different relationship of getting to giving. With mixed acquisitive desire, giving is only a means. Seeking the good of another is dispensable if what is sought for the self can be otherwise obtained. In some forms of self-interested benevolence, by contrast, the good sought for the self could not be realized if the primary aim of the desire were not another's good; the good sought for the self is inseparable from the good sought for the other.

Self-interested benevolence (itself a subordinate form of benevolent desire) seems to have five subordinate expressions. They may be designated by the terms "satisfaction," "moral improvement," "mutuality," "recognition," and "sharing." In each, the nature of the good intended for the self or the manner of its achievement differ. The first two of its expressions each involve two distinguishable goods; one for the other to whom the desire is directed, and a different though dependent good for the self. The next two also involve separate goods for self and other; but in these, what the self seeks it can get without being benevolent. The last expression of self-interested benevolence aims at only one good, intended for the other but shared by the self.

Satisfaction as an accompanying aim. The authors who claim that benevolence is humanly possible distinguish between the satisfaction that accompanies the fulfillment of a desire and the particular good at which the desire aims. As they analyze acquisitive desire, though the particular good sought and the satisfaction that accompanies its possession are both enjoyed by the self, they are distinct. In their view, benevolent desire points toward a good for someone else, while the satisfaction that accompanies the accomplishment of that good still remains in the self. The gratification of giving, though in one sense inseparable from the fulfillment of a benevolent desire, is existentially separate from what the desire aims at; the good sought is sought for another, while the satisfaction of accomplishing it remains in the self. It is, therefore, possible to anticipate the satisfaction of giving as a separate good for the self. When it is so anticipated, it is part of the conscious aim of a benevolent desire, making that desire not simply benevolent. There are authors who contend that an awareness that being benevolent will result in personal satisfaction to the benevolent person cannot be construed reasonably as casting doubt on the benevolent character of the desire.

Satisfaction, thus understood, takes its character, tone, and quality from the desire to which it attaches. The characteristic aim of benevolent desire, in all of its forms, is to give to another. The satisfaction of giving as a separate good for the self can be realized only when it attaches to a desire that points away from the self. Were one to anticipate it as a primary or final aim, the giving would become a means to it. The desire would cease to be benevolent; and the satisfaction would no longer be the satisfaction of giving, since it would no longer attach to a benevolent desire.

Thus, in the previously mentioned example (in the discussion of mixed acquisitive desire) of a man who gives to others in order to expiate a feeling of guilt, the satisfaction he experiences attaches to the particular good he seeks for himself—the amelioration of his pangs of conscience. Because his desire is to get, the satisfaction that attaches to it is not the satisfaction of giving. Were his desire to point toward another's good, not as a means but as an end, *i.e.*, were it to be a benevolent desire, it would be possible for him to anticipate the satisfaction of giving as a separate good for himself.

Moral improvement as an accompanying aim. Another good that authors say can be anticipated for the self while seeking the welfare of another is moral improvement for the benevolent person. Benevolent desire is often thought to be a humane impulse, a virtuous activity, not only an indication of a good moral character but also the way to a better one. Consideration for others sometimes even is said to be the key to a happy life.

A certain kind of ennoblement or moral improvement of self can be the primary aim of a desire, if such improvement can be realized apart from benevolence. Such a desire is acquisitive. But if a specific moral quality can be achieved only by being benevolent, then this quality, like the satisfaction of giving, can never be the primary goal of a desire. Such a moral quality is a good for the self. If it is viewed as the principal aim of a desire, the desire becomes, accordingly, an acquisitive one. But then the moral quality is precluded, since the very improvement in question derives from being benevolent, *i.e.*, in seeking primarily the good of another and not one's own good. A person who seeks his own moral improvement through benevolence must intend such improvement as a concurrent and subsidiary aim. The anticipation of derivative moral improvement is similar to the anticipation of satisfaction derived from benevolence, in that the realization of a separate good for the self depends on one's seeking the good of another. Both goods can be realized personally only by giving to another primarily for the sake of the other person.

However difficult, or, in ordinary procedure, impossible it may be to judge a given case, it is clear enough that, for example, a mother who seeks the welfare of her children in order to have the sense of doing her duty or in order to make herself happy is exhibiting an acquisitive desire. If, on the other hand, she seeks the welfare of her children primarily for their own sake and is, also and incidentally, aware that she will thus realize certain moral benefits, her animating impulse is a benevolent one, albeit self-interested.

This form of benevolence, attended by the anticipation of moral improvement, as well as the previous one, is sharply distinguished from mixed acquisitive desire by the authors who discuss them. Getting and giving are both present in all these desires. But whether getting a good for the self or giving a good to another is the controlling aim of a desire is the crucial sign by which it is identified as acquisitive or benevolent.

Mutuality as an accompanying aim. In this form of self-interested benevolence, the good anticipated for the self is of a different character than in the preceding two forms. What the self seeks is the return of the benevolence it extends; the giver wants reciprocity of some kind. He cannot give solely for the sake of this return and still be motivated benevolently; but when the hope for mutuality is not the basic but only a subordinated, accompanying reason for giving, the desire is self-interestedly benevolent.

Mutuality plainly is distinguishable from the accompanying satisfaction and accompanying moral improvement of benevolence. In this case, the personal good sought, *i.e.*, becoming the object of benevolence, can be realized without the seeker's being benevolently inclined toward the one in whom he wishes to arouse benevolence toward himself. The appearance of benevolence may be sufficient to arouse a benevolent desire in another. Authentic consideration may be returned for only apparent consideration. What arouses the desire to reciprocate in the other is action, and the other may be deceived about the motive of the action.

Recognition as an accompanying aim. The desire to help another is associated by some authors with the expectation that the one helped, or others, will be aware of who is the giver of that help. To want to see another helped and not care who is the giver of that help is disinterested benevolence; to want to see another helped and to want to be and be recognized as the giver of that help is a fourth form of self-interested benevolence. If the expectation of gratitude is the basic reason for extending the help, the giver is not benevolently motivated; if it is a subordinated, merely concomitant factor, then it does not change the assertion that he is benevolently motivated.

The personal good concomitantly anticipated, *i.e.*, acknowledgment of having done others good, can (as in the case of mutuality) be realized without actual benevolence. Recognition may be accorded someone who gives for other than benevolent motives. What is recognized is only the act of giving, and a benevolent motive is ascribed to that action. The recipient, however, may be deceived about the real motive behind the giving.

Sharing as an accompanying aim. Each of the preceding four forms of self-interested benevolence involves two goods: one for the recipient and a different and subsidiary one for the giver. But in sharing there is only one good; and because the desire is benevolent, it is a good sought for someone else. The desire is self-interested, not because the giver anticipates enjoying the separate goods of satisfaction, moral improvement, reciprocity, or recognition but because the benevolent person anticipates sharing what he seeks for someone else.

This sharing is either direct or vicarious. If it is direct, the giver anticipates an actual enjoyment of some part of the good he bestows or some result of it. A man who buys a dwelling to please his wife also knows he will live in it and enjoy it. If the sharing is vicarious, it is made possible by the sharer's "identifying" with the beneficiary. Such sharing reflects a condition in which one human being has achieved some sense of union with another. Because this union is never complete, because self and other remain distinguishable and existentially separate, the desire to aid the other is not acquisitive. Its principal aim is still another's good and not one's own. Nevertheless, because one person identifies with another and anticipates sharing vicariously what he gives and the other gets, the desire is not without self-interest.

A father may see in his son, or a teacher in his student, an image of himself. In seeking to do good for the one with whom he so identifies, he may anticipate, because of this sympathetic union, a vicarious enjoyment of the benefit he himself wishes to bestow. Benevolent desires that are accompanied by such a projection of the self are by no means necessarily limited to intimate relationships. A person may sense a strong similarity between himself and a perfect stranger. Another person may feel empathy for all the people he meets simply because they share with him the identity of being human. However large or small the unifying bond between two people may be, some obliteration of the sharp distinction between self and other must be felt by any person whose benevolence is self-interested in this way.

As this expression of self-interested benevolence depends upon an existing union between self and other, it is distinct from the desire for union. The desire for union signifies the tendency toward the very oneness that is here presupposed.[3] Were the person who exhibits this expression of self-interested benevolence not already united with the person for whom he seeks a good, he could not sympathetically share that benefit.

b. *Disinterested benevolence*

Even more than self-interested benevolence, disinterested benevolence must be understood on the level of deliberate intention, in terms of whatever awareness there is of one's own motive. On this level, disinterested benevolence points exclusively at the good of another, with no benefit for the self, even concomitant to the motivating intention.

The fact that a person seeks nothing for himself does not mean that he cannot realize a good as a *result* of this form of benevolent desire. One who has a disinterested benevolent desire may in fact experience the gratification of giving, be morally improved by such a desire, enjoy reciprocity, be accorded recognition, or even share in the good that he seeks exclusively for someone else. His desire is disinterested because no concurrent or shared goods for himself are any part of what he is consciously seeking. His single goal is the welfare of another.

In the literature on love the most frequently mentioned instances of disinterested benevolence are those that are not premeditated. An impulse to help someone trapped in a burning building or struck by an automobile is frequently said to involve no thought of self. The immediate concern is only to help the person afflicted.

What we are calling disinterested benevolence should not be confused with well-wishing that does not point to action. The word "disinterested" is meant in another sense here. All the notions in the order of tendency,

---

[3] See pp. 30 ff., *infra*.

including disinterested benevolence, signify intentions to act. Simply being well-disposed toward neighbors, countrymen, or even the whole human race without wanting to do anything for them is not what is meant by this notion. That disposition is disinterested in another sense. In the sense in which we use the term, "disinterested" means only that a person seeks nothing for himself.[4]

Acquisitive and benevolent desire are somewhat more complicated than the other notions in our analytical apparatus. As they are among the notions most frequently employed by authors in setting forth their theories of love, it may be useful to summarize the cardinal points made about them and their subordinate forms in the following outline:

Acquisitive desire—final aim is always to get
   Simple acquisitive desire—exclusive aim is to get
   Mixed acquisitive desire—final aim is to get through giving to
                                  another

Benevolent desire—primary or exclusive aim is to give
   Self-interested benevolence—primary aim is to give; concurrent and
                               secondary aim is to get

      Satisfaction as an accompanying aim.
      Moral improvement as an accompanying aim.
      Mutuality as an accompanying aim.
      Recognition as an accompanying aim.
      Sharing as an accompanying aim.

   Disinterested benevolence—exclusive aim is to give

Two terms remain in the sphere of tendency—sexual desire and the desire for union.

4. Sexual desire

Few authors have had a more decisive impact on the thinking about love and on the language of love than has Sigmund Freud. A good deal of the significance attached to the word "sex" (beyond the simple meaning of gender) can be traced to the popularization of his work. There is no doubt that the understanding and misunderstanding of Freudian writings have resulted in the term "sexual" meaning many different things. Freud

---

[4] Of course, all desires do not result in action. Conflict of desires, circumstantial obstructions, or lack of opportunity are only a few of the many factors that can affect their execution.

himself discusses the ambiguity of the word and comments on the difficulty of being precise about it:

> Seriously, it is not so easy to define what the term sexual includes. Everything connected with the difference between the two sexes is perhaps the only way of hitting the mark; but you will find that too general and indefinite. If you take the sexual act itself as the central point, you will perhaps declare sexual to mean everything which is concerned with obtaining pleasurable gratification from the body (and particularly the sexual organs) of the opposite sex; in the narrowest sense, everything which is directed to the union of the genital organs and the performance of the sexual act. In doing so, however, you come very near to reckoning the sexual and the improper as identical, and childbirth would really have nothing to do with sex. If then you make the function of reproduction the kernel of sexuality you run the risk of excluding from it a whole host of things like masturbation, or even kissing, which are not directed towards reproduction, but which are nevertheless undoubtedly sexual. However, we have already found that attempts at definition always lead to difficulties; let us give up trying to do any better in this particular case.[5]

For the purposes of dialectical inquiry we need not define the term "sexual"; we need only report the common understanding of sexual desire to be found in Freud's theory of love and in other theories. Some of these authors, like Freud, take a broader and more complicated view of this impulse than others. In order to include all of them, our formulation of the notion of sexual desire must reflect only a minimal understanding of this desire that is present in all the differing notions of it. We have found that the notion of sexual desire has the widest possible application in the literature on love when it is taken as the yearning for genital, or other directly related physical pleasures.[6]

Such a craving, insofar as it is directed to physical pleasure, must, of course, be in some degree biological. In certain views, it is thought to be entirely so. It also has been looked upon as the overt manifestation of a spiritual bond between two human beings. It even has been construed as an impulse to communicate. When sexual desire is directed to reproduc-

---

[5] *A General Introduction to Psychoanalysis,* Twentieth Lecture, pp. 312–313.

[6] This notion can be stretched to include related carnal pleasures, such as those that accompany erotic kissing or caressing, but it focuses on genital pleasure. Physical contacts of this kind can be included in the penumbra of sexual desire, if they produce genital pleasure, are pursued as preface to it, or are understood as closely connected with it by those who engage in them. Desires that aim at physical pleasure that is neither genital nor directly related to it are excluded from the notion of sexual desire for the purposes of this analysis. Thus, even though they are often understood as substitutes for the act of intercourse, impulses toward certain kinds of masochism or sadism, or even the "chaste kiss" mentioned in the literature on courtly love, are not taken here as instances of sexual desire.

tion, it has been thought of as aiming finally at race survival or personal immortality. Whatever ultimate significance is attributed to this impulse and whatever other inclinations are understood to be associated or combined with it, we call simple sexual desire any yearning the fulfillment of which involves genital pleasure achieved through contact between members of the opposite or the same sex.

In much of modern psychological literature, appetitive drives are distinguished according as they are unconscious or conscious. Conscious desires are thought to be functions of unconscious urges or needs. To say that such unconscious impulses are instances of sexual desire as we describe it is not to say that their conscious derivatives are necessarily instances of that desire. In the narrow sense in which we use the notion of sexual desire, it may not apply to sublimated or psychologically transformed conscious appetites, even though they may be understood as sexual in unconscious origin. Such conscious appetites may be so modified and transformed that they cease to qualify as instances of sexual desire as we describe that notion. Though business ambition, serious scholarship, artistic creativity, and even intense religious devotion often are held to be derived from unconscious sexual needs, they are not *in themselves* instances of sexual desire as we describe it, since they do not aim at genital pleasure.

The transformation or sublimation of sexual desire into a desire with another manifest aim must be distinguished from the deliberate use of distractions to frustrate the sexual impulse. Such frustration may not change the character of the desire at all but merely diminish its intensity. In the view of many psychologists—not to say poets—the frustration of the desire increases its intensity. The troubadors described in the literature of courtly love seemed to prefer the intense, sweet agony of self-imposed denial to the sexual fulfillment they believed would destroy their love. Whether the desire is diminished or increased by resistance to it, it is still present if such resistance does not transform but only modifies it.

5. *Desire for union*

What we shall call "desire for union" is an inclination that impels one human being to want to be together with another—to become, be, or remain one with the other in some way. In the literature about love, we find two forms of this desire corresponding to the two types of union sought: (a) the desire for the union of complementarity, and (b) the desire for the union of similarity. In the case of the former, the union sought is one in which self and other are, and remain, different. In the case of the latter, the union sought is one in which self and other are, to some degree, alike. The desire for either kind of union may be acquisitive or benevolent.[7]

a. *Desire for the union of complementarity*

Whenever those who are dissimilar or opposite come together to make a whole, their union is a complementary one. If the desire is acquisitive, the person wants to complete or fulfill himself by joining with another person who is what he is not or has what he does not have. If the desire is benevolent, the person wants to complete or fulfill another by joining with someone who is not what he is or does not have what he has. Though the desire need be neither mutual nor reciprocated in kind, in the clearest instances in which it is mentioned, the inclination is mutual and acquisitive. Each party lacks what the other possesses or offers, and does not feel complete alone. Conjoined, they constitute a balanced whole, complementing each other's characters, needs, or wants.

This notion is frequently applicable to the relationship between mother and child, sometimes to that between a leader and his people, and even, in a more extended sense, to the relationship of cooperating members of a team who perform different but complementary functions. The notion of the desire for the union of complementarity is not present in all views of the conjugal relationship, but it pervades many of them. It is particularly prominent in certain theories of love whose authors understand sexual intercourse between the genders as itself an obvious instance of the union of complementarity or as a symbol of such union.[8] These authors lay stress on the biological formulation of each sex as representing the differing but complementary masculine and feminine principles. The spiritual dimension of the union of complementarity between a man and a woman is a recurring theme in much of classical, medieval, and some modern literature. Complementary masculine and feminine viewpoints, emotional habits, duties, and virtues often are mentioned in treatises on marriage.

Perhaps the most celebrated and dramatic passage about the desire for the union of complementarity is the speech of the poet Aristophanes in

[7] In the literature, the term "union" is sometimes used to describe a relationship in which one person completely dominates or engulfs another. The desire for this kind of relationship has very little in common with the desires for the union of complementarity and for the union of similarity. Such desires may be acquisitive or benevolent. The desire to exploit another is, by contrast, always said to be acquisitive. A few authors even think of it as the paradigm of acquisitive desire.

[8] We distinguish between sexual desire and the desire for the union of complementarity. The former desire is identified by its aim: genital pleasure. The latter desire is identified by the manner in which whatever is being sought is sought. The two desires can obviously coexist.

Plato's dialogue *Symposium*. Asked to give a talk in honor of love, Aristophanes tells the others at a banquet of its origin. Originally, according to his myth, human beings were shaped in a circular fashion, with four arms and four legs. These beings were "of surprising strength and vigour, and so lofty in their notions that they even conspired against the gods." Concerned about the rebellious race, Zeus put forth an ingenious proposal to humble and weaken the recalcitrant humans:

> "I propose now to slice every one of them in two, so that while making them weaker we shall find them more useful by reason of their multiplication; and they shall walk erect upon two legs. If they continue turbulent and do not choose to keep quiet, I will do it again," said he; "I will slice every person in two, and then they must go their ways on one leg, hopping."

He sliced the beings in half, and commissioned Apollo to turn their faces to the cut side and to pull the skin over and fasten it at the navel. When Zeus saw that his division wrought such havoc among humans that they were perishing because they would not do anything apart, he took pity on them. To satisfy somehow their desire to be reunited, he moved their privy parts to the front so that they could beget on each other and not on the earth as previously.[9]

All human beings then, according to the Aristophanic myth, are incomplete, being but a part of their original and total selves. As the search for an appropriate partner is often a difficult one, many men and women are said to spend a good portion of their lives seeking a lost "other half." According to the myth, the anguished search must continue until a person achieves a complementary union with another, thus restoring the severed integrity of his original being and reverting to the primal estate.[10]

b. *Desire for the union of similarity*

The union of similarity is a condition in which the one to whom a person is united is not his "other half," but rather "another self." Those who are so united reflect each other's personality. Using this notion in his theory of love, Aristotle says that friends similar in virtue have "one soul in

[9] *Symposium*, 189A–193D, pp. 133–147, *passim*. In the myth there are three original sexes, only one of which is a combination of male and female. The cutting of this being in half explains the attraction of men for women and women for men. The other two original beings were wholly male or wholly female; their severance explains the attraction of man for man and woman for woman. Though the attraction of members of the same sex for each other also can be understood as a desire for the union of complementarity, it is not so clear a case as the attraction of members of the opposite sex.

[10] See *ibid*.

two bodies." The desire for this form of union leads to conversing with another in his manner, experiencing his problems and joys as he experiences them, meeting difficult tasks and dangers as he meets them, perhaps even to pursuing a common life.

In a much broader sense, this form of the desire for union has been viewed as a mass phenomenon, as the binding force among citizens in a commonwealth or soldiers in an army. When threatened externally, they are incited to draw closer together, to augment what they have and do in common, to reaffirm their collective identity, and to reenforce their sense of being among their own kind. However great the number involved, the desire for the union of similarity is present whenever individuals seek to fuse themselves into a shared identity.

The achievement of union, of complementaries or similars, does not necessarily terminate the desire for it. Those who achieve it may continue to desire it insofar as they seek to strengthen or perpetuate the ties that bind them to others. The achievement of union often is said to inspire an even stronger desire for it.

Two people who are alike cannot seek the union of complementarity in the respects in which they are alike since such union presupposes complementary differences in character or wants. Two people who are not alike may seek both types of union.

The compatibility of the two desires for union may be illustrated by considering the example of a possible relationship between a teacher and a student. Insofar as teacher and student are not only different but also have different functions and desires with respect to each other, their inclination to come together could be described as the desire for complementarity. The student listens to someone who knows more than he knows. The ignorance and eagerness of the student are also the *sine qua non* of the teacher's being able to realize his desire to instruct.

Yet, in another sense, their relationship may well exemplify a desire for the union of similarity. To the extent that the student wishes to advance himself in knowledge, he wants to become more like his teacher; insofar as the teacher seeks to help the student achieve this goal, he wants the student to become his intellectual equal. Even though only the student may change, they can both be said to be striving for a condition in which they are alike.

Since teacher and student are dissimilarly situated, the two desires for union are not mutually exclusive. If, on the other hand, teacher and student ever became identical, they would no longer be able to complement each other's desires to teach and learn. Though complete identity is impossible, it is true that, as their intellectual differences diminish, their desire for the union of complementarity, as far as teaching and learning go,

would necessarily decrease. (They could, of course, continue to complement each other in other respects.)

Finally, it must be stressed that mere interest in a common cause is not
an instance of the union of similarity, nor does it necessarily imply any
desire on the part of those who share this interest to want to become like
each other. Mortal enemies may have an identical stake in the outcome of a
business venture into which necessity or chance has thrown them, but
their desire to be as unlike and as far apart as possible could persist. A
father and a mother may have a common interest in the happiness and
welfare of their children. Pursuing this interest together need not incline
them to want to become like each other; its successful pursuit may even
impel them to retain their union of complementarity and to remain dissimilar.

B. JUDGMENT

In the sphere of judgment, the cognitive notions that are relevant to
theories of love are determinations or perceptions of some form of worth.
Our critical terms for these notions are "esteem" and "valuation"; the two
subordinate forms of esteem we call "admiration" and "respect." Esteem
signifies a judgment that someone is *good in himself*. Valuation signifies a
judgment that someone will be a means of acquiring a *good for me* or that
someone will be a recipient of a *good from me*. Esteem is a judgment of
intrinsic worth; valuation, a judgment that precedes a desire for the
possession or the accomplishment of a good. A few authors combine the
two judgments in their theories of love, but most keep them separate.

1. *Esteem*
a. *Admiration*

When the authors refer to the judgment of someone as exceptional, we
signify that judgment by the word "admiration." The person so judged is
measured in terms of the admirer's standards of goodness or greatness and
held in high regard because of moral qualities, social accomplishments, artistic talents, professional skills, or other merits. Those admired may be
heroes, prominent military or political figures, great artists, scholars,
athletes, or even criminal geniuses. Such admiration can range from unqualified veneration to the grudging approval extended to an ingenious
opponent.

As here described, the notion of admiration does not signify a judgment
that need give rise to desire. It signifies only a positive judgment or

approbation of another for an excellence that he possesses or exemplifies. A person may admire someone else and not want to emulate him. Admiration, so conceived, is neither a tendency nor is it necessarily causative of any desire.

b. *Respect*

Admiration signifies a high degree of approval of another human being; respect, as we use the term, signifies less. It is, like admiration, the judgment of the intrinsic worth of another; but, unlike admiration, it is not extended to another for any exceptional qualities he may possess or any excellence he may exhibit. Thus, someone who is judged to have intrinsic worth or inherent dignity that is not extraordinary—perhaps simply in virtue of his being human—is respected. He may also be admired for his wisdom, courage, or strength, or any such qualities that make him outstanding, but such is a judgment that goes beyond respect.

Respect, as that notion is employed in the literature, is tendered to someone because of the worth he is judged to have solely because of his membership in a group. It is one of the least individually discriminating of approbative judgments. There are people whom we do not admire, but for whom we have a certain regard because they are citizens of our country or members of our family. The special position they occupy in our judgment is not in virtue of any individual qualities but because they are members of a group, whether that group be the whole human species, the citizens of a country, the population of a city, or a family.

The notion of respect, like that of admiration, signifies a judgment that does not necessarily give rise to desire. A person may respect another from whom or for whom he wants nothing.

2. *Valuation*

We are using the term "valuation" to stand for the notion of a judgment that does elicit a desire. When someone is so valued, he is seen as a person either from whom we want or for whom we seek something, as the means of getting what we want or as the recipient of what we want to give. This evaluative judgment of another gives rise to a desire in regard to him or causes a desire to be directed toward him.

When a young man is attracted to a young woman (or vice versa), the desires he may have to caress, possess, be joined with, or benefit her are not often interpreted as related directly to admiration or respect. He may see her as good in herself, but he must also, according to many authors, single her out as someone from whom or for whom he will seek something; he must make another judgment.

Most authors place love entirely within the sphere of tendency. The inclusion of cognitive notions in our analytical scheme is necessitated by the fact that there are some theories in which love, or a certain type of love, is wholly or partly conceived in terms of the cognitive notions admiration, respect, and valuation. But, for most authors, the cognitive notions refer to elements that are prior to love, which they take to be wholly a tendency. The cognitive elements, therefore, have been understood variously as constituting the whole of love, a part of it, or a precondition of it.

We have adopted, then, in the tendential order, five basic terms: tendency in general, acquisitive desire, benevolent desire, sexual desire, and the desire for union; and, in the order of judgment, two basic terms: esteem and valuation. These seven, together with the terms for the subordinate forms, represent the relatively small number of critical notions employed by the leading writers about love in their effort to say what it is. We think we have found it possible to describe the core of any given author's conception of human love by one or more combinations of these notions. They constitute, therefore, the irreducible minimum for describing all the different conceptions of love we have been able to discover in the literature. We shall use them as our points of reference in the analysis and classification of theories in Part II. In the chapters immediately following, they will come into play in a number of the issues about the nature of love.

2

Controversies About Natural
Human Love

THE conceptions of love advanced in the literature range from notions of the simplest and most familiar of human phenomena to those
of the most complex and rarest. There are authors who hold that love is
omnipresent—that it is behind the propensities of everything that exists to
do whatever it does. Some refine this broad, cosmic theme. Plato, for example, mentions love only in relation to animate beings. Freud not only
restricts love to animate beings but also denies that love is the sole principle behind their actions. Some authors discuss love only as a human
phenomena, and one author, Reik, explicitly denies that there is any real
love outside of human relationships.

Within the restricted realm of human relationships, authors make
further distinctions. There are some who say that all tendencies among
human beings are acts of love. (A number of these divide all human
desires into acquisitive and benevolent ones, while a few of them hold that
human desires are all acquisitive.) Other authors narrow the range of love
among human beings by holding that only some acquisitive and benevolent
desires are instances of love. Some say that love is a relatively rare and
complex relationship involving both acquisitive and benevolent desires

37

together. Still others narrow the range of love even further by identifying it with sexual desire, while there are authors who ascribe to it the narrowest range of all in asserting that only genuine benevolence is love.

Despite the considerable and sometimes bewildering differences in the range and complexity of the various conceptions of love advanced, we assumed that we could find some kind of unity in the discussion as a whole. One way of testing this assumption was to see whether or not we could formulate significant questions about love for which there are sets of contrary answers in the literature. We believe we have found such questions, though their number is small in comparison with the vast number of differences in the views authors hold about love. Analysis reveals that few of these differences can be construed as real issues, *i.e.*, opposed answers to the same questions understood in the same way.

A difference that is not an issue can be suggested in the following simplified example. One author says that true love is always universal—that it is always for all men. Another says that true love is exclusive—that it is always for one and only one person. The apparent basic difference of opinion turns out to be nothing of the sort when we find out what each is referring to when he uses the word "love." Closer examination shows that the first author is concerned with the cultivation of a benevolent attitude toward all human beings—male and female. The second author, however, is talking about a certain combination of sexual desire and the desire for union in a relationship between a man and a woman. He asserts that both these desires must be focused on one person in order for love to come in being. Since each is referring to a different conception of love, the opposition between their two statements turns out to be verbal rather than substantive.

If there is a disagreement between these two authors, it is not on the question of how many persons can be loved at one time but on the more fundamental question of what love is. If the first writer says—or can be construed as saying—that the only meaning love has is the one that he affirms, while the second writer makes the same claim about his conception, then they are joining issue. The issues, however, are seldom as clear as this one.

Before issues about love can be discussed, it is necessary to describe the sense in which the authors who write about love are all concerned with the same subject. In seeking a general formulation of what *all* the diverse conceptions of love have in common, the critical notions set forth in the previous chapter must be considered. This common idea of love must reflect, on a higher level of generality, all the ways in which those notions are used to describe the different conceptions of love.

From the fact that the notions themselves are drawn from two distinct spheres, tendency and judgment, it is clear that the idea of love will reflect only a thin, common, minimal agreement among the authors who try to say what love is. Nevertheless, there is a definite sense in which all conceive it as having the same general characteristics. We find at least four such characteristics in all the conceptions of love advanced.

First of all, every author who writes of love either states or implies that the respect in which the lover loves the beloved is the respect in which the lover is interested in the beloved. Sexual desire is an expression of interest, as is the wish to help another. Any kind of approbative judgment—that another is good in himself, good for me, or a fitting recipient of a good from me—can also be understood as an expression of interest. All authors agree that indifference is incompatible with love in that respect in which one person loves another. It is true that one person may love another in one respect and be indifferent to that person in every other way. But the other respects are not those in which the lover is said to love the beloved.

Second, love always involves preference. The beloved may be preferred as a means or as an end—or both. Even if he is the object of an instinctive desire, he is "preferred" in the sense that the desire points to him for release. Or, as is more frequent, he may be consciously preferred as the object of a deliberate choice. To be loved, then, is normally to be singled out in the respect in which one is loved and for however long one is loved. This characteristic is obvious in theories of romantic love, where one woman assumes commanding importance in a man's mind. But the characteristic also holds for the love that is said to be directed toward humanity as a whole; for, even in such love, all human beings are valued and preferred in a way that animals and the rest of subhuman life are not.

Third, love points toward action—whatever the character of the love and whatever the character of the action. Another way of stating this is that esteem (the judgment that does not necessarily lead to action) is never regarded as constituting the whole of love. No author says that simply *admiring* someone or simply *respecting* him is equivalent to loving him.[1] In other words, love is said by all authors to be related to action, either as mental cause (valuation) or as one or another sort of interior inclination which precedes or causes overt action. Of course, such action need never occur. The common note is that love inclines toward action, not that it necessitates action. A lover can feel benevolence for another without ever doing anything for that other, either because he is unable or because an occasion for beneficence never arises. In either case, the inclination or

[1] Hume, who comes closest to taking this position, nevertheless admits that the judgment he calls love points toward desire and action.

readiness to act must exist before any of the authors would call the instance one of love.

Fourth, there is a sense in which all authors speak of love as either good in itself or as pointing toward some good.[2] Many mention bad loves, illicit loves, low loves, and insane loves; but almost always the discussion of the love condemned takes place in the context of contrasting such love with love praised, with love in its "higher forms." If an author does not think of love as invariably good, he does not fail to point out a type of it which he regards as invariably good. The capacity to love, or to love in a certain way, always is seen by him as a desirable or essential element in his notion of what life ought to be and how it ought to be lived. Love may be seen variously as aiming at the maximization of physical pleasure, as the human race's way of insuring its preservation, as the only possible escape from the torture of loneliness, or as the very essence of virtuous activity toward other men. Though many authors will admit that love can be destructive, such love is love gone awry; all of them eulogize it ideally as constructive. For this reason, love is never merely analyzed; all who theorize about love also moralize about it.

One would suppose that the principal characteristics that make up the general formulation of any basic idea would distinguish that idea from all others. The idea of love enjoys no such autonomy. The four characteristics listed above are applicable to a number of other ideas, all of them much more specific than love. The pervasiveness of the idea of love is necessitated by the fact that a number of ideas less general in range are included in its scope. As the friendship of utility has been called love, the idea of love and the idea of commerce must overlap. As both tendency and judgment have been called love, the idea of love must be broad enough to span both spheres. As both prayer and sexual desire have been called love, the idea of love must include both spiritual and physical desires. As both marriage and the fighting morale of an army are said to be effects of love, the idea of love must be applicable to relationships between two or among many. As everything from the craving for Cherries Jubilee to the will to lay down one's life for a friend has been called love, the idea of love cannot exclude any tendency. The general formulation of the idea of love distinguishes it only from all those ideas that have not been included, by one author or another, in love's compass.

The four characteristics common to all conceptions of natural love among human beings—that it implies interest, involves preference, inclines

---

[2] There is only one author who is a conspicuous exception to this statement: Lucretius. For him, the impulse of Venus, the attraction between the sexes (the only thing he calls love), is invariably a form of destructive madness which must be resisted constantly.

toward action, and is good or productive of good—form the nucleus of the idea of love. Whatever authors say more specifically about what love is, they share this general agreement. Such agreement provides the ultimate basis for whatever genuine issues divide them.

All of the issues that we discuss have been drawn from, or suggested by, the literature. With some of the questions, however, we find only one position taken in the literature. In such cases, we have not hesitated to suggest an opposed position that some author could take. In addition, we have not only set down the arguments advanced by authors in support of the positions they take but, here and there, have indicated possible lines of argument not actually found in the literature, though sometimes suggested there.

In this chapter we shall present little documentation of the positions and arguments we attribute to the authors involved. That documentation is presented in Part II, where the reader will find the full theories of each of the authors set forth. In those few cases where a passage is quoted in this chapter but not presented in Part II, the reference will accompany the quotation.

A. General Controversy: Issues About Love as Tendency

Probably the most basic and interesting set of issues centers on the question of what distinction, if any, authors make between human tendency as such—human desire of any sort—and love. Some of them, principally those authors who understand love as an all-pervasive cosmic influence behind the movement of everything inanimate and animate, make no distinction at all between human desire and human love. Many of these authors also hold binary theories of love; that is, they not only say that love is desire but that there are two sorts of human desire, acquisitive and benevolent, and that these are the two most general kinds of love. Still other authors, also holding binary theories of human love, agree that there is a kind of love that is acquisitive in character and another kind that is benevolent in character, but deny that *all* acquisitive desires or that *all* benevolent desires are forms of love. They add important qualifications which, in their view, are necessary to distinguish love from certain expressions of both types of desire. Still others say that love is always and only acquisitive in character, whether it includes all such desires on the part of man or only some (only sexual desires, for example). Finally, there are those who make a radical distinction between love and all desire by insisting that without benevolence there is no love. They deny that any acquisitive desire alone can be called love, no matter what form it takes.

Tendency or desire is the minimal generic meaning of love in all the above conceptions of it. Yet desire is an inclination toward a good for *someone.* Those who say that love is only acquisitive desire are saying, in effect, that love always has a good for the self as its controlling aim. Those who say that benevolence is essential to love are saying, in effect, that love always has a good for another as its controlling aim. And those who hold binary theories of love are saying, in effect, that love may have a good for the self or for another as its controlling aim, depending on which form it takes. The difference, then, among these three groups of conceptions of love, based as it is on the distinction between acquisitive and benevolent desire, directly reflects the polarity between self and other as objects of love. That polarity is basic to much of the discussion about love, not only in the literature but in everyday talk. Whether the actions of love are done for the self's sake or for another's sake is one of the most frequent and perplexing questions asked in regard to love, since, often, the same action may have an acquisitive or a benevolent aim.

The fact that the same action may have two different motives may account for some of the confusion in the language used to describe these two different desires. In any case, the ambiguity concerning the predication of love of or for someone is striking. More often than not authors will refer to both acquisitive desire *and* benevolent desire as "love for another" or as "love of another." To do so, however, is to use the phrases in different senses. Though love between human beings always *involves* another, with acquisitive desire the self is the person for whom a good is sought, while the other is a means of realizing it. With benevolent desire, on the other hand, the other is the person for whom a good is sought, while the self is the means of realizing it. In both cases, desire points to the person for whom the good is sought as the person loved, either self or other. Thus understood, love is always of the end and never of the means. But to refer to both kinds of desire as "love of another" or "love for another" involves predicating love both of the means and of the end. Such are clearly radically different uses of the phrases.

Returning, then, to the principal issue among authors who hold love to be tendency or desire, we can state the question as follows: In any act of love, who is the person loved? The answer given by those who claim that love is acquisitive desire is: the self only. The answer given by those who claim that love must involve benevolence is: the other, either only or primarily. (Some of these authors do not exclude self-interest from love, but they always subordinate it to the interest of the other.) The answer given by those who advance binary theories of love is: either the self or the other.

1. *Is benevolence possible?*

In seeking reasons why certain authors do not affirm any relationship between benevolence and love,[3] one is struck by the fact that only two of them, Charles Darwin and Andreas Capellanus, even discuss benevolence in the course of their analyses of love. The others do not mention it. For some of these authors, no firm conclusion can be drawn from this fact. The silence of others, however, does lend weight to the suspicion that they do not think benevolence to be humanly possible.

It is by no means certain that Stendhal would take this position, for he concentrates on only one love relationship—that between a man and a woman. He affirms that the romantic motivation is essentially an acquisitive one. One can only guess whether or not he would also view mother-love or friendship as acquisitively motivated. Denis de Rougemont also concentrates on the love relationship between a man and a woman, but does so in order to contrast romantic or erotic love with the love in Christian marriage. He makes the distinction between these two loves, in part, by contrasting the acquisitive and destructive impulses of erotic love with the benevolent and constructive impulses of Christian love. This latter love is supernatural, however; what we find in the way of a conception of natural love is characterized by acquisitiveness. Again, it is not entirely clear whether or not De Rougemont would assert that *all* natural human love is acquisitive. We only know for certain that this is how he conceives of romantic love.

The assertion of the predominance of the acquisitive motivation in human relationships is clearer in the theories of Plotinus, Ficino, Pico, and Bembo, but the evidence is inconclusive. These followers of Plato, all of whom see love as acquisitive, place their emphasis on the original Platonic definition of love as desire for goods for the self which are not yet possessed. One can only say that there is a strong possibility that these authors, unlike Plato himself and unlike the Platonist Castiglione, think that there is no human desire that does not spring from personal deficiency.

Evidence for the denial of the possibility of a naturally benevolent human motive is strongest in the theories of Spinoza and Anders Nygren. At several points in *The Ethics*, Spinoza affirms that all human actions are functions of the determinants of personal pleasure and pain. Nygren is emphatic in contrasting the disinterested benevolence of supernatural love with the totally self-centered motivation behind all natural human actions.

---

[3] We refer to those authors classified in Part II, Ch. 7, *infra*.

For both, therefore, natural actions, apparently beneficent, in fact proceed from underlying acquisitive motivations. All natural giving is ultimately for the sake of getting, since all such actions, however selfless they may appear, are, in fact, hedonistically or eudaemonistically motivated.

We can easily see why the adherents of the Spinoza-Nygren position deny that benevolence is a form of natural love. In their view, the condition of the human psyche is such that a natural desire that has as its final aim the good of someone other than the desirer is impossible. All natural inclinations must take the form of either simple acquisitive desire or mixed acquisitive desire. If natural love is tendential, it cannot be anything but acquisitive.[4]

The position that all human tendencies are acquisitive is obviously rejected both by those who claim that without benevolence there is no love at all and those who claim that, in addition to a kind of love that is characterized by acquisitiveness there is a kind that requires benevolence. They are, in this respect, joined in their opposition to those who take the view espoused by Spinoza and Nygren.

a. *Is personal satisfaction the controlling aim of all human desires?*

The nature and function of satisfaction is one of the points of contention among authors who differ on the question of the possibility of an authentically benevolent desire. Some of those who deny that benevolence is humanly possible do so because they think all actions originated by the self must aim at an alteration in the self that takes the form of satisfaction or pleasure. Many of the authors who assert the possibility of natural benevolence admit, as a matter of course, that every action by the self *involves* an alteration in the self. But they deny that such alteration is the sole reason for, or purpose of, the action. The question at issue is whether the fulfillment of a desire is merely accompanied by satisfaction or whether the desire aims solely at, or is pursued solely for, the sake of such satisfaction.

Though the nature and function of satisfaction has been the subject of extensive discussion in philosophical literature, it is far from having been explored fully in the literature on love. Of those who argue for the possibility of benevolence, Aquinas deals with this point most directly. First of

---

[4] A denial that benevolence is love need not rest on a denial that benevolence is possible. An author might not only admit but also affirm that benevolence is a possible natural motive and still not call benevolence love. This is, in fact, the position that Darwin seems to take. But Darwin does not argue that benevolence is not love; he simply never refers to it as such.

all, he distinguishes between carnal pleasure and the satisfaction that accompanies the fulfillment of nonphysical desires. He readily concedes that any purely biological impulse such as sexual desire has physical pleasure as its immediate aim. (In fact, as we define sexual desire, no author denies that it is always acquisitive. Furthermore, no author fails to recognize that such an uncomplicated impulse is seldom encountered in human relationships.) But Aquinas insists that desires that are not biological aim at goods that are distinct from the personal satisfaction that accompanies fulfillment—goods such as wisdom, justice, security, wealth, peace, etc. The good sought is not only distinct from the satisfaction that accompanies its achievement but is not to be understood solely as a means to satisfaction. The "delight" that accompanies the fulfillment of a non-carnal desire is not the aim of that desire but rather, in the language of Aquinas, a "proper accident."

In his analysis of both acquisitive and benevolent desire, Aquinas, following Aristotle, holds to the distinction between the object sought and the satisfaction concomitant with its attainment. Separating the particular good sought from the satisfaction attendant upon its realization enables him to claim that a desire may be benevolent. Though the satisfaction of realizing a desire is always in the self, the particular good sought may be sought for the self or for the other. For Aquinas, any desire aims at a good for someone—either self or other—whereas the occurrence of satisfaction in the attainment of the good desired is consequent to success in the effort following desire. Gratification occurs if the good desired—no matter for whom—is attained. Aquinas further maintains that the distinction between the good desired and the satisfaction attending its attainment affords the basis for denying that the anticipation of satisfaction concomitant to benevolence makes the motive behind the action a nonbenevolent one.

If, as is the case with Spinoza and Nygren, an author thinks that there is only one good that human beings seek—pleasure—and that everything else sought is but a means to it, it is clear that he consequently denies the possibility of natural benevolence. All giving is not only accompanied by getting but is, ultimately, done for the sake of getting. All love is self-love; it not only originates from personal deficiency but is always directed to the removal of that deficiency. According to this view, even sacrificing one's life for another has a self-centered motive. An author who takes this position no doubt would concede that a person may believe his motive to be benevolent, but he would maintain that the belief is an illusion. In short, his affirmation that love is tendentially acquisitive rests on his premise that all natural human tendency is, at root, acquisitive. Anything sought is sought as but a means to the one good—pleasure.

b. *Does the union of similarity make benevolence possible?*

Another argument for the possibility of benevolence is based on the notion of the union of similarity. The two principal proponents of this argument are Aristotle and Adam Smith. Both Aristotle, in his analysis of the friendship of virtue, and Smith, in his analysis of fellow feeling and sympathy, maintain that the basis of benevolence is the sense of communion that the lover feels with the beloved. The lover is able to transfer to another the attention and care that he normally gives to himself because he is able to relate the beloved's feelings, joys, and sorrows to his own. This projection of the self is possible because of an actual similarity between lover and beloved, or the desire for such similarity.

For Aristotle, the highest kind of friendship rests upon a degree of virtue that few achieve. The similarity that friends in virtue feel for each other rests on their moral and intellectual achievements and the mutual admiration those qualities evoke. This admiration gives rise to the mutual benevolence that characterizes that friendship. Smith also mentions friendship between two virtuous men, but, unlike Aristotle, he does not limit the benevolence of friendship to that relationship. For Smith, sympathetic identification between two human beings is a common enough human phenomenon, with the degree of love between them and its durability directly dependent on the degree of identification between them.

Despite this difference, both Aristotle and Smith believe that benevolence between friends is possible because one friend sees himself reflected in the other and thus is able and willing to do for his friend what he does for himself. Both Aristotle and Smith think that such desires do not constitute a kind of vicarious selfishness. Benevolent desires inspired by identification with another are not directed to the good of one's self but to the good of "another self." Aristotle, in effect, says that benevolence is self-love *transmuted* and *transferred* to another.

We find no direct address to this line of argument by those who deny that benevolence is possible. If an argument were to be made against this position, it would probably take the form of denying that desires arising only out of identification with someone else are truly transferred desires. The opponent would maintain that desires directed to the good of another, *only insofar as the other is an image of oneself,* not only derive from self-interest but also remain essentially self-interested. In contrast to the transitive act whereby the self exerts itself on behalf of another for his own sake, this desire requires the diminution, as far as possible, of the distinction between self and other. The opponent would accordingly maintain that what looks like benevolent desire is really acquisitive desire in disguise, a disguise made possible by an extension of the self rather than by a transfer of self-interest to another.

c. *Are desires that arise from excess rather than from deficiency benevolent?*

Still another argument that benevolence is possible is advanced by at least one author. According to this argument, there are certain human inclinations that spring from excess rather than deficiency and that are not only other-directed but have a creative purpose. Plato may be considered not only the originator but also the arch-exponent of this position. He argues that the desire to "beget upon the beautiful" is inherent in the very nature of love. When, for example, the desire for wisdom, which proceeds from lack of knowledge or ignorance, has been fulfilled, the lover no longer loves wisdom. The natural course of his desire is no longer directed toward the attainment of something that he now possesses; it is rather toward the fulfillment of the same lack in the soul of another who wishes to learn. In Plato's view, the fulfillment of the desire to know leads to the desire to have others know; the wise desire to "procreate" through teaching. Such a desire, proceeding from superabundance or "overflowing" and not from personal deficiency, does not aim at a good for the self but at a good for another.

There is little awareness of this position in the literature on natural love, and little, if any, confrontation of it. José Ortega y Gasset does refer to a "sentimental activity," a sort of veritable spontaneous overflow, which is the characteristic love inclination and which he sharply distinguishes from acquisitive desire; but he does not develop this observation at any great length. There are, of course, theologians who, commenting on the proposition that "God is Love," argue that God's goodness overflows to His creatures and to all creation, and that such benevolence certainly does not proceed from deficiency in Him; but these theologians do not argue that natural human benevolence is comparable.

C. S. Lewis, in discussing what he calls the "need to give," points out that there are instances, particularly in physical procreation, when beneficent actions have acquisitive motivations as their spur. The mother, he says, instinctively gives suck to her infants because she would otherwise experience pain. Plato himself also observes that the impulse to physical procreation creates a state of chronic unrest and discomfort until that desire is consummated. Such desires are, in their views, acquisitive.[5] But there is

[5] That Plato does not think that spiritual procreation, or teaching, is also acquisitive seems clear in his presentation of the model teacher, Socrates, not as a parental figure trying to perpetuate himself but as a "mid-wife" trying to aid the young in giving birth to ideas.

no direct argument in the literature that the desire for spiritual procreation, which proceeds from excess rather than deficiency, is also necessarily acquisitive.

If such an argument were to be made, it would probably take the form of a denial that there is any important difference between the desire proceeding from physical excess or overflow and the desire proceeding from spiritual excess or overflow. In other words, the desire to teach would be analyzed as just as much a personal need and as aiming just as much at a personal good as beneficent parental actions motivated by physical discomfort, by the desire to alleviate personal feelings of guilt, or by the desire for a kind of immortality. In order to deny the possibility of benevolence, the author making such an argument would have to maintain that, somehow, spiritual superabundance is just another acquisitive spur.

d. *Is benevolence possible because of the difference between unconscious and conscious desires?*

Another point of dispute arises with respect to the possibility of benevolence because of the often-asserted difference between actual and underlying motivation. For both those who assert and those who deny that benevolence is possible, the important issue to be examined is the degree of awareness of real motives on the part of the person desiring.

The problem here, of course, was posed most sharply by Freud. For him, all psychic inclinations not only originate in but are also sustained by bodily needs. Yet he claims that by a complicated process of transformation some human desires, which in their unconscious forms directly reflect physical appetites, approach benevolence as they become conscious. In addition, Freud holds that such conscious desires are functions of the unconscious demands upon which they depend completely and which are the basic psychic realities. If any person were to know his real motivations, he would see them all as acquisitive. Accordingly, Freud refers to "tenderness" or conscious benevolence as an "illusion." Yet, he makes conscious benevolence an essential element in what he calls "mature," "civilized," or "ideal" love. In experiencing that love, the lover is simply unaware of the acquisitive spur behind his "tenderness." As far as the lover is concerned, the benevolence he experiences is real. From the perspective of the conscious, benevolence is clearly a possibility in the Freudian theory. From the perspective of the unconscious, however, it is clearly precluded.

Those who would maintain that the possibility of benevolence is important for the Freudian theory of love would undoubtedly point out how crucial the distinction between unconscious and conscious motivation is for Freud. They would also argue that, because that distinction cannot be existentially erased, it lends a certain importance to the derivative, but nevertheless distinct, conscious desires. They would also note that benevolence, even though it is acquisitive desire in conscious disguise, is, in some sense, real as a psychological phenomenon. They might even argue that to describe the Freudian theory as one in which only acquisitive desires are called love is to distort it; to do so would preclude explaining Freud's conception of the best kind of love between a man and a woman.

The counterargument would necessarily stress the difference between real and merely apparent motivations. Those taking this position would insist that what the lover wants and why he *thinks* he wants it are different matters from why he *really* wants it. An analysis of love cannot, they would maintain, rest on the lover's fallible understanding of what is happening to him.

The point at issue here concerning real and apparent motivation is important for many theories. Nowhere, however, has the resolution of this point such serious consequences as in the Freudian theory. A number of authors freely admit that certain relationships, thought of as love, impair the lover's understanding of his real motives. Though many of them also say that the lover's enlightenment or disenchantment can destroy his desire or alter it in some respects, few of them also say, as Freud seems to say, that all benevolent inclinations are ultimately reducible to acquisitive ones.

There are, of course, other authors who would oppose the whole notion of a psyche in which the lover is unaware of his controlling motives. These authors, while admitting a distinction between unconscious and conscious desires, or perhaps between instinctive and deliberate desires, would deny that the latter merely reflect the former. They would argue that desires can originate consciously that do not have unconscious roots, and that some of these desires may be benevolent ones. This argument for the possibility of benevolence would hinge upon a measure of autonomy for the conscious mind.

2. *Is benevolence indispensable to love?*

In the previous issue about the possibility of benevolence, we presented three positions concerning the object of love. According to the first of them, the self is always the object of love; according to the second, both the self and the other are objects of love; and, according to the third, the other is always the object of love. In that issue, those who take the second and third positions were ranged against those who take the first; those who claim that benevolence is humanly possible were ranged against those who deny it. In this issue, those who take the first and second positions are ranged against those who take the third; those who claim that the self is an object of love (and deny, therefore, that benevolence is indispensable to love) are ranged against those who claim that only the other is the object of love (*i.e.*, that benevolence is indispensable to love).

Some of the principal authors who affirm the indispensability of benevolence to love are Reik, Erich Fromm, Ortega, Nicolai Hartmann, and Adam Smith. For different reasons, all of them deny that sexual desire alone is an instance of love, that any form of acquisitive desire alone is an instance of love. Though some of them are willing to say that certain love relationships, so-called romantic love, for example, involve acquisitive desire, the essential notion in all of their conceptions of love is benevolence.

a. Is love always and unqualifiedly good?

All of the authors who maintain that benevolence is indispensable to love lay great stress on how difficult and how precious love is. They do so primarily because they exclude from love any impulse that is deleterious, either in intent or in effect. Love, in short, is always praiseworthy and always good or productive of good. For these authors, the moment any inclination ceases to have a constructive aim it ceases to be love. Though they may admit some presence of acquisitive desire in a love relationship characterized by benevolence, they refuse to admit that the relationship can be totally acquisitive, that love and a complete indifference to the welfare of another are compatible. Thus, Reik, Fromm, Ortega, and Hartmann always see love as productive of good, particularly in the beloved. As their conceptions of love have a strictly moral dimension, there is for them, strictly speaking, no such thing as bad love.

Certain of the authors who hold broad theories of love would be obliged to oppose this position. They would have to argue that those who say that benevolence is indispensable to love are confusing a certain kind of praiseworthy love with love itself. Though they would concede that love is basically good, they would point out that, in fact, it very often not only has bad effects but also aims at "illusory" goods, the realization of which involves actual or intended harm to oneself or to another. For those who say that all human tendencies are instances of love, the man who seeks revenge in order to satisfy his sense of justice is, in some sense, involved in an act of love—self-love, to be sure, but love nevertheless. For such authors, the important moral distinction is not between love and nonlove but between high love and low love, moderate love and immoderate love, prudent love and imprudent love, good love and bad love.

Augustine, for example, is particularly emphatic on the point that all natural cupidities, all natural tendencies, whether acquisitive or benevolent, are inherently good. But he is far from saying that all human intentions and actions thereby are rendered good. Natural cupidities must be guided by knowledge, kept within the bounds of temperance, ordered hierarchically, and combined with virtue. Natural cupidities are good only in the sense that, if directed to their proper objects and combined with a right will, they can result in praiseworthy loves. Sexual desire is regarded by Augustine as a form of love and as inherently good. Yet it can result in a good love or a bad love, depending on whether or not it is controlled and kept within the institutional purposes of marriage.

Authors such as Plato, Augustine, Aquinas, Dante, and Freud could point out to those claiming that benevolence is indispensable to love that the distinction between desires that are potentially good and those that are actually good applies to both acquisitive and benevolent desires. Why, then, should love be predicated only of the benevolent desires?

b. *Does using another always involve harming another?*

Another version of the previous issue about the goodness of love arises because some authors imply that a person who is the object of acquisitive desire is used and, therefore, harmed. Since the result is injury to the other, such desire cannot be called an instance of love. Reik, Ortega, and Fromm often refer to acquisitive desire as an inclination by which someone is treated as a thing rather than as a person. All three authors maintain that things cannot be loved, nor can persons be loved as things. Things are used, and, in their view, when a person is desired as things are desired, he is perforce exploited or hurt. For this reason, they deny that sheer sexuality is a form of love. Acquisitive desire, by definition, implies an indifference to the good of the other (except insofar as the good of another is a means to one's personal good). Such indifference, these authors claim, is incompatible with love.

Arguments against this position are present by implication in the theories of authors who are willing to call forms of acquisitive desire love. Certain of them indicate their agreement that loving someone and harming him are incompatible. But they do not consider harm to be a necessary or even frequent corollary of the fulfillment of acquisitive desire. To use someone else is not necessarily to hurt him. These authors, therefore, deny that acquisitively desiring someone else necessarily involves desiring him as one desires food. Thus, a student who has only acquisitive desires toward a teacher uses that teacher for the sake of his own intellectual improvement. Yet, since he does not harm the teacher thereby, such desires can be called love.

It could also be argued that the fulfillment of any desire involves using someone—either oneself or someone else—and that such use can have beneficial effects. Benevolent desire aiming at the good of another can involve using the self in a certain way, but it need not involve self-sacrifice. A man may be the sole support of his family, and, out of benevolence, wish to enhance its material welfare. This desire, far from requiring him to sacrifice certain personal goods, even may require him to seek such goods. It may require him to take care of his health in order to remain able to work. His final aim is the financial security of his family—the good of others—and he uses himself to achieve that aim. Such use, instead of harming him, requires him to take care of himself as a means to an end. Accordingly, it could be argued that there is no necessary connection between use and harm.

There is another argument that could be put to the authors who say that benevolence is indispensable to love. Though such authors insist that harming someone else is incompatible with love, they do not also insist that harming oneself is incompatible with love. Not only do they say that the self must act in the interest of another through love but also that a great act of love may involve sacrificing the interest of the self, perhaps even one's own life. The question such authors then must answer is: What is the difference in principle between harming another for one's own good and harming oneself for the good of someone else? Why is one an act of love and the other not?

c. *Is real union only possible through benevolence?*

Fromm argues that benevolence is essential to love because of the kind of union that he says is of the very essence of love—a union in which two people preserve their integrity and autonomy. What he calls "symbiotic union" is "fusion without integrity" and consists of an unequal relationship. The motive of the dominating person is "sadistic" and that of the dominated person "masochistic"; the former "commands, exploits, hurts, and humiliates," while the latter is "commanded, hurt, exploited, and humiliated." Both the desire to exploit and the desire to be exploited spring from an all-powerful personal need to escape isolation. But when the fulfillment of that need takes the form of symbiotic union, it not only indicates that the two persons have little personal autonomy but also that the relationship is one that weakens and destroys what little autonomy they have. Symbiotic union is not love because it precludes the development of the parties to it into whole persons; it is not a process whereby the imperfect are perfected but one in which the imperfect are rendered even more imperfect through mutual acquisitiveness.

In Fromm's analysis, real or mature human union is also a condition sought because of personal need; yet it is one that is sustained by benevolence. Those involved in mature union, not only have achieved a certain individuality but also are able to sustain that individuality through mutual help. Fromm claims that this is the only way it can be sustained. For this reason he argues that benevolence is indispensable to love; it not only makes real union possible but also perpetuates it. It allows those who are parties to such union to retain and develop their own personalities instead of becoming totally absorbed in each other.

Fromm's position could be opposed in several ways. An author for whom benevolence is no part of love might cast his opposition in the form of a denial that union, or the desire for it, is any part of love. He might also reject Fromm's fundamental premise, namely, that the desire for "inter-personal fusion" is one of the most basic desires in human nature. Having denied the basis for the inclination to union, he would, in effect, be maintaining that there is no necessity for the benevolence that Fromm says makes a mature union possible.

A more direct confrontation would arise if such an opponent conceded that union or the desire for it is essential to love, but denied any necessary relationship between union and benevolence. Two persons, he could argue, can not only initiate but also maintain a lasting union or some union other than symbiotic union on completely acquisitive grounds. Moreover, the union need not be prejudicial to either party, and may even facilitate the development of each. Each can retain his autonomy and can improve himself more effectively since he can be presumed to know his own wants better than others know them and to have more interest in himself than others do. This is not to say that any giving on his part is precluded, but only that such giving need not be for the sake of the other person. Giving for the sake of getting and giving for the sake of the other person can have the same effects.

Another line of argument could be taken which would stress the relative reliability of acquisitive and benevolent motives. A union based upon mutual acquisitiveness might be asserted to be more durable, since those involved in a relationship based upon mutual need can rely on each other in a way that those involved in a relationship based upon mutual benevolence cannot. Because individuals more often and more consistently are motived by their own needs rather than someone else's, the basis for the union would be stronger.

It might also be held that mutual benevolence actually can be damaging rather than beneficial to both parties. Since human beings are always, in one way or another, in need, a requirement that they base a relationship on the help they can give each other may involve asking them to injure themselves. If they do not have a surplus of what they are asked to give, giving can involve self-deprivation. The parties to such a union run a serious risk of self-imposed injury as a consequence of mutual benevolence. The imperfect who give thereby may well be rendered more imperfect.

d. *Is benevolence indispensable because of the difference between real and apparent wants?*

In Hartmann's theory the kind of benevolence that is said to be the essence of love is directed, not merely to helping another satisfy his present wants but to helping him realize his full potentialities, his true nature. Such benevolence presupposes not so much an approbative judgment of the person as he really is as a prospective judgment of what he might become through the lover's help. Hartmann thinks that the lover is able to "see" (through love) the beloved in a way that he otherwise could not be seen. The lover can thus be presumed to know the beloved's "real" wants better than anyone else. Helping him satisfy those wants even may oblige the lover to frustrate some of the beloved's asserted wants.

One argument that could be leveled against this position would be based on a denial of the distinction between asserted and real wants. The opponent might agree that love precludes harm, and is in itself good or productive of good, but he would regard Hartmann's benevolence as not only based upon a fallacious distinction but as probably pernicious in effect. Helping someone measure up to what someone else considers to be his true self may involve not only persuasion but also coercion. And since, according to this criticism, the coercion is exercised on behalf of an illusory ideal, it is not likely to do the beloved any good. If enhancing the welfare of the beloved means helping him satisfy wants that he denies are his, the actions arising from this kind of benevolence would necessarily produce frustration and, often, harm. Such results are, accordingly, incompatible with love.

Another opponent might concede Hartmann the distinction between real and asserted wants, but still raise the question as to why this distinction is applied only to the beloved and not to the lover. If perception of the ideal for someone else is made possible by the love of that other, why is a comparable perception of one's own ideal self not made possible by self-love? If love is the only way to this kind of knowledge and if Hartmann denies that acquisitive desires are love, then this kind of self-knowledge is impossible. The opponent here could then go on to claim that such self-knowledge is obviously possible. He might not think that it is dependent upon self-love, but if he confronts Hartmann on his own terms he would, at least, point out what seems to him to be the inconsistency of associating two phenomena with regard to the other person and not associating them with regard to the self.

e. Is love a specific tendency rather than tendency in general?

Several of the authors who hold that benevolence is indispensable to love suggest that any conception of love that is less specific than the one they hold, e.g., that love is tendency in general, does not offer an adequate explanation of the special character of certain human relationships generally held to be instances of love. They imply that all other tendential relationships do not have enough in common with these special ones to group them all under a heading as important as love. In their view, the subject is thereby not only distorted but trivialized.

Some of them call attention to language to support their view that the identification of love and sheer tendency is conceptually inadequate. The very fact that all languages contain different words for love and tendency, or desire, suggests a conceptual difference among them. If the idea of love and the idea of tendency or desire are the same, one would feel no violence in substituting the word "love" for the word "desire" and the word "desire" for the word "love" whenever one uses either. Reik observes that the mind balks at agreeing that the word love means the same thing in the phrase, "I love pork chops," as in the phrase, "I love Jane."

The authors who oppose the view that benevolence is indispensable to love could counter this line of argument by pointing out that the limitation placed on what can be called love is an arbitrary one. Human tendency, they might argue, is never merely arbitrary or undirected inclination; it is always an inclination toward a good for someone, an inclination that aims at the enhancement of someone's welfare, at perfecting that someone, or at the fulfillment of someone's desires. If this is so, benevolent and acquisitive desire have more in common then sheer tendency.

These authors could point out, in addition, that the identification of love and tendency operates only as a generic definition and by no means constitutes a complete analysis of the subject; it is a necessary but not a sufficient explanation of love. Other distinctions not only can but should be added to further specify the various kinds of love, each of which has a number of distinguishing properties. Thus, one avoids superficiality by beginning but not ending one's description of certain loves with this most general statement.

The appeal to language on the part of those who claim that benevolence is indispensable to love might not only be dismissed but might actually be turned against them by the authors who hold binary theories of love. The latter could point out that since there are important differences between the mode and properties of an inclination toward food and the mode and properties of an inclination toward a woman, the use of a different word to describe the two tendencies is a reflection of those important differences. But they could also note that the same word, "love," *is* often used to describe both relationships as well as many others in which benevolence is not a factor. If the appeal is to usage, how is it possible to explain, according to the theory that love always involves benevolence, that sexual desire alone is frequently called love, that people can say "I love wine," "I love sleep," "I love to read," "I love my mother," "I love my son," etc., and be understood in all cases? These authors might go on to point out that such frequent and apparently disparate uses of the word "love" are all perfectly justified because they all have a minimal common meaning—tendency. If an author claims that love is only benevolent tendency, he is not only forced to reject the use of the word "love" when it is applied to acquisitive desires but he is also hard put to explain why the word is used so frequently.

3. *Is benevolence indispensable to a type of love?*

Authors who discuss a certain love relationship and do not include benevolence in it cannot be said to deny that benevolence is part of other love relationships not mentioned by them. The admission that benevolence is involved in mother-love or friendship need not alter the conceptions of male-female love advanced by Andreas, Stendhal, and Schopenhauer. These theorists conceive of the love relationship between a man and a woman as tendential and acquisitive. They are not necessarily at odds with the authors who hold binary theories of love and who say that there are love relationships that have nothing to do with benevolence. But, they are at odds with authors who hold that benevolence is indispensable to the type of love relationship with which they are concerned. And, of course, they are at odds with authors who affirm that without benevolence there is no love of any kind. The issue about the nature of male-female love is clearest when we contrast the conceptions of such love advanced by Andreas, Stendhal, and Schopenhauer with the conceptions of it advanced by Reik, Ortega, and Fromm. For the former authors, benevolence is no part of the love relationship between a man and a woman; for the latter group, benevolence is indispensable to that relationship. For both groups of authors, sexual desire is or can be part of male-female love. For none of the authors, however, is that desire unmixed with other elements, *i.e.*, for all, love is sexual desire plus. The disagreement is about whether or not the plus must be benevolence.

Reik, Ortega, and Fromm argue for the indispensability of benevolence in love between the sexes in terms of the discrimination which they say accompanies such love. Sheer sexuality, they claim, is indiscriminate; for what it seeks one woman is almost as good as another. Benevolence, on the other hand, since it follows from admiration or respect, implies some regard for another human being as a person who, particularly in love between the sexes, is singled out as someone special. Only by adding benevolence to sexual desire can one account for the exclusivity that is a frequent characteristic of the love between a man and a woman. If the love between the sexes were merely or basically a biologically acquisitive impulse, a woman would be regarded by a man as nothing more than a replaceable outlet for his passion. Although these authors would admit that there are relationships between men and women that involve nothing but sexuality, they point out that there are other relationships which can be understood only by adding something to sexuality. That something, in their view, must be benevolence.

There are two arguments against this position, one made by Schopenhauer and the other made by Andreas and Stendhal. Schopenhauer claims that sexual desire is anything but indiscriminate. Its purpose is not simply personal pleasure but the perpetuation and improvement of the species. The species pursues these goals through the desires of the individual by inclining him to be attracted sexually to someone with whom he can produce an offspring biologically superior to either parent. The inclination of sexual desire toward one person rather than another is, therefore, far from arbitrary. There are actual physical reasons why a man is attracted to a certain woman or type of woman and has little or no physical interest in others.

Andreas also opposes the view that a love between a man and a woman that involves no benevolence is necessarily indiscriminate. He concedes that sheer sexuality, a concern with "the solaces of the lower part" only, is compatible with promiscuity; but the pure love or courtly love, which is his principal concern, though not entirely sexual is entirely acquisitive and yet discriminate. A concern with the "solaces of the upper part" as well as of the lower implies no benevolence and not only permits but demands a high degree of discrimination. Such exclusivity is produced by a focusing and intensifying of all the acquisitive desires of the lover on one and only one woman. He not only yearns for the beloved's physical favors but also for the sheer ecstasy of being in her presence and of contemplating her beauty. The purest form of love, entirely acquisitive in character, involves desires that are spiritual as well as physical, though Andreas does say that the consummation of the spiritual desires depends upon the continued frustration (not the absence) of the physical ones. The acquisitiveness of this higher form of love not only admits admiration or respect, it depends for its continued existence upon a kind of adoring veneration of the lover for the beloved. Neither that veneration, beside which all other women pale, nor the durability of the relationship necessitates anything but a different form of acquisitive desire added to sexual desire. The relationship can, without benevolence, avoid being one of transitory, indiscriminate, physical indulgence.

Stendhal takes somewhat the same position concerning the love between a man and a woman. Sheer sexuality is of little interest to him. Yet the tendential aspect of real or true love involves no benevolence; real love consists simply in a broader acquisitive inclination which includes not only sexual pleasure but any pleasure derived from "seeing, touching, and feeling through all one's senses" the beloved. Admiration and exclusivity are also features of the relationship Stendhal describes, but neither of these, nor the extended duration of the love, seems to him to necessitate anything but a continual effort on the part of the lover to maximize his pleasure by ascribing to his beloved all sorts of imaginary perfections. Stendhal never says that this discriminating, intense, and relatively durable passion necessitates any benevolence.

Reik, Ortega, and Fromm do not confront these counterarguments directly. But they do say or imply two things: first, that certain things about love cannot be explained if love is interpreted as sexual desire only; and, second, that acquisitive desire generally (including sexual desire) must be tempered with, and governed by, benevolence in order for the relationship to be neither transitory nor destructive.

De Rougemont probably presses the points about transitoriness and destructiveness most forcefully. The momentary nature and harmful character of romantic love are central points in his description of natural love between a man and a woman; yet he makes these points about romance in the course of contrasting natural with supernatural love. Unlike Reik, Ortega, and Fromm, he understands the benevolence which is part of the true love between a man and a woman as a function of supernatural help. Even though, unlike these three, he is willing to call a certain relationship based on mutual acquisitiveness a kind of love, he stands with them in condemning that relationship. Like them, he also maintains that a mutually acquisitive relationship is often grounded in sexuality and that such sexuality is frequently indiscriminate and intense. Unlike them, however, he discusses, at some length, a completely acquisitive relationship such as the one described by Andreas and Stendhal. Such a relationship he considers transitory—not in the sense that it is always of brief duration but in the sense that it *can* cease at any moment. In this kind of love the lover is essentially passive; his "falling in" or "falling out" of love is a matter over which he exercises no great control. He can attempt to prolong the feeling, but the act of love itself is not deliberate.

De Rougemont argues for the destructiveness of romantic love in two ways. First, such love, since it proceeds solely from deficiency, is directed only to the fulfillment of that deficiency. Hence, he argues, like Reik, Ortega, and Fromm, that romantic love involves no recognition of the other as a person but as merely a means for the fulfillment of a lack. In this sense there is no discrimination, even though there may be preference for fulfillment's sake. Second, romantic love leads to the destruction and death of the individual (as individual) by inclining him to sublimate both himself and his beloved in a process in which neither retains his human identity. The attempt to feel at one with cosmic forces and principles leads to a total spiritual immersion that impoverishes the individual's own being. Such a spiritual immersion, in De Rougemont's view, points toward death rather than life and is the inevitable concomitant of any attempt to seek the eternal through temporal ecstasy.

The preceding issues revolve around the question whether some form of acquisitive desire alone can be said to be love or a kind of love, or, stated differently, whether some form of benevolence is indispensable to love or to a kind of love. That question is a pivotal three-sided disagreement. As we said earlier, authors who say that love is acquisitive desire are saying that the self is the object of love. Authors who say that benevolence is indispensable to love are saying that the other always must be the principal object of love in any love relationship. Authors who hold binary theories of love are saying that either the self or the other may be objects of love, that there are two kinds of love, not one. What all these authors dispute is the relationship of benevolence to love. The two principal points of divergence are, first, whether the notion of benevolence signifies a possible human motive, and, second, whether the notion of benevolence is conceptually necessary to explain what love or a kind of love is.

Among the authors who advance conceptions of love as some sort of tendency, there are, in addition to the aforegoing major issues, other general issues present in, or suggested by, the literature.

4. *Is there a type of natural love that is disinterested?*

None of the authors claim that self-interest is incompatible with natural love. Those who say that love is acquisitive in tendency obviously do not do so. Even those who say that benevolence is indispensable to love admit that the benevolence itself is self-interested. Though none explicitly denies that natural love can take the form of disinterested benevolence, they all say or imply that some self-interest is present in all the human motives they discuss—either as primary or concurrent. Some of them say that the personal good sought in conjunction with a benevolent desire is the satisfaction of giving, or the reciprocity such giving may produce. Others say that it is the moral improvement a man gains in being good to others, the actual sharing of the good he gives or the recognition of his gift. We find no author who denies that gaining some kind of personal good is compatible with natural benevolence, and none who denies that the anticipation of enjoying a personal good is also compatible with a benevolent intent.

If there were an author who included the notion of disinterested benevolence as a pivotal part of his theory of natural love among human beings, he would be obliged to set himself apart from all others who deal with natural love. Such an author would claim that a human being is capable of doing something for another without any personal spur at all. While we do find this claim made about supernatural human love, we do not find it made in the literature on natural love. The author who holds this position would be obliged to say either that satisfaction does not accompany the fulfillment of any desire or that such satisfaction cannot be considered a personal good.

What is more probable is that such an author would claim that disinterested benevolence is phenomenologically possible, that the anticipation of a personal good can be, in certain instances, no part of a person's conscious motive in helping another. In the literature there are suggestions that, in moments of quick decision when there is no time for reflection, a person may seek nothing for himself in helping another. Accordingly, this author might say that a man who rushes "spontaneously" into a burning house to save a person can think only of that person and not of any good that might come to himself.

Authors who maintain that natural benevolence is self-interested probably would concede the possibility of disinterestedness in this sense. But they would point out that such is not the case in normal circumstances and insist that, apart from the lover's awareness, self-interest or some residue of it is present in any natural human desire.

Thus, in the literature of natural love, the dispute about the relation of self-interest to benevolence is not in fact raised. Where it is a major issue, as we shall see, is in the dispute over the nature of supernatural human love.[6]

5. *Does love include all acquisitive and benevolent desires or only some?*

Among the authors who hold binary theories of love, there is an issue about whether all or only some acquisitive and benevolent desires are forms of love. The issue here is most clearly posed by contrasting Aristotle's

[6] See Ch. 3, *infra*.

theory of love with those of Aquinas and Dante. For the latter two, all human inclinations are forms of love. Aristotle, however, mentions only certain acquisitive and benevolent desires as forms of love, not all. The former are part of the inferior forms of friendship, the friendships of pleasure and of utility. The latter are primarily characteristic of the superior form of friendship, the friendship of virtue.

What the inferior and superior forms of friendship have in common is the absence of any intention to harm either the self or the other. Though the desires of friendships of utility and of pleasure aim finally at good for the self, they involve giving something to the person through whom the good is acquired, either in exchange for what is received or through reciprocation. Thus, for Aristotle, the commercial exchange of giving money for a service or product is an act of the inferior friendship of utility. Theft, however, is not an act of friendship, nor, presumably, is any act whereby personal good is acquired without giving something for it, or through injuring others. Not all acquisitive desires are forms of friendship or love, but only those that do not involve complete indifference to the welfare of the other.

Aristotle also implies that no act of love or friendship can involve complete indifference to the welfare of the self. The superior friendship of virtue, which is characterized by a concern for someone else for his own sake, is not without its admixture of self-interest. The virtuous friend in giving to another regards his giving as a moral action; he also anticipates some satisfaction in bestowing his gift; he may even look forward to sharing the good he bestows on someone else; and he looks forward to having his beneficence recognized and reciprocated by his friend. Even in the extreme cases such friendship precludes real harm to the self. Aristotle argues that a man who gives up his life for his friend gains thereby a good greater than life itself: honor. In no case does Aristotle say that the friend in virtue is obliged by his benevolence to do something unvirtuous for his friend's sake. Benevolence that involves indifference to the welfare of the self or total self-sacrifice also is precluded in Aristotle's theory.

Aquinas and Dante, though they mention and paraphrase Aristotle's analysis of the friendships of virtue and those of utility and pleasure, do not limit their conception of love accordingly. For them, love includes any and all tendencies, both acquisitive and benevolent. In their theories of love, harm is not precluded, either to the self or to the other. They do make emphatic distinctions between good loves and bad (often in Aristotelian terms), but still insist on the basic meaning of love as that which animates everything in the universe to do *whatever it does*. They imply that to restrict love not only to that which aims at a good either for the self or the other, but also to that which benefits, or causes no harm to, either the self or the other, is to confuse a moral with an analytical distinction. Love, for both Aquinas and Dante, is always to be identified in terms of its end, not its means. To seek a good for someone is to love that someone no matter how the good is acquired. Theft, thus, is an act of love in the sense that it is directed to the acquirement of a good for the self: money. It is bad love, but like every other human action, it is an act of love because it aims at a good—real or illusory—for someone.

6. *Are all the tendencies of love either acquisitive or benevolent?*

In setting forth their conceptions of love, many authors use the notions of the desire for the union of complementarity and the desire for the union of similarity. In all but one or two cases the desire for union is described fairly clearly as a form either of acquisitive or of benevolent desire. In Schopenhauer's theory, for example, the impulses on the part of a man and a woman to unite by complementing each other are understood as mutual acquisitiveness. Reik says that the desires for complementary union are initially a form of mutual acquisitiveness and subsequently express themselves as mutual benevolence. In Plato's theory the desire for the union of similarity is understood as taking both an acquisitive and a benevolent form. The student's desire to become like his teacher in wisdom is acquisitive; the teacher's desire to have the student become like him is benevolent.

A very important issue—perhaps the most important issue about love—would arise if there were an author who defined love only as desire for union and who further claimed that such desire is not reducible to acquisitive or benevolent desire. Its aim, in other words, is neither the good of the self nor the good of the other, but the good of a new, indivisible entity which transcends the distinction between self and other. No author makes such a claim. Without any exception, they affirm or assume that two people in love remain existentially separate and that spiritual similarity never reaches the point of identity. They all see the continuing desire to unite as primarily in the interest of the self or the interest of the other, even though such desire may include the interests of both. As analyzed in the literature, any desire for union can be described as acquisitive or benevolent.

Even Aristotle, who talks about "one soul in two bodies," uses that metaphor in discussing the perfect friendship of virtue to explain how one man may do so much for another, not only because the other is virtuous and deserving of his help but also because the other is so much like himself. Fromm, Pitirim Sorokin, and others talk about breaking down the walls of selfhood. The result of this effort, in their views, is a benevolent intention, an other-directed desire, rather than an obliteration of the distinction between self and other. Max Scheler emphasizes that the distinction between self and other is not a crucial one for understanding what love is. His point, however, is that love is exactly the same, whether it be directed to the self or to someone else.

Descartes comes closest to taking the position suggested above. For him, the essence of love lies in the judgment that there is a whole of which the lover and the beloved are parts—from which follows the decision to transfer to the whole the care and concern that a person normally reserves for himself. But, the tendencies that flow from that decision do not aim at the good of the whole as such, but at the good of each of the parts in proportion to the lover's esteem of each. The lover retains as much care for himself as is proportional to the estimation of his own worth in comparison to the worth of the beloved. Devotion is the result of esteeming the beloved as of greater worth than oneself. Friendship is the result of esteeming the beloved as of equal worth. Simple affection is the result of esteeming the beloved as of lesser worth than oneself. The proportions of benevolent to acquisitive desire vary accordingly. In all three cases the distinction between self and other remains.

7. Is love benevolence only, or a complex of acquisitive and benevolent desires?

Among the authors who agree that benevolence is indispensable to love, there is a possible issue about whether acquisitive desire has anything at all to do with love. Fromm, Reik, and Hartmann, though they affirm that without benevolence there is no love, are willing to include certain acquisitive desires in a *love relationship*.

In Fromm's theory, the original desire for interpersonal fusion and, in part, the desire that sustains the union is acquisitive. The individual seeks escape from the pain of isolation through association with another. What Fromm excludes are acquisitive desires in which escape from loneliness is sought through exploitation of another person. In Reik's view, also, the original and, in part, the sustaining impulse of those seeking union is a desire to add to oneself what one lacks through intimate association with another person. Even Hartmann, who strongly maintains that the characteristic love inclination is the opposite of the desire to possess or use, still allows acquisitive desire a place in some of the love relationships he analyzes.

An issue would arise if there were an author who maintained that benevolence alone is love and that acquisitive desires, though they may commingle with benevolent ones, are no part of the love relationship. To

concede that the love between a man and a woman is a mixture of
benevolence and sexual desire, such an author might argue, is to do
violence to the conception of love as caring for another for his own sake.
To admit that sexual desire or any acquisitive desire is an integral part of
any love relationship is to admit that self-love is a tenable conception of
love. If a desire that aims at a good for the self can be called part of love,
what then is the conceptual barrier against calling acquisitive desire alone
love? Conceding that sexual desire often accompanies benevolent inclinations in the love between a man and a woman, our hypothetical author
could insist that such a desire is only a property and not part of the essence
of that love. To admit sexual desire as part of the essence of a given love is
to admit it as part of the essence of any love, since the essence of love must,
in all instances, be the same. Yet, this author could note that sexual desire
is no part of other loves (*e.g.,* friendship or mother-love) discussed by
Fromm, Reik, and Hartmann.

The counterargument could run as follows: Fromm, Reik, and Hartmann could maintain that there is no conceptual inconsistency in including
acquisitive desire as part of a whole relationship called love. They could
argue that they have never maintained that benevolence alone is love, but
only that benevolence is the indispensable element in a complex of desires
which constitutes love. Acquisitive desire is also part of the essence of love
and not merely one of its properties, since it always accompanies benevolent desire in love; that is to say, *some form* of acquisitive desire always
accompanies benevolent desire in a love relationship. It takes the form of
sexual desire in the love between a man and a woman and other forms in
the loves among friends and between mother and child.

Further, the conceptual barrier against calling acquisitive desire alone a
form of love is found in the fact that benevolence is always associated with
such desire in love. There is, therefore, an implied recognition of the other
as an end and not only a means. Acquisitive desire alone does not necessarily imply any such recognition, though it does not preclude it. When
acquisitive desire is associated with benevolent desire in a relationship,
such recognition is necessarily implied. In the view of Fromm, for example,
this kind of recognition precludes acquisitive desires whose fulfillment
involves harming the other person.

8. *Is love, conceived as acquisitive, nothing but sexual desire?*

Whether love conceived as acquisitive desire is identical with sexual
desire or is broader in scope could be an issue, but it is one that is not
actually joined in the literature. There are a number of authors who
distinguish love from lust, but they almost always do so in terms of a

consideration for the other, which they say is present in a love relationship, as opposed to the desire merely to use the other, which they say is characteristic of a purely sexual relationship. The issue to which they are addressing themselves is whether or not benevolence is indispensable to love. The issue posed here is one in which the parties would agree that acquisitive desire is love but would disagree on the scope of that love. Such an issue might arise if an author claimed that, of all acquisitive desires, only sexual desire is love.

Freud comes closest to doing so in asserting that sexual desire is the prototype of all the desires of love. Though *eros* includes all the body's physical inclinations to perpetuate itself as well as its inclinations to procreate its kind, Freud says that the focus of *eros* is in sexual desire. Yet he also says that there are other human loves that are derived from sexual desire.

Schopenhauer says that love between the sexes is identical with sexual desire, but he does not affirm that, of all acquisitive desires, it is only one that should be called love. If any author affirmed this, he would probably argue that, of all acquisitive desires, sexual desire is the only one which aims at reproduction. Hence, it alone should be called love.

This position might be opposed in at least two ways. First, authors such as Plato might argue that sexual desire is merely one way in which human beings express their desire for what reproduction represents: permanence. Since it is not unique but merely one way in which human beings strive for immortality, love is broader in scope than sexual desire.

Second, and from a very different perspective, others who maintain that love is broader than sexual desire might deny that sexual desire is an inclination different from other physical desires, and that the natural aim of such desire is not reproduction but only or primarily pleasure. They might argue that the connection of the reproductive aim with sexual desire is an accidental association. Though sexual desire does, indeed, have something to do with reproduction, reproduction, they could contend, is not the reason why men seek sexual fulfillment. They do so for pleasure. They might argue, further, that if sexual desire has reproduction as its natural goal, we are hard put to explain why nature has implanted so much more of this desire than is necessary to realize that goal, and why this desire endures in women beyond the point where they are capable of reproduction and during periods when they are incapable of reproduction. In addition, they could point out that it is now possible to bypass sexual intercourse and its attendant pleasure by arranging for reproduction through artificial insemination.

Those who would defend the claim that sexual desire aims naturally and primarily at reproduction might argue in the following manner: As reproduction is nature's aim, it is not at all necessary that those who experience sexual desire be conscious of its aim. (Schopenhauer holds that the species often realizes its purpose through the individual without the individual being aware of the real reason behind his desire.) They could go on to say that if there is more sexual desire in human beings than is necessary to realize the goal of reproduction, there is also the fact that, though sexual desire may be ever present, sexual opportunity is not because of social and personal restraints. Furthermore, any natural appetite may be abused. A man may eat far in excess of what is necessary to maintain his health and even thereby impair his health. That he can abuse his appetite for food does not mean that his desire for food does not aim naturally at nourishment. They could also point out that what seems like an excess of sexual desire may not be so if looked at in historical perspective. Such apparent excess may well be nature's way of restoring the human race after its reduction by plague or other catastrophe. It may also be nature's way of maintaining reproductive possibilities where there is an imbalance of men or women. As for the fact that science has now made it possible to bypass sexual intercourse in reproduction, they could argue that the sexual instinct is a much more reliable motivation than a conscious effort of will. A decision by human beings to reproduce may, for many reasons, never be taken; but, with the powerful inducement of sexual pleasure, the gratification of sexual desire is much more likely to insure continual reproduction.

B. General Controversy: Issues About the Relationship of Judgment and Tendency

The literature on love would be easier to analyze if all authors presented theories of the subject in which love is described and discussed as some form of desire, wish, impulse, want, or inclination: if all the authors thought of it as something tendential. The disputes about what love is would all then be confined to the questions of what kind of inclination love is and to questions of what the properties are that accompany that inclination. The whole discussion and dispute would be carried on in one area of discourse. Such, however, is not the case. The majority of writers consider love tendential. But there are a few for whom it is scarcely tendential at all; there are also some for whom it is a complex of the tendential and the nontendential. A dialectical analysis of the idea of love must encompass such conceptions as well and deal with the issues that turn on the relationship of judgment to tendency, of cognition to desire, of perception to inclination, of "thinking to feeling."

There are those who agree that mental judgment precedes desire but disagree as to whether the preceding judgment, the consequent desire, or their combination should be called love. We also find important differences of opinion about the function of judgment that precedes the actual inclination. Most authors say that we see or decide, and that our seeing or deciding *causes* us to want. But Freud, for example, denies that the impression that someone is attractive actually gives rise to a previously nonexistent desire. He affirms, rather, that love in the form of undirected "libidinal energy" exists prior to the settling upon a loved object. Judgment, rather than causing love, is merely the occasion for the release of previously undirected desire. Ortega argues, similarly, that the function of the will is not to originate but only to correct and control the existing forces in the psyche.

Among those who agree that judgment is part of love, there are somewhat comparable differences. In maintaining his theory of "crystallization," Stendhal claims that the lover's idea of the beloved becomes completely illusory through his imputation of many perfections to her. Scheler and Hartmann agree with Stendhal that the beloved appears to the lover as she appears to no one else. Yet, they differ strongly with Stendhal on the question of whether what the lover, and no one else, sees is unreal. For them, love enhances rather than impairs vision.

There are disagreements of an even more fundamental kind. We find a few authors who insist that the judgment involved in love follows rather than precedes desire. Spinoza is probably the best example of an author who asserts that we do not desire something because we judge it in a certain way; we judge it in a certain way because we desire it. William James, in accordance with his theory of the "will to believe," also argues that a judgment about a beloved is more a consequence than a cause of a desire. Stendhal has it both ways. He says that there are judgments that precede and give rise to desire, as well as judgments that follow and are influenced, if not determined, by that desire. Scheler suggests that perception is inherent in and part of the very tendency that is love, rather than something sharply distinguished from it. This point is, to some extent, present in Fromm's theory when he discusses love as a way of knowing rather than something determined by knowledge. On the relationship of judgment to tendency, we find a wide and complex range of different opinions.

Disregarding for the moment the distinctions between the various kinds of judgment and the distinctions between the various kinds of tendency, the disagreements on this relationship can be divided into two groups. In the first group, the authors are more or less in agreement on the existential relationship of judgment to tendency, but disagree on how to understand that relationship and the elements that compose it; and this disagreement is sometimes reflected in what they choose or do not choose to call love. In the second group, the authors are in actual disagreement about the relationship of judgment to desire; and this disagreement is sometimes reflected in what they have to say about what love is. We say "sometimes reflected" in both cases because we have found no necessary and general correlation between an author's view of judgment in relation to desire and his conception of love.

1. *Is judgment a part of love?*
a. *When judgment is a cause of desire, is it a part of love?*

For most of the theorists on love, judgment precedes and gives rise to desire. A potential lover is "struck" by someone else (or a quality the other possesses) and the favorable impression is followed by some desire in regard to that person. This sequence, with the temporal priority of the cognitive to the tendential, is admitted as a matter of course by most of the authors from Plato to Reik. Though in existential agreement on this point, they still differ in their conceptions of love. Some say that love is primarily the perception or the judgment and not its tendential consequences; others say that it is a combination of the judgment and the desire; and still others (the large majority) say that love is exclusively a matter of tendency and that whatever awareness, perception, or judgment precedes (or even accompanies) the desire, impulse, or inclination they call love is no part of what they conceive love to be.

Some of these differences no doubt are explicable in terms of linguistic convenience, but some of the positions are necessitated by the authors' views of man's psyche. Without too much difficulty one can see why René Descartes and David Hume are obliged to conceive of love primarily as a matter of cognition rather than tendency. For both of them, thoughts are the only psychological realities. That is to say, their definition of love is necessitated by their view of the relationship between thinking and feeling. For Descartes, tendencies or feelings are merely confused thoughts; similarly, for Hume, impressions or feelings differ from ideas only in intensity. For both of these authors, the difference between the spheres of judgment and tendency is one of degree, not of kind. Both, therefore, present theories of love controlled by their prior tenet that tendencies are species of thoughts expressed or observed in a different way. Hence, love is to be understood as intellectual judgment. To call love a feeling or an emotion would amount to calling it a judgment, since all feelings and emotions are not only caused by judgments but *reducible* to them. Thus, if love is psychological, it must be something basically cognitive.

Authors who do not classify feelings, emotions, and desires as species of thought, identify love, on the whole, as more a matter of tendency than thought. Although some of these authors will admit cognitive aspects to their conceptions of love, there is almost unanimous agreement among them that the locus of love is in the sphere of tendency rather than that of judgment.[7] To the extent that these two groups of authors, regarding the same phenomena, arrive at different conceptions of love because of differences in psychological outlook, the dispute between them about the nature of love resolves itself into a dispute about the nature of man.

Of those who disagree with Descartes and Hume and place the emphasis on tendency rather than on judgment, some are obliged to do so for reasons inherent in their theories as a whole. This observation applies particularly to those who ascribe to love a cosmic dimension. If everything in the universe does whatever it does because of love or because of inherent propensities to do this or that, it is understandably difficult to call love a matter of judgment; many of the things said to love—stones, plants, particles of matter—do not possess the capacity for cognition, perception, or judgment. Yet, if both stones and men are said to love (in the same or an analogous sense of the word), what love is must be something of which both stones and men are capable. That something can only be tendency. It is no accident that we do not find natural human love discussed as a cognitive phenomenon within the cosmic theories propounded by authors such as Plato, Augustine, Aquinas, Dante, Castiglione, Freud, Plotinus, Ficino, and Pico. These authors do not even include a cognitive aspect in their conceptions of human love.[8]

Though the presence of a cosmic dimension in a theory of human love would seem to preclude a conception of it as thought, the absence of such a dimension (judging from the literature) does not imply anything about the presence or absence of cognitive notions in a conception of human love. In other words, some of those who do not propound a cosmic theory include a cognitive aspect in their conceptions of love and some do not.

Reik, for example, emphatically denies that love has a cosmic dimension. In fact, he is the only author who explicitly maintains that love is a term that has meaning only when applied to a human relationship. (Some others confine their discussion to human love but do not explicitly affirm that love can occur only among human beings.) Yet, even though he thinks of love as exclusively human, it is not the presence of judgment that

[7] An illuminating exception on this point is Vladimir Solovyev. Though he agrees that thoughts and feelings are different in kind, he nevertheless maintains that the essential element in love is respect rather than one or another kind of desire.

[8] The only author who has a cosmic theory of love and yet admits of a cognitive aspect in his conception of love among human beings is Sorokin. The core of his conception remains, however, the generic notion of the inclination toward union and harmony, which Sorokin says permeates both the inanimate and animate.

distinguishes it from nonhuman phenomena, but a certain complex of desires in a certain sequence of which only human beings are capable.

Hartmann, on the other hand, though he discusses love in terms of the same human relationships as Reik, nevertheless insists, unlike Reik, on a cognitive element as part of love itself and not merely as a preface to it. Both Reik and Hartmann affirm that love exists in a certain, specified relationship between a man and a woman. This relationship is characterized by the presence of a definite complex of desires, of which the essential one is benevolence. They further agree that, prior to the emergence of this complex of desires, the lover perceives something admirable in the beloved that attracts him. Reik, while laying great stress on the importance of that perception, nevertheless does not conceive of it as part of love. Hartmann does include it as part of his conception.

This clear difference about what love is could become a real disagreement if Reik were to maintain that there is no need to include the cognitive aspect of the process described above in order to distinguish it from all other phenomena. He would have to say that the characteristic complex of tendencies to which he refers is, in itself, unique; and, hence, there is no need to include the notion of its intellectual and originating cause as part of the very conception of love. Hartmann, on the other hand, would be obliged to counter that the complex of desires in a personal love relationship could also occur in a nonlove relationship not caused by a certain kind of judgment. He would argue, accordingly, that the notion of the judgment itself must be included in the conception of love in order to distinguish love from nonlove. As neither Reik nor Hartmann maintain these respective positions, we cannot judge whether the verbal difference between them does or does not reflect this real disagreement.

We do find, however, a real disagreement between these two authors which may well underlie the difference in their conceptions of love. That disagreement has to do with the character of the admiration that each says precedes the desires of love. For Reik, the admiration connected with love is a judgment about the person as he is; for Hartmann, the approbative judgment bears rather on the potential person, on the person as he or she might be. Reik's admiration is of the *actual* beloved; Hartmann's of the *ideal* beloved.

Reik holds that the lover must feel inferior vis-à-vis an actual person. He must admire her for what she has and he lacks, envy her, and then overcome his envy through a desire for complementary union, a desire directed initially to fulfilling his own deficiency. Through this union, the lover begins to feel tenderness and benevolence toward his beloved. They share a common destiny; his efforts, accordingly, are directed to the welfare of both parts of a whole. The benevolence he feels is less connected with the admiration he has for the beloved than with the fact that they are now united. Reik makes clear, in his discussion of the psychogenesis of love, that, at the point when the lover begins to care about the beloved for her sake, the admiration that originally drew his attention is far less pronounced, if present at all.

On this point, Hartmann's view is different. He sees a necessary connection between the lover's admiration and his benevolent desire, both before this desire arises and during the period it operates; the lover's benevolence is strictly dependent on the continued presence of admiration. The difference here is traceable to Hartmann's understanding of that judgment. In Hartmann's theory, as in Reik's, the original focus of attention of the lover on the beloved is admiration for the actual person. When love begins to stir, and perhaps even before, Hartmann argues that the lover begins to "see" beyond the existing person to his ideal personality and to be attracted to the existing person in terms of that ideal personality. That original and enduring attraction takes the form of benevolence, since the lover's characteristic desire is to aid the beloved in the achievement of his ideal personality.

The kind of admiration that Hartmann postulates, admiration for "the ideal in the empirical," produces the valuation, "the anticipation of the ideal," which gives rise to benevolence. For these are judgments about what *could be* for the other. The creative benevolence at the core of his conception of personal love, therefore, is integrally connected with and dependent upon the kind of admiration that precedes it and sustains it. (Brotherly love, which rests on respect rather than on admiration, in Hartmann's view, does not involve a productive benevolence but merely an ameliorating one—the attempt to ease the lot of other human beings; such love does not involve a vision of what others ideally might become.)

On the other hand, the result of the kind of admiration that Reik postulates is the valuation that leads to acquisitive desire. (In addition, Reik points out that such admiration may not lead to any inclination at all.) This kind of admiration is of the person as he or she is and does not point directly to a hoped-for change in the other. Only later, after the complementary union between lover and beloved has been realized, does Reik think benevolence emerges, a benevolence that can endure after the original admiration has faded or disappeared.

In view of the fact that both authors agree that benevolence is essential to love, we can understand the difference in their conceptions of love in terms of their differing conceptions of the judgment preceding that desire. For Hartmann, the admiration of the ideal and the particular kind of benevolence that he understands to be part of personal love are inseparable. Thus, he includes the notion of admiration as an aspect of his conception of love. For Reik, the admiration of the real and the benevolence that he sees as part of the love between a man and a woman are, though causally connected, existentially separable. Thus, he excludes the notion of admiration as an aspect of his conception of love.

A similar issue arises in comparing the conceptions of natural love among human beings advanced by Aristotle and by Kierkegaard. Both of these authors hold that there are loves that are essentially acquisitive desire and other loves in which benevolence is the indispensable element. They agree, further, that certain mental preferences of the lover give rise to these inclinations. Yet, Aristotle does not make those preferences or judgments part of his conception of love, whereas Kierkegaard does.

A key to the reason for this conceptual difference can be drawn from the fact that neither of these authors says that all desires are forms of love. In particular, they never mention an acquisitive desire, the fulfillment of which involves harming another, as a form of love. They both readily concede that self-love involves using someone else, but apparently draw the line between acquisitive desires that are love and those that are not in terms of the difference between use and harm. For both, love precludes deliberate harm of the other.[9] Aristotle makes this point tendentially, whereas Kierkegaard makes it cognitively.

For Aristotle, any love relationship involves some giving. In the friendship of virtue, what is given is given for the other's sake. In the friendships of pleasure and utility, what is given is given as an exchange. Yet in both cases the good of the other is not neglected. In love, simple acquisitive desire of any sort, and certainly desires that involve harming the other, are precluded. What the friendship of virtue and the friendships of utility and pleasure have in common is the desire to give, through benevolence in the former case and through mixed acquisitive desire in the latter. Though the friendship of virtue presupposes high mutual admiration, the friendships of utility and pleasure do not. Therefore, the cognitive notion of esteem is not part of Aristotle's general conception, since there are types of friendship which he says can exist without it.

For Kierkegaard, on the other hand, natural love need not involve giving. The only thing that love precludes is harming someone else; it need not involve any effort to enhance the welfare of the other. But since getting without giving is a possible form of love for Kierkegaard, what is it that, added to simple, direct acquisitive desire, precludes harming another in an act of love? For Aristotle, such harm is precluded by the fact that the acquisitive desire in the lower forms of friendship is mixed. In the acts of

---

[9] For Aristotle, love also precludes harming the self for the sake of the other. This is not so for Kierkegaard, who speaks of self-sacrifice as a possible corollary of natural benevolence.

self-love where the goals are pleasure or utility, one must give in order to get; both parties must gain something. Kierkegaard makes the distinction between acquisitive desires that are forms of love and those that are not in a different manner. He makes it in terms of esteem. Every desire that can be called love must be accompanied by admiration. This is so for Kierkegaard, whether the desire be benevolent or acquisitive; admiration is part of all "earthly" or natural love. Presumably, in his view, it is impossible to harm whomever one admires. Thus, the function served by giving in Aristotle's binary theory is served by admiration in Kierkegaard's. Natural benevolence clearly presupposes some sort of esteem; if the person whom one tries to help did not possess some kind of intrinsic worth, there would be no reason for helping him for his own sake. But, though acquisitive desire as such does not presuppose esteem, Kierkegaard maintains that only such desires as are combined with esteem may be called love.

In this way and for these reasons the theories of Aristotle and Kierkegaard differ. Both agree that tendencies or desires are preceded (and even caused) by certain judgments. Yet, for Aristotle, those judgments are no part of love itself, and for Kierkegaard, they are necessarily a part of the very essence of love. Each restricts the range of love as acquisitive desire for the same reason, yet each does so through the use of different notions.

b. *When judgment is a correlative of desire, is it a part of love?*

The authors who are party to the immediately preceding issues are agreed on the phenomena to the extent that they all affirm that judgment *precedes* tendency. They disagree on the question whether or not judgment is a part of love. The same conceptual question arises among those authors who agree existentially that judgment *accompanies* tendency.

Most of the authors who say that a certain judgment precedes desire also say or imply that such judgment remains when the desire comes into being and continues as long as the desire remains—that the judgment accompanies as well as precedes the desire. That act of approval is, in their opinion, distinct from the tendency they call love. However important cognitive notions are for understanding their full theories of love, they are no part of their conceptions of what love is. Thus, for Plato, the perception of a beautiful person both arouses and sustains a desire for that person. Yet only the desire is called love. The case is the same for many of the authors holding tendential theories of love, whether they are binary or not.

Three authors advance theories of love in which the relationship between the judgment accompanying desire and the desire itself is conceived differently. They are Scheler, Hartmann, and Fromm. For these authors, it is something obvious to say that one must be aware of someone else as attractive before one feels any desire toward him. For them, the much more revealing and important characteristic of cognition in relation to love is the lover's unique perception of the beloved. For each of these authors, this unique perception is made possible by and closely associated with the tendency of love. It certainly accompanies that tendency, and all of them consider it part of love itself.

In each theory there is a considerable amelioration, though not a complete obliteration, of the sharp distinction between a judgment or perception and a desire. In Scheler's theory, what he calls the movement toward value is distinguished from thought, on the one hand, and from emotion, on the other. Yet, some perception of value is a real part of that movement. For Hartmann, also, the perception of the beloved is not strictly a cognitive function. He calls it a kind of "emotional understanding." Fromm, too, thinks of the knowledge of the beloved gained by the lover as something more than, or something different from, a strictly mental perception.

It is clear that the inclusion of cognition in the conceptions of love advanced by authors such as these is explicable in terms of the very close existential relationship they see between what the mind sees and judges and what the whole person inclines toward. The "seeing" or choosing which is part of love not only is simultaneous with and dependent upon that inclination but is one that differs radically from other perceptions or judgments. For all these authors, love opens the eyes of the lover in a way that nothing else can. The lover, therefore, sees in the beloved what others do not see or sees the same things differently; he gets a unique and privileged view, different from the ordinary ones present in most human relationships. Thus, it is not the lover who is deceived but the rest of the world. These authors base this position on their rejection (at least as it relates to love) of the traditionally sharp distinction between thinking and feeling. For them, feeling is part of seeing and seeing is part of feeling; the two somehow blend into each other.

Many of the other authors who say that a mental act not only occasions love but accompanies and sustains it deny, at least by implication, that the distinction between perceiving or judging and desiring can be blurred. For these authors, thinking is one thing and desiring another. Many of them concede that the lover's judgment can be and often is affected by intense desire, particularly sexual desire. But love remains, for them, a combination of elements from two distinct spheres. Nor, for most of these authors, does the inclination of love or any other inclination offer, as part of itself, a privileged view of the beloved. On the contrary, most of them warn against being influenced by "passion" and advocate self-control and the most disinterested and searching examination of the beloved as precaution against blind impulses.

c. *When judgment is a consequence of desire, is it a part of love?*

Of the authors who agree that there is a judgment that is not the occasion but the consequence of a desire, some include that judgment in their conceptions of love and some do not. Spinoza is prominent among those who do, whereas Andreas, Schopenhauer, Freud, and Ortega are prominent among those who do not. Spinoza does not claim, in any significant sense, that judgment either causes or occasions a desire. What he does stress is that there is a judgment that follows and is determined by desire and suggests that this is the only judgment the lover makes. For the others, there are judgments preceding the specific desires called love, as well as judgments influenced by those desires. This difference of opinion on the phenomena themselves assumes some importance in the discussion of the next issue. Here, however, we are concerned only with explaining conceptual differences despite an agreement, up to a point, on the existential relationship of judgment and desire.

For Spinoza, desire is the attempt on the part of everything to "persist in its own being." It is "nothing else but man's essence, from the nature of which necessarily follow all those results which tend to its preservation." The fulfillment of some desires is pleasurable and of others, painful; the former perfect and the latter destroy. Love is "pleasure, accompanied by the idea of an external cause."[10] Whether such a cause is adequately or inadequately understood, love always presupposes consciousness. But consciousness for Spinoza means being aware, to some extent, of some referent for the pleasure one experiences. The pleasures that are not accompanied by such an awareness (the results of instinctive inclinations) are excluded from the realm of love. Spinoza uses a notion from the sphere of judgment or cognition to distinguish pleasure from love. He calls pleasure a primary emotion (along with desire and pain), while love is a secondary or derivative one. All love results in pleasure, but not everything that results in pleasure is love. By invoking the notion of valuation (anything deemed good is deemed "useful," *i.e.*, resulting in pleasure), Spinoza is able to give a greater degree of specificity to what he calls love.

Andreas and Schopenhauer also say that there is a judgment consequent upon and caused by the desire they call love, but they do not include that judgment in what they call love. Since the only love they discuss is based upon sexual desire, love is conceived by them as tendentially specific and hence distinct from tendency in general. Accordingly, they feel no need to

[10] William James might well be grouped with Spinoza here, as he defines love, at one point, as "the association of the agreeableness of certain sensible experiences with the idea of the object capable of affording them."

include in their conceptions a notion from the sphere of judgment to distinguish love from nonlove. Love aims at specific pleasures. What specifies love for Spinoza is not the character of the pleasure sought nor the nature of the object through which it is sought, since there are as many objects of love as there are objects capable of affording pleasure. Love is distinguished from pleasure when it is accompanied by the idea of an external cause. In short, Andreas and Schopenhauer distinguish love from nonlove in terms of tendency; Spinoza distinguishes them in terms of cognition.

Freud also distinguishes love from nonlove in terms of tendency, though he does not identify love, generically speaking, with a specific desire. Love encompasses all inclinations on the part of anything living to preserve and perpetuate itself; these inclinations of *eros* are distinct from those of *thanatos,* which are also inherent in a living being but which aim at its destruction. Though Freud, like Spinoza, affirms that human judgment is influenced or determined by desire, he does not include judgment in what he calls love. He does not regard the realm of love as limited by consciousness. Even the instinctive, biological efforts of the organism to perpetuate itself are also part of the love instinct. Since Spinoza admits that all desire is motivated by such an instinct, Freud could argue that Spinoza's limitation of love by consciousness is arbitrary.

Spinoza would no doubt reply that though everything does strive to preserve its own being, the desires of love point toward something more than pleasure, toward perfection, happiness, and "blessedness." For him, these can be achieved only through an intellectual love of God. Spinoza hesitates somewhat at using the term "pleasure" to describe this love, and, in any case, he distinguishes it from the love among human beings. But he does say that both are love and undoubtedly includes a cognitive notion in his conception of human love in order to explain the highest love of which he thinks human beings are capable. The love of God is a purely intellectual activity aiming at the "contentment of spirit, which arises from the intuitive knowledge of God." If such love is the paradigm of all love, all love must be to some degree conscious and cognitive.

2. *When judgment or perception is a part of love, is it a cause or consequence of desire?*

There is one overriding issue among the authors who say that love has a cognitive aspect and yet differ sharply on the existential relationship of judgment to tendency. The question on which these authors disagree can be stated most simply as follows: When human beings love, do they desire what they approve of or do they approve of what they desire? In other words, is judgment a cause or occasion of desire, or is desire a cause or occasion of judgment?

Three authors who may be taken as representative of the different positions on this question are C. S. Lewis, Spinoza, and Stendhal. Lewis affirms that there is a cognitive aspect to love but says that the judgment occasions and accompanies the desire. Spinoza affirms that there is a cognitive aspect but that the desire causes the judgment. Stendhal holds that there is a cognitive aspect but that there are two kinds of judgments, one causing desire and one that desire causes. All three agree that love implies consciousness.

The crux of their disagreement turns on their different views of the relationship of mind to body. Spinoza takes the most explicit stand on this relationship. In his theory of natural love among human beings, the mind does not originate motion; it is passive to the extent that it is affected by and aware of bodily movements and refers the pleasure or pain accompanying those movements to an external cause. However, the mind is not powerless. It progressively can gain control over the passions and lusts of the body through understanding. Only through understanding God can the mind become active rather than passive. Yet, its activity does not consist in originating tendencies but in controlling and channeling those presented to it by the body. Knowledge alone gives it this kind of power. Will is defined by Spinoza as the mind's consciousness of its own endeavor to control passion rather than as a separate faculty. Hence, in Spinoza's theory, it is the body that presents the tendential material that the mind is able to channel into virtuous activity.

Such is not the case for Lewis (nor, for that matter, for any of the authors who affirm that the mind is capable, to some extent, of determining its own tendencies as well as those of the body). In discussing friendship, Lewis makes it clear that mutual admiration is not only an integral part of this love but is that which makes possible and sustains the benevolent inclinations friends have for each other. Friends do not admire each other in order to rationalize their benevolent impulses; they care about each other because they admire each other. Lewis goes to some length to ridicule the notion that such benevolence is a form of sublimated sexual desire. It is not the body that originates these particular tendencies that the mind must find outlet for in either their original or disguised forms. In friendship, the rational principle originates and determines actions. Even in the love between a man and a woman, Lewis declares that sexual impulses must come after approval of the other human being as a person and not merely as a vehicle for the fulfillment of sexual desire. He admits that sexual desire can occur without the element of appreciation, but he does not call this love because he thinks such unmixed desire is indiscriminate. It seeks a woman, not this woman. The first stages of "falling in love" have, in Lewis' view, little to do with sexuality. They have to do, rather, with an "unspecified preoccupation" with the beloved, which grows into admiration and matures into a choice from which tendential consequences—both acquisitive and benevolent—flow. Desire need not follow judgment, but it can; and, in matters of love, it must.

Stendhal, analyzing love as a series of stages, mentions certain admiring judgments made by the lover which lead up to the decisive step when he is drawn toward the beloved. Those judgments, called respectively by him "admiration" and "loving admiration," occasion that desire; the desire does not occasion them. Stendhal even says that the process can be stopped before the desire arises, though it cannot be stopped after the desire arises. At that point, the process shifts. Now, instead of certain mental acts causing a desire, the desire in what he calls "passion love" causes and determines the subsequent evaluations of the beloved by the lover. His passion literally forces him not only to judge the beloved again and differently but to judge her as perfect, to impute to her, through a process Stendhal calls "crystallization," every flattering attribute he possibly can. Now, the lover judges the beloved as he does because he wants her.

The point at issue among these three authors is specific. Very few authors would deny, particularly in the love between a man and a woman or between a mother and a child, that the lover's evaluation of the beloved *can* be influenced, occasioned, or changed by desire or instinct, and that it is often thus affected. Whether or not this must always be the case is the point at issue. And on this issue, Stendhal stands with Lewis and against Spinoza in affirming that there are undetermined judgments which are part of love, and which preexist and cause the tendential part of love—the actual desires of the lover.

The argument against the position taken by Spinoza might take the following form: If we always approve of what we desire rather than desire what we approve of, what is it that directs our desires to one object rather than another? Even those (*e.g.,* Freud and Ortega) who say that specific desires are formed of preexisting psychic energy, which the mental apparatus only releases but does not originate, still affirm that such energy is directed to specific objects by that apparatus and in no other way. They still ascribe to it some directive function which precedes the desire's taking its final form, though such a directive function may not be free but determined by the structure of the psyche. If we always approve of what we desire, then thoughts and judgments are nothing but the mental residue or record of autonomous impulses that operate by preexisting plan, by instinct, or contain in themselves a species of perception that guides their movement in regard to objects.

Spinoza's answer to this argument is suggested in his reference to love both as an emotion and as a mode of thought. It is an emotion insofar as its essence is nothing but the endeavor to persist in its own being, *i.e.,* to seek pleasure. It is a mode of thought insofar as the mind is conscious of its own endeavor. Though Spinoza's theory of natural love is primarily a tendential one, there is a sense in which he, like Descartes, describes the same phenomena both analytically and existentially. Analytically, the mind's endeavor and its consciousness of its own endeavor are separable. Existentially, they are either not distinct or occur simultaneously. This also holds for the mind in relation to the body. Hence, though the mind does not guide the body in the sense that it originates motion, it is conscious of many bodily movements and inclinations. These inclinations, to the extent that the mind is conscious of them, are not blind. Spinoza's view of why these inclinations go in a certain direction rather than another is deterministic. He asserts that *"all things are conditioned to exist and operate in a particular manner by the necessity of the divine nature."*[11]

C. Special Controversy: Issues About the Properties of Love

All the issues so far treated in this chapter are variations on the question—What is love? Issues as to whether or not respect is part of love, whether sexual desire, benevolent desire, or the desire for union are essential to love all fall into the general rather than the special controversy. In the first phase of the general controversy, the primary issues were about the possibility of benevolence and its relationship to love. In those issues, as well as in the other issues dealt with in that phase, the authors share a general agreement that love is tendential, but disagree on the character or scope of the tendencies they call love. In the second phase of the general controversy, the issues were about the relationship of judgment to tendency and the relationship of both to love. All of these issues are part of the general controversy, because the parties to them advance conflicting definitions of love or claims about its nature.

The issues to be dealt with here in the special controversy are of a different character. Parties to these issues are not in disagreement about the nature of love but, rather, about some of the properties of the loves that they discuss and describe in their theories as a whole. Thus, two authors may be in full agreement in the general controversy that love and sexual desire are coextensive, and yet be in disagreement in the special controversy on other matters—on how this desire arises, on whether (in order to be

[11] *The Ethics,* Part I, Prop. XXIX, p. 68.

love) it must be between members of the opposite sex, on whether such a desire naturally aims at pleasure, procreation, or both, etc. Similarly, two authors may agree in the general controversy that what is essential to love is benevolence. They may agree even further that the most typical form of such love is that of the parent for the child. Yet, in the special controversy, one may claim that there is no important difference between the father's and the mother's loves. The other, on the contrary, may say that, though the father's and the mother's loves are benevolent in character, the former is, as a rule, mild and conditional, while the latter is, usually, intense and unconditional. The following are some of the more typical issues about the properties of love:

1. *How many others can or should be loved by one person?*

The questions of the number of those who can or ought to receive love from one person are seldom neglected by those who propound theories of love. The answer each author gives is often a good indicator of the kind of love he is discussing. When an author talks about one and only one beloved, he is, almost always, talking about love between a man and a woman. When he mentions more than one object of love but less than many, he usually is talking about familial bonds or of the fondness among tested and trusted friends. When a love that is universal in scope is mentioned, it is frequently described as a disposition on the part of one person to help all of his fellowmen insofar as he can. Despite the frequency of these correlations, we do find disagreements among authors who are discussing the same type of love on the questions of how many can or should receive love.

a. *Is exclusivity desirable in sexual love?*

Of those who agree that love, or a type of love, is essentially sexual desire, some differ sharply on the question of how many persons one may, or should, love at the same time. None of these authors would contest the fact that more than one love (*i.e.*, sexual) relationship can be carried on simultaneously, nor would they refrain from calling such relationships "love," but, for some of them, there is a marked inclination to focus on the exclusive love relationship as the normal or the best one.

For the writers on "courtly love," of whom Andreas can be taken as exemplary, anything other than exclusivity in the high form of love is unthinkable. The lover dotes on the beloved and yearns only for her; his fidelity is a point of honor attesting the purity and durability of his love. For Schopenhauer, the aim of sexual desire is animal procreation; hence, the love between a man and a woman lasts only until the aim is realized.

For a man, it ceases when he fulfills his function of impregnating the woman; he is then said to experience a complete "disillusionment." Prior to that, his desire is focused on one and only one woman "chosen" for him by the species. For a man, love comes and goes, but, while it is present, there is only one beloved. In Stendhal's view, the lover caught in the web of "passion love" finds it literally impossible to attend seriously to anyone or anything but his beloved.

Sexual exclusivity is argued for on many grounds, particularly by those authors who see love as involving components in addition to sexuality. For those who admit that there is a love that is basically sexual desire, the arguments for exclusivity are twofold. They say either that concentration on one and only one person as an object of sexual desire maximizes pleasure, or that such a relationship is most in accord with nature's procreative impulse. A man is attracted to a woman and a woman to a man in terms of the character of the potential offspring. Exclusivity, in other words, is dictated by what the union will produce and is perpetuated by the necessity for both male and female care of the offspring.

Plato affirms that there is a love relationship that is sexual, but denies that it should be an exclusive one. He does so because he understands the aim of homosexual love neither as pleasure nor as physical procreation. Plato construes this particular desire as a possible step in the ascent up the "ladder of love," the ascent from the physical to the spiritual. The young man ascending the ladder is to go through two stages of physical contact with beautiful bodies. In the first stage he has converse with one man only. But, in the second stage—the stage immediately before he leaves physical objects of love behind—the initiate has contact with a number of others. In Plato's view, such variety in sexual experience is better than exclusivity because it enables the initiate to see that the beauty that attracts him is not confined to one body; this insight is construed as capable of leading a young man on to a love of the spiritual beauty of the soul and, further, to a love of the eternal ideas. Plato advocates that the initiate experience a number of homosexual lovers because such variety should lead him on to a higher nonphysical love. If he experienced only one lover, presumably he would not be able to proceed up the ladder of love, or would find the transition from the physical to the spiritual much more difficult. For Plato, sexual desire involves pleasure and may involve procreation, but, as one step in an educational process, its principal aim is neither.

b. *How many should be loved benevolently? How many can be so loved?*

The disagreement about the desirable number of objects of sexual desire has its parallel among those who say that benevolence is indispensable to love. The parallel is not exact, however, since exclusivity is never advocated when human love is conceived as benevolent desire. Authors who consider benevolence essential to love differ among themselves on the question of whether human benevolence should be confined to some persons or be universal. Those who propound theories of supernatural love among human beings all agree that such love should be universal. But, with regard to natural love among human beings, there are disagreements.

Aristotle, in his discussion of the friendship of virtue, limits the extension of human care and concern to those who are worthy of it. A man is not a true friend, deserving of an undeviating benevolence, unless he is virtuous. The respect one human being has for another simply because he is human is sufficient grounds for occasional benevolence, but a continually benevolent disposition toward another person presupposes a high admiration for him. Adam Smith takes a similar position. Though Smith emphasizes that the high form of friendship characterized by benevolence is not limited to two persons, he does limit, with equal emphasis, such friendships to the wise and virtuous; in any case, to far fewer than all men.

Such is not the case of Sorokin and Fromm. Benevolence is not something that another person earns or merits. All men, in their views, are worthy of benevolence simply in virtue of being human regardless of their particular virtues or vices. The high standard of a love of all men by all men is proposed by Sorokin as unique therapy for many social ills, particularly war. He deplores any individual or group partiality when it comes to human concern for other human beings. Group partiality only increases the antagonism for those outside the group. The solution is to make love more and more "extensive," to include more and more people within the scope of one's benevolence until, finally, all are included. Fromm also stresses the importance of a universal "brotherly love" which, in his view, underlies all other loves. Brotherly love consists in a willingness or disposition to help all human beings. Fromm points out that there is an apparent conflict between this love and the exclusiveness of "erotic love," but denies that the conflict is real. He even maintains that it is impossible for a man truly to love a woman if it is only she whom he loves. Such an attachment is only an "egoism *a deux*," merely a form of collective or enlarged selfishness. The universality of brotherly love and the exclusivity of erotic love can be reconciled only when the lover loves all of humanity through his beloved, when, despite his unique relationship with her, he does not single her out to the extent that she monopolizes all of his affections; he must see her as a symbol of humanity. In this way, Fromm argues that an erotic attachment that has indifference to the rest of mankind as its corollary is not real love. Either someone loves all men, in some sense, or he loves no one.

Kierkegaard is in full agreement with both Sorokin and Fromm on the extent of ideal human love. Where he differs from them is in denying that a universal benevolence is naturally possible. To achieve such a range of benevolence, supernatural aid is required. Hence, for Kierkegaard, however far natural benevolence may be extended, it will always fall short of universality. It is beyond man's natural capacity to engender a benevolent affection for those who are either remote or hostile. Freud, who includes a type of love characterized by benevolence in his theory of love, also argues along this line in attacking the idea of a natural universal benevolence. He does not, like Kierkegaard, talk in terms of an ideal, supernaturally-aided love, but he does agree with Kierkegaard that talking about a natural universal benevolence is unrealistic. In his view, it is unrealistic for two reasons. First of all, only what is known and, to some extent, familiar can excite benevolence. One cannot feel benevolence for amorphous multitudes with whom one has no contact and with whom one shares nothing but the common destiny of being a "denizen of the earth." Such a thin bond of identity can excite little or no real disposition to act for another for his own sake.[12] Aristotle reinforces this assault upon the idea of a universal natural benevolence when he makes a distinction between mere "goodwill" and benevolence. He concedes that it is possible to be well-disposed toward relative strangers or even toward those whom one knows only through hearsay. But he sharply distinguishes goodwill from what he calls love since, for him, such goodwill does not readily incline one to beneficent action. It costs little to wish others well, but such a wish must be distinguished from an actual willingness to act on their behalf. In his view, only the latter should be called love.

Sorokin and Fromm might answer this attack by pointing out that the actual implementation of the ideal of universal benevolence is obviously impossible if such an ideal is interpreted literally. One man cannot benefit directly all other men since he comes into contact only with some of them. They (especially Fromm) could argue that universal benevolence does not mean an actual desire to act on behalf of any and all. But it does mean that there is a benevolence, potentially inclusive, which is actualized with any and all men with whom one comes into contact. Such benevolence may, in effect, be partial, due to human limitations; but it is universal in the sense that it does not deliberately involve discrimination between one man and another.

The point about the importance of discrimination made by Aristotle and Adam Smith is reiterated by Freud. Freud says that "If I love someone he must be worthy of it in some way or other." Loving those who have not

---

[12] See *Civilization and Its Discontents*, Ch. V, pp. 56 ff.

shown themselves worthy of benevolence is not only unrealistic but unjust. A man is indiscriminate if he bestows benevolence both upon those who are his friends and have tried faithfully to advance his interests and upon those who are either indifferent to his interests or hostile to him. Love, in short, must be earned, and simply being human is not sufficient inducement.

There is one author, Hartmann, who takes both sides of this issue by distinguishing between two kinds of benevolence, or rather between the kinds of goods at which each kind of benevolence aims. Hartmann mentions both the "love of the nearest" and the "love of the remotest." The former includes "brotherly love," a love that is essentially benevolent and a love, like those of Sorokin and Fromm, that is universal in scope. This love, however, has as its concern the empirical personalities of those loved. It is directed to the fulfillment of their actual needs as they experience them. It consists in the effort to relieve the immediate distress of all those whom one is able to help without regard to their qualities as human beings. The "love of the remotest," though also benevolent in tendency, is different in two respects. First, it is directed to the fulfillment of the potential of progress on the part of the race as a whole. Second, it is highly discriminating. Only a few—those who show a strong measure of human excellence and evoke admiration—are deemed worthy of it. It is extended only to individuals who are actually or potentially of great consequence in determining human history. Hartmann says that the two loves can and often do conflict. The "love of the nearest," directed as it is to the alleviation of misery, does little but "raise the fallen to the level of the average." It is even said to be a cause of "stagnation and regression," because it makes for a stultifying leveling. "Love of the remotest," however, springing as it does from inequality of worth, makes for progress. Hartmann denies that the conflict between the two loves is a serious one, however, because of the great disparity in their values. For him, the well-being of one's neighbor counts for little when measured against the "ideal value of humanity." Thus, if it is necessary to sacrifice one love for the other, the former must be sacrificed.

2. *Is love voluntary?*

To a very large extent the disagreement about the voluntariness of love is a byproduct of the position that the authors take on the question of free will. For some of them (*e.g.*, Freud and Spinoza) no act of love is free because no human act is free, *i.e.*, all are strictly determined by their preceding causes. But, even among those who affirm that man does possess the natural freedom of self-determination, there are some who say that certain aspects of human love are outside the sphere of the voluntary. Those who affirm that sexual desire is love or a type of love take it to be nonvoluntary in origin. Many of them think that it can be controlled or terminated indirectly by the action of an autonomous will, but no one says that a person can desire another sexually simply by willing it. Ortega insists that there is "choice" involved in whatever draws a man to a woman, but closer reading shows that he merely is emphasizing that the inclination toward one woman rather than another is not arbitrary and not that such an inclination is an expression of free will. In discussing friendship he does insist that there is an undetermined inclination toward another person, but regarding the acquisitive aspect of the love between a man and a woman he claims that the will is not originative but only corrective. Augustine claims that sexual desire was once a function of free choice—but, after man's fall in the Garden of Eden, it became involuntary.

The only real disagreement we have, then, in considering what authors say about volition in relation to love is among those who, agreeing that there is free will, disagree as to whether certain love inclinations (nonsexual acquisitive desires as well as benevolent ones) are or are not free.

We may take Aquinas as typical of those who assert that certain acquisitive and benevolent desires are free inclinations of the will. Kant opposes this view. For him, the most characteristically free inclinations of the will—those taken in obedience to the moral law—are matters of duty and not of instinctive or emotional tendency to which the will gives its assent. These latter actions are free in the sense that the will can cooperate with or oppose them, but they are not free in the sense that the will originates them. "Reason here occupies the place of a minister to natural inclination . . ." Such inclinations are acts of love precisely because they involve neither duty nor morality.

> *Love* is a matter of *feeling*, not of will or volition, and I cannot love because I *will* to do so, still less because I *ought* (I cannot be necessitated to love); hence there is no such thing as a *duty to love*.

Thus love is unfree in the sense that it is always an *influenced* inclination of the will. Whenever the will is the autonomous cause of its own action and whenever the will acts in accordance with the moral law, its actions are never instances of love. For Kant, "all duty is *necessitation* or constraint, although it may be self-constraint according to a law. But what is done from constraint is not done from love." When the will is completely free and when it is motivated solely by moral imperatives, it does not act out of love. Love, in a sense, must be spontaneous and not controlled by motivations of duty, obligation, or obedience to law. "Ought," which is the realm of freedom and "liking," which is the realm of love, are mutually exclusive.

The crux of the matter here would appear to be the question of whether or not one can ever be obliged to love. If love is subject to obligation, as Aquinas thinks it is, one must be free to love or not love. If love is unfree, in the sense of its being a matter of liking, emotion and feeling, as Kant thinks it is, it cannot be commanded. Thus, the marital vow according to which one promises to love would be acceptable to Aquinas but not to Kant. For Kant, one can promise to act in a certain way, but one cannot promise to love, *i.e.*, to feel like acting in that way.

Aquinas would not deny that there are involuntary inclinations, but he would insist that voluntary tendencies are also instances of love, even when they are matters of duty and even when they run counter to involuntary inclinations. He would insist on this, in part, because he has a different conception of morality than Kant. For Aquinas, natural morality aims at the perfection of men in all their faculties and has human happiness as its goal. It includes in its compass all natural tendencies, voluntary or not. Though blame can only be assigned to failures of will, all natural cupidities, however much error may occur in their prosecution, are inherently good. The perfectibility of man, which is the realm of morality considered broadly, must take account of them all. Morality must, therefore, look to experience for its prescriptions and proscriptions. It takes its bearings from the nature of man as that nature is discerned through reflection on human actions.

Kant counters that one cannot derive an "ought" from an "is." What men do is no guide to what they should do. Experience is, in fact, irrelevant. The only sure guide is the moral imperative which derives from the structure of the mind and is thereby rational and universal. It only can prescribe what all men should do. That such imperatives coincide with what men may want to do is happenstance. The inherent propensities of man to do this or that are instances of love but never can be said to be moral. An act is never judged to be moral or immoral by its consequences, by whether or not it results in greater or less happiness. An act is moral only if it is done in accordance with the principle of one's acting so that every other man may act in the same way, whatever the consequences of such action may be. Since every such action is completely different in motivation from those in which one is influenced by likes or dislikes, the former should not be called love. Love has to do with what a person wants to do, *i.e.*, what he is influenced to do through his experiences. Morality has to do with what a person ought to do regardless of his wants; it has to do with the inclinations of an autonomous will whose only motive is "a pure interest of practical reason alone, independent of sense."

3. *Does mutual benevolence presuppose equality or inequality?*

No author explicitly denies that both acquisitive and benevolent desire can occur between equals and unequals alike. There is, therefore, no general issue on this point. If, however, we limit the notions of equality and inequality to the matter of character or personality traits, we do find at least one dispute. The issue is between Reik, who explains the benevolence of friendship in terms of the complementary personalities of those who are parties to it, and several other authors who explain it in terms of the similar personalities of those who are parties to it. For Reik, it is imperative that friends be, to some extent, unequal; for the others, that they be, to some extent, equal.

Though Reik points out that friendship cannot occur between those who are markedly unequal, nonetheless, for him, the emergence of friendship presupposes differences rather than similarities in the parties involved. Like romantic love, or any love, friendship begins with the feeling of dissatisfaction with oneself vis-à-vis someone else. Friends are, originally, rivals or competitors. Each has something the other lacks. "As long as one person meets another and does not see him as a different individual with a different make-up, love is psychologically not possible." Friendship begins to arise when this feeling of rivalry turns into the acquisitive desire that the friend's qualities be added to one's own through association. Being united with a friend in this complementary way, in turn, gives rise to the benevolence essential to friendship. The differences in character remain throughout the friendship. One is not good to a friend because he is "another self"; one is good to him because certain of his traits constitute the desired complement to one's own personality.

The analysis of friendship is different for Aristotle and Adam Smith (as well as for Aquinas, Freud, and a number of others). These authors freely admit that friendships of sorts can and do occur between unequals. But they always refer such friendships to the most typical form of friendship that occurs between equals, of which all others are variants. Benevolence occurs in friendship because one friend sees in another an image of himself and thus is able to transfer the care and attention he normally expends on himself to the other person. The union between such friends is not one of complementarity but of similarity; their bond is based on their likeness not on their unlikeness to each other. Aristotle speaks of the likeness between friends in terms of virtue and common interests. For Smith, the likeness is broader. He mentions similarity in virtue as part of the highest kind of friendship, but such similarity is a function of "sympathy" or "fellow feeling," which is much wider in scope. According to Smith, love is the benevolent inclination arising from habitually sympathizing with the experiences and feelings of another. The condition presupposed is equality, not inequality.

Except for the appeal to experience, the argument between Reik and the other authors would probably center on the question of what kind of union is most consistent with benevolence. Aristotle and Smith would doubtless reject outright the notion that every kind of love, and especially friendship, must spring from some sort of resentment, envy, or competition. But here the argument would be conducted on grounds far afield from the subject of love and on grounds not entirely shared by both sides. There is more common ground on the question of union in relation to benevolence.

On this level, Reik, if he conceded that sympathetic identification with another person is possible, might argue that such identification really gives rise only to a vicarious selfishness and not to real benevolence. A desire is more clearly benevolent if the giving is to another who is not only different but, initially, also alien. Reik does not deny—indeed he affirms—that benevolence is in some way self-interested, and concomitant self-interest arises, in his view, because two human beings form a complementary whole, with each giving to the other something different because each part is different. They share the fruits of each other's benevolence because they share a common fate, not because one is a duplication of the other.

Smith confronts this argument directly. He argues that fellow feeling and sympathy do not consist in imagining oneself *as* someone else in detail. They consist, rather, in projecting into the situation of another who is sufficiently like oneself simply in virtue of sharing the same human fate. Thus, fellow feeling and sympathy do not presuppose a sense of similarity in terms of the total character of another person. They only presuppose enough similarity between human beings so that they can understand what the other is experiencing. Equality in this respect does not preclude inequality in many other respects.

Aristotle, because he insists on a strong similarity in character as the basis for benevolence, would be forced to argue differently. He could insist that the fact that benevolence derives in a certain way from self-love does not mean that such an inclination is any less truly benevolent. Since such benevolence is extended to those who have the same character and not only to those who share the same fate, a man may give something to his friend in which he has no personal interest at all, depending on the friend's wants and needs. In this sense, there is a radical difference between the love for "another self" and self-love.

Aristotle and Smith together might point out that the objection concerning the enlargement of the self can be made in connection with the union of complementarity as well as with the union of similarity. Reik maintains that the original impulse of the lover is to gain, through union, character traits that he lacks, would like to have, and that the other possesses. The beloved represents to him the part of his "ego-ideal" which he has been himself unable to achieve. The beloved then comes actually to replace the "ego-ideal." The beloved is the object of benevolence as a result of being the missing part of an imaginary and ideal self. If benevolence extended to an image of oneself is less than true benevolence, then why is not benevolence extended to an imaginary part of one's actual self less than true benevolence?

4. How does the gender of the participants affect the love relationship?
a. Is sexual desire between members of the same sex a form of love?

On the question of gender in relation to love we find few issues. There are two authors who agree that sexual desire is a form of love, but disagree whether such desire between men or women is a form of love. Both agree that homosexual desire is abnormal. Yet Freud is willing to call such desire love, whereas Andreas says emphatically that it is not.

The basis of Freud's position lies in his interpretation of homosexuality as a stage in the development of a person who eventually can become capable of a mature love. It is not abnormal in adolescence. An adult homosexual is one who has never advanced beyond this stage in psychic development. Such abnormal love is, for Freud, nothing but adolescent or infantile love. Yet he calls it a love precisely because it is, in normal development, one of the ways in which libidinal energy is expended upon an object. It does not, in itself, aim at the preservation of the individual or the procreation of the species (as Freud says all love does), but it can be called love because it leads to a love that does have such aims. Were the individual's development not arrested, he would have moved through the homosexual stage to the heterosexual one.

Andreas, in contrast, asserts that "two persons of the same sex are not at all fitted for giving each other the exchanges of love or for practicing the acts natural to it. Whatever nature forbids, love is ashamed to accept."[13] Andreas, of course, concentrates exclusively on courtly love between a man and a woman. But the fact that he chooses explicitly to exclude homosexual desire from the realm of love implies that he sees no generic connection between homosexual and heterosexual desire. In Andreas' theory, nature simply prohibits the former as a shameful deviation from love. Rather than leading to heterosexual love, it leads away from it.

[13] *The Art of Courtly Love*, Book I, Ch. II, p. 30.

b. *Is friendship between males the paradigm of all love relationships?*

No author says that friendship between a man and a woman is impossible. C. S. Lewis says that it is infrequent. Ortega thinks that it only is possible between a man and a woman if the woman sheds her femininity to some extent and takes on masculine characteristics. Though he does not say that friendship is or can be a substitute for love, Fromm maintains that love between a man and a woman is less frequent in contemporary society because of the attenuation of the differences between the sexes. Reik mentions a mature love between a man and woman as the culmination of the romantic love that interests him most, but does not make it clear whether this mature love is the equivalent of friendship. Certainly, none of these authors say that the love between a man and a woman ought to be a species of friendship.

Aquinas does say so, as does Aristotle. But the issue here is not as sharp as it seems. In fact, it is largely verbal, for, when Aquinas describes the friendship between a man and a woman, he describes a relationship that, essentially, is like that described by Lewis, Ortega, and Fromm; that is to say, he describes a complementary union of unequals in which each wishes the other well. Both Aquinas and Aristotle call this male-female relationship a species of friendship because they understand it as a form of the more typical friendship of a male-male relationship. That typical friendship has as one of its prime characteristics equality, symbolized by the participants' being of the same gender. How, then, can a male-female relationship of inequality be called a species of it?

Despite the fact that Aquinas sees the male-female relationship as one of superior to inferior, he argues that there is a sense in which inequality of gender does not preclude equality in another respect. For Aquinas, equality arises in marriage in the common devotion that both the man and the woman have to the furtherance of their union and to the care of their offspring. Though both parties are different and have different things to give to each other, they are equal in the sense that they are devoted to the same good, each giving what he can. The relationship thus approximates the typical friendship of equality and can be called friendship.

Aristotle makes the same point and develops it further. He not only says that equality is achieved through devotion to a common purpose but that an approximation to equality in all friendships involving unequals, including those of marriage, can be achieved through proportion:

> In all friendships implying inequality the love also should be proportional, i.e., the better should be more loved than he loves . . . for when the love is in proportion to the merit of the parties, then in a sense arises equality, which is certainly held to be characteristic of friendship.

If the issue between these two groups of authors is not merely semantic, it reduces to whether the love relationship of those equal in gender and in other ways is the pattern of all love relationships. Lewis, Ortega, and Fromm say that the common element in all loves is benevolence. They do not say that all loves are species of friendship, since, for them, friendship involves elements not present in other interpersonal loves. For Aquinas and Aristotle, all virtuous loves (of which marriage can and should be one) have not only benevolence in common but also, in some sense, equality, and therefore can be understood as different species of friendship.

In opposing Aristotle and Aquinas, Lewis, Ortega, and Fromm might argue that the asserted equality between man and wife is different from the equality present in the most typical form of friendship. In that friendship, not only is the gender of the friends the same but also their moral character, as well as the quality of their mutual love, since each gives the same thing to the other. In the love relationship of man and wife not only are the genders not the same but also the moral characters, as well as the quality of the love each has, since each gives something different to the other. To argue that equality is present because of the common devotion to the furtherance of the marital union or because of the proportionality of the love might seem, to these authors, an undue stretching of a point. In addition, it ignores what seems to be one of the most characteristic features of male-female love: the complementary union of unequals. It is more significant to point out that male-female love is built on the differences or inequalities between the sexes than on similarities or equalities, which are once removed from obvious equality. In their view, though male-female love has benevolence in common with friendship, it is not rightly understood as a species of friendship.

5. What brings love to an end?

No author claims that there is any form of natural love among human beings that cannot come to an end. Some loves are said to be capable of indefinite prolongation, but none is said to be immutable. What brings love relationships to an end is, however, an issue.

When love is conceived as acquisitive desire, springing from deficiency, such love terminates when the deficiency from which the desire springs is filled. (Here one must keep in mind Plato's notion of what constitutes a deficiency. A man may not only desire possession of something but continued possession of it. Hence, he can have something and still desire it acquisitively in the sense that he desires to retain it.) The differences concerning duration, then, among authors who conceive love or a love as acquisitive desire is directly reflected in their respective notions of what love as acquisitive desire seeks and how accessible its object is.

Though both Schopenhauer and Castiglione discuss one form of love as acquisitive sexual desire, they differ sharply on how long such love lasts. For Schopenhauer, the carnal appetite of a man for a woman ceases with the act of intercourse.[14] Though Castiglione admits that there is a momentary surcease, he argues that such a desire increases each time it is indulged, that sexual desire grows by what it feeds on. Their different opinions on the duration of such a love are direct consequences of their differing opinions on the aim of the desire. Both concede that genital pleasure is part of the incentive. But, for Schopenhauer, such pleasure is merely the way nature induces the individual male to fulfill his function in perpetuating the race. Whether the individual is aware of it or not, the aim of the desire is procreation; and such desire ceases in the male as soon as his procreative function is fulfilled. It may arise again but it will again have the same end, and it will again cease when that end is realized.

Castiglione does not think of procreation as the final aim of sexual desire. For him, sexual desire and a variety of other acquisitive desires called love have the possession and the enjoyment of the beautiful as their aim. As the consummation of sexual desire in intercourse is, for Castiglione, the least satisfactory way of enjoying beauty, the lover emerges from such experiences still full of desire. He has not gained in full measure what he lacks and seeks. The more he indulges his sexual desire the more he is conscious of his lack. Therefore, according to Castiglione, he must indulge such desire only in his youth and eventually abandon it. He must move through several stages up the ladder of love until he abandons the pursuit of beauty incarnate and pursues the spiritual beauty of the soul.

Castiglione might argue further against Schopenhauer that there is an integral connection between the pursuit of physical permanence (the perpetuation of the species) and the pursuit of spiritual immortality (the contemplation of the divine nature). As sexual desire is but one expression of the desire for permanence and the one least adequate to achieve it, sexual fulfillment does not end love. Sexual desire can and should be terminated in the sense that it can and should be transformed into desires for higher objects. But the mere fact of indulging sexual desire does not terminate it; on the contrary, it aggravates and increases such desire because the impulses of man's animal nature and his spiritual aspirations are all part of one pattern.[15]

[14] This is also true for Andreas. Were the courtly lover to consummate his sexual desire, his love would die.

[15] Because he thinks of male-female love as acquisitive and, in some measure, sexual or carnal, Stendhal can be considered a party to this issue. When love strikes, the lover seeks to perfect his beloved in his own eyes by imposing on her every sort of flattering attribute. His love cannot endure unless she is made perfect in his own eyes, for he can love only perfection. As his beloved is human and imperfect, the

If Schopenhauer were to oppose Castiglione, he would be forced to deny that sexual desire has any other aim or leads to anything other than procreation. He does not deny that the force of such desire can have tremendous effect on the thinking and judgment of the lover concerning the "exalted" love which he colors with "hyperphysical" clothing. But Schopenhauer is far from regarding exaltation as anything but a veil covering the strictly animal impulse to produce progeny. He appeals to experience in affirming that, after sexual fulfillment, the lover feels only disillusionment and indifference. His desire is gone because it has fulfilled its purpose. He construes that purpose as the perpetuation and the improvement of the species, not as personal immortality and certainly not as the enduring enjoyment of spiritual beauty.

On the side of benevolence we find no actual issue in regard to duration. Sorokin goes deepest into the matter, relating the duration of benevolence to its purity, extensity (or scope), intensity, and the degree to which it succeeds. However, the various assertions he makes concerning the duration of a love are not opposed directly in the literature. Cicero affirms that the benevolence of a virtuous person ceases, or rather should cease, when his friend shows himself to be unvirtuous. This view also is unopposed directly in the literature.

6. *Other points of possible disagreement*

There are several other properties on which authors, while agreeing on what love is, might disagree but do not actually do so. On the question of mutuality, Aristotle lays great stress on reciprocity, whether the love be acquisitive or benevolent desire. Yet he does not go so far as to say that unrequited desire is not, in some sense, love. We find in the literature mention of both one-sided and two-sided relationships, the latter covering relationships in which love is reciprocated in kind (friendship) as well as those in which love is reciprocated not in kind (mother and child). But in none of these discussions do we find any dispute among the authors—either with regard to acquisitive or benevolent desire—as to whether love is always or ought to be mutual.

There is a comparable absence of issue on the question of the age of those involved in a love relationship. Schopenhauer says that a man can only love from the age of puberty to the age of impotence. Anyone who holds, as he does, that love is sexual desire would hardly dispute the point.

---

reality, at some point, crushes his carefully nurtured illusion and the love ends. Here, however, the aim is not the achievement of immortality but the possession and enjoyment of someone perfect.

Plato only mentions benevolence on the part of an older and wiser man for a younger one. But he does not say that benevolence on the part of the younger for the older is impossible. In fact, no author denies that both acquisitive and benevolent desires are possible between almost any combination of ages. No author mentions an infant being benevolent to its parents, but, apart from such exceptions, the range is wide.

The same situation prevails concerning questions such as the proximity of lovers or their social status. Aristotle says that friends want to live together and share a common life, but he does not deny that friendship can endure and survive despite geographical separation. Andreas talks of the differences of love relationships in terms of the social classes of those involved, but the variations he discusses are largely matters of alterations in a lover's tactics. Either little is said about such matters by the authors or what little is said by them is not opposed by other authors.

We now turn, in the next chapter, to the disputes in the literature on supernatural love. Unlike the literature on natural love, the literature on supernatural love, or, rather, supernatural human love, contains disagreements that can be subsumed under one large controversy. That is to say, all the disagreements can be shown to be related aspects of a single theme. As the reader will see, the theme of that controversy not only has had a long history in religious literature but also is very much alive today.

3

The Controversy About
Supernatural Human Love

I n the previous chapter we were concerned with various controversies
about love among human beings in which superhuman power or influence was not affirmed to play a part. In this chapter the perspective
shifts in several ways. All the authors of the theories with which we are
here concerned hold that there is a supernatural realm; and they all claim
that there is a religious experience of love which is humanly impossible
without supernatural aid. In addition, the authors dealt with here invariably consider love among human beings as secondary and derivative.
As the principal lover or beloved, God is at the very focus of their theories.
Hence, it is really not possible to adhere strictly to the original limitation
laid down for this study: love among human beings. We have, however,
found it possible to concentrate on human love—whether such love be for
God or other humans—as it is affected by supernatural influence. Accordingly, we deal with God's love only to the extent that we must in order to
render intelligible an author's conception of supernatural human love.

We proceed as follows: First, we set forth the different ways in which
authors of theories of natural love and authors of theories of supernatural
love approach the subject. We also consider the main substantive distinc-

tion between all theories of natural love and all those of supernatural love. We then offer representative documentation for the principal positions taken in the literature on the nature of supernatural human love. Finally, we construct the controversy among the adherents of these positions by setting forth the arguments and counterarguments they advance.

As the reader will see, the controversy about supernatural human love reflects some of the differences between the Catholic and Protestant viewpoints. Those differences become clear, in a general way, when the position espoused by St. Augustine and Thomas Aquinas is compared with the position attributed to Martin Luther by Anders Nygren. However, all of the authors who are or could be parties to this controversy do not subscribe fully to one or the other of these positions. Within the Catholic tradition, men such as Miguel de Molinos and François de Fénelon hold views that are different, in important respects, from the traditional Church teaching on love. On the Protestant side, authors such as Søren Kierkegaard, Denis de Rougemont, C. S. Lewis, Reinhold Niebuhr, and Paul Tillich disagree, in different ways, with Nygren's sharp contrast between natural and supernatural love. In other words, between the position taken by Augustine and Aquinas, on the one hand, and the one taken by Nygren, on the other, there are gradations that underline the long history of theological differences about love.

Attempting to encompass all of the religious literature on Christian love not only goes far beyond the scope of this chapter but actually is unnecessary for our purposes. What we intend to do is highlight the central controversy about the nature of charity that pervades the whole literature. To do that, we believe, we need only present representative documentation of the principal positions that have been taken. As we see it, these basic positions recur, in a variety of forms, throughout the whole Christian literature, beginning with the interpretation of the Biblical revelation about love by John and Paul, through the writings of the early apostolic fathers, through the long tradition—inaugurated by Augustine—of reasoned explication of religious truths, through the meditations of Bernard of Clairvaux, Richard of St. Victor, and Bonaventure, through the medieval systemization of dogma that culminated in the work of Aquinas, through the efforts of Luther and other Reformation thinkers to show that the true import of Christ's teaching had been perverted by the attempt to harmonize faith and reason, through the counter-Reformation, and through the spirited modern renewals of the disputes that occurred within the Catholic tradition, as well as those that occurred between Catholics and Protestants.

In documenting the first position in the controversy, we think it is sufficient to present the views of Augustine and Aquinas, supplemented by a contemporary statement about charity from the *Dictionnaire de Théol-*

ogie Catholique. A presentation of the views of Fénelon and Bernard of Clairvaux is adequate to make clear the second position in the controversy. For the third position, Nygren's clear stand on the relationship between natural and supernatural love provides the necessary contrast with the position of Augustine and Aquinas. Following this, we set forth the views of several Protestant authors who qualify, in different ways, the position taken by Nygren.

The principles for structuring the controversy are logical rather than chronological. Though we begin the presentation of the debate with the arguments of M. C. D'Arcy (who engages Nygren directly on several crucial points), the arguments and counterarguments that flow from that beginning will be drawn from authors as separate in time as Aquinas, Fénelon, Pierre Rousselot, and Étienne Gilson.

A. Theories of Natural and Supernatural Human Love

1. The difference in approach

Many of the authors who write about natural love never advert to the supernatural. It might be argued that their silence implies a rejection of its reality. It would seem that if they accept the supernatural as real, they would accord it some consideration—if not the decisive role—in their theories of love. Hence, it might be thought that their approach is guided by the principle that all love is natural.

This interpretation ignores the fact that few of the authors explicitly claim to be giving a comprehensive account of love, *i.e.*, one that deals with every aspect of it. Most of them, in fact, clearly are dealing with only a part of the subject, with a kind of love that interests them particularly or that they think is especially in need of analysis and explication. To conclude that a writer who deals only with romantic love denies, by implication, that there is supernatural love is equivalent to concluding that he denies that there is friendship, paternal love, or filial love; in fact, he may be denying that such loves exist, but evidence for such a denial must rest on more than his silence about them.

The case is somewhat different when an author attempts, within his purely natural frame of reference, to arrive at a secular understanding of what is called human love for the divine. Attempts have been made to do this, particularly by some recent authors in psychology. The results are alternate explanations of phenomena understood by religious writers to be supernaturally inspired. The reality of divine influence thus is called into question within the context of a discussion of love. A dialogue concerning the adequacy or inadequacy of the competing explanations is, however, seldom pursued, because the crucial disagreement is not on the level of a discussion of love but, rather, is about the question of the reality of God and His influence. The issue of our knowledge of the existence or non-existence of God has certainly been debated in philosophical and theological literature. In that discussion those who take the atheist or agnostic position do not, for the most part, concern themselves with the consequences for love. And those who attempt to explain love from a purely natural perspective do not argue for the atheistic position on which the legitimacy of their approach depends; for the most part, they simply assume it.[1] Nevertheless, these authors do take the position that all love is natural—humanly possible without divine help—and, therefore, that what others called supernatural human love is explicable entirely in natural terms.

By contrast, no author of a theory of supernatural love makes the parallel claim, *i.e.*, that all love is explicable only in supernatural terms. There is a sense in which theologians claim that all love depends on God, since they affirm that all the love we experience is caused by Him. But no one takes the view that *all* human love is entirely devoid of human agency. According to that view, man would not love at all; he would be merely the vehicle for the expression of divine tendencies. This claim is made by some authors with respect to supernatural human love, but it is not made by any author with respect to the whole range of human love.

Between the two extreme positions—that there is no supernatural love and that there is no natural love—lies that of all the authors who actually propound theories of supernatural love.[2] According to them, there is natural *and* supernatural human love, and both are to be comprehended within a common genus. Verbally the two loves are most frequently distinguished as *eros* or *amor* and *agape* or *caritas*, love and charity, while some authors introduce a third term, *filia* or *amicitia*: friendship.[3]

That there is a distinction between natural and supernatural human love

[1] Some of them do claim that, in providing an adequate explanation of human behavior on natural grounds, they are rendering unnecessary the assumption of supernatural influence. Religious writers reject this claim for several reasons: some argue that the secular explanations provided are not and can never be adequate; others say that there is little conflict between both explanations since many secular explanations deal with phenomena while divine influence affects only motive; still others say that the secular assumptions concerning the nature of man are demonstrably incorrect.

[2] This statement is meant only to apply to those theologians who write within the Christian tradition. It may well apply to others, but the contrast between the natural and the supernatural is far less pronounced in Eastern thought.

[3] C. S. Lewis employs a fourth: *storge* or affection.

is not contested by the theological writers. How this distinction is made, however, is the subject of considerable disagreement. Before the positions in that controversy are set forth, it will be useful to explore the most general difference between all theories of supernatural love and all theories of natural love.

2. *The difference in conception*

All theories of supernatural love differ from all theories of natural love, whether the latter are advanced by those who accept or deny the reality of the supernatural or by those who ignore the whole question. Perhaps the best way of seeing the contrast here is to list the principal characteristics that all theories of supernatural human love have in common.

(a) The love is either divine or is directed to God in the sense of seeking harmony with His will.

(b) The love is always good; a morally bad supernatural love is a contradiction in terms.

(c) The love is, if not an act of free will, at least a love of which the lover is conscious. Purely instinctive or purely physical inclinations (such as sexual desire) are never instances of supernatural or supernaturally inspired love, though such inclinations often are said to be part of a relationship in which supernatural or supernaturally influenced love is involved.

(d) The love is never totally acquisitive. It is either exclusively benevolent or takes a benevolent form.

(e) The love must be for all men.

Since there are theories of natural love among human beings in which love is said to be always good, voluntary, or conscious in all of its forms, benevolent in tendency and universal in scope, only the first of the above characteristics constitutes the basis for a sharp distinction. As that characteristic does not involve the critical notions, they cannot be used to distinguish between what all the conceptions of supernatural human love have in common and all the conceptions of natural human love. It is true that all the theories of supernatural love exclude sexual desire as a form of supernatural love. But, as there are some theories of natural love in which sexual desire is said to be the antithesis of love, its exclusion is not a sufficient distinction here.

With the single exception of sexual desire, all of the critical notions are applicable to one or another of the theories of supernatural human love. But, though the critical notions often describe the core or focus of a

conception of supernatural love, they often require (as in the case of a
number of conceptions of natural love) supplementation or qualification in
order to constitute an adequate description. Thus, for example, benevolence often is called supernatural love only when the good one seeks for the
other is eternal salvation. The character of the good sought often is as
decisive as the character of the desire.

To say that there is only one way to distinguish theories of supernatural
human and natural human love on a general level does not mean that
specific theories of supernatural human and natural human love are not
distinguished in other ways. According to one theory of supernatural love,
any self-interested motive is excluded emphatically from the realm of such
love; whereas all theories of natural love include self-interested motives.
But the absence or presence of self-interested motives is not a sufficient
general distinction, since *all* theories of supernatural love do not exclude
them. More than one theory of supernatural love excludes acquisitive
desire, whereas a number of theories of natural love do not. But the
absence or presence of acquisitive desire is not a sufficient general distinction, since there are theories of supernatural love in which acquisitive
desire is not excluded. One theory of supernatural human love excludes
human agency from the realm of such love altogether, whereas all theories
of natural human love assume human agency. But the absence or presence
of human agency is not a sufficient general distinction, since *all* theories of
supernatural love do not exclude it.

The one general, distinguishing characteristic of all supernatural theories
of love—the absolutely central position accorded to God—is the one feature
that marks them off from all theories of natural love. By definition, a
theory of supernatural love is love in which an infinite and active deity, the
God of revealed religion, is either the principal object of love, the principal
lover, or both. Supernatural, or supernaturally influenced, human love is
one that is possible only through the action or grace of God.

B. Conceptions of Supernatural Human Love: Eros and Agape

The dispute about the character and the relationship of *eros* and *agape*
within the Christian tradition is one that is at the very core of the general
problem of supernatural human love and is the one most clearly documented in the literature. This dispute has several different aspects. There
is the question of whether an authentically benevolent tendency is possible
only within the realm of supernatural love, of whether all natural love is by
its very nature acquisitive. For some, the distinction between natural love
and supernatural love is made in terms of acquisitive and benevolent

desire; for these, the supernatural supplants or replaces natural love. For others, acquisitive and benevolent tendencies are present both within the realm of supernatural *and* natural love; the supernatural only supplements or crowns the natural. A related question is whether supernatural human love involves an admixture of self-interest even in its benevolent expression. Those who say that the supernatural is completely different from the natural also say that the benevolence of supernatural love is necessarily a pure or disinterested one. Some who say that the supernatural only completes or perfects the natural also say that the benevolence of supernatural human love is self-interested. Still others say that such love takes two forms: a self-interested benevolence and a disinterested benevolence.

None of the authors in this chapter deny that *eros*, or natural love, always involves a self-interested motive. (Indeed, some of them say that the aim of *eros* is exclusively the interest of the self.) Where they differ is on the question of whether or not human *agape* is not also always accompanied by self-interest. *We find three answers to this question: Supernatural human love is (1) always accompanied by a self-interested motive, (2) sometimes accompanied by a self-interested motive, and (3) never accompanied by a self-interested motive.*

The character of God's love for man—of supernatural love strictly speaking—is not in dispute among these authors. With some qualifications, they all agree that God's love for man is purely benevolent, since God is, by definition, perfect and in need of nothing.[4] The question of self-interest and *agape* arises primarily in the consideration of man's love for God and of man's supernatural love for his fellowmen. Is self-interest involved in these loves, and, if so, to what extent? Nowhere in the entire literature on love are the notions of self and other and the parallel notions of getting and giving more applicable or more crucial than in this dispute.

In this regard some important points must be noted concerning the critical notions of acquisitive and benevolent desire as they apply both to this controversy and to the literature on supernatural love generally. The notion of acquisitive desire as applied to theories of natural love was said to signify a tendency, the aim of which is a fulfillment of a deficiency in the self and which uses the other as a means to that end. The notion of benevolent desire was said to signify a tendency the aim of which is, at least primarily, the fulfillment of a deficiency in another and which uses the self as a means to that end. These notions, as explained in Chapter 1,

---

[4] Aquinas does say that God loves irrational creatures but not for their good. He adds, however, that He does not love them so for His own sake but because of their utility to man. Hence, God's acquisitive desire toward irrational creatures is benevolent desire for man. (See *Summa Theologica*, Part I, Q. 20, Art. 3, Reply Obj. 3, Vol. I, p. 116.)

are *not always applicable* to the theories of supernatural love, particularly as regards man's love for God, unless the following restrictions are placed on their significance: Acquisitive desire is a tendency, springing from need, which aims at a good for the self. But it no longer necessarily carries the implication that the other is used solely as a means to that end. This qualification is necessary since there are authors who say that there is a human love for God which has as its aim personal salvation, but who refuse to say that God can ever be used. Benevolent desire is a tendency that aims, at least primarily, at the other's good. But it no longer carries the implication that the other lacks or is in need. This qualification is necessary since there are authors who say that man's love for God is not for the sake of the self but for God's sake, but who deny that it is possible for God to lack or be in need.

1. *The position that supernatural human love always is accompanied by a self-interested motive.*

a. *Aurelius Augustine*

Augustine may be considered as one of the first authors within the Christian tradition who explicitly affirms that: (1) supernatural human love is intimately related to natural human love, since, in his view, the former perfects and does not simply replace the latter; (2) both forms of natural human love, acquisitive and benevolent desire, have their supernatural parallels; and (3) a self-interested motive is never absent from human love in its supernatural form, even when such love is benevolent.

Augustine says that all human love influenced by grace must be either a love for God or a love for one's fellowmen that is ordered or related to one's love for God. Human love for God has the ultimate good for the self, eternal happiness or salvation, as its goal. It would seem then that supernaturally aided love for one's neighbor, insofar as it is ordered or related to one's love for God, must be, to some extent, self-interested. Man, because he is fallen and in need, can only approximate but never achieve the pure benevolence of God's love.

To understand why man's supernatural love for man can never be purely benevolent, in Augustine's view, we must consider a pivotal and crucial distinction that he draws in his book *On Christian Doctrine*. It is the distinction between use (*uti*) and enjoyment (*frui*). He says that "to enjoy a thing is to rest with satisfaction in it for its own sake. To use, on the other hand, is to employ whatever means are at one's disposal to obtain what one desires."[5] Humanly speaking, both the desire to use as well as the

---

[5] *On Christian Doctrine*, Book I, Ch. IV, p. 9.

desire to enjoy aim, in part at least, at a good for the self: happiness. "Those things which are objects of enjoyment make us happy. Those things which are objects of use assist, and (so to speak) support us in our efforts after happiness, so that we can attain the things that make us happy and rest in them."⁶ The desire to use is ordered to the desire to enjoy, since the fulfillment of the former is a means to the fulfillment of the latter. Both desires indicate a deficiency in the self. We see this confirmed in Augustine's assertion that God does not enjoy men: "If He enjoys us, He must be in need of good from us, and no sane man will say that."⁷ God does not lack and, as a consequence, cannot desire to enjoy. Asserting further that God must either enjoy man or use him, since only in these two ways can He love, Augustine concludes that God indeed does use men. But he immediately adds that the use God makes of man is different from the use man makes of things. God uses men for *their* advantage since He uses them for each other's sake and not for His own. Divine use and ordinary human use are polar opposites. The former is benevolent and the latter is acquisitive desire.⁸

On the basis of these distinctions, Augustine sets forth the admonition that only God is to be enjoyed and everyone else is to be used by man:

> . . . it is a question whether man is to be loved by man for his own sake, or for the sake of something else. . . . For if a thing is to be loved for its own sake, then in the enjoyment of it consists a happy life, the hope of which at least, if not yet the reality, is our comfort in the present time. But a curse is pronounced on him who places his hope in man.⁹

Loving someone "for his own sake" does not mean, in Augustine's terminology, that we are seeking that person's good rather than our own; he is not referring to benevolent desire. For Augustine, when someone is loved "for his own sake," one hopes to achieve happiness through that person. Hence, the human desire to "enjoy" someone else is acquisitive in character. Since man cannot achieve real happiness by enjoying other men, he must love them in the sense of "using" them in order to enjoy God. Whatever a man enjoys, whatever he loves "for its own sake," is what he considers to be the highest good. The highest good is God. A man who enjoys another human being or even himself "is not occupied with anything unchangeable." He does not enjoy himself as fully as he could by keeping "his mind . . . fully fixed upon, and his affections wrapped up in, the unchangeable good."¹⁰

⁶ *Ibid.*, Ch. III ,p .9.
⁷ *Ibid.*, Ch. XXXI, p. 27.
⁸ *Ibid.*, Ch. XXXII, pp. 27–28.
⁹ *Ibid.*, Ch. XXII, p. 18.
¹⁰ *Ibid.*, pp. 18–19.

Commenting on the love of one human being for another, Augustine
says:

> If it is for his own sake, we enjoy him; if it is for the sake of something else,
> we use him. It seems to me, then, that he is to be loved for the sake of
> something else.[11]

This is a striking admonition. If Augustine is advising man to use his
neighbor in the sense of treating him only as a means of getting closer to
God, as a means of advancing his own happiness, he is advocating acquisitive desire. If, on the other hand, he is advocating that man approximate
divine use of men by trying to imitate divine love, he is advocating benevolent desire, though it will be a self-interested benevolence, since it must
fall short of divine love.

For Augustine, the presence of a self-interested motive in man's grace-
inspired love for man is, as we have already indicated, unavoidable. For
"whatever else is loved must be loved for the sake of the blessed life."[12]
However, if the obligation to "use" one's neighbor means that one does
good to them *only* in order to advance his own good, that he treats them
only as a means to his own salvation, that he gives to them, not primarily
for their sake but ultimately in order to get, then his desire is not benevolent but a mixed acquisitive desire. Yet, all of Augustine's writings are
filled with urgings to help our neighbors without reference to "love of self"
and to aid them in their endeavors to enjoy God.

> Let not those, then, who feed Christ's sheep be "lovers of their own selves,"
> lest they feed them as if they were their own, and not His, and wish to make
> their own gain of them.[13]

The difficulty can be resolved, in part, by considering Augustine's
comments on the Biblical precepts of charity: love God and one's neighbor
as oneself. In discussing these commandments, Augustine says:

> But as this divine Master inculcates two precepts, the love of God and the
> love of our neighbour,—and as in these precepts a man finds three things he
> has to love,—God, himself, and his neighbour,—and that he who loves God
> loves himself thereby, it follows that he must endeavour to get his neighbour

[11] *Ibid.*, p. 18.

[12] *The City of God*, Vol. II, Book XIV, Ch. 25, p. 44. Augustine addresses himself
to this point again, saying :"He [God] has compassion on us so that we may enjoy
Him completely, while we have compassion on another that we may completely enjoy
Him." (*Christian Instruction*, Book I, Ch. 30, p. 51.)

[13] *Lectures or Tractates on the Gospel According to St. John*, Vol. II, Tractate
CXXIII, p. 544. See also *ibid.*, Tractate LXXXIII, pp. 312–313; *Christian Instruc-
tion*, Book I, Chs. 28–29, pp. 98–102; and *On Christian Doctrine*, Book I, Ch.
XXIX, pp. 24–25.

to love God, since he is ordered to love his neighbour as himself. He ought to make this endeavour in behalf of his wife, his children, his household, all within his reach.[14]

The proper love of self consists in seeking the enjoyment of God, in seeking one's own happiness or salvation. To love one's neighbor as one loves oneself means seeking his enjoyment of God, his happiness and salvation. If this were not the primary motive in loving one's neighbor, then it would not be the same kind of love with which one loves oneself. In other words, if man's primary motive in helping his neighbor is to aid himself in his efforts to achieve personal salvation, to help his neighbor as a means to that end, he would not be obeying the commandment of love. Man's love for his neighbor must take a benevolent form. Yet, his very love for his neighbor also must involve a love for himself, since Augustine says that we cannot help loving ourselves in all our desires.[15] Man's motive, although benevolent, must also be self-interested.

Thus Augustine is able to say:

> When we take pity upon a man and care for him, it is for his advantage we do so; but somehow or other our own advantage follows by a sort of natural consequence, for God does not leave the mercy we show to him who needs it to go without reward. Now this is our highest reward, that we should fully enjoy Him, and that all who enjoy Him should enjoy one another in Him.[16]

The implication seems to be that one's immediate or primary intention is to help another, not for the sake of one's own happiness but for the other's advantage. Yet, because a person is obeying a commandment of God, he may also have an accompanying and secondary intention to advance himself morally. The primary good he seeks is the enhancement of the welfare of the other; the concomitant good he seeks is his own moral improvement.

Augustine goes even further in emphasizing the benevolent character of charity toward one's neighbor. In his commentary *Lectures or Tractates on the Gospel According to St. John,* he reminds the faithful that their obligation is not only to love each other as they love themselves but to try to love each other as God loves them.[17] The human attempt to imitate divine benevolence always will fall short, and is measured by the degree to which the giver is himself proximate to God. Emphasizing that the benevolent

[14] *The City of God,* Vol. II, Book XIX, Ch. 14, pp. 322–323.
[15] See *Christian Instruction,* Book I, Ch. 23, p. 43.
[16] *On Christian Doctrine,* Book I, Ch. XXXII, p. 28.
[17] See *Lectures or Tractates on the Gospel According to St. John,* Vol. II, Tractate LXXXIII, p. 311.

aspect of *agape* toward one's neighbor cannot spring from deficiency, Augustine says:

> . . . what charity does for one's own benefit is utility; what it does for our neighbor's good is called kindness. In this case, utility leads the way, for no one can give another a benefit from a supply which he does not have. The more the power of lust is destroyed, the more the power of charity is strengthened.[18]

A man's disposition toward his neighbor becomes more and more benevolent and more and more like divine love the closer he gets to God. His love for God is a love that springs from need; thus, "utility leads the way." He must have something to give before he can give. The degree to which that need is fulfilled is the degree to which he is able to imitate divine love in his supernatural love for his neighbors.

Another way Augustine confronts the difficulty of reconciling man's ever present need with the obligation to be benevolent is by stressing the unitive effect of charity. Love for God unites those who share it so that "all who enjoy Him should enjoy one another in Him."[19] All men are united in that they are all creatures of God and are united even more closely when they love God and aid each other to love Him more. Augustine says that we are obliged to desire that our neighbors "all love God with us, and all the assistance which we either give them or receive from them must be directed toward that one purpose."[20] The purpose is that all should love God *together*. In seeking the advantage of his neighbors by helping them to enjoy God, a man is simultaneously and indirectly fostering his own welfare, since he is seeking the collective good of all who love God.[21] Thus, because he is united with others as creatures of God, he can anticipate some sharing in the good he seeks for them. To the extent that he anticipates that sharing, his benevolence is self-interested.[22]

Supernatural love for one's neighbor, when it takes the form of benevolent desire, is self-interested in another way. Though charity is never extended to someone else for the sake of reciprocity, the desire for mutual love invariably accompanies it.[23] And the hope for reciprocity is self-interested.

---

[18] *Christian Instruction,* Book III, Ch. 10, p. 130. See also *Faith, Hope and Charity,* Ch. 32, p. 471.

[19] *On Christian Doctrine,* Book I, Ch. XXXII, p. 28. See also *On The Trinity,* Book IX, Ch. VIII, p. 234.

[20] *Christian Instruction,* Book I, Ch. 28, p. 48.

[21] See *The City of God,* Vol. II, Book XIX, Ch. 23, p. 339.

[22] See *On Christian Doctrine,* Book I ,Ch. XXIX, pp. 24–25.

[23] See *Lectures or Tractates on the Gospel According to St. John,* Vol. II, Tractate LXXXIII, pp. 312–313; and *Christian Instruction,* Book I, Ch. 29, p. 48.

In Augustine's view, all supernatural or grace-aided love has a self-interested aspect. In man's primary love for God, his motive is to achieve salvation, *i.e.*, his desire is acquisitive. In man's charity toward his neighbors, he not only aids them but also accepts their aid; acquisitive desire also is present here. Man is obliged to take as well as to give. The most typical form of charity among human beings is, however, self-interested benevolence.

b. *Thomas Aquinas*

Aquinas, with a somewhat different analysis, takes the same position as Augustine on the character of *agape*. Supernatural human love is different from, but closely related to, natural love; it takes both acquisitive and benevolent forms; its benevolent form is self-interested.

Just as with natural love, Aquinas maintains that the essence of supernatural love of an object is "nothing else than to will good to that thing."[24] He distinguishes between the way in which God loves and the way in which man loves. God's love precedes and causes the goodness in whatever is loved by Him; man's love does not cause the goodness in what he loves but is caused by that goodness. Aquinas puts it thus:

> . . . since our will is not the cause of the goodness of things, but is moved by it as by its object, our love, whereby we will good to anything, is not the cause of its goodness; but conversely its goodness, whether real or imaginary, calls forth our love, by which we will that it should preserve the good it has, and receive besides the good it has not, and to this end we direct our actions: whereas the love of God infuses and creates goodness.[25]

God's love for man is exclusively benevolent. Man's love for God, as well as his God-inspired love for other men, however, takes two forms: acquisitive and benevolent desire. Aquinas refers to both tendencies when he speaks of loving God "for His own sake." He is careful to point out that "to love one for his own sake can be understood in two ways. First, in such a way that one is loved as a final end; and thus only God should be loved for His own sake. Secondly, that we love him for whom we wish some good, as is proper to a friendship for a noble person."[26] God is loved by man in both ways. In the first way, man's love for God is acquisitive; in the second, benevolent with a self-interested aspect.[27]

Just as man's supernatural tendencies toward God are both benevolent

[24] *Summa Theologica*, Part I, Q. 20, Art. 2, Answer, Vol. I, p. 115.
[25] *Ibid.*
[26] *On Charity*, Art. VIII, Reply Obj. 16, p. 73.
[27] See pp. 109–110, *infra*.

and acquisitive, so also are his supernatural tendencies toward other men. Self-interest is involved in both relationships. But, since God should be loved more than self and self more than neighbor, benevolence must be the stronger love in man's relationship to God and acquisitiveness must be the stronger love in man's relationship to man. This does not mean that most of a man's desires toward other men should be acquisitive but only that his own salvation is more important to him than the salvation of others. (Though it is charity to give up one's life for one's neighbor's life, it is not charity to give up one's salvation for one's neighbor's salvation.)[28] In fact, to want to give rather than to get is, according to Aquinas, a better love, since he argues that to love another (benevolent desire) rather than wishing to be loved by another (acquisitive desire) is more proper to charity to one's neighbor.[29]

Aquinas distinguishes between the benevolence of supernatural and natural love among human beings in three ways. First, the benevolence of supernatural love is universal while natural benevolence is partial.[30] Second, the good one wishes one's neighbor is eternal beatitude. Third, in charity, one never is benevolent toward one's neighbor for his own sake, but always for God's sake.[31]

The difference between natural and supernatural love is not the difference between self-interested benevolence and disinterested benevolence. Self-interest is also present in supernatural human love. Since there is a sense in which "charity loves God in all fellow-men, for our neighbor is loved by charity because God is in him or God might be in him,"[32] man's charitable love for his neighbor is self-interested in the same way in which man's charitable love for God is self-interested.

Aquinas makes the same point in asserting that the "friendship of charity is based on the fellowship of happiness."[33] Just as there is a self-interested motive involved in loving God for His own sake, so also is that motive present in one's love of one's neighbor for God's sake. Just as in loving the whole (God) one benefits oneself as a part of that whole, so also

[28] See *Summa Theologica*, Part II-II, Q. 26, Art. 4, esp. Reply Obj. 2, Vol. II, p. 1297. See also Art. 5, p. 1298; *On Charity*, Art. XI, Reply Obj. 9, p. 93.

[29] See *Summa Theologica*, Part II-II, Q. 27, Art. 1, Vol. II, p. 1305.

[30] Though all men are included in the compass of charity (even sinners and one's enemies), Aquinas does say that some men are to be loved in charity more than others, depending on their relationship to the lover. (See *Summa Theologica*, Part II-II, Q. 26, Arts. 6–12, Vol. II, pp. 1298–1304.) And even though all are wished well in charity, in varying degrees, all are not actually the recipients of beneficence since no one can do good to all. (See *ibid.*, Art. 6, Reply Obj. 2, p. 1299.)

[31] See *ibid.*, Q. 44, Art. 7, p. 1378.

[32] *On Charity*, Art. IV, Answer, p. 43.

[33] *Summa Theologica*, Part II-II, Q. 25, Art. 12, Answer, Vol. II, p. 1294. See also Q. 24, Art. 3, Obj. 3, p. 1276.

in referring the good of a part of the whole (one's neighbor) to the good of the whole (God) one is also benefiting oneself. What makes the benevolence of supernatural love among human beings self-interested is the union of the good of all human beings in God.

> God is loved as the principle of good, on which the love of charity is founded; while man, out of charity, loves himself by reason of his being a partaker of the aforesaid good, and loves his neighbor by reason of his fellowship in that good. Now fellowship is a reason for love according to a certain union in relation to God.[34]

The three conceptions of love used by Aquinas in his analysis are: *amor* (love generically), *amicitia* (friendship), and *caritas* (charity). They are continuous even though the last is supernatural and the first two are natural. Friendship is a form of natural love (*amor*) and "charity includes friendship, as the perfect includes the less perfect."[35]

Charity in man (supernatural human love) is distinguished by Aquinas from the love that is God. Besides "that love which God is essentially, there is also in us a created love."[36] The movement of charity in the will is not the Holy Ghost Himself but is "from the Holy Ghost."

> For when the Holy Ghost moves the human mind the movement of charity does not proceed from this motion in such a way that the human mind be merely moved, without being the principle of this movement, as when a body is moved by some extrinsic motive power. For this is contrary to the nature of a voluntary act, whose principle needs to be in itself . . . love, of its very nature, implies an act of the will.[37]

Though "charity surpasses the proportion of human nature,"[38] and though it requires "divine infusion" not only in the beginning but through its whole duration,[39] its human expression is not the love that is God.

The principal reason for the presence of a self-interested motive in the various forms of supernatural human love is that such love does not replace natural love, but only perfects and supplements it. Grace-aided love, for Aquinas, is not so much supernatural as supernaturally inspired. Though such love requires divine aid, man is still the agent. And insofar as man

[34] *Ibid.*, Q. 26, Art. 4, Answer, p. 1297. See also Q. 25, Art. 12, p. 1294.
[35] *On Charity*, Art. VIII, Obj. 16, p. 68. See also *Summa Theologica*, Part II-II, Q. 23, Art. 1, Vol. II, p. 1269.
[36] *On Charity*, Art. I, Reply Obj. 5, p. 23.
[37] *Summa Theologica*, Part II-II, Q. 23, Art. 2, Answer, Vol. II, p. 1270. See also Q. 24, Art. 10, Reply Obj. 3, p. 1283.
[38] *Ibid.*, Q. 24, Art. 3, Answer, p. 1277. See also Art. 2, p. 1276.
[39] *On Charity*, Art. IV, Answer, p. 54.

acts, he acts, in some degree, for the sake of his own perfection. Therefore, self-interest is never entirely absent in any of his desires.[40]

c. *Dictionnaire de Théologie Catholique*

One of the better contemporary statements of the predominant Catholic position on the relationship of charity and self-interest occurs in the article on "Charité" in the *Dictionnaire de Théologie Catholique*. Reflecting mostly the view of Aquinas, but also drawing on the thought of Augustine, Bonaventure, and others, Dublanchy summarizes the position of the Church on this matter. Addressing the question directly, he says:

> The teaching of Scripture and tradition about the nature of charity toward God does not demand in the least that every motive other than God's infinite perfection be positively excluded. All that is required is that this infinite perfection be the ultimately predominant motive, to which other secondary motives such as hope, gratitude, or salutary fear have been or may be related, but with complete subordination.

He mentions the position that "the only charity that is really possible for us . . . is a love that has as its only object God's goodness towards us." He claims, however, that such a view "presupposes an unfortunate confusion between the motive of the act of charity toward God and something that is merely a condition necessary for the exercise of this act." Since every being loves itself and wills its own good in all that it does, "even as regards all love of benevolence, it is a necessary condition that the object, or the loved good, be previously perceived as in accord with our nature or our aspirations." Dublanchy adds:

> But once this condition that is demanded by our nature is realized, the motive of charity is really the infinite perfection loved for its own sake, in which we rest as in our ultimate end and to which everything else is completely subordinated.

Dublanchy then refers to Augustine and especially Bonaventure in developing the argument that in loving God for His own sake a human being also and necessarily is loving himself, since God, being the Supreme Good, encompasses his own personal good. According to Dublanchy, Bonaventure, "while admitting the specific unity of charity, the primary and only act of which is an adhering to God Who is loved for His own sake as the supreme good, asserts that this very same act is at once a love of

---

[40] It is also present even when the individual is united with God. "The blessed who already enjoy the possession of God desire the continuance of their enjoyment." (*Truth*, Q. 22, Art. 2, Vol. III, p. 42.)

friendship and a love of . . . [concupiscence]. It is a love of friendship inasmuch as it wills this good to God Himself. It is a love of . . . [concupiscence] inasmuch as it wishes or wills for itself this perfect good." Since the distinction between the love of friendship and the love of concupiscence is made "within the very act of charity itself," and since the self-interested aspect of charity is strictly dependent on the dominant love of friendship, the love of concupiscence in charity is not self-love in the ordinary sense. The self-love in charity presupposes not only that one loves "the gifts of the benefactor but his perfections themselves."

Summarizing his conclusions, Dublanchy says:

> Love of self, whether it be commanded by the virtue of charity or merely not opposed thereto, is readily compatible, in a given individual, with the motive of charity.
>
> a. This conclusion clearly follows from the principles already stated. When love of self, though not commanded by the virtue of charity, is nevertheless not opposed thereto, there is nothing to prevent an act of charity from subsisting parallel to a love of self, since the efficacy of the motive of charity is in no way affected, and a legitimate act of self-love simply goes along with it. The case is even stronger when a love of self is commanded by charity, *i.e.*, when one loves oneself only for God and in God, for on this hypothesis love of self is really just an act of charity. . . .
>
> b. Furthermore, if all love of self were necessarily incompatible with charity, we should be forced to conclude that the act of Christian hope that is strictly obligatory for all believers is also excluded by charity. This would be a mistaken conclusion, because the precept of Christian hope is imposed on all believers, either as a disposition necessary for justification, in the case of adults, according to the Council of Trent, session 6 c 6, or as an indispensable means of salvation, according to the constant and unanimous teaching of theologians.
>
> c. If all love of self were entirely opposed to charity, we should also have to conclude that charity is absolutely impossible in this life and even in the next life. For it is a universal law that every being, because it necessarily loves itself, cannot love with a love of benevolence any object situated outside itself unless this good is previously perceived as in harmony with its nature. . . .
>
> d. The Church is therefore right in disapproving the quietist propositions that assert the possibility, the existence, and even the obligation of a love of God which is entirely separated from all love of self, however pure it may be.

To explain the condemnation of self-love in religious writings, Dublanchy observes:

> As for the frequent and forceful disapproval of all self-love, especially in mystical and ascetical writings, what has to be noted is the unfavorable sense

in which this term is used. When self-love means merely the love of self whereby one locates one's ultimate end in oneself contrary to God's will, it is quite rightly condemned as is all disobedience to God's law.[41]

Claiming not only that self-interest is compatible with charity, Dublanchy also affirms that even perfect charity *cannot* be disinterested:

> The perfection of charity, no matter how intense it may be, can never bring with it an absolutely disinterested love of God, entirely free from all love of self.[42]

2. *The position that supernatural human love only sometimes is accompanied by a self-interested motive.*
a. *François de Fénelon*

Within the Catholic tradition one of the most important departures from the general view presented in the first section occasioned the dispute between François de Fénelon and Bishop Jacques Bossuet in the seventeenth century. Careful study of the materials that record the whole dispute has convinced us that a detailed presentation of all of them would add little to the structure of the argument over the possibility of "disinterested" or "pure" love. We shall, accordingly, limit our presentation to some cardinal passages from the work of Fénelon and to some propositions attributed to him in the Papal Brief of Innocent XII. As will be seen, Fénelon states clearly what he means by disinterested love and is concerned to show its reality. Bossuet, on the other hand, maintains that this view of Fénelon's is not only false but also inconsistent with the traditional teaching of the Church. He takes, roughly, the position set forth in the previous section and maintains that Fénelon's position amounts to a mitigated sort of "quietism."[43]

Fénelon's account of disinterested love occurs in the context of his explanation of the five loves whereby human beings can love God. The five constitute a kind of progression, the first being entirely interested and the fifth entirely disinterested. Of the first, Fénelon says:

> . . . We can love God not for His own sake, but for the goods that are distinct from Him and depend on His power, and which we hope to obtain from Him. Such was the love of the worldly Jews who observed the law in

[41] "Charité" in *Dictionnaire de Théologie Catholique*, Vol. II, Part 2, Cols. 2217 ff. (Our translation.)
[42] *Ibid.*, Col. 2236.
[43] Bossuet's writings on this particular dispute are found in Tome VI of *Oeuvres Completes de Bossuet*.

order to be rewarded by the dew from heaven and by the fertility of the land. This sort of love is neither pure nor filial, but simply servile. Strictly speaking, it is not loving God; it is loving oneself and seeking only for oneself not God but what comes from God.

The second love Fénelon mentions is like the first in that it is wholly self-interested, but unlike it in that it does not seek from God goods that are distinct from Him. It seeks God, but solely for the sake of personal happiness. Fénelon calls it the "love of faith" and argues that it has no degree of real charity in it. He says that when we have faith we know that God is our only happiness. But, then, he adds:

> If, in this state, we love God as the only instrument proper to our happiness and because of the impossibility of finding our happiness in any other object; if we consider God as a means of happiness and relate Him exclusively to ourselves as an ultimate end, this sort of love would be rather a love of faith than a love of God: at least, it would be opposed to order, for by considering God as the object or instrument of our happiness, it would refer God to ourselves and to our own happiness. Though such love would not make us seek any other reward but God alone, it would still be purely mercenary and come from pure concupiscence.

The third love that Fénelon discusses is not wholly self-interested. He calls it the "love of hope." This love is "mixed with the beginning of a love of God for His own sake. But the motive of our own interest is its principal and dominant motive."

The fourth love is a love of charity but not the love of pure charity. It is "still mixed with some remnant of self-interest, but is genuine justifying love because a disinterested motive is dominant in it." Fénelon remarks that as long as a self-interested motive prevails over a disinterested one, the love for God is deficient. Describing the shifting of the balance, he says:

> But when disinterested love, or the love of charity, begins to be prevalent over a motive of self-interest, then the soul that loves God is really loved by Him. Still, this genuine charity is not yet entirely pure, *i.e.*, free from any admixture; but since the love of charity prevails over the interested motive of hope, this state is called a state of charity. The soul then loves God for His own sake and for its sake, but in such a way that it loves the glory of God principally, and seeks after its own happiness only as a means, which it relates and subordinates to the ultimate end which is the glory of its Creator.

The fifth and highest love for God is entirely disinterested.

> . . . We can love God with a love that is pure charity without any admixture of the motive of self-interest. In this case we love God in the midst of suffering, in such a way that we would not love Him more even

when He loads the soul with consolations. Neither the fear of punishment nor the desire of rewards forms part of this love any longer. We no longer love God for the sake of merit, or for the sake of perfection, or because of the happiness we are bound to find in loving Him. We would love Him just as much even if, by an impossible supposition, He would inevitably be unaware that we love Him, or would will to make eternally unhappy those who loved Him.

Describing additional properties of this love, Fénelon says:

> The disinterested soul, in pure charity, awaits and desires and hopes in God as its good, as its reward, as that which is promised to it and is all for it. It wills Him for itself in order to conform itself to God's good pleasure who wills Himself for it. But it does not will Him for love of itself, because there is no longer any motive of self-interest that stimulates it.
>
> Such is pure and perfect love, that produces the same acts of all the same virtues as does mixed love: only with this single difference: it drives out fear as well as all unrest, and is also exempt from the pressures of interested love.[44]

Since Fénelon makes a distinction between what he calls "mixed" and "pure" charity, it is clear that he does not claim that supernaturally inspired human love always is disinterested. But he does claim that a disinterested love for God is possible. Essentially, it was this claim that gave rise to the Papal Brief "Cum Alias" (1699), in which a number of propositions attributed to Fénelon were condemned. The following are the statements in the Brief specifically covering the propositions that are relative to the dispute over disinterested love:

Errors concerning absolutely pure love for God

1. There is an habitual state of love for God that is pure charity, without any admixture of a motive of self-interest. Neither fear of punishments nor desire of rewards form part of this state any longer. God is no longer loved for the sake of merit, nor because of perfection, nor because of the happiness that is to be found in loving Him. . . .

4. In the state of holy indifference, a soul no longer has voluntary and deliberate desires for its own interests, except on those occasions on which it is not faithfully cooperating with all its grace.

5. In that same state of holy indifference, we will nothing for ourselves, but all things for God. We do not at all will to be perfect and blessed because of self-interest; but we will all perfection and blessedness insofar as God is pleased to accomplish this, so that we will these things under the impulse of His grace.

[44] *Explication des Maximes des Saints,* Tome II, pp. 4–6, *passim.* (Our translation.) Throughout his argument, Fénelon quotes liberally from François de Sales's *Traité de l'amour de Dieu.*

6. In this state of holy indifference, we no longer will salvation as our own salvation, as an eternal release from bondage, as a reward of our merits, as our own greatest interest; but we will it with all the strength of our will as God's glory and good pleasure, as something that He Himself wills and that He wills us to will for His sake.

On the relation of virtue to disinterested love, the Brief attributes these propositions to Fénelon:

18. In the passive state all the different virtues are practised without any thought of their being virtues. At every moment there is no other thought but to do what God wills, and zealous love at the same time prevents one from any longer willing virtue for oneself, and from ever being so possessed of virtue as when one is no longer attached to virtue.

19. In this sense it may be said that a passive and disinterested soul no longer wills even love itself insofar as love is its own perfection and its own happiness, but only insofar as love is that which God wills from us.

The following is the strongest of the propositions contained in the Brief:

23. Pure love itself alone constitutes the whole of the inner life; and in such a case it turns out to be the only principle and the only motive of all acts that are deliberate and meritorious.

The Brief's condemnation of the propositions is cast in the following terms:

Condemned and rejected, both in the obvious sense of their words and as regards their mutual relations, as rash, scandalous, not sounding right, offensive to pious ears, harmful in practice, and also individually erroneous.[45]

b. *Bernard of Clairvaux*

Insofar as Bernard takes the position that self-interest and supernatural human love are inseparable, he holds to the traditional, Catholic view. But he does mention a form of love for God that is totally disinterested. It is the

[45] According to the Latin version in Denzinger's *Enchiridion Symbolorum*, pp. 1327–49. (Our translation.) To understand the meaning of this condemnation, it is necessary to know the technical meaning of the "censures" listed at the end of the last proposition. These terms are defined as follows in the article on *Censures Doctrinales*: "rash (*temerariae*): opposed to a doctrine commonly held by theologians; scandalous (*scandalosae*): apt to be a source of spiritual harm to people; not sounding right (*male sonantes*): obviously open to a false interpretation; offensive to pious ears (*piis auribus offensivae*): so phrased as to indicate lack of reverence for something that is holy; harmful in practice (*perniciosae in praxi*): sure to cause damage if acted upon; erroneous (*erroneae*): opposed to a conclusion that follows logically from revelation but is not denied as a matter of faith." (*Ibid.*, Vol. II, Part 2, Cols. 2101–2113, esp. 2105–2110.)

fourth of the four degrees of love mentioned by him, the first of which is natural and the last three, supernatural.[46] In the second degree, man loves God not for God's sake but for his own. In the third degree, man loves God for His own sake, but also still loves himself. In the fourth degree, man loves not only God for His own sake but also himself for God's sake. When Bernard says that man loves God for His own sake and also himself for God's sake, he means that there is no self-interest involved. It is this love which he considers the culmination of supernatural human love, *but which he says is humanly impossible.*

Pointing out that God's love cannot "seek its own interest," since God is in need of nothing, Bernard contrasts it with human love by discussing what advantages can come to man from loving God.[47] In the second and third degrees of love, God is not loved for the sake of "reward" in the sense of being loved as a means to an end. "True love asks no reward but deserves one. It is when a man has not yet learned to love that a reward is set before him; it is due one who loves; it is awarded to him who perseveres."[48]

For Bernard, the movement up through the four degrees of love is a movement toward God and away from self-interest. Through the third degree, self-interest remains, since, in that degree, though God is loved for His own sake, the self is still not loved for God's sake. Of the fourth degree, Bernard says:

> Blessed and holy, I would say, is he to whom it has been given to experience such a thing in this mortal life at rare intervals or even once, and this suddenly and scarcely for the space of a single moment. In a certain manner to lose yourself as though you were not (Cf. *Galatians* II, 20), and to be utterly unconscious of yourself and to be emptied of yourself and, as it were, brought to nothing, this pertains to heavenly intercourse, not to human affection.[49]

Stressing the point that the fourth degree of love is a heavenly and not a human love, Bernard also says:

> . . . I know not if the fourth degree is attained in its perfection by any man in this life so that forsooth, a man loves himself only for the sake of

[46] Bernard's theory of natural love is a binary one.
[47] See *The Book of Saint Bernard On The Love of God*, Part I, Ch. I, p. 5, and Ch. 7, pp. 29 ff.
[48] *Ibid.*, Ch. VII, p. 30.
[49] *Ibid.*, Ch. X, pp. 43–44. With this love we "deliberately desire neither ourselves nor any other thing to have been in the past, or to be in the future, unless it be equally for His sake, to wit, for His sole will, not for our own pleasure." (*Ibid.*, p. 44.)

God. If there are any who have experience of this let them declare it; to me, I confess, it seems impossible.[50]

3. *The position that supernatural human love never is accompanied by a self-interested motive.*
a. *Anders Nygren*

No author is more concerned with the question of the relationship of supernatural love and self-interest than Nygren. In his work *Agape and Eros,* devoted largely to this problem, he claims that *eros,* or natural love, always is self-interested and that *agape,* or supernatural love, always is disinterested. He not only maintains that supernatural love is disinterested benevolence but also that there is no natural benevolence of any kind; all natural love is acquisitive.

Nygren's main thesis may be described as follows: With the advent of Christianity, a different and hitherto unknown love, called *agape* in the New Testament, was introduced into human history. Such love, being divine, differs in essential respects from all natural or earthly love. All conceptions of natural love are based upon the model of the "Platonic *eros.*" *Eros,* invariably springing from personal need, is reducible in all of its forms to self-love. Self-love is no part of the true Christian teaching. Every attempt made to reconcile *eros* and *agape* has been an attempt to reconcile the irreconcilable. The contrast between *eros* and *agape* is "a fundamental opposition between two whole attitudes to life."[51]

Aware of the long tradition in which efforts were made to harmonize the two, Nygren observes:

> Eros and Agape are Greek words, both of which are represented in our language by the one word "love." What, then, could be more natural than to assume that behind the one word there is one and the same idea, and to conclude that Eros and Agape stand for one and the same reality, or at any rate for closely related realities? . . . But the double spell cast upon us by tradition and language is broken as soon as we realise that Eros and Agape have originally nothing whatever to do with one another.[52]

Despite this, Nygren admits that, historically, both attitudes were frequently closely associated. Classical *eros* dominated the scene when *agape* appeared as a new idea. As the major alternative to *agape,* it forced Christian thinkers to come to terms with it, either through an outright

[50] *Ibid.,* Ch. XV, p. 63.
[51] *Agape and Eros,* Part 1, Ch. 3, Sect. II, p. 208.
[52] *Ibid.,* Introduction, Sect. I, p. 32.

repudiation of *eros* or through an attempt to incorporate it into the attitude of *agape*.[53]

> Hence arises the problem that has made itself felt in different contexts and in the most varied forms through the whole of Christian history ever since: the problem of Eros and Agape.[54]

This problem would not exist at all if the Platonic *eros* were conceived as nothing but sensual love. *Eros* directed only to the physical and *agape* to the spiritual would come into no conflict. The problem arises because, though Platonic love does have sensual roots, "its whole tendency is to seek deliverance from the merely sensual." It is the heavenly, not the vulgar or sensual, *eros* that "is the born rival of the idea of Agape."

> Agape displays a heavenly character from the beginning; it needs no spiritualising or sublimating to be recognised as divine and heavenly Agape. With Eros it is otherwise; only the highest form of Eros, Eros in the most sublimated sense, "heavenly Eros," is capable of entering the lists against Agape.[55]

Nygren says that the Platonic *eros* has three characteristics: (1) it is acquisitive, proceeding from deficiency; (2) it is man's way to the divine; and (3) it is "egocentric."[56] These characteristics sharply contrast it with the Christian *agape*, which is not an upward but a downward movement.

> Agape, Christian love, is of a wholly different nature. It has nothing to do with desire and longing. It "seeketh not its own," does not ascend, like Eros, to secure advantages for itself, but consists in sacrifice and self-giving. And it bears this character ultimately because its prototype is God's own love. The human is not here raised to the Divine, but the Divine, in compassionate love, descends to the human.[57]

Agape, properly understood, is entirely "dissociated from eudaemonism and utilitarianism";[58] it is totally disinterested. Insofar as *agape* involves no self-interested motive it is a serious error to represent it as a high, spiritual form

[53] "Of all the other views that have confronted the Christian idea of love, or *agape*, and have forced it to a decision—whether to the decision of a life-and-death struggle or of a settlement by compromise—by far the most important is that view of love which finds its most complete and classical expression in the Platonic conception of *eros*." (*Ibid.*, p. 30.)

[54] *Ibid.*

[55] *Ibid.*, Sect. III, p. 51, *passim*.

[56] In this connection, Nygren notes: "In order to prevent any misunderstanding . . . let it be clearly stated that the word 'egocentric' is not used here in any derogatory sense." (*Ibid.*, Part I, Ch. 2, Sect. II, p. 181.)

[57] *Ibid.*, Part 2, Introduction, p. 236.

[58] *Ibid.*, Introduction, Sect. II, p. 45.

of *eros*. "Agape stands alongside, not above, the heavenly Eros; the difference between them is not one of degree but of kind. There is no way, not even that of sublimation, which leads over from Eros to Agape."[59] Attempts to represent *agape* as a form of *eros* only amount to changing the object of love; such an approach fails to recognize that *agape* is exclusively an outgoing tendency that does not respond to value in an object but creates it. To see *agape* as but a higher form of *eros* directed to a more valuable object still is to understand it as an ingathering tendency and, therefore, to misunderstand it.[60]

Agape, unlike an acquisitive tendency that responds to value, is *"spontaneous and 'unmotivated' "* or *"indifferent to value."* God's love is groundless in the sense that there are no extrinsic grounds for it.[61] All the reasons for His motivation are in His nature, which *is* love,[62] and that nature includes no deficiency at all and, hence, no need to seek value outside itself. "To the question, Why does God love? there is only one right answer: Because it is His nature to love."[63] God is indifferent to value in the sense that the "distinction between the worthy and the unworthy, the righteous and the sinner, sets no bounds to His love."[64] Not only is the determinant of *agape* in God but His love is what creates value in the objects to which it is directed; men loved by God have no value except what is conferred by that love.

> God does not love that which is already in itself worthy of love, but on the contrary, that which in itself has no worth acquires worth just by becoming the object of God's love. . . . Agape does not recognise value, but creates it.[65]

Agape is also the initiator of fellowship with God since without it there would be no such fellowship at all. According to Nygren, *"there is from man's side no way at all that leads to God.* If such a thing as fellowship between God and man nevertheless exists, this can only be due to God's own action; God must Himself come to meet man and offer him His fellowship."[66]

---

[59] *Ibid.*, Sect. III, p. 52.

[60] See *ibid.*, Part I, Ch. 1, Sect. III, p. 157. *"Eros is the way by which man mounts up to the Divine not the way by which the Divine stoops down to man."* (*Ibid.*, Ch. 2, Sect. II, p. 178.)

[61] *Ibid.*, Part I, Ch. 1, Sect. I, pp. 75, 77.

[62] See *ibid.*, Introduction, Sect. II, p. 47. See also Part I, Ch. 1, Sect. III, p. 147; and Ch. 3, Sect. I, p. 201.

[63] *Ibid.*, Ch. 1, Sect. I, p. 75.

[64] *Ibid.*, pp. 77–78.

[65] *Ibid.*, p. 78.

[66] *Ibid.*, p. 80. See also Ch. 3, Sect. IV, pp. 220–221.

Nygren summarizes the differences between "the two fundamental motifs and their contrary tendencies" in the following table:

Eros is acquisitive desire and longing.	Agape is sacrificial giving.
Eros is an upward movement.	Agape comes down.
Eros is man's way to God.	Agape is God's way to man.
Eros is man's effort: it assumes that man's salvation is his own work.	Agape is God's grace: salvation is the work of Divine love.
Eros is egocentric love, a form of self-assertion of the highest, noblest, sublimest kind.	Agape is unselfish love, it "seeketh not its own," it gives itself away.
Eros seeks to gain its life, a life divine, immortalised.	Agape lives the life of God, therefore dares to "lose it."
Eros is the will to get and possess which depends on want and need.	Agape is freedom in giving, which depends on wealth and plenty.
Eros is primarily *man's* love; God is the *object* of Eros. Even when it is attributed to God, Eros is patterned on human love.	Agape is primarily *God's* love; God *is* Agape. Even when it is attributed to man, Agape is patterned on Divine love.
Eros is determined by the quality, the beauty and worth, of its object; it is not spontaneous, but "evoked," "motivated."	Agape is sovereign in relation to its object, and is directed to both "the evil and the good"; it is spontaneous, "overflowing," "unmotivated."
Eros *recognises value* in its object—and loves it.	Agape loves—and *creates value in its* object.[67]

As love expresses a relationship between a subject and an object, Nygren applies these contrasts to four such relationships: God to man, man to God, man to man, and man to himself. Again he charts his conclusions. Arranging the various relationships in the order of their importance for *eros* and *agape,* he gives three points to the relationship most important for each love and a zero to the relationship in which that love is absent.[68]

	Agape			Eros	
3	(Downward Movement)		God's love	(Upward Movement)	0
2			Neighborly love		1
1			Love for God		2
0			Self-love		3

On the side of *eros,* divine love for man is impossible. Since *eros* always implies deficiency, and since God does not lack anything, He cannot love

[67] *Ibid.,* Ch. 3, Sect. II, p. 210.
[68] *Ibid.,* Sect. III, p. 219.

man in this way. "Eros is the upward tendency; but there is no way upwards for God."[69] Regarding love among human beings, the erotic desire is not one through which the neighbor is sought for himself. Eros loves the neighbor "in so far as it can utilise him as a means for its own ascent." It is "its nature to be always detaching itself from its object and using it as a stepping-stone to higher things." It displays this characteristic most prominently in neighborly love, "which is never love pure and simple, but has always an ulterior motive in the thought that it is 'for God's sake.' "[70] Such a love is never extended to the neighbor for himself, but always for the sake of God. And, in this context, "for the sake of God" means ultimately for one's own sake. "The showing of love towards one's neighbour is regarded as a meritorious act, a step up on the way to God, and therein lies its justification."[71] *Eros* in the form of direct love for God also is acquisitively motivated. "Here the upward-striving tendency of Eros comes into its own: human want and need seeks for satisfaction in the Divine fullness."[72] In loving God, the highest personal advantages are sought. Self-love is the essence of *eros* and the prototype of its indirect forms: love for God and neighborly love.

The emphasis is reversed when the different relationships are viewed from the perspective of *agape*. Now, God's love is central. "All love that has any right to be called Agape is nothing else but an outflow from the Divine love. . . . Agape is a love that descends, freely and generously giving of its superabundance. . . ."[73] Neighborly love, accordingly, has the same benevolent character. It "is directed to the neighbour himself, with no further thought in mind and no sidelong glances at anything else."[74] Evidence for the absence of any ulterior motive is the fact that *agape* is directed to enemies as well as to friends, to those who offer nothing that incites love.[75] Such is the character of supernatural love which does not respond to value but creates it. Loving one's neighbor for God's sake in this sense "has no teleological but only a causal significance." It is not as the object of love but as the lover that God sets man's supernatural love for man in motion. As an extension of divine love, neighborly love has no other interest but the interest of the other. Unless "love for one's neighbour is directed to the neighbour alone, unless it is concerned exclusively with him and has literally no other end in view—not

[69] *Ibid.*, p. 212.
[70] *Ibid.*, p. 214.
[71] *Ibid.*, p. 215.
[72] *Ibid.*, p. 212.
[73] *Ibid.*
[74] *Ibid.*, p. 215.
[75] Loving one's enemies is a necessary feature of *agape* since it, unlike *eros*, is universal in scope. (See *ibid.*, Ch. 1, Sect. 1, p. 63.)

even that of gaining God's love—then it has no right to the name of neighbourly love."[76] Like God's love and like neighborly love, man's love for God bears the character of disinterested benevolence. Man gives not in the sense that he can add anything to God's perfection but in the sense that he willingly sacrifices himself and all of his interests to God. He gives in the sense that he submits himself to God's will and asks nothing. Such love amounts to "obedience to God, without any thought of reward."[77]

Self-love as a form of *agape* is excluded. "Christianity does not recognise self-love as a legitimate form of love." Self-love is the enemy of *agape* because it alienates man both from God and his neighbor. If he loves himself, he is unable to love God or his neighbor as commanded, even if a distinction is "drawn between a legitimate and a sinful self-love."[78] The movement of love is either for the sake of the other or for one's own sake; no compromise between these extremes is possible.

Nygren's justification for this interpretation of the Christian position is based, in part, on his understanding of the Biblical injunction to love one's neighbor as oneself. He argues that the attempt to find in this command a justification for self-love is motivated by a desire to impose on the commandment a meaning that is wholly alien to it. He claims that there is no need to dispute the fact that man does and must love himself by nature. The commandment points to an other-directed love which does not incorporate but excludes the natural tendency. It tells man to love his neighbor supernaturally as he loves himself naturally. It is indeed natural to love oneself.

> So, says the commandment of love, thou shalt love thy neighbour. When love receives this new direction, when it is turned away from one's self and directed to one's neighbour, then the natural perversion of the will is overcome. So far is neighbourly love from including self-love that it actually excludes and overcomes it.[79]

[76] *Ibid.*, Ch. 3, Sect. III, p. 216.
[77] *Ibid.*, Ch. 1, Sect. I, p. 95. Man's love for God is spontaneous and unmotivated, as is all *agape*. But it is not unmotivated in the sense in which God's love is unmotivated, since man can do nothing good without God's help. God supplies the motive for loving Him through His love for men. Spontaneity is present in man's love for God only by comparison with ordinary human love. It is unmotivated in the sense that it seeks nothing for itself. "All teleological motivation is excluded here. Love towards God does not seek to gain anything. It most certainly does not seek to gain anything other than God. But neither does it seek to gain even God Himself or His love. The very thought of gaining anything, even of gaining God's love, is fundamentally alien to it. It is the *free*—and in that sense spontaneous—surrender of the heart to God. When God gives His love freely and for nothing, there remains nothing for man to gain by loving God." (*Ibid.*, p. 94. See also pp. 91–95, and Ch. 3, Sect. III, pp. 212–214.)
[78] *Ibid.*, Ch. 3, Sect. III, p. 217.
[79] *Ibid.*, Ch. 1, Sect. I, p. 101.

As Nygren views the history of the Christian idea of love since its promulgation, it is a history of conflict and attempted syntheses with other basic approaches, primarily *eros*. He views Paul as the principal developer of the idea of *agape* as contained in the synoptic gospels. The Pauline explication is not an alien addition but "a logical, consistent development"[80] of the message of the gospels. That development consists in showing that Christian love, as exemplified by Christ's sacrifice on the cross, is always and essentially God's love and not man's. "Paul's entire religion and ethics are theocentric, and he cannot rest until he has referred everything to God."[81] Paul is interpreted as rejecting self-love as being any part of *agape*. Nygren also points to Paul's unwillingness to use the term *agape* to describe man's love for God. He understands the absence of this usage to mean that Paul is unwilling to attribute to man the same spontaneous, unmotivated love which is God's. According to Nygren, Paul distinguishes between God's love and man's love for God by calling the latter "faith." Faith is love, but a love characterized by "receptivity" rather than divine spontaneity. The term *agape* is reserved for divine love. Nevertheless, Paul has no reservation about describing supernatural love for one's neighbor as *agape*. His reason, according to Nygren, is that such love is God's love and not man's. Paul does not "conceive of man as a centre of activity independent of God. In the life that is governed by Agape, the acting subject is not man himself; it is—as Paul expresses it—God, the Spirit of God, the Spirit of Christ, the Agape of Christ."[82] With regard to his neighbor, the "Christian has nothing of his own to give; the love which he shows to his neighbour is the love which God has infused into him." Concerning Paul's interpretation of the relationship between God's love and neighborly love, Nygren declares:

> It is not that he uses Agape as the name of two different things—*God's* love for us and *our* love for our neighbour. When Paul speaks of Agape he always means the Divine love, never a merely human love. The Christian's love for his neighbour is a manifestation of God's Agape, which in this case uses the Christian, the "spiritual" man, as its instrument.[83]

In amplifying the teaching of love presented in the gospels, Paul extends the teaching of Jesus, "yet he does not thereby part company with Jesus."[84]

Much of Nygren's criticism of the theological position he opposes is woven into his account of the complex intellectual history of the relation-

[80] *Ibid.*, Sect. II, p. 126.
[81] *Ibid.*, p. 130.
[82] *Ibid.*, p. 129.
[83] *Ibid.*, pp. 129–130, *passim.*
[84] *Ibid.*, p. 126.

ship between the notions of *eros* and *agape*. As he sees that history, the movement begins with the introduction of the *agape* motif in the New Testament, particularly in the writings of Paul. The postapostolic period is characterized as one of interaction between the Hellenistic motif of *eros*, the Jewish motif of *nomos*, or law, and the new Christian motif of *agape*. This interaction prepared the way for the completion of the synthesis of *eros* and *agape* accomplished by Augustine. Nygren calls it the "caritas-synthesis." The notion of Christian love as *caritas*, or charity, became the Christian view from the time of Augustine, was extended and developed in the Middle Ages, and remained as the prevailing doctrine until the Reformation and Martin Luther's revival of the original *agape* motif.

> The Middle Ages made the best that could be made of the idea of Caritas; they followed the path of Caritas as far as ever it led. But it was reserved for Luther to see that this path was impracticable, to abandon the idea of Caritas and to rediscover primitive Christian Agape as the only legitimate point of departure for the Christian doctrine of love.[85]

The doctrine of *caritas* developed by Augustine is, according to Nygren, "not a simple interpretation of Agape, but a transformation of it."[86] It is a transformation insofar as Augustine claims that all human love, both natural and supernatural, involves self-interested motivation, since the interest of the self is always involved in any movement toward a good object, in any movement toward happiness. Nygren claims that the *eros* motif is basic to Augustine's doctrine of *caritas* because the fundamental distinction is not between acquisitive and benevolent tendency but between the higher and lower objects to which love can be directed. The fundamental contrast is between *caritas*, love of God, and *cupiditas*, love of the world, not a distinction of kind or mode but one of object.

> Love is desire and longing whether it is directed to temporal things or to God and the eternal. For Augustine love is a longing indifferent in itself, whose quality is determined by the object to which it is directed.[87]

Nygren does not deny that elements of Christian *agape* are present in Augustine's theory. But he does deny that the reconciliation of the *eros* motif, based on self-love, and the *agape* motif, based on self-sacrifice, is successful. He argues, for example, that neighborly love occupies an awkward position in a scheme in which self-love has such a central position. Benevolence for one's neighbor is said to follow from a proper love of oneself and of God. It "thus occupies an insecure position in Augustine:

[85] *Ibid.*, Part 2, Ch. 4, Sect. III, p. 641.
[86] *Ibid.*, Introduction, Sect. IV, p. 55. See also Part 2, Ch. 2, Sect. I, pp. 451 ff.
[87] *Ibid.*, Part 2, Sect. I, Sect. III, p. 494.

in principle there is no place for it in his scheme of love, yet the influence of the New Testament compels him to include it."[88]

In Nygren's view, Augustine runs into a similar difficulty when he introduces the *agape* motif in discussing God's love. The way to salvation for man is *eros,* the ascent to the heavenly, but man cannot make that ascent without divine help. God's love is benevolent; He gives to man the necessary help or grace to make the ascent. Thus, "a theocentric and an egocentric tendency are peculiarly interwoven in Augustine's doctrine of grace."[89]

According to Nygren, the same incompatibility arises in the medieval speculations about "unselfish love," prominent among which are those of Aquinas. Aquinas also tried to resolve the problem of reconciling the conception of acquisitive tendency (which reduces to self-love) with the conception of a love that "seeketh not its own." Like Augustine, Aquinas speaks of a natural tendency on the part of all things to seek their own perfection. The way to human perfection is love of God. He who "does not love God does not understand how rightly to love himself."[90] Aquinas tries to overcome the difficulty involved in the reduction of all love to self-love by distinguishing between *"amor concupiscentiae* and *amor amicitiae,* acquisitive love and the love of friendship."[91] But Nygren claims that the Thomistic doctrine of love suffered from the introduction of the concept of benevolence. Aquinas, feeling the tension between the *eros* motif and the *agape* motif, introduced the notion of *amicitia,* or friendship, to reconcile the two.

> It need hardly be said that this attempt was doomed to failure. Apart from the hopelessness of trying to express the meaning of Agape by the alien idea of "amicitia," it is obvious that this external corrective is unable to neutralise the egocentricity that is bound up with the very first premiss of the Thomistic doctrine of love.[92]

From the early interplay between the *eros* motif and the *agape* motif in postapostolic times, through the Augustinian *caritas*-synthesis, the elaboration of that synthesis in the Middle Ages, the revival of the *eros* motif in the neo-Platonism of the Renaissance, the original Christian doctrine of *agape* never held uncompromised sway. The revival of the *agape* motif of the New Testament had to wait until the Reformation and Martin Luther.

Though Nygren concedes that Luther did not use the terms *eros* and

[88] *Ibid.,* p. 553.
[89] *Ibid.,* p. 530.
[90] *Ibid.,* Ch. 4, Sect. III, p. 642.
[91] *Ibid.,* p. 644.
[92] *Ibid.,* p. 645.

agape and did not deal with the question of love in so many words, he nevertheless insists that Luther's objections to Church doctrine involve the matters at stake in the conflict between *eros* and *agape,* or, rather, in the conflict between the *caritas*-synthesis adopted by the Church and the original Christian doctrine of *agape.*[93] He ascribes to Luther a "Copernican revolution" in his insistence *"in opposition to all egocentric forms of religion, upon a purely theocentric relation to God."*[94] Luther opposes the inclusion of any vestige of the *eros* motif in the Christian notion of love. In particular, he opposes the *caritas*-synthesis adopted by the Church. "His criticism of the Catholic idea of love is radical and irrefutable."[95]

In contrast to the whole Catholic doctrine of love, which "displays an *egocentric perversion,"*[96] Luther maintains that only when all self-interest is totally rejected is love any good, *i.e.,* Christian, at all. "Thus the idea of good works as a heavenly ladder is rejected."[97] "Self-love is not to be ennobled and refined, but totally annihilated."[98] Even more emphatically, Nygren remarks:

> . . . Luther's conception can be described as a direct antithesis to . . . (certain) ideas of Augustine. When Luther brands selfishness, self-love, as sin and as the essence of the sinfulness of sin, he means what he says without any qualification. He knows no justifiable self-love.[99]

The principal reason Nygren interprets Luther as unqualifiedly opposed to the *eros* motif is that he sees "an inner connection and an exact correspondence between Luther's doctrine of justification and his view of love."[100] At the very center of Luther's doctrine of justification "stands his rejection of every idea of *merit."*[101] Man, through his own resources, can do nothing that merits anything from God. His justification before God is through faith, not works.[102] "Every attempt to make one's way to God by self-sanctification runs counter to the message of Christ's self-offering."[103] Man's efforts at salvation are worth nothing in the eyes of God. Hence, any effort on man's part to raise himself upward through an *eros* directed to the highest object is outside the pale of Christianity.

[93] See *ibid.,* Ch. 6, Sect. II, p. 692.
[94] *Ibid.,* Sect. I, p. 681.
[95] *Ibid.,* Sect. IV, p. 722.
[96] *Ibid.,* Sect. I, p. 683.
[97] *Ibid.,* Sect. III, p. 701.
[98] *Ibid.,* p. 709.
[99] *Ibid.,* p. 710.
[100] *Ibid.,* Sect. I, p. 683.
[101] *Ibid.,* Sect. III, p. 700.
[102] See *ibid.,* p. 716.
[103] *Ibid.,* Sect. I, p. 688.

For this intention, apparently so good and praiseworthy, has its deepest ground in man's unwillingness to live wholly upon God's "misericordia," in other words, upon God's Agape in Christ. In the will to purify oneself first, before one will take refuge in God, there lies a secret "praesumptio." By so doing, man ascribes to himself the work which God has reserved to Himself.[104]

Luther's contrast between faith and love is not to be understood as a contrast between faith and *agape*, but between faith and *eros*. *Agape*, which is God, is higher than faith.[105] It is rather the *eros* in the *caritas*-synthesis that carries with it the attendant notion of justification through good works that Luther contrasts with justification by faith alone.[106]

Accordingly, all acquistive tendency, all self-love is rejected by Luther whether it springs from a higher or a lower self. The New Testament distinction between spiritual and carnal is not parallel to the classical distinction between reason and sense. All man's natural inclinations, be they physical or spiritual, are of the "flesh." Even man's natural "righteousness, his religion and worship of God belongs to the realm of the 'flesh.' "[107] This is so because all of man's natural inclinations are acquisitive and, thus, the very antithesis of Christian love.

> There is nothing in the life and activity of the natural man which does not bear the marks of . . . seeking its own. It is therefore wholly under the dominion of sin, and on that basis there is no possibility of manifesting love in the Christian sense of the word, a love that seeketh not its own, but loves God with all its heart and its neighbour as itself.[108]
> Even *the very highest* which man can seek to attain—namely, fellowship with God itself—is polluted by the egocentricity which is inherent in everything human.[109]

In Luther's view, fellowship with God is not founded on holiness but, rather, on sin. In the Catholic view, fellowship with God depends, in part, on an approach to God by man, an approximation according to merit. In Luther's view, fellowship with God rests exclusively on God's unmotivated love for man. Because it does not rest on any human worth, nothing man does can enhance such fellowship.[110]

---

104 *Ibid.*, p. 685. "Luther cannot find words strong enough to warn us against this idea, apparently so godly but really so godless, of possessing our own holiness before God." (*Ibid.*, p. 686.)
105 See *ibid.*, Sect. III, p. 719.
106 See *ibid.*, pp. 716 ff.
107 *Ibid.*, Sect. I, p. 689.
108 *Ibid.*, Sect. IV, p. 723. See also pp. 724–725; and Sect. III, pp. 713–714.
109 *Ibid.*, Sect. III, p. 714.
110 See *ibid.*, Sect. I, p. 690.

In Nygren's view, as presented in his interpretation of Luther, the Christian is but a "channel" for God's love. "Christian love is not produced by us, but it has come to us from heaven. The subject of Christian love is not man, but God Himself, yet in such a way that the Divine love employs man as its instrument and organ."[111] Even the Christian's love for God has a downward, giving movement rather than an upward, getting one, since love for God reduces in its entirety to love for one's neighbor.[112]

4. *Other Protestant authors*

Nygren may be said to present the extreme Protestant view of the relationship of *eros* and *agape*. Other authors, of which the following are only a sampling, incline to some aspects of his view but reject others.

a. *Søren Kierkegaard*

Kierkegaard, for example, claims as strongly as Nygren that supernatural human love is totally disinterested. He also insists that it is universal. In fact, it is the nondiscriminating character of supernatural love that most sharply distinguishes it from earthly or natural love. The latter is "selfish" because it is not extended to all. It is also "selfish" because it is always, to some extent, self-interested. But Kierkegaard, unlike Nygren, does not claim that all natural love is acquisitive and evil. For him, natural benevolence is an authentic benevolence, even if it does fall short of the ideal of supernaturally disinterested benevolence. He does not disparage natural benevolence, but merely maintains that, with regard to Christian love, such natural love "remains standing at the halfway mark."[113]

b. *Denis de Rougemont*

De Rougemont, like Nygren, also insists on a radical difference in tendency and effect between *eros* and *agape*. He never mentions a natural benevolence. *Eros,* or natural love, is Platonic love, in its highest form a

---

[111] *Ibid.*, Sect. IV, pp. 733–734. "In relation to God and his neighbour, the Christian can be likened to a tube, which by faith is open upwards, and by love downwards. All that a Christian possesses he has received from God, from the Divine love; and all that he possesses he passes on in love to his neighbour. He has nothing of his own to give. He is merely the tube, the channel, through which God's love flows." (*Ibid.*, p. 735. See also Part 1, Ch. 1, Sect. I, p. 97; Ch. 3, Sect. III, pp. 212, 218; and Part 2, Introduction, p. 236.)

[112] See *ibid.*, Ch. 6, Sect. IV, p. 736.

[113] *Works of Love*, Vol. I, Ch. III, p. 107.

divine aspiration. *Agape* is Christian love, the giving impulse whereby, through obedience to God's will, the person affirms the individuality of his neighbor and does not use him as the "illusory excuse and occasion for taking fire."[114]

Two points, however, differentiate De Rougemont's approach from that of Nygren. First, he speaks of the sacrifice of Christ as opening to man a new way to love, what he calls (in contrast to Nygren) "the way of *holiness*." "To love according to this new way is a positive act and an act of transformation."[115] But, for Nygren, *agape* is not the way of human holiness, since the fellowship between God and man is based upon man's worthlessness, not upon human merit.

Second, though De Rougemont does speak of self-sacrifice in discussing *agape*, he never insists that *agape* has no element of self-interest. Indeed, one of his principal contrasts between the dark passion of boundless *eros* and the tendency of *agape* is that the former sublimates and destroys the individual as individual, whereas the latter "is the contrary of the sublimation that had been an illusory flight out of the concreteness of life."[116] He goes on to add: "Such a love, being understood according to the image of Christ's love for his Church . . . is able to be truly mutual."[117] For Nygren, no such mutuality is possible, since it is only God who can love with *agape*.

In addition, when discussing marriage, De Rougemont stresses the kind of union in which each party is recognized as an individual worthy of respect. Discussing that union, he says: "Fidelity . . . wants the good of the beloved, and when it acts in behalf of that good it is creating in its own presence the neighbour. And it is by this roundabout way through the other that the self rises into being a person. . . ."[118] Through loving another with Christian love, one makes oneself better. Nygren would not admit that such merit or improvement is possible nor would he admit that a benevolence blended with the motive for such improvement was admissible within the realm of *agape*.[119]

c. *Reinhold Niebuhr*

Niebuhr seems to agree with Nygren when he says that the perfection of love "implies an uncoerced giving of the self to the object of its

114 *Love in the Western World*, Book II, Ch. 3, p. 68.
115 *Ibid.*
116 *Ibid.*
117 *Ibid.*, p. 69.
118 *Ibid.*, Book VII, Ch. 4, p. 310.
119 De Rougemont's theory of natural love is characterized by acquisitive desire.

devotion." Yet he immediately adds that "this perfect love is, like God, in the realm of transcendence."[120] It is not present in the world as we know it. As Niebuhr asserts that "the ideal of love must relate itself to the problems of a world in which its perfect realization is not possible,"[121] he implies that the love human beings experience is less than the love which is God. "The self-forgetfulness of *Agape* is . . . no simple possibility in life."[122] Its presence in life, for Nygren, is, on the contrary, not only a possibility but a fact; whatever is seen of *agape* in life is God's love in its full perfection. But, for Niebuhr, that divine love is a norm toward which human *agape* aspires rather than a reality in human associations.

Niebuhr, unlike Nygren, also relates the benevolence of *agape* to self-improvement, or what he calls "self-realization," though he does say that its best expressions preclude any intention to improve the self:

> *Agape* is . . . the final law of human existence because every realization of the self which is motivated by concern for the self inevitably results in a narrower and more self-contained self than the freedom of the self requires. Consequently the highest forms of self-realization are those which are not intended or calculated but are the fruit of some movement of "grace" which draws the self out of itself despite itself into the love of God and the neighbor.[123]

In terms of his conception of supernatural human love, Nygren precludes any association of that love with self-improvement, even though such improvement be unintended.

Niebuhr does contrast *agape* with certain forms of acquisitive desire, which he calls "egoism," or "selfishness," and he seems to indicate that even natural egoism is sinful. Yet, in his discussion of the egoism he condemns, he does not lay negative stress on self-interest as such but on self-interest that is paramount, on self-interest seen in terms of the immediate or transient rather than the long range, and on various forms of political and social parochialism, which he contrasts with the universality of *agape*.[124] Clarifying his position, Niebuhr states that the law of love in the New Testament is not "a law which requires the destruction of the self," and goes on to explain:

> The Christian ethical norm has little relation to mystical concepts according to which the particularity of egohood is regarded as an evil and redemption is equated with the absorption of individual consciousness in universal

120 *An Interpretation of Christian Ethics*, p. 209.
121 *Ibid.*, p. 150.
122 *Faith and History*, Ch. XI, Sect. II, p. 175.
123 *Ibid.* See also p. 174.
124 See *An Interpertation of Christian Ethics*, pp. 114 ff.

consciousness. In contrast to such schemes of redemption from self, the Christian faith does promise self-realization.[125]

The self-realization to which he refers, however, seems to be one of the transcendent rather than the actual self, a realization that is achieved by "losing in order to find."[126] Such a self-realization requires the help of God or grace. In commenting on the work of Erich Fromm, Niebuhr observes:

> Fromm correctly discerns the weakness of a Christian moralism which regards the love commandment as the expression of a simple obligation which the self can, by sufficient will-power, obey. But in order to eliminate this error he falls into the more grievous one of making love of the neighbor a "phenomenon of abundance," a by-product of the overflowing vitality of the self which first loves itself. Such a view fails to measure the freedom of the self in its dimension of transcendence over self, which makes it impossible for it to be rich within itself.[127]

Though Niebuhr insists that benevolence is of the essence of Christian love and that the *"Agape* of Christ, which is the norm of Christian selfhood, is always finally defined as sacrificial love, as the love of the cross,"[128] he nevertheless (unlike Nygren) is concerned to preserve a connection as well as make a distinction between divine and human love. He claims that there is a "dialectic" between the highest form of love, divine love, and human loves which involve some self-interest:

> Mutual love (*philia*) is . . . a form of love, for the life of the other is enhanced. Yet, on the other hand, such expressions of love fall short of love in its ultimate form. For they are mixed with a careful calculation of interest and advantages in which the self always claims an equal share. The final form of love is bereft of such calculation and meets the needs of the other without calculating comparative rights. Sacrificial love is therefore a form of love which transcends the limits of love.

[125] *Faith and History*, Ch. XI, Sect. II, p. 175.

[126] Niebuhr refers to this as "the paradox of self-realization through self-giving." (*Christian Realism and Political Problems*, Ch. 10, Sect. III, p. 164.)

[127] *Faith and History*, Ch. XI, Sect. II, p. 177. Niebuhr admits that there are critical occasions when, without grace, a human being can transcend his natural inclinations and sacrifice himself for another. Such occasions "endow the individual with resources beyond his natural capacities. The mother who sacrifices her life for her child is enabled to do this by the heightening of the natural impulses of mother love in a moment of crisis. In soberer moments of reflection she could not give herself so completely for another life." (*An Interpretation of Christian Ethics*, p. 216.)

[128] *Christian Realism and Political Problems*, Ch. 10, Sect. III, p. 159.

Such sacrificial love "cannot be separated from the realm of natural love (whether *Eros* or *philia*) by a neat line. . . . Yet without an element of heedless love, every form of mutual love would degenerate into a calculation of mutual advantages."[129] In other words, it is incorrect to restrict benevolence solely to the realm of supernatural love.

It is in commenting on the relationship of love to law or justice that Niebuhr puts special stress on this point. He claims that Luther separates the two realms absolutely, and thus removes love as the final form of all human activity:

> Love . . . is only *Agape* in its purest and most unadulterated form, which means in a form in which it is known in human experience only in rare moments of evangelical fervor or crisis heroism. This is why the Lutheran formulation of the relation of love to law is so irrelevant to the broad area of common experience in which one must balance claims and counterclaims and make discriminate judgments about competing interests.[130]

In his comparable comment on Nygren he says:

> Nygren's exposition of the contrast between *Agape* and natural love is not so much concerned with the contrast between *Agape* and the positive law as in Luther. But his idea of an absolute contradiction between *Agape* and *Eros* contains the same error. It is the error of a too rigorous separation of the realm of grace and the realm of nature.[131]

Though disassociating himself from the view taken by Luther and Nygren, Niebuhr also makes clear that he is not in sympathy with the Catholic view as represented by M. C. D'Arcy. He says that "Catholic thought . . . is more inclined than the Reformation to interpret love as *pleroma* of everything intended in nature and in law. But it is also inclined to interpret love as yet a more rigorous law, thus obscuring the elements of ecstasy and spontaneity, which are the marks of 'grace.' "[132] Since law always involves the interest of the self as well as the interest of others, Niebuhr seems to be criticizing Catholic thought for affirming that all human love, grace-aided or not, must have an element of self-interest in it and cannot be disinterested, spontaneous, or ecstatic. On the other hand, he criticizes Luther and Nygren for affirming that love always has the opposite character and, hence, for making it irrelevant as a norm for all human activities.

Niebuhr summarizes his own position as between the Catholic position and Nygren's in the following way:

129 *Ibid.*, pp. 160–161, *passim.*
130 *Ibid.*, pp. 162–163.
131 *Ibid.*, p. 163.
132 *Ibid.*, Sect. I, p. 149.

Broadly speaking, the end of the law is justice. But we have already seen that justice is related to love. Thus there is a dialectical relation between love and law even as there is between love beyond law and love as law. It might be stated as follows: The law seeks for a tolerable harmony of life with life, sin presupposed. It is, therefore, an approximation of the law of love on the one hand and an instrument of love on the other hand. Consequently the distinction between law and love is less absolute and more dialectical than conceived in either Catholic or Reformation thought.[133]

d. *Paul Tillich*

Tillich also is unwilling to draw a very sharp distinction between *eros* and *agape* and even more unwilling to set up a sharp opposition between them. This unwillingness to follow Nygren in these two respects must be understood against the background of his theory of love as a whole.

Though Tillich says that "love is the moving power of life," he has a more specific conception of it than tendency in general. For him the essence of love is a tendency toward a certain kind of union. That union is not one that combines the absolutely alien with the absolutely alien. Insofar as it is not, "love cannot be described as the union of the strange but as the reunion of the estranged. Estrangement presupposes original oneness."[134] The impulse toward that original oneness is characteristic of love in all of its manifestations. Indeed, for Tillich, love is essentially indivisible. Viewed "ontologically," as he says a serious consideration forces us to view it, love is one thing. That is to say, in terms of the being or essence of love, all of its forms have in common the inclination to reunite the separated in a certain way.[135]

One of the ways of uniting rejected by Tillich as falling within the scope of love is the impulse that is completely "emotional." Though there is no love without emotion, to restrict love to the emotional is to misunderstand it.[136] It is to destroy its essential oneness.

> The ontology of love leads to the basic assertion that love is one. This contradicts the main trend in the recent discussions of the nature of love. They were useful in so far as they directed the attention to the different qualities of love. But they were and are misleading in so far as they consider the differences of qualities as differences of types.[137]

Tillich goes on to say:

[133] *Ibid.*, Sect. V, pp. 171–172.
[134] *Love, Power, and Justice*, Ch. II, p. 25.
[135] See *ibid.*, pp. 18–20, 23.
[136] See *ibid.*, pp. 24–27.
[137] *Ibid.*, pp. 27–28.

Traditionally *epithymia* ("desire") is considered the lowest quality of love.
. . . There is a strong interest on the part of philosophical and theological
moralists in establishing a complete gap between this quality and those
which are supposed to be higher and essentially different. On the other
hand, there is a tendency on the naturalist side to reduce all the other
qualities of love to the *epithymia* quality.[138]

Tillich opposes both of these positions. He argues, first of all, that the
attempt to reduce all love to "desire" is based on faulty psychology. It
assumes, as all hedonistic theories assume, that the aim of action is the
pleasure or satisfaction that action will produce in the person. But,
according to Tillich, it is not pleasure that man seeks but specific goods,
"food, movement, growth, participation in a group, sexual union, etc." and
the "fulfilment of these desires is *accompanied* by pleasure."[139] In short,
there is or can be, a difference between the aim of a desire and the
resultant pleasure that accompanies the fulfillment of that desire.

Tillich admits, in opposing the contention that *eros* and *agape* are totally
separate, that self-interest is involved in every manifestation of human love.
It is right to say that *"epithymia is a quality which is not lacking in any
love relation."*[140] It is only wrong, as the naturalists are wrong, to reduce
all love or even *eros* alone to *epithymia*. In Tillich's view, that reduction
plays an important role in the attempts radically to distinguish *agape* from
eros. As he says, the "attempts to establish an absolute contrast between
agape and *eros* usually presuppose an identification of *eros* and *epithymia*."
As part of his opposition to the asserted contrast between *agape* and *eros*,
Tillich denies that *eros* is reducible to or identical with *epithymia*. *Eros* can
only be understood as *epithymia* when the latter is pursued "for vital self-
fulfilment and not for . . . pleasure."[141] This is one reason that Tillich is
unwilling to call sheer, selfish acquisitiveness self-love or love in any sense
at all.[142]

Another reason why sheer acquisitiveness is ruled out by Tillich as a
form of love is that all love is "ecstatic." That is to say:

> The moment of love is a moment of self-transcendence. This implies the
> ecstatic character of Being in the sense of our transcending into the other
> Self while remaining within our own self.

He contrasts love, thus understood, with "loveless self-centeredness."[143]

Tillich distinguishes four types of love: "The *libido* type, culminating in

---

138 *Ibid.*, p. 28.
139 *Ibid.*, p. 29. (Italics added.)
140 *Ibid.*, p. 30.
141 *Ibid.*, *passim.*
142 See *ibid.*, pp. 33–34. See also *Being and Love*, Sect. IV, pp. 668 ff.
143 *Ibid.*, Sect. III, p. 666.

sex; the *eros* type, culminating in mystical union; the *philia* type, culminating in friendship; the *agape* type culminating in *caritas*."[144]

The libido type of love culminates in a kind of sexuality which is distinct from the "estranged form of sex" which aims at procreation or pleasure. In contrast, love that is sexual means "self-surrender not to the other being as such but to the other being as far as it is the other side of the love-unity." *Eros* "starts with sex ecstasy but elevates it beyond the vital self-transcendence." Such love strives for "the true and the beautiful itself" and "participates in the ultimate."[145] "The . . . *philia* type of love is bound to personality. It is self-transcendence toward the equal." With regard to the equal, ecstasy "is the participation in the self-realization of the friend in his changes and negativities. . . . Friendship depends on the participation of both sides as equals in an embracing unity."[146] The *agape* type of love "is self-sacrificing not for the sake of the other Self as such, but for the sake of the ultimate destiny of the other Self." Finally, the love toward God is "neither *agape* nor *philia* nor *eros* nor *libido* alone, but all of them united."[147]

Though Tillich stresses the benevolent character of *agape* when he describes it as the only thing that can overcome "the self-centeredness which contradicts the return to the unity,"[148] he also asserts that a self-interested motive (in the sense of self-transcendence) is of the essence of *agape*:

> The nearest to a meaningful idea of self-love seems to be in the *agape* type. . . . But the love of the *agape* type includes forgiveness and charity.[149]

Tillich, therefore, differs from Nygren in asserting that human *agape* is distinct from divine *agape* insofar as the former is either self-interested benevolence taking the form of a tendency to union or a blend of acquisitive and benevolent tendencies taking the form of a tendency to union.[150] In either case, *agape* does not exclude self-interest but incorporates it.

Tillich's view differs from the one set forth by Augustine and Aquinas in its denial that the merely acquisitive or "self-realization which is lacking the ecstatic self-transcendence"[151] is love at all. On the question of self-interest in relation to supernatural human love, however, he is closer to their view than to Nygren's.

---

144 *Ibid.*
145 *Ibid.*, p. 667, *passim.*
146 *Ibid.*, pp. 667–668.
147 *Ibid.*, p. 668.
148 *Ibid.*, Conclusion, p. 672.
149 *Ibid.*, Sect. IV, p. 669.
150 See *Love, Power, and Justice*, Ch. II, p. 25.
151 *Being and Love*, Sect. IV, p. 670.

e. *C. S. Lewis*

Though C. S. Lewis must also, finally, be classified as among those who
maintain that supernatural human love is always accompanied by a self-
interested motive, he maintains a position that does not exactly coincide
with that of Augustine and Aquinas. He differs from them in asserting (as
does Nygren) that the benevolence of supernatural human love is a disinterested one. Yet, insofar as he understands love as a *complex* of
acquisitive and benevolent tendencies, his theory includes a conception of
supernatural human love that involves self-interest.

Lewis makes his analysis of love, both natural and supernatural, in terms
of three notions: need-love, gift-love, and appreciative-love. In different
forms and in different proportions the elements signified by these notions
are all present in each of the natural loves of which he speaks: affection,
eros, and friendship. Supernatural loves are also a complex, and, insofar as
they all include some form of need-love (acquisitive desire), they are all, to
that degree, self-interested. In other words, what Lewis calls man's love for
God and his supernaturally-inspired love for other men are composed of a
tendency to get, a tendency to give, and admiration.

The only love that is totally disinterested is God's love. "This primal love
is Gift-love. In God there is no hunger that needs to be filled, only
plenteousness that desires to give."[152] In man, however, love includes both
benevolent and acquisitive tendencies. As regards natural love, Lewis says:

> God, as Creator of nature, implants in us both Gift-loves and Need-loves.
> The Gift-loves are natural images of Himself; proximities to Him by
> resemblance which are not necessarily and in all men proximities of ap-
> proach. . . . The Need-loves, so far as I have been able to see, have no
> resemblance to the Love which God is. They are rather correlatives, oppo-
> sites; not as evil is the opposite of good, of course, but as the form of the
> blancmange is an opposite to the form of the mould.[153]

Each of the natural tendencies in man has two parallels in the supernatural order: acquisitive tendencies both toward other men and toward
God, and benevolent tendencies both toward other men and toward God.
The supernatural forms of acquisitive and benevolent desire are only
possible with God's help or grace.[154]

With regard to the supernatural need-love for God, "Grace does not
create the need." It is already present "in the mere fact of our being

[152] *The Four Loves,* Ch. VI, p. 175.
[153] *Ibid.,* p. 176.
[154] See *ibid.,* pp. 176–179.

creatures, and incalculably increased by our being fallen creatures. What the Grace gives is the full recognition, the sensible awareness, the complete acceptance—even, with certain reservations, the glad acceptance—of this Need. For, without Grace, our wishes and our necessities are in conflict."[155]

In addition to transforming man's need for God, grace also transforms man's need for man and makes it charity.

> In reality we all need at times, some of us at most times, that Charity from others which, being Love Himself in them, loves the unlovable. But this, though a sort of love we need, is not the sort we want. We want to be loved for our cleverness, beauty, generosity, fairness, usefulness. The first hint that anyone is offering us the highest love of all is a terrible shock. . . .
>
> How difficult it is to receive, and to go on receiving, from others a love that does not depend on our own attraction.[156]

The ability to receive charity is, itself, a form of charity; grace transforms natural acquisitiveness so that man accepts charity, knowing that he is not naturally worthy of it.

According to Lewis, the benevolence that is part of supernatural human love is disinterested. Through grace, God gives men "a share of His own Gift-love."

> This is different from the Gift-loves He has built into their nature. These never quite seek simply the good of the loved object for the object's own sake. They are biased in favour of those goods they can themselves bestow, or those which they would like best themselves, or those which fit in with a pre-conceived picture of the life they want the object to lead. But Divine Gift-love—Love Himself working in a man—is wholly disinterested and desires what is simply best for the beloved.

Lewis adds that "Divine Gift-love in the man enables him to love what is not naturally lovable: lepers, criminals, enemies, morons, the sulky, the superior and the sneering."[157]

In addition to the supernaturally inspired benevolence among human beings, Lewis also considers a supernaturally inspired human benevolence toward God. By "a high paradox, God enables men to have a Gift-love towards Himself." He explains:

[155] *Ibid.*, p. 179. For natural acquisitive desire "Grace substitutes a full, childlike and delighted acceptance of our Need, a joy in total dependence. We become 'jolly beggars.' The good man is sorry for the sins which have increased his Need. He is not entirely sorry for the fresh Need they have produced. And he is not sorry at all for the innocent Need that is inherent in his creaturely condition. For all the time this illusion to which nature clings as her last treasure, this pretence that we have anything of our own or could for one hour retain by our own strength any goodness that God may pour into us, has kept us from being happy." (*Ibid.*, pp. 180–181.)

[156] *Ibid.*, pp. 181–182.

[157] *Ibid.*, p. 177.

There is of course a sense in which no one can give to God anything which is not already His; and if it is already His what have you given? But since it is only too obvious that we can withhold ourselves, our wills and hearts, from God, we can, in that sense, also give them. What is His by right and would not exist for a moment if it ceased to be His . . . He has nevertheless made ours in such a way that we can freely offer it back to Him.[158]

In Lewis' view, both the acquisitive and benevolent tendencies in charity do not supplant but rather supplement or transform their natural forms. In relating the human activities called "love" to the Love that is God, Lewis claims that "Divine Love does not *substitute* itself for the natural—as if we had to throw away our silver to make room for the gold. The natural loves are summoned to become modes of Charity while also remaining the natural loves they were."[159]

In order to understand the sense in which Lewis sees a relation between the natural and the supernatural, we must keep in mind his insistence that, though "our minds must divide and pigeon-hole," no one of the elements into which he divides the phenomena called love is love itself. One of the ways natural love is related to supernatural love is the presence of self-interest in both. Lewis holds that the benevolence of supernatural human love is disinterested. But, he includes both "Gift-love" and "Need-love" in supernatural human love and, therefore, includes self-interest in it.[160] This connection between the supernatural and natural is reflected in Lewis' repeated assertion that: "The highest . . . does not stand without the lowest." He goes on to add:

> It would be a bold and silly creature that came before its Creator with the boast "I'm no beggar. I love you disinterestedly." Those who come nearest to a Gift-love for God will next moment, even at the very same moment, be beating their breasts with the publican and laying their indigence before the only real Giver.[161]

Though he is in agreement with the preceding authors that supernatural human love always involves self-interest, he differs from them in his analysis of that love. Unlike Augustine and Aquinas, he asserts the possibility of a disinterested benevolence, but, also unlike them, he does not

[158] *Ibid.*, pp. 177–178. There is another indirect way of giving to God since "every stranger whom we feed or clothe is Christ." (*Ibid.*, p. 178.)

[159] *Ibid.*, pp. 183–184.

[160] *Ibid.*, p. 177. Lewis also includes in the complex love, "Appreciative love" or admiration. Three elements, then, go to make up what he calls love in both its natural and supernatural forms. "We murder to dissect. In actual life, thank God, the three elements of love mix and succeed one another, moment by moment." (*Ibid.*, Ch. II, p. 33.)

[161] *Ibid.*, Ch. I, p. 14. See also pp. 14–20, where Lewis discusses the distinction between the "nearness of likeness" and the "nearness of approach" to God.

conceive of benevolence alone as love; it is only one of the elements of a complex. He differs, also, from Bernard, who, although he discusses disinterested benevolence as a love, indicates that he does not think such a motive is humanly possible. Lewis, with Nygren, thinks that such a motive characterizes supernatural human love but he thinks, unlike Nygren, that it is always combined with "Need-love," with self-interest.

C. THE ARGUMENTS

As we have seen, the controversy about supernatural human love focuses sharply on the question of self-interestedness *vs.* disinterestedness. Perhaps because of this sharpness in the point at issue we find, in this dispute, as was not the case in the various disputes about natural love, rather wide agreement as to what the question at issue is. But, though there is a wide area of concord as to how a completely disinterested supernatural human love is conceived, there is a sharp existential disagreement as to whether such a love is possible. In other words, the question under discussion is not a conceptual question but rather a question of fact.

The representative authors presented in the previous section take their stands on the relationship between supernatural and natural love, and on the question of how divine influence affects natural love. As we have seen, some say that such influence perfects natural love but does not totally alter its character; others say that it perfects natural love and enables man to attain a state wherein he can transcend the self-interest that is inherent in natural love; still others say that supernatural love is devoid of self-interest, is completely alien to the natural, and that the former replaces the latter.

What arguments we find come principally from those who attack the orthodox Catholic view as represented in the theories of Augustine and Aquinas and those who defend that view.

As we have seen, a direct assault on that view is made by Nygren. Responding to Nygren, D'Arcy, in *The Mind and Heart of Love*, argues at length against his two principal theses: that there is no natural benevolence (all natural love being completely acquisitive), and that self-interest is no part of supernatural human love. D'Arcy summarizes Nygren's position by stating that Nygren thinks there are only two loves, the one "egocentric" and the other "theocentric,"[162] and that Nygren maintains "that self-centred love had crept into Christian thinking, been baptized by St. Augustine and as a result had contaminated medieval thought."[163]

---

[162] *The Mind and Heart of Love*, Ch. II, p. 66. D'Arcy also attributes this position to De Rougemont when he says that De Rougemont "allows for no kind of love in between the pagan passion of Eros and the Christian and supernatural love of charity." (*Ibid.*, Ch. I, p. 48. See also Ch. XIV, p. 350.)

[163] *Ibid.*, Preface, p. 12.

D'Arcy freely admits the contrast between acquisitive and benevolent desire. He also concedes that "the question to be answered is, how is egoism reconciled with altruism or how is possessiveness compatible with self-sacrifice?" [164] He asserts that the principle of self-interest is absolutely basic to human nature and that self-interest is present in natural and supernatural human love, since human agency is operative in both. He notes that "if this principle of self-love were totally true, then a grave difficulty would arise. For we should have to ask how it is possible to love others for themselves and how we can love God more than ourselves." D'Arcy adds: "Nygren stuck at this difficulty and resolved it by clearing away love of self."[165]

D'Arcy attacks Nygren's solution of the problem first by denying that natural tendency and acquisitive tendency are synonymous. He claims that the distinction between natural human benevolence and natural human acquisitiveness is reflected throughout nature:

> The simplest statement of the law which governs what is highest and lowest in the Universe can be called that of "Give and Take." In the most elementary changes in the physical world there is gain and loss, the taking on of something and the passing on of what once was and no longer is. . . . This principle is seen more clearly in the continuation of life. There is always a duality, of which one aspect is negative as compared with the other: one gives and the other takes. . . . The important point to notice is the universal fact of duality. What we meet in the animal world and in human beings has its analogies in art and literature and science.[166]

The analogy between subhuman and human inclinations must not be pressed too far. Man has a unique status. Human love is basically different from animal love. The higher actions of man have intrinsic value and he has a personal dignity.

> This dignity implies a radical difference between human love and any lower form of love. It forbids alike the brutal possessiveness which marks the positive, male surge of animal passion and the total self-yielding of feminine ecstasy . . . on the human level each self must grow in the taking and giving and each is a sacred life which must be respected.[167]

In human love, neither of the two tendencies totally possesses a human being. They are complementary rather than conflicting, both among human beings and within them. "Every human person has these two loves

[164] *Ibid.*, Ch. VIII, p. 228. See also Ch. III, p. 99.
[165] *Ibid.*, Ch. XIV, p. 359.
[166] *Ibid.*, Preface, pp. 14–15.
[167] *Ibid.*, pp. 15–16.

within him, with one usually predominant, but the sacrificial impulse has a new direction."[168]

D'Arcy summarizes this line of argument by saying:

> To give . . . as well as to take, is inherent in living organisms, and in the more developed animals we may well suppose that this mounts up into a desire equally strong as that of self-love and equally enjoyed. Two loves co-exist in every living thing.[169]

D'Arcy seems to mean two things when he says that the "principle of give and take has to be harmonized in all phases of love." The first is that benevolent desires as well as acquisitive desires are both natural human possibilities. An authentic benevolence does not require supernatural aid. (Nor does supernatural aid totally eliminate natural self-interest. "Grace perfects nature and does not undo it.") His second meaning seems to be that in a human (not an animal) love relationship, the two tendencies "balance" each other. On the one hand, the desire to get never goes to the point where the other is merely used or harmed as one would use or harm a thing, with no consideration for the person at all. On the other hand, the desire to give never goes to the point where the giver is indifferent to his own interest.[170]

Another sense in which the two tendencies "balance" each other is that no genuinely human love relationship involves one person doing all the taking and the other all the giving. "The principle of give and take has to be harmonized in all phases of love."[171] That harmony or combination is characteristic of a relationship involving human persons rather than a strictly animal relationship. The latter is characterized both by the separation of acquisitive and benevolent tendencies and by the unrestrained character of each. The former is characterized by the combination of these tendencies and the resultant check imposed on each.[172]

D'Arcy refers to the two tendencies in man in many ways, *e.g.*, intellect and will, masculine and feminine, egocentric and altruistic, but most frequently and most centrally he calls them the desires, respectively, of *animus* and *anima*. *Animus* is assertive and acquisitive. *Anima* is passive and benevolent.[173] Of the two D'Arcy says:

[168] *Ibid.*, p. 16. See also Ch. IX, p. 252.
[169] *Ibid.*, Ch. IX, p. 243.
[170] *Ibid.*, Ch. II, p. 83, *passim.* "Selfishness is only a vice if it means an undue regard for self; unselfishness is only a virtue if it is countered by self-respect. The two loves, therefore, so far from being opposites appear to require the presence of each other." (*Ibid.*, Ch. XIV, p. 348. See also Ch. III, p. 100.)
[171] *Ibid.*, Ch. II, p. 83.
[172] See *ibid.*, Ch. XIV, p. 362; Ch. IX, p. 244.
[173] See *ibid.*, p. 231; Ch. XIV, p. 358.

One love takes and possesses; the other love likes to be beside itself and give. One is masculine, the other is feminine. The two are necessary for one another, and together they tell us what we are and whither we are going. To neglect either is to court death.

If the self concentrates solely on its aggressive and acquisitive tendencies, an inflated egoism results, which, because not fed by external nourishment, collapses into "a period of melancholia and death." If the self concentrates on the opposite tendency, if it abandons itself to ecstatic love, "it moves like a moth to the candle . . . [choosing] to be a victim, to die of love and to find its sole joy in self-immolation."[174]

In contrast, D'Arcy advocates an ideal human love which is a combination of both tendencies checking and balacing each other:

> The ideal human life should consist in Animus and Anima composing their quarrels and coming together in amity. They are both human in their excellence and ought to be on the best of terms. The self to which both belong needs their combined help. They fill up each other's wants, and in the rise and fall and positive and negative rhythm of their interplay, they keep the self from lapsing into one opposite or extreme.[175]

Or, as he also says:

> The two serve each other's ends, and bring it about that perfect love is mutual giving and taking, possessing and being possessed.[176]

For D'Arcy, the true relationship of *eros* and *agape* must be understood in the light of friendship, which is the perfect love relationship.[177] That relationship, far from excluding self-interest, presupposes it in order to maintain the necessary balance between giving and getting.

Before going on to consider two other main lines of argument advanced by D'Arcy against the position taken by Nygren, it would be well to consider here the defense against this argument that is implied in the position Nygren takes and that could be taken by other authors who claim that all natural love is exclusively acquisitive.

In contrast to D'Arcy, Nygren insists that the two basic forms of natural love are the lower or carnal *eros* and the higher or spiritual *eros*. The difference between them is not one of mode but of object. The lover seeks in the former a lower good and in the latter a higher good, but in both he seeks goods for himself. Nygren even might concede D'Arcy's distinction between *animus* and *anima*, take and give, as a way of describing two basic

---

[174] *Ibid.*, p. 354.
[175] *Ibid.*, Ch. VII, p. 213.
[176] *Ibid.*, Ch. IX, p. 263.
[177] See *ibid.*, Ch. IV, pp. 118–139; Preface, pp. 9–10; and Introduction, p. 31.

tendencies inherent in all existing things. But, in line with his general position, he would be quick to point out that the difference between the tendencies is merely one of expression, not aim, of means rather than end. *Animus* takes without giving; *anima* gets through giving. Both tendencies are "motivated" in the sense that the spur for action springs from a disturbance or inadequacy in the self. Whatever the self inclines to naturally it has some sort of interest in; and, insofar as it has such an interest, the natural tendency is reducible to self-love. The movement of love is directly and indirectly for the sake of the self.

Nygren undoubtedly would insist that his position is, in fact, conceded in the descriptions D'Arcy gives of subhuman tendencies, particularly in the description of the procreative impulse. Commenting on the "universal fact of duality," D'Arcy says:

> This principle is seen more clearly in the continuation of life. There is always a duality, of which one aspect is negative as compared with the other: one gives and the other takes. The giving is a surrender and implies a certain passivity, perhaps even unto death and extinction. The desire which is felt by the two parties in this momentary or prolonged union accords with the role played. There is the whoop of triumph, the exultant mastery in the act of possession and on the other side there is a joy in self-surrender even to absorption and total extinction in the being of the other.[178]

He also adds that, "since there is in the lower forms of life no true individuality in either participant, there is nothing to prevent the owner of the instinct from rushing in joy to its death."[179] In Nygren's view, the reason for such passivity, surrender, or giving is clearly not the good of the other but the spur of the pleasure or joy the giver experiences. Its action aims at that pleasure or joy, and it only surrenders as a means of getting it. In giving, it is fulfilling its nature.

Nygren sees no alteration of this formula on the human level. Some human tendencies are admittedly different from animal impulses but they are no less acquisitive at root. All natural human desires are hedonistic or eudaemonistic; they aim finally at personal pleasure or happiness.

D'Arcy is at pains to show that there is a radical difference between animal and human love, but, in Nygren's view, that difference does not mitigate D'Arcy's claim that all human love is acquisitive. That in human love, brutal, complete, or aggressive acquisitiveness as well as total self-yielding are precluded, merely indicates to Nygren that certain extreme forms of getting and giving are precluded because of the presence of mutual human respect. It does not mean that an authentic benevolence is

[178] *Ibid.*, Preface, pp. 14–15.
[179] *Ibid.*, p. 15.

present. Nygren probably would point out that D'Arcy says that among humans the desire to give is as strong as the desire to get and "equally enjoyed."[180] To enjoy giving is to have an interest in giving, and interested giving is not benevolence but self-love.

D'Arcy freely admits that self-interest is involved in any human giving, but he does not see thereby why such giving should be called a mixed form of acquisitive desire. He even goes as far as to say that the "fundamental movement of love may be egocentric, but so far as we experience that movement and look at our motives we find that it is anything but selfish."[181] D'Arcy claims that there can be two aspects to a human motivation, a good for the self as well as a good for another; that the latter can characterize a human desire; that the two aspects are far from incompatible; and that the latter is not necessarily ordered to the former. If these claims are valid, a theorist of love can argue, and many do argue, that there is such a thing as a bivalent desire, that it is possible to perform one action for two motives that are not ordered one to the other. Thus, if a man gets satisfaction in giving to another, he need not be giving solely in order to experience that satisfaction, though the anticipation of that satisfaction can be one of his incentives. If a man anticipates reciprocity as a result of his beneficence to others, he need not be giving only for the sake of the expected return, though that expectation can be one of his incentives. It is precisely the possibility of this bivalence that Nygren contests. He says that "Agape-love is directed to the neighbour himself, with no further thought in mind and no side-long glances at anything else."[182] But even more important is his insistence that, if there is a "side-long glance," the love is not *agape*, not benevolent at all but acquisitive and self-interested basically and finally, as is all natural love.[183]

D'Arcy himself does not deal with this point at any length. He argues in a different manner. In addition to asserting that there is a necessary interplay of acquisitive and benevolent tendencies in all characteristically human love, D'Arcy offers at least two other main lines of argument; one, to support his contention that any human love, including supernatural human love, must involve the interests of the self; and, the other, to show how self-interest and benevolence can be reconciled.

The main thrust of D'Arcy's first line of argument is that supernatural human love ceases to be human in any sense at all if self-interest is elimi-

[180] *Ibid.*, Ch. IX, p. 243.
[181] *Ibid.*, Ch. III, p. 100.
[182] *Agape and Eros*, Part I, Ch. 3, Sect. III, p. 215.
[183] The opposed position taken by Aquinas and reflected in the position taken by D'Arcy is discussed and analyzed extensively in Louis B. Geiger's *Le Problème de l'Amour chez Saint Thomas d'Aquin.*

nated from it. In demanding that all traces of the self be removed, Nygren "is asking the impossible," because such a demand removes the person altogether from the stage of love as an actor or agent. "The consequence of uprooting what Nygren calls egocentric love would be, if only he were to follow out the logic of his thought, to extinguish human love altogether."[184] D'Arcy argues that in treating *agape* as solely a matter of disinterested benevolence, Nygren has reduced the human person to the status of a transmitter with no dignity at all. He adds nothing to the love that flows from him, since everything comes from God and nothing at all from him. D'Arcy admits that man needs God's help when he loves supernaturally, but he denies that nothing human is involved:

> Even though man's love in the new covenant of friendship with God is supernatural, that is to say, beyond his natural capacity, he does not become an automaton; he is not forced, not taken hold of willy nilly and made to love. The whole purpose of God's action is to give and not to take away, to restore and increase the dignity of the human person. This means that man must be left his freedom, his power to accept or refuse, and his power, consequently, to merit by co-operation with Divine love.[185]

Nygren not only would not deny the consequence D'Arcy draws from his position, he would and does insist that, because of the radically different nature of *agape*, nothing human, nothing of *eros* can be involved in it. All human tendencies spring from deficiency, have an upward movement, seek to possess and to gain, and are inspired by the quality of the object to which they are directed. All divine tendencies spring from excess, have a downward movement, seek only to give and create values in the object rather than react to values present in it. The latter are tendencies of which man, even with God's help, is incapable. In a real sense, supernatural love among human beings is not a love by human beings; it is God's love operating through them.

For this reason, Nygren frequently refers to the Christian as but a

---

[184] *The Mind and Heart of Love*, Ch. II, p. 80. "But if this theory is taken literally there is no one to respond. There is no need of that intercommunication which is essential to love. We are told that no Eros (in Nygren's sense) should enter into man's return of love, that it should be all Agape. But as we have seen, God is Agape. There is nothing human or personal in the response, nor can there be on this interpretation. In the elimination of Eros man has been eliminated." (*Ibid.*, p. 82.)

[185] *Ibid.*, Ch. II, Appendix 2, p. 90. "Nygren rejected the self-regarding love, and as a result mutilated the idea of a person." (*Ibid.*, Ch. XIV, p. 357.) A bit earlier, D'Arcy says that, when God does everything and man nothing and when self-regard and self-perfection are completely removed, the result is one deplored by Nygren himself. "Nygren," claims D'Arcy, "does not seem to see that what he says takes us away from Christianity and leads directly to the ideal of mystic fusion which so repels him. If man can do nothing, then extreme quietism is his lot, a quietism which must end in man being swallowed up in union with the godhead." (*Ibid.*, p. 353.)

channel, a receptacle, a means for the outflow of divine love.[186] The effect
of original sin is to remove any possibility of his contributing in any way to
the exercise of such love. As there is nothing good left in him, nothing
good can come from anything he originates.[187] With regard to *agape,*
though the love does flow through him, the Christian is totally passive. On
no other premise is supernatural love among human beings explicable.
Christianity enjoins the love of all men, whatever their character and
quality. A human love of all men, particularly of enemies, is inexplicable
since human love does not bestow and create value but reacts to value in
the object. "When my neighbour happens to be also my enemy, obviously
no reason for my loving him can be found in his own character or conduct."[188]

D'Arcy's replies to these claims, implied in the position he takes, take
several forms. First, he admits that man's nature, his capacity for good, was
injured by the fall in the Garden of Eden. Hence, he concedes the necessity for divine aid. But he emphatically denies that original sin left
nothing of any worth in man. As man retains some worth, he is capable of
doing some good to others. As his neighbors, even his enemies, have intrinsic worth by virtue of their having been created in God's image, he is
capable of reacting to the worth in them and not always for his own benefit
but sometimes for theirs. To speak of man as worthless, as capable of being
nothing but a channel or vehicle for divine love, is to remove the idea of
man as a person whose grace-aided actions are attempts to imitate divine
action. It is to remove completely the distinction between human *agape*
and divine *agape.*

Though it is precisely Nygren's intention to remove that distinction, he
does indicate awareness of the difficulties involved in eliminating human
agency altogether from supernatural human love. Those difficulties appear
in Nygren's struggles with the language he uses to set forth his position.
On the one hand, he refers to supernatural human love as God's love, and,
on the other, as a "reflection" of which God's love is the "prototype,"
"criterion," and "source."[189] He even distinguishes between the absolute
spontaneity of God's love and the relative spontaneity of man's love for
God and his neighbor.[190] He speaks of man's love for God signifying "that
man, moved by this Divine love, gratefully wills to belong wholly to
God,"[191] despite the fact that elsewhere he insists that man has no choice

186 See *Agape and Eros,* Part 1, Ch. 3, Sect. III, pp. 212, 218; Part 2, Ch. 6, Sect.
IV, pp. 734–735.
187 See *ibid.,* Part 1, Ch. 1, Sect. I, pp. 78–79.
188 *Ibid.,* Ch. 3, Sect. III, p. 215.
189 *Ibid.,* Part 1, Ch. 1, Sect. I, p. 97; Ch. 3, Sect. III, p. 218.
190 See *ibid.,* Ch. 1, Sect. I, pp. 94–95.
191 *Ibid.,* Ch. 3, Sect. III, p. 213.

at all in the matter and that neither his will nor anything of him is involved at all.[192] Nygren also observes that "the idea of appetitive desire can only be applied in a metaphorical sense to man's attitude to God,"[193] despite the fact that he consistently denies that the notion of desire is applicable to *agape* in any sense at all.[194]

The most striking difficulty Nygren faces—in claiming that supernatural human love is nothing but God's love operative in men—is explaining what sense there is in saying that man loves God. Obviously, there is a serious problem in saying that man's love for God is really God's love for Himself, since self-love of any kind is the one thing emphatically excluded from the realm of *agape*. In addition, *agape* does not respond to value, it creates it. But value cannot be created in God even by His own love channeled through men, since all the value there is comes from Him. Yet, in no other way can God be said to be the object of supernatural love in man since *agape*, by definition, "has no teleological but only a causal significance."[195] God does not excite love as the final end, or highest good, but only as the efficient cause having within Himself the only reason for loving.

Nygren's only resolution of this difficulty is found in his presentation of the view of Luther, to which he subscribes. That resolution consists finally in denying that there is any direct, literal meaning at all in speaking of man's supernatural love for God. Precisely because *agape* is always a downward, value-creating, spontaneous, and unmotivated movement, it cannot be directed by man or through man to God. In line with Paul's willingness to use the term *agape* in referring to man's love for God, Luther *reduces* love for God to love for neighbor. The commandment to love God has only one meaning: compliance with the divine will. The divine will is expressed in divine love, *agape*, flowing through the Christian as through a "tube" to other men. The commandment of love for God is, therefore, summed up in its entirety in the commandment of love for one's neighbor. There is only one *agape* and that is God's love bestowed directly on the Christian or on other men through the Christian. To love God means only to be open (even though such openness is involuntary) to the stream of divine love so that it can flow through to others.[196]

D'Arcy's second principal line of argument appears in response to

[192] See *ibid.*, pp. 213–214.

[193] *Ibid.*, p. 213.

[194] In Nygren's view, *eros* and *agape* do, however, have something in common: tendency. "Love . . . implies motion, a movement towards an object." (*Ibid.*, pp. 215–216.)

[195] *Ibid.*, p. 216.

[196] See *ibid.*, Part 2, Ch. 6, Sect. IV, pp. 734–737. See also Part 1, Ch. 1, Sect. II, pp. 124 ff.

Nygren's complaint that, if a self-interested motive is involved in man's love for God, such a motive involves reducing God to a means of human happiness. "Even though God is described as the *highest* good, this does not alter the fact that He is degraded to the level of a means for the satisfaction of human desire."[197] Nygren stresses this point in criticizing Augustine:

> The fact that love to God . . . receives an egocentric emphasis does not worry Augustine. He is satisfied so long as God is not "used" as a means to some other end, but is "enjoyed" as the final goal where we come to rest. This latter Augustine calls "loving God for His own sake," but he never considered the fact that the enjoyment itself is ultimately "for *our* own sake."[198]

Since, in his reply, D'Arcy rests heavily on the arguments advanced by Aquinas, and since Nygren refers directly to them, it will be useful to present those arguments here. Aquinas maintains that it is not primarily as a means that man's acquisitive tendency is directed to God, since God is the final end and not an intermediary one. Second, he maintains that a self-interested motive is compatible with human benevolence toward God.

According to Aquinas, the precept that God is to be loved includes "the precept that each one love himself. The reason for this is that as we are induced to love God, we are induced to desire Him, by which we especially love ourselves and wish for ourselves the highest good."[199]

When Aquinas refers to a sense in which human love for God is self-love, he clearly distinguishes this acquisitive tendency from the acquisitiveness of natural love in which the other is used *only* as a means. For Aquinas, God is not primarily a means to man's happiness; God *is* man's happiness in the sense that man's final happiness consists in union with Him. He is the last end of all things. In the sense in which man loves God "for His own sake," man seeks God as an end and not as a means to an end. Aquinas makes clear that this is his meaning when he discusses the meaning of the word "for" in the phrase "for His own sake." He points out that "for" denotes a causal relation and examines what he considers to be the four kinds of causes: final, formal, efficient, and material. According to these four causes, one thing is said to be loved *for* another. As regards the final cause, medicine is loved for the sake of health. As regards the formal cause, a man is loved for the sake of his virtue. As regards the efficient cause, someone is loved because he is the son of a father who is beloved for

197 *Ibid.*, Part 2, Ch. 2, Sect. III, p. 500. See also Part 1, Ch. 1, Sect. I, p. 92.
198 *Ibid.*, Part 2, Ch. 4, Sect. III, p. 641.
199 *On Charity*, Art. VII, Reply Obj. 10, pp. 63–64.

other reasons. As regards the material cause, someone is loved because of benefits received from him. After making these distinctions, Aquinas says:

> Accordingly, as regards the first three ways, we love God, not for anything else, but for Himself. For He is not directed to anything else as to an end, but is Himself the last end of all things; nor does He require to receive any form in order to be good, for His very substance is His goodness, which is itself the exemplar of all other good things; nor again does goodness accrue to Him from aught else, but from Him to all other things.[200]

There are, then, three senses in which God cannot be loved as a means; but there is a fourth in which He can be so loved.

> In the fourth way, however, He can be loved for something else, because we are disposed by certain things to advance in His love, for instance, by favors bestowed by Him, by the rewards we hope to receive from Him, or even by the punishments which we are minded to avoid through Him.[201]

There is even another sense in which Aquinas says that God can be considered as a means. He points out that God, the last end, may be considered in two ways: simply and in respect of the individual. To refer to the last end simply is to refer to the thing itself; to refer to it in respect of an individual is to refer to the attainment or possession of that thing. The last end simply is God; the last end in respect of the individual is the attainment of God. To the extent that one speaks of man's last end in the second sense, one may speak of God as a means.[202]

In addition to man's love for God out of need, there is also a love for God "for His own sake," which does not aim primarily at man's happiness. Aquinas affirms that God ought to be loved first and foremost, and oneself second. He is obviously, in this connection, not referring to the love for God that springs only from need, since such a love, aiming at personal salvation, is a form of self-love. He is referring to a nonacquisitive love, a form of benevolence which can be said, analogically, to apply to the relationship between man and God.[203]

Aquinas makes the distinction between the two kinds of love most clearly in the following passage:

> That a man wishes to enjoy God pertains to that love of God which is love of concupiscence. Now we love God with the love of friendship more than

---

[200] *Summa Theologica*, Part II-II, Q. 27, Art. 3, Answer, Vol. II, p. 1307.
[201] *Ibid.*
[202] See *ibid.*, Part I-II, Q. 16, Art. 3, Vol. I, pp. 654–655.
[203] In one sense, it obviously cannot apply strictly, since God is perfect and cannot be given anything, *i.e.*, "helped" by an imperfect creature. (See *ibid.*, Part II-II, Q. 27, Art. 3, Answer, Vol. II, p. 1307, where Aquinas asserts that nothing can be added to God's goodness.)

with the love of concupiscence, because the Divine good is greater in itself, than our share of good in enjoying Him. Hence, out of charity, man simply loves God more than himself.[204]

The love of friendship of man for God is nonacquisitive in the sense that it does not aim exclusively or primarily at man's good; it is not reducible to self-love. Aquinas makes it clear that such a love is not primarily self-interested when he says:

> The part does indeed love the good of the whole, as becomes a part, not however so as to refer the good of the whole to itself, but rather itself to the good of the whole.[205]

Yet, in loving the good of the whole, *i.e.*, God, man is also and incidentally loving himself, since he is part of that whole. Aquinas reinforces this point by distinguishing between "a certain good proper to each man considered as one person" and "a certain common good which pertains to this man or that man insofar as he is considered as part of a whole." In the first way "each one is the principal object of his own love." In the second way, "the principal object of love is that in which the good primarily exists; just as the good of the army is in the general, or the good of the state is in the king." It is in this way that "charity regards the divine good as its principal object, which pertains to every one according as he is able to be a sharer in beatitude."[206] The benevolence of this form of charity is a self-interested one. ". . . God ought to be loved out of charity as the root of beatitude; however each man ought to love himself in charity in order that he may share in beatitude."[207]

Naming the other possible objects of charity, Aquinas goes on to say, "He should also love his neighbor as his associate in the participation of beatitude, and his own body according as beatitude redounds to it."[208] In the order of charity, the objects to be loved are: God, self, neighbor, and one's own body.[209] (Aquinas includes the body as an object of charity because he says that on the last day it will be rejoined with the soul and hence will participate in eternal beatitude.)

[204] *Ibid.*, Part II-II, Q. 26, Art. 3, Reply Obj. 3, p. 1297.
[205] *Ibid.*, Reply Obj. 2, p. 1297.
[206] *On Charity*, Art. IV, Reply Obj. 2, p. 43, *passim.*
[207] *Ibid.*, Art. VII, Answer, p. 62.
[208] *Ibid.*
[209] See *Summa Theologica*, Part II-II, Art. 12, Vol. II, p. 1294. There is also a sense in which things can be loved in charity insofar as one wishes them for the sake of a person's welfare or beatitude. But this is love only in a secondary sense. Love, strictly speaking, means to wish someone well. Charity understood as wishing someone well can only be extended to those things "for which we are able to wish the good of eternal beatitude, for they are the things which were begotten to enjoy a good of this kind." (*On Charity*, Art. VII, Answer, p. 61.)

In commenting on the Thomistic solution to the problem of the reconciliation of self-interest with supernatural human love for God, D'Arcy discusses two different interpretations of it. The first is that of Pierre Rousselot; the second that of Étienne Gilson. Both interpretations affect the reconciliation by asserting that human good is always a function of divine good. Since there is a necessary association of the two goods, to love God is also and necessarily to love oneself. Though both positions are based on the unity of the divine and the human good, Rousselot and Gilson differ on the kind of unity each sees between God and man. According to D'Arcy, that difference is summarized in the emphasis that Rousselot places on the relationship of the part to the whole, on the one hand, and on the emphasis that Gilson places on the relationship of the image to the reality, on the other.

For Rousselot, the Thomistic solution to the problem is to be found in the special union between the part and the whole. The part that loves itself individualistically and solely as a part cuts itself off from the larger whole wherein it finds its true welfare. To look to the good of the whole is natural. For the part to sacrifice itself for that good, if necessary, also is natural. "Thus, it is natural that the hand is risked for the body, as it is also natural that an element moves into a place it would not normally go in order to avoid a vacuum."[210] The union of which Rousselot speaks, however, is one that is not indivisible but composed of parts differing in kind. It is in this sense that Rousselot says that "the total universe is more than any of its parts." An angel is more than a man and a man more than a stone, because each higher being has something that the lower ones do not have.[211] The love relationship between man and God is to be understood in these terms. The goodness of God's being transcends—as well as includes—the goodness of all beings below Him. Human love for the divine is self-interested because man is a part of the whole—the good of which he wills in willing the good of God.[212]

Gilson subscribes to the same Thomistic solution of the problem, but in a different way. For him, love for God is self-interested, not because man is a part of the whole in the sense in which the hand is part of the body. It is self-interested because man is an image of the divine reality.

In contrast to Rousselot, Gilson says:

[210] *Pour l'Histoire du Probleme de l'Amour au Moyen Age*, Ch. I, Sect. 1, p. 12. (Our translation.)

[211] See *ibid.*

[212] See *ibid.*, pp. 7–14. See also D'Arcy, *The Mind and Heart of Love*, Ch. III, pp. 102 ff. In making this argument, Rousselot is careful to note that man is not part of the whole which is God; he is part of the whole whose good is God. God is greater than the whole. He is not "the sum of beings in the universe; He is Being, infinite, separate." (*Pour l'Histoire du Probleme de l'Amour au Moyen Age*, Ch. I, Sect. 1, pp. 12–13.)

If we say that each good is but a particular good we can only mean, not that these particular goods are detached parts of a whole which would be Goodness, but that they are analogues of the creative Good that gave them birth.[213]

Gilson admits that there is some truth in the doctrine according to which "the relation of the divine to the human good is represented as the relation of a whole to its part." But he adds that, as soon as we leave the example of the hand and the body in the biological order and "seek one in the social order, then we can no longer hold to the same formula without risking a flagrant over-simplification."[214] Still less is the formula strictly applicable in describing man in relation to God.

> It is still true to say that God is the universal Good under which all particular goods are contained, but the relation of dependence in which man stands to God is no longer that of a part to its whole. God is not a whole of which man is a part; man is not a part of which God is the whole; the universal here in question embraces the particular in quite another manner than that in which the body contains the hand.[215]

Gilson adds:

> If . . . we say that God is the universal good, we can only mean that God is the sovereign good, the cause of all good. If we say that each good is but a particular good we can only mean, not that these particular goods are detached parts of a whole which would be Goodness, but that they are analogues of the creative Good that gave them birth.[216]

Applying the relationship of image to original, Gilson offers his solution of the problem of reconciling self-interest with love for God. "How reconcile love of self with love of God? There is no difficulty. Grant that a being is an image, and then the more it resembles its Original the more faithful it is to itself."[217] A little later on he is even more emphatic:

> In other words, it is impossible to love the image without at the same time loving the original, and if we know, as we do know, that the image is only an image, it is impossible to love it without preferring the original. What holds of the whole totality of creatures holds much more of man in particular. To will any object is to will an image of God, that is, to will God; to love oneself, then, will be to love an analogue of God, and that is to love God.[218]

213 *The Spirit of Mediaeval Philosophy,* Ch. XIV, p. 286.
214 *Ibid.,* p. 284.
215 *Ibid.,* p. 285.
216 *Ibid.,* pp. 285–286. See also Ch. XIV, Appendix, p. 302.
217 *Ibid.,* p. 297.
218 *Ibid.,* Ch. XIV, p. 286.

From this point of view it is impossible to sustain the claim that a self-interested motive involves using God as a means to one's own ends.

If . . . such and such a particular good is desirable only on account of its resemblance to the supreme Good, it is impossible to desire the supreme Good merely in view of this particular good; on the contrary, the particular good must always be desired for the supreme Good.[219]

Precisely because man's interest is inseparable from divine goodness, true love for God is "equally removed from the opposed extremes of utilitarianism and quietism." Though such love seeks no recompense in the sense of giving only in order to get, "neither should it be asked to renounce joy in the possession of the thing loved, for this joy is co-essential with love."[220]

Gilson goes further in denying that it is possible to love God merely as a means. A finite being desiring finite goods can have a merely utilitarian impulse toward them. "But the case is changed as soon as we admit the existence of an absolute good, such as that defined by Christianity. Human desire, henceforth, stands in the presence of an object such that it becomes quite impossible to desire it for anything other than itself."[221]

Gilson also says that "all human love is an analogical participation in God's own love for Himself." Hence, men must love God for His own sake just as He loves Himself for His own sake. If we love God otherwise, "our love is unfaithful to its own true essence."[222] Yet, precisely in loving God for His own sake, human need is best fulfilled, since a particular human good is contained in the divine good.

Of course, it is possible to misunderstand the relationship of human love to divine love and, hence, to love badly.

Man's misery lies in the fact that he can so easily deceive himself as to the true object, and suffer accordingly, without even suspecting that he does so; but even in the midst of the lowest pleasures, the most abandoned voluptuary is still seeking God; nay more, as far as regards what is positive in his acts, that is to say in all that makes them an analogue of the true Love, it is God Himself Who, in him and for him, seeks Himself.[223]

[219] *Ibid.* "To say that if man of necessity loves himself he cannot love God with disinterested love, is to forget that to love God with disinterested love is man's true way of loving himself." (*Ibid.*, p. 288.)

[220] *Ibid.*, p. 280. It is precisely in these terms that Gilson rejects Rousselot's critique of "Cistercian mysticism" and especially of Bernard's theory of love. For Gilson, Rousselot's claim that there are two forms of love presented in these devotional treatises—the physical or interested, and the ecstatic or disinterested—is an error. (See *ibid.*, Ch. XIV, Appendix, pp. 289 ff.)

[221] *Ibid.*, Ch. XIV, p. 278.

[222] *Ibid.*, pp. 278, 279.

[223] *Ibid.*, p. 274.

Though Gilson does say that "the end of human love is also its cause," he is far from denying that human agency is involved in supernatural human love. Man's love for God is not literally God's love channeled through men, it is only analogically God's love; it is an imitation of divine love by human will. Gilson says that "God is the cause of love inasmuch as He generates love in Himself, and causes it in other beings as an image and likeness of Himself."[224] Explaining in what sense God can be both the efficient cause of human love and its final object, Gilson goes on to say:

> As Being He is the sovereign good and the sovereignly desirable; therefore He wills and loves Himself; but since the good He loves is none other than His own Being, and since the love by which He loves this good is none other than His will, which is itself substantially identical with His being, God is His love. Now this love that God generates in Himself, and also substantially is, He causes in others by impressing on them a desire of His own perfection, analogous to the eternal act by which He loves Himself. Therefore we can, and, indeed, must, say that He moves His creatures to love Him; but here, as always in a Christian philosophy, the first motive cause differs from Aristotle's inasmuch as it is creative.[225]

Thus, Gilson takes sharp issue with Nygren in maintaining both that God is not only the efficient cause of love in men but also love's true object or final cause, and that human self-interest and love for God are not only compatible but inseparable.

With regard to the latter point, D'Arcy claims that all the strength of Gilson's argument "depends upon the analogy of image." Grant that man is an image of God in some strong sense and "the argument moves inevitably to the conclusion drawn."[226] But it is precisely on this point that Nygren most emphatically dissents.

Nygren bases his whole position on the subject of Christian love on the question of man's worth in relation to God, and opposes the position taken by Catholic theologians. By denying that after the Fall man is in any sense an "image" of God and that there is anything good in him, Nygren is also denying that any love that has any admixture of human motivation can be a good, *i.e.*, a Christian, love.[227] He does not deny that there is a fellowship of man with God. But he insists that this fellowship is one to which

[224] *Ibid.*, pp. 274–275. That image and likeness is present not only in men but in all existing things. "Born of love, the whole universe is penetrated, moved, vivified from within, by love that circulates through it like the life-giving blood through the body." (*Ibid.*, p. 276.)
[225] *Ibid.*, p. 275. For a parallel account of Gilson's position, see D'Arcy, *The Mind and Heart of Love*, Ch. III, pp. 108 ff.
[226] *Ibid.*, p. 111. For Jacques Maritain's comments on the relation of self-interest to love for God, see *Moral Philosophy*, Part I, Ch. 5, Sect. 7, pp. 76–79.
[227] See *Agape and Eros*, Part 1, Ch. 3, Sect. III, pp. 214 ff.

man does and can contribute nothing. It rests entirely on God's mercy. To hold otherwise is to perpetuate the "egocentric perversion" of the true Christian doctrine.

> Here everything centres upon man himself, upon what he does and what happens to him. Salvation, God's own work, which He has reserved to Himself and accomplished through Christ, is transformed more or less into a work of man; righteousness is transformed from something God gives into something man achieves. At the same time, everything also centres upon man's own *interest*. Through the idea of merit, the good which he does is put into intentional connection with eternal blessedness, so that it comes to be regarded less as obedience to God, than from the point of view of the profit which it yields for man. Everything is measured by the standard of human desire and judged by the importance it has for man. This applies even to God Himself. When He is extolled as the highest good, summum bonum, that is simply a way of saying that, when measured by the standard of human desire, He proves to comprise all the desirable things that man can possibly wish.[228]

Against this viewpoint, Luther's "Copernican revolution" restores the theocentric view according to which all fellowship between God and man is due entirely to God's love and not to any worth in man. Such a fellowship is not one of holiness, since man is incapable inherently of meriting anything in God's view, but a fellowship based upon sin, upon man's worthlessness.[229]

> The deepest difference between Catholicism and Luther can be expressed by the following formulae; in Catholicism: fellowship with God on God's own level, on the basis of holiness; in Luther: fellowship with God on our level, on the basis of sin. In Catholicism, it is a question of a fellowship with God motivated by some worth—produced, it is true, by the infusion of Caritas—to be found in man; in Luther, fellowship with God rests exclusively on God's unmotivated love, justification is the justification of the sinner.[230]

Nygren claims that Luther, by his insistence of justification by faith alone and not good works, takes an uncompromising stand against any notion of Christian love as an "upward tendency" and that at the center of his "struggle against the upward tendency stands his rejection of every idea of *merit*."[231] There are no "heavenly ladders" on which man can ascend

---

[228] *Ibid.*, Part 2, Ch. 6, Sect. I, pp. 681–682. Nygren admits of no compromise on this point. Any attempt to legitimize self-love within a Christian framework invariably leads to *agape* becoming a form of *eros*. (See *ibid.*, Part 1, Ch. 3, Sect. III, p. 217.)

[229] See *ibid.*, Part 2, Ch. 6, Sect. I, pp. 686 ff.

[230] *Ibid.*, p. 690.

[231] *Ibid.*, Sect. III, p. 700.

and make himself worthy of love. He can be lifted up only by the downward-reaching tendency of divine love. "God does not love that which is already in itself worthy of love, but on the contrary, that which in itself has no worth acquires worth just by becoming the object of God's love."[232]

It follows that, if man cannot make himself worthy, all his desire, all his self-love (be it directed to a high or a low object), is sinful.[233] Luther's idea of sin is thus governed by his idea of love. 'Love seeketh not its own.' As the opposite of this, the essence of sin is that man does seek his own. Judged by this standard, the whole of natural human life proves to be under the dominion of sin, since it has universally the character of a quest for 'its own.' " Hence, even the attempt to achieve fellowship with God "is polluted by the egocentricity which is inherent in everything human."[234]

D'Arcy agrees with Nygren that the difference between the Protestant and the Catholic views of love is a strict function of the difference between the two views of how much human nature lost as a result of original sin when he says that two prime representatives (Nygren and Gilson) of the differing views on love "differ because of their different view of the effects of the Fall. Nygren leaves nothing in man with which grace or Agape can collaborate, and so he can find no room for self-love in his concept of Christian Agape; Gilson agrees with St. Bernard and St. Thomas in holding that man is only wounded by the Fall and that therefore his high dignity remains. He naturally and rightly, therefore, loves himself."[235]

Closely connected with the question of the effect on human nature of original sin and the question of merit is the related question of whether or not justice is operative in the relationship between man and God. Nygren, of course, maintains that man can merit nothing from God and that there is no sense in which justice is involved in the relationship between man and God.

Fénelon also discusses the notion of merit. But in arguing for the possibility of a disinterested love for God, he seems to exclude any notion of justice as applicable to the relationship between man and God. He argues that any man's salvation is dependent on God's "arbitrary will." Accordingly, he maintains that "the kingdom of heaven is due to us only on the grounds of a purely gratuitous promise." One can only speak of "merit" when it is understood "that all our merits are not based on a strict right,

[232] *Ibid.*, Part 1, Ch. 1, Sect. I, p. 78.
[233] See *ibid.*, Part 2, Ch. 6, Sect. III, p. 710.
[234] *Ibid.*, pp. 713–714.
[235] *The Mind and Heart of Love*, Ch. III, pp. 109–110. It also might be noted that it is precisely this difference in regard to original sin that explains the presence of a natural benevolence in the Catholic view and its absence in the view presented by Nygren. Because something of human dignity is left in the former view, man can give benevolently of his own goodness to others. Because nothing of human dignity is left in the latter view, man, by himself, can try only to acquire.

but a promise made out of pure mercy." He then supposes "that God should will to annihilate my soul as soon as it is separated from my body," and goes on to say:

> A creature, that does not exist of itself, exists only insofar as the arbitrary will of the Creator makes it exist; to keep it from falling into its own non-being, the Creator has to renew incessantly the benefit of His creation, by preserving the creature through the same power which created it. I am therefore supposing something that is quite possible, for I am only supposing a simple exception to a purely gratuitous and arbitrary rule.

Fénelon puts himself into the position of someone who has but a moment to live and who knows that he "can no longer hope to possess God, or to see His face, or to love Him eternally, or to be loved by Him beyond this life." He then asks:

> Is it not evident that, under this quite possible supposition, I ought to love God solely for His own sake, without expecting any reward of my love, confronted with the certain loss of my beatitude; and as a consequence, this last instant of my life, which will be followed by eternal annihilation, must necessarily be taken up by an act of pure and fully disinterested love?

He answers that, under these conditions, he must love God none the less and that if he does not, he is "a monstrosity and an unnatural creature."

Fénelon summarizes his line of argument in the following passage:

> If eternal blessedness were due to us as a matter of perfect right, and if God, by creating men, incurred in their regard a strict indebtedness concerning eternal life, one might deny my supposition. But it cannot be denied without obvious impiety: the greatest of all graces, which is life eternal, would no longer be a grace; a reward would be due to us independently of the promise; God would owe eternal existence and happiness to His creature; He could no longer get along without the creature; the creature would become a necessary being. Such a doctrine is a monstrosity. On the other hand, my supposition clearly brings out the rights of God, and makes clear some possible cases in which love without interest would be necessary. The reason why it is not necessary in cases of the order established by the gratuitous promise is that God does not consider us worthy of such great trials, and is satisfied with an implicit preference of Himself and His glory to ourselves and our blessedness, which is, as it were, the seed of pure love in the hearts of all the just. But, finally, my supposition, by comparing a man ready to be annihilated with one who has received the promise of life eternal, conveys a sense of the way in which love that is mixed with interest is lower than disinterested love.[236]

The force of Fénelon's argument for the possibility (and superiority) of disinterested love hinges on the plausibility of his supposition that God

[236] *Oeuvres de Fénelon*, Tome I, pp. 329–330, *passim*. (Our translation.)

could deprive someone of eternal life by an arbitrary act of will, which implies that there is no justice operative in the relationship between man and God.

Aquinas, who mentions only a self-interested love for God and never a disinterested one, rejects the view that there is no sense in which justice is operative in the relationship between man and God.

Discussing the effect of sin on the good of human nature, Aquinas observes that the good of that nature is threefold:

> First, there are the principles of which nature is constituted, and the proper-
> ties that flow from them, such as the powers of the soul, and so forth.
> Secondly, since man has from nature an inclination to virtue . . . this
> inclination to virtue is a good of nature. Thirdly, the gift of original justice,
> conferred on the whole human nature in the person of the first man, may be
> called a good of nature.

He then argues that, with regard to the first good, sin has no effect at all. The properties of human nature and its powers remain the same. As regards the natural inclination to virtue, that good is "diminished." The good whereby man stood in a certain relationship of original justice to God was "entirely destroyed through the sin of our first parent."[237]

But though Aquinas does assert that the relationship of original justice, whereby man occupied a place in the eyes of God according to worth, was removed by original sin, he does not conclude that justice between man and God is thereby entirely removed and that the whole notion of human merit is thereby destroyed. He argues that even if a man is, after the Fall, naturally unable to merit eternal salvation without the gratuitous grace and mercy of God, salvation is not wholly dependent on such grace and mercy. The "first cause of our reaching everlasting life . . . [is] God's mercy. But our merit is a subsequent cause."[238] Salvation must be merited by man with the help of divine grace. And insofar as man can still merit salvation, insofar as he can earn it, some kind of justice between man and God still prevails.

As Aquinas explains it, merit and reward refer to the same thing, "something given anyone in return for work or toil, as a price for it." He goes on to observe that justice is related to equality and that simple justice occurs

---

[237] *Summa Theologica*, Part I-II, Q. 85, Art. 1, Answer, Vol. I, p. 966. Even the relationship of original justice was not one in which man could merit eternal life with divine help. Aquinas argues that "everlasting life is a good exceeding the proportion of created nature," and, hence, that even in that state of innocence, "no created nature is a sufficient principle of an act meritorious of eternal life, unless there is added a supernatural gift, which we call grace." (*Ibid.*, Q. 114, Art. 2, Answer, pp. 1154–1155.)

[238] *Ibid.*, Art. 3, Reply Obj. 2, p. 1155.

between those who are equal. Where absolute equality does not prevail, however, one cannot speak of absolute justice but only of justice in a relative sense. For "where there is no simple right, but only relative, there is no character of merit simply, but only relatively, in so far as the character of justice is found there, since the child merits something from his father and the slave from his lord." Applying this analysis to the relationship between God and man, Aquinas says:

> Now it is clear that between God and man there is the greatest inequality: for they are infinitely apart, and all man's good is from God. Hence there can be no justice of absolute equality between man and God, but only of a certain proportion, inasmuch as both operate after their own manner. Now the manner and measure of human virtue is in man from God. Hence man's merit with God only exists on the presupposition of the Divine ordination, so that man obtains from God, as a reward of his operation, what God gave him the power of operation for . . . differently, indeed, [than other beings] since the rational creature moves itself to act by its free-will, hence its action has the character of merit, which is not so in other creatures.[239]

Hence, since human merit or reward has two causes—first and foremost, divine ordination or grace, and, second, free will—man's salvation is not entirely gratuitous. As "the human mind's movement to the fruition of the Divine good is the proper act of charity,"[240] there is even some sense in which one may speak of debt in the human attempt to achieve salvation. Not that man may speak of God being man's debtor simply in regard to the reward for a virtuous life, since divine grace is what makes that virtue possible, but only insofar as "it is right that His will should be carried out."[241]

Since man merits in some sense and in some measure his own salvation, and since it is God's will that he should so merit it by doing what he should, freely, in cooperation with divine grace, Aquinas could argue that Fénelon's supposition is impossible. It would not be possible for God to withdraw the hope and the promise of salvation from a good man the moment before his death, because it would not be just to do so. And it is impossible for God to be unjust. It is possible for God to withhold grace altogether from an individual man, but in that case it makes no sense at all to speak of man's loving God, since, without grace, no good action, and certainly not a disinterested love for God, is possible.[242]

[239] *Ibid.*, Art. 1, Answer, p. 1154. See also Art. 4, p. 1156.
[240] *Ibid.*, Answer, p. 1156.
[241] *Ibid.*, Art. 1, Reply Obj. 3, p. 1154.
[242] For an extended discussion of the Thomistic theory of the relationship of divine grace and merit, see Reginald Garrigou-Lagrange's *Grace*, esp. Ch. XI, pp. 363–398. For his discussion of the question of "pure love," see *The Love of God and The Cross of Jesus*.

In this controversy one can fairly easily see how the differences on the question of self-interest in relation to supernatural human love are a direct function of the differences on the question of what the effect of original sin is. In other words, the different positions taken on the question of what kind of activity man is capable of are functions of more basic positions taken on the question of what human nature is and what worth it has. We find that this same relationship holds for a number of the issues about natural love; how love is understood follows from how human nature is understood. The fact that this relationship holds for much of the literature on natural love as well as for the literature on supernatural love suggests that, although it is possible to engage in controversy about love alone, the more basic issues about it must be resolved on another level. The idea of love or, rather, of human love, is less fundamental than the idea of man.

4

The Unity and Diversity of the
Literature on the Idea of Love

At the beginning of this inquiry we assumed that, in the entire systematic and discursive literature on love, we could find some general agreement about the subject and, accordingly, construct genuine issues to show that the contributors to the literature were addressing common problems, even though they often were not addressing each other. In other words, we assumed that what appeared to be mere *differences* could be shown to be real *disagreements* resting on some measure of agreement about the subject being discussed and the questions at issue. Despite the considerable diversity, behind much of which we found no conceptual agreement either on the subject or the question about the subject, we believe we have shown (primarily through the construction of the controversies) that there is enough unity to indicate that there is one idea being discussed throughout the whole literature and that there are real disagreements about it.

Our task was considerably more difficult in finding some unity within the great range of theories of natural love among human beings. Though the measure of general agreement we found is admittedly thin, and though the controversies are relatively few and poorly debated, discovering agreement and constructing controversies were not impossible. Our task was easier in constructing and, in some cases, simply reporting the comparatively rich controversy about supernatural human love. To the extent that we were successful in exposing and making explicit some degree of relevance not only within but also between the literatures on natural and supernatural love, we believe we have supported, if not verified, the assumption with which we began.

The controversies, however, do not show as well as can be shown the degree of unity and diversity within the whole literature on love since they are divided into those about natural love and those about supernatural love. We now propose to do this in two different ways. We first compare the literatures on natural and supernatural human love with an eye to the general points of similarity and difference between them. We believe this comparison shows that the degree of similarity is at least as great as the degree of difference. Indeed, we claim that the two literatures have more in common than do the various theories of natural human love.

Primarily to organize the diversity in the literature on natural love, we also discuss an analytical tool that can be used effectively for dialectical clarification. We propose five questions, which we term cardinal questions, that might be applied reasonably to each of the theories of love within the whole literature. They may serve, thus, not only as another way of assessing the unity of the literature but may be considered also as providing a kind of criterion for an "ideal" theory of love. All the authors treat at least one of these questions, and most treat more than one.

In general, documentation is not offered in the following. Here and there, specific authors are mentioned as dealing with one or another of the cardinal questions. For the most part, however, we consider hypothetical answers to the questions. These answers are not really hypothetical, because authors, in fact, say the things that we suggest they might say. But the analysis is simplified, and its explication made more readily comprehensible, if few authors are mentioned.

A. A Comparison of the Literatures on Natural and Supernatural Human Love

The distinction between natural and supernatural love and, consequently, between the controversies about them was not imposed by us for dialectical clarification. This distinction—perhaps the most basic in the whole literature—frequently is stressed by the authors themselves. The apparent result is not one but two literatures on love.

How important is this division? What are its implications and consequences? To what degree do the two literatures overlap? To what degree are natural and supernatural love separate subjects? What differences does the division make for those who analyze the idea of love? In pursuing our inquiry, some consideration of these questions is indicated.

Since the light of revelation is said so often to be different from the light of reason and experience, one would expect an enormous, perhaps unbridgeable, gap between the two literatures. Though there are obvious and important differences, there are also striking similarities that go deeper than the occasional, peripheral, and fragmentary likenesses resulting from the fact that both literatures must use terms comprehensible to human beings. Perhaps this is so because biblical writings did not take the form of systematic theology. Hence, when reason was used to explain the claims of faith, much of pre-Christian thinking reappeared—however much transformed—on the theological plane. Such thinking was also included in religious literature as the subject of adverse criticism because of the recurring suspicion that revelation was being perverted in the attempt to harmonize theories of natural and supernatural love. On the other side, much of the purely secular thinking about love has been affected deeply by the claims of revelation; certain features of theories of supernatural love—notably the ideal of universal love—have influenced many nonreligious thinkers who nevertheless rejected their attendant religious dogmas. Finally, many who reject completely the religious teaching on love have tried to explain its appeal and durability in nonreligious terms. But, whatever the causes, the discussions of love in both literatures display characteristics that transcend the difference between the natural and supernatural perspectives.

1. *Points of similarity*

We indicated, at the end of Chapter 3, that conceptions of human love are, in most theories, derived from or determined by conceptions of human nature. Though this point is most clearly shown in the controversy about supernatural human love, it is no less true of many of the theories of natural human love.

In addition, all theorists about love—be it natural or supernatural—conceive it in the realm of tendency. Though the specific conceptions differ greatly and though cognitive notions are often included in conceptions of both natural and supernatural love, there is universal agreement that, whatever love is, it is itself tendential or points to movement or inclination.

Many theorists of supernatural love agree with many theorists of natural love that love is a general tendency that is manifested in all things; in other words, the cosmic view of love is shared by a number of theologians and secular theorists. Theologians say that it is God's love that actively sustains everything in being, while secular theorists affirm that love is inherent naturally in all things.

All theorists about love agree that it is constructive, unifying, or simply good. This is particularly true of the theorists of supernatural love, for whom such love is always the basis of good activity. However, it is also true of the theorists of natural love who, though they often mention bad loves, always conceive of them as perverted forms of good loves.

On the human level, all theorists of supernatural love and many theorists of natural love agree that love itself is, in some way, the key to human happiness and the main factor influencing individual and collective human destiny.

These points of substantive similarity are supplemented by the similarity of the cardinal issues in both literatures. In both literatures, the question of the relationship of love, particularly human love, and self-interest is central. Directly or indirectly, the whole controversy about Christian love bears on the question of whether supernatural love and a self-interested motive are compatible—of whether supernatural human love replaces, or merely transforms, natural human love. In the literature on natural love, a great deal of attention is paid to the question of whether an authentic benevolence is possible, whether all love is reducible to self-love. That these issues are basic in both literatures indicates that, both for theologians and secular thinkers, love is primarily a relational concept—one in which the notions of self and other are pivotal.

2. *Points of difference*

Obviously the literatures differ. We indicated at the beginning of Chapter 3 the differences in approach and conception. As to approach, there are theorists of natural love who claim that all love is natural, while no theorist of supernatural love claims that all love is supernatural. As to conception, the one unqualified difference between all theories of natural love and all theories of supernatural love is the central position accorded, by definition, to the infinite God of revealed religion in the latter theories. In all such theories, God is the principal lover, the principal beloved, or both. Further, supernatural human love is only possible with divine help.

Between the two literatures the most arresting difference, however, is a formal one. As a whole, the literature on supernatural love contains more controversy and debate; there are more commonly understood questions and the frequency with which they are addressed with relevant arguments and counterarguments is greater. Not only the reported but also the constructed debates are richer than those discoverable in the literature on natural love. There is little doubt that the theorists on supernatural love are more conscious of all the literature that bears on their problems than the theorists on natural love are conscious of all the literature that bears on theirs. As a result, the literature on supernatural love has greater unity.

The formal difference between the literature on supernatural love and the literature on natural love might be explained in terms of the dimensions of each. The former is not only a smaller but also, in one sense, a narrower literature. Those who contribute to it operate within the limits of commonly accepted general principles or beliefs which preclude the kind of diversity one finds in the literature on natural love. In other words, in the literature on supernatural love one finds divergences within a single tradition, whereas in the literature on natural love one finds divergent traditions. Within each tradition of thinking about natural love there is some communication, but communication among these traditions is rare. That is to say, most of the positions taken against acknowledged intellectual opponents are taken by those who share in some way the general outlook of the opponents. For example, one finds fairly frequent and fruitful relevance within the modern psychological tradition of thinking about natural love initiated by Freud, but, except for Freud himself among its adherents, infrequent interest in, or sometimes even awareness of, other traditions of thinking about love. It is no exaggeration to say that, in general, the interplay among different traditions of thinking about natural love is less than the interplay between the whole literature on natural love and the literature on supernatural love.

B. Cardinal Questions Applied to Theories of Love

In addition to comparing different conceptions of, approaches to, and controversies about love, there is another way of assessing degrees of unity and diversity in the whole literature. Given the exigencies and difficulties of analyzing any basic idea, we would not expect to find consistent compliance with any one set of criteria of exposition in its literature. One way of finding out the degree of procedural irregularity in the whole literature on love (or in the part of it that treats natural love) is to apply a single set of reasonable questions to it. Thus, from a fixed perspective, we shall be able to measure the degrees of another kind of unity and diversity in the literature.

The questions to which we refer are formal not substantive; *theories containing different and even contrary conceptions of love can satisfy them.*

We shall concentrate on five such questions. These arise from the reasonable expectation that a theory of a subject will contain: a definition of the subject; a classification of it; an account of its relation to a larger subject if it forms part of the latter; an account of the causes and consequences of the subject; and some way of rendering intelligible the diversity of conceptions of the subject. As they apply to the subject of love, the questions can be stated as follows:

(1) What is love among human beings?

(2) Is love among human beings of one kind or more than one kind? If more than one, how can they be distinguished and classified?

(3) How is love among human beings related to other types of love? Is it the source of these loves or does it derive from them?

(4) What are the causes and consequences of human love?

(5) How is the fact explained that a wide range of phenomena are conceived as instances of love?

1. *What is love among human beings?*

This most basic of questions about love (or any other subject) calls for definition. In the theories examined, we found that the core of all of the conceptions of love advanced involves one, or some combination, of the critical notions discussed in Chapter 1. A theory that satisfies this question would contain a statement identifying or associating love with one or more of those notions (or with some other notion if an author presents an entirely novel conception of love). If an author, for example, associates love with sexual desire, the reader should be able to find out if love and sexual desire are identical in his view; if love or sexual desire is the genus of which the other is one mode or species; if love and sexual desire are coordinate but distinct modes or species of something else; or if love or sexual desire is a complex of which the other is a component part.

A statement relating an author's conception of love to one or more critical notions is necessary, but sometimes not sufficient, to satisfy this question. An author who thinks of love as completely physical may describe it as sexual desire. That he says that love is basically sexual desire does not necessarily mean that he thinks sexual desire is always love. In addition to saying that love is sexual desire, he might add that such desire must be between a man and a woman, or that it must aim at procreation, or that it must be of a certain intensity and duration, etc., in order to be love. Such qualifications are essential to his conception of love, though the indispensable part of that conception is the critical notion: sexual desire.

Though relatively few theories we examined contain explicit definitions, we were, in most cases, able to infer one. Most often, when we found definitions, they were of different types or kinds of love discussed within a single theory. In such cases, an author does not tell us directly what his general conception is. Yet he might refer both to romantic love and to friendship as forms of love and tell us (more or less) what he means by each of them. In addition, he might associate sexual desire with romantic love but explicitly exclude it from friendship. We know, then, that sexual desire, though part of his conception of one kind of love, is no part of his general conception of human love; it cannot be, since he mentions a love—friendship—from which it is excluded. In other words, what human love is, is what all human loves have in common.

Since it is not sexual desire, we then have to look for the common quality in romantic love and friendship (and all the other types of love he may mention). In the course of the discussion, we may notice that the author uses the notions of union or the desire for union to describe both the activities of friendship and romantic activities. In the case of friendship, the union he describes might be one in which the friends seek to strengthen the bonds and to enhance whatever similarity there is between them by doing the same things together in the same way. In the case of romantic love, the union he describes might be one of complementarity, one in which the parties to love are and remain different. The theme of union is, however, present in the discussion of both love relationships. The author may go further in his discussion of the desire to unite on the part of the romantic lovers as well as on the part of the friends. He may say that the desire for union takes acquisitive forms in both relationships. Between the romantic lovers each seeks from the other both physical pleasure and certain forms of spiritual satisfaction through union. So also among friends; their desire to become as much like each other as possible is, in some measure, a desire for personal improvement through emulation of an admired model. The author might go on, in each case, to point out that the acquisitive forms of the desire for union are not all there is to love. The desire for union, he may say, must also take the form of benevolence. Romantic lovers as well as friends must want to unite, not only for their own sakes but sometimes for the sake of the other. Both romantic love and friendship are conceived as a complex of two desires that occur sequentially: a desire for the sake of the self and a desire for the sake of the other. We find, then, a theory of love among human beings in which it is most generally conceived as a desire for union (either the union of complementarity or the union of similarity), which desire takes both acquisitive and benevolent forms in all instances of such love.

Some of the theories examined do not lend themselves easily to the kind of analysis indicated above. Sometimes we found a discussion in which something called romantic love and something called friendship are mentioned, but which are not joined by so specific a notion as the desire for union; though both are called love by the author, he does not make clear the conceptual justification for applying the same word to both. He may indicate that romantic love is primarily, if not exclusively, a matter of sexual desire, whereas friendship is a matter of caring about the other as much as (if not more than) oneself. The analyst's problem then becomes one of finding the common ground between the author's conception of romantic love as sexual desire and of friendship as benevolence. His theory of love among human beings is one in which both a form of acquisitive desire and a form of benevolent desire are, separately, called love. Since both sexual and benevolent desire are inclinations, we know that he thinks love is tendential. This much can be concluded, but we are then forced to look for clues to determine whether or not the author limits love only to the two instances he mentions, or would call all desires among human beings instances of love.

2. *Is love among human beings of one kind or more than one kind? If more than one, how can they be distinguished and classified?*

This question is taken up prior to the first question in many of the theories examined. Perhaps one of the reasons authors frequently bypass the first question and go right into a discussion of the kinds of love is that their general conception of love among human beings has no existential referent. That is to say, if an author does distinguish among kinds of love, he may not be referring to something experienced when he describes what these kinds have in common. For example, an author may begin by attempting to describe what he thinks the nature and properties of the romantic relationship between a man and a woman are, of friendship between men, as well as of both parental and filial love. Only then may he address the question of what they have in common. His procedure, in other words, is to go from the specific and observable to the general, rather than from a general conception either of love or love among human beings to conceptions of specific existential relationships.

When love is of one kind only, the core conception of it may be simple or complex, *i.e.*, composed of one critical notion or two or more such notions.

When love is of more than one kind it may be differentiated in several ways:

(a) It may be conceived in terms of one or more critical notions that are divisible into other notions. Thus, an author presenting a conception of love as tendency in general might differentiate kinds by distinguishing between acquisitive and benevolent desire; he might divide acquisitive desire further into sexual and nonsexual; and he might divide benevolent desire into its self-interested and disinterested forms. In this case, critical notions inherent in the general conception either differentiate or help to differentiate kinds.

(b) It may be conceived in terms of one or more critical notions, none of which is reducible to other critical notions. In this case, differentiation can be accomplished in one of two ways:

(i) In the first way, a critical notion that is not part of the core conception of love is added to that conception in order to distinguish a kind of love. Thus, love may be said by an author to be benevolence; but, though benevolence is the essential notion, he may add sexual desire to it in order to describe what he calls romantic love. He might add the desire for the union of similarity to benevolence to describe what he calls friendship. He might add admiration to benevolence to describe what he calls filial love. Though sexual desire, the desire for the union of similarity, and admiration are critical notions, they are used, in this instance, not to describe what love among human beings is but what certain kinds of love among human beings are.

(ii) In the second way, love is still conceived in terms of one or more critical notions that are not divisible or are not divided. The differentiation into kinds, however, is not accomplished by the addition of other critical notions but rather by the addition of certain qualifications or properties. Thus, an author may say that, although love is always sexual desire, it is of different kinds, such as romantic and conjugal, or homosexual and heterosexual. He may distinguish romantic love from conjugal love in terms of duration, maintaining that romance is characterized by brevity, while conjugal love endures. Homosexual love and heterosexual love are distinguished in terms of gender. This way of distinguishing kinds may also be employed when the core conception involves two critical notions instead of one. An author's general conception of love among human beings may be described by the two critical notions: respect and benevolence. He may distinguish kinds by the use of number, arguing that respect and benevolence for one person is one kind of love, and that respect and benevolence for the whole human race is another.

An author may use all of the ways mentioned to distinguish kinds. He may divide the critical notion or notions that constitute his core conception of love into their subordinate forms, add other critical notions to it or them, and also add other qualifications. He thus may describe love most generally as the desire for the union of complementarity. He may add, however, that such a desire takes two forms, which distinguish romantic love from friendship. In the former love, the desire takes an acquisitive form (say, sexual desire) and has admiration added to it. In addition, such a desire is involuntary and directed to only one person. In the second love, friendship, the desire for union takes a benevolent form and has respect added to it. In addition, it may be said that the desire must be voluntary, enduring, and, though it can be directed to more than one person, it cannot be directed to many.

3. *How is love among human beings related to other types of love? Is it the source of these loves or does it derive from them?*

As was said earlier, any author who discusses love also discusses interpersonal love. Many go on to discuss love that is not among human beings. The problem here is to discover the relationship between love that is among human beings and love that is not. That relationship is determined by the author's view of the principal object of love, the source of love, and the archtypical love relationship. Thus, for an author who thinks of God as love, love among human beings can be understood fully only by reference to God. So also for an author like Plato, who understands the human love for the enduring realities as that which makes love among human beings possible, since, in his view, they are attractive to each other only insofar as they reflect those realities. Other authors hold that love is an all-pervasive cosmic force. They, therefore, understand interpersonal love as but one expression of this force, though perhaps its most important. Still other authors who refer to cosmic phenomena as instances of love do so analogically. They assert that the human love relationship is the primary one, and that the understanding of nonhuman phenomena in terms of love is a way of proceeding from the known to the unknown. Others, who also assert the primacy of the human love relationship, maintain that the love of abstract ideals, of country, of mythical figures, etc., derives from the human love relationship; that such objects are images and substitutes for human beings or some qualities they exemplify.

Whatever its extent and whatever its focus, a theory of love answering this question would place love among human beings in perspective through relating it to the principal love relationship, the principal object of love, or the principal lover. When an author does this, his theory can be placed in one of the following classes:

(a) Love among human beings (or one love among them) is primary and all others are derivative; all other loves can only be understood by reference to the primary one.
(b) Love among human beings is derivative from another love.
(c) Love among human beings is but one of several coordinate types of love, each truly a species under the genus love.
(d) Love among human beings and all other loves stand to each other in a hierarchy, some more truly and some less truly love.

Of course, just as an author who answers the first question would tell the reader what the different kinds of love among human beings have in common, so also would he in answering this question tell the reader what love among human beings and all other loves have in common. This would amount to a statement of his most general conception of love.

If an author chooses to answer this third question first, his answer may cast light on the first two questions. It may contribute to a definition of interpersonal love insofar as he says that some particular property of love in its most general form is also a particular property of love among human beings. It also may contribute to the differentiation of the types that love among human beings can take through the stipulation that a certain kind of love involves admiration or the desire for union, or that it seeks requital, is voluntary or involuntary, or is directed to one or many.

4. What are the causes and consequences of human love?

There are many books—some of them major books—in which this question is dealt with first and foremost, often to the neglect of the other four. The area covered by this question includes the conditions under which love does or can arise, the conditions required for its preservation, and the conditions under which it ceases to be. It is a question that is applicable to all theories, since no author denies that human loves either are or can be mutable; that they have a beginning, run a certain course, and can end. Thus, if an author understands love as an inclination toward the beautiful, physical or spiritual beauty in the beloved obviously is the prime condition for the emergence of love. If love itself is understood as an evolving process rather than a stable condition, then the condition of possibility for its continuance is change. If luxury, comfort, and worldly pleasure are said to be the archenemies of a certain kind of love, then a degree of asceticism and renunciation of the world is required before that love can arise. If love is associated with physical or mental health, such states are conditions for its emergence. If age is said to be unfavorable to love, then the prolongation of youth is what preserves love. If a certain kind of love is a function of a good moral character, then the cultivation of virtue is a condition of its existence. If utility is the measure of love, then love dies when the object ceases to be useful. If love feeds on admiration, then the loss of admiration for the object kills love.

Explaining the origin of love, an author might make a distinction between the predisposing causes of love and its proximate or exciting causes. In Freud's theory, the predisposing cause is the existence of undifferentiated libidinal energy, and the proximate cause is contact with an object or person on whom this energy can be expended in a specific way. In Reik's theory, the predisposing cause is the existence of a feeling of inadequacy, and its exciting cause is contact with someone with whom, through union, one can remove that inadequacy. For Schopenhauer, the predisposing cause of love is species survival, and its exciting cause, contact with someone who arouses sexual desire and with whom one can fulfill the aim of the species. For Plato, the predisposing cause of love is the soul's contact with the enduring realities before birth; its exciting cause is encounter with someone who is the occasion for recalling those realities. For Fromm, the predisposing cause of love is the condition of agonizing loneliness into which he thinks every human being is born; this condition, coupled with a certain maturity in the lover and with exposure to someone with whom, through union, he can escape this loneliness, causes love. For Augustine, Aquinas, and Dante, God, Who is love, is the predisposing cause of all love, the proximate causes being the various and numerous opportunities for the exercise of the appetitive faculties in man.

A consideration of causes or conditions points to a consideration of effects. And the question of effects touches not only the lover but also the beloved. In confronting this question, most authors are concerned with the effect of love on the happiness of both lover and beloved. For some authors, romance is the great natural therapy; for others, it is the great natural disease. An author confronting this question would be concerned with the effect of love on the growth, change, activity, and well-being of both lover and beloved.

In this general area, a matter that strongly recommends itself to consideration, since it is mentioned so frequently, is the question of self-deception in relation to love. An author may consider himself obliged to clarify whether (and why) he thinks self-deception is a necessary, frequent, or possible characteristic of love. And in saying why, he would be obliged to decide whether self-deception precedes and makes that love possible or whether it follows and is caused by love.

5. *How is the fact explained that a wide range of phenomena are conceived as instances of love?*

Most of the theories of love advanced in the literature fall short of answering this question, and, in some ways, it is the most important one. For it is one thing to explain the univocal and equivocal uses of the term "love" in a given theory, and quite another to explain the wide uses of the term. If this question is reasonable, then the proponent of a theory of love is obliged, not only to tell the reader what he thinks love is but also how his conception renders intelligible the application of the word to different relationships, *whether his theory includes them or not.* An author may deny that sexual desire has anything to do with love. In answering this question, however, he would be obliged to explain why sexual desire so often has been called love and so often has been associated with a love relationship.

There are three main answers to this question in the literature. Those authors who identify love with tendency in general and see it as a cosmic force find no difficulty in accounting for almost all uses of the word, except perhaps for those that signify nothing but judgment. According to them, every action on the part of anything is inspired by love. Hence, applying the word "love" to all sorts of relationships—romance, friendship, paternal and filial affection, scholarly endeavors, pursuits of physical pleasure—is explicable. The authors of such theories often deny the word "love" to relationships or activities they consider bad; but when they do so, they are writing as moralists rather than analysts. For such authors, analytically speaking, good and bad loves are all still love, since love includes all movement. Identifying love with sheer tendency, they explain the various uses of the word in terms of the different kinds of tendency being referred to. The broad theories of love advanced by Plato, Augustine, Aquinas, etc., whether they be judged substantively as good or bad theories, are ones that come to terms with this question.

Another theory that answers this question is Freud's. Although Freud also holds that love is tendency in general, he is able to answer this question in another way. The narrower conception of human love advanced by Freud emphasizes the notion of sexual desire. Yet, according to Freudian psychology, sexual desire frequently is transformed into many desires that are not obviously sexual. Many conscious desires far from sexual in explicit intent, it is said, are sexual in unconscious origin and are sustained by that unconscious desire. Thus, by employing the distinction between unconscious and conscious, and by referring to such psychological mechanisms as sublimation and transference, Freud is able to explain the application of the word "love" to many phenomena that are not overtly sexual. His hypothesis enables him to explain why eating is called an act of love, why worldly ambition is called love, why friendship is called love, why, indeed, St. Francis' feeding of the birds is called love.[1]

Fromm's theory also renders intelligible the application of the term "love" to diverse phenomena. He is able to provide an explanation, in terms of his conception, of why different phenomena are called love, even though some of these phenomena are not what he would call real love. The essential notion in Fromm's conception of human love is "care," or what we call benevolence. By use of this notion he distinguishes between true and false or "symbiotic" love. Yet, what true and false love have in common is the human desire for union, or more specifically, the human desire to escape the wretched condition of loneliness and isolation into which, Fromm thinks, every human being is born. Hence, Fromm can understand why any attempt to escape this isolation is called love, even though all such attempts are not instances of real love. Only such attempts as involve care for the other person as well as for oneself, and only those which, to some extent, endure, should be included in love's compass. When a person simply uses another in order to diminish or temporarily erase the pain of loneliness, true love is not involved. What such a person is seeking, even though he may not realize it, is what only true love can offer. Thus, since "orgiastic" sexuality and true love have the same original motive, it is not surprising that both are called love. Further, since things as well as people can be used to supply temporary relief from the pain of human loneliness, Fromm is able to explain why people are said to love drink, food, clothing, etc. He can also explain fanatical attachment to a country, to a distant leader, or to an ideal being called love, since he views these objects as substitutes for a living human being with whom one can associate and unite in true love. Whatever its substantive value may be, Fromm's theory is able to account for what he regards as abuses as well as appropriate uses of the term "love."

Like the cosmic theories and Freud's and Fromm's theories, a theory of love answering this question would *either* include in its compass such generally recognized instances of love as romance, friendship, paternal and filial affection, *or*, excluding one or more such relationships, would include an explanation, in terms of the author's conception, of why they are commonly mistaken for love. What such a theory would do for some recurring

---

[1] "Even in its caprices the usage of language remains true to some kind of reality. Thus it gives the name of 'love' to a great many kinds of emotional relationship which we too group together theoretically as love; but then again it feels a doubt whether this love is real, true, actual love, and so hints at a whole scale of possibilities within the range of the phenomena of love." (*Group Psychology and the Analysis of the Ego*, Ch. VIII, p. 71. See also *Civilization and Its Discontents*, Ch. IV, p. 49.)

interpersonal relationships might also be done for phenomena that are not interpersonal but that frequently are or have been called instances of love.

We now turn to the actual theories of natural human love we found in the literature. These theories have been analyzed primarily through the use of the critical notions presented in Chapter 1, which also play a role in the way in which the theories are classified, as the reader will see from the following Introduction to Part II. However, the reader also may wish to examine the documentation by applying the five cardinal questions presented in this chapter to discover which each theory answers and which it ignores or confuses.

II

Natural Human Love:
The Documentation

The Basis of Classification

I N the following chapters we shall present the documentation for our analysis of the various theories of natural love (with emphasis on natural love among human beings). The critical notions that constitute our instrument for analyzing these theories are also the basis for classifying them. Through the use of these notions, we hope to effect a classification that will not only be simple despite the variety and complexity of the theories but one that will also feature their important similarities and differences.

The critical notions themselves do not dictate a single mode of classifying theories. Any one of them would suffice as a basis of classification. If the notion of sexual desire were taken as controlling, for example, we could group the theories as follows: those in which love and sexual desire are equated; those in which sexual desire is said to be part of love; and those in which love and sexual desire are said to be mutually exclusive. But this classification, as well as many others that are possible, results in little more than an orderly catalogue of theories that reveals little about their most important similarities and differences.

Our hope is for something more. Accordingly, we have made a judgment—confirmed, we believe, by a structure discernible in the literature—

that one mode of classification more illuminatingly sets forth the focal points of the controversies about love than any other. That mode of classification depends on taking the notions of acquisitive and benevolent desire as pivotal.

With few exceptions, theories of love can be classified under one of the three following headings:[1]

(1) Theories in which acquisitive and benevolent desire are each held to as separate types or kinds of love[2]

(2) Theories in which love or a kind of love is held to be wholly acquisitive in character

(3) Theories in which benevolence is held to be indispensable to love

This threefold classification, using two critical notions as pivotal, does not require us to neglect the other notions in the sphere of tendency. Tendency in general, sexual desire, and the desire for union, when applicable to theories in any of the three groups, will be used in their explication within the general taxonomic scheme. As our critical notions are not logically coordinate, some of them can be subsumed under others.

An author whose theory falls in the first group might maintain that all motion is love. Thus, the notion of tendency in general would apply to his theory. That notion could also apply to a theory that falls in the second group. An author might claim that all tendency is love and also hold that all human tendency is acquisitive in character.

Within the limits of our classification, the notion of sexual desire also will be involved where it is applicable. Since this notion is less general than the notion of acquisitive desire, it often is seen as a species of the latter. Thus, an author who says that all love is acquisitive desire may distinguish two types of love by using the notion of sexual desire. Love, he may say, is either physical, *i.e.*, sexual, or spiritual. Another author may say that love is nothing but sexual desire. His theory also would be classified in the second group. This does not mean that his theory is identical with all the others classified there. It only means that his theory has one thing in common with them: Love is conceived as acquisitive in character.

The notion of the desire for union has an even wider applicability, since it may take either an acquisitive or a benevolent form. One author may say that a man seeks a complementary union with a woman because he wants to help or complete himself. Another may say that he seeks such a union to

---

[1] Since the distinction is a tendential one, it obviously applies only to those theories in which love is conceived as primarily tendential. Those theories in which love is conceived exclusively or primarily as a matter of judgment will be dealt with separately.

[2] These theories we call "binary."

help or complete the other person. The notion of the desire for the union of similarity has the same ambivalence. An author may say that one person wishes to become like another to improve himself, or he may say that a person wishes another to become like him in order to improve the other. The purpose for which the union is sought determines whether the desire is acquisitive or benevolent. Accordingly, the notion of the desire for union may apply to theories in all three groups.

Once we have classified a theory according to the pivotal notions of acquisitive and benevolent desire, we shall employ as many of the critical notions and their subordinate forms as are necessary to describe it fully. We shall use these notions to give the theory greater articulation and to provide the additional qualifications, distinctions, and additions that the author thinks are important. For example, if we place a theory in the first group, we may find it necessary, in order to reflect all the variations on love that that theory contains, to employ the notions of simple and mixed acquisitive desire, self-interested and disinterested benevolence, sexual desire, and the desire for union. If we place a theory in the second group, we may find it necessary to note and stress that the only acquisitive desire the author mentions is sexual desire. If we place a theory in the third group, we may find it necessary to point out that benevolent desire always takes the form of the desire for union and that such benevolence is always self-interested.[3]

We shall proceed as follows: We shall deal with the theories that fall in the sphere of tendency in Chapters 5, 6, 7, and 8, and with the few theories that fall in the sphere of judgment in Chapter 9. We shall present the binary theories in Chapters 5 and 6, the theories in which love is characterized as acquisitive desire in Chapter 7, and the theories in which benevolence is said to be indispensable to love in Chapter 8.

The order of presentation of the theories within each chapter will not be undeviatingly chronological. Whenever, in our judgment, a theory can be made more intelligible by presenting it in close relation to some other theory, we shall associate the two theories even if they belong to two different periods in time.

[3] Though it is no part of the basis of our classification of theories, we shall also be concerned with the question of what it is that any author says a lover seeks—for himself or for others. Several authors lay greater stress on the result of loving, e.g., pleasure, immortality, happiness, than on the person loved (self or other) and the manner in which he is loved.

5

Love as Acquisitive and as
Benevolent Desire: I

THEORIES of love classified in this chapter and the chapter that follows have one principal feature in common—they all include a basic and tendential distinction between two broad kinds of love. One kind is completely acquisitive in character; the other, while not necessarily excluding acquisitive desire, is characterized by benevolence.

The theories differ considerably in other respects. In some, love is conceived as a universal principle; all things, or at least all living things, do whatever they do because of love. In other theories, love is, or is only discussed as, a human phenomenon. Within the sphere of love among human beings, some of the theories encompass all forms of acquisitive and benevolent desire, while others restrict the realm of love to specific forms of each kind of tendency, *e.g.*, sexual desire or the desire for union. The theories also vary regarding the character of what love seeks for the self or for another person.

Cognitive notions are not integral to the conceptions of love advanced in most of the theories in this group, though judgment is said to be a condition of love's emergence in most of them. In some theories, however, judgment is said to be a part of and not simply a preface to love. We shall deal directly with the cognitive aspects of such theories in Chapter 9.[1]

Insofar as the theories analyzed in this chapter and Chapter 6 have in common a basic tendential distinction between two kinds of love (however else they may differ), we have chosen to call all of them "binary." The authors holding binary theories of love treated in this chapter are: Plato, St. Augustine, Aristotle, Marcus Tullius Cicero, Thomas Aquinas, Dante Alighieri, Leone Ebreo, Baldesar Castiglione, and Bernard of Clairvaux. For convenience of arrangement, other authors holding binary theories of love will be treated in Chapter 6.

Plato

Plato's is one of the theories of natural love in which the focus is not on love among human beings. For him, interpersonal love is decidedly a derivative and not a primary theme.[2] The distinction between acquisitive and benevolent desire is but one aspect of the Platonic theory and far from the most significant one. Plato is less concerned with the generic definition of love as tendency and with the problem of distinguishing its modes than with the question of what are the highest things to which love can be directed. And, in his view, the most important objects of love, as well as those that reveal most about love's nature, are not human beings.

The distinction between the apparent and the real, the transient and the permanent, the mortal and the immortal is one of the most decisive in Platonic thought. It is so fundamental to Plato's theory that the love of one human being for another, *i.e.*, for what is transient and mortal, only can be understood in terms of a love for what is eternal, since the mortal is attractive only insofar as it reflects the eternal. Plato's famous ladder of love is, in effect, a spectrum of objects of acquisitive desire ranging from the most immediate and passing to the most permanent. The "fair-souled" who are capable of ascending this ladder must begin with the first objects of desire, and, pursuing a path of moral improvement or learning, gradually ascend from lower to higher loves. In this progression, the love of one

[1] It will not always be desirable to treat in different places the tendential and cognitive aspects of theories in which love is conceived as a combination of tendency and judgment.

[2] This is true despite the fact that Plato's theory does not involve what we call supernatural love. Although he writes of divinities and of a world of invisible realities, these are not supernatural in the sense in which the infinite God of revealed religion is supernatural. Furthermore, in Plato's theory, none of man's loves presupposes a power that lies beyond his own natural endowments. Supernatural human love, by our definition, depends upon active, supernatural help.

human being for another is left behind at an early stage; in the proper
ascent, love for another person is valuable only to the extent that it initiates
and prepares the lover for the next upward step.

The most direct presentation of the Platonic theory of love occurs in the
Symposium. The dialogue is a dramatic account of a series of speeches and
conversations said to occur after a banquet held at the house of Agathon, a
young poet. One of the guests, Eryximachus the physician, proposes that
each of those present make a speech in honor of love.

In the course of his speech, Socrates tells of a conversation he had as a
young man with a wise woman, Diotima, who introduced him to the
"mysteries" of love. During that conversation, Diotima affirms, as Socrates
agrees, not only the tendential character of love but also a general conception of it that can be described, in our terms, as tendency in general.
Having discussed love as a desire aiming ultimately at happiness, Diotima
asks Socrates:

> "Now do you suppose this wish or this love to be common to all mankind,
> and that every one always wishes to have good things? Or what do you
> say?"
>
> "Even so," I said; "it is common to all."
>
> "Well then, Socrates," she said, "we do not mean that all men love, when
> we say that all men love the same things always; we mean that some people
> love and others do not?"
>
> "I am wondering myself," I replied.
>
> "But you should not wonder," she said; "for we have singled out a certain
> form of love, and applying thereto the name of the whole, we call it love;
> and there are other names that we commonly abuse."
>
> "As, for example—?" I asked.
>
> "Take the following: you know that *poetry* is more than a single thing.
> For of anything whatever that passes from not being into being the whole
> cause is composing or poetry; so that the productions of all arts are kinds of
> poetry, and their craftsmen are all poets."
>
> "That is true."
>
> "But still, as you are aware," said she, "they are not called poets: they
> have other names, while a single section disparted from the whole of
> poetry—merely the business of music and metres—is entitled with the name
> of the whole. This and no more is called poetry; those only who possess this
> branch of the art are poets."
>
> "Quite true," I said.
>
> "Well, it is just the same with love. Generically, indeed, it is all that
> desire of good things and of being happy—Love most mighty and all-beguil-
> ing. Yet, whereas those who resort to him in various other ways—in money-
> making, an inclination to sports, or philosophy—are not described either as

loving or as lovers, all those who pursue him seriously in one of his several forms obtain, as loving and as lovers, the name of the whole."[3]

Each of the speakers preceding Socrates talks of love in an unusual and compelling way. Whether their views are interpreted as irreconcilable or compatible, they all agree on one point to which Socrates takes emphatic exception. All consider love a god who is good and beautiful. Just before Socrates makes his own speech, he has a short exchange with Agathon in which he makes clear his objection to this point.

During this exchange, Socrates forces Agathon to admit: (a) that love always has an object; (b) that love always implies a deficiency; (c) that love is of the good and beautiful; and (d) that, since love lacks these qualities, love itself is neither good nor beautiful. As he begins his speech—mostly a report of his conversation with Diotima—Socrates confesses that she forced him to admit the very things to which he had just compelled Agathon's assent. But she went even further, claiming that, since love is neither good nor beautiful, and since these qualities are possessed by all divinities, love is not a god.[4]

Socrates seems to insist that love and deficiency are inseparable. If this is so, love has as its final aim the fulfillment of the deficiency in the self from which it springs. It appears, at this point in the dialogue, that a theory of love is emerging in which, though love and tendency on the part of living things are coextensive, all such tendency is conceived as acquisitive, *i.e.*, that benevolent desire is impossible. To understand Plato's conception of benevolent desire as a form of love, we must consider how the point about love proceeding from deficiency is qualified in the perspective of the whole Platonic theory.

The first evidence that the notion of benevolent desire is present in the Platonic theory of love appears in the next part of Diotima's conversation with the young Socrates. Socrates suggests that, if love is not divine and immortal, it must be mortal. Diotima points out that just as whatever is not good is not necessarily bad, and just as whatever is not beautiful is not necessarily ugly, so also whatever is not divine is not necessarily mortal. She then says that love is an intermediary between the divine and the mortal, a spirit partaking of both.

[3] *Symposium*, 205A-D, pp. 185–189. This broad view of love as tendency in general first appears in the dialogue in the speech of Eryximachus. He says love is present in all living things and describes it as that which unites and harmonizes disparate and even antagonistic elements. After discussing the role of love in medicine, Eryximachus also says love is present in music, athletics, agriculture, and astronomy. (See *ibid.*, 185E–188E, pp. 123–133, esp. 187A, p. 127, and 188A–B, pp. 129–131.)

[4] See *ibid.*, 201D–202D, pp. 175–177.

To illustrate her meaning, Diotima tells a story about the parentage of love. When the goddess Aphrodite was born, the divinities held a feast to celebrate; among those invited was Resource, the son of Cunning. After dinner, Resource became intoxicated with nectar and went into the garden to sleep. Poverty, meanwhile, came begging at the door. Seeing Resource sleeping, she devised the scheme of having a child by him; and, laying down beside him, she conceived Love. Conceived on the birthday of Aphrodite, the goddess of beauty, Love is ever pursuing the beautiful. But, as the son of Resource and Poverty, he also has a dual heritage which shapes his peculiar character. On the one hand, "true to his mother's nature, he ever dwells with want." On the other hand, taking after his father, "he is brave, impetuous and high-strung, a famous hunter, always weaving some stratagem." Diotima goes on to add:

> By birth neither immortal nor mortal, in the selfsame day he is flourishing and alive at the hour when he is abounding in resource; at another he is dying, and then reviving again by force of his father's nature.[5]

Diotima also uses the notions of wisdom and ignorance to describe the intermediate character of love. The wise do not love or desire wisdom because they have it. Neither do the ignorant and self-satisfied because they do not know that they lack wisdom. Socrates then asks who the followers of wisdom are if they are neither the wise nor the ignorant. Diotima replies:

> Why, a child could tell by this time . . . that they are the intermediate sort, and amongst these also is Love. For wisdom has to do with the fairest things, and Love is a love directed to what is fair; so that Love must needs be a friend of wisdom, and, as such, must be between wise and ignorant. This again is a result for which he has to thank his origin: for while he comes of a wise and resourceful father, his mother is unwise and resourceless. Such, my good Socrates, is the nature of this spirit.[6]

Diotima's myth indicates that Plato's original point about love proceeding from deficiency has been qualified. Love is now depicted as somewhere between deficiency and fullness. If this means that love springs sometimes from emptiness and at other times from an overflowing, it suggests that the lover does not always want to get, but occasionally also desires to give. We begin to understand how benevolence is possible when Diotima affirms that love is not merely of the good and the beautiful, but that the lover necessarily seeks permanent possession of the good and the beautiful. The desire for immortality is integral to love's nature.

[5] *Ibid.*, 203D–E, p. 181, *passim.*
[6] *Ibid.*, 204B–C, p. 183.

Because this is something ever-existent and immortal in our mortal life. From what has been admitted, we needs must yearn for immortality no less than for good, since love loves good to be one's own for ever. And hence it necessarily follows that love is of immortality.[7]

The desire for immortality on the part of a mortal nature when it reaches maturity leads to "begetting upon the beautiful."[8] Reproduction of its own kind is the only way a mortal nature can approximate immortality; and it is naturally drawn to what is beautiful in order to effect that reproduction. But the desire to beget can be a physical desire or a spiritual one.

Most living beings, in Plato's view, seek to perpetuate their own kind through animal procreation. After an offspring is born, the parents have a strong desire to protect and preserve it. Diotima observes that "they are ready to fight hard battles, even the weakest against the strongest, and to sacrifice their lives; to be racked with starvation themselves if they can but nurture their young, and be put to any sort of shift."[9]

The beneficence implied is obvious. But, we may still question whether the desire to procreate and the resultant parental instinct to protect are benevolent. Since Diotima describes the amorously disposed as sorely troubled and sick, those who yearn to beget at a certain age may in fact do it to relieve themselves of a need. We must also take into account that the desire for permanent possession of the good and the beautiful when it expresses itself through the animal nature is a desire for personal immortality, for a perpetuation of the self. Such a desire is acquisitive. If parental protection of the young is also acquisitively motivated, the parent protects the vulnerable offspring instinctively or because he sees the latter as an image or perpetuation of himself.

It is necessary to consider the way in which Plato thinks the soul begets, to see more clearly how he conceives of benevolent desire as a form of love. For Plato, the spiritual begetting upon a beautiful soul is best understood in terms of teaching and learning. The notions of wisdom and ignorance are introduced early in Diotima's discourse on love.[10] Such notions point toward the heart of the Platonic theory. The desire for immortality achieves its highest expression in the desire to know the permanent realities. This desire is undoubtedly acquisitive. The fulfillment of the desire to know the permanent realities, however, leads to the desire to have others know them; the consummation of the desire to learn leads to the

[7] *Ibid.*, 206E–207A, p. 193.
[8] *Ibid.*, 206E, p. 193.
[9] *Ibid.*, 207B, p. 193.
[10] See *ibid.*, 202A, p. 175; and 204A, p. 183.

desire to teach. The inclination on the part of the wise to communicate their vision to the young is benevolent. But because teaching can only follow learning, benevolent desire is derivative from the fulfillment of acquisitive desire.

Neither the desire to know nor the desire to teach are completely intelligible unless we look beyond relationships among human beings. To do this, we must examine more thoroughly Plato's understanding of the relationship between love and knowledge, as well as his understanding of the human soul and its destiny.

Since the highest love in Plato's view—and in some sense the prototype of all love—is love of knowledge or philosophy, grasping his theory of love presupposes some understanding of his theory of learning or, as it is frequently called, the theory of recollection. According to this theory, all cognition is recognition; all learning is finding out or remembering what we once knew when our souls were not yet joined to our bodies. This view of learning presupposes the immortality of the soul—not only that it continues to exist after it is separated from the body in death but also, and more important, that it existed before it was joined to the body. During the period before the human soul is joined with the body, it beholds the enduring realities or eternal ideas directly and not through the medium of sense perception. When the soul joins the body, its vision or memory of these ideas is dimmed and blurred. The process of learning is one whereby these ideas are recognized through their images—the things in the visible world. Insofar as such things exist they participate in, or partake of, the being of the enduring realities and are therefore reflections of them. When the soul encounters the visible representations of the invisible ideas, it sometimes experiences tantalizing memories of its former existence. It then becomes excited and desires to return to a direct view of the ideas. This frenzied desire is love. Its highest and most revealing expression is the "divine madness" of philosophy to which Plato so often refers.[11]

In the dialogue *Phaedrus,* Socrates discusses the painful pilgrimage of a soul yearning for the upper regions while chained to the body. Again, Plato uses a myth to convey his meaning. Socrates relates the myth in the context of a conversation between himself and a young man, Phaedrus, about the advantages or disadvantages of associating with a calculating lover as opposed to a passionate one.

Phaedrus had been impressed with a speech of a famous teacher, Lysias, which emphasized the advantages of favoring a "non-lover" over a lover. The focus of Lysias' criticism of the passionate lover is that he is not in control of himself. He acts in the heat of passion and, after his ardor cools,

---

[11] *Phaedrus,* 245A–C, p. 469.

often repents of the kindnesses he extended to the beloved. In addition to being erratic, he is also often troublesome and jealous. The nonlover, or cold lover, by contrast, always acts in his own best interests, but does so in a reasonable and sensible way. He never acts in a fit of momentary passion and is, accordingly, less likely to injure the beloved. Since he considers the beloved a source, not only of present but also future pleasure, he acts with a view to what will preserve rather than destroy their relationship. The enlightened self-interest of the calculating lover brings more long-range benefits to the beloved than does the wild impulsiveness of the passionate lover.[12]

In his comment on the speech of Lysias, Socrates begins by agreeing that the nonlover is superior to the lover. Like Lysias, he bases his argument on the advantages of deliberate action over the compulsion of passion. Reason acts for gain through dispassionate deliberation rather than through blind impulse toward the intense pleasure of the momentary. Socrates mentions two guiding principles in the soul. One is the innate desire for pleasure that revels in excess. The other is the rule of acquired opinion that strives for long-range advantages and implies temperance. The former principle dominates the passionate lover; the latter controls the nonlover.[13]

The argument against the passionate lover is strengthened by Socrates when he points out that a lover of "unsound mind" is concerned only with having his own way. But he only can be sure of having his own way if he dominates the beloved. Thus, the lover, because of his unrestrained passion, either must reduce the beloved to an inferior position or, if the beloved is already inferior, keep him so. He cannot "endure a beloved who is better than himself or his equal."[14] Concluding his remarks in support of Lysias, Socrates says to Phaedrus:

> These things, dear boy, you must bear in mind, and you must know that the fondness of the lover is not a matter of goodwill, but of appetite which he wishes to satisfy.

And he adds:

> Just as the wolf loves the lamb, so the lover adores his beloved.[15]

It seems that Socrates supports the position of Lysias in order to add greater rhetorical force to his subsequent remarks. For, at this point, he abruptly reverses his position and tries to make Phaedrus understand Lysias' error. He even refers to the speech of Lysias and the remarks he

[12] See *ibid.*, 230E–234D, pp. 425–435.
[13] See *ibid.*, 237D–238C, pp. 445–447.
[14] *Ibid.*, 239A, p. 449.
[15] *Ibid.*, 241C–D, p. 457.

made supporting it as "shameless." He reminds Phaedrus that a man of noble and gentle nature, on hearing the speeches, undoubtedly would think he was listening to persons who had never known or seen a generous love.[16]

Socrates then presents the case in favor of the passionate lover by relating a myth in which the soul is described as having three parts, represented by a charioteer and two winged horses. The image applies both to the disembodied soul and to the soul that is joined to the body.[17] The state of the soul in the before-life is one of unrest; it moves around and sometimes toward the eternal ideas, guided by the charioteer, who represents reason. During the restless movement of the souls, certain charioteers try to keep a fixed gaze on the eternal ideas and aspire to move the whole soul closer and closer toward them. The two horses, representing emotion, that pull the chariot disturb the charioteer and often drag him away from the path he wishes to follow. Most souls, consequently, are unable to maintain a steady course toward the ideas. The soul that gets closest to them and gets the best view enters the body of a man who is to be a philosopher or lover of beauty. Those who are least successful enter the bodies of men who become sophists, demagogues, or tyrants. No soul, however, can enter human form unless it manages to see something of the realities.

The image depicts the charioteer as the natural guide of the horses, one of which is white, stately, and obedient, while the other is black, bent, and recalcitrant. When the soul is joined with the body, all three parts of it (the charioteer, the white horse, and the black horse) are animated by a desire to return to the upper regions. This desire means that the soul, whether it understands its predicament or not, yearns to escape the encumbering and restraining body and to return to its former proximity to the real and the permanent. Its plight is the plight of anyone imprisoned away from home. The only way it can begin its liberation is to follow the path of learning, by attempting to recollect the realities behind the images and illusions it perceives in this life. Socrates explains how difficult this task is, saying that

> it is not easy for all souls to gain from earthly things a recollection of those realities, either for those which had but a brief view of them at that earlier time, or for those which, after falling to earth, were so unfortunate as to be turned toward unrighteousness through some evil communications and to have forgotten the holy sights they once saw.[18]

16 See *ibid.,* 243C–D, p. 463.

17 It even applies to the souls of divinities which are never joined to bodies. (See *ibid.,* 245E–247C, pp. 471–475.)

18 *Ibid.,* 249E–250A, p. 483.

The soul can recall the idea of beauty most readily, since only the reflections of this idea can be perceived through sight, the sharpest of the physical senses. It is the idea, therefore, that can most easily arouse love, that is most frequently associated with love, and that puts the lover most often into a state of distraction. For, the lover,

> when he sees the beauty on earth, remembering the true beauty, feels his wings growing and longs to stretch them for an upward flight, but cannot do so, and, like a bird, gazes upward and neglects the things below.[19]

Socrates goes on to tell Phaedrus of the madness or frenzy caused by this recollection. He explains that the lover,

> when he sees a god-like face or form which is a good image of beauty, shudders at first, and something of the old awe comes over him; then, as he gazes, he reveres the beautiful one as a god. . . . And as he looks upon him, a reaction from his shuddering comes over him, with sweat and unwonted heat; for as the effluence of beauty enters him through the eyes, he is warmed . . . the whole soul, stung in every part, rages with pain; and then again, remembering the beautiful one, it rejoices. So, because of these two mingled sensations, it is greatly troubled by its strange condition; it is perplexed and maddened, and in its madness it cannot sleep at night or stay in any one place by day, but it is filled with longing and hastens wherever it hopes to see the beautiful one. And when it sees him and is bathed with the waters of yearning, the passages that were sealed are opened, the soul has respite from the stings and is eased of its pain, and this pleasure which it enjoys is the sweetest of pleasures at the time. Therefore the soul will not, if it can help it, be left alone by the beautiful one, but esteems him above all others, forgets for him mother and brothers and all friends, neglects property and cares not for its loss, and despising all the customs and proprieties in which it formerly took pride, it is ready to be a slave and to sleep wherever it is allowed, as near as possible to the beloved; for it not only reveres him who possesses beauty, but finds in him the only healer of its greatest woes. Now this condition, fair boy, about which I am speaking, is called Love by men.[20]

Socrates again discusses the conflict that the love of a beautiful person creates in the soul in terms of the image of the charioteer and the two horses. When the soul beholds a person through whom the idea of beauty is reflected, it feels an immediate desire to be close to that person. But the charioteer, remembering the true nature of beauty, is awed by the sight and does not move toward the beloved. The white horse, representing the orderly emotions, is constrained by modesty and obedience and also does

[19] *Ibid.*, 249D, p. 483.
[20] *Ibid.*, 251A–252B, pp. 487–491, *passim*.

not move forward. The black horse, by contrast, leaps impulsively and wildly forward and thus causes a great deal of trouble and embarrassment to both his mate and the charioteer. Feeling shy in the presence of the beautiful beloved, the charioteer holds himself back and, by exerting continual pressure on the reins, somehow manages to keep the black horse in check. It is, however, only because of the impulsive lunges of the black horse that the soul ever approaches the beloved. Finally, after much effort, the black horse is restrained and made subject to the wishes of the charioteer. Though the impulses of the black horse may be gratified later on in the relationship, they must not lead if "the better elements of the mind, which lead to a well-ordered life and to philosophy," are to prevail in love.[21] It is, therefore, through the image of the black horse that Socrates explains the madness or frenzy that is part of the very nature of love. He claims that this madness, when controlled, far from being something to be avoided can bring the greatest of blessings in its wake.

Farther along, Socrates discusses the protective and nurturing love of the older for the younger, the love of those in whom the charioteer subjugated the black horse for those in whom the battle still rages. He tells how each mature lover chooses his beloved according to his own character, which is, in turn, a reflection of the character of one of the gods. The followers of Zeus, the highest of the divinities, choose a beloved of a philosophic nature and do their utmost to form him according to the character of Zeus. No matter which god they honor and imitate, all true lovers

> seek for their beloved a youth whose nature accords with that of the god, and when they have gained his affection, by imitating the god themselves and by persuasion and education they lead the beloved to the conduct and nature of the god, so far as each of them can do so; they exhibit no jealousy or meanness toward the loved one, but endeavour by every means in their power to lead him to the likeness of the god whom they honour.[22]

The benevolent desire of an older lover for a younger person also may be interpreted as a desire for the union of similarity, particularly in a relationship in which philosophy is the prime interest. The lover himself is said to imitate a divinity. Insofar as he helps the beloved become like this divinity, he is also helping the beloved to become more like himself. However, the lover's aim is not to get something for himself but to aid and improve someone else. Thus Socrates is able to assert that a passionate lover can confer the greatest of blessings on the beloved. For, if the lover is a philosopher—if his passion is the divine madness of wanting to transcend the human condition by striving to know the eternal verities—his benevo-

[21] *Ibid.*, 256A–B, p. 501.
[22] *Ibid.*, 253B–C, p. 493.

lence takes the form of wanting to aid the beloved in the same effort. In view of this, Socrates concludes by telling the young man, Phaedrus, that great and divine blessings

> the friendship of a lover will confer upon you, dear boy; but the affection of the non-lover, which is alloyed with mortal prudence and follows mortal and parsimonious rules of conduct, will beget in the beloved soul the narrowness which the common folk praise as virtue; it will cause the soul to be a wanderer upon the earth for nine thousand years and a fool below the earth at last.[23]

The theme of the benevolence of a noble lover toward a beloved whose spiritual nurture he undertakes is also present in the later remarks of Diotima in the *Symposium*. The context is her description of the ladder of love. She speaks of a man who always has been concerned with the highest things. If such a man, on reaching maturity, chances upon a beautiful, younger person who is gifted, who is, in short, potentially a philosopher, his love for that person immediately prompts him to undertake the young man's education. In the course of his education, the initiate must ascend from one love to another, beginning with the love of a single beautiful body. From this stage he must be guided to converse with a number of beautiful bodies to permit him to see that beauty is not peculiar to any one individual. His next advance occurs when he is led to fasten his love on the beauty of the soul and to count such beauty as superior to bodily beauty. Then he must develop a love for beauty in the order and structure of the laws and institutions of society. Finally, he is to be led into the realm of knowledge, into discourse and conversation about the first things or ultimate realities. Diotima then says:

> When a man has been thus far tutored in the lore of love, passing from view to view of beautiful things, in the right and regular ascent, suddenly he will have revealed to him, as he draws to the close of his dealings in love, a wondrous vision, beautiful in its nature; and this, Socrates, is the final object of all those previous toils.[24]

At every stage on the ladder of love, the desire of the student is acquisitive, since his only aim is to improve and advance himself. The desire of his older lover, his teacher, is benevolent, since his aim is to help the student up the ladder. The teacher himself must already have climbed partway up the ladder of love and perhaps even have glimpsed the vision of the beautiful. Insofar as he has advanced, *i.e.*, knows beauty, he no

---

[23] *Ibid.*, 256E–257A, pp. 503–505.
[24] *Ibid.*, 210E, p. 205.

longer can be said to love the idea of beauty.[25] To the extent that he has seen the idea, he no longer lacks knowledge of it; nor can he possibly be said to have a benevolent desire toward the idea since it is eternal and self-subsistent. He may continue to have an acquisitive desire to know if his knowledge is only partial. But his love for another human being takes the form of wanting to convey the knowledge he possesses to a promising student. It is benevolent because it is directed toward the fulfillment of a deficiency in another person.

Socrates is Plato's prime example of a teacher, of someone who is concerned with helping the young and fair-souled to learn. A self-styled gadfly, he tries constantly to sting others out of their indifference by questioning them and prodding them to make the painful ascent of love.[26] He also calls himself a midwife, helping those with whom he converses to give birth to good thoughts. That he thinks of himself as a midwife rather than a parent strongly suggests the lack of any self-interested motive. Parents may seek to perpetuate themselves through procreation; Socrates seeks only to perpetuate the habit of learning through his own teaching so that the practice of philosophy and its fruition, wisdom, will not be lost. He seeks, therefore, to aid those who are or might become seekers after wisdom.

Socrates repeatedly denies that he is wise. He refers to himself as a student and not as a teacher. He prefaces almost every conversation with a statement that he does not know and that he talks and questions only to learn. These statements are, to some extent, a tactic of his teaching. For, at one point in the dialogue *The Apology,* in which Socrates explains and defends his way of life, he says that, although he does not know, he means he does not know in the sense of possessing absolute certainty about the ultimate realities. He adds that others to whom he has talked think that they really know when they do not. Socrates concludes that his own knowledge of his lack of certainty makes him wiser than those who mistake opinion for certainty.[27] From this, as well as from the whole picture of Socrates that we get in the dialogues, we must conclude that, if Plato thought that some degree of wisdom can be achieved in this life, Socrates is his exemplar. Plato always portrays Socrates as a philosophical hero and as the one who shows he has the greatest understanding of the subject under discussion. Despite his ironic or rhetorical posture of not knowing, Socrates' activity as a teacher throughout the dialogues is difficult to question, as is Plato's intention to teach his readers through the example of Socrates.

A dramatic illustration of Socrates' benevolent love for the young and untutored is given at the end of the *Symposium.* Just as Socrates finishes

[25] See *Lysis,* 218A, pp. 53–55.
[26] See *The Apology,* 30E–31B, pp. 111–113.
[27] See *ibid.,* 20D–23C, pp. 79–89.

his speech on love, Alcibiades enters in a drunken state. Agathon invites him to stay. Eryximachus tells him of the speeches in praise of love that each of the guests has already given. Alcibiades then also is encouraged to speak; but, instead of speaking in praise of love, he responds with a lover's speech in praise of Socrates.[28]

He refers to Socrates as one whose lips have the "power to entrance mankind by means of instruments." He goes on to describe the peculiar, entrancing effect of Socrates on him and frankly confesses that "there is one experience I have in presence of this man alone, such as nobody would expect in me—to be made to feel ashamed by anyone; he alone can make me feel it." Observing that Socrates always is amorously inclined to handsome persons, Alcibiades explains his own interest in Socrates:

> And believing he had a serious affection for my youthful bloom, I supposed I had here a godsend and a rare stroke of luck, thinking myself free at any time by gratifying his desires to hear all that our Socrates knew; for I was enormously proud of my youthful charms.[29]

He then tells the others how he devised several schemes to be alone with Socrates in order to seduce him. On one occasion, he succeeded in keeping Socrates up late, persuading him to sleep at his house. When Socrates agreed, Alcibiades confessed his intention:

> I consider . . . that you [Socrates] are the only worthy lover I have had, and it looks to me as if you were shy of mentioning it to me. My position is this: I count it sheer folly not to gratify you in this as in any other need you may have of either my property or that of my friends.

Alcibiades reports Socrates' reply:

> My dear Alcibiades, I daresay you are not really a dolt, if what you say of me is the actual truth, and there is a certain power in me that could help you to be better; for then what a stupendous beauty you must see in me, vastly superior to your comeliness!

Alcibiades relates how he lay down beside Socrates and offered himself. Socrates' only reply was to laugh scornfully at his youthful charms. Alcibiades concludes that he slept the night with Socrates as he would have slept with his father or elder brother.[30]

This story of Alcibiades and Socrates can be understood as illustrating Socratic love for the young, as illustrating the nature of the love of a true teacher. Socrates, by his indifference to the physical enticement offered

[28] See *ibid.*, 215A–222C, pp. 219–241.
[29] *Ibid.*, 215A–217C, pp. 219–225.
[30] See *ibid.*, 217A–219D, pp. 223–231.

him, is showing Alcibiades that he misunderstands the nature of Socratic desire or love. Alcibiades' love for Socrates is not reciprocated in kind. That Socrates does not have any sexual desire for Alcibiades suggests that his interest is not acquisitive. Socrates' love is benevolent insofar as he sees in Alcibiades a noble soul turned aside and distracted from its proper ascent up the ladder of love.

The distinction between love as acquisitive desire and love as benevolent desire corresponds in some way to the distinction between popular and heavenly love first introduced in the *Symposium* during the speech of Pausinias. Those who indulge in common or low love "are set on the body more than the soul," and "choose the most witless people they can find, since they look merely to the accomplishment and care not if the manner be noble or no." Such love is described by Diotima as being on the first rung of the ladder of love; it is the love of the black horse, decidedly acquisitive in character and most often taking the form of sexual desire.[31] Those who ascend beyond the popular to the heavenly love advance to a love also *initially* acquisitive in character, but one directed to the highest objects. This love, essentially the desire to learn, is not initially benevolent. Heavenly love only takes the form of benevolent desire when the desire to learn has, to some extent, been consummated. It characterizes the older and wiser man's love for the younger, not the younger's love for the older. The "elder of his plenty contributing" has benevolent desire for the younger. The "younger in his paucity acquiring" has acquisitive desire for the older.[32]

The parallel between acquisitive and benevolent desire and popular and heavenly love is not exact. Popular love is always acquisitive. Heavenly love is acquisitive as the lover ascends the ladder of love, but is transformed into benevolent desire when he becomes older and wiser and wants to aid a younger person in his ascent.

In both the *Symposium* and the *Phaedrus*, Plato implies that the parties to a love relationship are dissimilar. The difference between the older lover and the younger lover permits the former to give and the latter to take. This difference must be present in a relationship based on teaching and learning. The issue of the likeness or unlikeness of lovers or friends is taken up in a separate dialogue, the *Lysis*, in which Socrates converses with several young men about the nature of friendship. In the course of this short and complicated dialogue, a number of positions about who can be friendly with whom are taken up, considered, and rejected.

After a discussion of whether true love need be mutual and of the nature

[31] See *ibid.*, 181B, p. 109. See also 210A–211D, pp. 201–207; *Phaedrus*, 253D–254E, pp. 495–499; and *Laws*, Vol. II, 836E–837E, pp. 153–155.
[32] *Symposium*, 184D–E, p. 121.

of the affection a lover has for a beloved, the key problem of the equality or inequality of lover and beloved is raised. The first position considered is that like can be friendly to like, or, as it is alternately stated, that good can be friendly to good. Socrates argues that like cannot be friendly to like; for, in that case, what could be gained from, or what benefit could one bestow on, another who is exactly the same? He argues similarly that good cannot be friendly to good; insofar as a person is good he is self-sufficient. Those who are self-sufficient neither want anything from another nor are they able to bestow any benefit on another who is as self-sufficient as they are. The conclusion is that those who are alike, just as those who are good, cannot love each other.[33]

The alternative position is also taken up in the course of the dialogue. Love is the attraction of opposites. But the opposite of good is bad. Clearly the good cannot love the bad, nor the bad the good. Perhaps, then, the good can love that which is neither good nor bad, the neutral. Through a series of intricate arguments this position is also finally rejected. In the continuation of the dialogue, numerous other possibilities are considered, all of which suffer the same fate. The dialogue finally ends without any explicit conclusion, but this does not necessarily mean that Plato fails to suggest or point the way to an answer. As in some of his other dialogues, he may have been content to set the proper stage for the consideration of the question, thus inciting the reader to continue what he had begun. Or, as is more likely, he may have supplied the answer by implication. The lovers in the *Phaedrus* and the *Symposium* are unlike, but not as good is unlike bad, nor even as good is unlike what is neither good nor bad. They are related as good is to the potentially good, in a sense as knowledge is to opinion, rather than as knowledge is related to ignorance or no opinion. Whatever Plato's intention may have been in writing the *Lysis*, it is not without significance that Socrates never mentions the possibility that lovers are related as good is to potentially good, and that the affection of the former, though reciprocated, is not reciprocated in kind.

Aurelius Augustine

Augustine's whole theory of love is developed around four key terms: *caritas, amicitia, dilectio,* and *amor*. His use of these terms is highly flexible. He often employs them as synonyms, and argues, at one point, that some of them are so employed in Scripture. In other places, however, he draws very precise distinctions between them. On the whole, *caritas,* or

[33] See *Lysis*, 212A–213D, pp. 35–41; 215C–223B, pp. 45–71. Elsewhere Plato explicitly states the opposite conclusion: that love is "the affection of like for like, in point of goodness." (*Laws*, Vol. II, 837A, p. 153.)

charity, refers either to God's love for man or to man's love for God and his supernaturally aided love for other men. *Amicitia* is used least often and usually refers to friendship or affection as contrasted with lust or carnal desire. *Dilectio* and *amor* may be rendered into English as simply love. While *amor* is applied indifferently by Augustine to all the phenomena he calls love, *dilectio* usually is reserved for the loves that involve the free choice of the will.[34]

In Augustine's general remarks concerning love, he compares it to weight or gravity:

> For the specific gravity of bodies is, as it were, their love, whether they are carried downwards by their weight, or upwards by their levity. For the body is borne by its gravity, as the spirit by love, whithersoever it is borne.[35]

Or, as he says elsewhere:

> A body tends by its weight towards the place proper to it—weight does not necessarily tend towards the lowest place but towards its proper place. Fire tends upwards, stone downwards. By their weight they are moved and seek their proper place. Oil poured over water is borne on the surface of the water, water poured over oil sinks below the oil: it is by their weight that they are moved and seek their proper place. Things out of their place are in motion: they come to their place and are at rest. My love is my weight: wherever I go my love is what brings me there.[36]

In the course of universalizing love, Augustine makes clear that he thinks love can be predicated, strictly speaking, only of sentient and higher beings. The tendencies in the vegetative world (and presumably in the world of inanimate things) are quasi-appetites; one can only speak metaphorically of plants and inanimate things "craving" or "loving." Since Augustine says that "if we were beasts, we should love the fleshly and sensual life," he does not exclude animals from the realm of love.[37] Tendency in general, therefore, literally describes Augustine's conception of love for sentient creatures and the higher orders of being. It therefore describes his notion of natural love among human beings, since all human tendencies, including tendencies toward other human beings, are expressions of love.

The tendential, human faculty is the will. When Augustine refers to the motions of the soul, the motions of love, he says that "none of them is anything else than will."[38] All the inclinations or tendencies of man's will

---

34 See *The City of God*, Vol. II, Book XIV, Ch. 7, pp. 10–11.
35 *Ibid.*, Vol. I, Book XI, Ch. 28, p. 472.
36 *The Confessions of St. Augustine*, Book XIII, Ch. IX, pp. 326–327.
37 *The City of God*, Vol. I, Book XI, Ch. 28, p. 471.
38 *Ibid.*, Vol. II, Book XIV, Ch. 6, p. 9.

can be considered as forms of love, regardless of their moral quality. Though Augustine's principal and recurrent interest is the morality of love, he thinks of love itself as neither good nor evil. As he says:

> The right will is . . . well-directed love, and the wrong will is ill-directed love. Love, then, yearning to have what is loved, is desire; and having and enjoying it, is joy; fleeing what is opposed to it, it is fear; and feeling what is opposed to it, when it has befallen it, it is sadness. Now these motions are evil if the love is evil; good if the love is good.[39]

In Augustine's view, the moral quality of any love is determined exclusively by whether or not it is related to God.[40] Neither man's cupidities nor their objects are evil in themselves, since there are no intrinsically evil things in the whole of creation.[41] When Augustine says that all natural loves are deficient or evil, he means that they are not directed to God. Because of man's fallen nature, such loves, without grace, are nothing but illusory and futile searchings for happiness. They represent defections of will from its true and proper end.[42] The very same tendencies of natural love, through the power of grace, become good when directed to their proper end. Thus the form or type of love is no index to its moral quality. The love between a man and a woman may, for example, exist either as a natural and deficient love or as a supernatural and ordinate love, either as a bad or good love. Vice and virtue are but two sides of the same coin. Therefore, when Augustine says: "Love, and do what thou wilt,"[43] he is referring, not to love in its generic meaning but only to virtuous love, or, to be more precise, to the highest love of which man is capable: the love for God.

Augustine maintains that there are four possible objects of love; *i.e.*, four objects through which man may try to achieve happiness: what is above us, ourselves, what is equal to us (other human beings), and what is below us.[44] The love for what is above man is the love for God and is possible only through supernatural aid or grace. This love is the key to the good life, having not only a decided effect on how man loves his neighbors but

[39] *Ibid.*, Ch. 7, p. 11.
[40] "I define charity as a motion of the soul whose purpose is to enjoy God for His own sake and one's self and one's neighbor for the sake of God. Lust, on the other hand, is a motion of the soul bent upon enjoying one's self, one's neighbor, and any creature without reference to God." (*Christian Instruction*, Book III, Ch. 10, p. 130.)
[41] See *The City of God*, Vol. II, Book XIV, Ch. 3, pp. 4–6; Ch. 5, pp. 8–9; and Ch. 9, pp. 15–20.
[42] See *ibid.*, Vol. I, Book XII, Ch. 8, p. 491; and Vol. II, Book XIV, Ch. 7, pp. 10–11.
[43] *Homilies on the First Epistle of John*, Homily VII, Sect. 8, p. 504.
[44] See *Christian Instruction*, Book I, Ch. 23, pp. 42–43.

also moderating his love for himself and for what is below him. When the loves of self, neighbor, and of what is below man are not ordered to the love for God, they are natural or deficient. Whenever anything replaces God as the final object of love, love falls short of what it should be.[45]

God is central to Augustine's whole theory of love, since, in his view, God is love.[46] As a religious thinker, he is interested primarily in man's love for God and man's God-inspired love for man. This interest is not our principal concern here, since our focus is natural love among human beings. But Augustine does discuss natural love. In fact, the distinction between natural love and supernaturally aided love is directly reflected in his own distinction between the city of man and the city of God.

> Accordingly, two cities have been formed by two loves: the earthly by the love of self, even to the contempt of God; the heavenly by the love of God, even to the contempt of self. The former, in a word, glories in itself, the latter in the Lord. For the one seeks glory from men; but the greatest glory of the other is God, the witness of conscience.[47]

Augustine's "two loves," above all, imply a moral distinction. There is no parallel between his conceptions of love in the city of man as contrasted with love in the city of God and our notions of acquisitive as contrasted with benevolent desire. *Acquisitive and benevolent desire exist in both cities.* Loves in the city of man are distinguishable from loves in the city of God in terms of their moral deficiency.[48] In Augustine's view, natural loves are those that are directed to the good of the self or to the good of another without reference to God, whether they be acquisitive or benevolent.

Of the acquisitive form of natural love, or what he refers to frequently as inordinate love of self, Augustine writes at length. He takes sexual desire, "the greatest of all bodily pleasures," as the prototype of such love. Though he refers to such desire as of the flesh, or lust, the compass of natural acquisitive desire is much larger. He says that "lust may have many objects, yet when no object is specified, the word lust usually suggests to the mind the lustful excitement of the organs of generation."[49] Such loves are "not only those which concern the pleasure of the flesh . . . but also those which, though they be remote from fleshly pleasure, reveal the vices of the soul."[50]

Augustine's account of his life before his conversion is full of instances

---

[45] See *Lectures or Tractates on the Gospel According to St. John,* Vol. II, Tractate LXXXVII, p. 325.

[46] See *On the Trinity,* Book XV, Ch. XVII, p. 415.

[47] *The City of God,* Vol. II, Book XIV, Ch. 28, p. 47.

[48] For Augustine's theory of supernatural love, see Part I, Ch. 3, *supra.*

[49] *The City of God,* Vol. II, Book XIV, Ch. 16, p. 31, *passim.*

[50] *Ibid.,* Ch. 2, p. 3.

of deficient or illicit love. His most frequent failing was sexual desire, a hunger for "the limbs that carnal love embraces."[51] Augustine understands his desire for "the enjoyment of the body of the person who loved [him]," for carnal pleasure *as an end in itself,* as but a temporary palliative, an inadequate substitute for "incorruptible food." Since sexual pleasure could not satisfy his desire for happiness, and since the emptier and more unhappy he became the more he hated the thought of turning to God, his recourse was to indulge his desire more frequently. Thus he says that he was not in love with a person but only in love with love. He sought others only to consummate his ever mounting desire. He "did fall in love, simply from wanting to."[52]

Augustine's passionate denunciation of his earlier life, after his conversion, cannot be taken as a prohibition of any form of carnal indulgence, since he regards all natural cupidities as essentially good. He condemns sexual desire only when it is not related to the love for God—only when sexual pleasure is not enjoyed within marriage. Procreation is the purpose of sexual desire in marriage, and, in Augustine's view, it is so obviously a part of God's design that "it is great folly to oppose so plain a fact."[53] Referring in the *Confessions* to the mistress with whom he lived for many years, Augustine says:

> . . . I had but that one woman, and I was faithful to her. And with her I learnt by my own experience what a gulf there is between the restraint of the marriage-covenant entered into for the sake of children and the mere bargain of a lustful love.[54]

Despite the fact that it need not be sinful, sexual desire is one natural cupidity that Augustine thinks was altered decisively by the original sin of Adam and Eve. In man's original state, lust could not move the generative organs without the consent of the will:

> The honest love of husband and wife made a sure harmony between them. Body and spirit worked harmoniously together, and the commandment was kept without labour.[55]

After the Fall, sexual desire ceased to be voluntary. Sexual desire, no longer under the control of the will, is frequently at variance with it. Augustine observes that

[51] *The Confessions of St. Augustine,* Book X, Ch. VI, p. 215.
[52] *Ibid.,* Book III, Ch. I, p. 41, *passim.*
[53] *The City of God,* Vol. II, Book XIV, Ch. 22, p. 38.
[54] *The Confessions of St. Augustine,* Book IV, Ch. II, p. 62. Elsewhere, he says: "If material things please you then praise God for them, but turn back your love upon Him who made them." (*Ibid.,* Ch. XII, p. 72.)
[55] *The City of God,* Vol. II, Book XIV, Ch. 26, p. 44.

strangely enough, this emotion not only fails to obey the legitimate desire to beget offspring, but also refuses to serve lascivious lust; and though it often opposes its whole combined energy to the soul that resists it, sometimes also it is divided against itself, and while it moves the soul, leaves the body unmoved.[56]

As an additional part of man's punishment, sexual desire "requires for its consummation darkness and secrecy." Shame invariably attends it. Even in marriage, conjugal intercourse, "legitimate and honourable though it be . . . [seeks] retirement from every eye." Such intercourse is a right action and the effect of a good love, yet dreads being seen, "because that which is by nature fitting and decent is . . . accompanied with a shame-begetting penalty of sin."[57]

Though natural love among human beings most frequently takes the form of acquisitive desire, Augustine's theory also includes natural benevolence. This kind of benevolence is not charity. A person who is naturally benevolent is genuinely concerned with the welfare of another, but the deficiency of his love is that he is not concerned with the "supreme good" of the other person. Unlike charity, natural benevolent desire is not directed to helping another to love God. Augustine never tires of repeating that, for the Christian, "life eternal is the supreme good, death eternal the supreme evil."[58] This position leads him to say that "there is no true friendship unless You [God] weld it between souls that cleave together through that charity which is shed in our hearts by the Holy Ghost."[59]

However deficient natural friendship may be, Augustine views it as better than carnal love. Even before his conversion, he contrasted "the luminous line of friendship" with "the muddy concupiscence of the flesh."[60]

In commenting on his own hunger for the body of another, he writes: "Thus I polluted the stream of friendship with the filth of unclean desire and sullied its limpidity with the hell of lust."[61] By contrast, natural friendships are even good, though "through immoderate inclination to them . . . they are of the lowest order of good—things higher and better are forgotten."[62]

Accordingly, Augustine rejects the doctrines of certain philosophical sects, even though they "say that this happy life is . . . social, and loves the advantages of its friends as its own, and for their sake wishes for them

[56] *Ibid.*, Ch. 16, p. 32.
[57] *Ibid.*, Ch. 18, p. 34, *passim.*
[58] *Ibid.*, Vol. II, Book XIX, Ch. 4, p. 301.
[59] *The Confessions of St. Augustine,* Book IV, Ch. IV, p. 65.
[60] *Ibid.*, Book II, Ch. II, p. 27.
[61] *Ibid.*, Book III, Ch. I, p. 41.
[62] *Ibid.*, Book II, Ch. V, p. 32.

what it desires for itself."[63] He points out that, contrary to common belief, these sects do not really differ on the question of man's chief or ultimate good. All agree that man's ultimate happiness consists in philosophizing. Their principal disagreement is on the secondary question of whether a wise or virtuous man should associate with a friend in realizing that good and "whether the wise man will do this not for his own sake, but for the sake of his friend in whose good he delights as in his own."[64] But whether or not natural benevolence is viewed as part of the virtuous life, Augustine considers all such doctrines partial and in error, because in none of them is proximity to God viewed as man's ultimate good.

In the *Confessions*, the most poignant example of a genuine benevolence outside the realm of charity is Augustine's own feeling for his mother, Monica. Although in the years before his conversion he and his mother often were in conflict about his way of life, he admired and remained devoted to her. This is revealed clearly in Augustine's account of her last words to him:

> . . . when her illness was close to its end, meeting with expressions of endearment such services as I rendered, she called me a dutiful loving son, and said in the great affection of her love that she had never heard from my mouth any harsh or reproachful word addressed to herself.[65]

Though mutual giving is characteristic of friends, Augustine maintains that natural friendship is not entirely benevolent. He speaks of his own efforts to save his friend Alypius, who loved him because he was "kindly and learned."[66] He mentions "[doing] each other kindnesses"[67] as characteristic of his early friendships. But, early in the *Confessions*, he writes of his despair and grief when a dear friend became ill and died. He felt that he and his friend were "one soul in two bodies." After the friend's death, he says, "my life was a horror to me because I would not live halved."[68] In addition to being concerned about what he could give to his friend, he also was concerned about what he could derive from friendship. Most of his later reservations about mutual friendship spring from his realization that friends are vulnerable. They die, change, or are otherwise taken away.[69] Reliance on friendship is hazardous for,

---

[63] *The City of God*, Vol. II, Book XIX, Ch. 3, p. 301.
[64] *Ibid.*, Ch. 1, pp. 296–297.
[65] *The Confessions of St. Augustine*, Book IX, Ch. XII, p. 203. See also Book I, Ch. XI, pp. 14–15; Book V, Chs. VIII–X, pp. 94–96; Book VI, Chs. I–II, pp. 105–107; Book VIII, Ch. XII, p. 179; and Book IX, Chs. X–XIII, pp. 199–208.
[66] *Ibid.*, Book VI, Ch. VII, p. 114.
[67] *Ibid.*, Book IV, Ch. VIII, p. 69.
[68] *Ibid.*, Book IV, Ch. VI, p. 68.
[69] See *ibid.*, Ch. IX, p. 70.

the more friends we have, and the more widely they are scattered, the more numerous are our fears that some portion of the vast masses of the disasters of life may light upon them.[70]

In Augustine's view, man not only fears for his friends—benevolent desire—but also fears for himself—acquisitive desire—lest friendship as a source of comfort be taken from him. There is no comparable worry in the friendship of charity, since a man's happiness as well as that of his friends depends only on proximity to God—something immune to chance.[71]

To summarize: both acquisitive desire and benevolent desire are forms or types of love in each of the two parts of Augustine's theory; they are forms of supernatural as well as of natural love among human beings. The most frequent form of natural love is acquisitive desire, for which Augustine takes sexual desire as prototype. But he also affirms the existence of benevolent desire as a higher form of natural love as expressed in friendship and filial affection.[72]

Aristotle

Aristotle has all the requisites of a cosmic theory of love. He refers to a universal striving to participate in the eternal and the divine.[73] The generative tendencies of plants and animals, the movements of heavenly bodies, as well as the inherent desire of men to know, are all understood by him as different ways in which each being participates (according to the dictates of its nature) in this striving. Yet, only very rarely does he use the word "love," its synonyms, or its pseudo-synonyms in describing these tendencies as they manifest themselves in other than human beings.[74]

Almost all of Aristotle's account of love—or even reference to the subject—is found in Books VIII and IX of his *Nicomachean Ethics*. At the very beginning of Book VIII, in commenting on the efforts of his predecessors to understand love, he sets forth the scope of his own inquiry:

. . . they inquire for deeper and more physical causes, Euripides saying that "parched earth loves the rain, and stately heaven when filled with rain loves to fall to earth," and Heraclitus that "it is what opposes that helps" and

[70] *The City of God*, Vol. II, Book XIX, Ch. 8, p. 312.
[71] See *ibid.*, pp. 312–313.
[72] For a comparable account of Augustine's theory of love, see Étienne Gilson's *The Christian Philosophy of Saint Augustine*, Part II, Ch. II, pp. 132–142.
[73] See *On the Soul*, Book III, Chs. 9–10, 432b21–433a26, pp. 597–598. See also Ch. 12, 434a30–434b8, pp. 600–601.
[74] When Aristotle applies the word "love" to cosmic phenomena, he seems to be employing the word analogically, as for example, "The final cause, then, produces motion *as* being loved. . . ." (*Metaphysics*, Book XII, Ch. 7, 1072b3, p. 879. Italics added. See also *Nicomachean Ethics*, Book VIII, Ch. 1, 1155a16–19, p. 1058.)

"from different tones comes the fairest tune" and "all things are produced through strife"; while Empedocles, as well as others, expresses the opposite view that like aims at like. The physical problems we may leave alone (for they do not belong to the present inquiry); let us examine those which are human and involve character and feeling.[75]

Aristotle employs four principal terms in his analysis of human love: *philia, philotys, philesis,* and *eros. Philia,* or friendship, is by far the most important. Every reciprocal love relationship among human beings is interpreted by Aristotle as a variety of friendship, from the affections between parents and children to the feelings that constitute the bond among men in states. Aristotle distinguishes *philotys,* or goodwill, from friendship, both because it is not necessarily reciprocated and because it is an emotion or feeling that is not sufficiently intense to lead to action. Goodwill means, for him, being well-disposed toward someone else without necessarily really wanting to help him; it is a kind of substratum out of which friendship can develop. *Philesis,* or friendly feeling, is viewed as an instinctive and as yet unfocused affection for someone else. *Eros,* or love, has two meanings. In its generic sense, it refers to a number of human inclinations, passionate or deliberate, toward real or apparent goods. In this sense it is a much broader term than friendship. In its second sense, it is a much narrower term than friendship; for its signifies a reciprocal relationship between two persons that is "ideally" a sort of excess of friendship, which, because of its intensity, only can be felt for one person at a time.

Aristotle's theory of love among human beings is a tendential one. He distinguishes between the tendencies of love and the tendencies of friendship (which must be reciprocal) in the following way:

> Now it looks as if love were a feeling, friendship a state of character; for love may be felt just as much towards lifeless things, but mutual love involves choice and choice springs from a state of character; and men wish well to those whom they love, for their sake, not as a result of feeling but as a result of a state of character.[76]

By "wish" Aristotle means an inclination, or what we call tendency.

The character of friends and their activities are regarded by Aristotle as potential desire and actual desire. In this connection, he says:

> . . . those who live together delight in each other and confer benefits on each other, but those who are asleep or locally separated are not performing, but are disposed to perform, the activities of friendship.[77]

[75] *Ibid.,* Book VIII, Ch. 1, 1155b1–10, p. 1059. Aristotle does mention the "love" of humans for things but only to contrast it with his conception of love among human beings. (See *ibid.,* Ch. 5, 1157b29–30, p. 1064.)

[76] *Ibid.,* 1157b28–33, p. 1064.

[77] *Ibid.,* 1157b7–10, p. 1063.

Though friendship at its best is a virtue and virtue is an activity, men do not cease being friends when they are not performing the activities of friendship. Even during these intervals they are disposed or inclined to perform them; if opportunities to perform them arose, they would. Hence, the Aristotelian emphasis is on the activities of friendship and on the desires that are behind those activities.[78]

Aristotle's interest in love focuses on friendship, *i.e.*, reciprocal love among human beings. And the crux of his analysis of friendship is the distinction he makes among its three kinds. "There are therefore three kinds of friendship, equal in number to the things that are lovable. . . ."[79] They are: the friendship of virtue, the friendship of pleasure, and the friendship of utility.

Aristotle distinguishes among friendships by the good that is loved and by the manner in which a person loves, *i.e.*, by the mode of desire. The friendship of virtue has as its characteristic aim the good of the other, while the friendships of pleasure and utility have as their characteristic aim the good of the self. The former is benevolent in character and the latter are acquisitive. In describing the friendship of virtue, Aristotle says:

> Perfect friendship is the friendship of men who are good, and alike in virtue; for these wish well alike to each other *qua* good, and they are good in themselves. Now those who wish well to their friends for their sake are most truly friends; for they do this by reason of their own nature and not incidentally.[80]

By contrast, in commenting on the friendships of pleasure and utility, he says:

> Now those who love each other for their utility do not love each other for themselves but in virtue of some good which they get from each other. So too with those who love for the sake of pleasure; it is not for their character that men love ready-witted people, but because they find them pleasant. Therefore those who love for the sake of utility love for the sake of what is good for *themselves*, and those who love for the sake of pleasure do so for the sake of what is pleasant to *themselves*, and not in so far as the other is the person loved but in so far as he is useful or pleasant. And thus these friendships are only incidental; for it is not as being the man he is that the loved person is loved, but as providing some good or pleasure.[81]

[78] The tendencies of the best friendship, the friendship of virtue, seem to be exclusively matters of choice. Those of inferior friendships, particularly the friendship of pleasure, do not seem to be exclusively matters of choice, but also may involve, or originate in, emotion. (See *Rhetoric*, Book I, Ch. 10, 1369a1–5, p. 1360; and *Eudemian Ethics*, Book VII, Ch. 2, 1235b12–29.)

[79] *Nicomachean Ethics*, Book VIII, Ch. 3, 1156a7–9, p. 1060.

[80] *Ibid.*, 1156b7–11, p. 1061.

[81] *Ibid.*, 1156a10–20, p. 1060.

In addition to these basic differences, friendships of virtue are possible only among men of good character; those of utility and pleasure may arise among the participants regardless of their character.[82] Friendships of virtue require "time and familiarity"[83] to develop and such friendships endure; those of pleasure or utility can come into being quickly and last only as long as the parties involved find each other pleasant or useful.[84] Friendships of virtue are extremely rare; those of pleasure are frequent and most common among the young;[85] the friendship of utility "is of course that of the majority."[86]

The friendship of virtue is the prototype of the other two kinds of friendship. It is only by reference to the prototype that the relationships aiming at pleasure and utility can be called friendships. One of Aristotle's arguments for calling the relationships of pleasure and utility friendship is that the friendship of virtue, in addition to being morally good, is also pleasant and useful for those involved. Of the friendship of virtue, he says:

> This kind of friendship, then, is perfect both in respect of duration and in all other respects, and in it each gets from each in all respects the same as, or something like what, he gives; which is what ought to happen between friends. Friendship for the sake of pleasure bears a resemblance to this kind; for good people too *are* pleasant to each other. So too does friendship for the sake of utility; for the good are also useful to each other.[87]

Aristotle admits that the application of the term "friendship" to all three relations is not univocal, but neither is it equivocal. Common to all is that the tendency of friendship is toward some good. The real good of the friendship of virtue includes the goods of pleasure and utility, although in a virtuous friendship these goods differ from the pleasure and utility involved in the other two kinds of friendship. The friendship of virtue is essentially and properly called friendship. The friendships of pleasure and

---

[82] "For the sake of pleasure or utility, then, even bad men may be friends of each other, or good men of bad, or one who is neither good nor bad may be a friend to any sort of person, but for their own sake clearly only good men can be friends; for bad men do not delight in each other unless some advantage come of the relation." (*Ibid.*, Ch. 4, 1157a17–20, p. 1062.)

[83] *Ibid.*, Ch. 3, 1156b25, p. 1061.

[84] Such are "lovers not of each other but of profit." (*Ibid.*, Ch. 4, 1157a16, p. 1062. See also Ch. 3, 1156a19–24, p. 1060.)

[85] See *ibid.*, 1156b1–5, 24–26, p. 1061.

[86] *Eudemian Ethics*, Book VII, Ch. 2, 1236a32–33. It seems to be the friendship of utility that is the bond of men in states (since they group together because of mutual need), as well as the principle governing political alliances between states. "Friendship seems too to hold states together . . . it is not only necessary but also noble." (*Nicomachean Ethics*, Book VIII, Ch. 1, 1155a22, 29, pp. 1058–59.)

[87] *Nichomachean Ethics*, Book VIII, Ch. 4, 1156b33–1157a3, p. 1062.

utility only accidentally are called so, since in neither case is the other person loved for himself. Aristotle makes this point in the following way:

> For men apply the name of friends even to those whose motive is utility . . . and to those who love each other for the sake of pleasure, in which sense children are called friends. Therefore we too ought perhaps to call such people friends, and say that there are several kinds of friendship—firstly and in the proper sense that of good men *qua* good, and by analogy the other kinds; for it is in virtue of something good and something akin to what is found in true friendship that they are friends, since even the pleasant is good for the lovers of pleasure. . . .
>
> Friendship being divided into these kinds, bad men will be friends for the sake of pleasure or of utility, being in this respect like each other, but good men will be friends for their own sake, *i.e.*, in virtue of their goodness. These, then, are friends without qualification; the others are friends incidentally and through a resemblance to these.[88]

Or, as he also says in stressing the similarities and differences of real and incidental friendship:

> But it is from their likeness and their unlikeness to the same thing that they are thought both to be and not to be friendships. It is by their likeness to the friendship of virtue that they seem to be friendships (for one of them involves pleasure and the other utility, and these characteristics belong to the friendship of virtue as well); while it is because the friendship of virtue is proof against slander and permanent, while these quickly change (besides differing from the former in many other respects), that they appear *not* to be friendships; *i.e.*, it is because of their unlikeness to the friendship of virtue.[89]

Another feature common to all three friendships is that they are reciprocal relationships, even though those involved may not love each

---

[88] *Ibid.*, 1157a25–1157b4, pp. 1062–63.

[89] *Ibid.*, Ch. 6, 1158b5–11, p. 1065. Elsewhere, Aristotle says: "For springing from the perfect friendship which exists among the good there are also these forms of friendship, that which refers to the pleasant and that which refers to the useful. He, then, whose love is based on the pleasant does not love with the love which is based on the good, nor does he whose friendship is based upon the useful. And these forms of friendship, that of the good, the pleasant, and the useful, are not indeed the same, not yet absolutely different from one another, but hang in a way from the same head. Just so we call a knife surgical, a man surgical, and knowledge surgical. These are not called so in the same way, but the knife is called surgical from being useful in surgery, and the man from his being able to produce health, and the knowledge from its being cause and principle. Similarly, the forms of friendship are not all called so in the same way, the friendship of the virtuous which is based on the good, the friendship depending on pleasure, and that depending on utility. Nor yet is it a mere case of equivocation, but, while they are not actually the same, they have still in a way the same sphere and the same origin." (*Magna Moralia*, Book II, Ch. 11, 1209a16–32.)

other in the same way. Thus, one-sided affection—loving someone who either does not want to reciprocate or is unaware that he is loved—is, though an instance of love, not an instance of friendship, in Aristotle's view.[90]

A further feature of similarity is that in each friendship the other person is wished well in the respect in which he is loved. The friendship of virtue always involves being eager to seize an opportunity to enhance the friend's welfare *for his own sake*.[91] In the friendships of pleasure and utility, wishing the other well is also present. What distinguishes them from the true friendship of virtue is that the giving involved is always and only present for the sake of getting. As we shall see, "real" friendship—the friendship of virtue—is self-interested. But the *giving only for the sake of getting* of the friendships of pleasure and utility is logically distinct from the *giving and getting* of the friendship of virtue. This distinction is accurately reflected in the subordinate forms of acquisitive and benevolent desire: mixed acquisitive desire and self-interested benevolence.

In the typical instances of both inferior friendships, the persons involved are equal, and, in their mutual desires, each gets the same thing (or something like it) from the other. In a typical friendship of pleasure, both parties seek and get pleasure from each other, just as in a typical friendship of utility both parties seek and get a certain use out of each other. (Or, in a less typical instance, they may "exchange one thing for another, *e.g.*, pleasure for utility."[92]) Aristotle says of all three kinds of friendship that not only is there in each "a mutual and recognized love," but also that "those who love each other wish well to each other in that respect in which they love one another."[93] Probably the clearest example of giving in order to get is a commercial relationship, one possible form of the friendship of utility. One person gives money to the other in order to acquire an article or service; the other gives the article or renders the service in order to acquire the money.[94] Each gives only in order to get something for himself. Thus, Aristotle says:

> The man who has received a benefit bestows goodwill in return for what has been done to him, but in doing so is only doing what is just; while he who

[90] See *Nicomachean Ethics*, Book VIII, Ch. 4, 1156b33–1157a16, p. 1062; Ch. 8, 1159a33–38, p. 1067; and Ch. 13, 1162b32–1163a24, pp. 1074–75.

[91] "For those who are friends on the ground of virtue are anxious to do well by each other (since that is a mark of virtue and of friendship)." (*Ibid.*, Ch. 13, 1162b6–8, p. 1073.)

[92] *Ibid.*, Ch. 6, 1158b3–4, p. 1065.

[93] *Ibid.*, Ch. 3, 1156a8–10, p. 1060.

[94] "Now here a common measure has been provided in the form of money, and therefore everything is referred to this and measured by this." (*Ibid.*, Book IX, Ch. 1, 1164a1–3, p. 1076.)

wishes some one to prosper because he hopes for enrichment through him seems to have goodwill not to him but rather to himself, just as a man is not a friend to another if he cherishes him for the sake of some use to be made of him.[95]

Since the friendships must be mutual, the desires of both parties must be fulfilled. If pleasure or utility is the object of the friendship of two people, "it is dissolved when they do not get the things that formed the motives of their love."[96] Discussing the *quid pro quo* of inferior friendships, Aristotle says:

> Now if the friendship is one that aims at *utility*, surely the advantage to the receiver is the measure. For it is he that asks for the service, and the other man helps him on the assumption that he will receive the equivalent; so the assistance has been precisely as great as the advantage to the receiver, and therefore he must return as much as he has received, or even more (for that would be nobler). In friendships based on *virtue* on the other hand, complaints do not arise, but the purpose of the doer is a sort of measure; for in purpose lies the essential element of virtue and character.[97]

In contrast to the motives of the friends of utility or pleasure, the motive of the friends of virtue is the good of the other. Though benevolent desires distinguish the friends in virtue, Aristotle says that such desires are accompanied by a self-interested motive. Though the essential part of the friendship of virtue is a concern with the welfare of the other, an integral part of it is a concomitant concern with one's own welfare.

Aristotle says of friends of virtue that "those who have done a service to others feel friendship and love for those they have served even if these are not of any use to them and never will be."[98] But he also says, in various ways, that the benevolent person does—or rather can—gain a good for himself through being a true friend.

---

[95] *Ibid.*, Ch. 5, 1167a13–18, p. 1083.

[96] *Ibid.*, Ch. 1, 1164a9–10, p. 1077. One can imagine some cases in which simple acquisitive desire would suffice to keep the friendship alive. Two people who desire each other sexually may fulfill each other's desire by fulfilling their own. In seeking their own pleasure they give pleasure to another, not as a tactic but as a by-product. Apparently Aristotle thinks that such uncomplicated instances are rare. In most inferior friendships, "what each in fact wants is what he attends to, and it is for the sake of that that he will give what he has." (*Ibid.*, 20–21, p. 1077.)

[97] *Ibid.*, Book VIII, Ch. 13, 1163a16–24, p. 1075. See also Book IX, Ch. 1, 1164b7–13, p. 1078.

[98] *Ibid.*, Book IX, Ch. 7, 1167b32–34, p. 1085. The "good man acts for honour's sake, and the more so the better he is, and acts for his friend's sake, and sacrifices his own interest." A "man's best friend is one who wishes well to the object of his wish for his sake, even if no one is to know of it." (*Ibid.*, 1168a32–34, 1168b2–3, p. 1086. See also Book VIII, Ch. 13, 1162b5–13, pp. 1073–74.) We "prize friendship for itself, even though nothing else is likely to come to us from it." (*Topics*, Book III, Ch. 1, 117a3–4.)

Perhaps the benevolence of true friendship most obviously is self-interested in the giver's anticipation that his affection and concern will be returned in kind, even though his benevolence is not extended solely for the sake of its return. Though being a friend to someone means "wishing for him what you believe to be good things, not for your own sake but for his, and being inclined, so far as you can, to bring these things about," it means also that the friend "excites these feelings in return."[99] Love becomes friendship when it is recognized and returned. And the true friend wants to have his affection returned; however, for his desire to remain benevolent, reciprocity must be a concomitant and not a primary goal.[100]

Aristotle emphasizes the self-interested aspect of a virtuous friendship in discussing the part that such friendship plays in a good and happy life. He says that "without friends no one would choose to live, though he had all other goods."[101] For,

> if life is desirable, and particularly so for good men, because to them existence is good and pleasant (for they are pleased at the consciousness of the presence in them of what is in itself good); and if as the virtuous man is to himself, he is to his friend also (for his friend is another self):—if all this be true, as his own being is desirable for each man, so, or almost so, is that of his friend. . . .
>
> If, then, being is in itself desirable for the supremely happy man (since it is by its nature good and pleasant), and that of his friend is very much the same, a friend will be one of the things that are desirable. Now that which is desirable for him he must have, or he will be deficient in this respect. The man who is to be happy will therefore need virtuous friends.[102]

The absence of friends is a deficiency in the happy life, not because of the comfort friends give but because their presence makes it possible to exercise certain virtues; and, for Aristotle, happiness is activity in accordance with virtue.[103] What, Aristotle asks, "is the use of . . . prosperity without the opportunity of beneficence, which is exercised chiefly and in its most

[99] *Rhetoric*, Book II, Ch. 4, 1380b36–1381a2, p. 1386. ". . . we feel friendly to those who have treated us well, either ourselves or those we care for, whether on a large scale, or readily, or at some particular crisis; provided it was for our own sake." True benevolence inclines the recipient to feel the same. (*Ibid.*, 1381a12–14, p. 1387.)

[100] "This kind of friendship, then, is perfect both in respect of duration and in all other respects, and in it each gets from each in all respects the same as, or something like what, he gives; *which is what ought to happen between friends.*" (*Nicomachean Ethics*, Book VIII, Ch. 4, 1156b32–35, p. 1062. Italics added.)

[101] *Ibid.*, Ch. 1, 1155a5–6, p. 1058.

[102] *Ibid.*, Book IX, Ch. 9, 1170b3–8, 14–19, p. 1090. See also Book VIII, Ch. 7, 1158b24–28, p. 1066.

[103] See *ibid.*, Book I, Ch. 7, 1097b23–24, 1098a17–18, pp. 942–943.

laudable form towards friends?" Friendship, the essence of which is seeking
good for another, "is a virtue or implies virtue."[104] But, the good man who
has friends also aids himself in helping his friends by becoming more
virtuous and thereby happier.[105]

Aristotle also says that one of the most distinguishing marks of true
friendship is the delight friends take in each other. Part of this delight is
the satisfaction that each derives from helping the other.[106] Aristotle
maintains that it is better to love than to be loved; it is better to give
benefits than to receive them, not only because giving is nobler but also
because it produces greater delight than receiving. For this reason, Aristotle
says that a man still wants friends even if he is experiencing good fortune
and is happy in all other ways, for he also wants to share his good fortune
with others.[107]

Benevolent desire in the friendship of virtue is self-interested in another
way: through the similarity of friends. Typical friends are alike in character and interests. Aristotle says that

> your friend is the sort of man who shares your pleasure in what is good and
> your pain in what is unpleasant, for your sake and for no other reason. This
> pleasure and pain of his will be the token of his good wishes for you, since
> we all feel glad at getting what we wish for, and pained at getting what we
> do not. Those, then, are friends to whom the same thingss are good and
> evil.[108]

He who bestows a benefit on his friend participates in some way and to
some extent in the enjoyment of that good, since he grieves and rejoices
with his friend and finds the same things pleasant and the same things
painful.

In the typical case of the perfect friendship of virtue, the character of
the friends are alike, *i.e.*, they are, in this respect, already united. But this
existing union does not preclude a desire for the union of similarity both in

[104] *Ibid.*, Book VIII, Ch. 1, 1155a8–9, 3, p. 1058.

[105] ". . . the supremely happy man will need friends of this sort, since his
purpose is to contemplate worthy actions and actions that are his own, and the actions
of a good man who is his friend have both these qualities." (*Ibid.*, Book IX, Ch. 9,
1170a2–4, p. 1089.)

[106] The delight in giving is not, however, a conclusive sign of friendship. Mentioning the relationships of old men and "sour" people, Aristotle says: ". . . . such
men may bear goodwill to each other; for they wish one another well and aid one
another in need; but they are hardly *friends* because they do not spend their days
together nor delight in each other, and these are thought the greatest marks of
friendship." (*Ibid.*, Book VIII, Ch. 6, 1158a7–9, p. 1064.)

[107] See *ibid.*, Ch. 8, 1159a24–37, p. 1067. The man in bad fortune needs friends
more than the man in good fortune for "it is useful friends that one wants in this
case." (*Ibid.*, Book IX, Ch. 11, 1171a24–25, p. 1092.)

[108] *Rhetoric*, Book II, Ch. 4, 1381a4–8, p. 1386.

seeking to preserve their existing union and in wanting to pursue common activities. Probably the most characteristic mark of friends, for Aristotle, is their desire to live together. The relationship of friends is "realized in their living together and sharing in discussion and thought; for this is what living together would seem to mean in the case of man, and not, as in the case of cattle, feeding in the same place."[109]

Since benevolent desire is characteristic of perfect friendship, the desire for the union of similarity in it would have to take a benevolent form. Insofar as such a desire is present in inferior friendships, it takes an acquisitive form. Thus, in a friendship of pleasure, those who seek the same kind of pleasure may well do so through pursuing a common activity.

Just as the desire for the union of similarity may take a benevolent or acquisitive form so also may the desire for the union of complementarity. The clearest illustration of the desire for complementary union is in the relationship between man and wife.

> Between man and wife friendship seems to exist by nature; for man is naturally inclined to form couples—even more than to form cities, inasmuch as the household is earlier and more necessary than the city, and reproduction is more common to man with the animals. With the other animals the union extends only to this point, but human beings live together not only for the sake of reproduction but also for the various purposes of life; for from the start the functions are divided, and those of man and woman are different; so they help each other by throwing their peculiar gifts into the common stock. It is for these reasons that both utility and pleasure seem to be found in this kind of friendship. But this friendship may be based also on virtue, if the parties are good; for each has its own virtue and they will delight in the fact.[110]

In relationships in which mutual love takes the form of the desire for the union of complementarity, the two parties are different in character, as are the man and wife described above. Such relationships are atypical in Aristotle's view, however frequent they may be. The most typical friendships (whether they be those of virtue, pleasure, or utility) are those between persons of the same character who give and get the same thing from each other. Contrasting these typical friendships with those in which the persons are either dissimilar or do not reciprocate with the same kind of affection they receive, Aristotle says:

[109] *Nicomachean Ethics*, Book IX, Ch. 9, 1170b11–14, p. 1090. Sharing in discussion and thought is the characteristic common activity pursued by the friends in virtue. Other friends, however, do different things in common. Some "drink together, others dice together, others join in athletic exercises and hunting, or in the study of philosophy." (*Ibid.*, Ch. 12, 1172a3–5, p. 1093. See also 1171b30, p. 1093.)
[110] *Ibid.*, Book VIII, Ch. 12, 1162a16–27, p. 1073.

But there is another kind of friendship, viz., that which involves an inequality between the parties, *e.g.*, that of father to son and in general of elder to younger, that of man to wife and in general that of ruler to subject. And these friendships differ also from each other; for it is not the same that exists between parents and children and between rulers and subjects, nor is even that of father to son the same as that of son to father, nor that of husband to wife the same as that of wife to husband. For the virtue and the function of each of these is different, and so are the reasons for which they love; the love and the friendship are therefore different also. Each party, then, neither gets the same from the other, nor ought to seek it; but when children render to parents what they ought to render to those who brought them into the world, and parents render what they should to their children, the friendship of such persons will be abiding and excellent. In all friendships implying inequality the love also should be proportional, *i.e.*, the better should be more loved than he loves, and so should the more useful, and similarly in each of the other cases; for when the love is in proportion to the merit of the parties, then in a sense arises equality, which is certainly held to be characteristic of friendship.[111]

Equality—one of the identifying characteristics of friendship—is then possible in friendships between unequals through the proportion of their love. The dissimilarity between friends of an unequal character is compensated for by the inverse proportionality of their love.[112]

Aristotle does not mention the possibility of unequals desiring to become similar.[113] In a typical friendship between equals, whatever desire for union there is seems to be the desire for the union of similarity, at least in the friendships of virtue and pleasure. The friendships of utility, being less intimate than the other two, may involve no desire on the part of either party to become similar even if what each wants from the other is the same thing.

Of the tendential notions applicable to the Aristotelian theory of love,

---

[111] *Ibid.*, Ch. 7, 1158b12–28, pp. 1065–66.

[112] Aristotle concedes that there are cases where the inferior cannot love the superior as much as the superior deserves. But the friendship is preserved insofar as the inferior gives what he can. "For friendship asks a man to do what he can, not what is proportional to the merits of the case; since that cannot always be done, *e.g.*, in honours paid to the gods or to parents; for no one could ever return to them the equivalent of what he gets, but the man who serves them to the utmost of his power is thought to be a good man." (*Ibid.*, Ch. 14, 1163b14–18, p. 1076.) Thus, Aristotle says that the mother and child are friends, even though the love of a mother is the greatest love and cannot possibly be reciprocated by the child. (See *ibid.*, Book IX, Ch. 4, 1166a1–9, p. 1081.)

[113] A possible exception is the relation of parent to child. The parent, according to Aristotle, loves an image of himself in the child. His love for the child, therefore, may easily take the form of wanting to make the child more and more like himself. (See *ibid.*, Book VIII, Ch. 11, 1061b16–31, pp. 1071–72.)

the least germane is sexual desire. It is never explicitly discussed in the *Ethics* in relation to friendship or love, although there are several passages where sexual desire seems to be implied. Thus, Aristotle says: "Young people are amorous too; for the greater part of the friendship of love depends on emotion and aims at pleasure; this is why they fall in love and quickly fall out of love, changing often within a single day."[114] The only explicit reference to sexual desire in relation to love occurs in the *Prior Analytics*:

> To receive affection then is preferable in love to sexual intercourse. Love then is more dependent on friendship than on intercourse. And if it is most dependent on receiving affection, then this is its end. Intercourse then either is not an end at all or is an end relative to the further end, the receiving of affection.[115]

It seems clear that Aristotle regards a relationship that is based upon mutual sexual desire as an instance of a friendship of pleasure and thus as one of acquisitive desire.

Aristotle never mentions the possibility of disinterested benevolence in his discussion of the friendship of virtue. He does say that "friends on the ground of virtue are anxious to do well by each other (since that is a mark of virtue and of friendship),"[116] but he also says that "in loving a friend men love what is good for themselves."[117] The reconciliation of these statements seems to lie in Aristotle's insistence that in a friendship of virtue both men are equal and alike in virtue. Hence, "as the virtuous man is to himself, he is to his friend also (for his friend is another self)."[118] But a man, in Aristotle's view, wishes not only good for himself but the greatest goods. Since his friend in virtue is another self, does he also wish the greatest goods for his friend? Aristotle answers by saying that "we were right in saying that friend wishes good to friend for his sake . . . [and] that he will wish the greatest goods." He adds: "But perhaps not *all* the

---

[114] *Ibid.*, Ch. 3, 1156b1–3, p. 1061.

[115] *Ibid.*, Book II, Ch. 22, 68b3–6, p. 102. Aristotle apparently thinks of such relationships as involving reciprocal affection but as usually not involving reciprocation of the same kind of desire. After affirming that friendships of pleasure are more permanent when the friends get the same thing from each other, he indicates that this is not the case between lover and beloved. "For these do not take pleasure in the same things, but the one in seeing the beloved and the other in receiving attentions from his lover." (*Nicomachean Ethics*, Book VIII, Ch. 4, 1157a7–8, p. 1062.) Although sexual desire is not mentioned in this context, the relationship discussed is one that seems to involve such desire.

[116] *Ibid.*, Ch. 13, 1162b6–7, p. 1073.

[117] *Ibid.*, Ch. 5, 1157b32–34, p. 1064.

[118] *Ibid.*, Book IX, Ch. 9, 1170b6–7, p. 1090. See also Ch. 12, 1171b32–33, p. 1093, and Ch. 4, 1166a29–32, p. 1082.

greatest goods; for it is for himself most of all that each man wishes what is good."[119]

This statement is paradoxical in view of Aristotle's repeated insistence that the characteristic action of the friendship of virtue is done with a view to the welfare of the other. Aristotle deals with this problem in his discussion of self-love.[120] He points out that there is no conflict between seeking a good for a friend for the friend's sake and seeking the concomitant good of nobility for oneself. Someone's anticipation of the personal good he will achieve (and, perhaps, the recognition of his act by others) in sacrificing almost everything, even his life if necessary, for the sake of his friend does not compromise his intention to aid his friend for his friend's sake. If he performs such actions *only as a means* of acquiring honor, his motive is not benevolent. If, on the other hand, he aids his friend for the friend's sake (as Aristotle repeatedly insists a true friend must do) and is aware of a concomitant and greater good that he will achieve through helping his friend, his desire is benevolent, albeit self-interested. In short, a good friend will not use his friend's misfortune to enhance his own welfare, for he would cease to be virtuous and become a friend of utility, if a friend at all. In doing good to another, a virtuous man is not "selfless." He is not unaware of, nor unconcerned with, the particular personal good of nobility that will accrue to him in performing virtuous actions. The virtuous nobility that a man realizes even may be a greater good then what he gives or relinquishes, since no man can confer virtuous nobility on another. Thus, a good man's primary aim in giving to his friend is the welfare of the friend, even though his concomitant intention may aim at higher personal good. If it were otherwise, he would not achieve virtue in giving to his friend since the virtue of friendship is defined as helping the friend for his own sake. The good man's desire in helping his friend is benevolent, but it is also a self-interested benevolence.[121]

The relevance of Aristotle's analysis of love and friendship to political life is dealt with at the end of Book VIII of the *Ethics*. Of the three kinds of friendship, he clearly considers the friendship of utility to be the one of greatest moment in understanding the bond among men in states: ". . .

[119] *Ibid.*, Book VIII, Ch. 7, 1159a6–10, p. 1066.

[120] He says that self-love has two senses, one good and the other bad. The lover of self in the bad sense is simply selfish and properly condemned since he exclusively seeks his own good, but does not seek the highest good for himself: virtuous nobility. The lover of self in the good sense does constantly seek his own highest good. But, because he understands his own highest good to be virtuous nobility, it does not preclude helping others; it even requires it, since one of the activities of the friendship of virtue is benevolence. (See *ibid.*, Book IV, Ch. 8, 1168b1–1169b3, pp. 1086–88.)

[121] See *ibid.*, Ch. 8, 1169a11–1169b3, pp. 1087–88.

when men are friends they have no need of justice."[122] A man's friends of utility may include all of his fellow citzens. The analysis of the friendship of pleasure has political relevance insofar as it helps in the understanding of domestic relations and certain kinds of intimate social relationships, ranging from pleasant acquaintances to physical lovers.

Every friendship presupposes something in common among those who participate in it.[123] The closer the participants associate and the more they have in common, the more intense is the friendship. Thus, in the small communities, *e.g.*, a man's family or clan, his circle of acquaintances or comrades, his friendship (whatever its character) is stronger than his friendship for those who are related to him only as members of more distant communities, *e.g.*, the state. As indicated above, Aristotle seems to think that in the larger community the relationship of fellow citizens is understood best in terms of the friendship of utility:

> Now all forms of community are like parts of the political community; for men journey together with a view to some particular advantage, and to provide something that they need for the purposes of life; and it is for the sake of advantage that the political community too seems both to have come together originally and to endure.[124]

Marcus Tullius Cicero

Cicero's theory of love is found in his dialogue entitled *Laelius on Friendship* (*De Amicitia*). It differs from Aristotle's in a few respects, none of them cardinal. The theory of love presented by Laelius is a tendential one.[125] After indicating that human love is not necessarily directed to other human beings, and after relating love to friendship, he concentrates almost exclusively on the love among human beings.[126] Friendships are divided into two kinds: "true" and "ordinary," a distinction that corresponds basically to the one Aristotle makes between the friendship of virtue and the friendships of pleasure and utility. Laelius affirms

---

[122] *Nicomachean Ethics*, Book VIII, Ch. 1, 1155a25, p. 1059.

[123] ". . . the proverb 'what friends have is common property' expresses the truth; for friendship depends on community." (*Ibid.*, Ch. 9, 1159b30–32, p. 1068.)

[124] *Ibid.*, 1160a8–13, pp. 1068–69.

[125] There are, however, a few points in the dialogue where mutual admiration and accord, otherwise affirmed to be prerequisite to friendship, are actually said to be part of the love under discussion: "For friendship is nothing else than an accord in all things, human and divine, conjoined with mutual goodwill and affection." (*De Amicitia*, VI, 20, p. 131.) "But love is nothing other than the great esteem and affection felt for him who inspires that sentiment." (*Ibid.*, XXVII, 100, p. 207.)

[126] ". . . it is love (*amor*), from which the word 'friendship' (*amicitia*) is derived." (*Ibid.*, VIII, 26, p. 139. See also XXVII, 100, p. 207.)

that the highest form of friendship can occur only between men who are good and wise, that it must be mutual, that it involves equals and inclines them not only to want to be more like each other but to do things in common, that it is rare, that it must arise slowly, that it endures, that it is essentially a voluntary association, and that its prime characteristic is goodwill, benevolence, or concern for the other person for his own sake.

The constant theme of the dialogue is the contrast between the highest and most excellent friendship and those of the "frivolous" or the "ordinary kind." In distinguishing between them, Laelius stresses that real friendship is an affection or tendency that presupposes virtue. Such a "friendship cannot exist except among good men."[127] He says that virtue "both creates the bond of friendship and preserves it." When virtue "has raised her head and shown her own light and has seen and recognized the same light in another, she moves towards it and in turn receives its beams; as a result love or friendship leaps into flame."[128]

The tendencies or affections that characterize real friendship are essentially benevolent.[129]

> For friendship excels relationship in this, that goodwill may be eliminated from relationship while from friendship it cannot; since, if you remove goodwill from friendship the very name of friendship is gone.[130]

[127] *Ibid.*, V, 18, p. 127.
[128] *Ibid.*, XXVII, 100, p. 207. See also VIII, 27, p. 139.
[129] Cicero is not saying that all the tendencies in a real friendship are benevolent, but that benevolence is the affection that is essential to or characteristic of it. Thus, it is clear that friends need each other's help. Cicero does not think it any violation of friendship to ask for help from a friend. His point is that, if a person's primary or sole motivation toward a friend is to gain from him, then the friendship is not real. Real friendship is characterized by a concern for the good of the other. Laelius says that "mutual interchange is really inseparable from friendship" although it "springs rather from nature than from need." (*Ibid.*, VIII, 26, 27, p. 139.)
[130] *Ibid.*, V, 19–20, p. 129. The reference is only to real friendship; the generic name of friendship is not withheld from relationships characterized by acquisitive desire. Even in these relationships there seems to be some goodwill, though the giving involved is present only for the sake of getting. (See *ibid.*, XXV, 91–XXVI, 100, pp. 199–207.) It is possible to read *De Amicitia* in such a way that Cicero seems to be saying that friendship is a word that should be applied only to those rare relationships between human beings characterized by mutual benevolence. Thus Laelius says: "Wherefore it seems to me that friendship springs rather from nature than from need, and from an inclination of the soul joined with a feeling of love rather than from calculation of how much profit the friendship is likely to afford." (*Ibid.*, VIII, 27, p. 139.) And elsewhere he adds: "If people think that friendship springs from weakness and from a purpose to secure someone through whom we may obtain that which we lack, they assign her, if I may so express it, a lowly pedigree indeed, and an origin far from noble, and they would make her the daughter of poverty and want. If this were so, then just in proportion as any man judged his resources to be small, would he be fitted for friendship; whereas the truth is far otherwise." (*Ibid.*, IX, 29, p. 141.) The question is, of course, whether, in the above and other passages, Cicero is referring to

Or, as he adds:

> For friendship is nothing else than an accord in all things, human and divine, conjoined with mutual goodwill and affection.[131]

By contrast, the inferior or ordinary friendships are invariably acquisitive.

> Now they are worthy of friendship who have within their own souls the reason for their being loved. A rare class indeed! And really everything splendid is rare, and nothing is harder to find than something which in all respects is a perfect specimen of its kind. But the majority of men recognize nothing whatever in human experience as good unless it brings some profit and they regard their friends as they do their cattle, valuing most highly those which give hope of the largest gain. Thus do they fail to attain that loveliest, most spontaneous friendship, which is desirable in and for itself; and they do not learn from their own experience what the power of such friendship is and are ignorant of its nature and extent. For everyone loves himself, not with a view of acquiring some profit for himself from his self-love, but because he is dear to himself on his own account; and unless this same feeling were transferred to friendship, the real friend would never be found; for he is, as it were, another self.[132]

The distinction between benevolent and acquisitive desire is one that Cicero employs again and again to distinguish between the two kinds of friendship.[133]

---

a generic conception of friendship or to the real friendship with which he is primarily concerned. The difficulty may be merely a semantic one. Substantively the difference between a relationship in which the other is valued for his own sake and a relationship in which the other is valued for profit is quite clear. Cicero, unlike Aristotle, does not go into the question of the logical justification of applying the word friendship to both relationships. However, Cicero does not seem to deny that relationships characterized by acquisitive desire (or at least mixed acquisitive desire) are instances of love. (See *De Amicitia*, XX, 75–XXII, 82, pp. 185–189.)

[131] *Ibid.*, VI, 20, p. 131. The accord referred to here has a cosmic echo in Cicero's theory. For Laelius says at another point in the dialogue that "in nature and the entire universe whatever things are at rest and whatever are in motion are united by friendship and scattered by discord." (*Ibid.*, VII, 24, p. 135.) This statement identifies love as a universal harmonizing tendency, but nothing more is said in the dialogue to explain just what is meant by that. At another point in the dialogue, animals are said to love in ways "resembling" human love. (See *ibid.*, XXI, 81, p. 189.) Such remarks may indicate that Cicero's theory of love is a cosmic one, but the evidence seems to us to be insufficient.

[132] *Ibid.*, XXI, 79–80, pp. 187–189.

[133] The two kinds also are contrasted in other ways. True friendship is extremely rare. (See *ibid.*, XXI, 79, p. 187.) In contrast to ordinary and transient friendship, it can emerge only slowly. (See *ibid.*, XIX, 67–68, pp. 177–179.) Further, real friendship is always an affection of considered choice rather than a spontaneous feeling of goodwill. (See *ibid.*, XVII, 62–63, p. 173.)

The question arises as to whether the benevolence essential to true friendship is self-interested. On the one hand, Laelius says of the affection he had for his dead friend Scipio:

> Although many and great advantages did ensue from our friendship, still the beginnings of our love did not spring from the hope of gain.[134]

Posing the question, Laelius says:

> The oftener . . . I reflect on friendship the more it seems to me that consideration should be given to the question, whether the longing for friendship is felt on account of weakness and want, so that by the giving and receiving of favours one may get from another and in turn repay what he is unable to procure of himself; or, although this mutual interchange is really inseparable from friendship, whether there is not another cause, older, more beautiful, and emanating more directly from Nature herself.

Laelius' answer to his own question is that the affection of friendship inspired by virtue arises "rather from nature than from need."[135] Self-interest is not the primary motivation of a friendship based on virtue.

On the other hand, Laelius mentions a number of the advantages of real friendship, which, although precluded as a primary aim, are not necessarily excluded as concomitant aims.[136] "In the first place," asks Laelius, "how can life be what Ennius calls 'the life worth living,' if it does not repose on the mutual goodwill of a friend? What is sweeter than to have someone with whom you may dare discuss anything as if you were communing with yourself? How could your enjoyment in times of prosperity be so great if you did not have someone whose joy in them would be equal to your own?"[137]

Laelius, like Aristotle, even considers friendship an essential part of the happy life.

> Friendship was given to us by nature as the handmaid of virtue, not as a comrade of vice; because virtue cannot attain her highest aims unattended, but only in union and fellowship with another. Such a partnership as this, whether it is, or was, or is yet to be, should be considered the best and happiest comradeship along the road to nature's highest good. In such a partnership, I say, abide all things that men deem worthy of pursuit— honour and fame and delightful tranquillity of mind; so that when these blessings are at hand life is happy, and without them, it cannot be happy.

---

[134] *Ibid.*, IX, 31, p. 143.
[135] *Ibid.*, VIII, 26, 27, pp. 137–139.
[136] "It is not the case . . . that friendship attends upon advantage, but, on the contrary, that advantage attends upon friendship." (*Ibid.*, XIV, 51, p. 163.)
[137] *Ibid.*, VI, 22, pp. 131–133.

Since happiness is our best and highest aim, we must, if we would attain it, give our attention to virtue, without which we can obtain neither friendship nor any other desirable thing.[138]

Laelius goes on to say that it is not primarily from one's own need that friendship arises, and certainly not from a need for any extrinsic advantages that a friendship might bestow.[139]

And again, it seems to me at any rate, that those who falsely assume expediency to be the basis of friendship, take from friendship's chain its loveliest link. For it is not so much the material gain procured through a friend, as it is his love, and his love alone, that gives us delight; and that advantage which we derive from him becomes a pleasure only when his service is inspired by an ardent zeal.

Although Laelius asserts that friendship is best cultivated "by those least in need of another's help," he also says that "it is not well for friends never to need anything at all."[140] In such a case, they would have no opportunity to show their zealous affection for each other and their willingness to help each other. Furthermore "nothing gives more pleasure than the return of goodwill and the interchange of zealous service."[141]

The critical notion that applies to the notion of benevolence present in the above texts—*considered together*—is self-interested rather than disinterested benevolence. On the one hand, Laelius eschews the presence of an ulterior motive in real friendship.[142] A real friend does not give *only* in order to get—whether he seeks material gain or higher advantages. On the other hand, Laelius pictures real friendship as attended by advantages of the highest order, without which one cannot be happy, and he says every man wants a happy life.[143] Cicero's rhetorical emphasis on the benevolent aspect of true friendship strongly suggests the primacy of the aim of caring for another for his own sake. But his recurrent mention of the importance

---

[138] *Ibid.*, XXII, 83–84, p. 191. ". . . nature, loving nothing solitary, always strives for some sort of support, and man's best support is a very dear friend." (*Ibid.*, XXIII, 88, p. 195.)

[139] Love from a friend "is not sought because of material need or for the sake of material gain." (*Ibid.*, XXVII, 100, p. 207.)

[140] *Ibid.*, XIV, 51, p. 163.

[141] *Ibid.*, XIV, 50, p. 161. See also XXVII, 102, p. 209.

[142] He also eschews a calculatingly reciprocal relationship. "It surely is calling friendship to a very close and petty accounting to require it to keep an exact balance of credits and debits. I think true friendship is richer and more abundant than that and does not narrowly scan the reckoning lest it pay out more than it has received; and there need be no fear that some bit of kindness will be lost, that it will overflow the measure and spill upon the ground, or that more than is due will be poured into friendship's bin." (*Ibid.*, XVI, 58, p. 169.)

[143] See *ibid.*, XXIII, 86–87, pp. 193–195.

of friendship for a virtuous and happy life, together with his prudential warnings to weigh carefully potential friends so as to avoid disappointment, imply the presence of a concomitant motive.[144]

The theme of a friend as another self or as an image of oneself is important to Cicero's conception of ideal friendship. He "who looks upon a true friend, looks, as it were, upon a sort of image of himself."[145] The essential respect in which true friends are similar is virtue, for "friendship cannot exist except among good men."[146] Such similarity makes possible a friendship whose essence lies in "the most complete agreement in policy, in pursuits, and in opinions."[147]

An existing similarity of a definite kind is not only a prerequisite for ideal friendship but is the basis for a desire for further union. Friends want to pursue a common life. Laelius, recalling his dead friend Scipio, says: ". . . I feel as if my life has been happy because it was spent with Scipio, with whom I shared my public and private cares; lived under the same roof at home; served in the same campaigns abroad."[148] Later, Laelius observes that if "nothing so allures and attracts anything to itself as likeness does to friendship," then "it surely will be granted as a fact that good men love and join to themselves other good men, in a union which is almost that of relationship and nature. For there is nothing more eager or more greedy than nature for what is like itself."[149]

144 See *ibid.*, XXI, 77–78, pp. 185–187. The balance seems to be the following: A man ought not "to consider the goodwill of his countrymen a poor weapon in the battle of life, though to hunt after it with fawning and flattery is disgraceful." (*Ibid.*, XVII, 61, p. 171.) "Now the support and stay of that unswerving constancy, *which we look for in friendship*, is loyalty. . . ." (*Ibid.*, XVIII, 65, p. 175. Italics added.) Also, on the question of whether old friendships should be preferred to new ones, Laelius indicates a preference for the old, but adds: ". . . new friendships are not to be scorned *if they offer hope of bearing fruit*, like green shoots of corn that do not disappoint us at harvest-time." (*Ibid.*, XIX, 68, p. 179. Italics added.) ". . . there is one cause of offence which . . . may be preserved; for friends frequently must be not only advised, but also rebuked, and both advice and rebuke should be kindly received when given in a spirit of goodwill." (*Ibid.*, XXIV, 88, p. 197.)

145 *Ibid.*, VII, 23, p. 133.

146 *Ibid.*, V, 18, p. 127.

147 *Ibid.*, IV, 15, p. 125. Such sharing is undoubtedly one of the ways in which the benevolence of true friendship is self-interested. For just as whatever sorrow a friend experiences causes his friend to sorrow, so also whatever good a person experiences will cause his friend to rejoice. In other words, whatever good one seeks for another self, one also, in some sense, seeks for oneself. (See *ibid.*, VI, 22, pp. 131–133, and XIII, 48, p. 159.)

148 *Ibid.*, IV, 15, p. 125.

149 *Ibid.*, XIV, 50, p. 161. "Now if it is evident in animals, whether of the air, the water, or the land, and whether tame or wild, first, that they love themselves—for this feeling is born alike in every living creature—and, secondly, that they require and eagerly search for other animals of their own kind to which they may attach themselves—and this they do with a longing in some degree resembling human

The only form of the desire for union that Cicero discusses is the desire for the union of similarity.[150] Among those who are already equal, it takes the form of a desire to lead a common life. For those who are unequal, this desire requires the superior to "put himself on a level with his inferior, so the latter ought not to grieve that he is surpassed by the former in intellect, fortune, or position." So also should the superiors "in a measure . . . lift up their inferiors."[151]

The desire for the union of similarity is not necessarily a mark of the highest kind of friendship.

> For it seems clear to me that we were so created that between us all there exists a certain tie which strengthens with our proximity to each other. Therefore, fellow countrymen are preferred to foreigners and relatives to strangers, for with them Nature herself engenders friendship, but it is one that is lacking in constancy.[152]

The desire for the union of similarity, although it can take a benevolent form, is not coordinate with benevolent desire in a real friendship. In many instances a person who seeks good for his friend as he would seek his own also seeks to share that good insofar as he wants to be like his friend in every way possible. But Laelius also says that there is a dimension of benevolent desire that transcends the feelings a man has about his own welfare. He says that a real friend not only feels about his friend as he feels about himself but that he would do more for his friend than he would do for himself:

> For how many things we do for our friends that we never would do for ourselves! At one time we beg and entreat an unworthy man, and again we assail another too sharply or too loudly rail upon him—things not quite creditable in our own affairs, but exceedingy so in behalf of our friends; and there are numerous occasions when good men forgo, or permit themselves to be deprived of, many conveniences in order that their friends rather than themselves may enjoy them.[153]

---

love—then how much more, by the law of his nature, is this the case with man who both loves himself and uses his reason to seek out another whose soul he may so mingle with his own as almost to make one out of two!" (*Ibid.*, XXI, 81, p. 189.)

[150] It is indicated at one point that complementary characters and interests preclude friendship. "For difference of character is attended by difference of taste and it is this diversity of taste that severs friendships." (*Ibid.*, XX, 74, p. 183.)

[151] *Ibid.*, XX, 71, 73, p. 181. See also XIX, 69–70, p. 179. The desire present here is not so much the desire for the union of similarity but rather a desire on the part of the superior to appear equal to the inferior out of consideration for him.

[152] *Ibid.*, V, 19, p. 129.

[153] *Ibid.*, XVI, 57, p. 167.

The tendential notions applicable to Cicero's theory of love are: acquisitive desire (in the form of mixed acquisitive desire), benevolent desire (in the form of self-interested benevolence), and the desire for union (in the form of the desire for the union of similarity). Sexual desire is never discussed in relation to friendship or love.

Thomas Aquinas

The elaborate, systematic interconnection of Aquinas' theory of love with his detailed analysis of the whole of man's nature renders his discussion of love one of the most extensive. We shall not attempt an exhaustive presentation of his theory here. For to explain fully not only what Aquinas conceives love to be but also how he thinks it arises in man would require a presentation of nothing less than his whole psychology—particularly his position on satisfaction and pleasure—as well as his conception of the hierarchy of virtues and his theory of human passions and appetites. Some understanding of these matters is indispensable; but, insofar as it is possible, we shall concentrate on his theory of love and deal with these related subjects only when necessary for an adequate presentation of that theory. To do otherwise would involve us in an exposition of Aquinas' theory of man rather than his theory of love.

Like Augustine, Aquinas has a theory of supernatural and natural love. As theologians, both are concerned with the love that is God as well as man's supernaturally aided love for God and for his neighbor. Aquinas' theory of natural love, however, can be understood without reference to his theory of supernatural love, as he makes a sharp distinction between the two and treats natural love as a subject in itself.[154] He even deals with them in separate treatises. Though we shall not restrict ourselves to the *Treatise on the Passions,* in which Aquinas discusses natural love, we have found it possible to concentrate on our delimitation of the subject: natural love among human beings.[155]

The most general remark one can make about Aquinas on love is that he conceives it as a cosmic phenomenon in the sphere of tendency.

> Every agent acts for an end. . . . Now the end is the good desired and loved by each one. Wherefore it is evident that every agent, *whatever it be,* does every action from love of some kind.[156]

[154] Although natural love is intelligible for Aquinas without reference to supernatural love, the converse is not true, since Aquinas defines charity as the perfection of natural friendship. (See *Summa Theologica,* Part II-II, Q. 23, Art. 1, Vol. II, pp. 1269–70.)

[155] For Aquinas' theory of supernatural love, see Part I, Ch. 3, *supra.*

[156] *Summa Theologica,* Part I-II, Q. 28, Art. 6, Answer, Vol. I, p. 713. (Italics added.)

Since all tendencies to movement or action on the part of anyone or anything are expressions of love, all natural tendencies to action or movement among human beings are also expressions of love. The critical notion that we can apply to Aquinas' whole theory of love as well as to his theory of natural love among human beings is tendency in general.

In our terminology, natural love includes all love that is not inspired, aided, or transformed by an action of the transcendent God of revealed religion. Aquinas uses the phrase "natural love" in a more limited sense. Though he says that "it is common to every nature to have some inclination; and this is its natural appetite or love,"[157] he also clearly distinguishes natural love from sensual love and from rational or intellectual love. As these three loves are all outside the realm of supernatural love or charity, they are all included in what we call natural love.

Natural appetite, for Aquinas, is that innate tendency on the part of all existing things to incline toward something without perceiving it as a good. Thus, "the connaturalness of a heavy body for the centre, is by reason of its weight and may be called *natural love*." Sensitive appetite exists in all animals, including man, and, though it springs from the apprehension of a good, is a tendency that arises of necessity and not from choice. (In man the tendencies of the sensitive appetite are not a function of his will, but they can be subjected to the control of will. Thus a man perceiving food and experiencing hunger can control his indulgence of his hunger.) Rational or intellectual appetite in man springs from apprehension of a good, but is a tendency that is the freely chosen act of the will. Aquinas says that "in each of these appetites, the name *love* is given to the principle of movement towards the end loved." Love, therefore, is not only "something pertaining to the appetite"[158] but is common to all modes of appetite.

Love also "differs according to the difference of appetites."[159] Man has all three kinds of appetite and therefore loves in three different ways. As an existing thing, possessing dimension and weight, he has natural love. As an animal with bodily desires, he has sensitive love. And as a being with free will, he has intellectual or rational love, which distinguishes him from animals.

Man's love for other human beings is usually a matter of the will, of intellectual or rational appetite. The prominent exception is sexual desire. Normally, all the other sensitive appetites or physical inclinations are directed to animals or things. A person who is hungry seeks food; someone who is cold wants a garment to keep him warm.

[157] *Ibid.*, Part I, Q. 60, Art. 1, Answer, p. 297.
[158] *Ibid.*, Part I-II, Q. 26, Art. 1, Answer, p. 704.
[159] *Ibid.* See also Reply Obj. 3, p. 704; and Part I, Q. 19, Art. 1, Answer, p. 103.

Strictly speaking, only the tendencies or movements of the sensitive appetite are passions, since they are the only human tendencies that necessarily involve corporeal change. In this limited sense the word "passion" is being used as a synonym for involuntary inclinations or emotions. Accordingly, the only love among human beings that normally can be passionate, *i.e.*, that arises from the sensitive appetite and is accompanied by corporeal change, is sexual desire.

When Aquinas says that all human loves arising from the sensitive *or* the intellectual appetite are passions, he explains that he is using the notion of passion in a much more general sense. "Passion," he says, "is the effect of the agent on the patient." Since love consists in a change or tendency to movement in the appetite caused by the appetible thing,

> love is a passion: properly so called, according as it is in the concupiscible faculty [the sensitive appetite]; in a wider and extended sense, according as it is in the will.[160]

In other words, a man experiences a passion when action upon him draws him to an agent,[161] whether the reaction produced by the agent is an involuntary response of the sensitive appetite or a freely chosen inclination of the will. All human loves, then, are passions, because they all result from the effect of the attractive force that an agent or object exerts upon man's appetites. In this extended sense, all inclinations or appetites are passions.[162]

Since Aquinas discusses a number of other passions in addition to the passion of love, a qualification must be placed on the description of his

---

[160] *Ibid.*, Part I-II, Q. 26, Art. 2, Answer, pp. 704–705.

[161] See *ibid.*, Q. 22, Art. 1, Answer, p. 691.

[162] In another vein, Aquinas argues that all human loves are passions because, though they do not all originate in the sensitive appetite, they all involve the sensitive appetite. The movements of the will, though not themselves sensitive passions, express themselves in human love through the body. Possible objects of love are presented to the will through the senses. (See *ibid.*, Part I, Q. 20, Art. 1, Answer and Reply, Obj. 1, Vol. I, pp. 113–114.) The will's tendencies toward such objects also express themselves through the actions of the body. They are, therefore, all accompanied by bodily alteration, even though such alteration does not originate in the sensitive appetite and is not a bodily passion. In this sense, Aquinas is able to say that, in human passions, the effect of an agent upon a patient is always *accompanied* by corporeal change. (See *ibid.*, Part I-II, Q. 22, Art. 3, Answer, p. 693.) Aquinas even says that there are occasions when the body emotionally cooperates in the pursuit of a strictly intellectual love: "The craving for wisdom, or other spiritual goods, is sometimes called concupiscence; either by reason of a certain likeness; or on account of the craving in the higher part of the soul being so vehement that it overflows into the lower appetite, so that the latter also, in its own way, tends to the spiritual good, following the lead of the higher appetite, the result being that the body itself renders its service in spiritual matters." (*Ibid.*, Q. 30, Art. 1, Reply Obj. 1, p. 718.)

theory of natural human love as tendency in general. As the other passions are also tendencies or movements of appetite, how do such tendencies differ from love? Aquinas' answer is that all the other passions of the soul derive from, or are variations on, the one basic passion of love. As "love is the first movement of the will and of every appetitive faculty . . . all the other appetitive movements presuppose love, as their root and origin." Love is that basic passion that aims at "good universally."[163] Hence, it is the initial inclination of appetite toward an as yet unspecified good. The inclination is then transformed into specific tendencies or passions toward specific goods, or into specific tendencies or passions away from specific evils. The negative passions or tendencies away from repulsive objects are said to be derivative of the positive passions or tendencies toward attractive objects—Aquinas defines evil as the absence of good. Love underlies all the positive passions, and, hence, also, all the derivative, negative passions. All passions of the soul are, in effect, differentiated expressions of the general passion of love and are specified by the particular goodness or evil of their objects.[164]

Love, then, does not denote strictly the movements toward or away from objects, but rather the initial inclination in the appetite behind each of these movements.

> Although love does not denote the movement of the appetite in tending towards the appetible object, yet it denotes that movement whereby the appetite is changed by the appetible object, so as to have complacency therein.[165]

In other words, love is tendency in general in the sense that it is the basic tendency that underlies, precedes, and supports all other tendencies. Its expression depends upon the specific action of the object on the appetite and upon the character of the reaction or passion that the appetite produces. "Love is spoken of as being fear, joy, desire and sadness, not essentially but causally."[166]

Aquinas employs a number of distinctions in a variety of ways in his analysis of love. His first and major distinction is the one between natural love (*amor, dilectio,* and *amicitia*) and supernatural love (*caritas*).[167] As

---

[163] *Ibid.,* Part I, Q. 20, Art. 1, Answer, Vol. I, pp. 113–114. See also Part I-II, Q. 27, Art. 4, Answer, p. 709.

[164] See *ibid.,* Part I-II, Q. 23, Art. 4, Answer, p. 696.

[165] *Ibid.,* Q. 26, Art. 2, Reply Obj. 3, p. 705.

[166] *Ibid.,* Art. 1, Reply Obj. 2, p. 704.

[167] Aquinas' terminology for love parallels that of Augustine. *Amor* is his most general term for love and is applied to both natural and supernatural love. *Dilectio* signifies the inclinations of the free will or what he calls the love of choice as opposed to the love of bodily instincts. *Amicitia,* or friendship, is a form of *dilectio,* since

we have indicated, he mentions three kinds of appetite: natural, sensible, and rational. As love is appetite, he says that it differs according to the difference of its objects. For him, the passions fall into two classes: the concupiscible and the irascible. Those in the concupiscible power are immediate or direct reactions to an appetible object, while those in the irascible power are modified reactions caused by the presence of an obstacle or difficulty between the appetite and its object.[168] Aquinas also mentions the love of the spiritual or inner man and contrasts it with the love of the corporeal or outer man.[169]

Of all the distinctions Aquinas makes, the most basic and revealing is the distinction between the love of concupiscence and the love of friendship; it controls, to a very great extent, his entire analysis of human love. In the more frequent sense in which Aquinas employs this distinction (and which he himself says is the more proper use), it is parallel to the one we make between acquisitive and benevolent desire.

In a second sense, however, love of concupiscence is always and only a love of the means, while love of friendship is always and only love of the end, *i.e.*, the person for whom the good is sought. Whoever is wished well for his own sake is loved with the love of friendship, whether that person be oneself or another. Whoever or whatever is loved for the sake of someone else, whether self or other, is loved with the love of concupiscence. When the distinction is applied in this manner, the two loves are related as primary and secondary. Whatever is loved with the love of concupiscence is loved for the sake of whatever is loved with the love of friendship. For example, a man is hungry. His desire for food is the love of concupiscence, whereas his desire to nourish himself is the love of friendship *for himself*. If an acquaintance of his is hungry, the man's desire to

---

friendship is, for Aquinas, a matter of free choice. *Caritas*, or charity, is the name for supernatural love in all its forms, whether the lover be God or man. (See *ibid.*, Art. 3, Answer, p. 705.)

[168] Aquinas asserts that love is more properly in the concupiscible power than in the irascible power "because it regards good absolutely, and not under the aspect of difficulty." (*Ibid.*, Art. 1, Answer, p. 704.) Here he is using the word "love" in a more specific sense than previously. For, if love is the root of all passions, it is present in both the concupiscible and irascible passions. Hence, Aquinas must be saying that love is not only tendency in general but is also, in a more specialized sense, a specific passion in the concupiscible power. Concupiscence, like passion, is a word that Aquinas uses in both a limited and an extended sense. In its limited sense, the concupiscible passions are directed only to sensible goods. In its extended sense, the concupiscible passions are directed to any good, sensible or spiritual. (See fn. 160, p. 226, *supra*.)

[169] See *Summa Theologica*, Part II-II, Q. 25, Art. 7, Answer, Vol. II, p. 1291.

obtain food is also the love of concupiscence, whereas his desire to nourish his acquaintance is the love of friendship *for another.*

The love of friendship, when the distinction is applied in this sense, is the only name for the love of a substantial good, for the love of a person (self or other) for his own sake, for the love of the end and never of the means.[170] It is to this love, then, that Aquinas refers when he says: ". . . to love anything is nothing else than to will good to that thing . . ." But he also brings in the love of concupiscence when he says that the "act of love always tends towards two things; to the good that one wills, and to the person for whom one wills it: since to love a person is to wish that person good."[171]

The first sense in which Aquinas applies the distinction between the love of concupiscence and the love of friendship is less complex than the above one, involves a different application of these two phrases, but substantively amounts to the same thing. The simple application of the two terms ignores the distinction between the desire for the means and the desire for the end. In this sense, the love of concupiscence includes both the desire to enhance the welfare of the self and the desire to obtain the means of doing that.[172] Love of concupiscence now means self-love, and love of friendship now means love of another, where love ultimately is understood to mean wishing someone well. Thus, in the more frequent and basic sense in which Aquinas applies the distinction between the two phrases, love of friendship for the self is impossible; love of friendship is always for another.[173] Strictly speaking, one does not have friendship for oneself since friendship is a relation in which one wishes another and not oneself well.[174] Even though a man often wishes himself well through acquisitive desire, Aquinas says that

[170] Aquinas says that "the movement of love has a two-fold tendency: towards the good which a man wishes to someone—*to himself or to another,* and towards that to which he wishes some good. Accordingly, man has love of concupiscence towards the good that he wishes to another, and love of friendship, towards him to whom he wishes good." (*Ibid.,* Part I-II, Q. 26, Art. 4, Answer, Vol. I, p. 706. Italics added.) Or as he says in another place: ". . . a thing may be loved in two ways; first of all as a subsisting good; and secondly as an accidental or inherent good. That is loved as a subsisting good, which is so loved that we wish well to it. But that which we wish unto another, is loved as an accidental or inherent good. . . . This kind of love has been called by the name of *concupiscence,* while the first is called *friendship.*" (*Ibid.,* Part I, Q. 60, Art. 3, Answer, p. 299.)

[171] *Ibid.,* Part I, Q. 20, Art. 2, Answer, p. 115, and Art. 1, Reply Obj. 3, p. 114.

[172] See *ibid.,* Part II-II, Q. 25, Art. 3, Answer, Vol. II, p. 1288.

[173] Cf. fn. 168, p. 228, *supra.*

[174] See *Summa Theologica,* Part II-II, Q. 25, Art. 4, Answer, Vol. II, p. 1288.

not every love has the character of friendship, but that love which is together with benevolence, when, to wit, we love someone so as to wish good
to him. If, however, we do not wish good to what we love, but wish its good
for ourselves . . . it is love not of friendship, but of a kind of concupiscence.[175]

He notes this, not only because friendship "by its very nature, implies
mutual love and equality . . . which cannot be of one man towards
himself,"[176] but also because, at this point, he is predicating love only of
the end and never of the means. Love is, strictly speaking, only of the
person for whom a good is sought; and the love of concupiscence and the
love of friendship are, respectively, used to indicate self-love and love for
another. For, "although, properly speaking, friendship cannot be had for
self, on the other hand love is had for self."[177]

When Aquinas says "to love anything is nothing else than to will good to
that thing,"[178] he means that love is always of a person for his own sake,
whether such love be the love of concupiscence for the self or the love of
friendship for another. It is with this in mind that he is able to say that
"when a man loves his neighbor for his own profit or pleasure, he does not
love his neighbor *truly*, but loves himself."[179]

Friendships in which one person seeks only to use or to gain pleasure
from another are not true instances of the love of friendship. For, in such
cases, the other person is not loved or wished well for his own sake. To love
another human being truly means that

> we love him for whom we wish some good, as is proper to a friendship for a
> noble person; but not as the good which we wish for ourselves, as is proper
> to a friendship for a pleasant or useful person, in which we love a friend as
> our own good. For, it is not that we seek pleasure or utility for a friend, but
> that we seek pleasure or utility for ourselves from a friend; just as we also
> love things pleasing and useful for ourselves, such as food or clothing.[180]

Since Aquinas indicates that "friends" of utility and pleasure can be
treated as "food or clothing," he recognizes the possibility of love among
human beings taking the form of simple acquisitive desire (getting without
giving). Although Aquinas does say clearly that all such friendships are
instances of the love of concupiscence or acquisitive desire, he also indicates

[175] *Ibid.*, Q. 23, Art. 1, Answer, p. 1269.
[176] *Ibid.*, Q. 25, Art. 4, Reply Obj. 2, p. 1288.
[177] *On Charity*, Art. VII, Reply Obj. 11, p. 64.
[178] *Summa Theologica*, Part I, Q. 20, Art. 2, Answer, Vol. I, p. 115.
[179] *Ibid.*, Part II-II, Q. 44, Art. 7, Answer, Vol. II, p. 1378. (Italics added.) See
also Q. 25, Art. 1, Reply Obj. 1, p. 1286; and *On Charity*, Art. II, Answer, p. 29.
[180] *On Charity*, Art. VIII, Reply Obj. 16, p. 73.

that they may take the form of mixed acquisitive desire (giving in order to get):

> When friendship is based on usefulness or pleasure, a man does indeed wish his friend some good; and in this respect the character of friendship is preserved. But since he refers this good further to his own pleasure or use, the result is that friendship of the useful or pleasant, in so far as it is connected with love of concupiscence, loses the character of true friendship.[181]

Aquinas never explicitly mentions sexual desire in relation to love. But, as sexual desire is a passion of the sensitive appetite, and as all such passions are instances of love, he would consider sexual desire as an expression of love. As already noted, sexual desire is the only passion of the sensitive appetite that is an expression of love among human beings, since it is the only bodily appetite that is normally directed to persons and not to things. As it is an involuntary bodily appetite, and as benevolence is only possible through an act of will, sexual desire is acquisitive.

Aquinas' thoughts on sexual desire are found, for the most part, in his *Treatise on Marriage*, where he is concerned more with the question of the morality of sexual relations than with the problem of relating sexual desire to his conception of love. Like Augustine, he regards sexual desire as a deficient or evil love when its attendant carnal pleasure is pursued as an end in itself. Unlike Augustine, however, he does not affirm that the sexual impulse must be pursued within the bounds of charity or the love for God in order not to be sinful. As a natural love within the bounds of civil marriage such a desire is not necessarily sinful.

> For if the motive for the marriage act be a virtue, whether of justice that they may render the debt, or of religion, that they may beget children for the worship of God, it is meritorious. But if the motive be lust, yet not excluding the marriage blessings, namely that he would by no means be willing to go to another woman, it is a venial sin; while if he exclude the marriage blessings, so as to be disposed to act in like manner with any woman, it is a mortal sin. And nature cannot move without being either directed by reason, and thus it will be an act of virtue, or not so directed, and then it will be an act of lust.[182]

Though he concedes that "shamefulness of concupiscence . . . always accompanies the marriage act," he also maintains that such shamefulness is

[181] *Summa Theologica*, Part I-II, Q. 26, Art. 4, Reply Obj. 3, Vol. I, p. 706. Aquinas emphasizes that doing good to another may be an act either of real benevolence or of apparent benevolence, when he refers to the example of a man who gives alms either for the sake of God or for the sake of vainglory. (See *On Charity*, Art. III, Answer, p. 36.)

[182] *Summa Theologica*, Supplement, Q. 41, Art. 4, Answer, Vol. III, p. 2714.

"not of guilt, but of punishment inflicted for the first sin, inasmuch as the lower powers and the members do not obey reason." His statement, "it is impossible to maintain that the act of begetting children is . . . [such] that it be impossible to find the mean of virtue therein,"[183] suggests that he regards sexual desire within the bounds of marriage and controlled by reason, as a virtuous activity.

In addition to sexual desire, conjugal union involves other expressions of acquisitive desire. For, in speaking of the love of concupiscence, Aquinas says that a person is moved by intense desire "against all that hinders his gaining or quietly enjoying the object of his love. It is thus that husbands are said to be jealous of their wives, lest association with others prove a hindrance to their exclusive individual rights."[184]

Although the condition of union or likeness is an important prerequisite for the love of friendship or benevolent desire, the desire for union is not itself a frequent expression of love nor an important part of Aquinas' theory of love.[185] He does employ the notion of the desire for the union of complementarity to describe the mutual attraction of a man and a woman in marriage. In that connection he remarks that Aristotle mentioned the Aristophanic myth, in which lovers are depicted as striving to become one, but added that, if they succeeded completely, one or both would be destroyed. Hence, "they seek a suitable and becoming union—to live together, speak together, and be united together in other like things."[186] The desire of a man and a woman for such union springs, in part at least, from an existing biological dissimilarity, since they seek to be united in one flesh. Hence, the desire for the union of complementarity does take an acquisitive form.[187] But Aquinas also says that husband and wife are friends:

[183] *Ibid.*, Art. 3, Answer and Reply Obj. 3, pp. 2713–14.
[184] *Ibid.*, Part I-II, Q. 28, Art. 4, Answer, Vol. I, p. 712.
[185] The term "union" is very important for Aquinas' analysis of love. He says that union has a threefold relationship to love. There is the union that causes love, which is substantial union when it causes self-love, and the union of likeness when it causes love for another. Then there is the affective union, which is love itself, what he calls the first movement of the appetite whereby it is attuned to tend toward the object of love; Aquinas regards this as a connaturalness, or kind of union between lover and beloved. (See *ibid.*, Q. 32, Art. 3, Reply Obj. 3, p. 729.) Finally, there is a real union, which is the relationship that the lover seeks with his beloved. This last is what we call the desire for union, and the only example that Aquinas gives of it is one that strongly suggests the desire for the union of complementarity. (See *ibid.*, Q. 28, Art. 1, Answer and Reply Obj. 3, pp. 709–710.)
[186] *Ibid.*, Reply Obj. 2, p. 710.
[187] See *ibid.*, Part II-II, Q. 26, Art. 11, esp. Reply Objs. 2 and 3, Vol. II, pp. 1302–03.

> . . . there seems to be the greatest friendship between husband and wife, for they are united not only in the act of fleshly union, which produces a certain gentle association . . . but also in the partnership of the whole range of domestic activity.[188]

Though husband and wife are not equals, they are benevolent to each other. One of the ways in which they may seek to enhance each other's welfare is through the mutual fulfillment of complementary needs. In such a case, the intention of each in seeking a complementary union must be the good of the other person and not of himself or herself.[189]

More frequently than the desire for union, the benevolence in marriage takes the form of the desire to benefit the person to whom one is already united. To be more precise, the benevolence of husband or wife is to enhance the welfare of the other through contributing to the common good.

> . . . the object of marriage among men is not only the begetting and feeding of children, but also the partnership of a common life, whereby each one contributes his share of work to the common stock . . . as the offspring is reckoned a good of matrimony, so also should the communication of works.[190]

The benevolence involved is self-interested, since, by contributing to the common good of oneself and another, one contributes to one's own good. The welfare of the husband and that of the wife is interdependent.[191]

Aquinas calls love a "unitive force" in another sense; for he says that "inasmuch as we love ourselves, we wish ourselves good; and, so far as possible, union with that good."[192] But here he is talking about any and all acquisitive desires, including those in which a person may consume or destroy the good he seeks for himself. Our critical notion, the desire for union, applies only to those interpersonal relationships in which one person desires, acquisitively or benevolently, to become united with another while remaining existentially separate. So far as we can see, the only examples of

[188] *On the Truth of the Catholic Faith*, Book III, Part II, Ch. 123, p. 148. See also Ch. 124, pp. 150–152; and *Summa Theologica*, Supplement, Q. 42, Art. 2, Answer, Vol. III, p. 2716.

[189] See *Summa Theologica*, Supplement, Q. 64, Art. 5, Answer, p. 2803.

[190] *Ibid.*, Q. 49, Art. 2, Reply Obj. 1. p. 2737. In another place, Aquinas remarks: ". . . the accidental end of marriage is the binding together of mankind and the extension of friendship." (*Ibid.*, Q. 54, Art. 3, Answer, p. 2759. See also Q. 49, Art. 2, Reply Obj. 1, p. 2738; and Q. 55, Art. 1, Answer, p. 2762.)

[191] See p. 232, fn. 185, *infra*, for a fuller explication of the application of this notion to the theory of Aquinas.

[192] *Summa Theologica*, Part I, Q. 20, Art. 1, Reply Obj. 3, Vol. I, p. 114. See also Part I-II, Q. 28, Art. 1, Answer and Reply Obj. 2, p. 710.

such a desire that Aquinas discusses are the relationship of man and wife
and perhaps that of teacher and student.[193]

For the most part, Aquinas considers benevolent desire or the love of
friendship as a function of an existing condition of union. True friendship
presupposes not only virtue but also equality or similarity. Friends are of
one mind. "For the very fact that two men are alike, having, as it were, one
form, makes them to be, in a manner, one in that form. . . . Hence the
affections of one tend to the other, as being one with him; and he wishes
good to him as to himself."[194] Aquinas adds that, for this reason, a person
apprehends his friend as another self, insofar as he wills good to him as to
himself.[195] Hence, "the love with which a man loves himself is the form
and root of friendship."[196] Aquinas does not identify the love of friendship,
i.e., the desire of a person to benefit his friend, with the desire for the union
of similarity. The love of friendship, though based on the condition of
similarity, is not necessarily expressed as the desire to become like or remain
one with another.[197]

Throughout his theory, Aquinas employs most of the tendential notions
signified by our critical terms. Since he views love as a cosmic phenomenon, tendency in general applies. Since he mentions the possibility of
desiring others as one would desire things, simple acquisitive desire is
present. Both the friendship of utility and the friendship of pleasure are

---

[193] The relation of teacher and student is one of desire for union of complemen-
tarity. The teacher acts as the agent in causing knowledge; the student receives it.
This comes about through verbal communication, which can be an act of love. (See
Truth, Q. 11, Art. 1, Reply, Vol. II, pp. 82–83; Art. 2, Reply, p. 89; and *On
Aristotle's Love and Friendship*, Ch. 9, p. 36.)

[194] *Summa Theologica*, Part I–II, Q. 27, Art. 3, Answer, Vol. I, p. 708. Aquinas
does not hesitate to generalize the similarity that is presupposed when he says: "And
so everything loves another which is one with it in species, with a natural affection,
in so far as it loves its own species." (*Ibid.*, Part I, Q. 60, Art. 4, Answer, p. 300.)
And, in another place, "If we love someone on his own account, we love his entire
family, his relatives, his friends, inasmuch as they are related to him; but in all of
these, there is only one formal notion of love, viz., the good of the one whom we love
for his own sake. And, in a certain way, we love him in all these others." (*On
Charity*, Art. IV, Answer, p. 42.) Even a similar interest can be the basis of the love
of friendship since "in a political friendship . . . the object is the good of the state."
(*Ibid.*, Art. VII, Answer, p. 61.)

[195] See *Summa Theologica*, Part I-II, Q. 28, Art. 1, Answer, Vol. I, p. 709.

[196] *Ibid.*, Part II-II, Q. 25, Art. 4, Answer, Vol. II, p. 1288.

[197] Benevolence can also express itself in a relationship between dissimilars. For
"between those who are unequal there can be a greater love than between equals;
although there be not an equal response: for a father naturally loves his son more
than a brother loves his brother; although the son does not love his father as much as
he is loved by him." (*Ibid.*, Part I, Q. 96, Art. 3, Reply Obj. 2, Vol. I, p. 488.)
Although Aquinas' whole discussion of natural benevolence is focused on friendship,
the relationship of equals, it is with the above unequal relationship in mind that he
says that there is no greater love than a mother's. (See *ibid.*, Part II-II, Q. 27, Art. 1,
Answer, Vol. II, p. 1305.)

instances of mixed acquisitive desire. Sexual desire, arising as it does from the sensitive appetite, is a desire that is always acquisitive in character. The desire for the union of complementarity is present in the marriage relationship and may take either an acquisitive or benevolent form. Only the desire for the union of similarity, though certainly a possible tendency and therefore a possible expression of love, is not explicitly specified by Aquinas in his analysis.

Benevolent desire is clearly an instance of love for Aquinas. Is such benevolence self-interested or disinterested? Aquinas addresses this question most directly in an article entitled, *Whether Doing Good to Another Is a Cause of Pleasure.* He answers affirmatively, saying that

> doing good to another becomes pleasant, in so far as it arouses in man an imagination of abundant good existing in him, whereof he is able to give others a share.

He adds that another source of pleasure in doing good to others is a man's habitual inclination to do good, "by reason of which doing good becomes connatural to him: for which reason the liberal man takes pleasure in giving to others."[198] Hence, in wanting to give to another, a man can anticipate the satisfaction that accompanies such a desire or its fulfillment. Insofar as the satisfaction that he experiences is a good for him, his benevolence is self-interested.

Satisfaction accompanying a benevolent desire does not render it acquisitive. If doing good to another were only a *means* of achieving satisfaction, the desire would be acquisitive. But Aquinas denies that this is the case in a truly benevolent desire when he says:

> . . . there is a difference between a friendship for a noble person and a friendship for a pleasant person, because in a friendship for a pleasant person, the friend is loved for the sake of pleasure; but in a friendship for a noble person, the friend is loved for his own sake, although pleasure is a result of this.[199]

When satisfaction (or what he also calls delight or joy) is realized through an act of the intellectual appetite or will, it cannot be said to be the cause of the will's inclinations, but rather a "proper accident" that accompanies them.[200] Otherwise, Aquinas' distinction between the love of

[198] *Ibid.*, Part I-II, Q. 32, Art. 6, Answer, Vol. I, p. 731.
[199] *On Charity*, Art. XI, Reply Obj. 6, p. 91.
[200] *Summa Theologica*, Part I-II, Q. 2, Art. 6, Answer, Vol. I, p. 593. This is not so in the case of the sensitive or carnal appetite, where pleasure is the final cause of the body's inclinations. The problem here, as with passion and concupiscence, is that Aquinas uses the word "pleasure" in two senses. In the first sense it denotes bodily rest or satisfaction. Thus taken, the anticipation of carnal pleasure is the sole cause of any bodily appetite. (See *ibid.*, Q. 33, Art. 2, Answer, p. 734.) All physical inclina-

concupiscence and the love of friendship would not hold. If self-satisfaction or pleasure were the final cause of all desires, all desires would be instances of the love of concupiscence, *i.e.*, would have a good for the self as their final aim.

Since "a man can intend several things at the same time,"[201] he may have a self-interestedly benevolent desire; in the love of friendship he seeks a good for another as the final end of his desire, but he can also anticipate a secondary and concomitant good for himself, namely, the satisfaction of giving.

A benevolent desire can be self-interested in another way: through the moral improvement that the benefactor anticipates. Aquinas says that "we all naturally love that in which we see our own good. Now it is true that the benefactor has some good of his in the recipient of his benefaction . . . but the benefactor sees his virtuous good in the recipient."[202] He also says that "a man, from doing good to another, hopes to get some good for himself, either from God or from man."[203] Thus, a man can intend to do good for another while anticipating an increase of virtue or a recognition of his virtuous conduct without giving only for the sake of these personal goods.

Aquinas also says that benevolence can be self-interested because it is a function of the similarity that he claims is necessary for true human friendship. Friends are equal.[204] With this in mind, he argues that the

---

tions tend to it and give rise to actions that are done for the sake of it. This is why Aquinas does not and cannot admit of instinctive or physical benevolence; whatever the body or sensitive appetite inclines to, it inclines to only because of a good for the self: carnal pleasure. In the second sense in which Aquinas uses the term "pleasure," it signifies the satisfaction, joy, or delight that accompanies the exercise of the will or intellectual appetite. (See *ibid.*, Q. 30, Art. 1, Reply Obj. 1, p. 718; and Q. 31, Art. 5, Answer, p. 274.) But the will does not incline to an object for the sake of the satisfaction, joy, or delight that it can thereby achieve. It does so because of a substantive good (*e.g.*, health, virtue, knowledge) that it hopes to gain for the self (love of concupiscence) or for another (love of friendship). It does not seek that good for the sake of satisfaction, joy, or delight, though this personal good accompanies its inclinations. Therefore, in a benevolent desire, what the will seeks is *another's good* primarily; because such an inclination (like all of the will's inclinations) is accompanied by satisfaction, joy, or delight, the will may also anticipate a secondary and concomitant good for the self, namely, the satisfaction it takes in its benevolent action. (See *ibid.*, Q. 2, Art. 6, p. 593.)

[201] *Ibid.*, Q. 12, Art. 3, Answer, p. 641.

[202] *Ibid.*, Part II-II, Q. 26, Art. 12, Answer, Vol. II, p. 1303.

[203] *Ibid.*, Part I-II, Q. 32, Art. 6, Answer, Vol. I, p. 731.

[204] As we have already noted, Aquinas admits the possibility of benevolence outside of friendship, *i.e.*, in a relationship of inequality. (See fn. 195, p. 234, *supra.*) But Aquinas considers such a relationship an atypical friendship, if a friendship at all, since mutuality or reciprocation in kind is impossible. Benevolence between unequals is usually one-sided, normally from the superior to the inferior, as in the case of ruler and subject, or parent and child. (See *Summa Theologica*, Part II-II, Q. 25, Art. 4, Answer, Vol. II, p. 1288.)

love one has for a friend is based on the love one has for oneself.[205] Since "it is common to all for each one to love what he thinks himself to be,"[206] it is common for one to love another who possesses the same qualities and characteristics. For,

> when a man loves another with the love of friendship, he wills good to him, *just as he wills good to himself*: wherefore he apprehends him as his other self, in so far, to wit, as he wills good to him as to himself. Hence a friend is called a man's *other self*.[207]

But he who wills good to another because the other is similar to himself may anticipate sharing the welfare of the other, since friends, being "of one mind," are characterized by "rejoicing and sorrowing in almost the same things."[208] Or, as Aquinas says in greater detail when he discusses "mutual indwelling" in relation to the love of friendship:

> Whereas, in the love of friendship, the lover is in the beloved, inasmuch as he reckons what is good or evil to his friend, as being so to himself; and his friend's will as his own, so that it seems as though he felt the good or suffered the evil in the person of his friend. Hence it is proper to friends *to desire the same things, and to grieve and rejoice at the same*, as the Philosopher says. . . . Consequently in so far as he reckons what affects his friend as affecting himself, the lover seems to be in the beloved, as though he were become one with him: but in so far as, on the other hand, he wills and acts for his friend's sake as for his own sake, looking on his friend as identified with himself, thus the beloved is in the lover.[209]

Thus, self-interested benevolence also is present when a person anticipates sharing vicariously the good he wishes for his friend, just as he participates in his friend's sorrow.

The possibility of a disinterested natural benevolence is mentioned in passing by Aquinas when he says:

[205] He does not, of course, mean by this that love for another is but an indirect expression of the love of concupiscence (acquisitive desire). What he means is that one seeks the good of a friend in benevolent desire in the same way as one seeks one's own good in acquisitive desire.

[206] *Summa Theologica*, Part II-II, Q. 25, Art. 7, Answer, Vol. II, p. 1291.

[207] *Ibid.*, Part I-II, Q. 28, Art. 1, Answer, Vol. I, p. 709. (First italics added.)

[208] *Ibid.*, Part II-II, Q. 25, Art. 7, Answer, Vol. II, p. 1291.

[209] *Ibid.*, Part I-II, Q. 28, Art. 2, Answer, Vol. I, pp. 710–711. Aquinas stresses, in this regard, the anticipation of mutuality that accompanies the benevolent desire that characterizes friendship. Here again, though benevolence is not extended solely for the sake of having it returned (for this would be giving only in order to get), the anticipation of the return of love can accompany a benevolent desire, thus rendering it self-interested. "Some love on account of being loved, not so that to be loved is the end of their loving, but because it is a kind of way leading a man to love." (*Ibid.*, Part II-II, Q. 27, Art. 1, Reply Obj. 3, Vol. II, p. 1306. See also Part I-II, Q. 32, Art. 6, Answer, Vol. I, p. 731.)

. . . it is proper to the perfection of a friendship for a noble person that one who is occupied in serving a friend should sometimes even abstain from a pleasure which he experiences in the friend's presence for the sake of that friend. So according to this friendship, he who would absent himself from a friend for the friend's sake would love him more than he who would not wish to depart from the presence of that friend even for that friend's sake.

He immediately adds:

But if anyone be willingly and easily deprived of the friend's presence and be more pleased with other things, this proves that he loves the friend either not at all, or only a little.[210]

The question of benevolence as self-interested or disinterested in Aquinas' theory of supernatural love already has been discussed.[211] In his theory of natural love, self-interested benevolence would seem to be its only possible expression, particularly in the typical friendship of virtuous equals. Since friends are characterized by taking or wanting to take pleasures in each other's company, by their joy and sorrow in the same things, and by their desire to have their love reciprocated, self-interest normally would seem to be a part of any benevolent intention. Aquinas says that friends are necessary for whatever happiness a man can achieve in this life.

. . . the happy man needs friends . . . not, indeed, to make use of them . . . but . . . that he may do good to them; that he may delight in seeing them do good; and again that he may be helped by them in his good work.[212]

Some self-interest, therefore, necessarily would seem to be involved in every human desire. Man cannot avoid loving himself. The meaning of this love is that he seeks his own perfection or happiness in all that he does.[213] Hence, man must seek a good for himself in benevolent desire— indirectly, because benevolence precludes total or primary concern with one's own welfare—as well as in acquisitive desire.[214]

[210] *On Charity*, Art. XI, Reply Obj. 6, p. 91. In this connection, Aquinas notes that Aristotle remarked that "some women . . . entrust their children to a nurse; they do love them indeed, yet seek not to be loved in return, if they happen not to be loved." (*Summa Theologica*, Part II-II, Q. 27, Art. 1, Answer, Vol. II, p. 1305. See also *Nicomachean Ethics*, Book VIII, Ch. 8, 1159a29–32.)

[211] See Part I, Ch. 3, *supra*.

[212] *Summa Theologica*, Part I-II, Q. 4, Art. 8, Answer, Vol. I, p. 608.

[213] See *ibid.*, Part I, Q. 60, Art. 2, Answer, p. 298; Part I-II, Q. 4, Art. 3, Answer, p. 604, and Q. 5, Art. 1, Answer, p. 609.

[214] See Robert Johann's *The Meaning of Love*.

Dante Alighieri

Dante, like Stendhal, is one of the few authors who wrote both imaginatively and analytically about love. These two approaches to the subject are exemplified, to some extent, in *La Vita Nuova* and the *Convivio*, respectively; they are surely combined in *The Divine Comedy*. Though it is difficult to separate Dante the poet from Dante the analyst in these works, we have found it possible to distill from his writings a theory of love that is as simple and clear in its basic outlines as it is abundant in imaginative illustration.

Dante's interest in the subject of love has three foci. One theme is the morality of love. *The Divine Comedy* certainly attempts to depict a complete moral architecture of natural and supernatural love and to portray the manifold varieties of virtue and vice, *i.e.*, of good and bad love. Dante's own love for Beatrice is a persistent second theme. The third is a philosophical interest in the nature of love involving definition and certain logical distinctions. We shall concentrate on the third of these interests.

The skeleton of Dante's theory of love is not unfamiliar. It is, except for the prominent place now accorded to the figure of a woman, identical in essential respects with the theory of Thomas Aquinas (though by no means as fully elaborated). Like Aquinas, Dante conceives love as a cosmic phenomenon, an all-pervasive tendency, that even "moves the sun and the other stars."[215] Like Aquinas, he also distinguishes between natural and supernatural love.[216] The familiar scholastic distinction between man's sensitive appetite and his rational appetite or will is a pivotal one in his theory. Less pivotal, but present, is his distinction between love aiming at getting as opposed to love aiming at giving. When he speaks of benevolence, Dante frequently refers, as does Aquinas, to Aristotle's analysis of the friendship of virtuous equals. Like Aquinas, he stresses the need to control sexual desire, the only love of the sensitive or bodily appetite that

[215] *The Divine Comedy*, "Paradiso," Canto XXXIII, Line 145, p. 544.

[216] Dante makes the distinction in two ways. The first is figurative. Virgil, Dante's guide through hell and through part of purgatory, represents the best of natural love. But Virgil can lead Dante only so far in his ascent to God. At a certain point, Beatrice, who represents supernatural love, replaces Virgil. (See *ibid.*, "Purgatorio," Canto XXVII, Lines 32–54, pp. 328–329; Lines 124–142, pp. 331–332; and Canto XXX, Lines 25–145, pp. 345–349.) The second way Dante makes the distinction is through what Virgil says to Dante in terminating his explanation of the nature of love:

> . . . So far as reason plead
> Can I instruct thee; beyond that point, wait
> For Beatrice; for faith is here thy need.

(*Ibid.*, Canto XVIII, Lines 46–48, p. 279.)

normally is directed to other human beings. Further, his understanding of union and the desire for it in relation to love parallels that of Aquinas.

Though Dante very often lays more stress on what causes love than on what it is, there is no doubt that he conceives of it as tendency in general, as encompassing all inclinations on the part of anything. For he says that

> everything has its own special love; as, for instance, simple bodies have in themselves a love inspired by nature for their own proper place, and there- fore earth always tends downwards to the centre: fire has a natural love for the circumference above, adjoining the heaven of the moon, and therefore always leaps up towards that.[217]

Or, as Virgil says to Dante when asked about love:

> "Nor creature nor creator ever yet,
>   My son, was without love," continued he,
> "Natural, or of the mind: thou knowest it."

Virgil goes on to explain how all the natural appetites, *i.e.*, those tenden- cies that are not free inclinations of the will, cannot in themselves be the source of any moral condemnation, since they are inherently without blame. A love, any love, becomes good or bad because of free will. If the will inclines to the right things in the right way, and hence controls natural appetites through temperance, all of its various loves will be good. If, on the other hand, the inclinations of the will are not directed to the right things in the right way, they will be bad loves.

> The natural always is from error free;
>   But the other may, through a bad object, err
>   By too much force or its deficiency.
> While to the prime good 'tis resolved to steer,
>   And in the second keepeth measure due,
>   Of sinful joy it cannot be the spur.
> But should it swerve to evil, or pursue
>   The good with too strong or too feeble intent,
>   The creature to his Maker is untrue.
> Hence may'st thou understand how love is meant
>   To be in you the seed of virtue pure
>   And of all works deserving chastisement.[218]

---

[217] *Convivio*, Tractate III, p. 133.

[218] *The Divine Comedy*, "Purgatorio," Canto XVII, Lines 91–93, 94–105, p. 275. The phrase "Natural, or of the mind," in the first section of the quote, refers to involuntary or voluntary love, not to natural love as distinguished from supernatural love. In the next canto, Virgil reiterates the unique position of free will in determin- ing, by its inclination, the goodness or badness of any love. He makes the distinction clearly in saying:

> Now how the truth is hidden thou canst see
>   Plainly, from all those people who aver
>   That each love in itself is praiseworthy

Virgil explains to Dante that the sins of pride, envy, and anger, which are punished in a certain circle of purgatory, are but three perverted forms of love. The tendencies behind these three evils are inclinations toward proper goods, but have become evil because they were pursued intemperately. Virgil, then, in effect, identifies every good act and its opposite as an expression of love.[219]

Asked by Dante to make clearer just what love is, Virgil says:

> The mind which is created apt to love,
>   Soon as by pleasure it is stirred to act,
>   To every pleasing thing is quick to move.
> Your apprehension from a thing of fact
>   Draweth an image, shown to the inward view,
>   So that perforce it doth the mind attract.
> And if, being turned, it is inclined thereto,
>   *The inclination is love:* nature it is,
>   Which is through pleasure knit within ye anew.
> Then, just as fire to the upper region flies
>   By reason of its form which, where it best
>   Endureth in its matter, is born to rise,
> Even so the mind is with desire possessed,
>   Which is a motion of spirit, and cannot be,
>   Till the thing loved rejoiceth it, at rest.[220]

> Because perhaps its matter may appear
>   To be good always; but not every seal
>   Is good, however good the pressed wax were."
> (*Ibid.*, Canto XVIII, Lines 34–39, pp. 278–279.)

Virgil goes on to speak of love as the original tendency toward any object:

> . . . and this original bent
>   Desert of praise or blame admitteth not.
> Now, that with this will all wills else consent,
>   The power that judges is inborn in you
>   And ought to guard the threshold of assent.
> This is the principle that holds the clue
>   To merit in you, according as it can
>   Good loves and guilty garner and winnow true.
> Those reasoners who sought the Founder's plan
>   Have recognized this inborn liberty,
>   And therefore Ethic have they left to man.
> Wherefore suppose that from necessity
>   Arises every love that in you stirs,
>   You have the power to curb it in your fee."
> (*Ibid.*, Lines 59–72, pp. 279–280.)

[219] See pp. 198–199, *supra,* where Augustine also affirms the moral neutrality of love.

[220] *The Divine Comedy,* "Purgatorio," Canto XVIII, Lines 19–33, p. 278. (Italics added.)

There is no doubt that the Thomistic theory is reflected here. Love is not the actual movement or tendency toward the object, but the inclination of the appetitive faculty (in this case will) which is behind the movement or tendency.[221] In the passage above, Dante refers to "mind," or what he elsewhere calls intellectual appetite or will. But his definition of love applies to all the inclinations of living beings as well as to the innate tendencies of inanimate beings, since the latter have, in his view, natural propensities or "appetites."

Dante says there are five natures in the composite being—man—and that each has a distinctive mode of appetite or love. The first three, those of simple bodies, compound bodies, and vegetation, are not distinctively human, and give rise to tendencies not directed to other human beings. The fourth and the fifth natures, the animal and rational, do give rise to tendencies toward other human beings.

> And by the fourth nature, that of animals, I mean the sensitive nature, man has a different affection by which he feels love according to sensible appearances like the animals, and this love in man most of all has need of control on account of its excessive activity, chiefly in the pleasures of taste and of touch.
>
> And by reason of the fifth and last nature, that is, the truly human or, to use a better word, angelic, that is, rational, man has an affection for truth and virtue; and from this affection springs true and perfect friendship, derived from what is honourable; and of this the Philosopher [Aristotle] speaks in the eighth book of the *Ethics* when he treats of friendship.[222]

As with Aquinas, the only sensitive appetite that normally has other human beings as its object is sexual desire. Dante often refers to this appetite in describing the struggle between reason and "desire." In the fifth Canto of the "Inferno," in the second circle of hell, Dante depicts the lustful lovers. Their punishment is to be eternally united and blown about by stormy and violent winds, the winds of their own passion. Sins of the flesh are not, of course, all sexual. In the third circle of hell and the sixth terrace of purgatory, the gluttonous are punished. But unlawful sexual indulgence is *the* carnal sin. Those who so sin "let Desire pull Reason from her throne."[223] They allow their momentary and intense "love" of pleasure to overcome the restraints of their will. Dante mentions a number of

[221] See p. 227, *supra*.
[222] *Convivio*, Tractate III, pp. 134–135. See also pp. 133–134. Dante mentions five such modes of appetite, while Aquinas mentions only three. The reason for this is that Dante subdivides Aquinas' first mode of appetite, "natural" love, into three: the appetite of simple bodies; that of composite bodies; and that of plants. His fourth and fifth modes, sensitive appetite and rational appetite (or will), correspond precisely to Aquinas' second and third. To this extent the parallel is exact.
[223] *The Divine Comedy*, "Inferno," Canto V, Line 39, p. 27.

famous lovers whom he observes thus condemned to perpetual desire without hope: Helen of Troy, Paris, Semiramis, Cleopatra, Achilles. Dante says that more than a thousand pairs were named by Virgil. "Each lady of old, lost with her lovely knight."[224] Dante asks to speak with one such pair, Francesca da Rimini and Paolo Malatesta. Francesca tells Dante how they succumbed to temptation while reading about the romance of Launcelot and Guinevere:

> We were alone, and without any dread.
> Sometimes our eyes, at the word's secret call,
> Met, and our cheeks a changing colour wore.
> But it was one page only that did all.
> When we read how that smile, so thirsted for,
> Was kissed by such a lover, he that may
> Never from me be separated more
> All trembling kissed my mouth. . . .
> We read no more that day.[225]

In Dante's view, sexual desire, like any of the loves that are not matters of choice, may be good or bad depending on its subjection to reason. Adultery is against God's law. But sexual desire, when it occurs within marriage and is not pursued for the sake of carnal pleasure, is not condemnable.[226] Like any of the secondary goods, carnal pleasure must be kept in control by a will that inclines toward the "prime good," *i.e.,* the heavenly blessings.

Though human love must be related to the love for God in order to merit salvation, it is not always blameworthy if it is not so related. Thus, in the first circle of hell, limbo, Dante places the unbaptized, virtuous pagans who were born before Christ came to earth. Of them, Virgil says:

> These sinned not: but the merit that they achieve
> Helps not, since baptism was not theirs, the gate
> Of that faith, which was given thee to believe.
> And if ere Christ they came, untimely in date,
> They worshipped not with right experience;
> And I myself am numbered in their state.
> For such defect and for no other offence
> We are lost.[227]

[224] *Ibid.,* Line 71, p. 28. See also Lines 58–67.
[225] *Ibid.,* Lines 129–136, 138, p. 30.
[226] For example, the seventh terrace of purgatory is for the purging of lust. (See *ibid.,* "Purgatorio," Canto XXV, Line 112–Canto XXVI, Line 90, pp. 321–325.) Dante also speaks to married people in paradise. (See *ibid.,* "Paradiso," Canto III, pp. 378–382.)
[227] *Ibid.,* "Inferno," Canto IV, Lines 34–41, pp. 20–21.

Throughout the "Inferno" and the "Purgatorio," the prominent form of natural love among human beings is acquisitive desire. Every man has a natural and unavoidable love for himself; he seeks his own good in all that he does. Many sins result, not only from pursuing the wrong object or the right object in an intemperate way but also from pursuing an imaginary good exclusively while remaining indifferent to the good of others. Thus, the misers, the heretics, the traitors, the prideful, and the envious callously use others in order to gain what they want. Acquisitive desire, as a form of natural love among human beings, is not always an evil love in Dante's view. But it is clear that almost all of the evil forms of love presented in the "Inferno" and "Purgatorio" are acquisitive in character. In fact, benevolence as an expression of *natural* love among human beings is hardly mentioned in *The Divine Comedy*. One may suspect that the virtuous pagans in limbo had benevolent feeling for their friends, but no mention of this is made. It is likely that the lovers Paolo and Francesca had tender feelings for each other that went beyond their sexual desire, but Dante says nothing explicit on this point. If natural love is left behind when Virgil gives way to Beatrice as Dante's guide, any expression of benevolence is very difficult to find up to that point. In the realm of supernatural love, it is, by contrast, mentioned frequently. We see it on the part of Dante, Beatrice, the souls in paradise, and, of course, on the part of God, whose benevolence is pure.

The most explicit discussion of benevolent desire as an expression of natural love among human beings occurs in the *Convivio*. In that work, Dante refers to the Aristotelian analysis of friendship which Aquinas incorporated so much of in his own theory of love. In the third Tractate, during a discussion of what constitutes a philosopher, Dante introduces the familiar distinction between friendships of utility or pleasure (acquisitive desire) and friendship of worth or virtue (benevolent desire). He calls the former accidental friendships because, in them, the other person is regarded only as a means. True friendship consists in mutual "goodwill" not extended for the sake of advantage or pleasure.[228]

Since Dante does not mention divine aid in this discussion, the true friendship to which he refers can be assumed to be natural. In his theory, therefore, benevolence is an expression of natural human love. Like Aquinas, he seems to conceive of it as taking a self-interested form. Since friendship is based on self-love, the desire to do good to another is accompanied by a subsidiary aim of enhancing one's own welfare. True love for another is accompanied by the anticipation of reciprocity. It may

[228] Dante says that "true friendship, when considered in itself alone apart from the mind, has for its subject matter the knowledge of well-doing and for its form the desire for this." (*Ibid.*, Tractate III, pp. 166–167. See also p. 165.)

also be accompanied by the aim of personal moral improvement or by the aim of sharing in the good one does for another. Dante also mentions satisfaction and a "worthy delight"[229] that springs from the experience of two virtuous friends living together.

Like Aristotle and Aquinas, he asserts that all friendship presupposes an existing similarity or likeness between the friends. Like them, Dante admits that benevolence can exist among unequals and says that such friendship requires,

> if it is to be preserved . . . a certain ratio between them, which as it were reduces the unlikeness to likeness, as in the relation between master and servant. For although a servant when he receives a kindness from his master cannot repay him with a similar kindness, yet he ought to repay him as best he can, with so much solicitude and frankness that that which in itself is unlike becomes like through the display of goodwill, by which friendship is manifested and strengthened and preserved.[230]

With regard to the desire for union, the parallel with Aquinas' theory is close.

> Love, if we truly apprehend and nicely consider, is nothing else than the spiritual union of the soul with the object loved, to which union the soul of its own nature hastens quicker or slower according as it is free or obstructed.[231]

Dante means that whenever the appetite (or will) inclines to something as a good, this very tendency can be understood as a liaison between the person and the object loved. By virtue of this liaison, the two are, in some sense, united. But as we pointed out in discussing Aquinas, our notion of union and the desire for it is a much more limited one. What we mean by union is a condition in which two people, different in character, achieve a composite whole by coming together, *or* a condition in which two people are very much like each other in character or interests. For the two to be united, however, they must, in both cases, remain existentially separate. Thus, precluded, in the first case, is the total absorption of one person by the other; and, in the second case, the absolute identity of the two people involved. To this we must add that it is not the condition of union itself that is signified by our critical notion but the desire for it, whether or not that condition already exists.[232]

---

[229] *Ibid.*, p. 167.

[230] *Ibid.*, p. 127. See also Tractate IV, p. 285. Dante's point here is somewhat different than that of Aristotle. For Aristotle, benevolence among unequals approximates similarity when the superior's unequal relationship to the inferior is compensated for by his receiving more than he gives, in proportion to his superiority.

[231] *Convivio*, Tractate III, p. 129.

[232] See Part I, Ch. 1, *supra*.

With regard to the union of similarity, Dante states flatly that "no friendship can exist except where there is likeness."[233] From such similarity springs the desires of true friendship which Dante says are basically benevolent. But, though he holds that likeness is a prerequisite of friendship and lists "common aims" as one of the causes that increase it, he also says that love or friendship "is that which joins and unites the lover with the person loved."[234] In other words, friendship not only arises from an existing likeness but itself takes the form of a desire to strengthen and deepen the existing oneness or similarity, or lend to it a new dimension. Thus, Dante remarks:

> Hence when we speak of John as a friend of Martin, we do not mean to express merely that natural friendship which makes all men friends of all other men, but that friendship which is engendered over and above the former, and is peculiar and distinctive in individual persons.[235]

The natural similarity, then, between members of the same species is sufficient existing union for a real friendship to develop, which takes the form of a desire for a more personal union. Since Dante does not specify how the desire for union of similarity is related to the benevolent desire that characterizes true friendship, we can only say that both desires are coextensive in his theory.

The texts quoted above also point toward the inclusion of the notion of the union of complementarity in Dante's theory. While precise examples cannot be cited, the way Dante speaks of union indicates that he includes desires for both types of union in his theory of love.

As we have seen, the broad outlines of Dante's theory of love are the same as those of Aquinas. In short, the conceptual substratum of Dante's poetical writings on love is the traditional scholastic view. The striking addition to that view is the position occupied by Beatrice in Dante's thinking both about his own love as well as about his whole theory of love. The sonnets in *La Vita Nuova* are almost totally devoted to the theme of his love for Beatrice. The *Convivio* was written after the death of Beatrice and, although she is never mentioned in it by name, a figure of a lovely lady is introduced as the symbol of philosophy. (It is in this work, which he intended as a summary or compendium of philosophical and theological

---

[233] *Convivio,* Tractate III, p. 127.

[234] *Ibid.,* Tractate V, Canzone, p. 193. Dante goes further than this in describing the impulse of friendship as the desire for union: "And because things that are joined together do naturally interchange their qualities insomuch that *at times* the one is entirely transformed into the nature of the other, it comes to pass that the feelings of the person loved enter into the person who loves, so that the love felt by the one is communicated to the other." (*Ibid.* Italics added.)

[235] *Ibid.,* Tractate III, p. 165.

truths, that the scholastic influence on Dante is most apparent.)[236] Dante is reunited with his beloved Beatrice in *The Divine Comedy,* where she has become the focus of his spiritual and religious devotion and the means of his salvation as she leads him through the stages of paradise.

From the perspective of Dante's analysis of love in the *Convivio,* the character of Dante's love for Beatrice is as conceptually obscure as it is many faceted and compelling. We see her, through Dante's eyes, in *La Vita Nuova,* not only as a real woman but as the living personification of the highest virtue. At times she seems hardly human to him. He speaks of her even while she lived as

> so noble and praiseworthy that certainly of her might have been said those words of the poet Homer, "She seemed not to be the daughter of a mortal man, but of God."[237]

Throughout *La Vita Nuova* and even more after her death, Dante loves Beatrice, not only as a person but also as a symbol of all that he venerates. He depicts her as his muse, as an image of the cardinal Christian virtues of faith, hope, and charity, as a sacramental being incarnating all of God's graces, and, above all, as his mediator between earth and heaven. For these reasons, Dante's love for Beatrice is a love between human beings from one perspective only, and even from that perspective, never without a supernatural dimension. He certainly never thinks of her as inspiring anything but pure or purifying affections.

> And albeit her image, that was with me always, was an exultation of Love to subdue me, it was yet of so perfect a quality that it never allowed me to be overruled by Love without the faithful counsel of reason.[238]

If we ignore, for the moment, the distinction between natural and supernatural love, the application of the notions present in Dante's theory of love (and some concepts related to them) casts some light on his own love for Beatrice. For Dante, any love is always of the heart (his metaphor for appetite or tendency).[239] But love (and especially the love of a man for a woman) may be low or high depending on whether the heart controls the

---

[236] The *Convivio,* however, is both expository and metaphorical. Dante planned it around the metaphor of a banquet, as a sequence of courses of meat, or *canzone,* followed by bread. Of the fourteen projected *canzone,* only four were completed.

[237] *La Vita Nuova,* Ch. II, p. 548. In describing her elsewhere, Dante says in the same vein: "She went along crowned and clothed with humility, showing no whit of pride in all that she heard and saw: and when she had gone by, it was said of many, 'This is not a woman, but one of the beautiful angels of Heaven!' " (*Ibid.,* Ch. XXVI, pp. 593–594.)

[238] *Ibid.,* Ch. II, p. 548.

[239] See *ibid.,* Ch. XXXIX, p. 612.

reason or the reason, the heart. Since Dante's love for Beatrice is inspired by her beauty and her virtue, he always thinks of his love for her as a spiritual tendency, as a refined inclination of his will, as the yearning of a gentle heart (*gentil cor*).[240] Most of these desires toward Beatrice spring from Dante's own need. He loves Beatrice as his helper and comforter. His whole search for happiness is, in some way, bound up with her mediation.

Yet, even though he is basically a suppliant, he also has benevolent feelings for Beatrice. He and Beatrice are unequal in virtue and blessedness. Despite the fact that Dante allows for the possibility of friendship between unequals in his theory of love, he never refers to his love for Beatrice as a friendship.[241] This is not surprising when we consider that the intense veneration of the figure of a woman is alien to the Aristotelian-Thomistic analysis of friendship on which Dante drew so heavily in the *Convivio*. For a man to so honor a woman, however, is customary in the tradition of courtly love within which Dante lived and wrote. Still, his love for Beatrice, whatever its character, is devoid of the overt sexual desire that is fundamental to a large segment of that tradition.[242] If Dante's love for Beatrice is not friendship and not sexual, in just what ways does he have benevolent and acquisitive feelings toward her?

Of the two desires, Dante's need for Beatrice is the easier to understand. Initially, he wants to see her as much as he can to appreciate her beauty. Of his first encounter with Beatrice he says:

> And when I perceived her, all my senses were overpowered by the great lordship that Love obtained, finding himself so near unto that most gracious being, until nothing but the spirits of sight remained to me.[243]

This desire is so strong that he says: ". . . no sooner do I image to myself her marvellous beauty that I am possessed with the desire to behold her."[244] But Dante is not content merely with the appreciation of her beauty, nor even with his admiration of her virtuous excellence. He also wants very badly, and perhaps even needs, her recognition, her approval, her blessing, her "salutation."[245] That salutation is the recognition and praise of a supremely virtuous being. Dante's constant search for that blessing is essentially the desire to make himself worthy of her praise, by making himself more and more virtuous through her inspiration.

[240] Though Dante's love for Beatrice is a spiritual one, it is sometimes so intense that it produces physical effects in him. (See *ibid.*, Ch. IV, pp. 551–552.)

[241] In *La Vita Nuova*, Dante does comment on the relationship between Beatrice and her father by saying, "no other friendship is like to that between a good parent and a good child." (Ch. XXII, p. 580.)

[242] See *ibid.*, Ch. II, p. 548; and Ch. XI, pp. 559–560.

[243] *Ibid.*, Ch. XIV, p. 566.

[244] *Ibid.*, Ch. XV, p. 568.

[245] See *ibid.*, Chs. X–XI, pp. 558–563.

Dante's benevolent feelings for Beatrice are somewhat atypical. For, how can an imperfect and suppliant person intend to benefit someone whom he regards as the very model of virtuous perfection? Dante's answer is to want praise and exultation for Beatrice. In this way he can add to her glory. Love commands him from the beginning: "Do homage unto your mistress."[246] Since he cannot help her become more virtuous, the only thing he can give her is praise. Such praise is not without its admixture of self-interest before Dante has passed through the cleansing purgatorial fire. For, when questioned about his love for the living Beatrice, he says:

> Ladies, the end and aim of my love was but the salutation of that lady of whom I conceive that ye are speaking; wherein alone I found that beatitude which is the goal of desire.[247]

As he ascends with Beatrice through the stages of paradise, the two aspects of his love begin to merge. His love becomes more and more like the love of Beatrice for him and hence more and more like the divine benevolence that all good love reflects.

> Such love must needs stamp on me its imprint;
> For the good, soon as 'tis perceived as good,
>   Enkindles love and makes it more to live,
>   The more of good it can itself include.
> Therefore to the Essence, whose prerogative
>   Is, that what good outside of it is known
>   Is naught else but a light its own beams give,
> More than elsewhither must in love be drawn
>   The mind of him whose vision can attain
>   The verity the proof is founded on.[248]

Dante's final prayer to God is that he may be able to transmit to his fellowmen his own glimpse of the divine essence, that primal love with which his will is now in harmony.

Leone Ebreo

Ebreo's *The Philosophy of Love* (*Dialoghi d'Amore*) is presented in the form of three long conversations between two characters, Philo and

---

[246] *Ibid.*, Ch. XI, p. 559. See also Chs. XLII, XLIII, p. 618. It is in this sense that Dante's love for Beatrice may take the form of the desire for the union of similarity. Dante seeks his own salvation by striving to become more and more like Beatrice, whom he admires as the epitome of virtue.
[247] *Ibid.*, Ch. XVIII, p. 572.
[248] *The Divine Comedy*, "Paradiso," Canto XXVI, Lines 27–36, p. 502.

Sophia. They are cast in the roles of lover and beloved. Though the names imply a symbolic relationship between a friend, or lover (Philo), and wisdom (Sophia), the characters themselves are a man and a woman who discuss not only love itself but also their own human love relationship. Though much of the conversation is conditioned by this staging, Ebreo does not present Philo as saying only things that will please his beloved, but as striving to tell her the truth.

The three conversations, or dialogues (a promised fourth on the effects of love was never written), are entitled: "On Love and Desire," "On the Universality of Love," and "On the Origin of Love." In each, and principally in the last, the influence of Plato is apparent. Plato's theory is not simply reported; it is changed and combined with other concepts, some of them deriving from Aristotle and the scholastics. Thus, at one point, the Platonic emphasis on beauty in the beloved is stressed, while, at another point, persons who are loved are classified according to the Aristotelian distinction among pleasure, utility, and goodness or virtue.

Whatever its origins, the theory presented by Ebreo is one in which both acquisitive and benevolent desires among human beings are called love. Ebreo is most concerned with acquisitive desire and the objects to which it is directed. But as he also mentions benevolent desire in discussing true friendship, saying that true friendship cannot exist without it, his theory spans the distinction between the desire to get and the desire to give.

Despite the protracted discussion in the first dialogue of the possible difference between love and desire, Ebreo's general conception of love finally emerges as tendency in general. Love is the impulse behind the movements of the planets and that which preserves the celestial harmony. It is a cosmic or universal force operative in all things, living or inanimate; all things love because all things tend or incline to their natural ends.[249] They do so in three ways, depending on their nature. Inanimate things love through an innate natural inclination, animals through sensuous or physical inclinations, and man through the voluntary inclinations of his will. (Natural love among human beings is either sensuous or rational.)

What is common to the different kinds of human love is tendency or inclination. And tendency or inclination, whatever its character, is what we mean by our critical term "desire." Ebreo, however, uses the term "desire," initially, in a more limited sense than we do. For him, a desire is an inclination or impulse that always implies deficiency in the desirer. What he means by desire in the first dialogue is what we mean by acquisitive desire.

---

[249] At one point, Ebreo seems to include cognition even on the part of inanimate things in his generic conception of love. (See *The Philosophy of Love*, Dialogue II, pp. 74–75.)

Philo and Sophia distinguish in the first dialogue between two kinds of tendencies, called, respectively, "love" and "desire." In general, love is defined as the inclination to union with a good object, *whether it is possessed or not*. Desire, on the other hand, is the inclination toward a good object *not possessed*. Thus, love is a broader term than desire. In this connection, Philo tells Sophia that

> we could really define love as "desire to enjoy in union an object recognized as good"; though I told you before that desire presupposes the absence of its object. But now I add that even when the good exists and is ours, we may yet desire, not indeed possession thereof (for that is achieved already), but enjoyment of cognitive union with it; and such future enjoyment we may desire, because it is not yet actual. Such desire we call love: a desire to possess things we lack, or desire to enjoy in union those we have obtained: both of these may properly be called "desire," but the second more accurately—"love."[250]

In the third dialogue, the distinction between love and desire arises again, only to be treated somewhat differently. Philo concedes that there is some difference between the inclination to get something not possessed and the inclination to retain something already possessed. But he here insists that the two affections are really essentially the same, and that love and desire are synonyms. He also adds that love or desire is always accompanied by or associated with deficiency of some kind.[251]

Sophia then asks Philo how it is that God can love if love always implies deficiency. Philo answers that God's love is directed to the fulfillment of deficiency in His creatures and not in Himself. On a human level such love "which has its end in the beloved is called friendship and beneficence." He adds:

> Such is a part of the love of the father for the son, of the master for the disciple, and of one friend for another; and such, too, is the love of God for His creatures, the desire of their good but not of His. Both Plato and Aristotle allow the existence of this second form of love.[252]

The distinction between acquisitive and benevolent desire also is apparent in the discussion of friendship, in which Ebreo draws heavily on Aristotle. Friendships engaged in for the sake of pleasure or utility involve acquisitive desire; the other person is regarded and treated as a means to one's own end. The friendship of virtue, or true friendship, involves treating another as one would oneself, since the other is, ideally, another

---

[250] *Ibid.*, Dialogue I, p. 49.
[251] See *ibid.*, Dialogue III, pp. 241–249.
[252] *Ibid.*, pp. 254–255.

self. It also often involves doing more for another than one would do for oneself.[253]

Although union is essential to virtuous friendship, it is in the discussion of the relationship between a man and a woman (Philo and Sophia) that Ebreo stresses the desire for union. Philo claims that the physical expression of that desire is both compatible with and supports the desire for spiritual union.

> And this, my affection and love, has transformed me into you, begetting in me a desire that you may be fused with me, in order that I, your lover, may form but a single person with you, my beloved, and equal love may make of our two souls one, which may likewise [without distinction] vivify and inform our two bodies. The sensual element in this desire excites a longing for physical union, that the union of bodies may correspond to the unity of the spirits wholly compenetrating each other.[254]

Philo goes on to explain how physical union actually reenforces the desire for spiritual union. Though the "union of copulation" satisfies the physical appetite temporarily, it is an imperfect union which intensifies the desire for spiritual union.[255]

As in the other theories influenced by Plato's, we find the same insistence that the highest objects of love are not human beings, indeed, that human beings are not loved except insofar as they reflect these objects.

> Since our soul is formed in the image of the highest beauty, and by its nature desires to return to its divine origin, it is ever impregnated with this natural desire. When, therefore, it perceives a beautiful person whose beauty is in harmony with itself, it recognises in and through this beauty, divine beauty, in the image of which this person also is made. And the image of this beloved in the mind of the lover quickens with its beauty the latent divine beauty which is the very soul, and gives it actuality, as if it were to receive it from the beauty of the divine original itself.[256]

Baldesar Castiglione

Castiglione's *The Book of the Courtier* contains a theory of love in which many factors taken from the Platonic theory of love are blended with other factors decidedly non-Platonic. Some of the latter are present in theories of courtly love as well as in those scholastic in origin. Therefore, it

[253] See *ibid.*, Dialogue I, p. 31; and Dialogue II, p. 73.
[254] *Ibid.*, Dialogue I, p. 57.
[255] See *ibid.*, pp. 54–55, 62.
[256] *Ibid.*, Dialogue III, p. 465.

is only in a qualified sense that Castiglione can be described as a Platonist.[257]

On the one hand, Castiglione, like Plato, thinks of love as a cosmic force constantly mediating between the mortal and the immortal. In his view, love for the transient can only be understood in terms of love for the permanent. The path of moral improvement is a path of ascent from lower loves to higher ones, a movement up the so-called ladder of love. Central to his conception of human love is the attractiveness of beauty, which, in its invisible form, he associates with goodness. Despite his concern with the good manners of lovers, Castiglione, with Plato, thinks that what human beings love is less important than how they love.

On the other hand, Castiglione is non-Platonic insofar as the principal interpersonal love of which he speaks is the love between a man and a woman. The interpersonal love that is Plato's principal concern is the love between a man and a boy. Further, the ideal lover for Castiglione is less the philosopher than the courtier and the gentleman. In addition, the ultimate object of love is not the idea of the beautiful or the idea of the good but the omnipotent and omniscient God of revealed religion.[258]

There are four parts to Castiglione's work. Each is set in the dramatic form of a conversation on some aspect of love or the proper and improper ways of making love.[259] At the end of the whole work, Bembo, Castig-

---

[257] A number of other "Renaissance Platonists" wrote treatises that reflect Plato's views to some degree. Castiglione, unlike many of the others, is concerned not only with the practices of love, *i.e.*, the manner in which different loves ought to be pursued and the right order of pursuing them, but also with the theoretical question of what love is. *The Book of the Courtier* is not only a practical treatise for the masculine lover on the fine art of loving well, but also a treatise on the nature of love.

[258] Despite this, there is little of what can be called a theory of supernatural love in Castiglione's thought. He rarely mentions God's love for man. And the ascent of the courtier up the ladder of love is, apparently, accomplished without divine aid—at least there is no mention of such aid. *The Book of the Courtier* is not a religious book in the usual sense of the word.

[259] No one interlocutor is present in all four books. The views of the author are presented continuously by those five or six spokesmen who carry most of the conversation. The function of the other characters present seems to be exclusively one of asking the principal interlocutors the necessary questions about the subject. The presentation of *The Book of the Courtier* in a dramatic form seems to be an artistic device to create color and interest rather than an indirect manner of expressing the author's views. (See Book I, 1–3, pp. 11–14.) The problem of interpreting a serious disagreement among the participants arises several times, but the disagreement is resolved to the apparent satisfaction of all before the conversation moves on. The longest disagreement is one concerning the inferiority or the superiority of women. The Magnifico (who is the author's spokesman at this point) succeeds, after some difficulty, in refuting those who maintain that women are inferior. (See Book II, 90–98, pp. 188–195.)

lione's principal spokesman in the fourth book, eulogizes love as a universal force:

> Sweetest bond of the universe, midway between celestial and terrestrial things, with benign control thou dost incline the supernal powers to rule the lower powers, and, turning the minds of mortals to their source, joinest them thereto. Thou unitest the elements in concord, movest nature to produce, and movest all that is born to the perpetuation of life. Thou gatherest together things that are separate, givest perfection to the imperfect, likeness to the unlike, friendship to the unfriendly, fruit to the earth, calm to the sea, vital light to the heavens.[260]

Castiglione's most general conception of love seems to be some version of an all-pervasive tendency. Yet, shortly before this culminating statement, human love is defined as "nothing but a certain desire to enjoy beauty."[261] The inclination toward beauty, presumably, is the human tendency most easily identified as love.[262] In men, the inclination toward beauty most often expresses itself as an attraction toward a beautiful woman.[263] Yet the beauty men pursue and enjoy is not restricted to its expression in the feminine nature. The attraction of a virtuous man for a virtuous woman is understood by Castiglione as only a step in the courtier's ascent to the highest objects of love. Even the beauty men pursue in women may be enjoyed in different ways, depending on how such beauty is perceived and understood. Thus it is said that

> nature has ordained that to every cognitive power there shall be joined an appetitive power; . . . in our soul there are three modes of cognition, namely, by sense, by reason, and by intellect. . . . Being by nature rational and placed as in the middle between these two extremes, man can choose (by descending to sense or rising to intellect) to turn his desires now in one direction and now in the other. In these two ways, therefore, men can desire beauty.[264]

Castiglione is clear as to the way the courtier ought to proceed in loving. When the soul is seized with a desire to enjoy beauty, it must avoid allowing itself to be guided by the judgment of sense which leads one to believe that the origin of the beauty beheld is in the body itself. In order to

[260] *Ibid.*, Book IV, 70, p. 356. See also 69–70, pp. 355–357.

[261] *Ibid.*, 51, p. 336.

[262] As Castiglione thinks of friendship between men as a form of human love, the inclination toward beauty does not exhaust the capacity of humans to love.

[263] See *ibid.*, 52, p. 337.

[264] *Ibid.*, 51, pp. 336–337. Beauty, in whatever way it appears and however it is perceived, is thought to be "an effluence of the divine goodness . . . (shed, like the sun's light, upon all created things)." (See *ibid.*, 52, p. 337.)

enjoy that beauty, a person who so judges is moved "to join itself as closely to that body as it can." Such a person, misled by sensual appetite, mistakes the apparent beauty of the body for the real incorporeal beauty which is behind the appearance.[265]

The inclination toward the physical beauty of a woman takes the form of sexual desire. In Castiglione's view, it is an acquisitive desire that increases the lover's need each time it is indulged. Those who seek to fulfill their desire through the pursuit of physical beauty "feel pleasure at the moment, as sick men sometimes dream of a draught from some clear spring, still they are not satisfied or quieted." Deceived by a semblance of true beauty, "they soon return to their unbridled desire, and in the same turmoil they felt before, once more they experience that furious and burning thirst for what in vain they hope to possess perfectly."[266]

Castiglione maintains that "it nearly always happens that young men are wrapped up in this love which is sensual and is an outright rebel to reason; and so they make themselves unworthy of enjoying the graces and benefits which love bestows upon its true subject."[267] Nevertheless, he says that "since human nature in youth is so greatly given over to the senses, the courtier may be permitted to love sensually while he is young."[268]

Castiglione distinguishes the purely sensual lover from the courtier, who occasionally indulges sexual desire in the following way:

> I . . . excuse those who allow themselves to be overcome by sensual love, to which they are so much inclined by human weakness: provided that in such love they show gentleness, courtesy, and worth, and the other noble qualities which these gentlemen have mentioned; and provided that when they are no longer youthful, they abandon it altogether, leaving this sensual desire behind *as the lowest rung of that ladder by which we ascend to true love.*[269]

The ascent advocated is, as in Plato's theory, from the physical to the spiritual. The transition, however, is gradual. The lowest rung is the love of the courtier for his lady, in which sexual indulgence is permitted while the courtier is young. The next rung on the ladder of love is an ascent to a rational love that still focuses on the physical beauty of the beloved. However, the lover's interest at this stage is not tactile but visual. The

---

[265] See *ibid.*, Book IV, 52, p. 337. See also 62, p. 347.
[266] *Ibid.*, 52, p. 338, *passim.*
[267] *Ibid.*, 53, p. 339.
[268] *Ibid.*, 61, p. 346. Castiglione states that the young are much more susceptible to desiring the body of a woman, *i.e.*, mistaking physical beauty for true beauty, than are the old. Young people who love sensually "deserve more compassion than blame" whereas the older who love sensually "deserve more blame than compassion." (*Ibid.*)
[269] *Ibid.*, 54, p. 340. (Italics added.)

courtier, whose reason controls his emotions, "must consider that, just as one cannot hear with his palate or smell with his ears, so also beauty can in no way be enjoyed, nor can the desire it excites in our minds be satisfied through the sense of touch, but only by way of that sense whereof this beauty is the true object, namely, the faculty of sight."[270] The one tactile exception that is made for virtuous lovers is the chaste kiss. According to one of the spokesmen, Bembo, "the Lady may in reason and without blame go even so far as to kiss." The "rational lover sees that, although the mouth is part of the body, nevertheless it emits words, which are the interpreters of the soul, and that inward breath which itself is even called soul." He adds:

> Hence, a man delights in joining his mouth to that of his beloved in a kiss, not in order to bring himself any unseemly desire, but because he feels that that bond is the opening of mutual access to their souls, which, being each drawn by desire for the other, pour themselves each into the other's body by turn, and mingle so together that each of them has two souls; and a single soul, composed thus of these two, rules as it were over two bodies. Hence, a kiss may be said to be a joining of souls rather than of bodies, because it has such power over the soul that it withdraws it to itself and separates it from the body.[271]

Castiglione points out that even the chaste lover who pursues his love for one woman in an exemplary fashion still must fall short of what he is seeking. For he is made unhappy "as soon as his beloved lady, by her absence, leaves his eyes deprived of their splendor, and consequently leaves his soul widowed of its good."[272] In order to avoid this misery, the courtier finally must turn away from all beauty incarnate and focus his attention upon spiritual beauty. Such pure beauty, divorced of all matter, he need

[270] *Ibid.*, 62, p. 347. "Therefore let him keep aloof from the blind judgment of sense, and with his eyes enjoy the radiance of his Lady, her grace, her amorous sparkle, the smiles, the manners and all the other pleasant ornaments of her beauty. Likewise with his hearing let him enjoy the sweetness of her voice, the modulation of her words, the harmony of her music (if his lady love be a musician). Thus, he will feed his soul on the sweetest food by means of these two senses—which partake little of the corporeal, and are reason's ministers—without passing to any unchaste appetite through desire for the body." (*Ibid.*)
[271] *Ibid.*, 64, pp. 349–350, *passim*.
[272] *Ibid.*, 66, p. 351. "Hence, to escape the torment of this absence and to enjoy beauty without suffering, the Courtier, aided by reason, must turn his desire entirely away from the body and to beauty alone, contemplate it in its simple and pure self, in so far as he is able, and in his imagination give it a shape distinct from all matter; and thus make it loving and dear to his soul, and there enjoy it; and let him keep it with him day and night, in every time and place, without fear of ever losing it, remembering always that the body is something very different from beauty, and not only does not increase beauty but lessens its perfection." (*Ibid.*)

not fear losing. The preface to his concentration on spiritual beauty is his ceasing to focus his attention on one woman. The courtier must first realize "how narrow a bond it is to be limited always to contemplating the beauty of one body only." He then must bend his efforts to

> form a universal concept . . . of that single beauty which sheds itself on human nature generally. And thus he will no longer contemplate the particular beauty of one woman, but that universal beauty which adorns all bodies; and so, dazzled by this greater light, he will not concern himself with the lesser, and, burning with a better flame, he will feel little esteem for what at first he so greatly prized.

During this phase the courtier's love becomes one directed to the "universal beauty." He ascends by using his intellect to contemplate itself, then angelic beauty, and finally divine beauty.[273]

There are two stages of this intellectual love. First, the soul is purged by the study of true philosophy and turns inward to the contemplation of its own substance. It becomes blind to earthly things, and acquires a very keen perception of heavenly things. But this is not the highest stage of all, for the soul still but "senses a certain hidden savor of true angelic beauty, and, ravished by the splendor of that light, begins to kindle and to pursue it so eagerly that it is almost drunk and beside itself in its desire to unite itself to that beauty, thinking to have found the footprint of God."[274] It then rises to its noblest part, the intellect, and leaves all sense knowledge behind. This first stage is still imperfect, for it contemplates this beauty only within its own particular intellect. The final stage of love is attained when "love gives the soul a greater happiness; for, just as from the particular beauty of one body it guides the soul to the universal beauty of all bodies, so in the highest stage of perfection beauty guides it from the particular intellect to the universal intellect. Hence, the soul . . . not only completely abandons the senses, but has no longer any need of reason's discourse; for, transformed into an angel, it understands all things intelligible, and without any veil or cloud views the wide sea of pure divine beauty, and receives it into itself, enjoying that supreme happiness of which the senses are incapable."[275]

Despite the gentle way in which the courtier treats his lady during his ascent, the critical notion that identifies his continuing motive is acquisitive desire.[276] He is, above all, seeking his own happiness and perfection.

---

[273] *Ibid.*, 67, p. 352, *passim.* See also p. 353; and 53, pp. 338–339.
[274] *Ibid.*, Book IV, 68, pp. 353–354.
[275] *Ibid.*, p. 354.
[276] The courtier is obliged to "obey, please, and honor his Lady with all reverence, and hold her dearer than himself, and put her convenience and pleasure before his own, and love in her the beauty of her mind no less than that of her body. Let him take care therefore not to allow her to fall into any error, but through admonishment

Though Castiglione's emphasis is always on the courtier as lover, there is some evidence that the reciprocal love of his lady is comparable in motive to his own.[277]

Benevolence is most apparent in the relationship between a prince and a courtier, rather than in the bond between a courtier and his lady. According to Castiglione, "good princes do not fear for themselves but for those whom they rule." The life of a good prince must be "so ordered as to partake of both the active and the contemplative life, *in the measure that is suited to the welfare of his people,*"[278] Castiglione even conceives of the rule of the good prince as an image of divine rule. He says that

> just as in the heavens the sun and the moon and the other stars exhibit to the world, as in a mirror, a certain likeness of God, so on earth a much liker image of God is seen in those good princes who . . . show to the people the splendid light of His justice accompanied by a semblance of His divine reason and intellect.[279]

The benevolence that is advocated is not devoid of self-interest, for Castiglione says that, if the prince follows a virtuous course in regard to his people,

> his subjects will be good and the prince will be much more occupied in praising and rewarding than in punishing; and his rule will be a most happy one both for his subjects and for himself—not imperious, like that of master over slave, but sweet and gentle like that of a good father over a good son.[280]

Similarly, the good courtier (symbolizing the prince's subjects) has his prince's welfare at heart when he deals with him: ". . . to bring or help

---

and good precepts let him always seek to lead her to modesty, temperance, and true chastity, and see to it that no thoughts arise in her except those that are pure and free of all blemish of vice." It does not seem that Castiglione thinks of the courtier's motive as truly benevolent, however, for he adds that "thus, by sowing virtue in the garden of her fair mind, he will gather fruits of the most beautiful behavior, and will taste them with wondrous delight." (*Ibid.*, 62, p. 348. See also Book III, 63, p. 269.)

[277] In the third book, Castiglione's spokesman, the Magnifico, says of a woman's love relationship to a man that "even as she is perfected by him, she also perfects him; hence, they come together in procreation, which neither of them can effect without the other." (*Ibid.*, 16, p. 217.) Another of Castiglione's spokesmen, Bembo, says, in the fourth book, that by behaving solicitously the "Courtier will be most acceptable to his Lady, and she will always show herself obedient, sweet, and affable to him, and as desirous of pleasing him as of being loved by him; and the wishes of both will be most virtuous and harmonious, and so they will both be very happy." (*Ibid.*, Book IV, 62, p. 348.)

[278] *Ibid.*, 24, pp. 308–309. (Italics added.)

[279] *Ibid.*, 22, p. 307. See also 31–33, pp. 315–317.

[280] *Ibid.*, 27, p. 312.

one's prince toward what is right and to frighten him away from what is wrong are the true fruit of Courtiership."[281] Castiglione summarizes the duties of a good courtier toward his prince as follows:

> . . . the aim of the perfect Courtier . . . is so to win for himself . . . the favor and mind of the prince whom he serves that he may be able to tell him, and always will tell him, the truth about everything he needs to know, without fear or risk of displeasing him; and that when he sees the mind of his prince inclined to a wrong action, he may dare to oppose him and in a gentle manner avail himself of the favor acquired by his good accomplishments, so as to dissuade him of every evil intent and bring him to the path of virtue.[282]

The benevolence of the courtier toward his prince also seems to be self-interested, since Castiglione asserts that "there is no good more universally beneficial than a good prince, nor any evil more universally pernicious than a bad prince." Hence, the courtier who helps guide his prince toward a path of virtue also aims at a concomitant benefit for himself.[283]

Just as Castiglione condemns the ruler or tyrant who rules a people solely for his own good, he also condemns the courtier who manipulates a prince to his own advantage. There "is no punishment atrocious and cruel enough for those wicked courtiers who direct gentle and charming manners and good qualities of character to an evil end, namely to their own profit, and who thereby seek their prince's favor in order to corrupt him, turn him from the path of virtue, and bring him to vice."[284]

Unlike the relationship of the courtier to his lady, that of the courtier to his prince is a form of friendship. About friendship as such, Castiglione has little explicit to say. But he does say that two factors are essential. One is that friends be alike in some degree.

> . . . reason doubtless requires that persons who are joined in close friendship . . . must be alike in their desires, in their minds, their judgments, and talents.[285]

Second, the good friend must also be benevolent, *i.e.*, ". . . active and diligent in serving and caring for the welfare and honor of his friends."[286] In general he must try to lead his friend to the path of virtue, insofar as he

---

[281] *Ibid.*, 5, p. 290. "And because the real merit of good deeds consists chiefly in two things, one of which is to choose a truly good end to aim at, and the other is to know how to find means timely and fitting to attain that good end." (*Ibid.*)

[282] *Ibid.*, p. 289.

[283] *Ibid.*, 10, p. 294.

[284] *Ibid.* See also 24, p. 308.

[285] *Ibid.*, Book II, 29, p. 124. See also p. 125.

[286] *Ibid.*, 30, p. 126.

knows it. But in so doing the friend also gains a good—that of having a friend. Since it involves the hope of reciprocity, the friend's benevolence is self-interested.[287]

The Book of the Courtier reveals a theory of love in which acquisitive and benevolent desire are both conceived as types of love. The clearest example of a lover whose affections are acquisitive is the sensual lover whose motive is sexual desire. The true friend is the clearest example of a lover whose affections are essentially benevolent. In the spectrum between these two extremes a number of other possible types of love are mentioned that can be classified by mode, *i.e.*, as essentially acquisitive or as essentially benevolent. In this sense, the theory satisfies the requirements of being "binary."

One may question whether Castiglione thinks of any and all inclinations that human beings have toward each other as instances of love. For, though he proposes a theory in which love is generically conceived as tendency and though he refers to the intemperate indulgence of the purely sensual impulse of sexual desire as wicked love,[288] he never refers to the motives of a bad prince or a bad courtier as love, not even as bad love or self-love. The problem here may be only rhetorical, for Castiglione, like many authors, repeatedly uses the term "love" in two distinct senses: as a neutral identifying term, and as a term of praise. Analytically, he defines love as tendency in general, and then qualifies his definition in terms of the love relationship he is discussing. So conceived, love is neither good nor bad *in itself*. But, rhetorically, he often uses the terms "love" or "friendship" to apply only to relationships that he thinks are proper and virtuous. This problem recurs throughout the literature, but in this case the analytical evidence seems conclusive despite rhetorical deviations. Love is tendency in general and not only those tendencies that aim at the right objects.

Bernard of Clairvaux

Bernard's *On The Love of God* is essentially a devotional treatise, but it does include some analysis and contains a theory of love. Though primarily concerned with supernatural love, Bernard advances a conception of natural love. Natural love may take the form of both acquisitive desire and benevolent desire. However briefly stated, we find a binary theory of natural love among human beings.

[287] The "supreme degree of friendship" is described as that which "yields all the good that life holds for us." Without it, "man would be far more unhappy than all other creatures." (*Ibid.*, 30, p. 125, *passim*.) In this connection, see *ibid.*, 29–30, pp. 124–126.

[288] See *ibid.*, Book IV, 52, p. 338.

Bernard lists four "degrees" of love:

1. Man loves himself for his own sake. This love is called "carnal."
2. Man loves God for his own sake, not for God's sake.
3. Man loves God for His own sake.
4. Man not only loves God for His own sake but does not love anything else, especially himself, except for God's sake.[289]

These loves are distinguished as of the "flesh" (*i.e.*, natural) or of the "spirit" (*i.e.*, supernatural). Only the first of the four degrees of love is natural.

Love is most generally described as one of four basic affections or activities of the soul. (The other three are joy, fear, and sorrow.)[290] Bernard understands love, fundamentally, as a certain kind of tendency. Even though he uses the term "flesh" to distinguish natural love from supernatural love, he signifies by that term both physical and nonphysical tendencies. Thus, even natural benevolent tendencies toward another are a function of man's "carnal" nature. At the beginning of his discussion of the four degrees he says that

> BECAUSE WE are carnal and are born of the concupiscence of the flesh, it follows as a necessary consequence that our desire for personal gratification, or our love [*amor*] should have its source in the flesh.

He then adds:

> But if it is directed according to the right order of things, advancing by its several degrees under the guidance of grace, it will at last be consummated by the spirit because: *that was not first which is spiritual, but that which is natural; afterwards that which is spiritual.*[291]

In the first degree of love "man loves himself for his own sake; for, he is flesh and he can have no taste for anything except in relation to himself."[292] Bernard observes that the first commandment of Christian love is to love God. But he adds that "since nature is rather weak and feeble, it is impelled at the bidding of necessity to serve itself first. And there is carnal love by which before all other things man loves himself for his own sake, as

---

[289] See *The Book of Saint Bernard On The Love of God*, Part I, Ch. XV, pp. 62–63. The fourth of these loves Bernard doubts is humanly possible even with divine aid. For Bernard's theory of supernatural love, see Part I, Ch. 3, *supra*.

[290] Compare Augustine who says that desire, joy, fear, and sorrow are the four ways in which love, underlying them all, expresses itself. See pp. 199, *supra*.

[291] *The Book of Saint Bernard On The Love of God*, Part I, Ch. XV, p. 62.

[292] *Ibid.*

it is written: *first . . . that which is natural; afterwards that which is spiritual.*"[293]

Self-love, or acquisitive desire, can stay within the bounds of natural necessity; it can also become immoderate and "overflow" the limits of natural personal need. Moderate or immoderate, it can involve using other human beings for one's own ends. (The first degree of love is also directed to the use of things.) Bernard sees the overflow of natural love as "held in check by the commandment that opposes itself to it: *Thou shalt love thy neighbor as thyself.* It happens, very justly indeed, that the sharer in nature should not be excluded from a part in grace as well, especially in that grace which is inborn in nature itself."[294] Here Bernard is not alluding to supernatural grace, since God is first mentioned in relation to love in the second degree.

In the first degree of love, unlike the other degrees, a human self, one's own or another's, is loved for its own sake, *i.e.,* without reference to God. Both a moderate acquisitive desire and a natural benevolence are possible and meritorious without God's active help, though such kinds of loves are far from the highest of which human beings are capable. Bernard argues that consideration for one's neighbor is a result of moderating acquisitive desire:

> And if indeed, according to the advice of the wise man, you turn away from your own pleasures, and according to the teaching of the Apostle, content with food and raiment, you find it no burden to withhold your love for a little while *from carnal desires which war against the soul;* surely, I think, what you take away from your soul's enemy you will find no burden to bestow upon the sharer of your nature. Your love will then be both temperate and just if what is taken from your own pleasures is not denied to your brother's needs. Thus carnal love is made to belong to our neighbor when it is extended to the common good.[295]

He emphasizes, however, that such love, though good, falls short of supernatural love.

> Nevertheless, in order that it may be perfect justice to love one's neighbor, it is imperative that it be referred to God as its cause.[296]

[293] *Ibid.,* Ch. VIII, p. 37. He also adds: "And it is not imposed by a command but implanted in nature; for who *ever hated his own flesh?*" (*Ibid.*)
[294] *Ibid.*
[295] *Ibid.,* p. 38. See also *The Steps of Humility,* Ch. 3, p. 131.
[296] *The Book of Saint Bernard On The Love of God,* Part I, Ch. VIII, p. 39.

6

Love as Acquisitive and as
Benevolent Desire: II

Authors whose theories are presented here hold (as do the authors whose theories were presented in the previous chapter) that there are two broad kinds of love, one characterized by acquisitiveness and the other by benevolence. Those treated in this chapter are: Søren Kierkegaard, Immanuel Kant, Max Scheler, Pitirim Sorokin, Sigmund Freud, Karl Menninger, C. G. Jung, and William James.

Søren Kierkegaard

Throughout the *Works of Love*, Kierkegaard contrasts Christian, or supernatural love, with earthly, human, or natural love. This controlling distinction of his analysis is both moral and analytical. He sharply differentiates Christian love, which is eternal, from earthly love, which blooms and perishes. That supernatural love is the better love, while natural love is always deficient, is Kierkegaard's major thesis.

Supernatural and natural love are distinguished in a variety of ways. The first and most obvious way is that in supernatural love God always is intermediate in a relationship between two persons. In natural love, the relationship is a direct one.

> *Worldly wisdom* believes *that love is a relationship between man and man; Christianity teaches that love is a relationship between man—God—man, that is, that God is the middle term.*[1]

Despite the fact that God is not an intermediary in natural relationships among human beings, Kierkegaard does not withhold the word "love" from some of them. Since, in his view, God *is* love, God is somehow present even in relationships in which He is not explicitly included.

> Love's secret life is in the heart, unfathomable, and it also has an unfathomable connection with the whole of existence. As the peaceful lake is grounded deep in the hidden spring which no eye can see, so a man's love is grounded even deeper in the love of God. If there were at bottom no wellspring, if God were not love, then there would be no quiet lake or human love.[2]

However, Kierkegaard adds:

> There is really a conflict between what the world and what God understand by love. It is easy enough to bring about an apparent agreement (as is already apparent in the use of one and the same word, "love"); on the other hand it is more difficult really to detect the disagreement; but this difficulty is inevitable if we are to know the truth.[3]

The two sharpest distinctions between supernatural and natural love that Kierkegaard makes concern the number that is loved in each case, and the respective motives.[4] Christian love by its very nature is universal;

---

[1] *Works of Love*, Vol. I, Ch. III, p. 87. Kierkegaard explains elsewhere that God is not merely in the middle but is the focal point of the whole love relationship: "The world can never get this into its head, that God does not . . . merely become the third party in every love-relation, but really becomes the sole object of affection, so it is not the husband who is the wife's beloved, but it is God; and it is the wife who is helped by her husband to love God, and conversely, and so on. The merely human interpretation of love can never get any further than reciprocity: the lover is the beloved, and the beloved is the lover. Christianity teaches that such a love has not yet found its right object—God. A love-relationship is threefold: the lover, the beloved, the love; but the love is God. And, therefore, to love another man is to help him to love God, and to be loved is to be helped to love God." (*Ibid.*, p. 99. See also pp. 92 ff.)

[2] *Ibid.*, Ch. I, p. 8.

[3] *Ibid.*, Ch. III, p. 97.

[4] He mentions other differences, claiming, for example, that Christian love is always "eternal" while natural love (even the best natural love) is inevitably transitory. "All other love, whether, humanly speaking, it withers early and is changed, or cherished it endures throughout the temporal existence, is nevertheless perishable, it

it is extended to all men, even to one's enemy.[5] Any love that discriminates among human beings is no longer a truly supernatural love. *"Earthly love and friendship are partiality and the passion of partiality."*[6] Drawing the contrast even more sharply, Kierkegaard says:

> Christian love teaches love to all men, unconditionally all. Just as uncondi-tionally and strongly as earthly love tends toward the idea of there being but one single object of love, equally unconditionally and strongly Christian love tends in the opposite direction. If a man with respect to Christian love wishes to make an exception in the case of one man whom he does not wish to love, then such love is not "also Christian love," but it is unconditionally not Christian love.[7]

He sees a necessary and intimate connection between the partiality of earthly or natural love and what he regards as its "selfishness," saying flatly that "selfishness and passionate partiality are essentially one."[8] Kierkegaard does not mean that all natural human love is acquisitive in character. He concedes and even emphasizes the possibility of a natural benevolence. But he distinguishes this natural benevolence from supernatural love in two ways: It can never rid itself entirely of self-interest, and is never extended to all men. It is extended to wife, friends, family, or even one's nation but not to one's "neighbor," *i.e.*, everyone.

> "To love the beloved," says Christianity, "is that to love?" And it adds, "Do not even the heathen the same?" "To love one's friend, is that to love?" says Christianity. "Do not even the heathen the same?" If therefore someone were to believe that the distinction between heathendom and Christianity lies in the fact that the beloved and the friend in Christianity are loved with a wholly different loyalty and tenderness than in heathendom, then this is a misunderstanding. Does not paganism also show examples of love and friend-

---

merely blooms. In this lies precisely its fragility and its sadness; whether it blossoms for an hour or for seventy years, it merely blossoms. But Christian love is eternal." (*Ibid.*, Ch. I, p. 7.) Christian love transcends even death. "Death can deprive you of a friend, because in loving your friend you are really united with the friend; but in loving your neighbor you are united with God, and therefore death cannot deprive you of your neighbor." (*Ibid.*, Ch. II, p. 54.) Any strictly human love that aspires to permanence or that is pledged for eternity must fall short. For, "this immediate love contains the eternal in the form of a beautiful fantasy, but it is not consciously grounded on the eternal, and therefore it can be *changed*. Even if it does not change, it still retains the possibility of change, for it depends on good fortune." (*Ibid.*, p. 26.)

[5] See *ibid.*, Ch. III, p. 119.
[6] *Ibid.*, Ch. II, p. 43.
[7] *Ibid.*, p. 41.
[8] *Ibid.*, p. 44.

ship so perfect that the apprentice poet goes back to them? But no one in
heathendom loved his neighbor. . . . What heathendom, then, called love,
as distinguished from selfishness, was partiality.[9]

Kierkegaard understands supernatural love to be wholly a matter of
giving. "The inwardness of love must be sacrificial, and consequently must
not demand any reward."[10] In contrast, the benevolence of natural love is
accompanied by a self-interested motive, even if it is a vicarious one. Thus,
in union or the desire for union, Kierkegaard finds numerous examples of
the impossibility of erasing self-interest entirely. In friendship he finds that
the similarity that exists or is desired between two friends precludes the
elimination of self-interest. One may seek to enhance the welfare of a
friend primarily for his own sake; but precisely because the friend is "the
other I" with which one is united, the interest of the self is always
involved.[11] In discussing the natural inclination to help another, Kierkegaard says, "We by no means wish to disparage this. Oh, even this merely
human sacrifice is perhaps met with seldom enough. But from the Christian standpoint, we must say that it remains standing at the halfway
mark."[12] The worldly distinction between selfish and altruistic love falls
short, and must fall short, of the Christian measure.

> The merely human consideration interprets love *either* merely as purely
> immediate love, as impulse, inclination (earthly love), as affection (friend-
> ship), as emotion and affection with one or another discriminating additions
> of duty, natural relations, custom and so on, *or* as something which is to be
> aimed at and acquired, because the reason perceives that being loved and
> favored is an earthly good, just as having men one loves and favors is an
> earthly good. All this Christianity is not really concerned with, either with
> the immediate kind of love, or with the convenient kind.[13]

The world, according to Kierkegaard, calls the purely self-seeking
"selfish." It should also call "selfish" the inclination in union that involves
the slightest trace of self-seeking. Such "union also demands sacrifice and
devotion from the one whom it will call affectionate; it demands that he

[9] *Ibid.*
[10] *Ibid.*, Ch. III, p. 107. The "inwardness of Christian love is willing, as the
reward of its love, to be hated by the beloved (the object of affection). This proves
that this inwardness is a pure God-relationship; it has no reward, not even the reward
of being loved." (*Ibid.*)
[11] See *ibid.*, Ch. II, pp. 47–48. "In its strictest sense selfishness at bottom loves the
other I, for the other I *is himself*." (*Ibid.*, p. 48. Italics added.) "But can *devotion*
and *limitless submission* still be *selfishness*? Surely yes, when the devotion is to the
other I, the other self." (*Ibid.*, p. 45.)
[12] *Ibid.*, Ch. III, p. 107.
[13] *Ibid.*, pp. 116–117.

shall sacrifice a part of his own self-love."[14] Such a union is "selfish," not only because it excludes God and one's neighbor but also because "that sacrifice, which is understood by men, truly has its reward in their approbation, and insofar is not the true sacrifice which must unconditionally be without reward."[15]

Commenting further on benevolence in regard to union in natural love, Kierkegaard discusses the problem of self and other, or "I" and "you," of "mine" and "thine." He argues that "the more completely the difference of 'mine' and 'thine' disappears, the more perfect is the love." He concedes that there "does take place in love and friendship an overturning of the selfishness which is moved by self-love and by this stubborn 'mine' and 'thine.' " In love, one "feels beside himself, outside of the ego." But, Kierkegaard argues, though the "mine" and "thine" merge into an "our," to some extent they still represent a "collective" self-love. Other selves are still excluded. In addition, in "earthly love and friendship the revolution in self-love is by no means radically deep enough; therefore the obstinate difference between 'mine' and 'thine' of the primitive selfishness still slumbers within it as a possibility."[16] The "earthly lover still seeks in a certain . . . sense his own, and thus he has a 'mine.' . . . Only spiritual love has the courage to be willing to have no 'mine' at all."[17]

Kierkegaard contrasts the self-interestedness of the best natural love with the total disinterestedness of supernatural love by saying that it is important *"that in loving the individual, actual man, we do not slip in an imagined conception of how we believe or might wish that this man should be."*[18] He also says that "the greatest benefit cannot be bestowed in such a

[14] *Ibid.*, p. 98. "However beautiful a love-relationship has been between two or among many, however absolutely this love has been to them the source of all their happiness and all their blessedness in mutual sacrifice and renunciation, whether all men have praised this relationship—if God and the God-relationship have been neglected, then from the Christian viewpoint it has not been love, but a mutually enchanting illusion of love." (*Ibid.*, p. 87.)

[15] *Ibid.*, p. 98. "One will sacrifice this or that or everything, but one still hopes that this sacrifice will be understood and have sense and meaning for men, who then must recognize and rejoice at one's sacrifices. One is willing to forsake everything, but still one does not think that along with that his sacrifice should be forgotten in the conversation and understanding of men." (*Ibid.*, p. 107.)

[16] *Ibid.*, Vol. II, Ch. IV, pp. 215–216, *passim*. See also Vol. I, Ch. II, p. 45.

[17] *Ibid.*, Vol. II, Ch. IV, p. 217.

[18] *Ibid.*, Vol. I, Ch. IV, p. 133. See also Vol. II, Ch. IV, p. 219. Further emphasizing the disinterested benevolence of the highest love, Kierkegaard says: *"Love seeketh not its own. For the true lover does not love his own characteristics; on the contrary, he loves every man according to his own characteristics; but the phrase 'his own characteristics' is exactly the expression for his 'own'; hence the lover does not seek his own; just the opposite, he seeks the other's 'own.' "* (*Ibid.*, p. 218.) He also says: *"Love seeketh not its own; for it chooses rather to give so that the gift looks as if the gift were the recipient's own possession."* (*Ibid.*, p. 222.)

way that the recipient comes to realize that he owes it to me."[19] The greatest lover is inconspicuous.

For Kierkegaard, all natural love is of the "flesh." Yet not all love of the "flesh" is carnal. Natural love includes the sensuous and nonsensuous acquisitive inclinations as well as the self-interested benevolent ones. The realm of spiritual love, of Christian love, is distinguished from the realm of natural love, the love of the "flesh," by the total absence of any self-interested motive at all.[20] Kierkegaard's theory of natural love among human beings includes both a form of love in which benevolence is essential and a form which is acquisitive, the latter differing more sharply from supernatural love. But, even without reference to supernatural love, Kierkegaard distinguishes the two modes of natural love on the scale of getting and giving:

> The different factors constituting love may be combined in very different ways in the individual, so that love as it exists in one may not be the same as in another; the egoistic may predominate more, or the sympathetic.[21]

Kierkegaard discusses some nonphysical expressions of mixed acquisitive desire, but he devotes most of his attention to the sensual form of acquisitive desire: sexual desire. He stresses the sheer acquisitiveness of sexual love by contrasting it with "romantic" love:

> Romantic love . . . presents an analogy to morality by reason of the presumptive eternity which ennobles it and saves it from being mere sensuality. For the sensual is the momentary. *The sensual seeks instant satisfaction.*[22]

Don Juan is taken as the prototype of this type of lover. Kierkegaard sees him as animated by a purely sensual desire, by a love that is not "psychic." Though Hercules is said to have taken "his whole family, which numbered

[19] *Ibid.*, Vol. II, Ch. IV, pp. 222–223.

[20] See *ibid.*, Vol. I, Ch. II, p. 42. Such love can be combined with carnal love in marriage. (See *ibid.*, p. 44.) "The Christian may freely marry, freely love his wife, especially as he ought to love her, freely have friends and love his fatherland; but nevertheless there ought to be in all this a basic understanding between himself and God in the Christian sense, and this is Christianity." (*Ibid.*, Ch. III, pp. 117–118.)

[21] *Either/Or*, Vol. I, p. 147. "We know very well that there is a selfishness which one may call faithless selfishness." (*Works of Love*, Vol. I, Ch. II, p. 46.)

[22] *Either/Or*, Vol. II, p. 19. (Italics added.) Kierkegaard adds that in order to produce the eternity of true love "a determination of the will is called for," thus implying that the sensual is the instinctive. (*Ibid.* See also p. 18.) Though not *per se* a supernatural love, conjugal love is superior to romantic love since it does not rest in a naïve eternity. ". . . conjugal love has its conflict in time, its victory in time, its blessing in time." (*Ibid.*, p. 119. See also pp. 81–83, 114–118.)

some fifty daughters, and . . . had his way with all of them in a single night," Kierkegaard maintains that "he is still essentially different from Don Juan, he is no seducer." Hercules is, in some way, "faithful." In contrast, Don Juan "is a seducer from the ground up. His love is not psychical but sensual, and sensual love, according to his conception, is not faithful, but absolutely faithless; he loves not one but all, that is to say, he seduces all."[23] The force by which he seduces "is the power of desire, the energy of the sensual desire."[24]

Another way Kierkegaard distinguishes supernatural from natural love is through the notion of union. In supernatural human love, union is desired in the sense that its aim is that all men should love God together, inasmuch as "in being a neighbor . . . all unconditionally resemble one another."[25] The union thereby achieved is the union of all who "have human equality before God."[26] This union is different from the union that merely results in a larger self.[27] "Love to the neighbor is spiritual love, but two spirits can never become one self in a selfish sense."[28]

Kierkegaard summarizes the contrast between supernatural and natural love in the following way: "Christian love must not be regarded as a more precise definition of what in paganism and elsewhere has been called love, but as a fundamental change."[29] That fundamental change does not alter the essentially tendential character of love. "To love without passion is an impossibility; but the distinction between earthly and Christian love lies therefore in the one possible eternal difference of passion."[30] That difference is shown most strongly in the distinction Kierkegaard draws between the voluntary tendencies of supernatural love and the tendencies of natural love, which are, to some extent, a matter of chance.[31] Christian love is also a matter of the highest moral duty, whereas earthly love and friendship, "as the poet understands them, involve no moral problem."[32] It is in this

[23] *Ibid.*, Vol. I, p. 76. "Psychical love is a continuance in time, sensual love a disappearance in time." (*Ibid.*, p. 77.)

[24] *Ibid.*, p. 81.

[25] *Works of Love*, Vol. I, Ch. II, p. 73.

[26] *Ibid.*, p. 50.

[27] Though the union striven for in supernatural love is the union of similarity, it may be either the union of complementarity or the union of similarity in natural love. "In earthly love and friendship the two love each other by virtue of their dissimilarities, or by virtue of their similarities which underlie the differences." (*Ibid.*, p. 47. See also *ibid.*, Vol. II, Ch. IV, p. 219.)

[28] *Ibid.*, Vol. I, Ch. II, p. 47.

[29] *Ibid.*, Ch. III, p. 116. See also p. 119.

[30] *Ibid.*, Ch. II, p. 42.

[31] See *ibid.* "Worldly or merely human reflection," observes Kierkegaard, "is familiar with many kinds of love. . . . In Christianity the converse is the case. It really knows only one kind of love." (*Ibid.*, Ch. III, p. 116. See also p. 119.)

[32] *Ibid.*, Ch. II, p. 42.

sense, therefore, and not in the sense of denying that supernatural love is tendential, that Kierkegaard writes:

> *Love is a matter of conscience, and hence is not a matter of impulse and inclination; nor is it a matter of emotion, nor a matter for intellectual calculation.*[33]

In other words, supernatural love is a moral obligation and not merely a natural impulse that comes over someone. The task of a Christian is to love everyone as a neighbor, *i.e.*, to love them regardless of the presence or absence of endearing characteristics that inspire natural love.[34] As a result, the judgmental aspect of love is reduced in supernatural love, whereas it is a very important part of natural love. Kierkegaard says that "there must be admiration in earthly love." But he observes that "Christianity has never taught that one should admire the neighbor—but one must love him."[35] On the other hand, judgment is also present in supernatural love in the form of what we have called respect. Love of neighbor overlooks differences among men, regarding them as "only a disguise." Christianity does not abolish such differences; it only wants the differences "to hang loosely about the individual . . . [so] that [the] essential other is always glimpsed in every individual, that common to all, that eternal resemblance, the equality."[36]

Kierkegaard presents, then, a tendential and binary theory of natural love among human beings in which cognitive notions are present. The admiration that is a part of natural love may give rise either to acquisitive or to benevolent desires; benevolent desires are always self-interested, to some extent. The dream of eternity that accompanies natural love impulses only can be realized when they are mediated by God, when they become a Christian duty, when they are uplifted to the highest ethical level.

Immanuel Kant

Kant distinguishes a love that is acquisitive desire from a love that is benevolent desire in a number of ways. On the one hand, he says that "we are loved, because of the advantages we bring to others and the pleasure we confer. We love that by which we gain advantage."[37] On the other hand, he says: "It is a very beautiful thing to do good to men from love to them

[33] *Ibid.*, Ch. III, p. 116.
[34] See *ibid.*, Ch. IV, p. 129.
[35] *Ibid.*, Ch. II, p. 45.
[36] *Ibid.*, pp. 72–73.
[37] *Lectures on Ethics*, "The Two Impulses of our Nature and their Concomitant Duties," p. 186.

and from sympathetic good will."[38] He also mentions beneficence that is inspired by "friendly inclination (love) to others."[39] All loves, in Kant's view, are inclinations whose origins lie in feelings or emotions. In his terms, all love is "motivated";[40] that is to say, all the actions of love proceed from motives such as need, personal affection, and natural kindness.

Though Kant distinguishes between love as acquisitive and love as benevolent desire, he denies that *all* acquisitive and benevolent inclinations are instances of love. He particularly excludes from the sphere of love any moral inclination. Any moral tendency is always a matter of duty, *i.e.*, of an inclination of a man's free will in accordance with the dictates of reason. The prime dictate of the practical reason, the categorical imperative, is to act in such a way that all men may act in the same way.[41] Such actions when performed because of love rather than duty are not moral. The realm of love and the realm of morality (as he understands them) are mutually exclusive.

> *Love* is a matter of *feeling*, not of will or volition, and I cannot love because I *will* to do so, still less because I *ought* (I cannot be necessitated to love); hence there is no such thing as a *duty to love*.[42]

Kant's position that love is not a matter of will or volition does not mean that all love is physiological or instinctive. What he means is that love is distinct from the will's free inclination to do a moral action, *i.e.*, an act performed whether a person likes or dislikes the object of the action. Love is always a personal motive. Such a motive may well be conscious and wilful. "Reason here occupies the place of a minister to natural inclination, and the maxim which is assumed on that account has no reference whatever to morality."[43] Moral action, in contrast, is done out of a sense of duty and is not influenced by natural inclination. Kant emphasizes that "all duty is *necessitation* or constraint, although it may be self-constraint according to a law. But what is done from constraint is not done from love."[44]

There is a sense in which Kant concedes that duty can be a motive, but

[38] *Critique of Practical Reason*, Part I, Book I, Ch. III, p. 175.

[39] *Preface to the Metaphysical Elements of Ethics*, Ch. VIII, p. 303.

[40] See *Critique of Practical Reason*, Part I, Book I, Ch. III, pp. 176–177.

[41] ". . . *Act as if thy maxim of thy action were to become by thy will a universal law of nature.*" (*Fundamental Principles of the Metaphysic of Morals*, Sect. II, p. 39.)

[42] *Preface to the Metaphysical Elements of Ethics*, Ch. XII, C., p. 312.

[43] *Of the Bad Principle in Human Nature*, Ch. IV, p. 354, fn. 2 (continued from preceding page). See also *Critique of Practical Reason*, Part I, Book I, Ch. III, pp. 178–180.

[44] *Preface to the Metaphysical Elements of Ethics*, Ch. XII, C., p. 312.

he distinguishes this moral motive from the motives of love insofar as it is strictly rational and unaffected by other influences, particularly those of sense.

> From the notion of a motive arises that of an *interest,* which can never be attributed to any being unless it possesses reason, and which signifies a *motive* of the will in so far as it is conceived by the reason. Since in a morally good will the law itself must be the motive, the *moral interest* is a pure interest of practical reason alone, independent of sense.[45]

When the motive of an action is the law itself (*i.e.,* the categorical imperative), the inclination may be acquisitive or benevolent.[46] Men may act morally to enhance their own welfare as long as they act in such a way that all other men may act in the same way. Thus, the moral law does not eliminate self-interest; it "only *checks* selfishness." The only difference between self-love and the rational pursuit of self-interest is the "propensity to make ourselves in the subjective determining principles of our choice serve as the objective determining principle of the will generally."[47] In other words, in self-love we allow our natural inclinations rather than our duty to determine our actions. Kant also observes that benevolence, "as a mode of action, may be subject to a law of duty." When so subjected it is disinterested. Since the actions of benevolent love and benevolence willed out of duty can be the same, disinterested benevolence "is often called (though very improperly) *love*"; for it "is a duty *to do good* to other men according to our power, whether we love them or not."[48]

Love, for Kant, may then be described as encompassing inclinations, propensities, and impulses that aim either at a good for oneself or at a good for another, and *that do not originate in the will's devotion to the moral law, i.e.,* are not purely rational determinations.[49] The will devoted to

[45] *Critique of Practical Reason,* Part I, Book I, Ch. III, p. 172. That such a motive is not comparable to ordinary and natural motives is seen in Kant's statement that "the moral law, as a determining principle of the will, must by thwarting all our inclinations produce a feeling which may be called pain." (*Ibid.,* p. 165. See also *Preface to the Metaphysical Elements of Ethics,* Ch. VII, pp. 301–302.)

[46] Though Kant thinks that rational self-love is consistent with a will devoted to duty, he does not think of it as a meritorious love. "Provided that, in furthering my own, I do not hinder my neighbour in his pursuit of happiness, I commit no moral fault, although I achieve no moral merit." (*Lectures on Ethics,* "Friendship," p. 201.)

[47] *Critique of Practical Reason,* Part I, Book I, Ch. III, pp. 165–166.

[48] *Preface to the Metaphysical Elements of Ethics,* Ch. XII, C., p. 312, *passim.* See also A., p. 310, and *Critique of Practical Reason,* Part I, Book I, Ch. III, p. 167.

[49] There are other limitations on the sphere of love. Though Kant discusses legitimate and illegitimate sexual desire, he never refers to sexual desire as an instance of love. (See *Lectures on Ethics,* "Duties Towards the Body in Respect of Sexual Impulse," pp. 165–167.) Whatever its limits may be, love is tendential for Kant. (See *Critique of Practical Reason,* Part I, Book I, Ch. III, pp. 164–168.)

duty is always, to some extent, in conflict with a person's natural inclinations, propensities, and impulses. The conflict is particularly intense when self-love and the obligation to enhance the physical and moral welfare of others run counter to each other, or when duties are imposed toward those who are hated. The conflict between self-interest and duty never can be resolved completely.

> In fact, if a rational creature could ever reach this point, that he thoroughly *likes* to do all moral laws, this would mean that there does not exist in him even the possibility of a desire that would tempt him to deviate from them; for to overcome such a desire always costs the subject some sacrifice, and therefore requires self-compulsion, that is, inward constraint to something that one does not quite like to do; and no creature can ever reach this stage of moral disposition.[50]

Though he mentions parental love, conjugal love, and filial love, Kant's principal application of the distinction between acquisitive and benevolent desire occurs in his analysis of friendship. He begins by stating: "There are two motives to action in man. The one—self-love—is derived from himself, and the other—the love of humanity—is derived from others."[51]

Partly because of the distinction between these two different inclinations, Kant concludes that there are three kinds of friendship. He calls them: friendships of need, of taste, and of disposition. The ideal of friendship against which he measures all of them is a familiar one: "The greatest love I can have for another is to love him as myself."[52]

The friendships of need and disposition are characterized by self-interested benevolence. "The friendship of taste," which Kant refers to as "a pseudo-friendship," is characterized by mixed acquisitive desire.

"The friendship of need comes about when men can trust one another in the mutual provision for the needs of life." Kant sees this mutual need as the foundation of the development of a friendship whose "finest sweets . . . are its dispositions of good-will." Such a "friendship presupposes a benevolent disposition and a helping hand in need."[53] The true friend,

---

[50] *Ibid.*, p. 176. Kant adds, however, that such harmony "must be the constant though unattainable goal of his endeavours." (*Ibid.*, p. 177.) See also *Preface to the Metaphysical Elements of Ethics*, Chs. VII–IX, pp. 300–306.

[51] *Lectures on Ethics*, "Friendship," p. 200.

[52] *Ibid.*, p. 202. Kant adds: "I cannot love another more than I love myself." (*Ibid.*) He does not mean by this that benevolence toward a friend is impossible, since he mentions a number of examples in which a friend is so motivated. What he means is that such benevolence does occur in friendship, but that it presumably is impossible when to seek the welfare of another deprives one of life. "If I cannot secure the happiness of my neighbour otherwise than by refraining from satisfying the needs of life, no one can place upon me the obligation of looking to his happiness and showing friendship towards him." (*Ibid.*, p. 203.)

[53] *Ibid.*, p. 205.

even in need, does not take advantage of his friend's benevolence. As a measure of his own benevolence, he refrains from asking for help. As soon as one person desires the other as a means of satisfying his own needs, "the friendship becomes interested and ceases."[54] Although there is no request for assistance, the friendship that is extended is extended in the hope that it will be returned, and to this degree the friendship is self-interested.

"The friendship of taste is a pseudo-friendship. It consists in the pleasure we derive from each other's company." Kant understands such a friendship as acquisitive in tendency (and, because it is mutual, probably as mixed acquisitive desire). "I am not attracted to another because he has what I already possess, but because he can supply some want of mine by supplementing that in which I am lacking." Of necessity, such a friendship can arise only among those who are different. The acquisitive tendency, then, may well take the form of the desire for the union of complementarity.[55]

The third type of friendship, "the friendship of disposition or sentiment," is "friendship in the absolute sense." It occurs among those who are alike in character and interests, each of whom acts as a confidant for the other's innermost thoughts. To such a friend "we can disclose completely all our dispositions and judgments, from whom we can and need hide nothing, to whom we can communicate our whole self." To have such a friend "is to have one who will help us to correct our judgment when it is mistaken."[56]

This friendship requires that the friends' "intellectual and moral principles must be the same, if there is to be complete understanding between them." On the basis of this complete understanding the need of each friend to "confide unreservedly" in another may be fulfilled. Desires that spring from deficiency are part of this relationship. But all the desires of any real friendship cannot, in Kant's view, be acquisitive. He says that we "shun those who, under the cloak of friendship, make a convenience of us."[57] More important than the desire to be helped is the readiness of the friends of disposition to help each other. Such "good-will," though not the essence of the friendship of disposition, is essential to it. And insofar as we seek to make ourselves worthy of friendship through the development of good character and the extension of goodwill, the benevolence involved is self-interested.

Toward the end of his discussion of friendship, Kant observes that: "It is

[54] *Ibid.,* pp. 203–204, *passim.* "My friend is magnanimous in being well disposed towards me, wishing me well and being ready to help me in my need; I, again, must be magnanimous in refraining from making demands upon him." (*Ibid.,* p. 204.)
[55] *Ibid.,* p. 205.
[56] *Ibid.,* pp. 205–206, *passim.*
[57] *Ibid.,* pp. 205–207, *passim.*

not man's way to embrace the whole world in his good-will; he prefers to restrict it to a small circle." In short, "friendship is not universal." Yet Kant insists that "any tendency to close the heart to all but a selected few is detrimental to true spiritual goodness, which reaches out after a good-will of universal scope."[58] This is, as we have already noted, the goodwill of duty in obedience to the moral law rather than the goodwill of love. Such goodwill also is, in Kant's view, a disinterested benevolence as contrasted with the self-interested motives of love and friendship.

Max Scheler

In *The Nature of Sympathy*, Scheler explicitly denies that his conception of love can be understood in terms of the *precise* meaning of most of the notions signified by our critical terms—particularly acquisitive and benevolent desire; the theory he propounds is decidedly atypical. Nevertheless, we believe that the notions signified by our critical terms are sufficiently applicable to Scheler's theory to classify it. That is to say that, with all the qualifications duly noted, we find in Scheler's work an approximation of a binary, tendential theory of love with an approximation of a cognitive aspect.

One of the principal difficulties in applying the distinction between tendency and judgment to Scheler's theory of love is that he strongly opposes the classification of all interior or psychological phenomena as either reasonable or sensuous. He thinks there are kinds of perception and judgment that are not strictly intellectual; and tendencies that are not sensuous or physical. Scheler takes this position against what he regards as the traditional and mistaken dichotomy between "reason" and "the sensuous," because he claims that it requires us to assign our whole emotional life, including love and hate, to the sensuous sphere.[59] Scheler, in contrast, associates himself with Pascal in holding that there is a kind of logic of the heart. He sees a regularity in emotions which is not entirely reducible to intellectual regularity. For him, love and hate form the highest stage of our *intentional* emotional life, a life that is removed from neutral or passive feelings.

While he affirms that love is essentially a tendency, movement, or act, he excludes from it all sensuous feelings. And, while he affirms that an important part of love is the awareness or discovery of value, he denies that this awareness or discovery is strictly intellectual. Since our notion of

[58] *Ibid.*, pp. 206–207, *passim*. See also *Preface to the Metaphysical Elements of Ethics*, Ch. VII, pp. 300–302.

[59] See *Der Formalismus in der Ethik und die materiale Wertethik*, pp. 84–85, for example. This work is subsequently cited as *Form*.

tendency certainly is not limited to sensual feeling, we find no difficulty in applying it to Scheler's theory. However, we cannot apply unqualifiedly the notions of acquisitive and benevolent desire. And, because our cognitive notions are such that we conceive them to signify functions of intellect or functions closely related to intellect, we also cannot apply them unqualifiedly. For these reasons we are able to classify Scheler's theory of love only as an approximation of a binary, tendential one with an approximation of a cognitive aspect.

Scheler understands love as a movement or tendency toward value that is distinct, on the one hand, from instinctive feelings and even deliberate acts of the will,[60] and, on the other hand, from purely intellectual cognition or judgment. He says that "love is not a 'feeling' . . . but an *act* and a *movement*."[61] He speaks of love as "an emotional gesture and a spiritual act."[62] Love and hatred are "acts, and acts of an elementary kind." They are also distinct from "spheres of feeling, conation and affect."[63] Above all, love and hatred are "*spontaneous*."[64]

> They are entirely *primitive* and *immediate* modes of emotional response to the value-content itself; so much so that, phenomenologically speaking, they do not even disclose a process of apprehending value (e.g., feeling, preference, etc.), let alone the making of a value—judgement.[65]

Love and hatred also "represent a unique attitude towards objects of value, and it is certainly not just a cognitive function."[66] Scheler denies that love consists of purely intellectual functions and that it necessarily is preceded by such functions. The values toward which love is directed are values of "personality," which, according to Scheler, can never be grasped solely by the mind or by the feelings.

> Love and hatred necessarily fasten upon the individual core in things, the *core of value*—if I may be allowed the expression—which can never be wholly resolved into values susceptible of judgement, or even of distinct apprehension in feeling. On the contrary, our standards for the appreciation of value-attributes are governed by our love or hatred of the things exhibiting these values; it is not our appreciation that governs our love or our hate.[67]

---

[60] See *The Nature of Sympathy*, Part I, Ch. IV, p. 71.
[61] *Ibid.*, Ch. XI, p. 141.
[62] *Ibid.*, p. 142.
[63] *Ibid.*, Part II, Ch. I, p. 148.
[64] *Ibid.*, Part I, Ch. XI, p. 142.
[65] *Ibid.*, Part II, Ch. I, p. 149.
[66] *Ibid.*, p. 148. "Love and hatred afford an *evidence of their own*, which is not to be judged by the evidence of reason." (*Ibid.*, p. 150.)
[67] *Ibid.*, p. 149.

Though Scheler denies that love can be identified precisely in the tendential sphere or in the sphere of judgment, he nevertheless presents a conception of love which is, in essence, tendential and which has a dimension or aspect that involves "apprehension" of value.

"Love applies, in general, to the entire range of objects within the domain of value."[68] Love among human beings has a specific kind of value which distinguishes it from love taken generally, *i.e.*, moral value.[69] Moral value consists in never taking the other merely as an object but always as a person, as someone who has the value of "personality."

Scheler insists that the value of personality is not the sum of qualities that a person may possess; rather, in each individual there is an inherent and unique value which is discernible only through love. The "essence of individuality in another person, which cannot be described or expressed in conceptual terms . . . is *only* revealed in its full purity by love or by virtue of the insight it provides."[70] Scheler insists that it "is never values we love, but always something that possesses value."[71]

In addition to identifying love as a movement toward value, Scheler makes another cardinal point about love in relation to value, particularly moral value: it involves some kind of apprehension or *"vision"* of that value. In this regard he says:

> . . . love is a movement, passing from a lower value to a higher one, in which the higher value of the object or person suddenly flashes upon us.[72]

He also remarks that "it is just this *vision* of a higher value that is of the essence of love."[73] But emphasizing the tendential character of love, he immediately adds:

> Love does not simply gape approval, so to speak, at a value lying ready to hand for inspection. It does not reach out towards given objects (or real persons) merely on account of the positive values inherent in them, and already "given" *prior* to the coming of love.[74]

[68] *Ibid.*, Ch. II, p. 162. See also Part I, Ch. XI, p. 141.

[69] See *ibid.*, Part II, Ch. II, p. 165.

[70] *Ibid.*, Ch. I, p. 160. See also Ch. III, p. 168; Ch. IV, p. 171; Ch. VI, pp. 181–185; and Ch. III, p. 166. Commenting on the generally accepted opinion that the lover idealizes the beloved, Scheler observes that this exaltation is not always what it appears to be: "It is usually only the 'detached observer' who arrives at this conclusion, because he fails to recognize the particular *individual* values present in the object, but discernible only to the sharper eye of love. The 'blindness' then, is all on the side of the 'detached observer.'" (*Ibid.*, Ch. I, p. 160.)

[71] *Ibid.*, p. 148.

[72] *Ibid.*, pp. 152–153.

[73] *Ibid.*, p. 153.

[74] *Ibid.*

There is, then, a sense in which Scheler conceives of love as a tendency insofar as he calls it a movement and an act as well as a sense in which this movement or act is accompanied by a perception of value.[75]

Scheler also claims that love is not only directed to and perceptive of value but that it is creative of value:

> Love only occurs when, upon the values already acknowledged as "real" there supervenes a *movement,* an intention, towards potential values still *"higher"* than those already given and presented. These additional advantages are *not* yet manifested as positive qualities, being merely envisaged concurrently as potential ingredients of a corporate structural pattern. In so doing, love invariably sets up, as it were, an *"idealized" paradigm of value* for the person actually present, albeit conceiving this at the same time as an embodiment of his "true" nature and "real" value.[76]

The distinction between acquisitive and benevolent desire, though applicable to Scheler's theory of love, is not one that he regards as crucial. Love is the same whether the person to whom it is directed be oneself or someone else. ". . . the primary orientation of love is towards values, and towards the objects discernible, through those values, as sustaining them; whence it is essentially a matter of indifference whether the values concerned belong to the self or to others. The basic contrast is therefore between love, whether of self or others, and hatred, of self or others likewise."[77]

For Scheler, love and hatred appertain essentially to value. His most concise description of them is cast, accordingly, in terms of value. After rejecting several traditional conceptions of love, he says that

> love is that movement wherein every concrete individual object that possesses value achieves the highest value compatible with its nature and ideal vocation; or wherein it attains the ideal state of value intrinsic to its nature. (Hatred, on the other hand, is a movement in the opposite direction.) We are not concerned here with whether the love in question refers to oneself or to others, or with any other distinctions which might be drawn in this connection.[78]

[75] Scheler does not call this perception of value a judgment. For him, judgment implies preference and comparison, which is precisely what he says does not happen in love. (See *ibid*. See also *Form*, pp. 274–275.)

[76] *The Nature of Sympathy*, Part II, Ch. I, pp. 153–154. Scheler insists that this higher nonexistent value is nevertheless a real one. Love is directed to it whether it exists or not. "Love is certainly a movement towards positive value, but so far as the *nature* of love is concerned it makes no difference whether this value already exists or not." (*Ibid.*, Part I, Ch. XI, p. 141.)

[77] *Ibid.*, Part II, Ch. I, p. 151. See also p. 150.

[78] *Ibid.*, p. 161.

So far as the *nature* of love is concerned, Scheler does not regard the distinction between self and other as an important one. However, in analyzing types of love, he does apply the distinction. "Love," says Scheler, "calls explicitly for an understanding entry into the individuality of *another* person *distinct in character* from the entering self, by him accepted as such, and coupled, indeed, with a warm and whole-hearted endorsement of 'his' reality as an individual, and 'his' being what he is."[79]

In terms of this distinction, both self-love and love for another are admitted to be meaningful concepts. What Scheler denies emphatically is that self-love can be identified *simply* with acquisitive tendency and that love for another can be identified *simply* with benevolent tendency. Scheler considers that self-love is "distinct from mere egoism."[80] First of all, the egoist is not concerned primarily with the inherent value of his person. He is concerned rather with what he can get and how he rates in competition with others. "It is typical of Egoism," says Scheler, "that it implies a *glance at other people*."[81] Egoism is invariably social; self-love, invariably a private matter.

> The egoist is a man so taken up with his "social self" that he loses sight of his individual private self. It is not that he loves this social self; he is merely "taken up" with it, *i.e.*, *lives* in it. Nor is his concern for his own values, as such (for it is only by chance that he finds them in himself); it is for *all* values, in things or in other people, but only *insofar* as they are, or might come to be *his*, or have something to do with *him*. All of which is the very *opposite* of self-love.[82]

Still, that there is a self-love in Scheler's theory is clear from his definition of love itself. Love is the movement of passing from lower to higher value, whether the love be of oneself or of another. If the love is for the self, the passage is from a lower to a higher personal value. Hence, in this sense, the tendency involved can be called acquisitive, even though another person is not employed merely as a means in that transition.

To assert that there is a type of love in Scheler's theory whose essence is benevolent tendency necessitates comparable qualifications. The most important qualification is that the tendency of love for another is not benevolent in the sense that one, through an effort of will, *deliberately*

---

[79] *Ibid.*, Part I, Ch. IV, p. 70. Scheler adds that in love "there is built up, within the phenomenon itself, a clear-cut consciousness of two *distinct* persons. This consciousness is not merely a starting-point of love, for it only reaches full maturity as love pursues its course." (*Ibid.*, p. 71.)

[80] *Ibid.*, Ch. XI, p. 141.

[81] *Ibid.*, Part II, Ch. I, p. 152.

[82] *Ibid.* See also Part I, Ch. II, pp. 26 ff, for Scheler's denial that love is merely extended egoism.

wishes to change and improve the beloved. " 'Benevolence,' " as Scheler
understands the term, "includes an element of *remoteness* . . . on the part
of the well-wisher, a certain 'condescension.' "[83] For him, it is more closely
associated with pity than with love.[84] He also understands benevolence as
directed to the enhancement of the *material* welfare of another. Thus, it is
separate from love, which he understands to be connected with the values
of personality. Furthermore, benevolence is said always to involve an effort,
whereas love is spontaneous.[85]

These objections to identifying love and "benevolence" occur in the
context of Scheler's criticism of "the entire school of British moralists." He
says that their effort "to derive the facts of *love* and *hate* from fellow-
feeling" or sympathy was one of their "gravest errors."[86] It must be noted,
however, that the "benevolence" Scheler criticizes is not precisely the same
as the notion of benevolence signified by our critical term. Our notion of
benevolence does not necessarily involve remoteness, condescension, sacrifice, pity, material welfare of the other, or wilful effort. It does not even
necessarily involve attempting to change the other, since a tendency that
points toward the good of another may have as its aim the preservation of
the other as he is. Most simply it means to care about another; it may take
either the form of trying to realize a potential good in someone else, or the
form of seeking to perpetuate or merely rejoice in the presence of an
actual good possessed by another person.

Thus understood, our notion of benevolence does have some applicability to Scheler's conception of love for another. "Love . . . is a movement pointing from a lower value to a higher one, though it is *not*
necessary for *both* values to be *given* in the process."[87] The lower value is
the value of personality the lover discovers in the person as he actually is.
The higher value is not the value the lover strives to realize in the beloved.
(For this reason the lover does not necessarily try to change the beloved.)[88] The higher value toward which love moves is neither the actual
value the beloved has as a living personality nor a potential value the lover
would like to see the beloved realize. It is a "being" of a different nature.

The "being" we are concerned with here is that *"ideal* being" postulated in
love which is neither an empirical and existential one, nor one which it
"ought" to have, but a *third* thing, which is as yet indifferent with regard to

[83] *Ibid.*, Ch. XI, p. 140.
[84] See *ibid.*, p. 144.
[85] See *ibid.*, pp. 140–141.
[86] *Ibid.*, p. 140, *passim.*
[87] *Ibid.*, Part II, Ch. I, p. 156.
[88] Yet, beneficence is admitted by Scheler to be a very common effect of love. (See
ibid., Part I, Ch. XI, pp. 140–141.)

this distinction; the same being that is implied, e.g., in the phrase "Become what thou art," which means something quite different from "Thou shouldst be thus and thus," while it is also quite different from the being of empirical existence, for what one "is" in this latter sense, one does not need to *become*.[89]

That ideal being or higher value toward which love tends, after being aroused by the lower value, is what the beloved, in some sense, really is. But, since love's tendency, even though it involves no conscious effort to change the other, is constructive rather than destructive (for thus is love distinguished from hate), we feel justified in calling it benevolent. It is benevolent in its general tone even though it may lack a specific objective or higher value.[90]

> For in love there is no attempting to fix an objective, no deliberate shaping of purpose, aimed at the higher value and its realization; *love itself, in the course of its own movement,* is what brings about the continuous *emergence* of ever-higher value in the object—just as if it was streaming out of the object of its own accord, without any sort of exertion (even of wishing) on the part of the lover.[91]

Sexual desire, as such, is excluded by Scheler from the realm of love. However, he makes a distinction between sexual desire (which he denies is "sensual love") and sexual love. In order to understand how he does so, it is necessary to consider the levels of tendency in his analysis. There are four:

1. *Sensuous*—arising from sensations of various parts of the body.
2. *Vital*—arising from the body as a whole, and corresponding to the upgrade or decline of life and health.
3. *Mental*—arising from the success or failure of mental life in its striving for knowledge, beauty, etc.
4. *Spiritual*—arising from the highest personal level of value and concerned with what is "holy."[92]

Scheler distinguishes three "forms" or levels of love corresponding to the last three levels of tendency.[93] He emphatically rejects the first level,

[89] *Ibid.,* Part II, Ch. I, p. 159.
[90] See *ibid.,* pp. 156–159.
[91] *Ibid.,* p. 157.
[92] See *Form,* pp. 341–355.
[93] In addition to distinguishing "forms" of love, Scheler also mentions "kinds" and "modes" of love. "Kinds" of love are distinguished by different emotional qualities rather than different objects. Thus, a childless woman can experience mother love. "Modes" of love are distinguished according to the various social dispositions that are often associated with love. (See *The Nature of Sympathy,* Part II, Ch. IV, pp. 169–174.)

claiming that merely " 'pleasant' things cannot be suitable for love, seeing
that they are incapable of an enhancement of value in the sense implicit in
the nature of love." Accordingly, he says that

> there is no such thing as "sensual love," so far as the word "sensual" in this
> expression is taken to denote a particular kind of love, and not just a way of
> saying that love, in this instance, is accompanied and interspersed with
> sensual feeling and emotion. A purely "sensual" attitude to a person, for
> example, is at the same time an absolutely cold and *loveless* attitude. It
> necessarily treats the other as merely subservient to one's own sensual feel-
> ings, needs and, at best, enjoyment. But this is an attitude wholly incom-
> patible with any sort of intentional love for the other, as such.[94]

Sexual desire is an accompanying aspect or part of sexual love but it is not
identical with sexual love. To love sexually one must move from the realm
of the merely sensual to the realm of vital emotions, which, *although they
are bodily, express the whole person rather than one appetite.* Such vital
emotions ultimately aim at neither physical pleasure nor procreation.

> Pleasure and procreation *may* also be aimed at, but there is no ethical reason
> why they should be. Pleasure should not be the primary aim, and it is only
> as a by-product of love-making, not as a goal and object, that it attains a
> depth and power of passion sufficient to produce a genuine fusion and
> identity of feeling. If the pleasure pursued is entirely self-centred, the
> phenomenon of fusion and identification is invariably absent. The partner
> then becomes simply a means of auto-erotic satisfaction.[95]

Scheler adds: "There is equally little justification for treating procreation
as the object; for one thing, because it is doubly immoral in this sphere to
employ another human being as a means to an end."[96] He also points out
that reproduction—where reproduction means the bringing into the world
of merely a greater *number* of human beings—can be accomplished by the
sexual instinct alone and does not necessitate the vital form of bodily love.
"The selfish pleasure-seeking of the voluptuary, the most loveless couplings
of the bourgeoisie . . . [can] 'preserve' the species."[97] A qualitative aim
in reproduction is, however, consistent with love.

> But they merely *reproduce*, whereas love *creates*. For love is simply an
> emotional assessment of a value, anticipated as offering the likeliest chance
> for the qualitative *betterment* of mankind. It is a sort of emotional project
> for man as he might be—a better creature than those who have preceded

[94] *Ibid.*, p. 170.
[95] *Ibid.*, Part I, Ch. VII, p. 111. See also Part II, Ch. I, p. 157.
[96] *Ibid.*, Part I, Ch. VII, p. 111.
[97] *Ibid.*, p. 113.

him; already a visionary moment of contact with the Eros of universal life itself, in its eternal travail and endeavour to bring forth that which is new and better and fairer than what has gone before.[98]

Of sexual love itself, Scheler says: ". . . sexual love is not just one kind of vital love among others, but the *archetype and basis* of them all, and, as it were, the key-function among them."[99] This is so because true "sexual love . . . is a *creative life-force,* the nobility of life eternally blazing the trail upwards and outwards from its present level towards a higher form of existence."[100]

Vital love, of which sexual love is the principal expression among human beings, has a wide range in Scheler's theory. It is operative in all *living* things. Man, says Scheler, "like other organisms, owes his existence, in an ultimate and metaphysical sense, to a *creative act of universal life;* an act for whose occurrence the business of procreation and all its attendant processes are merely the physical occasioning causes."[101] He maintains that every project of this universal life "is a creation of Eros, the life-giving, body-building principle which animates all life everywhere; and it owes nothing whatever to human volition, or even to human agency."[102]

Despite the fact that Scheler considers vital love or "Eros" an operative force in all living things, he denies that mental and spiritual love can be derived from it. For this reason he takes strong exception to the Freudian conception of *eros* as an *all-inclusive* cosmic principle operative in all things living and as the *only* principle of love operative in man.

Against Freud and others, Scheler argues: "As a function of the vital soul . . . sexual love can never acquire a more-than-vital value, to which the whole of life could or should be subordinated. . . . It can be no more than the finest flowering, the absolute *climax,* summit and peak of man's career as a vital being."[103] This is because there are two higher levels in man, the mental and the spiritual, above the level of vital emotion, and these are not determined by the vital level.[104] Scheler maintains that these two levels are integral and separate parts of man's nature. Thus, he claims that Freud (and Schopenhauer) are wrong in holding that sexual love is a mere "*superstructure* reared by repression upon the massive foundation of

---

[98] *Ibid.* See also pp. 114–115, 118; and Part II, Ch. VI, p. 193.

[99] *Ibid.,* p. 204. Scheler is not saying, of course, that sexual love is the basis of all love but only of all vital (bodily) love. He emphasizes that vital love, mental love, and spiritual love operate independently and from separate causes. (See *ibid.,* Ch. IV, pp. 170–171; and Part I, Ch. VII, p. 115.)

[100] *Ibid.,* p. 117.

[101] *Ibid.,* p. 112.

[102] *Ibid.* See also p. 119.

[103] *Ibid.,* pp. 114–115.

[104] See *ibid.,* p. 118.

the sexual impulse. They recognize it, not as a *primary* emotional function of the vital soul, able to discriminate and select among values, but merely as a product of the inhibition of impulse, and a spiritual elaboration of these inhibitions."[105] Freud, Scheler argues, is right *within limits* in his emphasis on sex:

> For sexual desire and love are *primary* factors in the system of our vital instincts and in the corresponding system of love-impulses; and they are also *fundamental*—as Freud has, on the whole, rightly discerned—in the sense that as this central impulse of life declines there is a *corresponding* loss of energy and relapse into a certain degeneracy and decay on the part of all the other kinds of vital love and vital instinct.[106]

But Scheler emphasizes that "the Freudian attempt to derive the various qualities of love from that single quality he calls 'libido,' must be regarded as a complete failure."[107] Sexual desire and sexual love, then, differ in at least one cardinal respect. "Sexual desire, as such, has an undiscriminating reference to the opposite sex, whereas sexual love is essentially selective, opting, in principle, for the 'superior' qualities of life."[108] Sexual love invariably moves toward value. It cannot be understood as a desire for a specific pleasure or as a derivative of an undifferentiated yearning for pleasure. Therefore, Scheler argues that "*we must restore the idea of the sexual act to that true metaphysical significance,* which has been denied to it only during a single brief period in the history of the West."[109]

Though Scheler does not relate acquisitive and benevolent desire to the desire for union, he does so relate sexual love. He speaks of the "emotional identity of human beings in the unity of universal life, whose natural aim and end in the biological order of development is their *loving union in the sexual act.*" And he adds that he considers such a union as "the only case of *mutual* fusion into universal life which we have so far been able to identify as normal to human beings."[110] Union in human sexual love even points beyond to a sense of unity with all living things.

> Let this be granted: and let it be conceded also that man's sense of unity with the living cosmos is in general so bound up with the sense of union in sexual love that the latter is, as it were, the "gateway" to the former; for it is not so much the foundation thereof as the means, prescribed by Nature

[105] *Ibid.*, p. 115.
[106] *Ibid.*, Part II, Ch. VI, p. 204.
[107] *Ibid.*, p. 205. See also pp. 196–209 for the complete criticism of the Freudian theory. Scheler groups this theory with others that he calls "naturalistic."
[108] *Ibid.*, p. 204.
[109] *Ibid.*, Part I, Ch. VII, p. 110.
[110] *Ibid.*, p. 109.

herself, of *arousing* in man a capacity for identification with the cosmos, which is not, in itself, at all dependent upon sexual love.[111]

The notion of union is crucial to Scheler's attack on those who claim that "fellow feeling" or sympathy is love. A projection into the situation of another that results in fellow feeling or vicarious emotion "completely excludes the sense of unity or true identification" which he associates with love. Because the tendencies that derive from fellow feeling are not movements toward value, they are not love. The emotion of sympathy "being based on a fellow feeling which takes no account of value, is itself unmindful of distinctions of value or love-preference between one man and another."[112]

While he rejects an indiscriminate love of humanity based on fellow feeling, Scheler nevertheless admits the possibility of a "general" love. It is based on a "union in essence" between man's finite spirit and the divine spirit. Inclusion of the former in the latter "assuredly provides the metaphysical foundation for the *possibility of non-cosmic personal love;* and this, in our opinion, is the natural basis of the Christian love of our neighbour." Such a love is different from the general love of humanity based on fellow feeling because "it is . . . directed to the *individual centre of being* in every spiritual person."[113]

As we noted earlier, Scheler thinks that human love occurs on three levels, independent of each other and arranged in hierarchical order: vital love, mental love, and spiritual love. The love on each of these levels may be directed to other human beings. Sexual love is that expression of vital, passionate, or bodily love that is a love among human beings. Vital love, in general, is described as "a movement tending to the enhancement of value from the base to the noble."[114] And sexual love is said to "be no more than the finest flowering, the absolute *climax,* summit and peak of man's career as a vital being."[115] Though Scheler admits that sexual love may combine with "friendship and metaphysical love of the person as individual," he insists that "it is a simple, *unanalysable and genuinely vital form of love*" and not a "*mixtum compositum.*"[116] Though it involves sexual desire, Scheler's "sexual love" does not aim primarily at pleasure but at the

---

[111] *Ibid.,* p. 127. The frequent result of sexual union—parenthood—also promotes this sense of unity. Participation in the creation of a new human being "comes to conscious awareness in the *feeling* of fusion and identity, the phenomenon of sinking together into union with the eternal Mother of all things living." (*Ibid.,* p. 112. See also p. 120.)

[112] *Ibid.,* Ch. VI, p. 101.

[113] *Ibid.,* Ch. VII, p. 128.

[114] *Ibid.,* Part II, Ch. VI, p. 180. See also Ch. IV, p. 169.

[115] *Ibid.,* Part I, Ch. VII, pp. 114–115.

[116] *Ibid.,* pp. 114–115, *passim.*

personal value realized in this singular expression of life and at the production of a better individual. Therefore, in terms of the predominance of either of these aims, it may point primarily to a good for the self or for another. Sexual love is on the lowest of the three levels of love and may be sacrificed for higher values.[117]

Mental love of the individual self, also called "Love of Soul," is concerned with cultural values.[118] When it involves another individual soul, it is manifested most clearly in friendship, marriage, and the family.[119] Scheler says it often occurs in old couples after sexual love has disappeared.[120] It also may aim at the realization of a personal value or of a value in another.

Spiritual love of the person, also called "Sacred Love," is concerned with the values of the holy and the profane. As it is said to be summed up in the scriptural command to love God and neighbor,[121] it obviously includes love among human beings. Scheler gives no indication that it presupposes supernatural aid. The sacred transcends all vital and mental values.[122] Nevertheless, as it conforms to the generic definition of love, it may also aim at the realization of a personal value or of a value in another.

Pitirim Sorokin

Sorokin treats love as a separate subject in a treatise devoted exclusively to it. His elaborate discussion and analysis of love, its causes and effects, its human and universal significance, its higher and lower forms, and its implications for other subjects constitute one of the most extensive treatments to be found in the systematic literature about love. *The Ways and Power of Love* is an ambitious attempt to subject to analytical schema a phenomenon that Sorokin claims has both a human and a cosmic dimension. Of "its many forms of being" he explicitly mentions the following: "religious, ethical, ontological, physical, biological, psychological, and social."[123] Sorokin's theory of natural love among human beings is found principally in his comments on the biological, psychological, and social aspects of love.

[117] See *ibid.*, p. 118.
[118] See *ibid.*, Part II, Ch. IV, p. 169.
[119] See *ibid.*, p. 171.
[120] See *ibid.*, Ch. VI, p. 184.
[121] See *ibid.*, Ch. IV, p. 171. For Scheler's discussion of Christian and humanitarian love, see *Ressentiment*, Ch. IV, pp. 114–136; and *On the Eternal in Man*, pp. 357–402.
[122] See *The Nature of Sympathy*, Part II, Ch. VI, p. 181.
[123] *The Ways and Power of Love*, Part I, Ch. 1, p. 3.

In his remarks on the ontological aspect of love, Sorokin contrasts it as a universal force with the force of chaos and strife; these fundamental forces constitute, for him, the basic polarity operative in all existing things. Love may be described broadly as tendency in general in the sense that it is all-pervasive. Described more precisely, it is all inclinations toward union. "Ontologically love is . . . one of the highest forms of a *unifying, integrating, harmonizing, creative energy or power.*" It is operative everywhere and everything is dependent upon it for its very existence.

> Everywhere in the inorganic, organic and psychosocial worlds the integrating and uniting role of love functions incessantly. Untiringly, it counteracts the dividing and separating forces of chaos and strife. Without the operation of love energy the physical, the biological, and the sociocultural cosmos would have fallen apart; no harmony, unity, or order would have been possible; universal disorder and enmity would have reigned supreme.[124]

The desire for union among human beings can take many forms. One of the principal ways Sorokin distinguishes these forms is in terms of the difference between acquisitive and benevolent inclinations. He employs this distinction not only as an analytical but also as a moral one. To go toward another for the purpose of gaining something for oneself is, though a genuine love, a love of a low order.

Sorokin applies this distinction most sharply in his discussion of the "supraconscious." The supraconscious is absolutely indispensable for the practice of "sublime love," the essence of which is benevolence. This love can be achieved only by identifying with, or striving to become like, the supraconscious. Sorokin describes this effort as follows:

> Widely varying in forms and details, the *essential part of this procedure consists in a progressively growing awareness by the maturing altruists that their true self is neither their body, nor their unconscious, subconscious, or preconscious energy, nor their bioconscious or socioconscious egos with all their trappings, but rather the supraconscious, whatever name and properties they give to it. The supraconscious is the embodiment of the altruist's very highest ideal. It is his highest value.* In this sense it is his Absolute. As to the name, the supraconscious is called by widely different names by various altruists.[125]

The names given to the supraconscious vary from personal to metaphysical to mystical to psychological and ethical. One of the most frequent names is

---

[124] *Ibid.*, p. 6. In this connection Sorokin notes: "According to Solovyev and others, the physical counterpart of love in the inorganic world is shown in all physical forces that unite, integrate, and maintain the whole inorganic cosmos in endless unities, beginning with the smallest unity of the atom and ending with the whole physical universe as one unified, orderly cosmos." (*Ibid.*, pp. 8–9.)

[125] *Ibid.*, Part III, Ch. 9, pp. 145–146.

God. To say then that God is love is to say that God is the disinterested benevolence to which *"maturing altruists"* aspire. These men strive for progressive identification with the supraconscious.

Every normal man has the supraconscious in him to some degree. Every individual has moments when he is dominated by it, when his ego is forgotten "in the sublimest altruistic sacrifice."[126] Some men have it to a very high degree. Sorokin calls these men "the inspired apostles of love . . . the great moral teachers of humanity . . . [the] founders of all genuine religions . . . the true sages, seers, and prophets of practically all countries, cultures, and periods." Of these he says:

> In slightly different terms like love, compassion, sympathy, mercy, benevo-
> lence, reverence, friendship, Eros, Agape, the Golden Rule, mutual aid, co-
> operation, and so on, they unanimously affirm the supreme love as the
> highest moral value and its imperatives as the universal and perennial moral
> commandments.[127]

The benevolence of supreme love is contrasted in a number of ways with the acquisitiveness of "ego-centered" love:

> Supreme love transcends our conscious egos and their rational—hedonistic,
> utilitarian, and eudaemonistic—interests. If it remains ego-centered it is not
> supreme altruistic love but its low-grade modicum. Supreme love often urges
> a sacrifice of the important interests of our egos. Once in a while it dictates
> even a free sacrifice of the life of the individual.[128]

There is little doubt that the notion of disinterested benevolence characterizes the supreme love which is the touchstone of Sorokin's morality.[129]
There is, however, some problem in classifying this disinterested benevolence as a supernatural or a natural human love. Supernatural human love
is, as we describe it, a love of which human beings are incapable without
divine aid (in theological terms, without the gift of grace from an infinite
and personal God). Sorokin does say that *"supreme love can hardly be
achieved without a direct participation of the supraconscious,"*[130] yet he
does not specify just what form the "participation" of the supraconscious
takes. Further, he claims that the transcendent God of revealed religion is
only one form that the supraconscious has taken in the minds of men. For

126 *Ibid.*, Part II, Ch. 6, p. 113.
127 *Ibid.*, Part V, Ch. 23, p. 485.
128 *Ibid.*, Part III, Ch. 8, p. 126.
129 *"The purity of love ranges from the love motivated by love alone—without the
taint of a 'soiling motive' of utility, pleasure, advantage, or profit, down to the 'soiled
love' where love is but a means to a utilitarian or hedonistic or other end."* (*Ibid.*,
Part I, Ch. 2, p. 17. See also Part III, Ch. 8, p. 126.)
130 *Ibid.*, p. 125.

him, the supraconscious is also the *sine qua non* of not only the highest love but the highest achievement in philosophy, in science, in the fine arts, and in other fields of human endeavor.[131] Though Sorokin says that the "forces of the unconscious (in man) and of the conscious egos cannot generate supreme love as they cannot produce the supreme achievements in other fields of creativity," we are unable to determine whether the transcending of the conscious by man is accomplished by his own efforts or through the *active* help of a power greater than he.[132] We are, accordingly, unable to classify the supreme love that Sorokin discusses as either a supernatural or a natural human love.

At one point in his discussion of the religious aspect of love, Sorokin does identify the supreme love made possible by the supraconscious as a supernatural love, *i.e.*, as a love by the infinite God of revealed religion or as a human love made possible by divine help. In commenting on the sharp distinction made by Anders Nygren between *agape* (God's love springing from His fullness) and *eros* (human love springing from deficiency and need), Sorokin observes that this distinction has seldom been made so incisively in describing the proper love for human beings. In general, he claims, the view has been taken that the proper religious love is a combination of both *eros* and *agape*. That is, man by his own efforts can get closer to God but he also needs God's grace in the process.[133]

> To sum up: properly understood, self-centered love, as an effort of man to liberate in himself his real and divine self and to reach union with God, and God-centered love, as divine grace helping man in this endeavor, are given in practically all true systems of love, oriental and occidental, though some systems stress the Agape, and others the Eros.[134]

Yet Sorokin does not say that supreme love is exhausted by religious love, nor does he say that the human achievement of supreme love always presupposes supernatural aid.

Whether or not the disinterested benevolence, which identification with the supraconscious makes possible, is a natural love among human beings does not change the classification of Sorokin's theory as binary. It includes a type of love that is strictly acquisitive in tendency, as well as a type of love that is benevolent in tendency yet distinct from the supreme love at the apex of his system.

Acquisitive desire is mentioned in relation to love in at least two forms:

[131] See *ibid.*

[132] *Ibid.*, p. 126. See also Part II, Ch. 6, pp. 98–100, 112–114, where characteristics of the supraconscious are discussed.

[133] See *ibid.*, Part I, Ch. 1, pp. 3–5.

[134] *Ibid.*, p. 6.

sexual desire and mixed acquisitive desire. Any biological process that aims at the preservation of life is an act of love. "The biological counterpart of love energy manifests itself in the very nature and basic processes of life."[135] And the principal biological process that occurs among human beings is the sexual process.

> Co-operation of two organisms in sexual reproduction of multicellular organisms, accompanied by the passion of biological attraction between them, is a visible form of this "biological love" necessary for the maintenance of all such species and, through that, of life itself.[136]

Sorokin regards such biological love, *i.e.*, sheer sexuality unconnected with enlightened, psychological love, as impure.[137] It is a love "motivated by utilitarian considerations, hedonistic expectations, and other selfish advantages," and lasts "only as long as these utilities, pleasures, and advantages are forthcoming."[138] In the same vein, he says:

> Heterosexual love motivated exclusively by sex pleasure lasts, as a rule, only as long as the libidinal pleasure continues. When it fades, or when erotic pleasure from copulation with another person becomes more attractive, such sexual love dies. Marriages based on it crumble; "romances" fade.[139]

Sorokin by no means limits "soiled" love, *i.e.*, acquisitive desire, to physical relationships among human beings. As he sees it "millions of cases of love . . . invariably are a variety of 'soiled love' in which selfish, utilitarian, and hedonistic motivations are conspicuous. . . . By their very nature these are selfish and almost always are planned to get as much as possible for as little as possible."[140] In their social rather than personal expression such impulses take the form of convenient friendships in which whatever is given is given reluctantly or only as a necessary price for getting. "There are millions of superficial friendships motivated merely by threat of punishment, by conscious considerations of convenience, utility, pleasure, or profit.[141]

---

[135] *Ibid.*, p. 9.

[136] *Ibid.* Sorokin also comments on what he considers another biological relationship: "The parental care of the offspring, during its period of helplessness—the care that in some species, like *Homo sapiens*, must last several years—is a still more explicit manifestation of biological love energy." (*Ibid.*)

[137] See *ibid.*, Ch. 2, p. 34. Nevertheless, Sorokin says that "without the operation of a biological counterpart of love energy, life itself is not possible, nor its continuity, nor the preservation and survival of species, nor life evolution, nor the emergence and evolution of *Homo sapiens*." (*Ibid.*, Ch. 1, p. 9.)

[138] *Ibid.*, Ch. 2, p. 34.

[139] *Ibid.* See also pp. 28–29.

[140] *Ibid.*, p. 28.

[141] *Ibid.*, Part III, Ch. 8, p. 125.

Prominent among such social loves or convenient friendships Sorokin finds the impulse toward social cohesion for the sake of a personal good. These relationships are entered into for the sake of what one can get out of them and last only as long as they provide what is expected of them. "Any love or alliance of persons or groups that is based on the hatred of a common foe is . . . short-lived. Once the common enemy has disappeared that 'love,' 'alliance,' or 'mutual aid' of the previously allied parties quickly dies out." Sorokin adds: "For the same reason many . . . 'brotherhood' communes, communities, associations, and sects turn out to be short-lived as soon as the profits, pleasures, and advantages of their 'love' and 'brotherhood' fade."[142]

The natural love in Sorokin's theory which is distinct, on the one hand, from the "soiled" or "low" forms of love mentioned above (acquisitive desire) and, on the other hand, from the complete altruism of supreme love (disinterested benevolence) is a love characterized by a benevolence not unmixed with self-interest. In discussing this love, Sorokin speaks frequently in terms of union and the desire for union.

In true love, it is through the higher form of the desire for union that a good for another *and* for the self are realized. Sorokin leaves little doubt as to whose good is primary in such love. He says that *"love as a psychological experience is 'altruistic' by its very nature."* But he also says that:

> In any genuine psychological experience of love, the ego or I of the loving individual tends to merge with and to identify itself with the loved Thee. The greater the love, the greater the identification. The joy or sorrow of the loved person becomes joy and sorrow to the loving person. Genuine sharing of all the values of life follows. Sacrifice for the loved person becomes a sacrifice for the person himself.

Hence, there is a sense in which the true love of which Sorokin speaks, though essentially benevolent in character, has also, through the sharing of goods made possible by union, an admixture of good for the self. While maintaining strongly that in "a genuine love the loved person is experienced always as the *end* value" and that "in the egoistic experience the other person is always only the *means* value,"[143] Sorokin does not entirely exclude self-interest in the higher love. However, the lover can anticipate a personal good for himself without tarnishing his love only if such anticipation is of sharing the good he does for another, and if such anticipation is subsidiary to his altruistic motive.

[142] *Ibid.,* Part I, Ch. 2, p. 34.
[143] *Ibid.,* Ch. 1, p. 10, *passim.*

In a love relationship, the egos of the parties are freely merged into one "we"; the joys and sorrows of one party are the joys and sorrows of the other(s). . . . Each party gladly does and gives anything for the well-being of the other party. There is no bargain, nor calculation of profits, pleasures, and utilities.[144]

Or, as Sorokin also says:

. . . *love is a meaningful interaction—or relationship—between two or more persons where the aspirations and aims of one person are shared and helped in their realization by other persons.* A loving person not only does not hinder the realization of the wise aims of the loved person but positively helps it. So far as he helps, he does not cause pain or sorrow to the loved person, but increases his happiness. It is the joy of giving and the joy of receiving; it is fulfilling oneself in others and by others.[145]

Sorokin specifies several goods that the lover can achieve through the uniting and altruistic tendencies of his love. First of all, he can escape his own loneliness and thus enhance and enrich his own life by participating in "the highest life of humanity." Second, love will beautify his life since he will beautify that which he loves and has become united with. Third, because *"love is goodness itself"* loving will make him *"noble and good."* Finally, he will experience *"freedom at its loftiest,"* since "to love anything is to act freely, without compulsion or coercion."[146]

The range of love in Sorokin's theory is from the disinterested benevolence of "sublime love" to the self-interested benevolence of higher or "true" love to the acquisitiveness of "soiled" or "low" love. Natural love among human beings seems to encompass two types of love: self-interested benevolence and acquisitive desire, either simple or mixed. Psychological love may be either benevolent or acquisitive in tendency. Physical or biological love is always acquisitive in tendency and its prime expression is sexual desire. Encompassing all of these tendencies is the notion of the desire for union. Anyone who loves another person seeks union with him, either for his own or the other's good.

The principal form of love among human beings is psychological love. Of this form, Sorokin says: "Psychologically the experience of love is a complex consisting of emotional, affective, volitional, and intellectual elements." Since Sorokin mentions admiration and respect as elements that "color" love as a psychological experience, his theory of natural love among

[144] *Ibid.,* Ch. 4, p. 76.
[145] *Ibid.,* Ch. 1, p. 13.
[146] *Ibid.,* p. 11, *passim.*

human beings, though primarily a tendential one, also has a judgmental aspect.[147]

As part of his analytical schema, Sorokin sets out five categories (or "dimensions"), which he says helps us to classify and understand better the phenomena included under psychological love: "(1) the intensity of love; (2) its extensity; (3) its duration; (4) its purity; (5) the adequacy of its objective manifestation in overt actions and material vehicles in relation to its subjective purpose."[148] By the "adequacy" of love Sorokin means the degree to which the intention of the lover and his actions are in harmony. In other words, the lover may have genuine benevolent intentions but the actions to which these give rise defeat their own aims. Thus, mothers often spoil their children. Conversely, a person may have no benevolent intentions at all and yet do things that are highly beneficent. Thus, a researcher, motivated only by interest in his work, may discover a drug that alleviates a great deal of human suffering. The "intensity" of love is the degree to which it dominates and excites the energies of a person. The "extensity" of love is the number of people loved. The "duration" of love is, of course, how long it lasts. The "purity" of love is the degree to which it approaches the disinterested benevolence of sublime love.[149]

Sorokin sets up a number of possible relationships between these factors. For example, with a given love and under certain circumstances the intensity of love varies inversely with its extensity: love is often very intense toward a small group (*e.g.*, one's own family).[150] He also says that, when love is not replenished (*e.g.*, by reciprocity), its intensity tends to decrease with its duration.[151] Perhaps his most revealing application of

---

[147] See *ibid.*, pp. 9–10. The judgmental aspect of love can include not only admiration and respect but also valuation. In true love, for example, the lover must not only esteem the beloved but make the additional judgment that the welfare of the other is important to him, *i.e.*, that he or she is someone for whom he, the lover, would extend himself. (See *ibid.*, Part III, Ch. 10, pp. 175–178. See also Part I, Ch. 2, p. 35.)

[148] *Ibid.*, p. 15.

[149] *Ibid.*, pp. 15–19.

[150] See *ibid.*, pp. 19–20.

[151] See *ibid.*, pp. 24–25. Taking only intensity and extensity, Sorokin draws seven applications: "1. There are many persons whose love is very intense toward a small in-group (their family, their friends, their clique or sect or faction), but whose love for anybody beyond this little universe is nonexistent. The extensity of their love is thus very low. 2. There are many persons who profess to love the whole of humanity. The extensity of their love is thus enormous. But their love of humanity rarely goes beyond speech-reactional declarations, and shows little in their deeds. This is *love of low intensity combined with vast extensity*. 3. There are persons who most intensely love their little in-group, then love *but in a decreasing degree of intensity* various larger groups: their neighbors, their village or town, their occupational or political or religious or national or state groups, then all humanity. This is a type of love decreasing in intensity as it increases in extensity. 4. We all know love actions of the *highest intensity* but of *very short duration*. A soldier impulsively risking his life to

this device is his analysis of the nature of conflict among human beings in relation to the extensity of their love.

Given reasonable purity, intensity, duration, and adequacy of love, Sorokin understands "intergroup warfare" to result from the lack of extensity. The "tragedy of tribal altruism" is that "an exclusive love of one's own group makes its members indifferent or even aggressive towards other groups and outsiders."[152] An "in-group altruism" inevitably means "an out-group egoism." Sorokin emphasizes the human need to move from tribal egoism to universal altruism, and considers parochial love, even if it is true love, to be among the most serious of continuing human problems.

> The result is a relentless intergroup struggle for existence and domination. Whether in the form of a cold or a hot war, this intergroup warfare has gone on incessantly in human history, and has filled its annals with the most deadly, most bloody, and most shameful deeds of Homo sapiens. An exclusive tribal solidarity—known also as tribal patriotism, tribal loyalty, and tribal altruism—has mercilessly set man against man, and group against group. It has killed more human beings and destroyed more cities and villages than all the epidemics, hurricanes, storms, floods, earthquakes, and volcanic eruptions taken together. It has brought upon mankind more suffering than any other catastrophe. Tribal solidarity has been the greatest curse and the most merciless Nemesis of humanity's tribal egoism and moral stupidity. It has been responsible for all the interstate and interreligious wars, and for all the interracial, interethnic, intertribal, intercaste, and interclass wars, as well as for all the cold wars between masters and slaves, patricians and plebeians, nobility and serfs, the rich and the poor, the privileged and the underdogs, the rulers and the ruled, capitalists and proletarians, labor and management, "the chosen" and "the inferior people," and for hundreds of other intergroup conflicts. Mountains of corpses and seas of human blood have been sacrificed to the Moloch of warfare of exclusive tribal solidarities. In an endless rhythm of today's victors and tomorrow's victims, the groups have been succeeding one another in this

---

save his comrade on a battlefield is such a case. Many are heroes of love for a short moment; only a few are such for a long time! 5. There are persons *who love for a long time but with a low intensity*. Persons who for years contribute their reasonable donation to a community fund are examples of this type. Most 'American Good Neighbors' in my collection of some 1,000 cases belong to this type. 6. There are persons who love intensely, and for an indefinitely long time, either a small or an extensive human universe. 7. We have love activities in which *high purity* is combined with high or low intensity, small or vast extensity, short or long duration, low or high adequacy; and similar combinations of *low purity* with other dimensional values. Which of these combinations is more frequent in an ordinary human universe remains unknown and can be learned only by systematic studies as have yet hardly been begun." (*Ibid.*, pp. 19–20.)

[152] *Ibid.*, Part V, Ch. 23, pp. 459, 461, *passim*.

process of mutual extermination. And as long as tribal altruism–egoism continues, the intergroup warfare is bound to continue also.[153]

Sigmund Freud

We must distinguish, at the outset, between Freud's discussion of human love and his discussion of love as a cosmic force. In most of his works, Freud, writing as a clinical psychologist, is concerned with the problems of understanding the nature, development, deviations, and perfection of human love. Accordingly, most of his discussions of love are cast in human terms. But in his works *Beyond the Pleasure Principle* and *Civilization and Its Discontents,* he extends his conception of love—or rather its applicability—to all forms of life.[154] In short, love is not just a psychic phenomenon. Or, if it is, Freud considers a metaphorical application of the concept to nonhuman life as perfectly justifiable. He refers to the life instinct in any being as *eros,* or love. *Eros* includes all tendencies on the part of all living things to preserve life. Through *eros* all organic beings strive to retain their living unity, to avoid the destruction of, or separation of, their component parts and to resist the return to the primal estate of inorganic matter. *Eros* "holds together all things living."[155]

Two qualifications must be placed on the description of the Freudian theory of love as tendency in general. First, love is only present in living things; it is never predicated of the natural tendencies of inorganic matter. Second, not all tendencies of living beings are instances of love, but only those that have the preservation or strengthening of life as their aim.

Freud postulates the existence of two basic tendencies in all living beings. One, the life instinct, is love; the other, the death instinct, is not love.

> After long doubts and vacillations we have decided to assume the existence of only two basic instincts, *Eros* and *the destructive instinct.* . . . The aim of the first of these basic instincts is to establish ever greater unities and to preserve them thus—in short, to bind together; the aim of the second, on the contrary, is to undo connections and so to destroy things. We may suppose that the final aim of the destructive instinct is to reduce living things to an inorganic state. For this reason we also call it the *death instinct.*[156]

[153] *Ibid.,* p. 461. See also Part I, Ch. 3, pp. 36–46, esp. pp. 42–43.
[154] See *Beyond the Pleasure Principle,* Chs. V–VI, pp. 41–79; and *Civilization and Its Discontents.*
[155] *Beyond the Pleasure Principle,* Ch. VI, p. 64. See also Ch. V, pp. 11–17.
[156] *An Outline of Psychoanalysis,* Part I, Ch. 2, p. 20. "If we suppose that living things appeared later than inanimate ones and arose out of them, then the death instinct agrees with the formula that we have stated, to the effect that instincts tend toward a return to an earlier state." (*Ibid.,* pp. 20–21.)

The battle between the life and death instincts is the principal touchstone employed by Freud to explain not only human development but also the whole range of living phenomena from the mechanics of the cell structure of the lowest forms of organic life to the highest peaks of human civilization. He names this opposition *"Eros-Thanatos,"* the struggle between love and death.

In commenting on the whole course of human history, Freud says:

> It must present to us the struggle between Eros and Death, between the instincts of life and the instincts of destruction, as it works itself out in the human species. This struggle is what all life essentially consists of.[157]

Freud actually puts forth two conceptions of love. The first of these is identical with his conception of love as a cosmic principle and is much the broader of the two. It includes all the tendencies that strengthen and preserve life in man; it signifies, basically, primitive, undifferentiated human energy, or what Freud calls "libido."[158] Using this conception, Freud discusses a number of the phenomena that colloquially are called love or are associated with love, and he approves of gathering them under a single term. Within the context of his own work he gives a number of examples of what he considers love: the discontent of a hungry or uncomfortable infant, the impulse toward the sexual act, perversion, conceit, patriotism, artistic creation, religious worship—indeed, the very course of human civilization. In commenting on the differing manifestations of love, he says:

> Libido is an expression taken from the theory of the emotions. We call by that name the energy (regarded as a quantitative magnitude, though not at present actually mensurable) of those instincts which have to do with all that may be comprised under the word "love." The nucleus of what we mean by love naturally consists (and this is what is commonly called love, and what the poets sing of) in sexual love with sexual union as its aim. But we do not separate from this—what in any case has a share in the name "love"— on the one hand, self-love, and on the other, love for parents and children, friendship and love for humanity in general, and also devotion to concrete objects and to abstract ideas.

He concludes by saying:

> We are of the opinion, then, that language has carried out an entirely justifiable piece of unification in creating the word "love" with its numerous

157 *Civilization and Its Discontents*, Ch. VI, p. 75.
158 See *An Outline of Psychoanalysis*, Part I, Ch. 2, pp. 22–24.

uses, and that we cannot do better than take it as the basis of our scientific discussions and expositions as well.[159]

Libido is invariably acquisitive. For Freud, acquisitive desire is the most fundamental and controlling tendency in human beings. Hence, love, in the sense of the psychic energy that is the ingredient of all the life instinct tendencies—whatever complicated form it may finally take—is acquisitive in origin; all loves, in fact, derive ultimately from biological wants or needs.

The notion of benevolent desire also is present in the Freudian theory. Benevolence is the essential ingredient in what Freud refers to as "real, true, actual love."[160] This is Freud's second and much narrower conception of love among human beings, and is considered by him as the best kind of human love. It signifies a mature relationship between two adults, male and female, and is reserved for this relationship alone. To understand this love, particularly how the benevolence essential to it is derived from the more basic acquisitive human impulses, it is necessary to have some grasp of Freud's conception of the structure of the human psyche as well as some familiarity with his theory of human psychological development.[161]

Freud speaks of the individual human being as consisting of a *psyche* and a *soma*. This distinction corresponds roughly to the familiar one between mind and body. However, the psyche has no being apart from its somatic locus, since it is only a function of the soma.[162] The purpose of the psyche, in a broad sense, is to mediate between the actual bodily tissues, or soma, and the environment in every instance where the needs of the tissues can be met only with something from the environment. A great deal of Freud's thought is devoted to the mechanism by which these needs, originating in the body, are transmitted from the soma to the psyche and disposed of by the psyche in one way or another—e.g., immediate gratification, partial gratification, delayed gratification, or repression. The dynamic aspects of this transmission and disposition of needs must be

---

[159] *Group Psychology and the Analysis of the Ego*, Ch. IV, pp. 37–38. Freud explains his extension of the term thus: "Our justification lies in the fact that psychoanalytic research has taught us that all these tendencies are an expression of the same instinctive activities; in relations between the sexes these instincts force their way towards sexual union, but in other circumstances they are diverted from this aim or are prevented from reaching it, though always preserving enough of their original nature to keep their identity recognizable (as in such features as the longing for proximity, and self-sacrifice)." (*Ibid.*, p. 38.)

[160] *Ibid.*, Ch. VIII, p. 71.

[161] Freud's discussion of love is more genetic than analytic. He is much more concerned with describing the stages of human growth—and their corresponding phases of love—than with formulating a theoretical and abstract definition of love. Invariably, he answers any question concerning a static theory of love in terms of the progressive stages of growth and love.

[162] See *An Outline of Psychoanalysis*, Part I, Ch. 1, pp. 13–14.

understood in terms of Freud's new conception of the structure of the psyche.

The *id* is the most primitive part of the psyche and the part in which somatic needs are first registered. A shortage of salt in the body become a "wish" for salt in the id. The id in no way transforms or alters the character of somatic needs; it merely reflects them. The id urges upon the rest of the psyche the instantaneous gratification of the needs it reflects. It has no regard for the circumstances prevailing in the environment because it knows nothing of them. Conversely, it demands instantaneous cessation of all somatic pain or discomfort. The functions of the id are never any immediate part of an individual's conscious psychic life.[163]

The *ego* is that part of the psyche in which somatic needs presented by the id are weighed against the circumstances prevailing in the environment, and in which both these influences are weighed against limitations advocated by the superego, or "conscience." The ego is the mediator among these three influences; it tries to find the course of action that will best balance all three. Since it is the part of the psyche most directly concerned with and affected by the environment, the ego operates partly on the basis of the *reality principle*. This does not mean that the ego consistently denies or limits somatic satisfactions, for it is concerned with the good of the whole organism and responds to the id by seeking as much pleasure as possible (pleasure principle). Nor does it mean that it consistently ignores the limitations imposed by the superego, since it would thereby suffer anxiety at a conscious or unconscious level. Rather, the ego acts as a bridge between internal tensions and external forces.[164]

The *superego* is that part of the psyche that presents to the ego opinions and judgments acquired from parents or other influential persons during an individual's childhood. Freud did not establish a principle for the superego, but it is clear from his remarks that it operates on a social-moral basis.[165]

The distinction between the *unconscious* and the *conscious* is crucial in Freud's theory, since he thinks the individual is unaware of his most basic psychic activities. Conscious means aware *now,* and is only predicable of a portion of the ego. Preconscious means that which can be normally and easily recalled into consciousness.[166] Unconscious means outside the awareness of the conscious portion of the ego, but still within the psyche. Unconscious is a condition of the id as a whole, most of the superego, a portion of the ego, and most of the interactions among them.[167]

[163] See *ibid.*
[164] See *ibid.*, pp. 14–17.
[165] See *ibid.*, pp. 16–18.
[166] Usually, when Freud refers to the "conscious," his words include and apply to the preconscious.
[167] See *An Outline of Psychoanalysis,* Part I, Ch. 4, pp. 33–45, esp. pp. 37–40.

Instinct is a collective name for many individual somatic needs having a broad, common objective. As already noted, Freud finally concludes that there are two basic instincts: the life instinct and the death instinct. *Eros* (sometimes referred to as the "sexual" or "synthetic" instinct) has as its dual goal the survival of the individual human being and the survival of the human species. The goal of *thanatos* is the natural death of the individual, i.e., death from old age rather than death from accident or disease.[168]

The needs of the life instinct that permeate the psyche are involved in what Freud calls *psychosexual development,* a process that begins at birth and continues throughout life.[169] The pursuit of the objectives of *eros* (individual and racial survival) takes place within it. It is divided temporally into three main phases, in each of which a particular type of relationship is of extreme importance to the individual. There is, first, the *oral phase,* in which the crucial relationship is between the infant and his mother's breast; second, the *anal phase,* in which the crucial relationship is between the infant and his own feces; and, finally, the *genital phase,* which includes a series of relationships ending, ideally, with a relationship between the individual and a member of the opposite sex.[170]

In normal cases, the genital phase of psychosexual development (which begins at age 2 or 3) has several distinct subphases: first, the *phallic period* (when the male genitalia are the libidinal object for children of both sexes); then, the *Oedipal period* (during which the libidinal object is the parent of the opposite sex); then, the *latency period* (during which the libidinal objects are children of the same sex); and, finally, the truly *genital*

---

[168] See *ibid.,* Ch. II, pp. 19–20; *Civilization and Its Discontents,* Ch. VI, pp. 73–75; and *Beyond the Pleasure Principle,* Ch. V, pp. 47–51.

[169] *Eros* exists in the soma as well as in the psyche. Some of its component somatic needs are met without reference to the psyche. A new arterial system may develop if one of the original arteries becomes constricted, without involving the psyche at all. However, many if not most of the component needs of *eros* can be met only through some interaction between the individual and his environment, and these must involve the psyche. (See *An Outline of Psychoanalysis,* Part I, Ch. 2, pp. 20–23.)

[170] The genital phase subsumes and does not terminate the oral and anal phases. But, though the oral and anal phases continue during the genital phase, their somatic objectives are no longer primary. In each of the three phases the object of desire is not the real, external entity but rather its representation in the psyche. Breast is the focal object during the oral phase, yet the somatic needs of this period of life are numerous: food, warmth, cuddling, relief from skin irritation, etc. The focal object of the genital phase is a member of the opposite sex, yet the actual somatic need is to obtain genital pleasure through sexual intercourse. The somatic objective during the anal phase, the experience of pleasurable sensations while defecating, is perhaps more directly reflected in its focal object: the feces. However, the somatic objective of the anal phase has a far less clear connection with individual and race survival than the somatic objectives of the oral and genital phases. (See *A General Introduction to Psychoanalysis,* Twentieth Lecture, pp. 322–325; Twenty-First Lecture, pp. 337–338; and *An Outline of Psychoanalysis,* Part I, Ch. 3, pp. 28–30.)

period, beginning at puberty (when the libidinal objects are members of the opposite sex). In Freud's view, only those who reach the truly genital period are capable of mature or normal love. Those who, for whatever reason, are arrested in their development, exhibit loves that are deviations from the norm. For Freud, such perversions are nothing but instances of infantile love, *i.e.,* examples of the stage at which an individual's psychosexual development was arrested.[171]

Freud notes that the infant, during most of the oral phase, does not make the distinction between self and other; the breast, mother, and even the rest of the world are nothing but an undifferentiated extension of himself. Hence, since the loved object in the anal phase is not another person, we may say that the focus of Freud's theory of love among human beings is in his discussion of the genital phase.[172]

As we have indicated, Freud has two conceptions of human love. According to one, human love is libido, *i.e.,* all tendencies (whether unconscious or conscious) that aim at self-preservation or race preservation. According to the other, love is the optimal relationship between two adult human beings of opposite sexes. We shall return to this relationship in a moment. First, we must explain Freud's understanding of how the ideal love between a man and a woman develops out of modifications of love that encompass all life-preserving tendencies.

The earliest form of gratification toward which all libidinal tendencies aim is pleasurable physical sensation. In Freud's view, such sensations remain as the basis of all human striving throughout life.

[171] See *A General Introduction to Psychoanalysis,* Twentieth Lecture, p. 325; and Twenty-Second Lecture, pp. 348–352.

[172] In those cases in which a person does not reach the final stage of the genital phase of psychosexual development, he (as a rule) does not engage in genital, heterosexual intercourse. Instead, he engages in some type of substitute activity, from which he can obtain a substitute pleasure. For example, there can be a neurotic preoccupation with something inanimate, such as boots or corsets (fetishism); or there can be a perverse sexual relationship involving the use of the genitals (homosexuality); or there can be exclusive preoccupation with cultural or religious matters (sublimation). In some of these cases the individual enters psychoanalysis for the purpose of advancing, through therapy, to the truly genital phase. (See *ibid.,* Twentieth Lecture, pp. 313–316; and also Twenty-Seventh Lecture, pp. 439–443.) Freud applies distinctions in his analysis of love in many ways according to his rhetorical or pedagogical purpose. One of the most basic of these distinctions is between normal and perverse love. However, since our basic distinction between acquisitive and benevolent desire applies to both normal and perverse loves, Freud's distinction need not play a major role in this presentation. (Indeed, many types of perverse human love are not types of love among human beings.) In his discussion of possibly the most frequent type of perverse love among human beings, homosexuality, Freud certainly does not exclude benevolent desire from that relationship.

As we see, it is simply the pleasure-principle which draws up the programme of life's purpose. This principle dominates the operation of the mental apparatus from the very beginning.[173]

In other words, all psychological tendencies derive from bodily wants or needs and, in their original form, aim at the fulfillment of these wants or needs. Since these tendencies seek an outlet through the ego, which is the only part of the psyche that has conscious contact with the environment, at one point Freud defines love "as the relation of the ego to its sources of pleasure."[174] He also refers to the object of this relationship as a "sexual" one.

Freud employs the term "sexual" in both an extended and a limited sense. In its broad sense it applies to all the tendencies of the life instinct, both as they occur in the body and as they are represented in the psyche. Thus, in this sense, sexual impulses cover those desires for food, heat, etc. (which aim ultimately at self-preservation), as well as those that are directed to genital pleasure (and aim ultimately at race survival). In this sense, sexual and libidinal are synonymous, since they both involve all impulses that aim at somatic pleasure.

In his discussions of the genital phase of psychosexual development, Freud often employs the term "sexual" in a more limited sense; he applies it only to those impulses that aim at genital pleasure and not, as elsewhere, to all libidinal impulses. The two usages are connected by the fact that, in both senses, sexual desires are those that aim at somatic pleasure. But an even more important connection is that the desire for genital pleasure is *the* dominant human desire, since genital pleasure is the prototype of all somatic pleasure;[175] thus Freud considers sexual desire in the narrow sense of the desire for genital pleasure as a focus of sexual desire in its

[173] *Civilization and Its Discontents*, Ch. II, p. 16.

[174] *Instincts and their Vicissitudes*, p. 78. Earlier in his work, Freud distinguished between ego drives (aiming at self-preservation) and libido (aiming at race preservation). In *Civilization and Its Discontents*, however, he affirms that ego drives develop out of libido and that the ego "remains to some extent its permanent headquarters." In other words, libidinal energy, seeking outlet through the ego, is the source of tendencies that aim at self-preservation as well as of those that aim at race preservation. (*Op. cit.*, Ch. VI, p. 69.) Freud goes on: ". . . we do not customarily say that the single sexual component-instinct loves its object, but see the most appropriate case in which to apply the word 'love' in the relation of the ego to its sexual object." (*Instincts and their Vicissitudes*, p. 80.)

[175] Genital pleasure is the prototype of physical pleasure not only in the unconscious but also in the conscious. ". . . one of the forms in which love manifests itself, sexual love, gives us our most intense experience of an overwhelming pleasurable sensation and so furnishes a prototype for our strivings after happiness. What is more natural than that we should persist in seeking happiness along the path by which we first encountered it?" (*Civilization and Its Discontents*, Ch. II, p. 24.)

broader sense. The turning point of development in the genital phase is, according to Freud, "the *subordination of all the sexual component-instincts under the primacy of the genital zone.*"[176] The importance of the desire for genital pleasure in Freud's theory of love is indicated in the following passage:

> . . . the word "to love" becomes shifted ever further into the sphere of the pure pleasure-relation existing between the ego and its object and finally attaches itself to sexual objects in the narrower sense and to those which satisfy the needs of sublimated sexual instincts.[177]

All bodily needs, from which all psychological impulses ultimately derive, are acquisitive desires. Hence, when love is defined as libido (the mental side of the sexual, *i.e.*, somatic impulse),[178] as the desire for bodily pleasure, it is defined as acquisitive desire. The basic reality in the Freudian theory of love is not merely tendency but sheer acquisitive appetite.

Though an individual always is animated by his desire for sensual gratification, his love object changes as he develops and grows. In the oral phase, the focus of his desire for somatic pleasure is his mother's breast. But he soon finds additional sources of pleasure in his own body and in the world around him. More important than his discovery of new ways to achieve pleasure is the frustration he naturally experiences throughout his development in attempting to gratify his desires. The environmental obstacles he meets continually force him to change his object choice or to redirect his instinctual urge—or both. These changes, known as *instinctual viscissitudes*, take several forms, the most important of which are: *identification, transformation* (the reversal of an instinct into its opposite), *sublimation* (unconscious redirection of the instinctual urge to another object or mode of gratification), and *repression* (unconscious refusal to gratify the urge because it conflicts with what a person believes to be proper behavior).[179]

It is in terms of these changes, particularly sublimation, that benevolent desire must be understood. *Benevolence is never an original or basic human motive in Freudian theory.* The only reality it has is on the conscious level of psychic activity, and all such activity is derivative. And on the conscious level it does not directly reflect the acquisitive need it represents. Benevolence is not only derivative from an underlying desire for genital pleasure

[176] *A General Introduction to Psychoanalysis*, Twenty-First Lecture, p. 337.
[177] *Instincts and their Vicissitudes*, p. 80.
[178] See *A General Introduction to Psychoanalysis*, Twenty-First Lecture, p. 339.
[179] See *Instincts and their Vicissitudes*, pp. 68–69; and *Thoughts for the Times on War and Death*, pp. 296–297.

but is itself a transformed version of that acquisitive desire. Because the underlying desire for genital pleasure is "inhibited," for any one of a number of reasons, it must find conscious release in other forms, one of which is benevolence.

> We have to conclude that all the feelings of sympathy, friendship, trust and so forth which we expend in life are genetically connected with sexuality and have developed out of purely sexual desires by an enfeebling of their sexual aim, however pure and non-sensual they may appear in the forms they take on to our conscious self-perception. To begin with we knew none but sexual objects; psycho-analysis shows us that those persons whom in real life we merely respect or are fond of may be sexual objects to us in our unconscious minds still.[180]

Or, as Freud says more briefly:

> Love with an inhibited aim was indeed originally full sensual love and in men's unconscious minds is so still.[181]

Freud most frequently describes the result of such aim-inhibition as a feeling of "tenderness," but he does not hesitate to associate this feeling with clearer indications of benevolence. In any case, the inhibition of a desire for somatic pleasure (caused ultimately by environmental obstacles or by the influence of the superego) is an indispensable condition for the emergence of conscious tendencies that are benevolent or approach benevolence. This applies whether such benevolence is extended to one's mate, to one's family or friends, or to men at large. Even of the protective concern of parents for their children, Freud says: "Parental love, which is so touching and at bottom so childish, is nothing but parental narcissism born again and, transformed though it be into object-love, it reveals its former character infallibly."[182]

The original *narcissism* to which Freud refers is present in the earliest phase of the infant's development. The first (and most basic) object of love is the self; all the psychic tendencies of a newborn child are acquisitive. Initially, he is only aware of his body and its needs. With the development of the *reality principle*, he gradually acquires the ability to associate his pleasure with the person who helps him acquire it. His mother is usually his first object of love, *i.e.*, of his acquisitive desire to fulfill his own needs.

> . . . a child loves himself first and only later learns to love others and to sacrifice something of his own ego to them. Even the people whom he seems

---

[180] *The Dynamics of the Transference*, p. 319.
[181] *Civilization and Its Discontents*, Ch. IV, p. 49. See also *Group Psychology and the Analysis of the Ego*, Ch. VIII, pp. 71–72.
[182] *On Narcissism: An Introduction*, p. 49.

to love from the outset are loved in the first instance because he needs them and cannot do without them—again therefore, from motives of egoism. Only later does the impulse of love detach itself from egoism: it is a literal fact that the child learns how to love through his own egoism.[183]

The child's love remains acquisitive even after he has learned to distinguish others from himself, since he loves them only in order to gain their services. As he develops, he seeks an ever widening field of pleasure and discovers simultaneously an ever greater number of barriers to the realization of his desires. On encountering these barriers, the child's libidinal energy turns back on itself and is transformed. He learns that he will get more of what he wants if he behaves in accord with the dictates of authority; as a result, he may try to make himself lovable. This development is by no means entirely conscious. The original acquisitive desire is more and more held under the conscious mind. It may be directed to the same person, but more and more it comes to take an aim-inhibited and consciously acceptable form. The result of this change, and of other instinctual vicissitudes, can give rise to feelings described by Freud as tender, kind, and altruistic:

> Love for oneself knows only one barrier—love for others, love for objects.
> . . . The libido props itself upon the satisfaction of the great vital needs,
> and chooses as its first objects the people who have a share in that process.
> And in the development of mankind as a whole, just as in individuals, love
> alone acts as the civilizing factor in the sense that it brings a change from
> egoism to altruism.[184]

It must be remembered that all aim-inhibitions resulting in conscious tenderness or benevolence are, from the perspective of the acquisitive and controlling unconscious, tactical. The more the aim of a desire is inhibited the less the person is aware of the real aim of his tendency. In other words, from the perspective of the unconscious, conscious benevolence, however sincere, is really giving only in order to get. It is thus that Freud is able to describe the most altruistic feelings as inspired ultimately by motives of self-interest:

[183] *A General Introduction to Psychoanalysis,* Thirteenth Lecture, p. 214.
[184] *Group Psychology and the Analysis of the Ego,* Ch. VI, pp. 56–57. This change is accomplished, according to Freud, in the following way: "By the admixture of *erotic* components the egoistic instincts are transmuted into *social* ones. We learn to value being loved as an advantage for which we are willing to sacrifice other advantages. . . . Civilization is the fruit of renunciation of instinctual satisfaction, and from each new-comer in turn it exacts the same renunciation. . . . The influences of civilization cause an ever-increasing transmutation of egoistic trends into altruistic and social ones, and this by an admixture of erotic elements." (*Thoughts for the Times on War and Death,* p. 297.)

A small minority are enabled . . . to find happiness along the path of love; but far-reaching mental transformations of the erotic function are necessary before this is possible. These people make themselves independent of their object's acquiescence by transferring the main value from the fact of being loved to their own act of loving; they protect themselves against loss of it by attaching their love not to individual objects but to all men equally, and they avoid the uncertainties and disappointments of genital love by turning away from its sexual aim and modifying the instinct into an impulse with an *inhibited aim.* The state which they induce in themselves by this process— an unchangeable, undeviating, tender attitude—has little superficial likeness to the stormy vicissitudes of genital love, from which it is nevertheless derived.[185]

Most desires show considerable modification when they appear in the conscious. But only in some cases does the modification result in the transformation of an acquisitive desire into a benevolent one. In other words, though unconscious desires are invariably acquisitive, conscious desires may be acquisitive or benevolent.[186] Freud's optimal definition of love between the sexes includes both types of desire. Ideal love is a relationship between a mature man and a mature woman in which acquisitive desires (of which the most important is sexual desire) and tender feelings of concern or benevolent desires are both present. Ideal love can be characterized as a combination of direct and aim-inhibited acquisitive desires. The direct sexual impulses are a necessary condition for such love, but they are not sufficient.

To ensure a fully normal attitude in love, two currents of feeling have to unite—we may describe them as the tender, affectionate feelings and the sensual feelings.[187]

Or, as Freud also says:

The depth to which anyone is in love, as contrasted with his purely sensual desire, may be measured by the size of the share taken by the inhibited instincts of tenderness.[188]

[185] *Civilization and Its Discontents,* Ch. IV, p. 48.

[186] The desire for sexual intercourse may, for example, be modified to the desire for sexual intercourse with a certain type of woman. In this case, the modification has resulted only in a more discriminating desire, not a transformed one.

[187] *Contributions to the Psychology of Love. The Most Prevalent Form of Degradation in Erotic Life,* p. 204.

[188] *Group Psychology and the Analysis of the Ego,* Ch. VIII, p. 73. Freud indicates that the conscious feeling of tenderness even serves a function in regard to reproduction, since it preserves the man-woman relationship during the intervals when conscious sexual desire is dormant: "In one class of cases being in love is nothing more than object-cathexis on the part of the sexual instincts with a view to

The conscious feeling of benevolence does not always totally disguise what lies behind it. There is considerable evidence that Freud thinks such total disguise is infrequent. There are times when those who wish well to others, are concerned for them and act tenderly toward them, are somehow dimly aware that they do these things for their own good. But Freud does not deny, and, in fact, frequently implies, that a sincere benevolent intention is humanly possible. Since the line between the conscious-preconscious and the unconscious is indistinct and seldom stable in any human being (particularly during the decisive phases of growth), he emphasizes that it is difficult to tell whether any given instance of the desire to give is a desire to give for the sake of getting or whether the desire is sufficiently cut off from its roots by the limits of consciousness to qualify as benevolent.

Aim-inhibition resulting in tenderness and concern for another is a typical path of instinctual gratification and utilizes much of the libidinal energy that was originally sexual. These benevolent feelings are not only present in a mature relationship between a man and a woman but are also extended to one's children, relatives, friends, and sometimes even to humanity at large.

In Freud's view, it is this process of aim-inhibition that has built up and now sustains civilization. Not only does it take the form of kindness and social responsibility but also the form of devotion to ideals or abstract concepts. Patriotism, interest in the arts, philanthropy, religious devotion, the pursuit of knowledge are all, for Freud, examples of aim-inhibited desires, though not all are instances of benevolence. In short, all culture is built upon the renunciation of instinctual needs.[189]

The progress of the human race in society reflects the progress of man through his states of infantile sexuality. If a child progresses or matures normally, he renounces the objects of his infantile desires (and infantile modes of attaining them) and gains the adult balance between gratification and repression. Such a personal balance, in the relationship of a man to a woman, is considered by Freud as normal, adult, and healthy. The aim-inhibited ingredient of this love is also present, in a variety of forms, in all other instances of civilized love among human beings.

---

directly sexual satisfaction, a cathexis which expires, moreover, when this aim has been reached; this is what is called common, sensual love. But, as we know, the libidinal situation rarely remains so simple. It was possible to calculate with certainty upon the revival of the need which had just expired; and this must no doubt have been the first motive for directing a lasting cathexis upon the sexual object and for 'loving' it in the passionless intervals as well." (*Ibid.*, pp. 71–72. See also p. 78.)

[189] See *Thoughts for the Times on War and Death*, p. 297; and *Civilization and Its Discontents*, Ch. III, p. 43.

Elaborating this idea still further, Freud explains that such aim-inhibited desires form the unifying bonds that hold together all human relationships. The desire for union is basic, therefore, to Freud's understanding of love among human beings. Though Freud does not discuss the desire for union in terms of acquisitiveness or benevolence, it seems reasonable to suppose from his examples that it may take either form. A person may unconsciously or consciously wish to unite with another for his own good; a person may consciously wish to unite with another for the other's good. But whatever the character of the motive, there is no doubt that Freud sees love as a unifying force.

In discussing love as the desire for union, Freud again takes the relationship between a man and a woman as a prototype. Of such a relationship he says:

> At its height the state of being in love threatens to obliterate the boundaries between ego and object. Against all the evidence of his senses the man in love declares that he and his beloved are one, and is prepared to behave as if it were a fact.[190]

Or, as he says later:

> In no other case does Eros so plainly betray the core of his being, his aim of making one out of many.

Freud goes on to say that love's propensity to unite is not restricted to the drawing together of a man and a woman:

> . . . in actuality culture is not content with such limited ties as these; we see that it endeavours to bind the members of the community to one another by libidinal ties as well, that it makes use of every means and favours every avenue by which powerful identifications can be created among them, and that it exacts a heavy toll of aim-inhibited libido in order to strengthen communities by bonds of friendship between the members. Restrictions upon sexual life are unavoidable if this object is to be attained.[191]

On this broader scale love impels men to seek the union of similarity, to become more and more like each other by strengthening their common aim. In Freud's view, love

> aims at binding together single human individuals, then families, then tribes, races, nations, into one great unity, that of humanity. Why this has to be done we do not know; it is simply the work of Eros. These masses of

---

[190] *Ibid.*, Ch. I, pp. 3–4.

[191] *Ibid.*, Ch. V, p. 57. The union to which Freud refers here is the union of complementarity. Only this type of union applies to normal romantic love since man and woman are unlike and therefore complement one another.

men must be bound to one another libidinally; necessity alone, the advantages of common work, would not hold them together. The natural instinct of aggressiveness in man, the hostility of each one against all and of all against each one, opposes this programme of civilization. This instinct of aggression is the derivative and main representative of the death instinct we have found alongside of Eros, sharing his rule over the earth.[192]

The few people who are able to carry the process of sublimation to a very high degree accomplish this by

attaching their love not to individual objects but to all men equally, and they avoid the uncertainties and disappointments of genital love by turning away from its sexual aim and modifying the instinct into an impulse with an *inhibited aim*. The state which they induce in themselves by this process— an unchangeable, undeviating, tender attitude—has little superficial likeness to the stormy vicissitudes of genital love, from which it is nevertheless derived.[193]

All the principal tendential notions signified by our critical terms are applicable to the Freudian theory of love among human beings. All psychic energy or libido in the unconscious, reflecting actual bodily needs and wants, takes the form of direct and simple acquisitive desire. Following the genital phase of psychosexual development, these basic acquisitive desires are almost all transformed into, or colored by, sexual desires. And in the conscious, such desires may remain acquisitive desire, in either its simple or mixed form.

Benevolent desire is present in the Freudian theory only in the conscious and always as a result of the aim-inhibition of an original and basic acquisitive desire. The ideal love between a man and a woman is a combination of sexual desires and tender concern which is or approaches benevolence. But beyond this, aim-inhibition of sexual desire can produce benevolence or desires akin to it in other relationships, from the familial to the political. Such benevolence may be more or less self-interested, depending on the degree of sublimation to which the original acquisitive desire is subjected.[194] Freud implies that conscious benevolent desires are less frequent than acquisitive ones.

---

[192] *Ibid.*, Ch. VI, pp. 74–75. See also Ch. IV, p. 49; and *An Outline of Psychoanalysis*, Part I, Ch. 2, p. 20.
[193] *Civilization and Its Discontents*, Ch. IV, p. 48.
[194] Thus, for example, Freud notes that a neighbor is worthy of love "if he is so like me in important respects that I can love myself in him; worthy of it if he is so much more perfect than I that I can love my ideal of myself in him." (*Ibid.*, Ch. V, p. 58.) Such a relationship would permit self-interested benevolence by doing good for another and anticipating sharing that good through identification with the other. Though Freud makes no mention of the forms of self-interested benevolence where

Finally, the notion of the desire for union is also present in the Freudian theory. In the case of the relationship between a mature man and woman, the union sought is the union of complementarity. The union fostered by love as the cohesive force of civilization is the union of similarity.

Though Freud does claim that the binding force of love gives society whatever cohesion and culture it has, he denies that civilizing tendencies have had very great success. He insists that the ideal of civilized society, "Thou shalt love thy neighbour as thyself,"[195] is "completely at variance with original human nature"[196] and is, accordingly, impossible to realize. Referring to benevolence, Freud claims that no one can extend it to everyone. To be loved, a person, "must be worthy of it in some way or other." To be "worthy" of love, in Freud's view, a person must be similar to the lover, personify his ideals, or be related or united to him in some way.[197] "But," Freud says, "if he is a stranger to me and cannot attract me by any value he has in himself or any significance he may have already acquired in my emotional life, it will be hard for me to love him."[198] Freud also claims that the mere fact that another man is also a living being is not a sufficient basis on which to make the ideal of universal love operative.

> But if I am to love him (with that kind of universal love) simply because he, too, is a denizen of the earth, like an insect or an earthworm or a grass-snake, then I fear that but a small modicum of love will fall to his lot and it would be impossible for me to give him as much as by all the laws of reason I am entitled to retain for myself.[199]

The ultimate basis for Freud's rejection of the ideal of universal love is his claim "that men are not gentle, friendly creatures wishing for love, who simply defend themselves if they are attacked, but that a powerful measure

---

the concomitant goods for the self are the satisfaction of giving or the moral improvement of the self, he nevertheless does talk about the extension of benevolence that, though not done for the sake of mutuality, is accompanied by a hope or anticipation of its return. (See *ibid.*, Ch. V, pp. 56–67; *Thoughts for the Times on War and Death*, pp. 296–300; and *Group Psychology and the Analysis of the Ego*, Ch. VI, pp. 52–59.)

195 *Civilization and Its Discontents*, Ch. V, p. 57.

196 *Ibid.*, p. 62.

197 *Ibid.*, p. 58.

198 *Ibid.* Freud adds: "I shall even be doing wrong if I do, for my love is valued as a privilege by all those belonging to me; it is an injustice to them if I put a stranger on a level with them." (*Ibid.*)

199 *Ibid.*

of desire for aggression has to be reckoned as part of their instinctual endowment."[200]

Karl Menninger

Menninger is a Freudian disciple. The pivotal distinction employed in his book *Love Against Hate* is between the life instinct and the death instinct, the constructive and the destructive tendencies, "Eros and Thanatos," love and hate. Menninger asserts:

> It was Freud who related these two contrary laws to the innate nature of human beings; it was he who recognized that the destructiveness of human beings is not the result of some passing fever, some incidentally occasioned accident in the normal course of life, but the expression of a deep persistent instinct.[201]

He adds that

> it was also Freud who showed us that the impulse to live and love is likewise an instinctual endowment of human beings and a source of strength in opposition to the self-destructiveness. Die we must, ultimately, but in the meantime we can live, if we can love.[202]

Menninger is concerned almost exclusively with human love, and particularly with the problems of how the life instinct, or love, in human beings can be made to overcome, incorporate, or neutralize the death instinct, or hate. He regards love as a tendency much broader in scope than sexual desire, as in fact covering all inclinations that aim at the preservation of life.

> The erotic instinct, properly conceived of, does not refer solely to impulses toward physical contact, but to the drives in the direction of social and biological life, with the ultimate object of race preservation. A better term for it is simply love.[203]

---

[200] *Ibid.*, pp. 60–61. For a few of the many theories of love that reflect the Freudian one in whole or part, see Franz Alexander's *Fundamentals of Psychoanalysis*; Karl Abraham's *Selected Papers on Psychoanalysis*; Havelock Ellis' *Psychology of Sex*; E. R. Matthews' *Sex, Love and Society*; and Oskar Pfister's *Love in Children and Its Aberrations.*

[201] *Love Against Hate*, Ch. I, p. 5. Although Menninger's main concern is love among human beings, he considers that "the investment of love in nonhuman objects is . . . a form or variety of love" and should be encouraged within limits. Love of inanimate objects is made possible through "personification" in childhood; in adult life such love continues, although the personification is repressed. (See *ibid.*, Ch. 10, pp. 263–266.)

[202] *Ibid.*

[203] *Ibid.*, Ch. 3, p. 46.

Menninger seems to go even further when he says that a careful "scientific" study of human desires reveals that "the scientific theory of love has become the theory of the interaction and fusion of the erotic and destructive instincts."[204] However, although in his attempt to understand the phenomena called love Menninger emphasizes the fusion of the two instincts, he still identifies love, properly speaking, with the positive or life-preserving instinct rather than with the combination of that instinct and the negative or life-destroying instinct. He uses the idea of "fusion," or what he also calls "sublimation," primarily to show that there is "no such thing as pure love (or pure hate)."[205]

In civilized society both the death and the love instincts undergo modification. "Primitive man could kill what he liked and could gratify his love instinct without reference to any restrictions. Contemporary man can do neither." The modification undergone by the death instinct in civilized society is effected by love. Love, says Menninger, "is capable of modifying the hate impulses and bringing them within the range of social acceptability and usefulness."[206] He adds, however, that the love instinct itself, which is originally acquisitive, also undergoes modification. The result is the expression of "love" in three forms. The first is "in the partial or complete neutralization of the destruction instinct—in other words, in the accomplishment of sublimation." The second form of love "is expressed in diffuse extensions of love to nonsexual objects, or to objects that are not sexual in the ordinary sense of the word." Such objects include human beings. Menninger, following Freud, asserts that the basic impulse behind such attachments derives from physical, primarily sexual, desire. But he adds that "the object selected and the feelings experienced for it are not consciously recognized as pertaining to sexuality." Finally, love expresses itself in the form of sexual desire.[207]

The third form of love, being directly physical in origin and aim, is acquisitive in character. The first two forms of love, though they derive from impulses that are and remain acquisitive on the unconscious level, are expressed consciously as either acquisitive or benevolent desires. In other words, though not all human tendencies are love (since destructive tendencies are excluded), acquisitive tendencies (on the unconscious or conscious level) and benevolent tendencies (always conscious and the essential part of a love relationship also involving acquisitive tendencies) are both separately called love. Menninger's theory, therefore, is binary.

204 *Ibid.*, Ch. 10, p. 262. See also pp. 260–261.
205 *Ibid.*, p. 263.
206 *Ibid.*
207 *Ibid., passim.*

The range of Menninger's theory perhaps is best expressed in the following passage, where he discusses love in terms of the desire for union:

> I am aware that some readers unfamiliar with psychological science will find it difficult to believe that the feelings of positive attraction that bind the members of groups and that bind doctor and patient are identical in nature with those bonds which exist between a lover and his sweetheart, or a man and his wife. They will fall back upon the conventional distinctions between liking and loving. But there is no scientific justification for this distinction; liking and loving differ only in intensity. If we leave aside large groups of people and think for a moment of those intimacies which spring up between friends, let us say between two friends, there will be less difficulty in accepting the thesis. Whether it is between father and son, or father and daughter, or the fathers of two sons, the esssential nature of the positive attraction and feeling is the same. It is true that it will be differently expressed.[208]

For Menninger, the basic life instinct or life-preservative tendency may be directed to the preservation of one's own life or another's; the tendency may be acquisitive or benevolent. "Love is the reflection of the instinct of life, and the love of ourselves is of the same texture as the love of others."[209]

Since Menninger initially associates the instinctive life-preservative tendencies with physical pleasure, he sees love beginning "not in adolescence nor in maturity but in infancy." The child begins to love, to desire things it needs or wants, from the time it begins to breathe. The original expressions of love are impulses toward physical gratification. "Using all the organs of his body, he attaches himself with pleasure to a succession of love objects in response to the satisfactions they offer and afford him. His mother, his father, later his brothers and sisters, still later his playmates and teachers, and finally his adult companions, become successive foci of the direction of his love."[210] In the early stages the love impulse takes the form of simple acquisitive desire; the infant seeks directly what he wants. Later, however, the child discovers that he can acquire certain physical pleasures as well as the satisfaction of parental approval and care only if "he gives up a socially disapproved habit or attitude." He gives the parents what they request of him in order to gain something.

> The encouraging smile of the mother when the baby remembers her prohibitions, his parents' beaming pride in observing his efforts to use a spoon

[208] *Ibid.*, pp. 270–271.
[209] *Ibid.*, Ch. 6, p. 136.
[210] *Ibid.*, Ch. 10, p. 261.

instead of his fingers—these are tangible rewards for which the child barters his naive ideas of comfort and selfish ease.[211]

The habit of mixed acquisitive desire, of giving in order to get, colors and modifies the directly acquisitive character of the sexual impulse at the onset of puberty. The child has "learned" that the gratification of his instinctive urges must be accomplished within the limits of the restrictions and prohibitions not only of his parents but of society at large. In Menninger's view, the effectiveness of these restrictions and prohibitions in the past accounts in part for the "curious fact that until relatively recent times love was not considered an aspect of the sexual life."[212] The presence of the sexual impulse in a love relationship between a man and a woman is, in Menninger's view, the reason it is often regarded as "the most intense expression of the life instinct."[213]

In Menninger's theory, as in Freud's, it is the inhibition of the primary acquisitive tendency that gives rise, on the conscious level, to benevolent desires.[214]

> The mature love object, in so far as it is selected for its own sake and not as a symbol of some reluctantly abandoned earlier object, receives the unalloyed affection, protection, and confidence of the one-time child, now the mature adult.[215]

Benevolence takes a number of forms since love "is expressed in material ways such as protection and support, and in psychological-physiological ways such as tenderness and caresses."[216]

Stressing mutuality, Menninger says:

> It is a part of the function of marriage for the partners to supply to each other that amount of support and encouragement which is necessary to assuage the wounds and frustrations encountered in the daily lives of each.[217]

Menninger refers to a passage of Joan Riviere in which she mentions the two factors essential to a normal and healthy love relationship: the capacity to receive and the capacity to give. Again stressing the need for reciprocity with regard to both factors, he says:

[211] *Ibid.*, Ch. 2, p. 23. See also p. 24.
[212] *Ibid.*, Ch. 10, p. 279. See also p. 292.
[213] *Ibid.*, Ch. 3, p. 47.
[214] See *ibid.*, Ch. 10, pp. 280-281.
[215] *Ibid.*, Ch. 5, p. 129.
[216] *Ibid.*, Ch. 3, p. 47.
[217] *Ibid.*, Ch. 4, p. 107.

When the balance between these two elements in the love bond is unequal, when one party or the other is deficient in his capacity to give love, the other partner is imposed upon and unconsciously resents it.[218]

In one sense, the development of love in a human being is the gradual process by which the tendencies of love shift, from a total concern with the welfare of the self to, at least, a partial concern with the welfare of another that is still accompanied by a concern for the self. The movement is from the simple acquisitiveness of the infant to the mixed acquisitive desire of the adolescent and of the adult to the self-interested benevolence that sometimes is present in love relationships among adults. Though he does not call benevolence an illusion as does Freud, he maintains that the desire remains an acquisitive one in unconscious origin; that it is seldom if ever a disinterested benevolence, and that, though the giver may not consciously intend it, he is, in giving, enhancing his own welfare in the most effective way.

> The gift expresses love because it symbolizes the giver himself or an important part of himself; it may even be his life—"greater love hath no man than this."
>
> Thus the gift is more than a bribe, a purchase price offered for love; we rebel in our minds against the thought that love is "bought" or "earned" or "repaid"; nevertheless, it is a fact that a certain exchange is made and a certain balance is inevitably established. We do measure love and weigh it, even if not accurately. We are most inaccurate when we assume that the balance is in the favor of the recipient rather than the giver. That it is more blessed to give than to receive is psychologically true because giving stimulates love while expressing it.[219]

In other words, those who love often believe that their intentions are, at least primarily, to enhance the welfare of another. On the conscious level their motive often is benevolent, but they are in fact unconsciously intending their own welfare and in fact enhancing it more than the other's through the satisfaction they get in giving and through the love they stimulate on the part of the recipient.

In his analysis of love, Menninger lays considerably more stress on the desire for union than does Freud.[220] On the whole, he refers to the union

---

[218] *Ibid.*, p. 108.

[219] *Ibid.*, Ch. 10, pp. 273–274. See also Ch. 4, p. 107.

[220] Menninger quotes Shelley's definition of love and says that it is one "of the best": "That profound and complicated sentiment which we call love is the universal thirst for a communion not merely of the senses, but of our whole nature, intellectual, imaginative and sensitive. . . . The sexual impulse, which is only one, and often a small part of those claims, serves, from its obvious and external nature, as a kind of type of expression of the rest, a common basis, an acknowledged and visible link." (*Ibid.*, Ch. 10, pp. 280–281.)

sought in love as the union of similarity or "identification," the desire for which may take either an acquisitive or a benevolent form.[221] According to Menninger, love and union, or "identification," go together. "Identification leads by extension to a wish for fusion. This fusion may be idealistic, it may be intellectual, it may be social, it may be physical. . . . To accomplish this fusion is the object of the love impulse. . . . We have spoken of the function of eating together, exchanging gifts, talking and listening to one another for the furtherance of this mutual identification."[222] Menninger also says:

> Love is experienced as a pleasure in proximity, a desire for fuller knowledge of one another, a yearning for mutual identification and personality fusion. This we show to one another by our efforts to be understood, and by indulging the less imperious longing to understand.[223]

He sees this desire for union, for "identification" and "fusion" as pervasive in society, as therefore behind the organizing of "clubs, societies, associations, unions, and the like,"[224] as the essential cohesiveness of the human community. The multiple forms of this cohesiveness, provided they are directed to good ends, *i.e.*, the preservation and enhancement of life, is what Menninger hopes will overcome the destructive instinct in men. He asks for an extension of "our identifications to include more brothers, more sisters, more sons and daughters in a vastly wider family concept." In his view, the extension of "love is the medicine for the sickness of the world, a prescription often given, too rarely taken." On it he bases his hope for the preservation of the human race as well as "for the promotion of human happiness."[225]

C. G. Jung

There is little doubt that Jung conceives love as tendential. Since he mentions loves that are acquisitive in character, loves that are benevolent in character, and love relationships that involve both desires, his theory is binary.

The problem of love, according to Jung, is "one of immense scope and intricacy." It is a problem ethically, socially, and psychologically, and is a collective as well as an individual problem. Its forms or manifestations

---

[221] Menninger also mentions the male-female union of complementarity but does not stress it as much. (See *ibid.*, Ch. 4, p. 106, and Ch. 10, p. 277.)

[222] *Ibid.*, p. 277. See also pp. 272 ff.

[223] *Ibid.*, p. 272.

[224] *Ibid.*, p. 267.

[225] *Ibid.*, p. 294, *passim.*

range from the highest and most refined spiritual impulses of sacrifice and benevolence to the most obvious and most direct sexuality and acquisitiveness. It can express itself in the form of "compassion, philanthropy, and social service." Jung also discusses filial love and parental love, especially mother love. He says that we "speak of 'love' to cover the sexual act on all possible levels." The love in which acquisitive and benevolent desires are both involved is conjugal love.

> When we come to conjugal love we leave the purely spiritual realm behind, and enter that between-world that stretches between mind and instinct, where on the one hand the pure flame of Eros sets fire to sexuality, and where, on the other ideal forms of love, such as parental love, love of country and love for one's neighbour become contaminated with lust for personal power and the will to possess and command.[226]

Conjugal love can be understood as the intermediate between the extremes of "brutish" sexuality[227] and the disinterested benevolence of total sacrifice. Both of these extremes are very rare. Normally, men and women seek a psychic as well as a physical relationship with one another,[228] and they are also seldom without some concern for themselves.

> Have we not seen countless people who love and believe in their love, and then, when their purpose is accomplished, turn away as though they had never loved? And finally, is not this the way of nature herself? Is "disinterested" love at all possible? If so, it belongs to the highest virtues, which in point of fact are exceedingly rare.[229]

Jung also relates the desire for union (both that of complementarity and that of similarity) to love. Complementary union is mentioned principally in the relationship of a man and a woman, which *ideally* involves both acquisitive and benevolent desires.[230] The union of similarity is discussed as a phenomenon of "transference," leading men to project their feelings onto others, thus rendering "brotherly love" possible.[231]

Despite the applicability of our critical notions to Jung's thought on love, his work on psychology, taken as a whole, cannot be said to contain a developed theory of love. At no point does he say exactly what he conceives it to be. In fact, he mentions love only when it touches upon his principal

[226] *Contributions to Analytical Psychology*, pp. 204–206, *passim*. See also pp. 176, 185, 78 ff.

[227] "Sexuality is . . . purely animal, recognizing no psychic distinctions." (*Ibid.*, p. 215.)

[228] See *ibid.*, p. 185. See also pp. 175–176. "Sexuality released as sexuality is brutish. But as an expression of love sexuality is hallowed." (*Ibid.*, p. 224.)

[229] *Two Essays on Analytical Psychology*, p. 37.

[230] See *Contributions to Analytical Psychology*, pp. 180–181, 195–198.

[231] See *Psychology of the Unconscious*, Part I, Ch. III, pp. 77–78.

interests, which he sees as closely related to, but still distinct from, love.[232]
As a result, most of what Jung says about love is tangential. To a very great
extent his comments are occasioned by his desire to place qualifications on,
modify, or oppose certain featues of the Freudian theory.

The closest to a definition of love in Jung's work is contained in the
following passage:

> Logically, the opposite of love is hate, and of Eros, Phobos (fear); but
> psychologically it is the will to power. Where love reigns, there is no will to
> power; and where the will to power is paramount, love is lacking.[233]

In the same context, he places a further restriction on the scope of the
tendency that is love by explicitly denying that love can be identified with
the life instinct. Jung even refuses to concede the validity of the distinction
between the life instinct and the death instinct, the two basic forces
operative not only in man but in all living things according to Freud.

> It was a concession to intellectual logic on the one hand and to psychological
> prejudice on the other that impelled Freud to name the opposite of Eros the
> destructive or death instinct. For in the first place, Eros is not equivalent to
> life; but for anyone who thinks it is, the opposite of Eros will naturally
> appear to be death. And in the second place, we all feel that the opposite of
> our own highest principle must be purely destructive, deadly, and evil. We
> refuse to endow it with any positive life-force; hence we avoid and fear
> it.[234]

Probably the strongest objection Jung makes to the Freudian theory of
love is the position he takes in regard to Freud's original identification of
love with sexual desire. Jung does not exclude sexual desire from the realm
of love, and to the extent that sexual desire can be considered a form of, or

[232] Jung was interested in neurosis, introversion, and extroversion, in bringing the
conscious and the unconscious into cooperation, and in libido as a multiform repository of energies. He opposed the Freudian notion that there is a single kind of
energy, namely, sexual, to which all human motives and characteristics can be traced,
and developed other explanations of human motives. He explained neurosis as having roots in past experience, principally in frustrated attempts to contend with
reality. He did not explain neurosis as emanating only from sexual frustration. His
comments on love, then, are a result of his attempts to explain sensation and emotion
on hypotheses different from those of Freud.

[233] *Two Essays on Analytical Psychology*, p. 52. See also p. 34.

[234] *Ibid.*, p. 53. Jung emphasizes this point in his parallel objection to Freud's use
of terminology. Freud, says Jung, used the word "libido" to signify *eros*, or the life
instinct, thus excluding from its scope the tendency of the death instinct. Jung prefers
to use the term "libido" for all psychic energy, particularly since he does not admit
the distinction between the life instinct and the death instinct. "Since the so-called
destructive instinct is also a phenomenon of energy, it seems to me simpler to define
libido as an inclusive term for psychic intensities, and consequently as sheer psychic
energy." (*Ibid.*, p. 52, fn. 6.) Libido taken either in its restricted Freudian sense or in
the wider Jungian sense is never identified with love by Jung.

part of, love he concedes that "Freud's sexual theory of neurosis is grounded on a true and factual principle." But he immediately adds that such a theory "makes the mistake of being one-sided and exclusive; also it commits the imprudence of trying to lay hold of unconfinable Eros with the crude terminology of sex. In this respect Freud is a typical representative of the materialistic epoch, whose hope it was to solve the world riddle in a test-tube."[235] Jung extends his indictment concerning the misunderstanding of the relationship between love and sexuality when he says that "most men are blind erotically. They commit the unpardonable mistake of confusing eros with sexuality."[236]

Jung indicates what his own position is in saying:

> Eros is a questionable fellow and will always remain so. . . . He belongs on one side to man's primordial animal nature which will endure as long as man has an animal body. On the other side he is related to the highest forms of the spirit. But he only thrives when spirit and instinct are in right harmony.[237]

This passage suggests that Jung conceives the ideal or best love as a combination or balance of both physical and nonphysical desires. Generically speaking, however, he often discusses love as purely physical or sexual (though he denies that all love has its origin in such impulses), and again as a purely spiritual phenomenon. In other words, he distinguishes between the question of what the best love is and the question of what love is. Considering the statements he makes concerning what tendencies are not love (hate, fear, will to power, life instinct, etc.), it is far from clear what he thinks the character of the basic love tendency is. *Eros*, says Jung, "is not the whole of our inward nature, though he is at least one of its essential aspects."[238]

William James

James is another author in psychology who, though he does not subject love to full analytical treatment, nevertheless discusses it here and

[235] *Ibid.*, p. 27. Jung also notes: "Freud himself, with advancing years, admitted this lack of balance in his theory, and he opposed to Eros, which he called libido, the destructive or death instinct." (*Ibid.*)

[236] *Contributions to Analytical Psychology*, p. 176. See also *Two Essays on Analytical Psychology*, p. 17, fn. 8.

[237] *Ibid.*, p. 27.

[238] *Ibid.* Jung does say that the object to which love is directed is not an index to the character of love: "One loves a Beethoven sonata but one loves caviar also. . . . It is a common error for one to judge the longing according to the quality of the object. . . . The longing is the same; the object changes." (*Psychology of the Unconscious*, Part I, Ch. IV, p. 94.)

there in analyses of other subjects.[239] The theory that emerges from these
various remarks is one in which love is conceived as primarily tendential
and as taking both acquisitive and benevolent forms.[240]

James' "functional" psychology is heavily influenced by the Darwinian
notions of struggle for existence, adjustment to environment, adaptation,
etc.; he does not concentrate on an analysis of the psyche as such, but
rather on the whole man as a functioning organism in relation to his
environment.[241] On the other hand, where psychology is stressed in his work,
the crucial notion is the "stream of thought" or "stream of consciousness" in
which all psychic elements—sensations, perceptions, feelings, emotions,
even acts of will are said to occur in combination from moment to
moment. Human love, according to James, occurs in this complex.

The separation of self and other in regard to tendencies (as well as
judgments of worth) is a crucial problem for James. In discussing "the
facts of self-love and self-seeking," he distinguishes, as a matter of course,
between tendencies whose aim is one's own good and those whose aim is
the good of another. "A man in whom self-seeking of any sort is largely
developed is said to be selfish. He is on the other hand called unselfish if he
shows consideration for the interests of other selves than his own."[242] The
problems James concentrates on in this regard are: which of the multiple
selves in any given man is seeking a good, how that seeking is made
possible, and to what extent volition is involved in each case.

Generally speaking, James distinguishes three selves that make up the
composite man: the material self, the social self, and the spiritual self.
Each self is capable of acquisitive and benevolent desires, which James
identifies as forms of love. With regard to acquisitive desire, he says:

> The *kind* of selfishness varies with the self that is sought. If it be the mere
> bodily self; if a man grabs the best food, the warm corner, the vacant seat;
> if he makes room for no one, spits about, and belches in our faces—we call

[239] James is interested principally in the sources of vitality in human life. He
considers as main areas of concentration: instinct, emotion, will, perception, etc. At
the same time he exposes their very concrete relationships to the self, so that he
presents, in his *Psychology*, a thorough consideration of forces as well as detailed
development of their physical and psychic manifestations. The whole breadth of the
subject matter is traversed and penetrated by his method of considering whatever
level of thought, emotion, and experience is involved in a variety of human actions.
So we find love, not a separate subject but discussed as it is linked with emotion, will,
the self-consciousness, instinct, etc.

[240] At one point, James does say that love "is the association of the agreeableness
of certain sensible experiences with the idea of the object capable of affording them."
(*The Principles of Psychology*, Vol. I, Ch. XIV, p. 599.)

[241] For this reason, he, like Darwin, talks quite freely of animal love. (See *ibid.*,
Vol. II, Ch. XXIV, pp. 386 ff.)

[242] *Ibid.*, Vol. I, Ch. X, pp. 317–318.

it hoggishness. If it be the social self, in the form of popularity or influence, for which he is greedy, he may in material ways subordinate himself to others as the best means to his end; and in this case he is very apt to pass for a disinterested man. If it be the "other-worldly" self which he seeks, and if he seeks it ascetically,—even though he would rather see all mankind damned eternally than lose his individual soul—"saintliness" will probably be the name by which his selfishness will be called.[243]

James claims that there is a natural propensity in men to see the maximum good for each of the selves;[244] he also maintains that the tendencies of the three are often in conflict and that the conflict is often heightened by the hierarchy in which they are arranged:

A tolerably unanimous opinion ranges the different selves of which a man may be "seized and possessed," and the consequent different orders of his self-regard, in an *hierarchical scale, with the bodily Self at the bottom, the spiritual Self at top, and the extra-corporeal material selves and the various social selves between.*[245]

None of these forms of love as acquisitive desire depend solely or even primarily on the perception that there is an ego or an I which is thought to deserve attention. On the contrary, James insists that self-love in any of its forms invariably is activated by the perception of another thing or another person who offers the possibility of a specific good. In other words, a person eats, not because he knows he must in order to live but because there is a certain food that excites the anticipation of the pleasure of eating. He socializes, not because he thinks he must or should but because someone he meets draws him into sociability. He seeks his own spiritual advancement, not because it is an obligation or duty but because some particular occasion or experience incites him to do so. The tendencies of the three selves spring from certain instincts activated, for the most part, by specific and individual causes. Such causes or objects make self-love possible.

243 *Ibid.*, pp. 317–318, fn. See also chart on p. 329, and see pp. 307–309.
244 "Our merely natural self-seeking would lead us to aggrandize all these selves; we give up deliberately only those among them which we find we cannot keep. Our unselfishness is thus apt to be a 'virtue of necessity'. . . ." (*Ibid.*, pp. 313–314.) Understanding that this process is not totally a matter of profit and loss, James adds that a "direct ethical judgment unquestionably also plays its part" in the sacrifice of interest. (*Ibid.*, p. 314.)
245 *Ibid.*, p. 313. He later says: "*In each kind of self, material, social, and spiritual, men distinguish between the immediate and actual, and the remote and potential,* between the narrower and the wider view, to the detriment of the former and advantage of the latter. One must forego a present bodily enjoyment for the sake of one's general health; one must abandon the dollar in the hand for the sake of the hundred dollars to come; one must make an enemy of his present interlocutor if thereby one makes friends of a more valued circle; one must go without learning and grace, and wit, the better to compass one's soul's salvation." (*Ibid.*, p. 315.)

To have a self that I can *care for,* nature must first present me with some *object* interesting enough to make me instinctively wish to appropriate it for its *own* sake, and out of it to manufacture one of those material, social, or spiritual selves, which we have already passed in review.[246]

To make this point clearer, James adds:

When I am led by self-love to keep my seat whilst ladies stand, or to grab something first and cut out my neighbor, what I really love is the comfortable seat, is the thing itself which I grab.[247]

Acquisitive desire has its origin in, and is most obvious and most undiluted in, bodily appetites.

My own body and what ministers to its needs are . . . *the primitive object, instinctively determined, of my egoistic interests. Other objects may become interesting derivatively* through association with any of these things, either as means or as habitual concomitants; *and so in a thousand ways the primitive sphere of the egoistic emotions may enlarge* and change its boundaries.[248]

James stresses this point in regard to sexual desire, which he discusses under the heading of love. "Of all propensities, the sexual impulses bear on their face the most obvious signs of being instinctive, in the sense of blind, automatic, and untaught."[249]

Because James seldom analyzes human actions as inspired solely by instinctive tendencies, emotional tendencies, or wilful tendencies, it is impossible to claim that he thinks sexual actions are all acquisitively motivated. He thinks a great many such actions are promoted by a blend of different desires. Though he stresses the instinctive aspect of sexual impulses, he freely admits that such desires are connected with emotional ones and claims that they can be indirectly controlled by the will.[250]

Furthermore, James, as Darwin, sees ample evidence of instinctive and

[246] *Ibid.,* p. 319. The phrase "for its own sake" does not mean in Jamesian terminology what it means in ours. What it means is that an object desired "for its own sake" has distinctive qualities that appeal to a particular person, as opposed to an object that is one of many indistinguishable ones, all of which can fulfill a given desire. (See *ibid.,* Ch. VIII, p. 206.)

[247] *Ibid.,* Ch. X, p. 320. "To sum up, then, *we see no reason to suppose that self-love is primarily, or secondarily, or ever, love for one's mere principle of conscious identity.* It is always love for something which, as compared with that principle, is superficial, transient, liable to be taken up or dropped at will." (*Ibid.,* p. 323.)

[248] *Ibid.,* p. 324. "The most palpable selfishness of a man is his bodily selfishness; and his most palpable self is the body to which that selfishness relates." (*Ibid.,* p. 319.)

[249] *Ibid.,* Vol. II, Ch. XXIV, p. 437.

[250] See *ibid.,* Ch. XXV, pp. 461 ff.

emotional beneficence.[251] Parental love is, for example, described as an instinct.[252] James emphatically denies "that altruistic passions and interests are contradictory to the nature of things." On the contrary, he claims:

> The phenomenon of passion is in origin and essence the same, whatever be the target upon which it is discharged. . . . I might conceivably be as much fascinated, and as primitively so, by the care of my neighbor's body as by the care of my own. . . . The sympathetic instincts and the egoistic ones are thus co-ordinate. They arise, so far as we can tell, on the same psychologic level. The only difference between them is, that the instincts called egoistic form much the larger mass.[253]

It is doubtful, however, that such tendencies can be described as benevolent since James relates instincts and emotions, unaffected by the influence of will, to personal pleasure or pain.[254] Whether or not such tendencies can be classified as benevolent, James does present a theory of love we can classify as binary, for he asserts that conscious and deliberate tendencies of the will may be acquisitive or benevolent. He explicitly denies that such tendencies can be understood in terms of the determinants of pleasure and pain.[255]

James defines instinct as *"the faculty of acting in such a way as to produce certain ends, without foresight of the ends, and without previous education in the performance.* That instincts, as thus defined, exist on an enormous scale in the animal kingdom needs no proof."[256] No judgment is required to produce an instinctive tendency, but one is required in the case of emotional tendency. James asserts that judgment or perception often gives rise to bodily change directly and that our awareness or feeling of these changes is an emotion.[257] Will, on the other hand, is the faculty of actively determining that a "desired feeling, having, or doing shall be real." Unlike instincts and emotions, such wilful impulses are free.[258]

That James thinks voluntary acquisitive tendencies are present in human love relationships is clear from the following celebrated passage:

> Romeo wants Juliet as the filings want the magnet; and if no obstacles intervene he moves towards her by as straight a line as they. But Romeo and Juliet, if a wall be built between them, do not remain idiotically pressing their faces against its opposite sides like the magnet and the filings with the

---

[251] See *ibid.*, Vol. I, Ch. X, pp. 324–325; also Vol. II, Ch. XXIV, pp. 410–411.
[252] See *ibid.*, pp. 439–440.
[253] *Ibid.*, Vol. I, Ch. X, p. 325.
[254] See *ibid.*, Vol. II, Ch. XXVI, pp. 549 ff.
[255] See *ibid.*, pp. 549–553, esp. fn. on pp. 551–552.
[256] *Ibid.*, Ch. XXIV, p. 383.
[257] See *ibid.*, Ch. XXV, p. 449.
[258] *Ibid.*, Ch. XXVI, p. 486. See also pp. 569 ff.

card [in between]. Romeo soon finds a circuitous way, by scaling the wall or otherwise, of touching Juliet's lips directly. With the filings the path is fixed; whether it reaches the end depends on accidents. With the lover it is the end which is fixed, the path may be modified indefinitely.[259]

It is primarily in terms of the notion of union (and not the desire for it) that James discusses benevolence. He remarks on the projection of a person's self, or rather self-interest, onto that of the beloved. Though existentially separated from the other, the lover does everything possible to enhance the welfare of the beloved and to minimize his sorrow and pain. He does this because he feels a sense of union with, and interest in, the other's welfare. The beloved represents, in a sense, the lover's "social" or other self.

> The most peculiar social self which one is apt to have is in the mind of the person one is in love with. The good or bad fortunes of this self cause the most intense elation and dejection—unreasonable enough as measured by every other standard than that of the organic feeling of the individual. To his own consciousness he *is* not, so long as this particular social self fails to get recognition, and when it is recognized his contentment passes all bounds.[260]

James mentions the unlikely possibility of a projection of oneself onto another so complete as to preclude any self-interested motive at all:

> Were my mental life dependent exclusively on some other person's welfare, either directly or in an indirect way, then natural selection would unquestionably have brought it about that I should be as sensitive to the social vicissitudes of that other person as I now am to my own. Instead of being egoistic I should be spontaneously altruistic, then.[261]

He concludes that such a projection does not seem humanly possible, adding that all human benevolence has some self-interested aspect to it:

> Probably no one can make sacrifices for "right," without to some degree personifying the principle of right for which the sacrifice is made, and expecting thanks from it. *Complete* social unselfishness, in other words, can hardly exist.[262]

In *The Varieties of Religious Experience,* James bases his analysis of love (*i.e.,* benevolence) for one's fellowmen on a projection of the self

---

[259] *Ibid.,* Vol. I, Ch. I, p. 7. See also Ch. X, pp. 307–309, for a discussion of the ways in which men engage in bodily self-seeking, social self-seeking, and spiritual self-seeking, all of which can and often do contain an element of volition.

[260] *Ibid.,* Ch. X, p. 294. See also pp. 291–293.

[261] *Ibid.,* p. 324.

[262] *Ibid.,* pp. 316–317.

made possible by the universal paternalism of God: awareness of a higher and personified active principle that tends to unify men as brothers. He suggests more than once that this is the way "to explain both the humility as to one's self and the charity towards others which characterize spiritual excitement, as results of the all-leveling character of theistic belief."[263] "Brotherly love," he says, "would follow logically from the assurance of God's friendly presence, the notion of our brotherhood as men being an immediate inference from that of God's fatherhood of us all."[264] In describing the love or charity made possible by this identification with other human beings, James says:

> The shifting of the emotional centre brings . . . increase of charity, tenderness of fellow-creatures. The ordinary motives to antipathy, which usually set such close bounds to tenderness among human beings, are inhibited. The saint loves his enemies, and treats loathsome beggars as his brothers.[265]

James is convinced that love for enemies is a rare and difficult human achievement. Though not denying the possibility of such a love, he says that such a love, taken to an extreme,

> would involve such a breach with our instinctive springs of action as a whole, and with the present world's arrangements, that a critical point would practically be passed, and we should be born into another kingdom of being. Religious emotion makes us feel that other kingdom to be close at hand, within our reach.[266]

[263] *Ibid.*, Lectures XI, XII, and XIII, p. 279.
[264] *Ibid.*, p. 278.
[265] *Ibid.*, p. 274.
[266] *Ibid.*, pp. 283–284. See also Lectures XIV and XV, pp. 355–359.

7

Love as Acquisitive Desire

THE authors whose theories are classified in this chapter discuss love only as tendentially acquisitive, as a desire that aims ultimately at something for the self. Beyond this, they differ in a number of ways. Some do not even mention benevolent desires. Others discuss benevolent desires but withhold the name of love from them. Some indicate that they do not believe benevolence to be humanly possible even as a conscious illusion. Still others allude to such impulses and call them illusions, but do not attach decisive importance to them in their theories of love. Several maintain that love is a universal force or influence; others discuss it only in the context of human relationships. Some authors deal primarily with the sexual relationship between a man and a woman and regard this relationship as the focal point of their theory of love. There are also some who, while admitting that sexual desire is an expression of love, understand love as a much broader acquisitive tendency. Most of the authors whose theories are classified in this chapter see love as totally a matter of tendency, but a few include judgmental aspects in their conceptions of love.

Our primary concern is to show that love is conceived as tendentially acquisitive in each theory presented. Among the authors who conceive

325

natural love among human beings thus are: Plotinus, Marsilio Ficino, Giovanni Pico della Mirandola, Pietro Bembo, Ibn Sina, Andreas Capellanus, Marie-Henri Beyle (de Stendhal), Arthur Schopenhauer, Denis de Rougemont, George Santayana, Charles Darwin, Jean-Jacques Rousseau, Benedict de Spinoza, and Gottfried Wilhelm Leibniz.

Freud could well be listed with the authors who affirm that love is essentially acquisitive in tendency. The reader will recall that in characterizing Freud's theory of love as one that includes the notions of both acquisitive and benevolent desire, our interpretation rested entirely on the crucial distinction he makes between unconscious and conscious inclinations. Unconscious desires are invariably acquisitive for Freud. And all conscious desires derive from the unconscious ones. Many conscious tendencies are also acquisitive, though most of them have been altered, to a greater or lesser degree, in the process of becoming conscious. However, Freud also maintains that some conscious desires can be benevolent. Of those he mentions, the ones that most clearly approach what we mean by benevolent desire are those that result in the tenderness Freud understands as an essential part of mature love between a man and a woman. Freud, however, refers to this inclination as an illusion, since it remains acquisitive in its unconscious and original form.

Thus it is certainly possible to interpret Freud's theory as one in which love, ultimately and basically, is conceived as totally acquisitive in character. For, in the Freudian view, the unconscious origin of all desires is such—and remains such—that true benevolence is not really possible. Desires that appear to be benevolent are merely useful illusions.

Despite the fact that benevolent desire has acquisitive roots in the Freudian theory, we believe the theory will be better understood if classified as binary.[1] If we viewed the Freudian theory only from the perspective of the unconscious, it would be classified in this chapter.

Plotinus

In all but one important respect the theory of Plotinus is very close to that of Plato. The reader will recall that we interpreted the desire for *intellectual* procreation, *i.e.*, the desire to teach, in the Platonic theory, as a benevolent desire even though it resulted from the fulfillment of an acquisitive one, *i.e.*, the desire to learn. Plotinus makes no mention of this

---

[1] It might be argued that Schopenhauer's theory should also be so classified. Though he does mention the lover's misunderstanding of his own motives, he does not specify that benevolence is one of the lover's illusions and certainly does not make it a requisite for the type of love he discusses. (See pp. 356 ff., *infra*.)

form of benevolent desire nor, indeed, of any giving in relation to love; he discusses only loves that are acquisitive in character.

In other respects the Platonic influence is not only obvious but acknowledged by the author. The ultimate objects of love are the everlasting forms or eternal ideas, true "Beauty" or the "Good."[2] As these eternal forms or ideas have worldly images or reflections, love among human beings must be understood as the soul's desire to draw closer to the ultimate realities by getting closer to their images. Thus, for Plotinus as for Plato, interpersonal love is of secondary importance and significance.

Plotinus says there are two kinds of love: the love of worldly appearance (which includes love among human beings) and the love of spiritual realities. Both loves, as he understands them, involve the same mode of tendency.

> Lovers here mould themselves to the beloved; they seek to increase their attraction of person and their likeness of mind; they are unwilling to fall short in moral quality or in other graces lest they be distasteful to those possessing such merit—and only among such can true love be. In the same way the soul loves the Supreme Good.[3]

In each case the tendency is an acquisitive one, for "there is in it [Love] the lack which keeps it craving."[4]

Like Plato, Plotinus understands the path of human perfection as the ascent from the lower love of appearance (which includes carnal love) to the higher love of invisible reality.

> The soul in its nature loves God and longs to be at one with Him in the noble love of a daughter for a noble father; but coming to human birth and lured by the courtships of this sphere, she takes up with another love, a mortal, leaves her father and falls.

[2] The relationship between beauty and goodness as objects of love is best described in the following passage: "The perception of Beauty and the awe and the stirring of passion towards it are for those already in some degree knowing and awakened: but the Good, as possessed long since and setting up a natural tendency, is inherently present to even those asleep and brings them no wonder when some day they see it, since it is no occasional reminiscence but is always with them though in their drowse they are not aware of it: the love of Beauty on the contrary sets up pain when it appears, for those that have seen it must pursue. This love of Beauty then is later than the love of Good and comes with a more sophisticated understanding; hence we know that Beauty is a secondary: the more primal appetition, not patent to sense, our movement towards our good, gives witness that The Good is the earlier, the prior." (*The Enneads*, Ennead V, Tractate 5, pp. 412–413. See also Ennead I, Tractate 6, pp. 59–60.) Beauty, however, differs from goodness and is discussed more often in relation to love because it can be perceived through the senses, particularly the sense of sight. (See *ibid.*, Ennead VI, Tractate 5, p. 538.)

[3] *Ibid.*, Ennead VI, Tractate 7, p. 585.

[4] *Ibid.*, Ennead III, Tractate 5, p. 200.

But one day coming to hate her shame, she puts away the evil of earth, once more seeks the father, and finds her peace.[5]

Once the soul has ascended to the point where it can glimpse the ultimate and highest object of love, it leaves its earlier, terrestrial love behind.

And one that shall know this vision—with what passion of love shall he not be seized, with what pang of desire, what longing to be molten into one with This, what wondering delight! If he that has never seen this Being must hunger for It as for all his welfare, he that has known must love and reverence It as the very Beauty; he will be flooded with awe and gladness, stricken by a salutary terror; he loves with a veritable love, with sharp desire; all other loves than this he must despise, and disdain all that once seemed fair.[6]

Plotinus illustrates the distinction between the love of the highest and the love of the worldly by commenting on Plato's *Symposium*. He recalls that the Platonic myth tells of the parentage of *Eros,* or love. He notes that *Eros* was born on the birthday of Aphrodite and that "Eros is described as being either her son or in some association with her." But Plotinus says that Aphrodite is twofold. There is the heavenly Aphrodite, which is—or rather represents—the intellectual principle in the soul inclining always to strive for the higher and more enduring objects. And there is the other Aphrodite "who presides over earthly unions."[7]

The principal followers of the latter Aphrodite are those who "desire earthly procreation [and] are satisfied with the beauty found on earth, the beauty of image and of body; it is because they are strangers to the Archetype, the source of even the attraction they feel towards what is lovely here." They seek the engendering of beauty through "copulative love." This desire is acquisitive, for its purpose is self-perpetuation. The desire to reproduce "is the expression of a lack; the subject is conscious of insufficiency and, wishing to produce beauty, feels that the way is to beget in a beautiful form." Those who indulge sexuality for the sake of procreation and not "against the purposes of nature" are expressing "a desire of such immortality as lies within mortal reach."[8]

[5] *Ibid.,* Ennead VI, Tractate 9, p. 623. Love "takes two forms, that of the good whose devotion is for beauty itself, and that other which seeks its consummation in some vile act." (*Ibid.,* Ennead III, Tractate 5, p. 191.)

[6] *Ibid.,* Ennead I, Tractate 6, p. 62. See also Ennead VI, Tractate 7, pp. 585–586.

[7] *Ibid.,* Ennead III, Tractate 5, pp. 192–193, *passim.*

[8] *Ibid.,* pp. 191–192, *passim.* Plotinus admits that followers of the lower Aphrodite include those "that love beauty of person [and] without carnal desire love for beauty's sake." (*Ibid.,* p. 192.) He places these under the lower Aphrodite because their love is still directed to persons, *i.e.,* to beauty incarnate, rather than to beauty itself.

The followers of the heavenly Aphrodite are those "to whom earthly beauty is a leading to the memory of that in the higher realm and these love the earthly as an image." They aspire, through an intellectual ascent, to get closer and closer to beauty itself, and to fuse themselves as far as possible with it.[9]

Though love is always an acquisitive tendency, its characteristic expression, on both levels, is the desire for union. Love "rises in souls aspiring to be knit in the closest union with some beautiful object."[10] With the lower love the desire for union is expressed either as sexual desire or as a desire to contemplate and appreciate the beauty of the beloved. With the higher love the desire for union is the desire for the union of similarity, the tendency of the soul to make itself more and more like the ultimate objects toward which it strives.

Plotinus also mentions Plato's striking image of the dual parentage of love, born of Poverty and Possession (or Plenty) and combining both in its nature. But, whereas Plenty is the basis for benevolent desire in Plato's theory, it is interpreted by Plotinus as only reenforcing love's basic acquisitive tendency:

> On the one hand there is in it the lack which keeps it craving: on the other, it is not entirely destitute; the deficient seeks more of what it has, and certainly nothing absolutely void of good would ever go seeking the Good.[11]

Marsilio Ficino

Another author who presents his theory of love in the form of a commentary on Plato's *Symposium* is Marsilio Ficino. Again, there are strong similarities to the Platonic theory as well as variations on it and deviations from it.

The theory presented in the *Commentary on Plato's "Symposium"* is a cosmic one. But it hinges upon a conception of an active and supernatural God rather than upon the impersonal ultimate realities postulated by Plato. The tendencies of God are benevolent, in Ficino's view, but, of course, such tendencies are no part of his theory of natural love among human beings. Acquisitive desire as a cosmic principle is explained in two connections: the love of the inferior for the superior and the love of like for like. The former love animates the body's attachment to the soul, the soul's desire for the bliss of "heavenly beings," and the heavenly beings' worship of the "supreme divinity." Love of like for like holds the elements

---

[9] See *ibid.*, p. 191.
[10] *The Enneads*, Ennead III, Tractate 5, p. 191.
[11] *Ibid.*, p. 200.

together; it also draws animals of the same kind to flock together instinctively.[12]

Love is the author and preserver of everything, not only in the sense that
it is behind the procreative impulse of all living things but also because it
provides a natural balance among the nonliving elements, each of which
seeks its natural place. Love also preserves all things since it strives to keep
together the constitutive parts of anything and works to prevent them from
dispersing.[13]

Ficino's most general definition of love involves the notion of beauty:
"When we say Love, we mean by that term the desire for beauty, for this is
the definition of Love among all philosophers."[14] The beauty to which
Ficino refers, and to which all love is ultimately directed, is an invisible
reality that is reflected in corporeal forms. Its source is God, the final object
of all love. Though "Goodness is said to be the outstanding characteristic of
God," Ficino says that "Beauty is a kind of force or light, shining from Him
through everything." Beauty, emanating from a divine source and reflected
in different ways, incites love. The emanation of divine beauty filters down
in stages through the universe. The first receiver of it is a purely intellectual substance, the angelic mind, in which the eternal ideas reside. Beauty
also "fills the Soul with a series of Concepts; it sows Nature with Seeds;
and it provides Matter with Forms. In much the same way, in fact, that the
single light of the sun lights up four bodies, fire, air, water, and earth, so
the single light of God illumines the Mind, Soul, Nature, and Matter."[15]

Ficino makes the familiar and fundamental distinction between spiritual
and physical love in terms of the traditional metaphor of the two Venuses.
He says, in summary, that

> Venus is two-fold: one is clearly that intelligence which we said was in the
> Angelic Mind; the other is the power of generation with which the World-

[12] See *Commentary on Plato's "Symposium,"* pp. 148, 153.

[13] See *ibid.,* pp. 149–150, 153, 192. Under the general category of the love of the
superior for the inferior, Ficino also mentions the love of the "heavenly beings" for
the soul and that of the soul for the body, both presumably benevolent. Ficino does
mention the teaching impulse, but in a context that inclines one to interpret it as an
acquisitive rather than a benevolent desire, since its aim seems to be personal
immortality. (See *ibid.,* p. 204.) And, at another point, his description of the love of
an older man for a younger clearly involves an acquisitive impulse on the part of the
older, since the older uses the younger in his ascent up the ladder of love. (See *ibid.,*
p. 199.)

[14] *Ibid.,* p. 130.

[15] *Ibid.,* p. 140, *passim.* See also pp. 168, 179, 183. "If we love bodies, the Soul, or
the Angelic Mind, we do not really love these, but God in them: the shadow of God
in bodies, the likeness of God in the Soul, and the Image of God in the Angelic
Mind." (*Ibid.,* p. 215.)

Soul is endowed. Each has as consort a similar Love. The first, by innate love is stimulated to know the beauty of God; the second, by its love, to procreate the same beauty in bodies.

One Venus is called "the Heavenly, the other the Earthly."[16] Both of these loves ultimately are attracted by the reflections of divine beauty, but each seeks the beautiful in a different way. The higher love is directed to the nonhuman, to the highest. The lower love is directed to the procreation of physical beauty.

Although these two loves are in conflict, Ficino stops short of saying they are mutually exclusive. He maintains only that each is engaged in a struggle with the other. The one pushes a man "down to the animal and voluptuous life," while the other urges him to raise himself "on high to the angelic and contemplative life."[17] But, as long as sensual love is controlled and limited to procreation, Ficino maintains that "both loves are honorable and praiseworthy, for each is concerned with the divine image." In fact, he says that the mind "through the first" of these loves "is frequently aroused to the second," as long as physical love involves the pleasure of sight as well as touch.[18]

Love among human beings, especially when it takes the form of the desire for union, always seeks reciprocity. When this aim is frustrated, Ficino says that "the lover is completely dead, for he neither lives in himself . . . nor does he live in his loved one, since he is rejected by him."[19] On the other hand, if the love is returned, the two lovers

> watch each other constantly, and also try to please each other. Inasmuch as each is watched by the other, they abstain from all evil, for they never lack a witness. Inasmuch as they try to please each other, they are always under-

[16] *Ibid.*, p. 142. See also p. 191. At another point, Ficino makes a threefold rather than a twofold distinction. Instead of the distinction between heavenly and earthly love, he speaks of contemplative, practical, and voluptuous love, or, as he also says, divine, human, and animal love. Divine love is the desire to know, through the use of the mind, the divine being, and animal love is the desire to procreate physical beauty. Human love is also on the physical level but is limited to the pleasures of sight. It seeks only the delight one takes in viewing a beautiful person. Ficino also makes the point that animal or sexual love is not really love if *all* that it seeks is physical pleasure. If it does not aim at procreation through physical intercourse, it is only "lust and madness." (See *ibid.*, pp. 130, 146–147, 193, 204.)

[17] *Ibid.*, p. 217. "Pleasures and sensations which are so impetuous and irrational that they jar the mind from its stability and unbalance a man, love does not only not desire, but hates and shuns, because these sensations, being so intemperate, are the opposites of beauty. A mad lasciviousness drags a man down to intemperance and disharmony, and hence seems to attract him to ugliness, whereas love attracts to beauty. Ugliness and beauty are opposites." (*Ibid.*, p. 130.)

[18] *Ibid.*, p. 143, *passim.*

[19] *Ibid.*, p. 144.

taking great tasks with a burning zeal, so that they may not appear contemptible in the eyes of the beloved, but may seem worthy of an exchange of love.[20]

Ficino understands this desire toward another person in terms of the Aristophanic myth about the original nature of man. Before he was cut in half by the gods, man was a whole creature. Love seeks to restore the original unity and draw two beings, appropriate to each other, into union.[21]

> Hence mutual love, the restorer of their original nature, is innate in all men, striving to make the two one again, and to heal the natures of men.[22]

Ficino's interpretation of the Platonic myth about the parents of love, Poverty and Plenty, is similar to that of Plotinus. Poverty accounts for the element of deficiency in love and Plenty for the lover's desire to fulfill that deficiency. In other words, love can occur only when the lover has *only in some measure* what he wants. He cannot love if he has no contact with the object of his love; and he cannot love if he has the object completely.

> Since the soul so long as it has received no image of a beautiful thing does not yet love that thing, which is still unknown, as it were; so also one who possesses the whole beauty is not vexed by the prickings of love. For who desires what he has?

Love, therefore, "is a certain mean passion between beauty and absence of beauty, sharing in both." Plenty offers the soul of the lover a "foretaste" to excite its desire for full possession of whatever is beloved. Poverty means that the lover, while he loves, does not have what he wants. The function of Plenty is to make possible and reenforce love's acquisitive tendency.[23]

Ficino says that the benefits of love, or rather of love fulfilled, are threefold: first, it makes us whole by repairing the original division made in human nature; second, it arranges us in our proper and natural place so that we are content with our lot; and third, it constantly offers us new delights by enticing us to different and attractive things we do not possess fully. The fullness in love "perpetually" spurs us on to these delights, and

[20] *Ibid.*, p. 131.
[21] Ficino puts the emphasis on similarity rather than complementarity. The enchantment resulting from love "is the attraction of one thing by another because of a certain similarity of their nature." (*Ibid.*, p. 199. See also p. 146.) Hence, in terms of the myth, he is thinking of those beings who were originally all male or all female rather than of mixed sex. The impulse of love for the former beings seems to be different from the procreation in beauty that can only be accomplished by the union of a man and a woman.
[22] *Ibid.*, p. 154.
[23] *Ibid.*, pp. 183–184, *passim.*

the deficiency in love assures us that these delights will be continual, since, "banishing all repletion," it makes the search for beauty never ending.[24]

Giovanni Pico della Mirandola

Pico is still another author whose theory of love is influenced decisively by Plato. His theory is found principally in a small work entitled *A Platonick Discourse upon Love*. At the beginning of the second book, Pico mentions a number of meanings attached to the word "love." These, he says, "we exclude, and admit no other signification, but 'the desire to possesse what in it self, or at least in our esteem is fair.' " Such is "of a different nature from the love of God to his Creatures, who comprehending all cannot desire or want the beauty and perfections of another." The love he is considering, therefore, is not of a benevolent character. Rather, it is always the tendency of a being striving to fill a deficiency in itself. Pico defines love "with Plato" as the desire for beauty.[25]

Pico treats four varieties of the desire for beauty or for union with beauty. Three of the four are human loves, but only two are loves among human beings. Consideration of the one nonhuman love helps us to understand Pico's conception of love among human beings.

The highest and purest desire for beauty occurs in a being that Pico calls the "Angelick Minde," a pure intelligence. It is the only being *immediately* created by God and is thus free of the taint of all matter. This being, however, is not divine because it is imperfect. The angelic mind receives its form from God. ". . . this form is Ideas, the first Beauty; which in this descent from their divine Fountain, mixing with a different nature, become imperfect. The first Minde [the Angelick Minde], by its opacousness eclipsing their lustre, desires that Beauty which they have lost; this desire is Love." In other words, the completely disembodied intelligence (which is presumably not a person in any sense) is still somehow separate from the divine essence. It lacks something, and is therefore capable of love. Pico calls this love celestial, "an Intellectual desire of Ideal Beauty."[26]

It is in terms of the ideal of this purely intellectual love that he makes a broad threefold distinction with regard to human love. Human beings may love beauty intellectually, they may love it humanly, or they may love it sensually. He calls these three human loves (all of which are acquisitive in

[24] See *ibid.*, p. 163.
[25] *A Platonick Discourse upon Love*, Book II, p. 21, *passim*. "Desire is an inclination to real or apparent good. As there are divers kinds of good, so of desire. Love is a species of desire; Beauty of good." (*Ibid.*) See also p. 22 where a kind of cosmic theory of love seems to be implied.
[26] *Ibid.*, pp. 30–31, *passim*. See also p. 33.

tendency) "Angelical" love, "Humane" (human) love, and "Sensual" love, adding that the latter two "are conversant about the same object, Corporeal Beauty."[27] Angelic love is a purely intellectual love which has nothing to do with the physical senses. Pico says it is the love of celestial beauty, but, because it is a human love, it is not the celestial love of the "First Minde" (or "Angelick Minde") but only the barest image of it. Human love and sensual love (or "Bestial Love") are directed to sensible beauty and are the two loves that occur among human beings. Explaining the difference between them, he says that

> when the species of sensible Beauty flow into the Eye, there springs a twofold Appetite of Union with that whence this Beauty is deriv'd, one sensuall, the other rational; the Principles of Bestial and Humane Love.[28]

He goes on to say that the observed corporeal beauty appeals only to the senses in bestial love and hence gives rise to the desire for sexual union with a beautiful person. In human love, on the other hand, a man, by use of his reason, tries to separate the visual image of the beautiful person from that person's body. Since it is not the body that is loved, human love is called an image of celestial love (though still obviously a fainter image than human angelic love).

Pico's ascent in love differs in some details from Plato's ladder of love. He does not begin with bestial love or sexual desire, but rather with the first stages of human love, the mind's love of the visible beauty in another person. The "Soul through the sight represents to her self the Beauty of some particular Person, inclines to it, is pleased with it, and while she rests here, is in the first, the most imperfect material degree." Through the use of the imagination the soul is then able to separate the image of the beautiful person from the physical matter or body of that person, making the image "a little nearer Ideal Beauty" by "making it more perfect as more spiritual." The next step, still concerned with sensible beauty and therefore still within the range of human love is described as follows:

> By the light of the agent Intellect abstracting this Form from all singularity, she considers the universal Nature of Corporeal Beauty by it self: this is the highest degree the Soul can reach whilest she goes no further than Sense.

Moving up from the level of sense, the soul next looks into itself, examining its own activity, and finds in itself "the Image of Ideal Beauty

[27] *Ibid.*, p. 47, *passim.* Pico also makes a twofold distinction with regard to love by human beings. On the one hand, there is the human love of the mind alone for invisible beauty. On the other hand there is the human love for visible beauty ("Vulgar Love"), which can be either human or sensual. (See *ibid.*, pp. 42–43, 45. Pico also refers to these two loves as two Venuses on p. 28.)
[28] *Ibid.*, p. 43. See also p. 47.

communicated to her by the Intellect, the Object of Celestiall Love." From this stage the soul then proceeds upward from the particular idea of beauty it has, striving to unite itself with "the first Minde, the chiefest of Creatures, and general Habitation of Ideal Beauty."[29] As the union between the individual soul and the "First Minde" can never be complete, human intellectual love of beauty always will fall short of celestial love.

Pico also mentions the parentage of *Eros*, or love, described in Plato's *Symposium*. He applies the metaphor of Poverty and Plenty somewhat differently than Plato. For Pico, Plenty (*porus*) represents the pure realities that descend from God. Poverty (*penia*), on the other hand, represents the deficient natural matter in which they inhere, from the matter of the angelic mind all the way down to the matter of physical bodies. The union of ideas and matter is necessarily imperfect and the pure luster of the ideas is dimmed. Love is the desire to view the ideas in their original clarity.

Again the function of Plenty is only to reenforce acquisitive desire.

> It is the Property of every desiderative Vertue, that he who desires, possesseth in part the thing he desires; in part not: for if he were wholly deprived of its Possession, he would never desire it.[30]

It may be said of Pico's theory, as of the Platonic theory, that there is a sense in which love among human beings is not really included. What is loved in all cases, *i.e.*, what the lover wants to get closer to, is an idea that human beings reflect. A beautiful person is only an imperfect image of the idea of beauty, which is what the lover is really seeking. "Love transforms the lover into the thing loved" in the sense that it urges him to achieve, through his mind, the closest possible union with beauty in itself.[31] In Pico's view, a beautiful person is merely the occasion for the rousing of this desire. Yet, since other human beings necessarily are involved in bestial and human love, in this sense it is possible to classify them as loves among human beings.

Pietro Bembo

Pietro Bembo's *Gli Asolani* is another work of "Renaissance Platonism," a phrase often applied to different approaches to the subject of love. Some of the men who wrote in this tradition presented theories of love very close to the Platonic original. Others took substantial parts of the Platonic theory

---

[29] *Ibid.*, Book III, pp. 73–74, *passim*.
[30] *Ibid.*, Book II, p. 24.
[31] See *ibid.*, p. 69.

and turned them to their purpose by blending them with or superimposing them on concepts of different origin. Still others adopted a few of the more striking parts of the Platonic theory and something of its manner of presentation and, against this background, wove discussions of love that have a resemblance to Plato's that is more literary than substantive. Bembo's work perhaps is accurately described as one of these.[32]

Participants in the discourses composed by Bembo are three maids of honor to the Queen of Cyprus and three young noblemen: Perottino, Gismondo, and Lavinello, the author's spokesmen in Books I, II, and III, respectively. The work begins with a talk on love by Perottino in which he stresses the uncertainties, pains, and misfortunes that constitute the lot of all lovers. In Book II, Gismondo, by contrast, eulogizes love as that which brings more delight to human beings than anything else in their lives. Up to this point the love under discussion is the love between a man and a woman.[33] The final talk is given by Lavinello whose audience now includes the Queen herself. Lavinello begins by referring to the two previous speakers (Perottino and Gismondo) in order to make the principal point of his own discourse:

> To put in brief what they took hours to expound: one of them wished to persuade us that love is always evil and never can be good, the other that it is always good and never can be evil. But if they had simply said that it is good and that it is evil, without going further, Your Majesty might well have spared yourself the trouble of listening to me; for the love which they describe may be both good and evil, as I shall try to make clear to them.[34]

Lavinello then goes on to explain that love, since it is nothing but tendency, is in itself morally neutral; the goodness or badness of a love depends on its object and on how it is pursued. Lavinello divides human desires into two classes: natural and wilful or rational. The natural, instinctive, involuntary desires cannot be bad. The wilful or rational desires can be bad either when they are directed to the wrong objects or when they do not exercise sufficient control over the natural desires. A man who loves a good woman in the right way is a happy lover. A man who

[32] Bembo himself influenced the work of another author already treated, *The Book of the Courtier* by Castiglione, since he appears as one of Castiglione's principal spokesmen. The theories of the two men are different, however, particularly since Castiglione's theory covers both acquisitive and benevolent desire, while Bembo's is limited to the former. See Part II, Ch. 5, *supra*.

[33] During his speech, Gismondo does mention in passing that love is the basic passion that is behind all others and also describes it as that which animates and harmonizes everything in the universe. (See *Gli Asolani*, Book I, p. 45; and Book II, pp. 110, 113.)

[34] *Ibid.*, Book III, p. 153.

loves either a bad woman or a good woman in the wrong way is an unhappy lover. The former lover enjoys virtuous love, since it is "a desire for beauty of mind no less than body."[35]

Lavinello then explains how he learned these and other truths about love earlier that morning when, while out for a walk, he met an old man with whom he conversed. The old man first told him that love was broader than desire since one could love both what is possessed and what is not possessed, while one could only desire what is not possessed. However, shortly after, he said:

> Yet, Lavinello, I would not reason or dispute with you as closely as with school philosophers; and I am willing, if you wish, to call love and desire the same thing.[36]

The old man next divided the objects of love into those of reason and those of sense, and immediately pointed out:

> If reason is proper to men and sense to animals . . . and if reason, as there is no doubt, is a more perfect thing than sense, then those who follow reason in their love act like men in following the more perfect thing; and those who follow sense act like animals in following the less perfect.[37]

Reason's love, furthermore, is only initially a love among human beings. It begins with such love in its ascent to God only if the soul, "imprisoned in the body," does not forget "its divine origin."[38] The soul must ascend to God through virtuous love, which "is not merely desire of beauty . . . but desire of true beauty, which is not of that human and mortal kind which fades, but is immortal and divine."[39]

After stressing the inestimable benefits, among them immortality, that follow from pursuing reason's love of God, the old man told Lavinello:

> Therefore, your friends will do wisely if they will henceforth court this Prince as they have wooed their ladies hitherto, and if remembering that they are in a temple, they will now dispose themselves to pray since they have had enough of vanities, and casting aside false, earthly, mortal love, will clothe themselves in that which is true, celestial, and immortal. And this it would be well for you to do likewise.[40]

[35] *Ibid.*, p. 157.
[36] *Ibid.*, p. 175. Here again the distinction originally affirmed does not imply that love is not tendential. The desire to retain possession of something, to continue to enjoy it, is different from the desire to possess something one does not have, at least in one sense. Yet, both are seen by all the authors who make this distinction as inclinations or tendencies.
[37] *Ibid.*, p. 177.
[38] *Ibid.*, p. 179. See also pp. 180, 187.
[39] *Ibid.*, p. 182. See also pp. 183–184.
[40] *Ibid.*, p. 192.

The old man ended his speech shortly thereafter with a similar remark and with it, Bembo ends Lavinello's own speech and the work as a whole.

The core of Bembo's theory of love comes in the third book, particularly in Lavinello's account of his exchange with the old man, in which Bembo summarizes almost all that was previously said. For our purposes it is important to stress that neither in that talk nor anywhere else in the whole work is love characterized as an inclination that is benevolent or even approaches benevolence. What we find is a variation on the Platonic theory in which the only inclinations that are discussed as love are acquisitive and aim at perfecting or pleasing the lover.

Ibn Sina

In *A Treatise on Love*, Ibn Sina is not primarily interested in love among human beings. He mentions such love but only in the context of showing that love pervades all beings, and that all beings tend by love toward the "Absolute Good" or "First Cause," which both originates and sustains it. Ibn Sina begins his treatise by affirming the universality of love:

> Every being which is determined by a design strives by nature toward its perfection, *i.e.*, that goodness of reality which ultimately flows from the reality of the Pure Good, and by nature it shies away from its specific defect which is the evil in it, *i.e.*, materiality and non-being,—for every evil results from attachment to matter and non-being. Therefore, it is obvious that all beings determined by a design possess a natural desire and an inborn love, and it follows of necessity that in such beings love is the cause of their existence.[41]

Some have achieved their perfection and some have not. The latter are in an intermediate stage between nonbeing and being. Love holds the perfect beings in their state and inclines the imperfect ones to strive for a state of perfection. The loving subject is naturally impelled toward what is good. Love "is the source of its yearning for it when it is absent . . . and of its unification with it when it is present."[42]

Arguing for the existence of love in simple inanimate entities, Ibn Sina points out that the two principal effects of love always are present in all things. First, all matter "yearning" for form of some kind, "whenever it is deprived of a form it will hurry to receive another form in its stead." All beings naturally are repelled by "absolute non-being," which is nothing but unformed matter. Second, every being adheres "to its perfections and natural places when it happens to be at them"[43] and moves toward them when it is separated from them.

[41] *A Treatise on Love*, p. 212.
[42] *Ibid.*, p. 213. See also p. 214.
[43] *Ibid.*, p. 215, *passim*.

Love in "vegetative souls" manifests itself in three ways, corresponding to the three faculties such souls possess. Because of the vegetative soul's faculty of nutrition, it desires food in order to maintain itself. Because of its faculty of growth, it increases its size in the proper proportions. Because of its faculty of procreation, it produces "a new principle similar to the one from which it derives itself."[44]

A nonrational animal shows all the manifestations of love in the vegetative soul, as well as a few additional ones. In addition to the faculties of nutrition, growth, and procreation, the "animal soul" also has the faculty of sense perception. This faculty operates both externally and internally. Externally, the faculty "functions by way of seeking familiarity with some sense-objects in preference to others, and by finding some more repulsive than others." Internally, the faculty "functions by way of finding rest in the enjoyment of restful imaginations and suchlike when they are present, and by striving for them with desire when they are absent." A part of the animal soul also displays "anger." This, says Ibn Sina, "results from the animal's desire for revenge and mastery and from its shying away from weakness and humiliation and what resembles them."[45]

Regarding animal appetite, Ibn Sina makes a distinction between natural and spontaneous love. All the vegetative faculties fall into the category of natural love. An animal will nourish itself naturally, grow, and procreate as long as no impeding force stops it, in the same way that a stone will move to its natural resting place unless obstructed. When the love is spontaneous, its "possessor will sometimes turn away under its own initiative from the object of its love. . . . Thus, for instance, when a donkey sees from afar a wolf approaching, he will stop crunching barley and run away in flight."[46]

The faculty peculiar to man is the rational faculty. In most human loves this faculty operates in conjunction with the lower vegetative and animal faculties.[47] The lower faculties should be guided by reason. Thus "sense-perception, imagination, sexual intercourse and the spirit of aggression and warfare," though functions of the animal soul, are, when guided by the rational faculty, pursued "in a nobler and more refined manner." The animal soul, then, "pursues among the objects of sense those which are of a

[44] *Ibid.,* p. 216.

[45] *Ibid., passim.*

[46] *Ibid.,* p. 217. Ibn Sina observes that there are instances when natural and spontaneous love have the same object: "Quite often the appetitive animal faculty resembles the vegetative one by reason of the absence of free will in it, while, on the other hand, the vegetative faculty sometimes resembles the appetitive one, because it reaches its aim through free will." (*Ibid.*)

[47] Ibn Sina argues that higher faculties often enlist the lower ones in gaining their ends and thus raise the lower faculties to a higher excellence. (See *ibid.,* pp. 218–219.)

better constitution and have a sounder composition and relationship,—things of which the other animals are not mindful, let alone that they pursue them."[48] The rational faculty uses sense perception "in order to derive universals from the particulars by way of induction." It imposes on sexual desire the aim of procreation rather than simple pleasure. It guides the appetite to "strive for food and drink not at random" but at times and in ways that contribute to health. The rational faculty also "makes the faculty of anger wish to fight heroes and to embrace war for the sake of turning an enemy away from a flourishing city or a righteous people." Harmony among the faculties is present only when reason controls. When it does not, "the pursuit of . . . worldly good often interferes with the acquisition of a good which is of greater value."[49]

Of the manifestations of love among human beings, Ibn Sina mentions three: the urge to embrace, the urge to kiss, and the urge for conjugal union. These are functions of the animal soul, yet can be pursued rationally if the animal faculty is subdued by the rational faculty. The aim of conjugal union can be rational, *i.e.*, the propagation of the species.[50] Embracing and kissing are also animal in expression and their purpose "is to come near to one another and to become united." Ibn Sina explains these actions in the following way:

> The soul of the lover desires to reach the object of his love with his senses of touch and sight, and thus he delights in embracing it. And he longs to have the very essence of his soul-faculty, his heart mingle with that of the object of his love, and thus he desires to kiss it.

These actions are not in themselves bad, but must be watched and controlled by reason since "feelings and actions of excessive lust happen to follow them frequently."[51]

The "First Cause" is the principle of all order in the universe, and, thus, for all things, is the final object of love. The rational soul's love of the "First Cause" is nourished by a perception of this order.

> Both the rational and the animal soul—the latter by reason of its proximity to the former—invariably love what has beauty of order, composition and harmony, as for example harmonious sounds, harmoniously blended tastes of well-prepared dishes and suchlike. But, whereas in the animal soul this is due to natural instinct, in the case of the rational soul it results from its occupation with the conception of the ideas which are higher than nature. It recognizes that the closer a thing is to the First Object of love, the more

[48] *Ibid.*, p. 219, *passim.*
[49] *Ibid.*, pp. 219–220, *passim.* See also p. 221.
[50] See *ibid.*, pp. 221–222.
[51] *Ibid.*, p. 222, *passim.*

steadfast is it in its order, and the more beautiful in its harmony, and that what follows It immediately attains a greater degree of unity and of such qualities as result therefrom, *viz.*, harmony and agreement,—whereas, on the contrary, the more remote a thing is from It, the nearer is it to multiplicity and such characters as follow it, *viz.*, contrast and disharmony.[52]

Leaving the level of love among human beings, Ibn Sina lays great stress on the desire for the union of similarity. He says:

. . . whenever it is evident to a being that it is conducive to an increase in excellence and rank to imitate a certain being, to come close to it and to establish a special relation with it, then the former will invariably love the latter by its very nature.[53]

Thus, in the relationship of inferior to superior, the rational part of the human soul invariably loves the "First Cause," *i.e.*, strives to become like it. Ibn Sina calls the rational part of the human soul and the souls of angels "divine" because, unlike all other souls, they are able to seek their perfection through a direct imitation of the "Absolute Good." Their perfection lies in two things:

(i) the conception of those intelligible beings to which they have a possible relation,—each according to its capacity; this is in an effort to become assimilated to the essence of the Absolute Good—, and (ii) in the consequent emanation from them of such actions as are in harmony with their nature, and as are just in relation to the latter.[54]

The love of divine souls (human and angelic) for their perfection is unceasing. Human souls are always in a state of "preparation," one in which they strive for what they do not have. Angelic souls are always in a state of "perfection," in which they seek to retain the perfection they have already achieved.[55]
In the conclusion of his short treatise, Ibn Sina says that

since every being has a natural love for its perfection,—and "perfection" means the acquisition of its goodness—it is obvious that the term by reason of which its goodness results to the thing—no matter what the situation and form of realization—should of necessity be loved as the source from which its goodness stems. But as far as this function is concerned, there is nothing more perfect than the First Cause and nothing prior to It. It follows that It is loved by all things.[56]

[52] *Ibid.*, pp. 220–222.
[53] *Ibid.*, p. 222.
[54] *Ibid.*, p. 224, *passim*.
[55] See *ibid.*, pp. 224–225.
[56] *Ibid.*, p. 225.

The love for the "First Cause," which all existing beings have, is acquisitive in character, since it is a tendency whereby each thing strives to achieve, or persist in, a state of perfection. Each strives to imitate the "First Cause" within the limits of its nature. The human and angelic souls strive to do so directly, while other beings strive to do so indirectly by imitating the "First Cause" in their aims though not in their activities. Although nutrition and sexual intercourse resemble nothing in the "First Cause," their aims, preservation of the individual and of the species, are imitations of it.[57] As all less than divine loves proceed from deficiencies, the theory of love presented is not binary. Ibn Sina never mentions benevolence as a form of natural human love.[58]

The "First Cause" has no privation or deficiency; its love for everything below it is benevolent.[59] The "Absolute Good," says Ibn Sina, "desires in Its wisdom that things should obtain some of Its gifts, even though the degree in which they will be obtained will not reach perfection. Thus, the Exalted King desires that others should imitate Him, in contrast with earthly kings."[60] Divine love, proceeding from perfection, and human love, proceeding from imperfection, are opposites.

Andreas Capellanus

The Art of Courtly Love by Andreas Capellanus is one of the central documents in what has come to be called the tradition of "courtly love."[61] This tradition concentrates on a special kind of love relationship between a man and a woman.[62]

Writings on courtly love are overwhelmingly poetic, but there are a few prosaic treatises, such as Andreas', in which the character and code of this variety of love are set down. These treatises are less analytic than they are

[57] See *ibid.*, p. 227.
[58] Even the doing of "noble deeds" is said by Ibn Sina to have "no other purpose than to make possible an approximation to the Absolute Good, and in order that from this proximity excellence and perfection should result." (*Ibid.*, p. 224.)
[59] See *ibid.*, pp. 223–224.
[60] *Ibid.*, p. 228.
[61] The work is also titled the *Treatise on Love*.
[62] See Maurice Valency's *In Praise of Love*, pp. 26 ff, and John Charles Nelson's *Renaissance Theory of Love*, pp. 107, 141, 167, 170. The basic pattern of the story told in the literary tradition of courtly love (which has many variations) may be briefly described as follows: A wandering troubadour, who writes and sings songs of love, falls in love with a lady who is invariably the wife of someone else, usually the poet's lord and feudal master. The husband is jealous, cruel, and dangerous. The love of the poet and the lady, if not hopeless, is extremely difficult and fraught with continual frustration. It is this frustration upon which the poet's love as well as his poetic inspiration feeds.

prescriptive of the intricate and refined manners of the art of lovemaking. Yet, Andreas' work does contain a conception of love among human beings. In it the notion of sexual desire is fundamental. One of the constant themes in Books I and II is the contrast between low love, lust, or unmixed sexual desire and the love between gentle men and women, which is sexual only in part.[63]

At the very opening of his treatise Andreas defines love:

> Love is a certain inborn suffering derived from the sight of and excessive meditation upon the beauty of the opposite sex, which causes each one to wish above all things the embraces of the other and by common desire to carry out all of love's precepts in the other's embrace.[64]

Or, as he later says in commenting on the word "love":

> Love gets its name (*amor*) from the word for hook (*amus*), which means "to capture" or "to be captured," for he who is in love is captured in the chains of desire and wishes to capture someone else with his hook.[65]

In setting forth his conception of love between a man and a woman, Andreas makes a basic distinction between animal love, or lust, and rational or courtly love. The tendency common to both forms of love is sexual desire. The way in which this desire is pursued and, among other things,

---

[63] Book III, entitled "The Rejection of Love," contrasts markedly with Books I and II in its view of the place of love in human life. In Books I and II the view taken of love between a man and a woman is a very sympathetic one, to say the least. In Book III, Andreas says that love is contemptible, sinful, animal, disgusting, awful, the cause of all human ills including the Fall, and something to be avoided by all virtuous men. (There are no virtuous women.) This view is absolutely contradicted in Books I and II. There, love is seen as the highest human pleasure and one of the important human goods. It is praiseworthy from the human point of view, and even "God cannot be seriously offended by love, for what is done under the compulsion of nature can be made clean by an easy expiation. Besides, it does not seem at all proper to class as a sin the thing from which the highest good in this life takes its origin and without which no man in the world could be considered worthy of praise." (*The Art of Courtly Love,* Book I, Ch. VI, Dialogue 8, p. 111.) Women, in Books I and II, instead of being considered as the source of all evil, are viewed as the cause of virtue and the repository of goodness. The question immediately arises as to which of these positions is Andreas' own. Most of his commentators understand Book III as a necessary repudiation of love written to satisfy Andreas' ecclesiastical superiors and thereby to escape blame and punishment. Whatever the explanation of the contrast in views between Books I and II and Book III, it should be noted that the difference is exclusively a moral one, *i.e.*, a difference as to the sinful or virtuous quality of a certain variety of love between a man and a woman. The conception of what such a love is—apart from its goodness or badness—is the same in Book III as it is in Books I and II.

[64] *Ibid.*, Book I, Ch. I, p. 28. "For what is love but an inordinate desire to receive passionately a furtive and hidden embrace?" (*Ibid.*, Ch. VI, Dialogue 7, p. 100.)

[65] *Ibid.*, Ch. III, p. 31.

whether or not it is consummated, distinguish one love from the other.

Unadulterated sexual passion, when excessive, indiscriminate, and un-controlled, is a barrier to the development of courtly love. Of men so overcome by "Venus," Andreas says:

> men who, after they have thought long about some woman or even en-joyed her, when they see another woman straightway desire her embraces, and they forget about the services they have received from their first love and they feel no gratitude for them. Men of this kind lust after every woman they see; their love is like that of a shameless dog.[66]

Of women so possessed, he has similar remarks to make:

> . . . for when a woman is so passionate that she cannot confine herself to one man, but desires to gratify the passion of many, there love can find no place at all. For true love joins the hearts of two persons with so great a feeling of delight that they cannot desire to embrace anyone else; on the contrary they take care to avoid the solaces of everybody else as though they were horrible things, and they keep themselves for each other. This readi-ness to grant requests is, we say, the same thing in women as overvoluptu-ousness in men—a thing which all agree should be a total stranger in the court of Love. For he who is so tormented by carnal passion that he cannot embrace anyone in heart-felt love, but basely lusts after every woman he sees, is not called a lover but a counterfeiter of love and a pretender, and he is lower than a shameless dog.[67]

The marks of true love include the fidelity of the lovers, the durability of the love, and the exclusive relationship of the lovers. Frustration and difficulty must also be present, for Andreas says that "where you find it easy to attain your desire you may be sure there is no love."[68] Sexual desire

[66] *Ibid.*, Ch. V, pp. 32–33, *passim.* "They should rather, I believe, be compared to asses, for they are moved only by that low nature which shows that men are on the level of the other animals rather than by that true nature which sets us apart from all the other animals by the difference of reason." (*Ibid.*)

[67] *Ibid.*, Ch. X, p. 149. See also p. 148.

[68] *Ibid.*, p. 149. In a dialogue that Andreas presents between a man of the nobility and a woman of the middle class, the woman says that "love seems to be nothing but a great desire to enjoy carnal pleasure with someone, and nothing prevents this feeling existing between husband and wife." The man replies that at least one important element is lacking, jealousy, which, if it occurs between husband and wife, will destroy love, but which preserves love between unmarried lovers. (Ch. VI, Dialogue 7, p. 102.) Andreas is more emphatic at a later point when he says that "if the parties concerned marry, love is violently put to flight." (Book II, Ch. IV, p. 156.) Throughout the whole treatise he stresses the necessity of obstacles and diffi-culty in the emergence of love. ". . . whenever the possession of some good thing is postponed by the difficulty of getting it, we desire it more eagerly and put forth a greater effort to keep it. Therefore if one has difficulty in obtaining the embraces of one's lover and obtains them rarely, the lovers are bound to each other in more ardent chains of love and their souls are linked together in heavier and closer bonds of affection." (Book I, Ch. VI, Dialogue 7, p. 99.)

itself, though it may be a low form of love in Andreas' view, is only a prerequisite, but not a sufficient condition for the development of courtly love.[69]

That sexual desire is necessary for love is clear from Andreas' remarks about who can love:

> Now, in love you should note first of all that love cannot exist except between persons of opposite sexes. Between two men or two women love can find no place, for we see that two persons of the same sex are not at all fitted for giving each other the exchanges of love or for practicing the acts natural to it. Whatever nature forbids, love is ashamed to accept.
>
> Every attempt of a lover tends toward the enjoyment of the embraces of her whom he loves; he thinks about it continually, for he hopes that with her he may fulfill all the mandates of love—that is, those things that we find in treatises on the subject. Therefore in the sight of a lover nothing can be compared to the act of love, and a true lover would rather be deprived of all his money and of everything that the human mind can imagine as indispensable to life rather than be without love, either hoped for or attained.[70]

The above passage not only affirms that sexual desire is fundamental to love but also rules out sexual passion between members of the same sex as an instance of love. More important, it distinguishes a special love between a man and a woman from conjugal affection, feelings between kinsmen, friendship, and charity, all of which Andreas mentions. These phenomena are, presumably, outside the realm of love.[71]

The two types of rational or courtly love mentioned by Andreas are mixed love and pure love. Mixed love "gets its effect from every delight of the flesh and culminates in the final act of Venus . . . mixed love, too, is real love, and it is praiseworthy, and we say that it is the source of all good things, although from it grave dangers threaten, too." Pure love, on the other hand, is said to consist "in the contemplation of the mind and the

[69] The question of whether or not unalloyed sexual desire or "animal passion" is or is not a form of love for Andreas is not easily resolved. There are times when he uses the word "love" as a synonym for "sexual desire," as when he advises a nobleman who has fallen in love with a peasant woman not to hesitate to take what he seeks by force. (See *ibid.*, Book I, Ch. XI, p. 150.) There are also times when he emphatically denies that sexual desire by itself can be called love. The resolution of this question, however, does not affect our classification of his theory. For love, whether it includes courtly love only or courtly love and unalloyed sexual desire, is essentially acquisitive in character—at least insofar as it is tendential.

[70] *Ibid.*, Book I, Ch. II, p. 30. To reenforce his point, Andreas goes on to maintain that those who have not yet attained puberty and those who are approaching senility are incapable of love. (See *ibid.*, Ch. V, p. 32.)

[71] For his remarks on conjugal affection and the affection among kinsmen, see *ibid.*, Ch. VI, Dialogue 7, pp. 100, 101. Most of his remarks on friendship and charity are in Book III, pp. 187–212. (See also Book I, Ch. VI, Dialogue 8, p. 121.) These subjects are very casually considered and are not related to the love between a man and a woman as Andreas conceives it.

affection of the heart; it goes as far as the kiss and the embrace and the modest contact with the nude lover, omitting the final solace, for that is not permitted to those who wish to love purely."[72] Andreas points out that the two are not so different as they seem:

> For although pure love and mixed love may seem to be very different things, if you will look at the matter properly you will see that pure love, so far as its substance goes, is the same as mixed love and comes from the same feeling of the heart.[73]

These loves are first mentioned in a dialogue between a man of the high nobility and a woman of the same class, both of whom, because of their breeding and social status, are qualified to enter love's court. The problem of love is posed to the man, who answers by distinguishing between the "solaces of the upper part" and the "solaces of the lower part." He maintains that the true lover seeks the former solaces because they are "attributes peculiar to the nature of man," whereas the latter are "in no wise differentiated from [those of] brute beasts." The woman replies that his remarks are "very far from the truth." She says:

> Whatever solaces men use to drive away their cares always take their beginning from that which lies hid in the lower part, and thence is derived the origin of all of them.

In her view, the lower part is "the efficient cause of love."[74]

The man replies that "it would seem a very shameful and improper use of the body and a great disgrace for women to practice the lower solaces without the upper. Indeed [he adds], it seems impossible to enjoy the delight of the lower part without that of the upper, unless we are to have too indecent and shameful a use of the body." He proceeds by affirming that "the rational order in love requires that one should first, after much urging, obtain the wanton solaces of the upper part, and after that go on step by step to the lower ones." He adds that "the man who chose the upper part should be the preferred lover." The woman finally concedes that his position is correct:

[72] *Ibid.*, pp. 122–123, *passim.*
[73] *Ibid.*, Book II, Ch. VI, p. 164. Andreas goes on to say: "The substance of the love is the same in each case, and only the manner and form of loving are different, as this illustration will make clear to you. Sometimes we see a man with a desire to drink his wine unmixed, and at another time his appetite prompts him to drink only water or wine and water mixed; although his appetite manifests itself differently, the substance of it is the same and unchanged. So likewise when two people have been long united by pure love and afterwards desire to practice mixed love, the substance of the love remains the same in them, although the manner and form and the way of practicing it are different." (*Ibid.*)
[74] *Ibid.*, Book I, Ch. VI, Dialogue 8, pp. 135–136, *passim.*

Although your opinion may seem to be opposed by many arguments, still, because I see that all justice is on its side and that it is defended with the more rational firmness, I think I ought to assent and follow it as the one that has the truth back of it.[75]

If love feeds on the frustration of sexual desire, then "pure" love, which permits many physical embraces but omits "the final solace," would seem to be a high degree of love between a man and a woman. The "mixed" love, though it does not preclude the fulfillment of sexual desire, requires, in order to be distinguished from simple animal passion, that sexual intercourse be approached in stages and that it be mixed with spiritual affection.[76]

Although there is little doubt about what Andreas means by the solaces of the lower part, it is not too clear what he means by the solaces of the upper part, except that such solaces seem to be nonphysical. One strong possibility emerges from the treatise in regard to the spiritual dimension of courtly love. It is the desire for the union of similarity. Andreas claims that:

Just as a skillful fisherman tries to attract fishes by his bait and to capture them on his crooked hook, so the man who is a captive of love tries to attract another person by his allurements and exerts all his efforts to unite two different hearts with an intangible bond, or if they are already united he tries to keep them so forever.[77]

In regard to the characters of the lovers and their inclinations toward each other, the union to which Andreas refers is the union of similarity. "Love seeks for two persons who are bound together by a mutual trust and an identity of desires."[78] Or, as he says more directly: "A person of good character draws the love of another person of the same kind."[79] The desire for the union of similarity, whether it occurs between unequals or equals, is itself an equalizing tendency.

There is no evidence that Andreas thinks that benevolence is essential to love. The only emphatic mention of it occurs in a dialogue between a man and a woman of the higher nobility, when the woman says:

. . . God forbid that anyone should ever buy love for a price. For love is a gracious thing, arising only out of nobility of the heart and pure liberality of

[75] *Ibid.*, pp. 137–138, *passim.*
[76] See *ibid.*, p. 122, *passim.*
[77] *Ibid.*, Book I, Ch. III, p. 31.
[78] *Ibid.*, Book II, Ch. IV, p. 156.
[79] *Ibid.*, Book I, Ch. VI, p. 35. In another of the dialogues of love, a nobleman says to a middle-class woman: "For, as you yourself have well said already, no matter how much nobler one of the lovers is than the other, after they have begun to love they should walk in Love's court with equal steps." (*Ibid.*, Dialogue 6, p. 87. See also Dialogue 1, p. 38.)

the mind, and so should be given to everybody without cost and with no idea of payment, although lovers may, for mutual solace, honor each other with certain gifts. But if they are found to be engaged in the service of Love solely with an eye to the payment, after that their love is considered, not true love, but feigned love.[80]

We may say then that benevolence is possible in this relationship (and perhaps in others), but that it is not necessary for love, since the notion of benevolence is no part of Andreas' own conception of love.

Essentially, Andreas thinks of love as a type of refined—even frustrated —sexuality that is *mutually* acquisitive. It can endure if unrequited since lack of reciprocity is a frustration and love feeds upon frustration. In mentioning his own love to the young man for whom he has written the treatise, Andreas says:

> We have fallen in love with a woman of the most admirable character, although we never have had, or hope to have, any fruit of this love. For we are compelled to pine away for love of a woman of such lofty station that we dare not say one word about it, nor dare we throw ourself upon her mercy, and so at length we are forced to find our body shipwrecked.[81]

One of the recurrent and characteristic themes in the literature on courtly love is the idealization of the woman and the lover's subsequent veneration of her. Although present in Andreas' treatise, this notion is less important for his theory than for the theories of some of the other courtly writers. Andreas is not unmindful of the importance of the judgment of the lover in the emergence of love. (The first step in falling in love is to be struck by the beauty or excellence of character of a member of the opposite sex.) But he seems to be saying that such judgment is prior to and not part of love. Love is an "inborn suffering *derived from* the sight of and excessive meditation upon the beauty of the opposite sex."[82] However important the judgmental notions of admiration, respect, or valuation are for his theory of love, it is an essentially tendential theory. Love is a desire.

Marie-Henri Beyle (*de Stendhal*)

In the original preface to his work *On Love*, Stendhal informs the reader that he is departing from novel writing to compose a "scientific treatise on a type of madness."[83] "This book," he goes on to say, "explains simply, rationally, mathematically, as it were, the different emotions which

80 *Ibid.*, Dialogue 8, p. 131. See also pp. 108–109; and Book I, Ch. II, p. 31.
81 *Ibid.*, Book II, Ch. VI, pp. 163–164.
82 *Ibid.*, Book I, Ch. I, p. 28. (Italics added.)
83 *On Love*, First Preface, p. xi.

follow one after the other and which taken all together are called the passion of Love."[84]

The passion of love, to the analysis of which Stendhal devotes most of his book, is only the first of four types of love he mentions at the outset: passion love, sympathy love, sensual love, and vanity love. Though there are important differences between the principal love—passion love—and the other three, all of them occur in the context of the one relationship in which Stendhal is interested: the relationship between a man and a woman. As all four types of love "obey the same rules," Stendhal takes the most important of the four (what he, at one point, calls "real" love) to trace the operation of these rules.[85] Though he says that the other three types are instances of actual love, he treats them as if they had little significance, discussing them not only casually but disdainfully.

Early in his work, Stendhal offers what appears to be a definition of love:

> To love is to derive pleasure from seeing, touching and feeling through all one's senses and as closely as possible, a lovable person who loves us.[86]

This definition, however, is set forth to describe only the fourth step in a *process*, the sum total of which Stendhal thinks love, *i.e.*, passion love, to be. That process combines both tendencies and judgments in the following phases or steps:

1. Admiration
2. Loving admiration
3. Hope
4. Love is born (as defined above)
5. The first crystallization
6. Doubt is born
7. The second crystallization.[87]

We shall return to this sequence.

The tendential aspect of love, in Stendhal's theory, is less complex than the judgmental. Yet the theory is a tendential one at its core, even though a passion is not considered to be love unless certain characteristic judgments are present. What the four types of love most clearly have in common is a

---

[84] *Ibid.*, p. xv. See also Book I, Ch. III, p. 11, fn. 1.

[85] These rules are applicable fully only to passion love; they apply only in part to the other three types of love.

[86] *Ibid.*, Ch. II, p. 5. Though mutuality is one of the properties of love, Stendhal says that the degree of love on the part of two people who love each other is hardly ever equal. (See *ibid.*, Ch. XXXVI, p. 124.)

[87] See *ibid.*, Ch. II, pp. 5–9.

kind of desire; the tendency that is characteristic of love, in all of its expressions, is acquisitive desire.

Passion love (which Stendhal understands as a highly complex phenomenon) and sensual love (which, by contrast, he understands as a relatively simple phenomenon) are distinguishable most clearly in terms of judgment. Yet there is also a tendential distinction. In its tendential aspect, passion love involves a very broad acquisitive tendency; the lover seeks pleasure in many different ways. Sensual love is narrower in tendency; it is basically sexual desire. It is what happens when a man "out shooting" meets "a fresh, pretty country girl who darts away into a wood. Every one knows [he adds] the love founded on pleasures of this kind."[88] Even sexual desire in passion love is different, in at least one way, from the sexual impulse in sensual love. The former always is directed to one person only.

> In love [*i.e.*, passion love] there is no pleasure in slaking one's thirst except at this chosen spring. Fidelity, in that case, becomes natural.[89]

Vanity love also is essentially acquisitive desire though not completely sexual. It is rather what impels men to "desire and possess a fashionable woman as they would possess a fine horse, as a necessary luxury for a young man." Though she cannot be just anyone, the fashionable woman is chosen and enjoyed solely as a means of pleasing the man. In Stendhal's view, the "most agreeable form of this rather insipid relationship" occurs when it is combined with sensual love and when "sensual pleasure is increased by habit."[90]

The same kind of desire is also present in sympathy love, which is the mildest and most refined of the loves mentioned. It contains no surprises and never risks "infringing custom, fashion, refinement, etc." It is completely and coldly voluntary and "always knows how to adjust itself to [one's own interests]."[91]

The tendential aspect of passion love, as we have said, is also acquisitive.

[88] *Ibid.*, Ch. I, p. 2.
[89] *Ibid.*, Book II, Ch. LVI A, p. 242, fn. 1. "When we have just seen the woman we love, the sight of any other woman is distasteful to us and actually hurts our eyes; I can see the reason for this." Stendhal also says: "Perfect naturalness and intimacy can only exist in passion-love, for in all other forms of love one feels the possibility of a favoured rival." (*Ibid.*, "Miscellaneous Fragments," CLVIII and CLIX, p. 337.)
[90] *Ibid.*, Book I, Ch. I, p. 2.
[91] *Ibid.*, p. 1. "It is true that if you strip this poor form of love of its vanity, very little remains; without its vanity, it is like a feeble convalescent who is scarcely able to drag himself along." (*Ibid.*, pp. 1–2.) "Nothing is so interesting as passion, because everything in it is unexpected and its originator is his own victim. Nothing is so insipid as sympathy-love, in which everything is done by calculation as in all the prosaic affairs of life." (*Ibid.*, "Miscellaneous Fragments," XI, pp. 276–277.)

Though Stendhal says that it "carries us away against all our interests," he clearly does not mean that its motive is one of benevolence or self-sacrifice.[92] What he means is that the love is so powerful and so all-consuming that it forces us to do things that, though offering us great momentary pleasure, are detrimental to our long-range or real interests. In Stendhal's view, human actions—and especially involuntary human actions—are governed by the expectation of pleasure or the dislike of pain. Passion love is the most striking illustration of the operation of these determinants, since Stendhal regards it as the most powerful passion that can affect man and thus the one that causes him the greatest pleasure and pain.

The course of love can be arrested at its outset. But once a man is in the grip of this passion he is powerless.

> Man is not free to refuse to do the thing which gives him more pleasure than any other conceivable action. Love is like a fever; it comes and goes without the will having any part in the process.[93]

The acquisitive desire, though involuntary, is a complicated and changing one in passion love. Sexual desire is involved, but the desire of passion love is never wholly sexual. Stendhal says that to love is to derive pleasure "through all one's senses."[94]

Probably the most important physical sense for passion love is sight; for beauty, which plays such a decisive role in this love, is perceived through sight. Beauty is described by Stendhal as "only the promise of happiness,"[95] and as "a new faculty for giving . . . pleasure." He goes even further in saying:

> The crystallization of a man's mistress, or her BEAUTY, is nothing more than the collection of ALL THE SATISFACTIONS and of all the desires that he has successfully formed in respect of her.[96]

[92] *Ibid.*, p. 1. Stendhal does say: "Where there is a perfect naturalness, the happiness of the two people becomes commingled." (*Ibid.*, Book I, Ch. XXXII, p. 108.) He also clearly implies the presence of the desire for union, but such a desire must be presumed to be acquisitive since there is no mention of benevolence in this context or elsewhere. (See *ibid.*, Ch. III, p. 12; Ch. XXXII, p. 102; and Book II, Ch. LIX, p. 264.)

[93] *Ibid.*, Book I, Ch. V, p. 16. See also Ch. XII, p. 33; Ch. XXXIX B, p. 147; and "Miscellaneous Fragments," CXL, pp. 328–330. One of the primary distinctions between passion love, on the one hand, and sympathy love and vanity love, on the other hand, is that the former is involuntary and takes the whole person completely in its grasp, whereas the latter are voluntary, calculating loves and are relatively weak in emotional force.

[94] *Ibid.*, Ch. II, p. 5.

[95] *Ibid.*, Book I, Ch. XVII, p. 44, fn. 1.

[96] *Ibid.*, Ch. XI, pp. 31–32.

In sensual love, beauty arouses the expectation of sexual pleasure. In passion love, however, the scope is broader. This emotion arouses "as many different kinds [of pleasure] as there are individuals."[97] The range of pleasure is from the aesthetic to the physical, since love derives pleasure "from seeing, touching, feeling."[98] There is the visual pleasure of delighting in the beauty of the beloved. "The greatest happiness that love can give is the first hand-pressure of the woman one loves."[99] And, of course, there is the pleasure that sexual intercourse gives.

The notion of beauty is central to the most striking feature of Stendhal's theory of love. One of the principal aims of his treatise is to explain a cognitive phenomenon he thinks peculiar to love.

> I call crystallization that process of the mind which discovers fresh perfections in its beloved at every turn of events.[100]

Crystallization plays an extremely important role in passion love. Once the process has begun, each new beauty or perfection the lover discovers "is a cause for fresh rapture."[101] The lover projects so far that he sees his beloved in everything that strikes him as beautiful. More important, however, is the lover's propensity to *impose* on the beloved all the beauty and perfection that he possibly can. It is this that distinguishes passion love from every other emotion.

> In the case of other passions, one's desires have to accommodate themselves to cold realities; but in the case of love realities model themselves enthusiastically on one's desires.[102]

Crystallization is Stendhal's explanation of what people mean when they say that love is blind. It is the process whereby the lover increases his own pleasure (or perhaps the anticipation of pleasure) by adding to the beloved's qualities perfections that she does not possess. The peculiar passion of love necessitates this process and feeds upon it. Thus Stendhal concludes: "Love is the only passion which pays itself in a coin which it mints itself."[103] The lover must embellish the beloved in order to keep his love alive. Stendhal uses a metaphor to explain what he means:

[97] *Ibid.*, p. 31.
[98] *Ibid.*, Ch. II, p. 5.
[99] *Ibid.*, Ch. XXXII, p. 105.
[100] *Ibid.*, Ch. II, p. 6.
[101] *Ibid.*, Ch. XI, p. 31. See also Ch. XXXI, p. 105; and Book II, Ch. LIX, p. 264.
[102] *Ibid.*, Book I, Ch. XII, p. 33. Stendhal qualifies this assertion at another point when he admits that hatred and the passion involved in gambling also can produce some crystallization. (See *ibid.*, Ch. VI, pp. 18–19.)
[103] *Ibid.*, "Miscellaneous Fragments," CXLV, p. 332.

In the salt mines of Salzburg a bough stripped of its leaves by winter is thrown into the depths of the disused workings; two or three months later it is pulled out again, covered with brilliant crystals: even the tiniest twigs, no bigger than a tomtit's claw, are spangled with a vast number of shimmering, glittering diamonds, so that the original bough is no longer recognizable.[104]

Love does not begin with crystallization. The first step in the process is admiration. The beloved, or future beloved, is singled out at this stage because of certain *real* qualities she possesses, and those qualities are neither distorted nor embellished. It is certainly possible to make an error at this stage and admire someone for qualities that she does not possess. Yet this is not crystallization, for no qualities have yet been projected onto the beloved. Crystallization is still absent in the second stage, that of loving admiration. This stage is also one of judgment. It differs from the stage of simple admiration in that the lover brings himself into the picture. He no longer simply admires the beloved for herself; he now values her in relation to himself. "One says to one's self: 'How delightful to kiss her, to be kissed in return.' "[105] He imagines the pleasure he would enjoy in having this woman as his own. For the first time he thinks of her as good for him, as a possible object of his love.

This judgment leads to what Stendhal calls the third stage of love: hope. The lover begins to think he has a chance, that the woman would not only be a delightful beloved but may be his. A very small degree of hope is sufficient to cause the birth of love. Although this stage may be very brief, it is an essential catalyst for the crucial fourth stage. "Hope may subsequently fail at the end of two or three days, but love is none the less born."[106]

In the fourth stage "love" is born. It is at the stage of passion that the lover feels an intensifying desire for a particular woman. He quickly reaches the point where little else matters but satisfying this passion. This stage is decisive because, once it is reached, the subsequent ones follow of necessity. Up to this point the process might have been aborted.

The first crystallization begins immediately after the decisive fourth step. Stendhal describes it as follows:

We take a joy in attributing a thousand perfections to a woman of whose love we are sure; we analyze all our happiness with intense satisfaction. This

104 *Ibid.*, Book I, Ch. II, p. 6.
105 *Ibid.*, p. 5.
106 *Ibid.*, Ch. III, p. 10. The principal distinction between the way men love and the way women love is made by Stendhal in his discussion of this stage. Both must entertain hope in order for the love to be mutual but the man does so aggressively and the woman reluctantly—at least in appearance. (See *ibid.*, Ch. VIII, p. 25.)

reduces itself to giving ourselves an exaggerated idea of a magnificent possession which has just fallen to us from Heaven in some way we do not understand, and the continued possession of which is assured to us.[107]

This step in the process is so fundamental to Stendhal's theory of love that he denies that passion love can exist without it. At one point he even defines love as "that act of folly which makes us attribute every beauty and every kind of perfection to the woman we are beginning to love."[108] Stendhal thinks the lover is actively engaged in a process of elaborate self-deception. However prudent or realistic a man may be in all his other affairs, once caught in the grip of this relentless development, he is unable to do otherwise. The beloved must be perfect in his eyes, and his judgment obediently carries out the command to make her so. As the crystallized perfections are all the product of his imagination, no one else sees them.[109]

Though the first crystallization goes far in imposing perfections on the beloved, it is not sufficient to perpetuate the love. Even if crystallization is so complete that a man sees *only* perfection in his beloved, it still produces ennui and wandering attention. Such perfection and its resultant happiness is monotonous; in order for love to continue, doubt must be born. This is the sixth stage.

There is an obvious connection between this doubt and the deliberate frustration of desire that is such an important part of courtly love. Modesty in women, for example, is said by Stendhal to be essential.[110] Passion love is a civilized love. The savage cannot experience it, for his habit is to grasp blindly for his transient pleasures. Impatient with obstacles, he allows no time for the process to take hold. The best he can achieve is an indifferent lust (or perhaps a low form of sensual love) since "man does not as a rule put a very high value on what is offered to him freely, whatever it may be."[111]

Stendhal does not say the beloved must give cause for doubt; he says only that for love to develop fully and become strong doubt must be present. Thus, if the beloved gives no cause for doubt, the lover will still somehow find cause. The doubt does not concern the perfections of the beloved, but rather her constancy. On this doubt the second crystallization feeds. "Always some little doubt to calm, that is what keeps one ever eager, that is what keeps alive the spark of happy love."[112] Once a lover begins to doubt the fidelity of the source of his happiness he begins a second and more vigorous crystallization.

[107] *Ibid.,* Ch. II, p. 5.
[108] *Ibid.,* Ch. III, p. 12, fn. 1.
[109] See *ibid.,* "The Salzburg Bough," p. 367.
[110] See *ibid.,* Ch. XXVI, p. 73.
[111] *Ibid.,* Ch. X, p. 30. See also Ch. II, p. 6; and Ch. III, p. 11.
[112] *Ibid.,* Ch. XXXIII, p. 112.

Now begins the second crystallization, producing as its diamonds various confirmations of the following idea:

"She loves me."

Every quarter of an hour, during the night following the birth of doubt, after a moment of terrible misery, the lover says to himself: "Yes, she loves me"; and crystallization sets to work to discover fresh charms; then gaunt-eyed doubt grips him again and pulls him up with a jerk. His heart misses a beat; he says to himself: "But does she love me?"

Since the lover now hovers constantly "between an appalling abyss and the most perfect happiness,"[113] the second crystallization is more important than the first. It is the last of the stages of the process the lover goes through. After it, love may (and, in Stendhal's view, often does) die.

Stendhal sets no fixed time for this whole process, but he does relate the stages temporally. Between admiration (the judgment that the beloved is good in herself) and valuation (the judgment that the beloved would be good for the lover) a year may elapse; between valuation and hope, a month. Between hope and the birth of love "there is but the twinkling of an eye." There is no appreciable interval between the birth of love and the first crystallization. A few days may elapse between the first crystallization and the beginning of doubt. And, again, there is no appreciable interval between the beginning of doubt and the second crystallization. The second crystallization continues as long as love lasts.[114]

If we take the whole process as Stendhal's conception of love, we see at once that love involves both tendential and judgmental elements and, indeed, is identified as the interaction of these elements. This interaction is particularly evident at the stages of crystallization.

This phenomenon which I have allowed myself to call *crystallization*, arises from the promptings of Nature which urge us to enjoy ourselves and drive the blood to our brains, from the feeling that our delight increases with the perfections of the beloved, and from the thought: "She is mine."[115]

The first judgments the lover makes in passion love, admiration, and valuation do not involve crystallization. They are—seen either as preface to or part of love—relatively uninfluenced by desire of any kind. After the fourth stage, however, the first and second crystallizations are determined decisively by the pleasure-seeking tendency of love. The first crystallization permits the lover to maximize his pleasure by allowing him to think that the one he loves is (at least visually) perfect. The second crystallization

113 *Ibid.*, Ch. II, p. 8. "The lover hovers incessantly amongst these three ideas: 1. She is perfect in every way. 2. She loves me. 3. How can I get the strongest possible proof of her love for me?" (*Ibid.*, p. 9.)
114 See *ibid.*, Ch. IV, pp. 14–15; and Ch. VI, p. 17.
115 *Ibid.*, Ch. II, p. 6.

permits the lover to maximize his pleasure by assuaging continually his doubt that his love is not returned. The first crystallization reenforces his admiration and the second his valuation.

Arthur Schopenhauer

In his essay *The Metaphysics of the Love of the Sexes*, Schopenhauer repeatedly asserts that love is sexual desire and sexual desire is love. He mentions friendship once or twice, but does not include it in his conception of love because he regards it as "a feeling of an entirely different origin."[116] For him, love is a purely instinctive and biological impulse aiming at procreation. As it is essentially a physical inclination, he finds no difficulty in extending his theory to cover the procreative impulses throughout the animal realm.

There are, however, some distinctive accompanying characteristics of sexual desire as it occurs in human beings. A man in love, Schopenhauer says, has

> the feeling that he is acting in affairs of such transcendent importance which raises the lover so high above everything earthly, nay, even above himself, and gives such a *hyperphysical* clothing to his very physical desires, that love becomes a poetical episode even in the life of the most prosaic man.[117]

In such a state, "he seems to lose sight altogether of his real, very physical aim."[118] That physical aim is, at base, not merely a desire for sexual pleasure, though such pleasure is involved. Rather, it is the relentless effort of the species to perpetuate itself. This instinct is present in every individual, *whether he is aware of it or not,* and is behind his desire for sexual gratification.

> For all love, however ethereally it may bear itself, is rooted in the sexual impulse alone, nay, it absolutely is only a more definitely determined, specialised, and indeed in the strictest sense individualised sexual impulse.[119]

Despite all appearances to the contrary, then, the essential matter in love is "possession, *i.e.,* with the physical enjoyment" that serves the interest of the species. "The growing inclination of two lovers," he says, "is

[116] *The World as Will and Idea*, Vol. III, Ch. XLIV, p. 372. See also pp. 345, 347–349.
[117] *Ibid.*, p. 367. (Italics added.)
[118] *Ibid.*, p. 366.
[119] *Ibid.*, p. 339.

really already the will to live of the new individual which they can and desire to produce."[120]

Schopenhauer accounts for the illusions that often accompany passionate or romantic love by stressing two points: the tremendous force of love, and the fact that the interest of the species and the interest of the individual (through whose instinctive urge the species realizes its aim) are seldom in harmony. The latter point is crucial, for the illusions accompanying passionate love are attempts to reconcile, or rather conceal, the conflict between the competing interests of the species and the individual. Schopenhauer indicates no doubt about which of these interests is more basic:

> Because the passion depended upon an illusion, which represented that which has only value for the species as valuable for the individual, the deception must vanish after the attainment of the end of the species.[121]

Thus, the sexual instinct always operates in accord with the sovereign demands of the species. As these demands are always made on behalf of the good (*i.e.*, the preservation) of the whole, the individual (or his happiness) may well be sacrificed in the course of fulfilling them.

The individual frequently cooperates in the fulfillment of those demands by blinding himself to their real nature. The overwhelming power of the reproductive instinct reenforces this propensity to self-deception. Schopenhauer says that sexual desire ranks with self-preservation (and sometimes higher than self-preservation) as "the strongest and most powerful of motives."[122] While conceding that the desire is controllable, he points out that it

> may rise under certain circumstances to a passion which exceeds all others in vehemence, and which then sets aside all considerations, overcomes all obstacles with incredible strength and perseverence, so that for its satisfaction life is risked without hesitation, nay, if that satisfaction is still withheld, is given as the price of it.[123]

The instinct is so strong that no man is immune from danger. Many are forced to give up happiness, wealth, honor, life—even forced to "crimes such as adultery or rape, all merely in order to serve the species in the most efficient way."[124] It is so powerful that many men love, *i.e.*, sexually

---

[120] *Ibid.*, pp. 341–342. See also p. 340. Love can occur only between people who are sexually potent. For "every individual loses attraction for the opposite sex in proportion as he or she is removed from the fittest period for begetting or conceiving." (*Ibid.*, p. 352.)
[121] *Ibid.*, p. 370. See also p. 365.
[122] *Ibid.*, p. 339.
[123] *Ibid.*, p. 337. See also pp. 361, 364–365, 369.
[124] *Ibid.*, pp. 347–348. See also pp. 364, 368.

desire, those whom they otherwise hate. Frustration of the desire only increases its intensity.

Self-deception is the inevitable corollary of the focusing of sexual desire on one and only one beloved. When contact occurs between a man and a woman whose combined physical qualities would produce a healthy off-spring, the intensity of the desire increases and the individuals accede to it, believing that it is in their own interest to do so. But, though it is in the interest of the species for the individual to do so, it is not in the individual's interest. Schopenhauer regards the insistence upon one and only one beloved as, in fact,

> an unparalleled illusion, on account of which such a lover would give up all the good things of this world to enjoy the possession of this woman, who yet can really give him nothing more than any other.[125]

Marriages made out of love turn out to be unhappy as a rule, since they are made in the interest of the species and not of the individual. In any marriage, "either the individual or the interests of the species must come off a loser."[126]

These remarks apply to the male lover rather than to the female. According to Schopenhauer, a man naturally desires a variety of women in sequence. He is not by nature faithful because his reproductive function is completed during the sexual act. Hence, his love dies when his desire is satisfied and only begins again when that desire again is roused. The woman, however, since she must bear the child, continues to love, *i.e.*, to pursue the aim of reproduction. The male, having anticipated "an infinite blessedness . . . for him in the union with this female individual,"[127] becomes disinterested. Schopenhauer says that the male "will experience a marvellous disillusion after the pleasure he has at last attained, and will wonder that what was so longingly desired accomplishes nothing more than every other sexual satisfaction."[128] Not only "has the unsatisfied passion of love sometimes a tragic issue, but the satisfied passion also leads oftener to unhappiness than to happiness."[129]

Schopenhauer also discusses love, or sexual desire, in relation to the desire for the union of complementarity:

[125] *Ibid.*, p. 362. See also pp. 360–361.
[126] *Ibid.*, p. 372. Schopenhauer says that marriages of convenience usually are in the interest of the individual since they are made on the basis of reality and not illusion.
[127] *Ibid.*, p. 367. See also pp. 350–351.
[128] *Ibid.*, pp. 348–349.
[129] *Ibid.*, pp. 367–368.

For such a truly passionate inclination to arise something is required which can only be expressed by a chemical metaphor: two persons must neutralise each other, like acid and alkali, to a neutral salt.[130]

Again, this propensity is understood in terms of the interest of the species. The instinctive sexual desire naturally fixes upon one who has certain perfections that the lover does not have. The species more fully realizes its purpose when offspring are produced that are better than the parents, *i.e.*, combine the best features of both. Hence, since the sexual instinct is guided by the aim of the species, "each one loves what he lacks."[131] The desire for union points beyond the lovers themselves to their child.

They feel the longing for an actual union and fusing together into a single being, in order to live on only as this; and this longing receives its fulfilment in the child which is produced by them, as that in which the qualities transmitted by them both, fused and united in one being, live on.[132]

[130] *Ibid.*, p. 356.
[131] *Ibid.*, p. 355. See also pp. 347, 360–361.
[132] *Ibid.*, p. 342. Lucretius also speaks of love as an all-pervasive mating impulse present in all living things:

> . . . [Venus] through seas and mountains and swift streams,
> Through leafy homes of birds and greening plains,
> Kindling the lure of love in every breast,
> Thou bringest the eternal generations forth,
> Kind after kind. (*Of the Nature of Things,* Book I, p. 3.)

Of the power of the mating impulse and its effect on the mind, Lucretius is fearful.
> As when the thirsty man in slumber seeks
> To drink, and water ne'er is granted him
> Wherewith to quench the heat within his members,
> But after idols of the liquids strives
> And toils in vain, and thirsts even whilst he gulps
> In middle of the torrent, thus in love
> Venus deludes with idol-images
> The lovers. (*Ibid.*, Book IV, p. 176.)

In Ovid's *The Art of Love,* the word "love" stands for a sexual relationship between a man and a woman—nothing more. How to conduct such a relationship is an intricate art that can be taught and perfected. (See *ibid.*, p. 105.) This art covers not only the matters of proper and pleasing appearance and manners but also includes rules concerning how to choose a love mate, how to court, how to make love endure and how to recover from unrequited love. Dissimulation is absolutely essential to the art of love. There is a prescribed deception for every occasion. If infidelity is practised— Ovid regards this as highly likely—the deceptions must multiply rapidly. Not only is deceiving the other a regular feature of love but self-deception also occurs.

> . . . Folly, Illusion, and Madness,
> All that undisciplined crew dance their attendance on . . . [love]. (*Ibid.*, p. 17.)

Love comes into being and endures largely by means of illusion. Along with deception, habit imparts to love what little duration it has.

Denis de Rougemont

The "central purpose" of *Love in the Western World* (alternately titled *Passion and Society*) is "to describe the inescapable conflict in the West between passion and marriage."[133] At the root of this conflict, De Rougemont sees a fundamental antagonism between what he variously calls passive and active love, destructive and constructive love, romantic and true love, *eros*, or "boundless desire," and *agape*, or Christian love. He asserts categorically that "passion and marriage are essentially irreconcilable. Their origins and their ends make them mutually exclusive."[134] De Rougemont describes the conflict between these two basic forces, pleads the moral superiority of *agape*, and argues its importance for the health of the institution of marriage.

The author concentrates on love among human beings, actually only on the love between a man and a woman. His primary concern throughout the work is to distinguish conceptually and historically between romance (*eros*) and Christian love in marriage (*agape*). Though he conceives of both loves as tendencies, he contrasts them in numerous ways. They are distinguished primarily as natural and supernatural. "We are," says De Rougemont, "unendingly and incessantly in the thick of the struggle between nature and grace."[135] Natural human love is always a function of *eros* and is, in terms of true human ends, an inadequate form of love. Unless *eros* is "rescued" by *agape*, by supernatural love, the love between a

---

Love comes into the mind by habit, and habit expels it;
He who can counterfeit sense comes to his senses in time. (*Ibid.*, p. 196.)

Love and the sexual desire are coextensive for Rémy de Gourmont also. As far as love is concerned, man differs from the other animals only in degree and detail. "Man will then find himself in his proper and rather indistinct place in the crowd, beside the monkeys, rodents, and bats." (*The Natural Philosophy of Love*, p. 6.) When "we follow the love act, it is truly, in the idiom of theologians, *more bestiarum*. Love is profoundly animal." (*Ibid.*, p. 10.) The aim of love or sexual desire is procreation, though such an aim is often disguised. "The flowers we have strewn upon love may disguise it as one disguises a trap for wild beasts . . . the aim of human life is the continuation of human life . . . man is in his whole condition subject to the sexual tyranny. . . . In principle the sole occupation of any creature is to renew, by the sex act, the form wherewith it is clothed." (*Ibid.*, pp. 14–15, *passim.*) It is for this reason that De Gourmont resists the notion that love is for the sake of sexual pleasure. "One must dissociate the idea of pleasure and the idea of love, if one wants to understand anything of the tragic movements which perpetually beget life at the expense of life itself." As such, pleasure is but the means and not the end of love; by itself, it "explains nothing." (*Ibid.*, p. 149.)

[133] *Love in the Western World*, Preface, p. 8.
[134] *Ibid.*, Book VI, Ch. 1, p. 277. See also *The Crisis of the Modern Couple*, p. 109.
[135] *Love in the Western World*, Book VII, Ch. 7, p. 323.

man and a woman only can be acquisitive, transitory, passionate, or emotional, nourished only by obstacles and frustrations, directed to the imaginary rather than real, and pointed toward destruction and death. By contrast, the love between a man and a woman, under the influence of grace, can be benevolent, lasting, deliberate, unimpeded, directed to the real and pointed toward life.

Eros springs from personal need and is acquisitive. In contrast to *agape*, it treats "a fellow-creature as but an illusory excuse and occasion for taking fire."[136] In marriage, when "a man is faithful to one woman, he looks on other women in quite another way, a way unknown to the world of Eros: other women turn into persons instead of being reflections or means."[137]

Natural love, thus understood, is totally self-centered. Because it is a love between a man and a woman, it is very often sexual in character, though not entirely so. De Rougemont observes that, "if we try to treat passionate love as a mere matter of sex, it is evident that we then do not know what we are talking about. If conversely we seek to connect this love with anything *alien* to sex it will have queer results."[138] Romantic passion, though based in large measure on "physiological factors," is a more ambitious desire. Unlike the pure sexual instinct, it seeks to perpetuate itself. Pure sexual "instincts are manifested as a hunger, and this hunger, like that for food, tends to obtain satisfaction at any cost. The more ravenous, the more indiscriminate it becomes."[139] Romance is no less acquisitive than unadulterated sexual desire but is more complex in its demands.[140] Passion seeks "something that will alter my life and enrich it with the unexpected, with thrilling chances, and with enjoyment ever more violent and gratifying."[141] Sexuality is often the occasion for seeking that something.

Though De Rougemont denies that passion and sexuality are synonymous, he uses the example of sexual love to contrast the acquisitiveness of *eros* with the benevolence of *agape*:

> Savage and natural love is manifested in *rape*. . . . But rape, like polygamy, is also an indication that men are not yet in a stage to apprehend the presence of an actual person in a woman. This is as much as to say that they do not know how to love. Rape and polygamy deprive a woman of her equality by reducing her to sex. Savage love empties human relations of personality. On the other hand, a man does not control himself owing

136 *Ibid.*, Book II, Ch. 3, p. 68.
137 *Ibid.*, Book VII, Ch. 5, p. 313.
138 *Ibid.*, Book III, Ch. 1, p. 142.
139 *Ibid.*, p. 141.
140 See *ibid.*, Book II, Ch. 2, p. 64; and Book VII, Ch. 5, p. 314.
141 *Ibid.*, Book VI, Ch. 3, p. 282.

to lack of "passion" (meaning "power of the libido"), but precisely because he loves and, in virtue of his love, will not inflict himself. He refuses to commit an act of violence which would be the denial and destruction of the person. He thus indicates that his dearest wish is for the other's good.[142]

De Rougemont never mentions natural benevolence in his discussion of human love between a man and a woman. He always associates the benevolent tendency with a love for God, *i.e.*, as derivative of man's love for God. The "Love of God," he says, "has opened an entirely new way to us—the way of *holiness*."

> For to love God is *to obey* God, Who has commanded us to love one another. *To love your enemies* is to shed selfishness and the desirous and anxious self; it means the death of the solitary human being, but it also means the birth of our neighbour. In reply to the ironical question: "Who is my neighbour?" Jesus answered: "Whoever has need of you."[143]

Though De Rougemont writes of "losing the self" in Christian marriage, the benevolence of supernatural love is not disinterested. In regard to marriage, he speaks of a "life *allied* with mine, for the rest of our lives—that is the miracle of marriage. Another life that wills my good as much as its own, because it is united with mine." The lasting union of marriage makes it possible for a human being to achieve a personal good through being good to another. "Fidelity . . . wants the good of the beloved, and when it acts in behalf of that good it is creating in its own presence the neighbour. And it is by this roundabout way through the other that the self rises into being a person."[144]

While conceding that certain kinds of passion, or *eros*, may last, De Rougemont claims that romance (a species of passion) is transitory by definition. Marriage, which should be a lasting relationship, must be founded on a more durable form of love; indeed, it cannot be founded sucessfully on romance. Romance is "by its very nature incapable of establishing a durable marriage, and . . . it is not an act of courage but one of absurdity to marry someone forever because of a fever that endures for two months."[145] De Rougemont even goes as far as to indict the whole of contemporary Western civilization for attempting the impossible:

[142] *Ibid.*, Book VII, Ch. 5, p. 315. The characteristic tendency of true love is benevolence. But such benevolence presupposes respect for the other human being as a person. De Rougemont says that respect "means that we recognize in a being the fullness of a person. A person . . . is what cannot be used by man as an instrument or thing." (*Ibid.*, p. 313, fn. 1.) Respect, however, is not a part of *agape* but a prerequisite to it.

[143] *Ibid.*, Book II, Ch. 3, pp. 68–69.

[144] *Ibid.*, Book VII, Ch. 4, p. 310.

[145] *The Crisis of the Modern Couple*, p. 116.

> We are in the act of trying out—and failing miserably at it—one of the
> most pathological experiments that a civilized society has ever imagined,
> namely, the basing of marriage, which is lasting, upon romance, which is a
> passing fancy. Of all the possible motives for the marriage act . . . we are,
> practically speaking, embracing only the most unstable and ephemeral.[146]

The current emphasis laid on romance is the principal cause of the rapidly
increasing divorce rate. De Rougemont stresses again and again that the
only antidote for this trend is to rely in marriage on a higher and more
durable form of human love, one that is derivative of God's love for man
and man's love for God.[147]

Romance is transitory in character partly because it is emotional and not
wilful or deliberate. Romance is something that happens to a person,
something that he suffers passively, something not subject to command. "It
would be altogether absurd," says De Rougemont, "to demand of a man a
state of sentiment. The imperative, 'Love God and thy neighbour as
thyself,' creates structures of active relations. The imperative, 'Be in love!'
would be devoid of meaning; or, if it could be obeyed, would deprive a
man of his freedom."[148] Romance is totally a matter of feeling; *agape*
need not involve feeling at all.

Romance, proceeding as it does from deficiency, dies when the romantic
desire is fulfilled. The romantic lover (who is in love with love rather than
with the beloved) strives to perpetuate his love through the creation of
obstacles; the condition of its continuation is the perpetual frustration of
the romantic desire.

> Romance feeds on obstacles, short excitations, and partings; marriage, on the
> contrary, is made up of wont, daily propinquity, growing accustomed to one
> another. Romance calls for "the far-away love" of the troubadours; marriage,
> for love of "one's neighbour."[149]

De Rougemont imagines the romantic lover saying: ". . . I must devise
fresh obstructions if I am to go on desiring, and if I am to magnify my
desire to the dimensions of a conscious and intense passion that shall be
infinitely thrilling. And only suffering can make me aware of passion; and
that is why I like to suffer and to cause to suffer."[150] Such love is "an

---

146 *Ibid.*, p. 107. De Rougemont is quick to add that romance has a certain role to
play in a good marriage. He insists, however, that "it should play the minor and final
role of a catalyst" and not be the sole or primary basis for entering conjugal union.
(See *ibid.*)
147 See *Love in the Western World*, Book VII, Ch. 5, pp. 313–314; Book VI, Ch.
6, p. 292; and *The Crisis of the Modern Couple*, p. 108.
148 *Love in the Western World*, Book VII, Ch. 4, p. 311.
149 *Ibid.*, Book VI, Ch. 6, p. 292; and Book IV, Ch. 4, p. 182. See also *The Crisis
of the Modern Couple*, pp. 115–116.
150 *Love in the Western World*, Book VI, Ch. 4, p. 284.

inability to enjoy the present without imagining it as absent, a never-ending flight from possession."[151]

The deliberate placing of obstacles in the path of the fulfillment of desire is connected with another feature of romance: illusion. Illusion "thrives upon absence, dream, and nostalgia"; whereas true love depends on "presence, familiarity, and actual exchange of experience and emotion." De Rougemont adds that "romance is a narcissistic love, addressed to the image of the other and not to his real being, a projection of unconscious and intimate nostalgia, not a real dialogue."[152] He asks, then, what constitutes the link between a man and a woman in this kind of love, and answers as follows:

> It is essentially an imaginary one. For there is no real communication from being to being, but rather a double make-believe, a projected complicity in the creation of eternal obstacles and resistances keenly calculated to arouse passion while refusing to permit the culmination which would assuage it. . . . We are justified in saying that Tristan does not love the real Isolde, nor Isolde the true Tristan, but rather that both of them are really in love only with the love they themselves feel—the actual pain of that burning feeling in the heart—and that all else is but a pretext to nourish the flame.[153]

Though the romantic lover perpetually is seeking "illusory" goods for the self, like anyone caught in passion love, he actually is aiming at destruction and death, his own and that of his beloved. The end of *eros* is death, because *eros*, springing from deficiency, aims at its removal, and hence at the removal of desire and life altogether. The creation of obstacles to the fulfillment of desire can postpone this process but the process itself points toward inertia and extinction. "The supreme soaring of desire ends in non-desire."[154]

To strengthen his claim that *eros* aims at death, De Rougemont describes the way in which the tendency of *eros* seeks the annihilation of the individual. The sublimest "soaring" of *eros* "carried to its loftiest pitch"[155] in natural religion aims at total (spiritual) immersion in and identity with

---

[151] *Ibid.*, p. 285. See also *The Crisis of the Modern Couple*, p. 110. "Romance is by its very nature incompatible with marriage even if the one has led to the other, for it is the very essence of romance to thrive on obstacles, delays, separations, and dreams, whereas it is the basic function of marriage daily to reduce and obliterate these obstacles, for marriage succeeds only in constant physical proximity to the monotonous present." (*Ibid.*, p. 108.)

[152] *Ibid.*, pp. 109–110, *passim*.

[153] *Ibid.*, p. 109. See also *Love in the Western World*, Book VI, Ch. 3, p. 282, Ch. 4, p. 286; Book VII, Ch. 5, p. 313; Book IV, Ch. 17, p. 225.

[154] *Ibid.*, Book II, Ch. 2, pp. 61–62.

[155] See *ibid.*

principles and realities higher than the individual person; it aims at "an impoverishment of one's being"[156] and at the destruction of the individual as individual.[157] The "wish for complete union is indissolubly linked with a wish for the death that brings release."[158] Natural religion "tends *to sublimate* man, and culminates in condemning his 'finite' life. Our desires are intensified and sublimated by the god Eros through being embraced in a single Desire whereby they are abolished. The final goal of the process is to attain what is not life—the death of the body."[159] Of the believer in natural religion, De Rougemont says:

> He was condemned to put his faith in Eros—to trust in his most powerful desire and to expect release through this desire. Yet Eros could lead him but to death. But a man who believes the revelation of Agape suddenly beholds the circle broken: faith delivers him from natural religion.[160]

In natural religion "men can only achieve salvation by ceasing to be, by being 'lost' in the bosom of the divine."[161]

In Christianity "this process is completely inverted."

> Death, from being the last *term*, is become the first condition. What the Gospel calls dying to self is the *beginning* of a new *life* already *here below*—not the soul's flight out of the world, but its return in force into the midst of the world. It is an immediate recreation, a reassertion of life—not of course of the old life, and not of an ideal life, but of our present life now repossessed by the Spirit.[162]

[156] *Ibid.*, Book VI, Ch. 4, p. 285.
[157] See *ibid.*, Book II, Ch. 2, pp. 61–62; Book III, Ch. 2, pp. 145–146.
[158] *Ibid.*, Book IV, Ch. 12, p. 207; Book V, Ch. 1, p. 243.
[159] *Ibid.*, Book II, Ch. 3, p. 67. See also p. 66.
[160] *Ibid.*, Book VII, Ch. 5, p. 312.
[161] *Ibid.*, Book II, Ch. 3, p. 67.
[162] *Ibid.*, p. 68. A number of religious writers agree with De Rougemont. Not only do they contrast the acquisitiveness of natural love between a man and a woman with benevolence made possible by supernatural aid, they also assert that all natural love is acquisitive and cannot be otherwise. All human motives, unless aided by grace, have a good for the self as their final aim: whatever natural giving there is, is always for the sake of getting. Such writers do not say that all natural love is evil but only that natural love does not include benevolence. Albert the Great may be taken as typical of this group. He says: "The ancients, Praepositinus and Gulielmus Altisiodorensis, have said that there is a twofold love or dilection of the will, namely, love (*dilectio*) of friendship and love of concupiscence. Love of friendship tends toward the other, and of it Gregory says that 'it cannot be between less than two.' Love (*dilectio*) of concupiscence is of nature, which always turns back on itself (*curva est in seipsa*), and whatever it loves turns to itself, *i.e.*, to its own and private good; and unless grace elevated it above itself, all that it loved it would turn to its own good and love for its own self so as to seek (in the beloved object) its own advantage. However, in this there is nothing evil (*perversa*), since farther than this nature cannot go unless aided by grace. For it is natural to all that is to love and

If we consider the basic contrasts between *eros* and *agape*, we see that the natural love among human beings discussed in this theory of love is acquisitive in character; and when it takes the form of romance, partly sexual. This love is sharply contrasted with *agape*, which, when manifested in Christian marriage, is a love relationship that also involves acquisitiveness in the form of sexuality, but is *characterized* by benevolence. *Agape*, however, is not a natural love; it requires grace. De Rougemont does not mention benevolence without connecting it with grace; the only natural love he discusses is tendential and totally acquisitive.

George Santayana

The love with which Santayana is concerned is between a man and a woman and has an animal basis.[163] Existentially speaking, "love does not itself appear until a sexual affinity is declared."[164] The sexual instinct in man, however, "is entangled in many cross-currents of desire," which go beyond the desire for physical gratification. Though always tendential and though always rooted in sexual desire, the inclinations of love are acquisitive in more than an animal sense.[165] The love between a man and a woman, though based on physical impulses and drives, aims in its characteristic expression at the achievement of the "ideal" rather than the actual.[166] Such "spiritual interests are supported by animal life."[167] Their aim, however, is not only nonphysical but also not directed toward the acquisition of the individual as individual. Rather, they point toward the ideal that the individual embodies.

---

delight in things naturally advantageous to them, as Plato and Boethius have said." (Albert the Great, *Summa Theologica*, II, iv, 14, in 4, a. 2, Vol. 32, p. 200. Our translation.) The view that benevolence is naturally impossible, of course, is not confined to religious writers. Among his few remarks on love, the stoic Epictetus, for example, says: "For be not deceived, every creature, to speak generally, is attached to nothing so much as to its own interest. Whatever then seems to hinder his way to this, be it a brother or a father or a child, the object of his passion or his own lover, he hates him, guards against him, curses him. For his nature is to love nothing so much as his own interest; this is his father and brother and kinsfolk and country and god." (Epictetus, *Discourses*, Book II, Ch. 22, p. 322.)

[163] *The Life of Reason*, Vol. II, Ch. I, p. 9. See also p. 14.

[164] *Ibid.*, p. 21.

[165] *Ibid.*, p. 16. Just as Santayana says that physical pleasure alone cannot be the aim of love, so also does he claim that procreation is not its characteristic aim. Reproduction "will offer no basis for love if it does not require a union of the two parent bodies." (*Ibid.*, p. 10.)

[166] See *ibid.*, p. 8. See also p. 31.

[167] *Ibid.*, p. 33.

That the true object is no natural being, but an ideal form essentially eternal and capable of endless embodiments, is far from abolishing its worth.

It is this ideal form that is loved and that inspires love. "Whenever this ideality is absent . . . there is a friendly and humorous affection, admirable in itself, but no passion or bewitchment of love."[168]

Santayana admits that the "soaring" impulse toward the ideal perceived in a beloved is seldom if ever unmixed with other tendencies. He says that love "will often be merely an ingredient in an actual state of feeling; friendship and confidence, with satisfaction at being liked in return, will often be mingled with it."[169] However, it can be singled out; for "love, while it betrays its deep roots by the imperative force it exerts and the silence it imposes on all current passions, betrays also its ideal mission by casting an altogether novel and poetic spell over the mind."[170] The blindness associated with falling and being in love is a manifestation of this spell. Santayana says that the lover "loves what he imagines and worships what he creates." Concerning the cause of the love itself, he remarks:

> Nine-tenths of its cause are in the lover, for one-tenth that may be in the object. Were the latter not accidentally at hand, an almost identical passion would probably have been felt for someone else; for although with acquaintance the quality of an attachment naturally adapts itself to the person loved, and makes that person its standard and ideal, the first assault and mysterious glow of the passion is much the same for every object.[171]

Because the real object of love is the ideal and not the actual, Santayana denies that the lover is completely deceived. "Love is . . . only half an illusion; the lover, but not his love, is deceived. His madness, as Plato taught, is divine; for though it be folly to identify the idol with the god, faith in the god is inwardly justified."[172] The love, in other words, is irresistibly drawn to the ideal even though the lover may dote on an actual person who falls far short of it.[173]

Santayana stresses the intensity of love between a man and a woman, its "absolute sway over happiness and misery,"[174] and its capacity to effect a "re-arrangement of the soul."[175] Love, says Santayana,

---

[168] *Ibid.*, p. 31. "Love could not be called divine without platitude if it regarded nothing but its nominal object." (*Ibid.*)

[169] *Ibid.*, p. 7, fn.

[170] *Ibid.*, p. 7.

[171] *Ibid.*, p. 22.

[172] *Ibid.*, p. 30. See also pp. 31 ff.

[173] See *ibid.*, p. 20.

[174] *Ibid.*, p. 21.

[175] *Ibid.*, p. 24.

must become a principle of action and an influence colouring everything that is dreamt of; otherwise it would have lost its dignity and sunk into a dead memory or a domestic bond.[176]

It "can be wholly satisfied only by a happiness which is ultimate and comprehensive," and "is . . . most truly love when it is irresistible and fatal."[177] This, and not "contemplation, sense, and association" nor "a moral bond, the sympathy of two kindred spirits or the union of two lives,"[178] is the essence of love.

Charles Darwin

Darwin never defines love and has relatively little to say about it. One of his main points of interest in the subject is to show that there is no essential qualitative difference between human and animal love. For both men and animals, love is instinctive, *i.e.*, an ingrained "habit" of behavior, formed by a process of "natural selection" among those competing to survive.[179]

Although he does not say what love is, Darwin consistently and sharply distinguishes it from sympathy. Sympathy is the ability to identify, wholly or in part, with the feelings of another. Both men and animals feel it for their own kind. It impels animals of the same species to aid each other. It also impels men to rejoice at each other's pleasure, and both to commiserate with and attempt to remove another's pain or danger. In short, it is the impulse behind most beneficent action. While love and sympathy together help to make up the social or gregarious instincts, sympathy is the more important factor in the development of those instincts.[180]

Darwin mentions several love relationships common to different species when comparing the mental powers of men and the lower animals. Among the instincts they have in common are "that of self-preservation, sexual love, [and] the love of the mother for her new-born offspring."[181] He also mentions love relationships between species. "Every one," he says, "has seen how jealous a dog is of his master's affection, if lavished on any other creature; and I have observed the same fact with monkeys. This shews that animals not only love, but have desire to be loved."[182] Probably his most

[176] *Ibid.*, p. 26.
[177] *Ibid.*, p. 32.
[178] *Ibid.*, p. 21. Such passion "may be merely momentary, or it may be perpetual: a Don Juan and a Dante are both genuine lovers." (*Ibid.*, p. 24.)
[179] For Darwin's discussion of instinct, see *The Origin of Species*, Ch. VIII, pp. 184–208, esp. pp. 184–185.
[180] See *The Descent of Man*, Part I, Ch. IV, pp. 471–475.
[181] *Ibid.*, Ch. III, p. 446.
[182] *Ibid.*, p. 450.

striking comparison of human and animal love occurs in a discussion of religious devotion. Of that devotion he says:

> . . . we see some distant approach to this state of mind in the deep love of a dog for his master, associated with complete submission, some fear, and perhaps other feelings. The behaviour of a dog when returning to his master after an absence, and, as I may add, of a monkey to his beloved keeper, is widely different from that towards their fellows. In the latter case the transports of joy appear to be somewhat less, and the sense of equality is shewn in every action. Professor Braubach goes so far as to maintain that a dog looks on his master as on a god.[183]

The most obvious way in which both men and animals love their own kind is sexually. Sexual desire is acquisitive because it is biological, both in origin and expression.[184] The several forms of dependent love that Darwin mentions—the love of a child for its parents, a dog for its master, men for God—are also acquisitive. The problematic love in Darwin's theory is the protective love of the superior for the inferior, of which the prototype is parental or motherly love. Though such love gives rise to beneficent actions, there is a question as to whether the human desire behind the action is benevolent. In considering the beneficent actions of the lower animals, Darwin is clear about the acquisitive impulse behind them:

> With respect to the impulse which leads certain animals to associate together, and to aid one another in many ways, we may infer that in most cases they are impelled by the same sense of satisfaction or pleasure which they experience in performing other instinctive actions; or by the same sense of dissatisfaction as when other instinctive actions are checked.[185]

Noting, however, that many human and animal instincts differ in degree, he points out that the "motive to give aid is likewise much modified in man."[186]

The best way to understand this modification of motive in regard to benevolence is to examine the instinct of sympathy, which differs from the instinct of love.[187] Darwin relates all animal and most human beneficent

---

[183] *Ibid.*, p. 470.

[184] See *ibid.*, p. 446.

[185] *Ibid.*, Ch. IV, p. 477. "Of the various instincts and habits, some are much stronger than others; *that is, some either give more pleasure in their performance, and more distress in their prevention, than others.*" (*Ibid.*, p. 479. Italics added.)

[186] *Ibid.*, Part III, Ch. XXI, p. 913.

[187] "The all-important emotion of sympathy is distinct from that of love. A mother may passionately love her sleeping and passive infant, but she can hardly at such times be said to feel sympathy for it. The love of a man for his dog is distinct from sympathy, and so is that of a dog for his master." (*Ibid.*, Part I, Ch. IV, p. 478.)

actions to the social instincts of which sympathy is the most dominant.[188] Sympathy not only "forms an essential part of the social instinct," but "is indeed its foundation-stone."[189]

The social instincts are, in themselves, "highly beneficial to the species,"[190] since "they have in all probability been acquired through natural selection." They enable both the individual and the species to survive. They are also the basis of man's moral sense, which, in Darwin's view, most sharply distinguishes man from animal. Though not identical with the social instincts, this moral sense is, in large part, a result of their "enduring and ever-present nature." The moral sense itself, however, arises because man "is capable of reflecting on his past actions and their motives —of approving of some and disapproving of others."[191] Its emergence is, in short, coincident with the emergence of self-consciousness.

In elaborating on what he means by a moral sense, Darwin says:

> Notwithstanding many sources of doubt, men can generally and readily distinguish between the higher and lower moral rules. The higher are founded on the social instincts, and relate to the welfare of others.[192]

Explaining how this capacity arose, he says:

> . . . as man gradually advanced in intellectual power . . . he regarded more and more, not only the welfare, but the happiness of his fellow-men; as from habit, following on beneficial experience, instruction and example, his sympathies became more tender and widely diffused, extending to men of all races, to the imbecile, maimed, and other useless members of society, and finally to the lower animals.[193]

Human beneficence is seldom inspired by the higher moral rules, *i.e.*, by a conscious concern for the welfare of another for his own sake. Darwin says that human beings, like animals, often help each other, not only out of blind instinct but that they very often consciously give only in order to get

---

[188] For Darwin, the manifestations of sympathy are most obvious among men, but he also believes that sympathy occurs among animals of the same species, and is most apparent in their immediate community. (See *ibid.*, Ch. IV, pp. 474–475; and Part III, Ch. XXI, p. 913.)

[189] *Ibid.*, Part I, Ch. IV, p. 472.

[190] *Ibid.*, Part III, Ch. XXI, p. 912. The instinctive impulse to help the species survive is not what we mean by benevolence. Benevolence implies some consciousness of one's own motive. Darwin says that an action "performed by many individuals in the same way, without their knowing for what purpose it is performed, is usually said to be instinctive." (*The Origin of the Species*, Ch. VIII, p. 184.) Instinctive beneficence does not imply benevolence.

[191] *The Descent of Man*, Part III, Ch. XXI, p. 912.

[192] *Ibid.*, Part I, Ch. IV, p. 491. See also p. 481.

[193] *Ibid.*, p. 493.

something for themselves. Thus, a man often is motivated in helping another by a desire to gain the approval and praise of his fellowmen, by a desire to avoid the moral discomfort of remorse, and "unfortunately very often by his own strong selfish desires."[194]

"But," he adds, "as love, sympathy and self-command become strengthened by habit, and as the power of reasoning becomes clearer . . . he will feel himself impelled, apart from any transitory pleasure or pain, to certain lines of conduct."[195] It is then that man is able to say that he is the supreme judge of his own conduct. In view of this, Darwin rejects the school of morals that affirms "that the foundation of morality lay in a form of Selfishness."[196] We may infer, therefore, that Darwin believed that a conscious benevolent motive is possible for men who have achieved a high moral development.

But, though Darwin believes benevolence possible, he does not explicitly include it in his theory of love, nor does he mention it in relation to love. Each time he discusses love and its actions—including mother love—he does so in terms of blind instinct, or in terms of the immediate determinants of pleasure and pain. By implication, the lover's motive seems to be acquisitive. Thus we suggest—since the evidence is far from conclusive—that love is essentially acquisitive in character in Darwin's theory.

Jean-Jacques Rousseau

Rousseau's conception of human love seems to parallel Darwin's. His understanding of human love, as well as of most other human phenomena, is conditioned by the controlling distinction he makes between man as he is in the state of nature and man as he is in political or civilized society. It is in terms of this distinction that Rousseau mentions "the physical and moral ingredients in the feeling of love." The former is unqualified sexual desire. The latter is sexual desire focused on one person and intensified by the restrictions of civilized life.[197] This love, both in its physical and moral aspects, is essentially acquisitive in character.

In addition, Rousseau mentions and discusses such things as conjugal love and parental love.[198] In his remarks on these loves and in his discussion of love of country we do not find sufficient evidence to justify an interpretation suggesting that there is a type or kind of love for which benevolence is essential. Although he does discuss the affection of a

[194] *Ibid.*, p. 481.
[195] *Ibid.*
[196] *Ibid.*, p. 489. See also pp. 490–491.
[197] See *A Discourse on the Origin of Inequality*, Part I, pp. 227–229.
[198] See *ibid.*, Part II, p. 239.

"country" for its "citizens," it is not at all clear that such love is among human beings. A country or state, in Rousseau's thought, is something different from those who comprise its government or the aggregate of its citizens. Even the "love" that Rousseau urges the citizens to have for each other is not clearly benevolent. For, he urges civic virtue on the basis of the "common interest" of the citizens; respect for the law and patriotism will promote these interests. Rousseau does not specify whether the motive behind this devotion is the promotion of one's own interest through promoting the interest of all as a group, or whether it is the promotion of the interest of the group first and, secondarily, one's own interest. In other words, he does not specify whether the love to which he refers is one that takes the form of collective acquisitiveness or of self-interested benevolence.[199]

The most explicit discussion of benevolence that we find is one in which Rousseau mentions it, not in relation to love but rather in relation to "compassion" (what he elsewhere calls sympathy):

> Compassion must, in fact, be the stronger, the more the animal beholding any kind of distress identifies himself with the animal that suffers. Now, it is plain that such identification must have been much more perfect in a state of nature than it is in a state of reason.[200]

He adds:

> It is . . . certain that compassion is a natural feeling, which, by moderating the violence of love of self in each individual, contributes to the preservation of the whole species. It is this compassion that hurries us *without reflection* to the relief of those who are in distresss.[201]

Such compassion is not voluntary but an "innate repugnance" of which even "benevolence and friendship" are only the effects. Rousseau also includes, as a result of compassion, "the tenderness of mothers for their offspring and the perils they encounter to save them from danger."[202] Such impulses have their root in the identification or union that living creatures (and particularly human beings) feel for other such creatures.

Though the actions to which compassion gives rise are clearly beneficent, the motives behind them may or may not be benevolent. In the case of Darwin, such instinctive desires were said to be controlled by pleasure and pain. Rousseau does not go into this question. But, like Darwin, he

---

[199] See *ibid.*, Appendix, pp. 281–282; and *A Discourse on Political Economy*, pp. 300–308.
[200] *A Discourse on the Origin of Inequality*, Part I, pp. 225–226.
[201] *Ibid.*, p. 226. (Italics added.)
[202] See *ibid.*, pp. 223–255.

distinguishes compassion or sympathy (whether or not it is benevolence) from love.

Benedict de Spinoza

That Spinoza's theory of love is an atypical one is to be explained partly in terms of his method. Taking as his model mathematical demonstration, specifically geometry, he begins each part of his *Ethics* with definitions and axioms and then proceeds to state and argue for a whole series of propositions about God (Part I), the mind (Part II), the emotions (Part III), the emotions in regard to human bondage (Part IV), and the understanding in regard to human freedom (Part V). He states his methodical principle very succinctly when he says: "I shall consider human actions and desires . . . as though I were concerned with lines, planes, and solids."[203]

At the end of Part III, Spinoza offers his definition of love: "Love is pleasure, accompanied by the idea of an external cause."[204] To understand this definition it is necessary to consider the meaning ascribed by Spinoza to several basic terms.

The most general thing that can be said about love is that it is an emotion. Of the emotions that occur in both body and mind, Spinoza gives the following definition:

> By *emotion* I mean the modifications of the body, whereby the active power of the said body is increased or diminished, aided or constrained, and also the ideas of such modifications. . . . If we can be the adequate cause of any of these modifications, I then call the emotion an activity, otherwise I call it a passion.[205]

Hence, emotions are divided into two classes: those that are passions and those that are activities. Love can be either a passion or an action.

The tendencies or emotions that are activities are distinguished from those that are passions by what Spinoza calls "adequate cause." The movements or happenings in us that we understand clearly, distinctly, and rationally, we are said to be the adequate cause of and, thus, are activities. Those happenings, however, of which we have an inadequate idea, we are said to be the inadequate cause of and, hence, are passions.[206]

For the most part, natural loves among human beings are passions.

203 *The Ethics,* Part III, p. 129.
204 *Ibid.,* Def. VI, p. 175.
205 *Ibid.,* Def. III, p. 130.
206 Spinoza is a determinist, emphatically denying freedom of the will. Hence, when he uses the phrase "adequate cause" to distinguish actions from passions, he is not distinguishing self-determined from other-determined movements. The distinction concerns only the degree of our understanding of what is happening, which is itself determined by the unalterable chain of divine causality that pervades the entire universe and all of the substances within it.

Laying stress on the mental aspect of such an emotion, Spinoza refers to it as a *"confused idea,"* which implies a certain passivity in the soul.[207] Insofar as they are ideas, they are mental; insofar as they are the mental counterparts of bodily change and insofar as they determine the mind not only to think of one thing rather than another, but also to strive for one thing rather than another, such emotions are tendencies. Hence, the theory presented by Spinoza is essentially a tendential one, in which love is conceived as a desire.

For Spinoza, all psychic activity is mental. Mental *tendencies,* however, do not fall into the sphere of judgment. But, since Spinoza refers to a judgment in his definition of love, his conception of love does have a cognitive aspect. Since he does not, unlike Descartes, reduce all emotions to thoughts or ideas, the conception of love advanced by him is not primarily or entirely cognitive.

Though Spinoza never says so explicitly, the idea of an external cause which he mentions in his definition of love must be a judgment of something as good. Since the good is defined as whatever is thought to be useful,[208] the judgment implied is valuation. This judgment, however, is not *prior* to love. Spinoza states emphatically "that in no case do we strive for, wish for, long for, or desire anything, because we deem it to be good, but on the other hand we deem a thing to be good, because we strive for it, wish for it, long for it, or desire it."[209] Since the idea of an external cause is essential to love, love is an emotion that presupposes consciousness. Using Spinoza's analytical distinction between mind and body, we may say there are, first, physical changes or movements in the body of which the mind is either simultaneously or subsequently aware. When these changes are, or tend toward, what is pleasurable and the mind refers them to an external cause, they constitute the emotion of love. In short, that emotion is always *accompanied by* the judgment of valuation.

While Spinoza presents a tendential theory of love, he does not claim that love and tendency are identical. Only some tendencies are love. Spinoza argues: *"Everything . . . endeavours to persist in its own being,"* and that this endeavor really constitutes the essence of anything that exists.[210] It makes its endeavor through the emotions. All secondary emotions (of which love is one) derive from and are attributable to three primary emotions: desire, pleasure, and pain. Desire "is, in fact, nothing else but man's essence, from the nature of which necessarily follow all those results which tend to its preservation."[211] It is any striving, wishing, or longing

207 *Ibid.,* "General Definition of the Emotions," p. 186.
208 See *ibid.,* Part IV, Def. I, p. 190. See also Prop. VIII, p. 195.
209 *Ibid.,* Part III, Prop. IX, Note, p. 137.
210 See *ibid.,* Prop. VI-VII, pp. 136–137.
211 *Ibid.,* Prop. IX, Note, p. 137.

for whatever one thinks will be useful to that end. Some of these inclinations, or their fulfillment, are pleasant or joyful; some of them are painful or sorrowful. *Only those that result in pleasure are called love.* There are, then, as many varieties of love as there are objects that produce, or can produce, pleasure. *"There are as many kinds of pleasure, of pain, of desire, and of every emotion compounded of these . . . such as love, hatred, hope, fear, &c., as there are kinds of objects whereby we are affected."*[212]

Therefore, love must be understood in terms of the endeavor to preserve being. It is in these terms that pleasure and pain are defined:

> . . . *Pleasure* is the transition of a man from a less to a greater perfection.
> . . . *Pain* is the transition of a man from a greater to a less perfection.[213]

Perfection is "each thing's essence, in so far as it exists, and operates in a particular manner."[214] Perfection is the same as reality; the more perfection the more reality and *vice versa*. Pleasure is that which increases the number of modes that a person can be affected by and increases the number of modes with which he can affect external bodies.[215] Not only is the body's power of acting increased by pleasure but the mind's range of understanding is also extended. Correspondingly, the body's power of acting and the mind's range of understanding is reduced by pain. Love is related to pleasure or joy, which is its sole motivation.

Pleasure and pain are directly coordinate with good and evil. *"Pleasure in itself is not bad but good: contrariwise, pain in itself is bad."*[216] Pleasure, however, is a *personal* good. The end of all human love is the transition from being less perfect to being more perfect; the final referent is always the self. According to Spinoza, one does good to another only if one will gain pleasure thereby or if one would suffer pain by not doing so. His theory of love, then, is one in which love is conceived as totally acquisitive.

Spinoza denies that benevolent desire is possible. If one does good to another only because one will gain pleasure thereby, or because one would suffer pain by not doing so, the motive is mixed acquisitive desire. Spinoza

---

[212] *Ibid.*, Prop. LVI, p. 168.
[213] *Ibid.*, Def. II-III, p. 174. Spinoza says elsewhere that pleasure is *"a passive state wherein the mind passes to a greater perfection,"* and pain *"a passive state wherein the mind passes to a lesser perfection."* (*Ibid.*, Prop. XI, Note, p. 138.
[214] *Ibid.*, Part IV, Preface, p. 190.
[215] See *ibid.*, Part IV, Prop. XXXVIII, p. 215.
[216] *Ibid.*, Prop. XLI, p. 217. Spinoza does make something of a qualification on this general statement. He even gives examples of pleasures that are not good or may not be good, viz.: hope, partiality, pride, titillation, lust, etc. Pleasure can be excessive; it can be disproportionate to its object, and produce fixations that preclude a person's being affected by more modes of experience. Spinoza distinguishes between pleasures that activate and emancipate the mind and those that narrow and impede it. To say that pleasure can be excessive and harmful, however, does not mean that it is, in itself, bad. (See *ibid.*, Prop. XLIII, pp. 217–218; Part III, "General Definition of the Emotions," pp. 185–186; Part IV, Prop. XXXVIII-XXXIX, pp. 215–216; and Part III, Prop. LVIII, p. 171.)

makes this point most clearly when he asserts that "benevolence" is derivative from compassion. To be compassionate a person must think of himself as similar to another in some sense.

> By the very fact that we conceive a thing, which is like ourselves . . . to be
> affected with any emotion, we are ourselves affected with a like emotion.[217]

He goes on to say: "This imitation of emotions, when it is referred to pain, is called *compassion*."[218] Compassion gives rise to *"benevolence."*

> This will or appetite for doing good, which arises from pity of the thing
> whereon we would confer a benefit, is called *benevolence*, and is nothing
> else but *desire arising from compassion*.[219]

Pity, however, is defined by Spinoza "as *pain arising from another's hurt*."[220]
The relief of the pain, sympathetically experienced, is the spur of the beneficent action.[221] The desire is finally and basically acquisitive.[222]

At the very point in his work where he defines love, Spinoza denies that the desire for union is essential to love or to a type of love. He says that "the definition given by those authors who say that love is *the lover's wish to unite himself to the loved object* expresses a property, but not the essence of love."[223] Spinoza is not here stating that the inclination to unite with someone is never an instance of love. He is merely emphasizing that it is the emotion of pleasure that distinguishes the tendencies of love from other tendencies (*e.g.*, hate); as the desire for union may result in pleasure or pain it may or may not be an instance of love.

Spinoza calls sexual desire a love, but does not dwell on it, since it is but one among many forms of pleasure. Of it he says: *"Lust is desire and love in the matter of sexual intercourse."*[224] Sexual desire is part of marriage

---

[217] *Ibid.*, Part III, Prop. XXVII, p. 148.
[218] *Ibid.*, Note I.
[219] *Ibid.*, Note II, p. 149.
[220] *Ibid.*, Prop. XXII, Note, p. 146. He adds: "What term we can use for pleasure arising from another's gain, I know not." (*Ibid.*)
[221] The desire for personal pleasure can also be a spur to beneficent action. (See *ibid.*, Prop. XXXIX, p. 156.)
[222] All emotions, in Spinoza's view, are acquisitive, since their originating cause is always to achieve a good (gain pleasure) or avoid an evil (reduce pain) for the self.
[223] *Ibid.*, Def. VI, "Explanation," p. 175.
[224] *Ibid.*, Def. XLVIII, p. 184. Spinoza does make a rather veiled comment on the danger of excessive sexual desire: "Localized pleasure or stimulation (*titillatio*) is pleasure, which, in so far as it is referred to the body, consists in one or some of its parts being affected more than the rest . . . ; the power of this emotion may be sufficient to overcome other actions of the body . . . , and may remain obstinately

and is in "harmony with reason" if engendered not only by physical beauty but also by the desire to have children.[225]

None of the loves possible among human beings is the highest of which man is capable. The highest love must be directed to the highest good. Since Spinoza says: "We call a thing good or evil, when it is of service or the reverse in preserving our being . . . that is . . . when it increases or diminishes, helps or hinders, our power of activity,"[226] the highest good to which human love can be directed is that which will maximize human perfection. Spinoza devotes a good portion of Part V of *The Ethics* to showing that the highest good is God and that the highest human love is the intellectual love of God (*amor intellectualis Dei*). It is the climax of his whole ethical view.

Spinoza stresses the point that the love of the highest good, God, is an intellectual love. Because it is an intellectual love, it cannot be a bad love. "Our actions, that is, those desires which are defined by man's power or reason, are always good. The rest may be either good or bad."[227] To contemplate the eternal, substantial, and real being of God, to gain an idea of Him that is as adequate as possible is to maximize one's own perfection through the highest endeavor of the human mind.

Thus in life it is before all things useful to perfect the understanding, or reason, as far as we can, and in this alone man's highest happiness or blessedness consists, indeed blessedness is nothing else but the contentment of spirit, which arises from the intuitive knowledge of God: now, to perfect the understanding is nothing else but to understand God, God's attributes, and the actions which follow from the necessity of his nature. Wherefore of a man, who is led by reason, the ultimate aim or highest desire, whereby he seeks to govern all his fellows, is that whereby he is brought to the adequate conception of himself and of all things within the scope of his intelligence.[228]

---

fixed therein, thus rendering it incapable of being affected in a variety of other ways: therefore . . . it may be bad." (*Ibid.*, Part IV, Prop. XLIII, Proof, p. 217. See also Appendix, XIX, p. 240.)

[225] *Ibid.*, Appendix, XX, p. 240.

[226] *Ibid.*, Prop. VIII, Proof, p. 195. Earlier, Spinoza offers a broader definition of good: "By *good* I here mean every kind of pleasure, and all that conduces thereto, especially that which satisfies our longings, whatsoever they may be." (*Ibid.*, Part III, Prop. XXXIX, Note, p. 156.) But just as Spinoza qualifies his description of pleasure as an unqualified good so also does he qualify this definition. That is to say, certain pleasures, if indulged in excessively, may not contribute to growth and development but may actually hinder it.

[227] *Ibid.*, Part IV, Appendix, III, p. 237.

[228] *Ibid.*, Appendix, IV, p. 237. In this vein, Spinoza adds that "whatsoever things hinder man's perfecting of his reason, and capability to enjoy the rational life, are alone called evil." (*Ibid.*, Appendix, V, p. 237.)

Spinoza notes that intellectual love of God "is pleasure, if we may still use that term,"[229] but it is not the desire to use, which characterizes lower loves. Rather, one may say that the love of God *is* the fulfillment of human nature since it is the essence of the effort to persist in being. *"Blessedness* [which consists in loving God] *is not the reward of virtue, but virtue itself."*[230] In other words, the intellectual love for God is acquisitive only in an atypical sense. God is not loved as a *means* to happiness. God is loved *as* man's perfection, or, rather, as perfection itself. It is in this sense that Spinoza can say that man's intellectual love for God is the same as God's love for Himself.[231]

Gottfried Wilhelm Leibniz

Leibniz's theory of love is brief and clear. For him, love is always an interpersonal phenomenon, always tendential and always acquisitive. ". . . to *love* is to be inclined to take pleasure in the complete perfection or happiness of the object loved."[232] Elsewhere, Leibniz adds to this definition: ". . . to love or to cherish is to find pleasure in the happiness of another, or, what amounts to the same thing, to accept the happiness of another as one's own."[233] Though the happiness or good of another is absolutely essential to love, it, like any other human tendency, has as its final aim a personal good. The key word is "pleasure." Everyone loves because of the good that accrues to himself, *i.e.,* the pleasure that he derives. (God is therefore the most lovable of all objects; since His happiness is the greatest, loving Him gives us the greatest pleasure.)[234]

Leibniz makes the point about the self-centeredness of all love in several different contexts. It is particularly evident when he argues that the traditional distinction between acquisitive and benevolent desire is, in fact, only a distinction between simple acquisitive desire (getting without giving) and mixed acquisitive desire (getting through giving):

> Philosophers and theologians even distinguish two kinds of love, viz: the love which they call the *love of complacency,* which is nothing but the

---

229 *Ibid.,* Part V, Prop. XXXVI, Note, p. 265.

230 *Ibid.,* Prop. XLII, p. 270.

231 See *ibid.,* Prop. XXXVI, pp. 264–265.

232 *New Essays Concerning Human Understanding,* Book II, Ch. XX, pp. 167–168. The definition is repeated a number of times with small variations. See also *Philosophical Papers and Letters,* Vol. I, Part I, Ch. 10, p. 232; Part II, Ch. 32, p. 432, and Ch. 35, p. 467; and Vol. II, Part IV, Ch. 66, p. 1042.

233 *Ibid.,* Part III, Ch. 44, p. 690.

234 See *ibid.,* Vol. I, Part I, Ch. 10, pp. 232–233; and Vol. II, Part III, Ch. 44, p. 691.

desire or feeling which we have for the one who gives us pleasure, without concerning ourselves whether he receives it; and the *love of benevolence*, which is the feeling that one has for the one who, by his pleasure or happiness, gives us some. The first makes us have in view our pleasure and the second that of another, but as making or rather constituting ours, for if it did not reflect upon us in some way we could not concern ourselves with it since it is impossible, although they affirm it, to be separated from the good proper.[235]

Leibniz is careful to emphasize that the self-interest he sees in connection with love is not merely an accompanying and secondary motive but the basic spur from which all love arises. At one point he refers explicitly to the controversy about whether the desire that "seeks the well-being of the beloved, nevertheless depends upon the impulsion toward one's own well-being. . . . Who [asks Leibniz] seeks the well-being of the beloved for its own sake, since we will nothing except for the sake of our own good?" He answers by affirming that whoever denies that self-interest is the basis of all love is in conflict "with the nature of things, for the impulse to action arises from a striving toward perfection, the sense of which is pleasure, and there is no action or will on any other basis." He goes on to add that no one can "renounce (except merely verbally) being impelled by his own good, without renouncing his own nature."[236]

Reiterating that "we do nothing deliberately except for our own good," Leibniz nevertheless makes a distinction concerning the way that good is achieved:

> There is a twofold reason for desiring the good of others; one *is* for our own good, the other *as if* for our own good. The former is calculating, the latter loving. The former is the affection of a master for his servant, the latter that of a father for his son; . . . the former for the sake of some expected good, the latter for its own sake. But, you ask, how is it possible that the good of others should be the same as our own and yet sought for its own sake?

Leibniz's answer is that the only thing sought for its own sake is pleasure. Hence, whenever we seek the pleasure of another, we are seeking a good for its own sake, as an end, even though that pleasure is a means to our own.[237] The giving involved in love is the giving of a good for its own

---

[235] *New Essays Concerning Human Understanding*, Book II, Ch. XX, p. 168. "For the happiness of those whose happiness pleases us is obviously built into our own." (*Philosophical Papers and Letters*, Vol. II, Part III, Ch. 44, p. 690.) In love "while each benefits the other as much as he can, he may increase his own happiness in that of the other." (*Ibid.*, pp. 692–693.)

[236] *Ibid.*, pp. 695–696, *passim.*

[237] See *ibid.*, Vol. I, Part I, Ch. 7, pp. 212–214, *passim.*

sake in the sense that *what* we give is pleasure, but it is giving for the sake of getting in the sense that we give, ultimately, for the sake of *our own* pleasure, which depends on the happiness or pleasure of the beloved.

> For we try to learn the wishes of the person whom we love and to conform to them. A true lover has regard for the slightest movements of the person on whom his happiness depends.[238]

[238] *Ibid.*, Part II, Ch. 23, p. 328.

8

Benevolence as Indispensable
to Love

THE authors of the theories classified in this chapter agree that without benevolence there is no love of any kind. Some of them hold that love and benevolence are identical (thus excluding acquisitive desire from love altogether), but others merely assert that benevolence is an essential part of any love relationship, even though such a relationship may include both the desire to get and the desire to give.

None of the authors in this chapter asserts that acquisitive desire alone can be called an expression of love. They differ, therefore, both from the authors in Chapter 7, who discuss love only as acquisitive desire, and from those in Chapters 5 and 6, who hold binary theories of love. To be sure, the latter authors hold that there is a kind of love in which benevolence is essential; but they also assert that some form of acquisitive desire *in and by itself* is a kind of love. For them, acquisitive and benevolent desire (either alone or as part of a relationship involving other elements) are *separate* kinds of love.

For many of the authors in Chapters 5, 6, and 7, sexual desire alone may be an expression of love; for the authors in this chapter, sexual desire alone can never be a form of love. When some of them mention sexual desire (or other forms of acquisitive desire) in relation to love, they invariably add that sexual desire can be considered an aspect of love only when it is part of a wider relationship, that is, when it is accompanied by benevolence.

Authors whose theories of natural love among human beings may be so described include Adam Smith, Georg Wilhelm Friedrich Hegel, Georg Simmel, Nicolai Hartmann, C. S. Lewis, José Ortega y Gasset, Theodor Reik, and Erich Fromm.

Adam Smith

In *The Theory of Moral Sentiments,* Adam Smith refers to love as an affection, an emotion, a feeling, a sentiment, and a desire. There is little doubt that all of these terms signify something tendential. All human tendencies, Smith claims, fall into two groups: "The great division of our affections is into the selfish and the benevolent."[1] For Smith, love is always a benevolent affection.

The key to Smith's theory of love is in his analysis of sympathy, or "fellow feeling," through which he finds the human capacity to love intelligible. He argues that the only way one human being can care about another for the other's sake is by vicariously experiencing the other's joys and sorrows. "As we have no immediate experience of what other men feel," he says, "we can form no idea of the manner in which they are affected, but by conceiving what we ourselves should feel in the like situation." Only thus is it possible to appreciate what the other person is experiencing. "By the imagination we place ourselves in his situation, we conceive ourselves enduring all the same torments, we enter as it were into his body, and become in some measure the same person with him."[2]

Smith delineates the narrow and the broad sense in which sympathy may be defined:[3]

> Pity and compassion are words appropriated to signify our fellow-feeling with the sorrow of others. Sympathy, though its meaning was, perhaps, originally the same, may now, however, without much impropriety, be made use of to denote our fellow feeling with any passion whatever.[4]

From this notion of sympathy and fellow feeling, Smith draws his conception of affection:

---

[1] *The Theory of Moral Sentiments,* p. 394.

[2] *Ibid.,* pp. 3–4, *passim.* See also pp. 7–8, 321.

[3] "The word sympathy, in its most proper and primitive signification, denotes our fellow-feeling with the sufferings, not that with the enjoyments, of others." (*Ibid.,* p. 60.)

[4] *Ibid.,* p. 5. See also pp. 97 ff.

What is called affection is in reality nothing but habitual sympathy. Our concern in the happiness or misery of those who are the objects of what we call our affections; our desire to promote the one and to prevent the other, are either the actual feeling of that habitual sympathy, or the necessary consequences of that feeling.[5]

Love is the affection that arises from sympathizing neither only with the sorrow nor any one emotion but with *all or most* of the feelings of another; it is a benevolent tendency that habitually inclines us to diminish all the sorrows and increase all the joys of someone else. The stronger identification with another is, the more sympathy inclines to love and the more intense the emotion we feel. When "we *entirely* sympathize and go along with the motives of the agent, the love which we conceive for him upon his own account, enhances and enlivens our fellow-feeling."[6] All love rests on a large measure of identification with another and is continuously benevolent in tendency.[7] But all benevolence, since it may be momentary and rest on but a partial identification with another, is not love.[8] The ideal of love is mutual sympathy in all things. "We expect less sympathy from a common acquaintance than from a friend; we cannot open to the former all those little circumstances which we can unfold to the latter."[9]

A considerable part of Smith's treatise is devoted to the refutation of the position that all human desire, including the tendency of love, is basically acquisitive. Smith holds benevolence to be one of the "original passions of human nature." In the very first words of his treatise he asserts:

How selfish soever man may be supposed, there are evidently some principles in his nature, which interest him in the fortune of others, and render their happiness necessary to him, though he derives nothing from it, except the pleasure of seeing it.[10]

Also, concerning the reality of benevolent tendencies, he later says:

When I condole with you for the loss of your only son, in order to enter into your grief, I do not consider what I, a person of such a character and

---

[5] *Ibid.*, p. 323.
[6] *Ibid.*, p. 103. (Italics added.)
[7] See *ibid.*, p. 43.
[8] One may sympathize with another person's love of a third without loving the other person. That is to say, one may identify with a particular emotion such as love in another and not identify with his other emotions. To the extent to which identification is so restricted, love is not present, despite the fact that love easily arouses sympathy for itself. (See *ibid.*, pp. 39, 42, 52–53.)
[9] *Ibid.*, p. 24.
[10] *Ibid.*, p. 3.

profession, should suffer, if I had a son, and if that son was unfortunately to die; but *I consider what I should suffer if I was really you; and I not only change circumstances with you, but I change persons and characters.* My grief, therefore, is entirely upon your account, and not in the least upon my own. It is not, therefore, in the least selfish.[11]

Though Smith emphasizes the interest in the other to the exclusion of self-interest, there are passages that indicate that some self-interest, as an accompanying aim, may be present in benevolent desire.[12] In the passage cited earlier, Smith mentions the "pleasure of seeing" the effects of one's own benevolence. He also says that we may seek mutual love.[13] His clearest reference to self-interest occurs when he discusses benevolence as a moral virtue.[14] According to him, "to feel much for others, and little for ourselves . . . to restrain our selfish, and to indulge our benevolent affections, constitutes the perfection of human nature."[15] Though such perfection cannot be the primary aim of the benevolent desire, it presumably may be an accompanying aim.[16]

Though Smith's conception of love is tendential, he does not distinguish types of love in terms of different kinds of tendencies but rather on the basis of the judgment that precedes and gives rise to love, as well as upon the love's durability and extent. In other words, though love between "young people" and the friendship of the wise and virtuous are both benevolent in tendency, they differ in origin, duration, and in the number involved. Thus, friendship based on virtue is "the happiest, as well as the most permanent and secure" of loves. Smith also contrasts friendship with adolescent love in terms of number:

> They who would confine friendship to two persons, seem to confound the wise security of friendship with the jealousy and folly of love. The hasty, fond, and foolish intimacies of young people, founded commonly upon some slight similarity of character altogether unconnected with good conduct, upon a taste, perhaps, for the same studies, the same amusements, the same diversions, or upon their agreement in some singular principle or opinion not commonly adopted; those intimacies which a freak begins, and which a freak puts an end to, how agreeable soever they may appear while they last, can by no means deserve the sacred and venerable name of friendship.

11 *Ibid.*, p. 466. (Italics added.) See also pp. 465, 10 ff.

12 Speaking of our willingness to help someone we love, Smith says: "Our love, however, is fully satisfied, though his good fortune should be brought about without our assistance." (*Ibid.*, p. 95.)

13 See *ibid.*, p. 331. See also p. 166.

14 See *ibid.*, p. 214.

15 *Ibid.*, p. 27.

16 See *ibid.*

Friendship, says Smith, "may safely embrace all the wise and virtuous with whom we have been long and intimately acquainted, and upon whose wisdom and virtue we can upon that account entirely depend."[17]

Georg Wilhelm Friedrich Hegel

Hegel deals with love most directly and extensively in his early theological studies, particularly in *The Positivity of the Christian Religion, The Spirit of Christianity and Its Fate,* and a fragment on *Love.* The conception of love in these writings (and, for the most part, in his later works) is one in which the notions of the benevolent tendency and the desire for union are stressed. Though he never explicitly equates love with benevolence, Hegel strongly implies that there is no genuine love without it, nor without the inclination toward union.[18]

Denying that love is a matter of reason or understanding, Hegel asserts: "It is a feeling, yet not a single feeling."[19] Rather, it is a complex of tendencies that are not "isolated feelings" but are merged in "a single and unified self."[20] The focal tendency is the desire for union.

> Love means in general terms the consciousness of my unity with another, so that I am not in selfish isolation but win my self-consciousness only as the renunciation of my independence and through knowing myself as the unity of myself with another and of the other with me.

Hegel immediately adds: "Love, however, is feeling. . . ."[21] He goes on to observe:

[17] *Ibid., passim.* At one point Smith discusses the notion of universal benevolence. In that discussion it is not clear whether it requires divine assistance or not. Smith does connect it with a belief that all men are under the care of God, but he makes no mention of God's help in attaining universal benevolence. At another point he says that "the care of the universal happiness of all rational and sensible beings, is the business of God, and not of man. To man is alloted a much humbler department . . . the care of his own happiness, of that of his family, his friends, his country." (*Ibid.,* pp. 345–348.)

[18] We understand the Hegelian theory to be one of natural rather than supernatural love. Though these essays are heavily theological in content, Hegel seems to be trying to win a secular and natural understanding of the phenomena of religion. Though he employs the idea of divinity in these works (and retains it in his later works), he uses it here in a different sense from the active and personal infinite God of revealed religion. In Hegel's view, the reality of such a divinity is, to say the least, doubtful. (See *The Spirit of Christianity and Its Fate,* Sect. iii, p. 240. See also p. 247, for the pantheistic view.)

[19] *Love,* p. 304. See also *The Spirit of Christianity and Its Fate,* Sect. iii, p. 247.

[20] *Love,* p. 305.

[21] *Philosophy of Right,* Addition 101, p. 261, *passim.* Hegel emphasizes the natural tendential character of love in the context of criticizing Kant's understanding

The first moment in love is that I do not wish to be a self-subsistent and independent person and that, if I were, then I would feel defective and incomplete. The second moment is that I find myself in another person, that I count for something in the other, while the other in turn comes to count for something in me.[22]

Hegel is concerned particularly with the union of love among human beings. "True union, or love proper, exists only between living beings who are alike in power and thus in one another's eyes living beings from every point of view; in no respect is either dead for the other."[23] Since love tries to annihilate the distinction between self and other, it presupposes differences between self and other.

In love man has found himself again in another. Since love is a unification of life, it presupposes division, a development of life, a developed many-sidedness of life. [24]

Hegel points out that the unifying tendency between two persons (or in a small group) tends to exclude others as it grows stronger. Also, the more people it includes, the less its intensity.

The more extended the multiplicity of the relations and feelings of the lovers and the more deeply love is concentrated, the more exclusive it is and the more indifferent to the life of other persons. . . . The love which a large group of people can feel for one another admits of only a certain degree of strength or depth and demands both a similarity in mind, in interest, in numerous relationships of life, and also a diminution of individualities.[25]

When love is diluted beyond a certain point, it ceases to be love though it may retain the form of love.

By love's extension over a whole community its character changes; it ceases to be a living union of individualities.[26]

---

of the Biblical imperative to love God and one's neighbor as oneself. Hegel rejects what he believes to be Kant's understanding of that statement, "as a 'command requiring respect for a law which commands love.'" On the other hand, both Hegel and Kant separate the realm of love from the realm of duty. (*The Spirit of Christianity and Its Fate*, Sect. ii, p. 213. See also Sect. i, p. 187; Sect. iii, p. 225; and Sect. ii, pp. 216–217. See pp. 270 ff., *supra*.)

[22] *Philosophy of Right*, Addition 101, p. 261. See also 173–176, pp. 290–291.

[23] *Love*, p. 304. See also pp. 305 ff.

[24] *The Spirit of Christianity and Its Fate*, Sect. iv, pp. 278–279. See also *Love*, pp. 303, 308.

[25] *The Spirit of Christianity and Its Fate*, Sect. iv, p. 279.

[26] *Ibid.*, Sect. v, p. 289. "Exemption from fate through flight into an empty life was made easier for the members of the community because they constituted a community which kept itself aloof from and opposed to all forms of life or else

Love stretches beyond its bearable limits when a complex of families becomes a race or a people. When this transition has been accomplished, the bond uniting the people "has already ceased to be simply a bond of love and confidence, and has become one of plighted service."[27]

The family has its origin in sexual desire, which is compatible with love as long as it and the tie it carries with it are "elevated . . . to a spiritual significance—the unanimity of love and the temper of trust."[28] "Marriage," says Hegel, "as the immediate type of ethical relationship, contains first, the moment of physical life. . . . But, secondly, in self-consciousness the natural sexual union—a union purely inward or implicit and for that very reason *existent* as purely external—is changed into a union on the level of the mind, into self-conscious love."[29]

Although Hegel describes the tendential character of love as "a mutual giving and taking,"[30] he places greater emphasis on benevolence; and says of love "that its essence is not a domination of something alien to it," and that "self-love is a word without meaning."[31] More emphatically he argues:

> Where the sentiment of love exists, there is an equal *abandon*—love the most fervid. The ruler who loves the slave, glorifies the object of his love by laying at his feet all his magnificence, power and honor—forgetting sceptre and throne for him. . . . This reckless fervor shows itself also in the glowing warmth of the Arab and Saracen poetry. That glow is the perfect freedom of fancy from every fetter—an absorption in the life of its object and the sentiment it inspires, so that selfishness and egotism are utterly banished.[32]

But, though benevolence is primary in Hegel's conception of love, self-interest is not absent. The loving family, for example, "live . . . in a unity of feeling, love, confidence, and faith in each other." Each "lives out of self"; yet "in this mutual self-renunciation each regains the life that had been virtually transferred to the other; gains, in fact, that other's existence and his own, as involved with that other."[33]

---

determined their character solely by the universal spirit of love, i.e., it did not *live* in those forms." (*Ibid.*) See also Sect. iv, p. 280 and Sect. v, p. 294, where Hegel refers to the idea of a universal philanthropy as "a shallow idea and an unnatural one."

27 *The Philosophy of History*, Introduction, pp. 41–42.
28 *Philosophy of Mind*, Sect. 518, p. 254. See also Sects. 519–522, pp. 254–255.
29 *Philosophy of Right*, Par. 161, pp. 111. See also *The Phenomenology of Mind*, pp. 468 ff.
30 *Love*, p. 307.
31 *The Spirit of Christianity and its Fate*, Sect. iii, p. 247. See also pp. 250 ff.
32 *The Philosophy of History*, Part IV, Sect. I, Ch. II, pp. 358–359.
33 *Ibid.*, Introduction, p. 42, *passim*.

Georg Simmel

Insofar as our critical notions apply to Simmel's theory of natural love among human beings, his conception can be classified as completely tendential and benevolent. Love excludes any inclination to use another merely to realize one's own ends. At certain points in the *Fragmente über die Liebe,* however, Simmel indicates that his conception of love transcends the distinction between acquisitive and benevolent desire.

Love, for Simmel, is a tendency or feeling, "a dynamic arising, so to speak," resulting in a "form of behavior." The feeling does not originate in the lover but only is transformed by an external object from latency to actuality; "it does not come *from* the object but goes *to* it." And, at least in its original stage, love is "closely and unconditionally bound to its object."[34]

The object of love, according to Simmel, is never fractioned. Whoever is loved is loved in his totality. Correspondingly, "love . . . is the only form in which [many] can give their ego in its totality."[35] Unlike other human feelings, love "is under all conditions a function of the relatively undifferentiated unity of life." To explain precisely how love differs from other feelings, Simmel says:

> This feeling [love] is more bound up with the unity of life than many, or most. The majority of our feelings, of joy and sorrow, of respect and contempt, of fear and interest, arise and live at a greater distance from the point where the streams of subjective life unite, or more correctly, from the center from which they spring. Even when we "love" a lifeless object we do not designate it as useful, pleasant or beautiful. We mean, rather, that there is a central feeling (which may however have different degrees of strength) which it releases in us, while those other evaluations represent more peripheral responses.[36]

The outgoing feeling of love has two prominent characteristics: it does not go toward the object on the lover's behalf, and it is ultimately not "teleological." In denying that the beloved is ever simply used, Simmel is able to distinguish love from sexual desire, though he concedes that a love relationship often involves sexual desire. "The frequently heard contention," says Simmel, "that the erotic and the sensual are incompatible is, I

[34] *Fragmente über die Liebe,* pp. 19–20, *passim.* (Our translation.)

[35] *The Secret and the Secret Society,* Ch. II, Sect. 6, p. 325. This point applies whether the relationship be "romance" or friendship. (See *ibid.*)

[36] *Fragmente über die Liebe,* p. 19. Love "is absolutely bound up with its object and not merely associated with it . . . love, and the total conduct of the lover, is plainly something unitary, not composed of independent elements." (*Ibid.,* pp. 18–19.)

think, groundless. What love excludes is rather *isolated* sensuousness, *sensuous enjoyment for its own sake.*" Sexual desire, as such, is "an entirely unindividualized desire, the object of which is always replaceable. This is obvious since replaceability is always of the nature of a *means,* the means to the attainment of a solipsistic purpose—which is the harshest contradiction to the *love* of this object that could be imagined."[37]

Though Simmel asserts that it is "of the utmost importance to acknowledge love as an immanent . . . formal function of *spiritual* life,"[38] he affirms that the root of love lies in instinct and nonspiritual tendencies:

> That love develops out of [instincts concerned with the propagation of the species] cannot be doubted. For the typical concurrence of the epoch of sexual activity and the arousal of love cannot be a mere accident, nor would the passionate aversion (though this is not without its exceptions) to sexual relations with anyone but the beloved, and the equally passionate longing for relations with this particular person, be otherwise explicable.

This drive in human beings is finally "singularized," *i.e.,* directed to one person. Yet "the individualization of the drive does not add up to love; for this can be either hedonistic refinement or a vital-teleological instinct for the partner fitted to produce the best children."[39] Nevertheless, the fact that there is only one beloved makes it possible for love to arise, *i.e.,* for the physical impulse to be transformed in the consciousness of the lover. Sensuality may be "carried over the threshold of genuine love,"[40] but "spawning life which has established the attraction of the sexes as mediation between two of its wave crests, undergoes now that powerful revolution whereby this attraction becomes love."[41] That revolution consists in making the "hedonistic" or "genetic" fulfillment of the sex drive subservient to love itself.

> But at the very moment at which love appears as a natural development the picture changes; as soon as love is realized in this species-teleological sense, it has already become something different, having a status beyond that. To be sure, it always remains life, but it is now seen as of a special sort. The real dynamic, the natural evolving process of life, is there for its own sake; it becomes a definitive and makes itself free from that teleology and, indeed, in so far as it remains in connection with it, actually reverses it: the lover feels that life must now serve love, must lend its forces to conserve it.[42]

As a result love finally *excludes* not only the aim of physical pleasure but also "a concern for the propagation of the species."

[37] *Ibid.,* p. 25.
[38] *Ibid.,* p. 19. (Italics added.) See also p. 24.
[39] *Ibid.,* pp. 22–23, *passim.*
[40] *Ibid.,* p. 25.
[41] *Ibid.,* p. 27.
[42] *Ibid.,* pp. 22–23, *passim.*

Just as the loving man, as loving, who has freed himself from all actual purposefulness (with regard to the love-object), from the hedonistic and egoistic, as also from the moral and altruistic, *can* attach himself to a state of being but not to a life of conduct, so for him also the purpose of propagating the species is alien. He is no transition-point but an end-point, or more correctly, his being and self-feeling are beyond ways and goals, beyond means and the making of means.[43]

Judgment is also excluded from the realm of "genuine" love (though not from the substrata out of which it grows). Simmel admits, as a matter of course, that a "man must naturally exist externally and in the temporal order and be known before he is loved."[44] He adds: "When I venerate anyone this is mediated by the general property of worthy-to-be-venerated which, together with more particular characteristics, continues to adhere to the image of this man as long as I venerate him." Simmel adds, however, that from "love, once it has arisen, is to be excluded the mediating, always relatively universal quality which permitted it to arise." Genuine love "has left behind it all the qualities of the beloved which were its original inspiration."[45]

Probably the most accurate way to describe Simmel's conception of love is to call it a tendency of a very vital nature, which, in some way, is identified with the basic life force itself.[46] The first expression of that tendency that Simmel discusses in his *Sociology* is an unrestrained giving (in friendship and particularly in marriage). The desire is "to let oneself be completely absorbed by the other, to send the last reserves of the soul after those of the body, to lose oneself to the other without reservation." Simmel observes that for most men such abandon threatens the love relationship. Few can indulge in it safely.

> Only those individuals can give themselves *wholly* without danger who *cannot* wholly give themselves, because their wealth consists in a continuous development in which every abandon is at once followed by new treasures. Such individuals have an inexhaustible reservoir of latent psychological possessions, and hence can no more reveal and give them away at one stroke than a tree can give away next year's fruits with those of the season.

Most men are not equipped to abandon themselves in this way.

> With every flight of feeling, with every unconditional abandonment, with every revelation of their inner life, they make inroads (as it were) into their capital, because they lack the mainspring of ever renewed psychic affluence

[43] *Ibid.*, p. 26. See also pp. 21, 27–28.
[44] *Ibid.*, p. 18.
[45] *Ibid.*, pp. 20–21, *passim*.
[46] See *ibid.*, pp. 27–28.

which can neither be exhaustively revealed nor be separated from the ego. In these cases . . . the Dionysian bliss of giving may leave behind it an impoverishment.[47]

Simmel affirms that it is essential, particularly in marriage, that the "other individual must give us not only gifts we may accept, but the possibility of our giving *him*—hopes, idealizations, hidden beauties, attractions of which not even *he* is conscious." Giving is indispensable to an interpersonal love relationship. In the few instances where inexhaustible personal resources exist, no limits need be placed on giving. Otherwise, restraint is imperative. "It is highly probable that many marriages founder on this lack of reciprocal discretion—discretion both in taking and in giving."[48] For Simmel, even taking is benevolent, since one takes to give another an opportunity to give.

Despite Simmel's suggestion that the final stage of love transcends all motives, his observations, taken as a whole, indicate that benevolence is essential. He explicitly excludes judgment, acquisitive desire, and sexual desire. Little is said about union. The only critical notion explicitly related to love (*i.e.*, friendship and marriage), beyond unspecified tendency, is giving.

Nicolai Hartmann

Hartmann's conception of love is benevolent desire (or a relationship in which the essential tendency is benevolent), with a judgmental aspect. He deliberately withholds the word "love" from completely acquisitive tendencies or relationships. The greater part of his analysis consists of various contrasts between tendencies aiming at another's good and those aiming at one's own good.

The two types of natural love among human beings that are discussed at greatest length are personal love and brotherly love. "EVERYONE," says Hartmann, ". . . is well aware that besides universal love of one's neighbour, and of the far distant, and besides the love which dispenses spiritual gifts, there is another, closer and richer, an intimate love directed exclusively to one individual person."[49]

In such love, the lover is devoted less to the empirical personality of the

[47] *The Secret and the Secret Society*, Ch. II, Sect. 6, pp. 328–329, *passim*.
[48] *Ibid.*, p. 329. Simmel adds that "the place where we deposit all this, which *we* produce, but produce for *him,* is the indistinct horizon of his personality." (*Ibid.*)
[49] *Ethics*, Vol. II, Sect. VII, p. 368. Exclusiveness is the trait that most clearly distinguishes personal love from brotherly love. Personal love "creates an ethical situation of a special kind, an intimate, absolutely reciprocal union between two human beings. A third person requires again a new and equally special commitment. Distributed among several, love loses its personal character." (*Ibid.*, p. 370.)

beloved than to the ideal he has of him. The lover attempts to raise the real
beloved to the level of the ideal. According to Hartmann, "it inheres in the
essence of personal love, to pierce through the empirical person to his ideal
value." He adds:

> Thus we can understand how it may attach itself to one who is morally
> undeveloped and imperfect, indeed to one whose ideal ethos is deficient. Its
> commitment merges into the ideal of personality; it lets this stand for the
> empirical individual, accepting him as equivalent to his highest possibilities,
> as raised to a power above his actual being. It loves in him what inheres in
> his essential tendency, the axiological idiosyncrasy of his Ideal, yet not as an
> Ideal, but as a trend toward actuality, just as if it were already actualized in
> him. In this way, looking back from the Ideal upon its imperfect carrier, it
> loves the empirical individual in his characteristic peculiarity.[50]

Most characteristics of personal love are what Hartmann calls "altruism."
It is "the positive trend, the kindness and devotion which place oneself at
the service of the other—a tendency of the will, *which is the reverse of the
desire to possess."* In other words, "it is a pure Being-for-thee on my part,
irrespective of any Being-for-me on thy part, and stands in perceptible
contrast and occasionally in acute conflict therewith."[51] Since Hartmann
speaks of superficial loves in which the will to possess rather than to give
dominates, relationships can still qualify as loves even if the benevolent
desire is not primary.[52] Yet, for love to exist, benevolence is essential,
though it may be overshadowed or even temporarily eclipsed by a strong
acquisitive tendency such as sexual desire.[53]

Self-interest is not entirely excluded from personal love, though seeking
the interest of the beloved is primary in the characteristic love tendency.
Hartmann freely admits that "all personal love looks forward to a return of
love," and that the lover is disappointed if his affection is not reciprocated.
He adds that "its emotional value by no means depends on the response."[54]
Unreciprocated love can, and often does, endure, since it is not extended
primarily or exclusively for the sake of such return or any other personal
good. Its tendency may be self-interestedly benevolent but it is not acquisitive.

[50] *Ibid.*, p. 369. The tendency to enhance the empirical personality of the beloved
is in part wilful, in part not. Hartmann argues that if love were a wilful effort, it
would be "planned and not genuine." But though it cannot be originated by will, "an
element of will rightfully subsists in love." The wilful part of love is the volitional
effort made to make love's benevolent tendencies more effective, as well as to nourish
them with the "volitional energy." (*Ibid.*, p. 372, *passim.* See also p. 374, and Sect.
VI, p. 271.)
[51] *Ibid.*, Sect. VII, p. 373, *passim.* (Italics added.)
[52] See *ibid.*, p. 376.
[53] See *ibid.*, p. 377.
[54] *Ibid.*, p. 376.

The self-interested aspect of the benevolence of love manifests itself in two other ways. The first is the "proverbial bliss" or accompanying satisfaction that the lover can experience in loving.[55] The second is the vicarious joy the lover can experience in sharing the good bestowed upon the one with whom he feels united; for Hartmann claims that the union of personal love transcends the existential union of empirical personalities. It is, in addition, a "union of two kinds of ideal ethos."[56] "Personal love," says Hartmann, ". . . unites forthwith innermost depth to innermost depth, overleaping the surfaces."[57] This is why, though the lover does not always perceive it, "that it is precisely the ethical nature of himself *and* the other person which in his love is struggling for fulfillment."[58] The lover, insofar as he is aware of this struggle, may anticipate a personal good along with his desire to enhance the welfare of the beloved.

In Hartmann's view, the judgment in personal love "is the least recognized" of its elements. Love is often said to be blind. Yet, Hartmann asks: "How can love move to the ideal value of personality, even find its way to the real Being of the man, unless it somehow comprehends it?" A "cognitive element," he argues, "is always contained in love," even though this element is closer to "emotional understanding" than to "a thinking, reflective, rational consciousness of an object."[59]

This cognitive element takes two forms: admiration and valuation. In the lover's view of the beloved, "only the lover knows personality as a value. There is no way of understanding it, except through the insight of love." Since the lover sees beyond the actual person and "discovers the ideal in the empirical," and as he is the only one able to do this, his view of the beloved is unique. He sees something more, or, at least, something potential, and hence often is regarded as "blind." Valuation, "an anticipation of the ideal" that "precedes its actualization" is the judgment that precedes the "constructive work of love," the determination of the lover to make the empirical object of his love more and more like the ideal.[60]

Although the tendential dominates in personal love, there is a sense in which judgment, particularly the admiration of the ideal, is regarded by Hartmann as more valuable. Because personal love allows the lover not only to participate in the enhancement of an ideal but also to perceive it, such love,

> like radiant virtue, gives an ultimate meaning to life; it is already fulfillment in germ, an uttermost value of selfhood, a bestowal of import upon human

[55] *Ibid.*, p. 377.
[56] *Ibid.*, p. 371.
[57] *Ibid.*, p. 377.
[58] *Ibid.*, p. 371. (Italics added.)
[59] *Ibid.*, pp. 378–379, *passim.*
[60] *Ibid.*, pp. 379–380, *passim.*

existence—useless, like every genuine self-subsistent value, but a splendour shed upon our path.[61]

The tendential aspect of brotherly love also is benevolent. But Hartmann emphasizes that the "altruism of personal love is essentially different from that of brotherly love, which looks primarily to the empirical Being of another, to his welfare, happiness and the like."[62] Furthermore, it usually looks to the welfare of more than one beloved.

Hartmann understands brotherly love, or love for one's neighbor, as having come from Christianity, though he considers it divorced from its religious underpinnings. As he understands it, this love is directed primarily "towards whoever is nearest, towards the other person, and it is a positive affirmative tendency, the transference of interest from the I to the Thou."[63] He goes on to add:

> The modern word, altruism, which admittedly is much misused, gives exact expression to this fundamental tendency in its opposition to all egoism—and by no means to its more blatant forms only. In altruism the centre of one's whole sphere of interests is transferred from oneself to the other person. It is the abrogation of the self-centred tendency and a transference of interest to the being of another for his own sake.[64]

Hartmann notes that because love of one's neighbor frequently is understood as the desire to help the needy and the deprived, it is often confused with pity.[65] Denying that they are identical, he says: "The essence of neighbour-love is not pity at all nor suffering, but a feeling, a striving, which approves another person as such." He distinguishes brotherly love from pity in at least two ways. First, it tends to be an enduring and comprehensive interest, not a transient and partial one. "As a basic tendency love is not at all a reaction to the person's momentary condition, but is a spontaneous, original interest in him as a person, including all that concerns him, like the interest one has in oneself and all that concerns oneself."[66] Second, unlike pity, brotherly love necessarily includes the element of respect. Such respect consists in a recognition of the worth of common humanity. Respect makes it possible, theoretically at least, to

---

[61] *Ibid.*, p. 381.

[62] *Ibid.*, p. 373.

[63] *Ibid.*, Sect. VI, p. 268. Though Hartmann denies that such love is self-interested in the sense that one can seek moral improvement or reward through it (see *ibid.*, pp. 278–279), he does not deny that a certain "sympathetic delight in another's welfare, still remains." (*Ibid.*, Sect. VII, p. 314. See also p. 313.)

[64] *Ibid.*, Sect. VI, p. 268. "Brotherly love is the living sense of another's worth; and in so far as this is endangered—whether from without or from within—it comes to the rescue." (*Ibid.*, p. 273.)

[65] See *ibid.*, p. 272.

[66] *Ibid.*, p. 273.

extend the scope of brotherly love indefinitely,[67] though it is, in fact, always restricted to those with whom one comes into contact.[68] Of the judgmental elements in brotherly love, respect may be tendered to all men, whereas valuation (the actual decision to help someone) is restricted to those with whom one actually has associations.

> Neighbourly love . . . places one's own ego on a level with that of others, concerning itself merely with those who are nearest at hand, those accidentally present, with the narrow circle of those who are within reach. Indirectly, of course, it applies to the whole community.[69]

Both the respect and the valuation in brotherly love contribute to the sense of oneness the lover has with the beloved. These judgments make possible "a curious invasion of one ego into the experience, the emotional life and even the moral being of another ego, an ethical communication between the two worlds, otherwise eternally separated, of the Self and the Not-Self."[70] Hartmann again makes clear that such judgments do not have, strictly speaking, the character of intellectual functions, when he states that there is "an emotional apriorism of love which pierces through the dividing wall," a movement that "forces its way . . . into the sphere of another's inner experience, his feelings, struggles and failures, his happiness and sufferings." But he adds: "Indirectly, of course, it has the character of knowledge."[71] Love, as well as "any real knowledge of human nature which deserves the name, rests upon the emotional act of transcending one's own ego."[72]

A third kind of love among human beings Hartmann calls "love of the remotest" as distinguished from "love of the nearest" (which includes personal as well as brotherly love). Love of the remotest is essentially a benevolent tendency, which, though it may also be directed to an existing person, is "a love for the man who is to be." Hartmann describes this love thus:

> It is a love which knows no return of love, which radiates only, gives only, devotes, overcomes, sacrifices, which lives in the high yearning that cannot be fulfilled for the one who loves, but which knows that there is always a future and that indifference to it is a sin.[73]

[67] See *ibid.*, p. 279.
[68] See *ibid.*, Sect. VII, p. 373.
[69] *Ibid.*, Sect. VI, p. 269.
[70] *Ibid.*, p. 274.
[71] *Ibid.*, p. 275, *passim.*
[72] *Ibid.*, p. 276.
[73] *Ibid.*, Sect. VII, pp. 317–318, *passim.* As in all loves, the lover transcends his own ego. The transcendence of the love of the remote, however, "lies in another dimension of life; it does not tend to fellowship with individuals nor even to union with the community, but is prospective towards some future time which is still asleep in the non-existent." (*Ibid.*, p. 315.)

This love (which Hartmann associates with both Plato and Nietzsche) perpetuates an ideal that will benefit both the living and the unborn.

> Love of the nearest does not go beyond one's contemporary. Its effect does not endure, it dies with its object; it is not adapted to the continuation of its object, but to his present existence. Love of the remotest seeks a different measure of efficiency, an efficacy which will last.[74]

These two loves are not entirely mutually exclusive. The love of the remotest must work through the love of those at hand. "But its aims do not centre in the nearest."[75] It aims primarily at benefiting posterity rather than the person through whom posterity may be benefited. In this way, those who are near are loved in part as means, not to one's own good but to the good of posterity.

> Love of the remotest, as such, does not require that the nearest should be treated "merely" as a means. It allows him scope as an end in himself. It only insists that he should "also" be regarded as a means to a farther end.[76]

As love of the remotest is the impetus to progress, it presupposes that the actual or potential (not yet existent) beloved be admired, that he be a person of great consequence. Such individuals make human progress possible. Because ordinary altruism is based only on respect not admiration, it at best "raises the fallen to the level of the average. And from the point of view of general progress this is of no use." Neighbor-love by itself "leads to a levelling of mankind, it is a cause of stagnation and of retrogression— since there is never an arrest of change. Levelling makes selection impossible, it leads to an inversion of development, past recovery."[77]

Regarding judgment, Hartmann says that the love of the remotest "must unearth again the principle of selection which love of the nearest has buried." Though all men are worthy of respect and love of the nearest, only the best are worthy of admiration and the love of the remotest. Only the best can love in this way just as only the best are worthy of being so loved. Love of the remotest "must reinstate the worthiest, the ethically strong and aspiring, and favour him at the cost of the man who is sinking."[78] "Love of the remotest," says Hartmann, "goes a step farther: not only are men ethically unequal, but they also ought to be. The more unequal they are, so much the more movement there will be in the process

[74] *Ibid.*, p. 318.
[75] *Ibid.*
[76] *Ibid.*, p. 320.
[77] *Ibid.*, p. 319.
[78] *Ibid.*

of development, and so much the higher will be the ends aimed at."[79] Love of the remotest is not of "the nearest but the best."[80]

Although Hartmann says that love of the remotest and love of the nearest differ little in regard to the value of their benevolence, he leaves no doubt as to which he thinks aims at the higher good.

> The situation which love of the remotest strives for is incomparably greater than that which neighbour-love aims to achieve; as for height of value the well-being of one's neighbour cannot be weighed in the great scales in which the ideal value of humanity, as always understood, must be weighed. If the whole value of the two lay in the values aimed at, their axiological relation would prove so utterly unfavourable to neighbour love that one could never speak of a conflict between them. Love of the nearest would need to withdraw from comparison with love of the remotest.[81]

C. S. Lewis

C. S. Lewis' *The Four Loves* focuses on human love. Except for a few references to animal love[82] and for a discussion of God's love, the whole book is about man as lover. And of all human loves, Lewis is most concerned with love among human beings.[83]

In setting forth Lewis' theory, it is essential to distinguish between his four major love relationships and the three principal elements of those relationships. Lewis applies the word "love" to all. That is to say, the relationships of "Affection," "Eros," "Friendship," and "Charity" are all called kinds or types of love. And the principal elements of these relationships he calls "Gift-love," "Need-love," and "Appreciative love."

After defining the three basic elements present in any love relationship, Lewis uses them to explain the composition of the four principal love relationships and how they differ from each other. Of the four, charity is by definition not a natural but a supernatural love. Accordingly, we shall concentrate here on affection, *eros*, and friendship, each of which is a type of natural love among human beings.[84]

Lewis begins by acknowledging that in his original meditations he had assumed that he could reserve the word "love" for benevolent desires, or what he calls "Gift-love." Noting that such a restriction led him to "puzzles

---

[79] *Ibid.*, p. 322. "As can be easily seen, the nature of love for the remotest is akin to nobility of character. It is preferential in its discrimination." (*Ibid.*, p. 325.)

[80] *Ibid.*, p. 319.

[81] *Ibid.*, p. 331.

[82] See *The Four Loves*, Ch. III, pp. 53–55.

[83] In the second chapter, he does discuss two forms of love "for what is not personal." (See *ibid.*, Ch. II, pp. 33–35.)

[84] For Lewis' conception of supernatural human love, see Part I, Ch. 3, *supra*.

and contradictions," he concludes: "I cannot now deny the name *love* to
Need-love."[85] But need-love is only one element in the several relationships called love. Lewis' general conception of love includes the notions of
both acquisitive desire and benevolent desire. It also includes a notion from
the cognitive order, what Lewis calls "Appreciative love." "This judgment
that the object is very good, this attention (almost homage) . . . can go
out not only to things but to persons. When it is offered to a woman we
call it admiration; when to a man, hero-worship; when to God, worship
simply."[86]

Lewis bases his analysis of human love on three of our critical notions:
benevolent desire, acquisitive desire, and esteem.

> Need-love says of a woman "I cannot live without her"; Gift-love longs to
> give her happiness, comfort, protection—if possible, wealth; Appreciative
> love gazes and holds its breath and is silent, rejoices that such a wonder
> should exist.[87]

Since Lewis' conceptions of the three natural love relationships—affection,
eros, and friendship—each involve all three basic notions, benevolent desire
is, in Lewis' view, essential to any natural love among human beings. His
distinction among the three elements signified by the three basic notions is
analytical rather than existential.

> We murder to dissect. In actual life, thank God, the three elements of love
> mix and succeed one another, moment by moment. Perhaps none of them
> except Need-love ever exists alone, in "chemical" purity, for more than a
> few seconds. And perhaps that is because nothing about us except our
> neediness is, in this life, permanent.[88]

Need-love always aims at a good for the self. It may involve complete
indifference to the welfare of the one from whom that good is sought. On
the other hand, need-love, when joined with appreciative love, may seek a
personal good only in ways not injurious to the other party.[89] This limita-

[85] *Ibid.,* Ch. I, pp. 11–12, *passim.* Lewis offers three reasons for including acquisitive desire in the realm of love. First, although admitting that language is not an
infallible guide, he is impressed that such desires are called love. Second, he denies
that need-love and selfishness are synonymous. Third, he sees most of man's desires
toward God as springing from need. (See *ibid.,* pp. 12–13.)

[86] *Ibid.,* Ch. II, p. 33.

[87] *Ibid.*

[88] *Ibid.*

[89] Lewis makes this distinction in two contexts. In the first, he discusses the
different expressions of need-love or acquisitive desire in regard to things. Though
both desires are acquisitive, a man's desire for water and his desire for a quality wine
differ. (See *ibid.,* Ch. II, pp. 28–29.) In the second context, Lewis distinguishes
sharply between the sheer sexuality that is "without Eros" and that sexuality that is
"part of Eros." (See *ibid.,* Ch. V, p. 132.)

tion on need-love can occur whether it takes the form of simple or mixed acquisitive desire. The prime example of giving in order to get, in Lewis' analysis, is instinctive mother love. Of a mother's "Gift-love" he says: "She gives birth, gives suck, gives protection. On the other hand, she must give birth or die. She must give suck or suffer. That way, her Affection too is a Need-love. There is the paradox. It is a Need-love but what it needs is to give. It is a Gift-love but it needs to be needed."[90]

Gift-love is benevolent desire, but, in its natural form, it is not disinterested benevolence. The only disinterested benevolence is divine love or divinely aided love.[91] The sole aim of such love is the good of the other. By contrast, natural gift-loves "never quite seek *simply* the good of the loved object for the object's own sake. They are biased in favour of those goods they can themselves bestow, or those which they would like best themselves, or those which fit in with a pre-conceived picture of the life they want the object to lead."[92] But even natural gift-love because it is benevolent—although a self-interested benevolence—"must work towards its own abdication," for, "the proper aim of giving is to put the recipient in a state where he no longer needs our gift."[93] In other words, the primary aim of even natural benevolence must be the fulfillment of the need of another for his own sake and never the personal good one may achieve in fulfilling that need. In this sense, need-loves and gift-loves are "opposites . . . as the form of the blanc-mange is an opposite to the form of the mould."[94]

Affection

Affection is the humblest of the natural loves and is the least distinctively human.[95] Lewis explains it largely in his discussion of family rela-

---

[90] *Ibid.*, Ch. III, p. 54. Lewis says that the maternal instinct has no power, in itself, to fulfill the law of true benevolence. "The instinct desires the good of its object, but not simply; only the good it can itself give. A much higher love—a love which desires the good of the object as such, from whatever source that good comes—must step in and help or tame the instinct before it can make the abdication. And of course it often does. But where it does not, the ravenous need to be needed will gratify itself either by keeping its objects needy or by inventing for them imaginary needs." (*Ibid.*, pp. 76–77.) Lewis adds that not only mothers feel the need to be needed. (See *ibid.*, p. 77.)

[91] "But Divine Gift-love—Love Himself working in a man—is wholly disinterested and desires what is simply best for the beloved." (*Ibid.*, Ch. VI, p. 177.)

[92] *Ibid.* (Italics added.) Lewis also points out that natural gift-love always presupposes admiration or respect. Divine gift-love, on the contrary, may be directed to those whom one neither admires nor respects for any human excellence or quality.

[93] *Ibid.*, Ch. III, p. 76.

[94] *Ibid.*, Ch. VI, p. 176.

[95] ". . . Affection is the most instinctive, in that sense the most animal, of the loves." (*Ibid.*, Ch. III, p. 71. See also pp. 56–57.)

tionships, particularly mother love. He characterizes affection as consisting of a great deal of need-love, some gift-love, and a barely discernible amount of appreciative love. But he also says that affection extends far beyond familial ties: "This warm comfortableness, this satisfaction in being together, takes in all sorts of objects. It is indeed the least discriminating of loves."[96] In its extrafamilial expression affection seems to be little more than liking someone.[97]

Within the family, however, the intensity of affection often goes beyond mere liking. The child's need for its mother is an instance of affection as is the mother's need to protect the child. Lewis uses King Lear as a striking example of one "devoured with a ravenous appetite for Affection." Desperately wanting his daughters to care for him, he "is half-crazy with it."[98] In Lewis' view, such desires are perfectly normal. It is only when they dominate that they become destructive; this is most likely to happen when affection is the only love a person experiences.

There is a parallel in the gift-love present in affection. Lewis does not claim that all mother love is acquisitive in character, *i.e.*, that it is animated by a need to be needed. Parental love can be truly benevolent, but only when the basic instinct is controlled. Bringing it under control requires " 'common sense,' that is, reason . . . 'give and take'; that is . . . justice . . . [and] 'decency.' There is no disguising the fact that this means goodness; patience, self-denial, humility, and the continual intervention of a far higher sort of love than Affection, in itself, can ever be. That is the whole point. If we try to live by Affection alone, Affection will 'go bad on us.' "[99]

The appreciative love in affection is atypical. Affection demands neither admiration nor respect, strictly speaking, but it does require familiarity. And affection, insofar as it involves judgment, rests on the belief that what is familiar (or one's own) is somehow better than what is not. The appreciative love in affection probably is described best as the difference in our attitude toward an "old" friend and one recently acquired, both of whom are good friends.[100]

Affection "is indeed the least discriminating of loves." Lewis claims that the criterion of familiarity is the great equalizer here. Since a person can become pleasantly familiar with almost anyone, "almost anyone can become an object of Affection."[101] Affection does not depend on the merits of its

[96] *Ibid.*, p. 54.
[97] See *ibid.*, p. 25.
[98] *Ibid.*, pp. 63–64, *passim*. See also pp. 54, 82–83.
[99] *Ibid.*, pp. 81–82. See also pp. 76–77.
[100] See *ibid.*, p. 55. This is true only after affection has proceeded beyond its imperceptible initial stages. "To become aware of it is to become aware that it has already been going on for some time." (*Ibid.* See also pp. 57–59, 63.)
[101] *Ibid.*, p. 54. See also p. 58.

object. It is in this sense that the appreciative love in affection is atypical. It is not typically admiration or respect (though these are not precluded); it is rather the awareness that another person is a member of the family, lives in the same neighborhood, is a long-standing acquaintance, is not a stranger.

Eros

However important sexual desire (a variety of need-love or acquisitive desire) may be for *eros,* Lewis denies that the two are identical. "Sexuality may operate without Eros or as part of Eros." As he also says:

> That sexual experience can occur without Eros, without being "in love," and that Eros includes other things besides sexual activity, I take for granted.[102]

The distinction between sexual desire and *eros* is made most clearly when Lewis contrasts the strictly sexual impulse toward another person, who is treated as a "necessary piece of apparatus" for the attainment of physical pleasure, with the desires of *eros. Eros* incites a man to desire a woman as a person and hence to want and need her as more than a sexual object.[103]

The difference between the desire for a woman as a mere vehicle for the fulfillment of sexual desire and the desire for her as a person seems to be appreciative love. Lewis speaks of the first stages of *eros*—"to fall in love with her"—as usually having little to do with sex. He speaks rather of "a delighted pre-occupation with the Beloved—a general, unspecified pre-occupation with her in her totality."[104] The growth and full development of *eros* is contingent upon the transformation of this unspecified preoccupation into admiration or veneration. "It is the nature of a Need-pleasure to show us the object solely in relation to our need, even our momentary need." In *eros,* however, another judgment is essential; the joining of need-love with appreciative love. For,

> Eros, a Need, at its most intense, sees the object most intensely as a thing admirable in herself, important far beyond her relation to the lover's need.[105]

To the elements of need (which is only partly sexual desire) and appreciation, Lewis adds gift-love, though he does not think of this last as playing as decisive a role as the other two. Yet, it is undeniably important for his conception of *eros.* Of *eros* fully developed he says:

[102] *Ibid.,* Ch. V, pp. 131–132.
[103] *Ibid.,* p. 135. See also p. 134.
[104] *Ibid.,* p. 133.
[105] *Ibid.,* p. 136.

In one high bound it has overleaped the massive wall of our selfhood; it has made appetite itself altruistic, tossed personal happiness aside as a triviality and planted the interests of another in the centre of our being. Spontaneously and without effort we have fulfilled the law (towards one person) by loving our neighbour as ourselves.[106]

Lewis also mentions other characteristics of *eros. Eros,* unlike sexual desire, is an exclusive love.[107] A man who claims he loves two women at the same time loves neither. On the other hand, since *eros* "is notoriously the most mortal of our loves," it is possible to love more than one woman at different times.[108]

The metaphors "falling in" and "falling out" of love suggest to Lewis a certain involuntariness,[109] but he also maintains that man's will is not totally powerless in controlling and channeling *eros.* For the sake of a good love, he counsels that we "must not give unconditional obedience to the voice of Eros," for "Eros, honoured without reservation and obeyed unconditionally, becomes a demon."[110] Lewis recognizes that married persons may fall out of love. When this happens, the absence of *eros* does not invalidate the marriage nor taint the sincerity of those who took the marital vows.[111]

One final point Lewis makes in regard to *eros* is the importance of the desire for the union of complementarity. In *eros* the "man does play the Sky-Father and the woman the Earth-Mother; he does play Form, and she Matter."[112] In a sense, this complementary union desired by both is the most striking and puzzling characteristic in Lewis' conception of *eros.* The desire for it does not seem to be necessarily either acquisitive or benevolent. It is not guided by any consideration of happiness—either one's own or another's—at least happiness as usually understood. Hence, whenever a person who is under the influence of *eros* is faced with the prospect of nothing but misery for both himself and his beloved if he persists in pursuing his love, Lewis says his answer must be: "Better this than parting. Better to be miserable with her than happy without her. Let our hearts break provided they break together." He adds: "If the voice within us does not say this, it is not the voice of Eros."[113] We might conjecture that,

[106] *Ibid.,* p. 158.
[107] See *ibid.,* Ch. IV, p. 91.
[108] *Ibid.,* Ch. V, p. 158. *Eros* is not doomed by its very nature to be transitory. Lewis merely remarks how often it is transitory, and ironically notes the contrast between the "fickleness" of *eros* and "his protestations of permanency." A lover's *eros* always is thought by him to be eternal. (See *ibid.,* pp. 158–159.)
[109] See *ibid.,* Ch. IV, p. 126.
[110] *Ibid.,* Ch. V, pp. 153–154.
[111] See *ibid.,* p. 132.
[112] *Ibid.,* p. 145. See also p. 144.
[113] *Ibid.,* p. 150.

because such lovers prefer being together as better than separation, they might be more miserable apart and, therefore, choose the union despite pain and obstacles. But even if that is assumed we still have no clue as to whether they make such a choice primarily for their own benefit or for the benefit of the other.

Friendship

Of the three basic notions in Lewis' analysis of love, appreciative love or esteem is most readily identifiable in his conception of friendship and is the most essential to it. If friendship "is not full of mutual admiration, of Appreciative love, it is not Friendship at all."[114] This admiration either causes or arises from the discovery of mutual interests, shared opinions, or common tastes. It is distinct from "Companionship," which can exist without this union, but companionship is the usual basis out of which friendship develops.

> Friendship arises out of mere Companionship when two or more of the companions discover that they have in common some insight or interest or even taste which the others do not share and which, till that moment, each believed to be his own unique treasure (or burden).

When two people "share their vision," friendship is born;[115] this union and the desire to strengthen it through the pursuit of common activities is the essence of friendship. Lewis sharply distinguishes this intimacy from that of *eros* in the following way: Lovers talk about each other and about their love with endless interest; friends discuss the interests that bind them together and seldom discuss each other or their friendship.[116]

Gift-love is part of friendship also. "A Friend will, to be sure," says Lewis, "prove himself to be also an ally when alliance becomes necessary; will lend or give when we are in need, nurse us in sickness, stand up for us among our enemies, do what he can for our widows and orphans." But Lewis also adds that "such good offices are not the stuff of Friendship."[117] Benevolence, though important, is not the most important part of friendship.

[114] *Ibid.*, Ch. IV, p. 124. See also p. 104. Lewis is not implying here that only virtuous men can be friends. In fact, he explicitly denies this. (See *ibid.*, p. 115.) What he is emphasizing is that friends must admire something in each other, whether that quality be good or bad.

[115] See *ibid.*, pp. 96–97. See also p. 91.

[116] See *ibid.*, pp. 91, 102.

[117] *Ibid.*, pp. 101–102. Lewis is quite clear on this point. He says that "the role of benefactor always remains accidental, even a little alien, to that of Friend." (*Ibid.*, p. 102.)

Lewis says that the "very condition of having Friends is that we should want something else besides Friends." Those who simply want friends can never make any; they must want something else out of which friendship develops.[118] He also says that friendship "has no survival value." But he adds that "it is one of those things which give value to survival."[119] Whether or not one can want friendship even in some partial way, Lewis seems to imply that it is possible to want something from a friend after friendship has developed. One way in which need-love may express itself in friendship is through the desire for the union of similarity. But here, as in the case of the desire for the union of complementarity in *eros*, Lewis does not specify whether the uniting impulse is acquisitive or benevolent.

Lewis sharply distinguishes in terms of volition the motivations of friendship from those of affection and *eros*. He refers to friendship as "the least *natural* of loves; the least instinctive, organic, biological, gregarious and necessary." Friendship is the only natural love among human beings that exists "in that luminous, tranquil, rational world of relationships freely chosen."[120]

Not only do the three elements of love relationships "mix and succeed one another,"[121] but the natural love relationships may also coexist. ". . . Affection, besides being a love itself, can enter into the other loves and colour them all through and become the very medium in which from day to day they operate."[122] Affection can, though it need not, coexist with both *eros* and friendship. *Eros* and friendship can similarly coexist, though their coexistence is not so frequent. *Eros* is a love relationship that can occur between members of the opposite sex as well as between members of the same sex. The former relationship Lewis regards as normal, the latter, abnormal. Friendship also can occur among members of the opposite sex and members of the same sex. Lewis regards the latter as the more typical, but he also says that friendship between a man and a woman occurs more

[118] *Ibid.*, p. 98.
[119] *Ibid.*, p. 103.
[120] *Ibid.*, pp. 88–89. See also pp. 125–126. Another distinction between friendship and the other two natural love relationships is made in terms of number. *Eros* can occur only between two persons. Affection can occur between one person and as many others with whom he is familiar. Friendship, however, is necessarily limited to a few. Lewis says that, although two friends will welcome a third, friendship "must exclude" others. (See *ibid.*, pp. 91–92, 97, 122.)
[121] *Ibid.*, p. 33.
[122] *Ibid.*, Ch. III, p. 57. Lewis adds that such loves would probably not wear very well without affection: "To make a friend is not the same as to become affectionate. But when your friend has become an old friend, all those things about him which had originally nothing to do with the friendship become familiar and dear with familiarity. As for erotic love, I can imagine nothing more disagreeable than to experience it for more than a very short time without this homespun clothing of affection." (*Ibid.*)

frequently in modern times than it did in the past. All three relationships, then, may coexist.[123] Yet they are distinct. Lewis emphatically denies, for example, that sexual desire (whether conscious or not), so essential to *eros*, is any part at all of the motivations of friendship.

José Ortega y Gasset

Though he concentrates on human love (especially on the love between a man and a woman), Ortega acknowledges that love itself is much vaster in scope. It has a cosmic as well as a psychological dimension.

> The ideology of recent times has lost cosmological inspiration and has become almost exclusively psychological. Refinements in the psychology of love, by multiplying subtle casuistry, have drawn away our attention from this cosmic dimension, which is elemental to love. We too are about to enter the psychological zone, although attacking what is most essential to it. We must not forget, however, that the multiform history of our loves, with all their complications and incidents, lives finally from that elemental, cosmic force, which our psyche—primitive or refined, simple or complex, from one century to another—merely administers and models in varied ways.[124]

Even within the range of human love he finds great variety. "The word 'love,'" says Ortega, "so simple and with so few letters, is used to label innumerable phenomena which differ so widely that it would be well to doubt if they have anything in common with each other. We speak of 'love for a woman'; but also of 'love of God,' 'love of country,' 'love of art,' 'maternal love,' 'filial love,' etc. One and the same word embraces and names the most varied fauna of emotions." He also says that, in order to "avoid uttering the usual nonsense on the subject of love," it is necessary, first of all, to find out whether certain of its usages are equivocal.

> Is there some important similarity which exists between "love for a woman" and "love of science"? When we examine both states of mind we find that almost every element in them differs. There is, however, one identical ingredient, which a careful analysis would enable us to isolate in both phenomena. If we saw it freed and isolated from the remaining factors which make up both states of mind, we would understand that, strictly speaking, it alone deserves the name of "love."[125]

---

123 "This blending and overlapping of the loves is well kept before us by the fact that at most times and places all three of them had in common, as their expression, the kiss." (*Ibid.*, p. 58.)

124 *On Love*, "Love in Stendhal," p. 41. See also *ibid.*, "Features of Love," p. 12.

125 *Ibid.*, "Love in Stendhal," pp. 44–45, *passim*.

That critical ingredient is a tendency, an inclination, a "going forth toward" an object or a person. He calls it a "psychic" flow, a "centrifugal" movement, a "sentimental" activity.[126] This inclination or tendency must have a definite aim in order to be love. Love must be "a cordial, affirmative interest in another person for himself."[127] It is by its nature "a transitive act in which we exert ourselves on behalf of what we love."[128] "In hate . . . one goes toward the object but against it. In love, one also goes toward the object but on its behalf."[129] For Ortega, benevolence is of the essence of love.

Emphatic as Ortega is about what love is, he is more emphatic about what love is not. He stresses repeatedly that the activity of love must not be confused with any inclinations to get something for oneself. For him, "desire," the inclination to get, and love, the inclination to give, are in separate domains.[130]

> Desire enjoys that which is desired, derives satisfaction from it, but it offers nothing, it gives nothing, it has nothing to contribute.[131]

Or, as he says elsewhere:

> A glass of water is desired, but is not loved, when one is thirsty. Undoubtedly, desires are born of love; but love itself is not desire.[132]

Though Ortega excludes any form of acquisitive desire from the essence of love, he does not exclude certain acquisitive desires from relationships in

---

[126] *Ibid.*, "Features of Love," pp. 16–17, *passim*. See also *ibid.*, "Love in Stendhal," p. 46. Loving "something is not simply 'being,' but acting toward that which is loved." (*Ibid.*)

[127] *Ibid.*, p. 47. He adds that such an interest "can equally be directed toward a woman, a piece of land (one's country), a branch of human activity such as sports, science, etc." (*Ibid.*)

[128] *Ibid.*

[129] *Ibid.*, "Features of Love," p. 16. "This characteristic of finding oneself psychically in motion, en route *toward* an object and continually on the march from our inner being toward another is essential to love and hate." (*Ibid.*, p. 15.)

[130] What Ortega means by "desire" is what we mean by "acquisitive desire." "Desiring something is, without doubt, a move toward possession of that something ('possession' meaning that in some way or other the object should enter our orbit and become part of us)." (*Ibid.*, p. 12.) We have taken the word "desire" as merely a synonym for "tendency." In our usage, it is, therefore, applicable to both the inclination to give as well as the inclination to get. We have distinguished these tendencies by the adjectives "acquisitive" and "benevolent."

[131] *Ibid.*, p. 18.

[132] *Ibid.*, "Love in Stendhal," p. 46. "Of course, in some manner or form we also want what we love; but, on the other hand, we obviously want many things that we do not love, things which leave us indifferent on a sentimental plane. Desiring a good wine is not loving it, and the drug addict desires drugs at the same time that he hates them for their harmful effect." (*Ibid.*, "Features of Love," p. 11.)

which love is present. Thus, while sexual desire cannot be benevolent and therefore is not of the essence of love, it exists in the relationship called romantic love. "There is no [romantic] love, for example, without sexual instinct."[133]

In addition to benevolence and sexual desire, a certain mental paralysis is characteristic of romantic love.

> Romantic poses aside, let us recognize that "falling in love"—I repeat that I am not talking about love *sensu stricto*—is an inferior state of mind, a form of transitory imbecility. Without a paralysis of consciousness and a reduction of our habitual world, we could never fall in love.[134]

While maintaining that the essence of love is always an outgoing activity of concern for another *for his own sake*, Ortega is able to distinguish types of love by adding other factors to the basic love inclination. Between man and woman, sexual desire, though no part of love, is compatible with it and gives this type of love a distinguishing characteristic. In this way, Ortega is able to distinguish between the "sexual instinct" and "sexual love."[135]

Ortega also frequently associates the desire for union with certain love relationships.

> What does this union mean? It is not merely physical union, or even closeness. Perhaps our friend (friendship must not be forgotten when love is generically considered) lives far away and we do not hear from him. Nevertheless, we are with him in a symbolic union—our soul seems to expand miraculously, to clear the distance, and no matter where he is, we feel that we are in essential communion with him.[136]

He also claims that the desire for union is present in mature love between man and woman. Scarcely does genuine love begin when

> the lover experiences a strange urgency to dissolve his own individuality in that of the other and, vice versa, to absorb the individuality of his beloved into his own. A mysterious longing! Whereas in every other situation in life

---

[133] *Ibid.*, "Love in Stendhal," p. 55.

[134] *Ibid.* In some sense, this might be said to be Ortega's principal concern in writing of love. He has a great interest in the psychological conditions and judgments that precede and accompany love. (See Ch. 9, *infra*.)

[135] See *ibid.*, p. 39. "If it is an absurdity to say that a man's or woman's true love for one another has nothing sexual about it, it is another absurdity to believe that love can be equated with sexuality." (*Ibid.*, "The Role of Choice in Love," p. 95.) "All one has to do is observe the inalterable fact that a man, with varying degrees of intensity, feels sexual desire for innumerable women, whereas his love, no matter how excessive and prolific it may be, is only focused upon a few. It becomes impossible, therefore, to equate the two impulses." (*Ibid.*, p. 107.)

[136] *Ibid.*, "Features of Love," p. 18.

nothing upsets us so much as to see the frontiers of our individual existence trespassed upon by another person, the rapture of love consists in feeling ourselves so metaphysically porous to another person that only in the fusion of both, only in an "individuality of two," can it find fulfillment.[137]

Ortega suggests that, in the love between man and woman, this desire is the desire for the union of complementarity:

> The over-rational in a woman smacks of masculinity and, rather than love, he feels friendship and admiration for her.[138]

He writes that both a man and a woman in love are alike in that they love *only* each other. Yet, in the course of a lifetime, man and woman differ in the number of times they love. A man, unlike a woman, "is almost always pluralistic in love." But he adds that, since he is discussing "the pure forms of this sentiment, the simultaneous existence of several love affairs is excluded and we are left with those which occur successively."[139]

At one point, Ortega takes up the question of the degree to which love is voluntary. Two extremes are mother love, which he says flows from "a deep-rooted instinct," and friendship, which he says involves "a clear decision" of will.[140] The love between man and woman lies between these two extremes.

But, for Ortega, volition can never be an originating power. The role of the will "is not creative, but merely corrective."[141] "We all realize," he says, "to some extent that the kind of life to which we are committed is already determined in areas deeper than those in which our will is active."[142] Specifying the function of the will, he affirms:

> The fact is that, except for the superficial intervention of our will, we live an irrational life, which empties into our consciousness and which originates from our hidden source, the invisible depths which really define us.[143]

Therefore, the impulse of love "which springs from the most profound depths of our beings," is not originated by the will. The will can consent to or resist an impulse that came into being prior to its action and it can also,

[137] *Ibid.*, "Love in Stendhal," p. 40. See also pp. 35, 38; and "The Role of Choice in Love," p. 120.

[138] *Ibid.*, "Landscape with a Deer in the Background," p. 166.

[139] *Ibid.*, "The Role of Choice in Love," p. 100. Cf. "Love in Stendhal," p. 35.

[140] *Ibid.*, "Toward a Psychology of the Interesting Man," p. 190.

[141] *Ibid.*, "The Role of Choice in Love," p. 90.

[142] *Ibid.*, p. 93.

[143] *Ibid.*, p. 91. "To say that man is rational and free is, I think, a statement very close to being false. We actually do possess reason and freedom; but both powers form only a tenuous film which envelops our being, the interior of which is neither rational nor free." (*Ibid.*)

to some extent, control its direction and intensity, but no one can love by deciding to.[144]

Theodor Reik

Though all authors who analyze love discuss it as an interpersonal phenomenon, Theodor Reik is the one author who explicitly states that the use of the term in any other context is inappropriate.[145] His theory of love lies within our delimitation of the subject: natural love among human beings; since love can only have real meaning in a relationship among persons, "love of mankind" and "love of country" are figurative phrases only—metaphorical misapplications of the term.[146] Tendencies toward things, which are often called love in ordinary usage, also are differentiated sharply by Reik from the desires among human beings which are properly called love:[147]

> I presuppose love to be possible only as an emotion of one person for another person. I do not mean the same thing when I say, "I love pork chops," as when I say, "I love Jane." . . . If I say, "I love ice cream," I extend the significance of the word unjustifiably.[148]

Reik, of course, is writing within the context of modern psychological analysis, and frequently acknowledges the influence of his teacher and contemporary, Freud. Yet, at the very outset of his principal work on love (*A Psychologist Looks at Love*), he departs from the Freudian view on a point he regards as absolutely pivotal: the relationship between love and sex.

Pointing out that Freud's view changed during the course of his life, Reik says that the younger Freud took sex in the narrow sense of the craving for genital pleasure, identifying it with love. The search for a love partner was understood as nothing but the direct or indirect search for a sexual partner. Later, however, Freud broadened his concept of sexuality, which then became the basis for the Freudian hypothesis of *eros*, "the great power that creates life, keeps united that which is separated and secures its renewal against the powers of destruction." Reik understands the Freudian conception of *eros* as "a mixture of the biological sexual need, of certain ego-

---

[144] See *ibid.*, pp. 88–90.

[145] See *A Psychologist Looks at Love*, Ch. I, Sect. 2, p. 7.

[146] See *ibid.*, Ch. III, Sect. 13, pp. 182, 187.

[147] Reik does distinguish varieties or types of love among human beings, but most of his analysis is devoted to the understanding of the love relationship between a man and a woman, which he calls romance or romantic love. (See *ibid.*, Sect. 14, p. 189.)

[148] *Ibid.*, Ch. I, Sect. 2, p. 7. See also Sect. 3, pp. 9–10; and Ch. III, Sect. 13, p. 182.

drives and of the yet unknown substance, love." He breaks away from both
the earlier and later Freudian conceptions of love in stating categorically
that sex and love are not only distinct but also have nothing to do with
each other. Though Reik admits "that sex and love are frequently united
and directed to the same object," he nevertheless emphatically affirms that
they are "different in origin and nature . . . [and are in] two separate
domains, which must be distinguished."[149]

Reik contrasts sexual desire and love in numerous ways. Sex is a biological need and instinct, one of the great drives, like hunger and thirst. Its
chief aim is release from a physical tension. Love is not a biological need,
for it is not found in all men or all societies. The sexual object must have
certain physical qualities that excite or arouse. The object of love must
have certain highly valued psychical qualities not demanded of a sexual
object. Sex is a passionate interest in another body. Love is a passionate
interest in another personality and in his whole life. There are many
possible sex objects at any time and one can easily be replaced by another.
At any time, there is only one person who is loved and that person is not
easily replaced. Sex originally is objectless; it acquires objects for its drives
to ease the tension of the sexual urge. Love always has a specific object; it is
an emotional relationship between a "Me" and a "You." Sex is undiscriminating; it wants "a woman." Love is highly discriminating; it insists on "this
woman." Sex does not always involve a personal relationship. There is no
such thing as an impersonal love. Sex can be casual about its object. Love
cannot be casual at all about its object. The sex urge is subject to fluctua-
tions. Love is far less subject to fluctuation. There is need for variety in sex.
There is need for constancy in love. Except when the individual is sexually
aroused, the sex object is not desired and its absence is not regretted; on the
contrary, its absence is often desired. Love regrets the absence of the other
and feels lonely and deprived without the other. The object of sex may
become of no account, boring, or even hateful immediately after sexual
tension has been reduced. The object of love does not undergo a similar
transformation. Sex seeks momentary physical pleasures. Love seeks enduring happiness in the form of contentment with life itself. The peak of sex
gratification is ecstasy. The peak of love is beatitude. In sex, it is possible
to possess another person unilaterally; the other person, so possessed, is an
object used. In love, you cannot thus possess another person. Instead you belong to another person as the other person in turn belongs to you. Use is excluded. Sex is utterly selfish, using the other person only in order to get
pleasure. Love is not without some self-interest, but such an interest is

[149] *Ibid.*, Ch. I, Sect. 4, pp. 12–18, *passim.* "Whiskey," says Reik, "is usually taken
with soda, but the mixture of the two does not change whiskey into soda nor soda
into whiskey." (*Ibid.*, p. 17.)

sought in being happy in the happiness of another. Love can never be completely self-seeking; it always involves a concern with the welfare of another. You can force another person to sexual activity. You cannot force another person to love.[150]

In making all these contrasts, Reik, of course, uses the notion of sexual desire in the narrow sense—the desire for genital pleasure. Though love and sexual desire are not mutually exclusive existentially (a person who is loved may *also* be sexually desired), Reik insists that the question of what love is, is logically distinct from the question of what sexual desire is. This distinction is one of the cardinal points on which his whole analysis of love rests. The critical notion, sexual desire, is illuminating only in its negative application to Reik's theory.

Reik departs most obviously from Freud in his emphasis on ego-drives rather than sexual drives in his analysis of the psychogenesis of love. According to Reik, each human being, in the course of his development, builds up an "ego-ideal," or image of himself as he would like to be. Most human beings fall short of this ideal because of the frustrations, compromises, disappointments, and failures forced on them by reality. The result is not an alteration of the ego-ideal but an awareness of the gap existing between the ego-ideal and one's own accomplishments. Feelings of dissatisfaction with the self, *i.e.*, awareness of this gap, are an absolute prerequisite for the emergence of love; no one who is completely satisfied with himself can love.[151]

Since love presupposes a feeling of inadequacy, it is an emotion that definitely springs from need *at its beginning*.[152] Reik lays great stress on the acquisitive aspect of love, the effort to fulfill or perfect the self. In terms of one of the basic polarities that recurs throughout the literature on love, the opposition between love as therapy and love as disease, Reik

---

[150] See *ibid.*, pp. 17–24. See also *Psychology of Sex Relations*, Part III, pp. 192–193; and Part II, pp. 100–102. Elsewhere, he says: "Duty contradicts the spontaneity which is a necessary condition of love." (*A Psychologist Looks at Love,* Ch. III, Sect. 9, p. 156.)

[151] See *A Psychologist Looks at Love,* Ch. II, Sect. 3, pp. 43–44. See also Ch. III, Sect. 4, pp. 121–122, 124–125. Such a gap does not necessarily lead to love; if the gap between a person and his ego-ideal is large enough, it precludes love. "No one can say 'I love you' who feels as a nobody." (*Ibid.,* Ch. II, Sect. 7, p. 71. See also Ch. III, Sect. 4, pp. 121–122.) Love is an achievement requiring an effort of will and some self-confidence, courage, and self-respect. (See *ibid.,* pp. 126–127. See also Sect. 8, pp. 147–149.)

[152] See *ibid.*, Ch. II, Sect. 1, p. 32; Sect. 2, p. 40; and Sect. 5, pp. 55–57. This is why Reik says "that love is only possible when you attribute a higher value to another person than to yourself, when you see her or him as a personality who is, in certain directions at least, superior to you." (*Psychology of Sex Relations,* Part II, p. 86.)

places himself with those who claim that love is (or can be) beneficial to the lover:[153]

> All love is founded on a dissatisfaction with oneself. It is an attempt to escape from oneself in search of a better, an ideal self.[154]

Reik understands love, especially romantic love, as an "attempt to fulfill the demands of our ideal ego," as a drive that takes "the place of the original striving for self-perfection."[155]

In view of this, a potential lover must sense himself as lacking certain definite traits which he admires and would like to have as his own. He encounters someone (in the case of romantic love, someone of the opposite sex) who apparently personifies the very characteristics he so admires.[156] The other person represents his ego-ideal and is, accordingly, admired. But, because he feels inferior to her, the admiration extended contains an element that is "dissenting, recalcitrant, even begrudging." Such admiration is an essential step in the development of love.

> In order to love someone we have to admire him or her. We need not always know what we admire in the object; we need not even know that we do admire, but only that we feel attracted or fascinated. It seems, however, that admiration is a necessary feeling of incipient love. I do not assert, of course, that admiration must lead to love, but only that it is a preliminary condition which is absolutely essential.[157]

[153] See *A Psychologist Looks at Love*, Ch. II, Sect. 5, pp. 58 ff.

[154] *Ibid.*, Ch. III, Sect. 14, p. 190. "Love is, I think, the most successful attempt to escape our loneliness and isolation. It is an illusion like every search for human perfection, but it is a necessary illusion. It comes nearest to the ego-gratification we all need in pushing the ego aside. To connect one's life in thoughts and deeds with others is the only way to make it worth living." (*Ibid.*, p. 194.) "Love is an escape from oneself, an antidote for the self-dislike and sometimes even for the self-hate which a person feels." (*Psychology of Sex Relations*, Part II, p. 89.)

[155] *A Psychologist Looks at Love*, Ch. II, Sect. 8, p. 86.

[156] See *ibid.*, Sect. 3, p. 50.

[157] *Ibid.*, pp. 44–45, *passim*. Reik goes on to describe the character of this judgment: "What kind of admiration is this, anyhow? Certainly not a cool, dispassionate, impersonal kind of appreciation. It is of a decidedly different character; much nearer the core of one's own personality. It strikes a chord in one, stirs something, makes one restless or desirous. It arouses certain dark wishes, makes mysterious claims. There is something in it of the nature of a challenge. It is the kind of admiration that makes one feel small, inferior, unworthy by comparison with the object. At the same time it stimulates wishes to be like the object or to take possession of her; either to be endowed with similar qualities or to own such a personality. It is not a high respect or regard or like other kinds of appreciation. It has a provoking, even an alarming nature. It is not only exciting but also inspiring; not only inspiring but also irritating." Reik here seems to be describing what we have set forth as two judgments: admiration and valuation. Admiration we have called the judgment that someone is good in himself and valuation the judgment that he is good for me. Both are present in what Reik calls admiration. (See *ibid.*, See also pp. 50–51.)

The next step in the process follows from the kind of admiration present. Reik points out that the admiration that inclines us to "feel inferior" to someone inevitably has "a covetous characteristic in it somewhere." He adds:

> When you follow this thread to the realms of the unconscious processes you will find there a feeling which is otherwise termed envy or jealousy. *In other words, the reverse or wrong side of this admiration for the love-object is envy.*[158]

Reik adds to the prerequisites for love when he says that "he who cannot be envious is unable to love."[159] At another point, he explains why this is so:

> Of course love need not develop from envy and hostility. There are other fields of action for these repressed emotions, but they are the unconscious perquisites for deep affection. In other words, if you cannot hate you cannot love. If you cannot bite you cannot kiss. If you cannot curse you cannot bless. Who cannot be a good hater will be a poor lover.[160]

Reik believes that at the point of envying, it is an open question whether a person will love or hate.[161] If the emotion of love is aroused, the beloved is taken as a substitute for one's own ego-ideal. Instead of envying, the lover tries to make the other person part of himself through union. There is no doubt that, for Reik, the initial impulse of love is acquisitive.

> The transfer of the ego-ideal to a person is the most characteristic trait of love. The development thus starts as a striving after self-perfection, which is frustrated. It ends in finding the perfection which we could not reach within ourselves in this second self.[162]

The end is union and the path of love is the ever growing desire for that union.

> In this wish to change one's personality into the other's there appears, although in a dim light and scarcely recognizable, an essential feature that

158 *Ibid.*, p. 45, *passim*. See also p. 47, and Sect. 5, p. 57. A little later on, Reik notes: "But why choose the word envy at all, rather than the word emulation? If it were only a choice of words I would not object to the expression emulation instead of envy. But it is more than that. The connotation of emulation is different from envy. It does not signify the awareness of one's own inferiority to the other person, nor does it imply that the other possesses something which one misses and covets." (*Ibid.*, Sect. 3, p. 48.)

159 *Ibid.*, Ch. III, Sect. 4, p. 122.

160 *Ibid.*, Ch. II, Sect. 5, p. 60.

161 See *ibid.*, Sect. 3, p. 49. Admiration and envy, strictly speaking, precede and are not part of love. These are stages in what Reik refers to as the incubation period. (See *ibid.*, Sect. 5, p. 58.)

162 *Ibid.*, Sect. 2, p. 43.

will be felt as fulfilled later on, when love has taken the place of envy: the wish to be one with the beloved person, to be united with her, to melt and merge into one being.[163]

This desire for union presupposes an existing difference between lover and beloved.[164] "As long as one person meets another and does not see him as a different individual with a different make-up, love is psychologically not possible."[165] The tendency toward union, however, seems to be twofold. The difference between lover and beloved corresponds to the gap between the lover and his ego-ideal, once the lover has transferred his ego-ideal to the beloved and taken her as a substitute for it.[166] And because he strives to become like his ego-ideal, he strives to become like his beloved in the ways in which he admires her. In this respect, then, his desire for union is a desire for the union of similarity.[167] On the other hand, Reik insists that what is unique about love is the vicarious achievement of one's ego-ideal through a complementary union with one who has been taken as a substitute for it. The beloved is somehow added, through union, to the lover's personality. "The object does not become identified with the ideal better self, but it so complements the ego that the drive for self-perfection becomes superfluous."[168] Or as Reik also says:

> We do not forget that this merging is the most tender form of taking possession of the other person, even though it accompanies the surrender of oneself. In this roundabout way the individual has fulfilled his original desire to own the other person or to be the other person.[169]

The first desire is to become like the beloved, who represents the lover's ego-ideal.[170] This desire is satisfied indirectly through complementary union in the consummation of love.

Though Reik excludes the notion of sexual desire from his conception of love, he obviously conceives another form of acquisitive desire as an important part of it. Yet, he denies that the combination of desires he calls love are *all* acquisitive ones. Indeed, *unless some of these acquisitive desires are overcome and replaced by benevolent ones love does not exist at all.*

[163] *Ibid.*, Sect. 3, p. 50.
[164] "Love cannot start from the feeling of oneness. It only arrives there." (*Ibid.*, Ch. III, Sect. 10, p. 159.)
[165] *Ibid.*, Ch. I, Sect. 2, p. 8.
[166] See *Psychology of Sex Relations*, Part III, pp. 117 ff, for a discussion of the ways in which a man wants to be like a woman and a woman like a man.
[167] See *A Psychologist Looks at Love*, Ch. II, Sect. 2, p. 42. "Two people who love each other are inter-changing their ego-ideals. That they love each other means they love the ideal of themselves in the other one." (*Ibid.*)
[168] *Psychology of Sex Relations*, Part II, p. 115.
[169] *A Psychologist Looks at Love*, Ch. II, Sect. 7, p. 73.
[170] See *Psychology of Sex Relations*, Part II, p. 108.

What happens to envy and jealousy? When the emotional reaction-movement reached flood tide it swept those impulses away in a mounting, encircling wave of tenderness. They are as conspicuous by their absence as the contrary tendencies by their presence and prominence. The last remnant of the sense of property expresses itself sometimes in an unwillingness to share the company of the object with others.[171]

Or, as he says elsewhere:

Who loves wants to give, and his appetite in giving seems never to be appeased. Hostility has given place to tenderness; envy, to kindness.[172]

Far from denying the original acquisitive character of the benevolent desires in love, Reik states:

Love which does not tire in giving was once, in its hidden origin, an urge to take away, to take possession of and to own for oneself the physical and the psychical excellencies of the object. Love is thus the overcoming of these unconscious tendencies of envy, jealousy, and greed.[173]

Contrasting the benevolence of love with what he considers the most obvious acquisitive desire, sexual desire, Reik says that

sex is utterly selfish, using the object only in order to get satisfaction. Love is not unselfish, but it is very difficult to name its selfish aims, other than that of being happy in the happiness of the beloved person. In no case can love be only selfish, or as selfish as sex. Then it would not be love. It is always concerned with the welfare or happiness of the other person, regrets the other's absence, wants to be together with the object, feels lonely without it, fears calamity or danger for it.[174]

Reik means two things when he says that love is not unselfish. The first is that love consists of two kinds of desires taken together, the desire to give *and* the desire to get. "Love itself is a blend of tenderness and domination, of surrender to and taking possession of the object." The second is that the very benevolence, which is so essential to love, is not disinterested. Because

[171] *A Psychologist Looks at Love*, Ch. II, Sect. 7, p. 76. He adds: "The deep and hard compulsion of envy gave way to the desire to give and to enjoy the gifts and achievements of the mate, the second and better self. You cannot be envious of yourself." (*Ibid.*)

[172] *Psychology of Sex Relations*, Part II, p. 98. See also pp. 107–109; and Part III, p. 152.

[173] *Ibid.*, Part II, p. 94. "*Love is in its essential nature an emotional reaction formation to envy, possessiveness and hostility.*" Reik adds: "It rejoices in the happiness, achievements and fine qualities of the object. Love is not hostile but the supreme expression of tenderness." (*A Psychologist Looks at Love*, Ch. II, Sect. 6, p. 66.)

[174] *Ibid.*, Ch. I, Sect. 5, p. 20.

love is a desire for union the interest of the beloved and that of the lover are related. Though in the giving that characterizes love the good of the other is primary, the lover is not unaware that his own good is involved.[175]

Reik emphasizes benevolence, but not to the exclusion of the self-interested aspect of love. He says, for example, that love "is as selfish as breathing," but adds that "this self has changed; it has incorporated another being." He makes it clear that the delight one takes in giving to a beloved is a personal delight, since the other has become fused with the self. He rejects the idea of personal deprivation, of self-sacrifice as integral to love; the lover need not and should not hurt himself in giving.[176] Reik makes this point particularly emphatic when he discusses altruism in sex: "He who is altruistic in sex, who always consciously renounces his own enjoyment and considers only how to give pleasure to the partner, will give satisfaction neither to the partner nor to himself."[177] On the other hand, he deplores sheer sexuality. His point (and he considers it a very important one) is that, as in other desires of a love relationship, the lover must be concerned both with the good of the beloved and his own good. If he is concerned only with the good of the beloved, he will fail to enhance it in the long run. Though he may consider his own good secondary to that of the beloved, he must not ignore it (or, under normal circumstances, sacrifice it). His benevolence should be self-interested; it should involve a concomitant desire to share the good that he bestows on his beloved. As Reik puts it: "Whether or not sex relations are selfish or altruistic depends entirely on whether the sex act is accompanied by love. If sex and love relations coexist, the problem is nonexistent, for the enjoyment of one partner is at the same time the pleasure of the other."[178]

Reik points out the self-interested aspect of love in still another way. The lover, in giving, seeks to have his love returned. "In showing tenderness and affection, we indicate what the other person should give to us."[179] He claims that the lover's motive, whether he is aware of it or not, in caring about another and in treating that person with tenderness and kindness is, in part, his desire to be treated in the same way.[180] However, he does not maintain that love need be mutual in order to last.

Reik understands romantic love as one high point in a process of

[175] See *ibid.*, Ch. II, Sect. 7, pp. 76–77. "The old desire for self-improvement, for a better, nobler self, has disappeared or rather is realized in the beloved person." (*Psychology of Sex Relations*, Part II, p. 98. See also Part III, pp. 152 ff.)
[176] *A Psychologist Looks at Love*, Ch. II, Sect. 7, p. 79. See also pp. 77–78.
[177] *Psychology of Sex Relations*, Part III, p. 200. See also pp. 201–204.
[178] *Ibid.*, p. 199.
[179] *Ibid.*, Part II, p. 85. See also Part III, p. 223.
[180] See *A Psychologist Looks at Love*, Ch. III, Sect. 2, p. 114. See also p. 103.

continuing development.[181] He goes as far as to say that it "can be evaluated as a kind of preparation for true love, as child-talk is for the speaking of adults." True love or mature love, however, is not discussed at any length. Reik does contrast the "frenzy," "intensity," and "emotional extravagance" of romance with the calmness of mature love. He also notes that the mature lover has a less idealized view of his beloved. And he says that, for the most part, romance is characteristic of youth, while true love comes with age.[182] With maturity comes a deepening care and a moderation of the acquisitive impulses that are a strong part of romance.

> Perhaps love is as a Frenchman said, *"l'ombre d'une ombre,"* the shadow of a shadow. But this shadow which our ego-phantom casts gains substance and reality in time. Romance appears sometimes as a kind of rehearsal. The real performance comes much later. Age knows love without too much possessiveness, with more care for the real welfare of the beloved.[183]

Reik notes the tendency in romantic literature to make love, sympathy, and compassion "flow into each other." He says:

> Like everyone else I have seen instances in which pity for the object seemed coupled with admiration, yes, even with a certain envy of the sufferer because of his superior courage, patience or dignity. But every penetrating psychological analysis proves that such coexistence of pity and love only marks a transition phase and leads to an unconscious conflict in which one emotion eventually conquers the other.[184]

Therefore, "pity and love are incompatible . . . they cannot coexist." Given the premise that any lover seeks his ego-ideal and transfers this image to the loved object, he cannot pity that same object, because he regards it as superior. "Unconsciously we feel privileged when comparing our own circumstances or happier lot with the situation of the afflicted person."[185] Pity is looking down. If love and pity occasionally can be seen

---

[181] See *ibid.*, Sect. 14, pp. 190–191. Reik says that his approach is a genetic or biological one: "I would like to present my concept in the form of a clinical description, in the cool and dispassionate spirit of psychological research. In studying this passion, passion is out of place. I should like to set forth the premises, the genesis and development of love as a botanist describes the soil on which a plant grows, the way it puts forth buds, and blossoms, and fades. I know, of course, that such a treatment will not always be possible, but it is the aim toward which I strive." (*Ibid.*, Ch. I, Sect. 2, p. 9.)

[182] See *ibid.*, Ch. III, Sect. 14, pp. 191–192, *passim*. Though time is an important factor for mature love, Reik does not think that it is essential in distinguishing infatuation, which he does not regard as a love, from romance. (See *ibid.*, Ch. II, Sect. 8, pp. 80 ff.)

[183] *Ibid.*, Ch. III, Sect. 14, pp. 192–193.

[184] *Ibid.*, Sect. 9, pp. 151, 153.

[185] *Ibid.*, pp. 151–152, *passim*.

in the same person, *directed to* the same object, one will have to predominate soon; one cannot look down and up at the same time.

Both romantic and mature love, in Reik's view, share the basic character of all love. In distinguishing them, he points out that the "distinctions are not differences in the essential character of love but in the proportions of the underlying emotions."[186] The importance of these differences, however, are very great.

> Romance is not identical with love. Affection and tenderness can exist and work outside romance. Love can outlast passion. It need not die. It can survive, but only if it changes its character or, rather, if it gains its real character.[187]

When Reik says that "Romance is not identical with love," he has in mind not only mature love but also at least two other types. Although he denies that romantic love is the most important, he nevertheless concentrates his analysis on it because he regards it as love's most conspicuous expression; in it he can most easily identify the elements he thinks are common to all loves. " 'Romantic love' is not different in its origin from others but in its density and intensity."[188] Reik does not hesitate to apply the basic pattern he discovers in his analysis of romantic love to friendship and mother love. Since Reik categorically asserts that all "love is founded on a dissatisfaction with oneself,"[189] his task is to show how friendship and mother love proceed from that basis.

First, he points out some obvious differences between friendship and romance, the most obvious being the difference in intensity. "Could you speak of a 'passionate friendship'? It sounds a bit gaunt, exaggerated or ridiculous." Friendship, he concludes, is a much "cooler" affection than romance. Friendship, like mature love, does not idealize. "You appreciate the excellent qualities of your friend but you also know his shortcomings and faults."[190] Friendship can be extended to more than one person, unlike romantic love, though Reik claims it cannot be a "mass article."[191] Friendship rarely occurs between the sexes. Though friends may want to

---

[186] *Ibid.,* Ch. II, Sect. 10, p. 92.

[187] *Ibid.,* p. 93.

[188] *Ibid.,* Ch. III, Sect. 14, p. 190. The intensity of romantic love is accounted for by Reik partly in terms of its exclusivity. In such a love, a man and a woman focus all their loving powers on one person, often to the temporary exclusion of all other loves. (See *ibid.,* Sect. 11, pp. 171–172.)

[189] *Ibid.,* Sect. 14, p. 190.

[190] *Ibid.,* Sect. 11, pp. 168–169, *passim.* This is one of the characteristics that differentiates friendship from mature love. In many other respects, however, friendship and mature love are very similar.

[191] See *ibid.,* p. 171.

become like each other in certain respects, friendship does not feature a desire for union.

What, then, is the common ground between friendship and romance? Reik's answer is the parallel between the rivalry at the beginning of friendship and the envy at the beginning of romance. Although he claims that friendship can only flourish on a level of equality which precludes *marked* inferiority and superiority, he nevertheless stresses the differences between friends. In friendship, the other person is taken as a substitute for the ego-ideal. But, whereas in romantic love the substitution is complete, in friendship it is only partial. We originally admire only some traits of a potential friend. Hence, instead of the intense feeling of envy through which romance begins, the much milder feeling of rivalry is the origin of friendship.

> Love is a reaction-formation to envy, jealousy and greed. Friendship is a reaction to original feelings of rivalry and competition which were aroused by the unconscious acknowledgment of certain qualities of the object.[192]

The overcoming of the feelings of rivalry makes a friend a partial supplement to oneself. The complete "melting of two human beings . . . does not take place in friendship."[193]

Like romantic love, friendship involves benevolence.

> In fully developed friendship the results of the emotional reaction appear on the surface; kindness in the place of hostility, the tendency to spare the friend, to support him instead of the impulse to harm him, a successful effort to help him reach his aims instead of a desire to frustrate him.[194]

Also like romantic love, it involves acquisitive desires. These range from the simple conscious desire for help to the occasional desire to emulate, which Reik says is the conscious form of the suppressed rivalry.[195]

The touchstone between mother love and the other types of love is also a basic feeling of dissatisfaction. Before he presents his analysis, Reik claims that what is usually called mother love is a combination of two elements, only one of which is love. The original and enduring feeling between mother and child is an instinctive or biological one which should not be called love. Only later does a psychological and parallel relationship grow

[192] *Ibid.*, p. 171. After these first steps, the development of friendship is, in general, parallel to that of romantic love.
[193] *Ibid.*, p. 173.
[194] *Ibid.*
[195] See *ibid.*, Sect. 11, pp. 166–177.

up between mother and child which Reik is willing to call love.[196] Here again, particularly with the mother, the beginning of love is envy and jealousy.

> A mother is also unconsciously envious and jealous of her child, of its better opportunities, future chances in life and greater endowments. . . . This unconscious envy also leads to a kind of resentment or hostility which contrasts strongly with the deep affection for the child. The reaction sets in and the complete rejection of the negative tendencies results in an intensified tenderness as in other cases. But what may be called love in a mother's feelings is an addition to the one woven much earlier, the biological tie for which I have no name.[197]

As with the other loves, Reik stresses the importance of benevolent desires, pointing out again that these alternate with acquisitive ones. The mother does care for her baby for its own sake, but also wants her child to do well in life as a mark of her own success.[198]

In examining the various types of love analyzed by Reik, particularly romantic love, we find a completely tendential conception of love. However important admiration and valuation may be for the understanding of the emergence of love, Reik claims that these judgments are prior to and not part of love. In each type of love, both acquisitive and benevolent desire are present. Though neither one alone is called love, both together, when certain other conditions are fulfilled, are present in any love relationship. Benevolence, therefore, is an essential notion in Reik's generic conception of love.

One condition for the emergence of love is the psychological as well as the instinctive or biological ego-drives. In fact, it is by contrasting the sexual urge with the rather complicated psychological inclinations of love that Reik explains his hypothesis about the emergence of love in history.

Reik holds that sex and not love is coextensive with the existence of man. Sex can occur anywhere and has occurred everywhere throughout time. But Reik claims:

> You cannot call love an instinct like hunger or sex. It is the fruit of a late psychical development. Love is decidedly a product of culture.[199]

[196] See *ibid.*, Sect. 10, p. 162. The child's love for the mother develops much later than the mother's love for the child, since the child does not perceive the mother as a separate entity for some time and even for a longer time does not feel hostile toward her.

[197] *Ibid.*

[198] See *ibid.*, pp. 157–166. Of the father's love for the child Reik says: "One guesses that it must be, so to speak, a diluted or weaker solution of the same mixture without its biological factor." (*Ibid.*, p. 162.)

[199] *Ibid.*, Ch. I, Sect. 2, p. 8. "Love is justifiably considered as an upstart in the family of instincts, as an outsider and intruder. It is, as a matter of fact, a product of

Reik rests this claim on two premises. The first is his belief that primitive peoples are incapable of social consciousness, of singling out a person as more than a mere member of a group, and of placing great value on personal diversity. Since love depends both on an awareness of the difference between, as well as of the intrinsic superiority of, one person and another, love is not possible for those not profoundly aware of personal differences and their value.[200]

More elaborately discussed as a reason for the late emergence of love in history are the restraints placed upon the sexual impulse. Though Reik argues that such restraints make the emergence of love possible, he denies that love is a sublimation of sexual desires. Love between men existed long before love between the opposite sexes, since envy and hostility (the prerequisites of love) were possible between men before they were possible between man and woman. In most primitive societies the woman was too low to be admired or envied; she was simply used.

Love between man and woman began to emerge when women set up certain restraints against being used sexually. This development (taking place over a very long period of time) did not cause a sublimation of the sexual desires into love. Rather it made possible the turning of the masculine ego-drives onto the woman. Because she withheld herself sexually, she gradually assumed value as a possible substitute for a masculine ego-ideal. She became more valuable because she became, sexually, more difficult to obtain. She gradually acquired other values in masculine eyes, which clustered around and were reinforced by her sexual reluctance. Through this tactic, she gave birth to romance.

> Romance was originally introduced into the relationship between men and women, not as a result and consequence of sex, as psychoanalysts imagine, but in opposition to sex, as a hurdle which had to be taken before sexual gratification was granted.[201]

Reik further argues that, although women reaped great material and emotional rewards from this development, they did not reciprocate. They dreaded not being loved, but, because they did not love in return, the very love they cherished was difficult to sustain. Women "threw a weapon at men, and it turned into a boomerang which hit themselves."[202] Reik

---

civilization which worked as long as necessary in opposition against more primal instincts until it obtained a place among them." (*Psychology of Sex Relations*, Part II, p. 132.)

[200] See *A Psychologist Looks at Love*, Ch. I, Sect. 2, p. 8. See also *Psychology of Sex Relations*, Part II, p. 122.

[201] *Ibid.*, p. 131.

[202] *Ibid.*, p. 133.

points out that the emergence of romance (which he considers primarily a masculine affection) has sometimes, of late, been replaced by mature love. He says, in summary, that

> love was originally opposed to sex, that it emerged as a counterpower to it, and that their conflict resulted later in the glorious reconciliation and amalgamation of the two enemies.[203]

But his principal point about the history of love is that it began with the feminine rebellion against indifferent lust.

> Here is the seed of the passionate emotion we observe today, the germ of what we call romance. I want to point out—most politely, most politely— that love, whether it is evil or good, is an invention of the ladies, not of men.[204]

Erich Fromm

Fromm, like Reik, is an author who considers love beneficial or therapeutic. Though he does not think of love as a panacea for all human ills, he does view it as the only real solution for the most basic problem of human existence: personal isolation. "The deepest need of man . . . is the need to overcome his separateness, to leave the prison of his aloneness."[205] For Fromm, love, "the only sane and satisfactory" solution for this problem, is far less possible in contemporary society than ever before.[206]

The most important notion in Fromm's analysis of love is the desire for interpersonal union.[207]

> This desire for interpersonal fusion is the most powerful striving in man. It is the most fundamental passion, it is the force which keeps the human race together, the clan, the family, society. . . . Without love, humanity could not exist for a day. Yet, if we call the achievement of interpersonal union

[203] *Ibid.*, p. 136.

[204] *Ibid.*, p. 129. For a discussion of the whole theory, see pp. 120–136; and Part III, pp. 149–156.

[205] *The Art of Loving*, Ch. II, Sect. 1, p. 9.

[206] See *ibid.*, Ch. IV, p. 133. See also Ch. II, Sect. 2, p. 40. "No objective observer of our Western life can doubt that love—brotherly love, motherly love, and erotic love—is a relatively rare phenomenon, and that its place is taken by a number of forms of pseudo-love which are in reality so many forms of the disintegration of love." (*Ibid.*, Ch. III, p. 83.)

[207] The focus throughout *The Art of Loving* is on love between human beings. At one or two points, Fromm says that we see "love or rather, the equivalent of love, in animals." (*Ibid.*, Ch. II, Sect. 1, p. 7.) He also says, in the course of discussing the love between a man and a woman, that the masculine-feminine polarity exists in nature (both in animate and inanimate nature). (See *ibid.*, p. 34.) These remarks, however, are casual asides. There is nothing in Fromm's work that suggests a fully developed theory of love as a universal or cosmic principle.

"love," we find ourselves in a serious difficulty. Fusion can be achieved in different ways. . . . Should they all be called love? Or should we reserve the word "love" only for a specific kind of union . . . ?

. . . Do we refer to love as the mature answer to the problem of existence, or do we speak of these immature forms of love which may be called *symbiotic union?* . . . I shall call love only the former.[208]

He explains symbiotic union between human beings, using the pattern of the biological relationship between the pregnant mother and the fetus, a physical relationship of complete domination and dependence. Translated into the psychic level, Fromm sees this relationship as representative of two forms of symbiotic union, the active (or sadistic) and the passive (or masochistic).

The sadist seeks escape from personal isolation by making another totally dependent on him. But, he is as dependent on the other person as the other person is on him. "The difference is only that the sadistic person commands, exploits, hurts, humiliates, and that the masochistic person is commanded, exploited, hurt, humiliated." The masochistic person is submissive. He "escapes from the unbearable feeling of isolation and separateness by making himself part and parcel of another person who directs him, guides him, protects him."[209] He renounces his integrity and allows himself to be totally manipulated by another.

These two people, seeking union, have in common "fusion without integrity." They are involved in a symbiotic and not a real relationship. "In contrast to symbiotic union, mature *love* is *union under the condition of preserving one's integrity,* one's individuality." Love allows one to overcome his sense of isolation while allowing him a personality in his own right. "In love the paradox occurs that two beings become one and yet remain two."[210]

Fromm discusses other forms of symbiotic escape. He mentions the executive who tries to escape by burying himself in his work. He sees alcoholism, drug addiction, and sheer sexuality as kinds of "orgiastic fusion," which, because they are transitory solutions, only aggravate the problem. He also observes that social conformity is a way in which individuals choose to identify with others and thus mitigate the torture of isolation.[211] Of these forms of escape, Fromm says:

[208] *Ibid.,* p. 18. Actually, Fromm does call the impulses of immature or symbiotic union "love" throughout the book. The distinction between these impulses and mature or real love, however, is not merely verbal. Fromm dwells on substantive differences which preclude a decisive conceptual bond between the desire for symbiotic and real union. He includes only the latter in his theory of love.

[209] *Ibid.,* pp. 19–20, *passim.*

[210] *Ibid.,* pp. 20–21, *passim.*

[211] See *ibid.,* pp. 12–18.

The unity achieved in productive work is not interpersonal; the unity achieved in orgiastic fusion is transitory; the unity achieved by conformity is only pseudo-unity. Hence, they are only partial answers to the problem of existence. The full answer lies in the achievement of interpersonal union, of fusion with another person, in *love*.[212]

However important it is, the desire for union, in any form of real love, cannot be understood as benevolent.[213] The individual is seen as miserable, isolated with his innermost thoughts, feelings, hopes, fears, and ambitions. Love is, in part, the effort to free oneself from this isolation. To that extent, it involves acquisitive tendencies. But Fromm distinguishes the desire for the union of love and the desire for symbiotic union most frequently in terms of the difference between an acquisitive desire, which does not involve exploitation, and an acquisitive desire, which does. The acquisitive desires of real love never are realized intentionally at the expense of the beloved.

Fromm states repeatedly that there can be no real love in which benevolent desire does not predominate:

> In the most general way, the active character of love can be described by stating that love is primarily *giving*, not receiving.[214]

A woman who says she loves flowers and does not water them does not, in fact, love them. "*Love is the active concern for the life and the growth of that which we love.*"[215] Although the helpless person "loves" his master and the child its parents, it is only "in the love of those who do not serve a purpose, [that] love begins to unfold."[216]

Though the controlling aim of love is another's welfare, Fromm does not deny that the lover's good also is involved. Having asserted that the selfish person is unable to love, he asks: "Does not this prove that concern for others and concern for oneself are unavoidable alternatives? This would be so if selfishness and self-love were identical. But that assumption is the very fallacy which has led to so many mistaken conclusions concerning our problem."[217] He argues that

---

[212] *Ibid.*, p. 18.
[213] This is true whether the desire takes the form of wanting to be like someone else or the form of the desire for the union of complementarity.
[214] *Ibid.*, p. 22.
[215] *Ibid.*, p. 26.
[216] *Ibid.*, Sect. 3, p. 48. Fromm maintains "that the ability to love as an act of giving depends on the character development of the person. It presupposes the attainment of a predominantly productive orientation; in this orientation the person has overcome dependency, narcissistic omnipotence, the wish to exploit others, or to hoard, and has acquired faith in his own human powers, courage to rely on his powers in the attainment of his goals. To the degree that these qualities are lacking, he is afraid of giving himself—hence of loving." (*Ibid.*, Sect. 1, p. 26.)
[217] *Ibid.*, Sect. 3, p. 60.

the attitudes toward others and toward ourselves, far from being contradictory, are basically *conjunctive*. With regard to the problem under discussion this means: love of others and love of ourselves are not alternatives. On the contrary, an attitude of love toward themselves will be found in all those who are capable of loving others.[218]

Fromm means at least three things in saying that self-love and love for another are compatible. First, since all love implies union, whatever good one does for another is done also and indirectly for oneself.[219] The lover "in giving . . . cannot help bringing something to life in the other person, and this which is brought to life reflects back to him; in truly giving, he cannot help receiving that which is given back to him."[220] The giver consciously affects his own welfare by altering for the better the person with whom he has achieved "interpersonal fusion." Since the barriers of separateness have been broken down, what affects one affects the other.

Second, he means that true giving is always accompanied by an "exquisite joy." Though the lover "does not give in order to receive," he nevertheless derives a personal and unique satisfaction in helping another.[221]

> Giving is the highest expression of potency. In the very act of giving, I experience my strength, my wealth, my power. This experience of heightened vitality and potency fills me with joy. I experience myself as overflowing, spending, alive, hence as joyous. Giving is more joyous than receiving, not because it is a deprivation, but because in the act of giving lies the expression of my aliveness.[222]

Third, Fromm means that the lover seeks mutual love. Though he does not give only for the sake of this return, he, nevertheless, tries "to make the other person a giver also."[223]

That the self-interest involved in love cannot be a primary motive Fromm makes clear when he says:

> The *selfish* person is interested only in himself, wants everything for himself, feels no pleasure in giving, but only in taking. The world outside is looked at only from the standpoint of what he can get out of it; he lacks interest in the needs of others, and respect for their dignity and integrity.

---

[218] *Ibid.*, p. 59. "The love for my own self is inseparably connected with the love for any other being." (*Ibid.*)

[219] Fromm argues that those who sacrifice their own interest for others, who never want anything for themselves, who seem to be "disinterested" in their giving are really basically selfish. (See *ibid.*, pp. 60 ff.)

[220] *Ibid.*, Sect. 1, p. 25.

[221] *Ibid.*

[222] *Ibid.*, p. 23.

[223] *Ibid.*, p. 25.

He can see nothing but himself; he judges everyone and everything from its usefulness to him; he is basically unable to love.[224]

Fromm specifically discusses four types of interpersonal love: brotherly, erotic, motherly, and fatherly.[225] He says that there are, in addition to the desire for union and benevolence, four elements "common to all forms of love. These are *care, responsibility, respect,* and *knowledge.*"[226]

Care seems to be a particular kind of benevolence. Fromm says that this element is most evident in a mother's love for her child. It is a concern for the welfare of another but more particularly it is an active concern for the *growth and development* of that other.[227] Closely connected with care is responsibility. ("To be 'responsible' means to be able and ready to 're-spond.'") In the case of the mother and child, the mother is responsible because she makes the child's physical needs her own worry. In the love between adults, responsibility is taken for the psychic needs of the other person. "Respect means the concern that the other person should grow and unfold as he is." It implies not only the absence of exploitation but also that help is given to another so that he may develop *in his own ways.*[228]

Whatever Fromm means by knowledge, it is not simply a cognitive element, not merely an intellectual judgment or perception. "The only way of full knowledge lies in the *act* of love: this act transcends thought, it transcends words." This knowledge apparently is a kind of illumination achieved through union. "Love is active penetration of the other person, in which my desire to know is stilled by union. In the act of fusion I know you, I know myself, I know everybody—and I 'know' nothing."[229]

As three of the four elements in all loves are varieties of, or imply, benevolence, we may say that they serve to emphasize the importance of this critical notion for Fromm's conception of love. There is no doubt that he thinks there is no love without it.

"The most fundamental kind of love, which underlies all types of love, is *brotherly love.*"[230] Fromm speaks of it as a love among equals, *i.e.,* a love that can exist among men simply because of their common humanity. Because they all are human, they all are, from time to time, in need of help. But love of those who are in need of help is only the beginning of brotherly love. Its true expression is in the love for the stranger and even

224 *Ibid.,* Sect. 3, p. 60.
225 Fromm also mentions "self-love." In this connection he makes two points. The first is that without self-respect one cannot love another. The second is that caring for another does not preclude caring for oneself. (See *ibid.,* pp. 57–63.)
226 *Ibid.,* Sect. 1, p. 26.
227 See *ibid.,* pp. 26–27.
228 See *ibid.,* p. 28.
229 *Ibid.,* pp. 30–31. See also Ch. III, p. 103; and Ch. II, Sect. I, p. 32.
230 *Ibid.,* Sect. 3, p. 47.

for the enemy. It is not discriminating; the degree to which it does discriminate is the degree to which it is not love. "If a person loves only one other person and is indifferent to the rest of his fellow men, his love is not love but a symbiotic attachment, or an enlarged egotism."[231] Brotherly love is, by definition, a universal love.

In one sense, erotic love is and must be not a universal but an exclusive love, since it is the desire for the union of complementarity.[232] In another sense, Fromm insists that, if erotic love is not a universal love, if it is not based on brotherly love, it is not love at all:

> One can often find two people "in love" with each other who feel no love for anybody else. Their love is, in fact, an egotism *à deux;* they are two people who identify themselves with each other, and who solve the problem of separateness by enlarging the single individual into two. They have the experience of overcoming aloneness, yet, since they are separated from the rest of mankind, they remain separated from each other and alienated from themselves; their experience of union is an illusion.

He then adds:

> Erotic love is exclusive, but it loves in the other person all of mankind, all that is alive. It is exclusive only in the sense that I can fuse myself fully and intensely with one person only. Erotic love excludes the love for others only in the sense of erotic fusion, full commitment in all aspects of life—*but not in the sense of deep brotherly love.*[233]

Sexual desire is present in an erotic love relationship, but in and by itself is insufficient for real love. A purely sexual desire is a desire for symbiotic union. "Because sexual desire is in the minds of most people coupled with the idea of love, they are easily misled to conclude that they love each other when they want each other physically." But Fromm claims that if "the desire for physical union is not stimulated by love, if erotic love is not also brotherly love, it never leads to union in more than an orgiastic,

---

[231] *Ibid.,* p. 46. See also pp. 47–48. Fromm does not mean that brotherly love implies active concern for every living man. He speaks of this love rather as an attitude or orientation of character which disposes one to want to help all those with whom one comes into contact. (See *ibid.,* p. 46.)

[232] Fromm obviously connects the union of complementarity with erotic love. He notes at an early point that the "polarity of the sexes is disappearing, and with it erotic love, which is based on this polarity." (*Ibid.,* Sect. 1, p. 15.) He concedes that the masculine-feminine polarity is most obviously a biological one, but affirms that it is more than physical: "The polarity between the male and female principles exists also *within* each man and each woman. Just as physiologically man and woman each have hormones of the opposite sex, they are bisexual also in the psychological sense." (*Ibid.,* p. 33.)

[233] *Ibid.,* Sect. 3, p. 55. (Second italics added.) See also pp. 52–57.

transitory sense."[234] Sexual desire is a part of erotic love only when it "is blended with tenderness."[235]

The prime characteristic of mother love is that it is unconditional. The mother cares for and will protect her child, not primarily because the child is gifted, strong, beautiful but because the child is her own. She loves him without reservation despite his defects.[236]

The paradigm of mother love is love for the helpless. In contrast to brotherly and erotic love, the relationship between child and mother is one in which one person constantly needs help and the other constantly gives it. "It is for this altruistic, unselfish character that motherly love has been considered the highest kind of love, and the most sacred of all emotional bonds." Fromm adds that one must distinguish two phases of such love: the love for the helpless infant and the love for the growing child. The love for the helpless infant is by far the easier; almost all mothers experience it instinctively. They eagerly care for the infant "in spite of the fact that they do not 'get' anything in return from the child, except a smile or the expression of satisfaction in his face." But the mother is put to trial as the child begins to grow. For now her loving function is to help him grow and "eventually become a completely separate human being." The mother must seek the child's proper separation from her and her total care. As Fromm puts it: "In erotic love, two people who were separate become one. In motherly love, two people who were one become separate."[237] Separation often is difficult. In Fromm's view, many mothers fail to achieve it. "Only the really loving woman, the woman who is happier in giving than in taking, who is firmly rooted in her own existence, can be a loving mother when the child is in the process of separation." He adds that "a woman can be a truly loving mother only if she can *love;* if she is able to love her husband, other children, strangers, all human beings."[238] Mother love, as erotic love, cannot be completely exclusive and still be real love.

Father love, unlike mother love, is conditional. The father loves the child

---

[234] *Ibid.*, p. 54. Fromm observes earlier that "in many individuals in whom separateness is not relieved in other ways, the search for the sexual orgasm assumes a function which makes it not very different from alcoholism and drug addiction. It becomes a desperate attempt to escape the anxiety engendered by separateness, and it results in an ever-increasing sense of separateness, since the sexual act without love never bridges the gap between two human beings, except momentarily." (*Ibid.,* Sect. 1, p. 12.)

[235] *Ibid.,* Sect. 3, p. 54. The sexual desire is stimulated by love and not vice versa. (See *ibid.*)

[236] See *ibid.,* Sect. 2, p. 41. Of this love, Fromm says: "Unconditional love corresponds to one of the deepest longings, not only of the child, but of every human being." (*Ibid.*)

[237] See *ibid.,* Sect. 3, pp. 50–51, *passim.* There is still the desire for union in the late phase of motherly love. However, it is no longer the union of total dependence.

[238] *Ibid.,* p. 52.

because the child deserves it; it is a love that the child can lose if he fails to measure up to expected standards. Fromm says that the balance between the "mother's and the father's attitudes toward the child correspond to the child's own needs."[239] The mother, if she makes the proper transition and does not perpetuate the child's dependence, gives the child the necessary security he must have in life. The father, on the other hand, because he places demands on the child, assumes the function of teacher, the one who introduces him to the world. In the order of time, maternal love precedes paternal love. Fromm places great importance on the sequence and merging of these two influences.

> In this development from mother-centered to father-centered attachment, and their eventual synthesis, lies the basis for mental health and the achievement of maturity. In the failure of this development lies the basic cause for neurosis.[240]

In all cases the hallmarks of real love are the desire to escape one's loneliness in a mature (*i.e.*, nonexploiting) union, coupled with the desire to enhance the welfare of the beloved primarily for his own sake. The theory, then, presented by Fromm is one in which, though acquisitive desires are present, benevolence is indispensable to love. [241]

Fromm discusses not only the nature of love but also the question of how men can learn to love, or love better, than they do. He speaks of love as an art that men can practice or not, according to their own knowledge, decision, and powers. He, therefore, thinks of loving as, in some sense, voluntary, since it is something over which men can exercise some control, either directly or indirectly.[242]

Fromm makes the point about the voluntary character of love in his discussion of erotic love, a love generally thought to be the least voluntary: "Love is supposed to be the outcome of a spontaneous, emotional reaction, of suddenly being gripped by an irresistible feeling." If this view is taken, Fromm argues:

[239] *Ibid.*, Sect. 2, p. 43.

[240] *Ibid.*, p. 44. Filial love is dealt with briefly by Fromm. He does not seem to think that the infant is capable of real love before the age of eight-and-a-half to ten. At this point, however, a new factor enters the child's life. "For the first time, the child thinks of *giving* something to mother (or to father). . . . It takes many years from this first beginning to the maturing of love. Eventually the child, who may now be an adolescent, has overcome his egocentricity; the other person is not any more primarily a means to the satisfaction of his own needs. The needs of the other person are as important as his own in fact, they have become more important." (*Ibid.*, p. 40.)

[241] There is also the element of knowledge. However, the theory presented by Fromm is primarily a tendential one.

[242] See *ibid.*, Ch. I, p. 5; and Ch. IV, p. 118.

One neglects to see an important factor in erotic love, that of *will*. To love somebody is not just a strong feeling—it is a decision, it is a judgment, it is a promise. If love were only a feeling, there would be no basis for the promise to love each other forever. A feeling comes and it may go. How can I judge that it will stay forever, when my act does not involve judgment and decision?[243]

Perhaps more decisive than the wilful act of love are the deliberate preparations a person can make enabling him to love better. Claiming that the ability to love depends on the development of a person, Fromm specifies the character traits love presupposes: discipline, concentration, patience, interest in mastering the art, the overcoming of narcissism, the cultivation of reason, the development of humility, faith in oneself, and courage.[244] The cultivation of these traits enables a person to be actively concerned for others.

According to Fromm, the pressures of contemporary society make such traits increasingly difficult to acquire; hence, true love today is a rare and difficult achievement. More pointedly he argues that these pressures (particularly the economic ones) force individuals to develop acquisitive rather than benevolent habits, thus diminishing the incidence of love:

> If our whole social and economic organization is based on each one seeking his own advantage, if it is governed by the principle of egotism tempered only by the ethical principle of fairness, how can one do business, how can one act within the framework of existing society and at the same time practice love?[245]

Fromm does not claim that the social and economic organization precludes love but only that it makes it more difficult. Men are still free to love if they decide to conduct their life, or some part of it, in opposition to contemporary currents. He argues, however, that, if love is to become a social rather than a highly individualistic phenomenon, "important and radical changes in our social structure are necessary."[246]

[243] *Ibid.*, Ch. II, Sect. 3, p. 56. See also Ch. I, p. 4, where Fromm contrasts the experience of falling in love with the state of being in love.
[244] See *ibid.*, Ch. IV, pp. 107–128.
[245] *Ibid.*, pp. 130–131.
[246] See *ibid.*, p. 132.

9

Love and Judgment

I N this chapter we apply the cognitive or judgmental notions to three groups of theories. In the first and smallest of the three, love is conceived primarily in terms of the nontendential notions of esteem or valuation. In the second group, the judgmental notions in the sphere of cognition are conceived as an aspect of love. That is to say, love is understood as primarily tendential but as having an element of judgment in it. For the third and largest of the three groups of theories, the notions of esteem (as admiration or respect) and valuation are important for understanding how love emerges rather than for understanding what love is, since most authors conceive of love in the sphere of the tendential. The authors of these theories understand the cognitive elements as necessary or important conditions prior to love, as concomitant with love or as effects of love, but as separate from love itself.

The three parts of the chapter, corresponding to the three groups of theories, may be described as follows:

A. *Love as Wholly or Primarily Judgment.* The principal authors of these theories, presented here for the first time, are: René Descartes, David Hume, John Locke, Vladimir Solovyev, and Blaise Pascal.

431

B. *Judgmental Aspects of Primarily Tendential Conceptions of Love.*
These theories already have been presented in previous chapters. Hence,
we shall concentrate on the features of them that involve judgmental
notions. Their principal authors are: Søren Kierkegaard and William
James (from Chapter 6); Marie-Henri Beyle (de Stendhal) and Benedict
de Spinoza (from Chapter 7); and Nicolai Hartmann, Erich Fromm, and
C. S. Lewis (from Chapter 8).

C. *Judgmental Notions in Relation to Wholly Tendential Conceptions
of Love.* These theories also have been presented in previous chapters.
Hence, we again shall concentrate on the features of them that involve
judgmental notions. The principal authors of these theories are: Plato,
Aurelius Augustine, Marcus Tullius Cicero, Aristotle, Thomas Aquinas,
Dante Alighieri, Baldesar Castiglione, and Sigmund Freud (from Chapters
5 and 6); Plotinus, Marsilio Ficino, Giovanni Pico della Mirandola,
Andreas Capellanus, Arthur Schopenhauer, and Denis de Rougemont
(from Chapter 7); Theodor Reik and José Ortega y Gasset (from Chapter 8).

A. Love as Wholly or Primarily Judgment

René Descartes

Descartes expresses his thought on love in his discourse on *The Passions
of the Soul* and in the *Letter to Chanut.* Though the former contains a
much more extended analysis of love, the latter is nevertheless the guiding
document in understanding Descartes's conception. The *Letter to Chanut*
(a) focuses exclusively on love; (b) deals directly and at length with the
question of what love is; and (c) sets forth the *essentials* of the theory of
love.

The problem of classifying Descartes's theory in regard to the judgmental and tendential spheres is caused by the fact that he discusses love in
three different ways: as purely intellectual, as passion, and as a combination of elements from both spheres.

Love "commonly" understood is a combination of intellectual love and
love as passion. Love analytically understood is either "purely intellectual
or reasonable" or "a passion."[1] The analytical approach is used by Descartes
because of his radical distinction between the functions of the mind (or
soul) and the functions of the body,[2] which appears "clearly and distinctly" in his bifocal view of human phenomena. This controlling distinc-

1 *Letter to Chanut*, pp. 654–655. (Our translation.)
2 See *The Passions of the Soul*, Part I, Arts. 4–26, pp. 109–121.

tion underlies the opening remark of his *Letter to Chanut:* "I distinguish between love which is purely intellectual or reasonable and love which is a passion."[3] He goes on to discuss and describe both ways of looking at love. In *The Passions of the Soul*, however, Descartes deals with love primarily as a passion. Since the letter and the treatise exhibit a generally uniform vocabulary, they complement (and at times even overlap) each other.

Our classification of Descartes's theory of natural love among human beings as judgmental, or primarily judgmental, rather than tendential, rests on the position he takes concerning the relationship between thought and tendency. That tendency is but a species of thought is brought out clearly in several controlling texts in the *Letter*, of which the following is perhaps the most significant:

> But when our soul is joined to the body, this reasonable love is ordinarily accompanied by the other, which one can call sensual or sensitive, and which I have said generally of all the passions, appetites, and sentiments, *is nothing else but a confused thought*, aroused in the soul by some movement of nerves, which inclines it toward this other, clearer thought in which reasonable love consists.[4]

Although Descartes's conception of love involves notions from both the cognitive and tendential spheres, the judgmental crowns the tendential. Intellectual love can exist in the soul apart from the body, whereas the love that is a passion *presupposes* the body's connection with the soul as well as the soul's ability to love intellectually.

> And all these movements of the will in which love, joy, sadness and desire consist, insofar as they are reasonable thoughts and not passions, can be found in our soul, even if it did not have a body.[5]

By itself, intellectual love is totally a matter of approving judgment. It occurs "when our soul, perceiving some good, whether it is present or absent, which is suitable (*convenable*) to it, joins itself voluntarily to that thing; that is to say, the soul considers itself with that good to be a whole of which it is one part and the good the other."[6]

In this context, suitable (*convenable*) means referred to the soul.[7] The

---

[3] *Letter to Chanut*, p. 654–655.

[4] *Ibid.*, p. 656. (Italics added.)

[5] *Ibid.*, p. 655.

[6] *Ibid.*, p. 654. Descartes adds that, if the good already is possessed, the movement of the will that accompanies the judgment (*connaissance*) is joy. If the good is not possessed, the movement is sadness. Furthermore, if the good is not possessed, the movement of the will accompanying the judgment that the object would be good to possess is desire. (See *ibid.*, pp. 654–655.)

[7] See *The Passions of the Soul*, Part I, Art. 27, pp. 121–122.

judgment bears on the worth of the object as compared with the estimation
one has of oneself,[8] and is distinct from the inclination toward that object.
Descartes affirms that, "sometimes love is found in us, without our will
inclining to anything because we do not find an object that we think is
worthy."[9] Elsewhere, he refers to "the reasonable thoughts by which we
love that which we judge to be worthy."[10]

In general, men judge the objects of their love to be less worthy, as
worthy, or more worthy than themselves. In terms of these judgments,
Descartes distinguishes among affection, friendship, and devotion:

> We can, it seems to me, more rightly make distinctions in love according to
> the esteem we feel for what we love as compared to ourselves: when we
> esteem the object of our love less than ourselves, we have only simple affection
> for it; when we esteem it as much as ourselves, we feel what is known as
> friendship; and when we esteem it more than ourselves, the passion we have
> may be called devotion.[11]

The characteristic common to these expressions of love is esteem.[12]

Love is best realized in "true magnanimity"[13] or self-esteem and is
assumed "to exist, or at least to be capable of existing, in all other men."[14]
Hence, for the virtuous man, the esteem in love among human beings is
most often respect and sometimes admiration.

Another judgmental element, valuation, is part of virtuous love. Descartes explains what he means in his definition of intellectual love by the
phrase "to will to join itself"[15] when he describes the soul's approval of the
beloved object. He says: ". . . I do not here intend to speak of desire,
which is a passion apart and relates to the future, but of the consent by

[8] There is only one reason men properly can esteem themselves: the possession and
proper use of free will. Only free actions properly are subject to praise and blame.
Those actions Descartes thinks properly are praised and for whom men properly may
esteem themselves are inspired by "good will" toward others. (See *ibid.*, Part III,
Arts. 152–154, pp. 182–183.)

[9] *Letter to Chanut*, pp. 655–656. Descartes adds that "the contrary can also occur,
that we perceive a good which is worth a great deal, and our will inclines to it, but
without any passion for it, since our body is not so disposed." (*Ibid.*, p. 656.)

[10] *Ibid.*, p. 658.

[11] *The Passions of the Soul*, Part II, Art. 83, p. 147. See also *Letter to Chanut*,
pp. 661–662. Making his distinction more specific, Descartes says: "Thus we may
have affection for a flower, a bird or a horse, but unless we have a seriously deranged
mind, we can have friendship only for men. And they are so truly the object of this
passion that there is no man so imperfect that we cannot feel very perfect friendship
for him if we think he loves us and if we have a truly noble and magnanimous soul."
(*The Passions of the Soul*, Part II, Art. 83, p. 147.)

[12] See *ibid.*, Part III, Art. 150, pp. 181–182.

[13] *Ibid.*, Art. 153, p. 182.

[14] *Ibid.*, Art. 154, p. 183.

[15] *Ibid.*, Part II, Art. 79, p. 145.

which we consider ourselves as henceforth joined to what we love, so that we imagine a whole with ourselves as one part and what we love as another."[16] Valuation consists in the determination to act for the sake of the whole of which the lover and beloved are parts (which is separate from the tendency that follows this determination).

> The nature of love [is] that one transfers such cares as one is accustomed to have for oneself to the conservation of the whole, that one retains as much for oneself as small or as large a part of them as one believes one is a small or large part of the whole to which one has given his affection.[17]

For those objects of love judged to have intrinsic worth, the tendency that follows valuation (the shift of caring only for himself to caring for a whole of which the self is a part) depends on the relationship between the esteem the lover has for himself and the esteem he has for the object or person loved. If the lover esteems the object more than himself, he will care for it more (devotion); if he esteems the object as he esteems himself he will care for it as much (friendship); if he esteems the object less than himself, he will care for it less (affection).

The principal tendential result of the valuation is benevolent, except in affection, where benevolence is outweighed by the tendency to care for ourselves more than for the beloved object. Contrasting affection with devotion, Descartes says:

> As for devotion, its principal object is no doubt the sovereign Divinity, to whom we cannot fail to be devoted when we know Him as we should. But we may also be devoted to our ruler, our country, our city, and even to a private individual, when we esteem him much more than ourselves. Now the differences among these three kinds of love appear to lie chiefly in their effects; for inasmuch as in all three of them we regard ourselves as being joined to and united with the object of our love, we are always ready to abandon the lesser part of the whole which we compose with it in order to preserve the other part, which means that in simple affection we always prefer ourselves to what we love, and that, on the contrary, in devotion we so prefer the object of our love to ourselves that we are not afraid to die in order to preserve it. Examples of this have often been seen in those who have exposed themselves to certain death for the defense of their ruler or their city, or sometimes even for private individuals to whom they were devoted.[18]

[16] *Ibid.*, Art. 80, p. 145.
[17] *Letter to Chanut*, p. 661.
[18] *The Passions of the Soul*, Part II, Art. 83, pp. 147–148. See also *Letter to Chanut*, pp. 661–662.

Intellectual love is an act of valuation grounded in esteem, which may have tendential *effects* that can be benevolent or acquisitive; love's essence is judgment and not tendency.

Descartes explicitly rejects the traditional distinction between concupiscent and benevolent love. He says "that this distinction concerns only the effects of love, and not its essence,"[19] and adds that a love for any object, no matter what it is, always is followed by a desire to give it things believed beneficial to it, which is one of the principal effects of love. He also says that, "if we judge that it is good to possess it or to be associated with it in some way other than through the will, we desire it, which is also one of the commonest effects of love."[20]

In discussing love as a passion, Descartes mentions loves that seem to involve little or no esteem and result in little or no benevolence. He contrasts these with the love of a good father for his children, which he takes as a high example of devotion:

> There is also no need to distinguish as many kinds of love as there are diverse objects which we may love, because, for example, although the passions of an ambitious man for glory, of a miser for money, of a drunkard for wine, of a brutal man for a woman he wants to rape, of a man of honor for his friend or his mistress, and of a good father for his children, are very different from one another, they are all similar in that they share some of the characteristics of love. But the first four have love only for the possession of the objects to which their passion is related, and have none for the objects themselves, for which they have only desire mingled with other particular passions, whereas the love of a good father for his children is so pure that he does not desire to obtain anything from them and does not wish to possess them otherwise than he does, or to be joined with them more closely than he is already; regarding them as an extension of himself, he seeks their good as his own, or with even greater care, for, considering that he and they form a whole of which he is not the best part, he often places their interests before his and is not afraid of losing himself in order to save them.[21]

What the passions "of a brutal man for a woman he wants to rape" and "of a good father for his children" have in common seems to be valuation. Since "they share some of the characteristics of love," Descartes understands them both to involve that assent of the will (or valuation) to the welfare of a whole of which the lover and the beloved in each case form a part. The

[19] *The Passions of the Soul*, Part II, Art. 81, p. 146. See also *Letter to Chanut*, p. 658.

[20] *The Passions of the Soul*, Part II, Art. 81, p. 146.

[21] *Ibid.*, Art. 82, pp. 146–147. Descartes adds: "The affection which men of honor have for their friends is of this nature, although it is seldom so perfect, and that which they have for their mistresses is of a closely similar nature, although it also has some characteristics in common with the other kind." (*Ibid.*, p. 147.)

difference is that, for the rapist, the woman attacked forms but a transitory and negligible part of that whole. This is why Descartes says that such a man does not have love for her but for the possession of her. She is valued merely as a means to his pleasure, and whatever is done for her is done solely to facilitate that pleasure; the tendential effect is necessarily acquisitive since the man cares little or not at all for the woman for her own sake. The opposite is true of the father in relation to the children. He values the children much more than himself; they form, in his opinion, the larger and more valuable part of the whole of which he and they are parts. Hence, the tendential consequence of his valuation is benevolence. Though the love of virtuous men for those whom they judge their equals or their betters has both esteem (either as respect or admiration) and valuation, there are loves mentioned by Descartes that do not seem to involve esteem. The prime characteristic of intellectual love, therefore, is valuation.

Though all love is grounded in intellectual love (since, for Descartes, passions, emotions, and sentiments are but confused thoughts), the love that is a passion, together with other passions of the soul, is found in the mind *as joined to the body*.[22] Because of this, passions of the soul often are accompanied by a physical change in the body.[23]

Some discussion of how Descartes applies the distinction between action and passion is essential for grasping his conception of love as a passion. The distinction is set forth clearly in the following statement:

> To begin with, I observe that whatever takes place or happens anew is generally called by philosophers a passion with regard to the subject to which it happens, and an action with regard to what causes it to happen, so that although the agent and the recipient are often quite different, the action and the passion are always one and the same thing which has these two names because of the two separate subjects to which it can be referred.[24]

The same phenomenon, then, may be called an action or a passion, depending on whether one views it from the perspective of the agent or the recipient.

Applying this distinction, Descartes then says "that what is a passion in the soul is usually an action in the body."[25] That is to say, most of what

[22] See *ibid.*, Part I, Art. 17, p. 117; and Art. 27, pp. 121–122. In this sense, love, which is a passion, is peculiar to human beings; other animals, like human bodies without mind, are machines with no passions, and hence no love. (See *ibid.*, Arts. 6 and 7, pp. 110–111.)

[23] See *ibid.*, Part II, Art. 97, p. 154; Arts. 106 and 107, pp. 158–159; Art. 111, p. 160; and Art. 137, p. 173. The single exception to this rule is the passion of wonder. (See *ibid.*, Art. 71, pp. 141–142.)

[24] *Ibid.*, Part I, Art. 1, p. 108.

[25] *Ibid.*, Art. 2, p .109.

occurs in the soul is occasioned by physical change in the body.[26] Occurrences in the soul that are not occasioned by bodily changes originate in the soul, and may terminate in it (such as when one wills to love God) or in the body (such as when, without physical stimulation, one determines to walk). These are actions and not passions, properly speaking, since they are not occasioned by change in the body.

As physical stimuli do not determine the soul to act in a certain way (because the will is free) but merely occasion some action on the part of the soul, their effect on the soul is not a passion.[27] For this reason, Descartes says that, since "it is certain that we cannot will anything without perceiving by the same means that we will it; . . . [nevertheless] although with respect to the soul it is an action to will something, we can say that it is also a passion in it *to be aware that it wills.*" He adds:

> However, since this perception and this volition are actually the same thing, and since it is always named from what is the more noble, it is customary to call it an action rather than a passion.[28]

The "principal effect [therefore] of all the passions in man is to incite and dispose the soul to will the things for which they are preparing the body."[29] Descartes immediately adds, however, that "the will is by nature so free that it can never be constrained."[30]

Through action of the will occasioned by a physical stimulus is never a passion, perception by the will of its own action always is.

Descartes asserts that only thought can be attributed to the soul. Thoughts are of two kinds: "those which are the actions of the soul, and those which are its passions." Explaining the difference, he says:

> I name all our volitions its actions, because we experience them as coming directly from our soul and seeming to depend on it alone; on the other hand, we can generally give the name of passions to all the different forms of perception or awareness that are in us, because often it is not our soul which makes them what they are, and because it always receives them from the things they represent.[31]

[26] The body experiences certain sensations which are transmitted to the soul through the mediation of "animal spirits." These are imperceptible, small bodies that carry these sensory impressions to the pineal gland in the skull where they are registered by the soul. (See *ibid.,* Art. 50-Part II, Art. 51, pp. 134–135.)

[27] Descartes excepts illusions, dreams, and daydreams and calls them passions caused directly by the body since they do not involve exercise of will. (See *ibid.,* Part I, Art. 21, p. 119.)

[28] *Ibid.,* Art. 19, p. 118. (Italics added.)

[29] *Ibid.,* Art. 40, p. 128. "Thus the feeling of fear arouses a will to flee, that of boldness the will to fight, and so on with the others." (*Ibid.*)

[30] *Ibid.,* Art. 41, p. 128.

[31] *Ibid.,* Art. 17, p. 117.

Distinguishing between perceptions "which we refer to our body . . . hunger, thirst, and our other natural appetites . . ." and "perceptions which we refer to the soul . . . joy, anger, etc.,"[32] Descartes says they are all passions "when we take the word in its most general meaning," but adds that "it is customary to restrict it to mean only those which are related to the soul itself, and it is these alone which I have undertaken to explain here under the name of passions of the soul."[33] He then proceeds to define the passions of the soul (of which love is one) "as those perceptions, sensations or emotions of the soul which we refer specifically to it, and which are caused, maintained and fortified by some movement of the animal spirits."[34]

Thus Descartes distinguishes passions from bodily change, on the one hand, and from free movements of the will, on the other. For him, passions always are forms of perception by the soul occasioned by sensory stimuli, and which consist in the soul's simultaneous awareness of its own free inclinations. In this way Descartes is able to distinguish the intellectual love that can occur apart from the body from love as a passion, which, because it is thought, is grounded in intellectual love, but which is "confused and obscure" because of the soul's association with the body. Of all passions, he says:

> We may call them perceptions when this word is used generally to signify all thoughts which are not actions of the soul or volitions, but not when it is used only to signify clear cognitions, for experience shows that those who are most agitated by their passions are not those who know them best, and that the passions are to be counted among the perceptions made confused and obscure by the close alliance between the soul and the body.[35]

There are six primary passions from which all others derived: wonder, love, hatred, desire, joy, and sadness. Love and hatred are sharply contrasted according to whether the object is seen as good or bad.[36] Descartes also is most careful to distinguish love from desire. Love as a passion is the perception of the will's judgment that an object or a person has value, which perception is separate from whatever tendential consequences arise from it. The primary distinction between love and desire is made in terms of time; love looks to the present and desire to the future. Of love as a passion, he says:

[32] *Ibid.*, Arts. 24–25, p. 120, *passim*.
[33] *Ibid.*, Art. 25, p. 121.
[34] *Ibid.*, Art. 27, pp. 121–122.
[35] *Ibid.*, Art. 28, p. 122. Descartes also says that they may be called sensations because they are received into the soul from the outside "and are not otherwise known by it." He adds that they may be called emotions because they are the most moving thoughts the soul can have. (*Ibid.*)
[36] See *ibid.*, Part II, Art. 56, p. 137.

Love is an emotion of the soul, caused by the movement of the animal spirits, which incites it to will to join itself to objects which appear to be beneficial [*convenable, i.e.,* suitable] to it.[37]

Stressing that the essence of this passion is not tendency, he adds: "By the word 'will' [*volonté*], I do not here intend to speak of desire, which is a passion apart and relates to the future, but of the consent by which we consider ourselves as henceforth joined to what we love."[38] Of the passion of desire, he says:

The passion of desire is an agitation of the soul caused by the animal spirits which dispose it to wish for the future those things which it represents to itself as agreeable [*convenable*]. Thus we desire not only the presence of an absent good, but also the preservation of a present good, and, further, the absence of evil, whether it be that which we have already, or that which we believe may come to us in the future.[39]

Because Descartes is careful to distinguish love from desire, he rejects the notion that the attraction between the sexes (which he understands as the acquisitive desire for the union of complementarity) can be included under love. In his view, it springs from the passion of delight. After mentioning several tendencies caused by delight, he says:

But the principal one is that which comes from the perfections we imagine in a person who we think can become another self to us; for with the difference of sex which nature has placed in men as well as in animals without reason, it has also placed certain impressions in the brain which, at a certain age and at a certain time, *cause us to regard ourselves as incomplete and as though we were only half of a whole of which a person of the opposite sex ought to be the other half.* The acquisition of this other half is confusedly represented by nature as the greatest of all goods imaginable. And although we see many persons of the opposite sex, we do not wish to have many of them at the same time, since nature does not make us imagine that we need more than one half. But when we observe something in one person which is more pleasing than what we observe in others at the same time, it determines the soul to feel for that one alone all the inclination which nature gives it to seek the good that is represented to it as the greatest which can be possessed; *and the inclination or desire that thus arises from delight is more commonly given the name of love than the passion of love* which has been described above. It also has more extraordinary effects, and it is what serves as the principal material for novelists and poets.[40]

[37] *Ibid.,* Art. 79, p. 145.
[38] *Ibid.,* Art. 80, p. 145.
[39] *Ibid.,* Art. 86, p. 149. See also Art. 57, p. 137; and Art. 87, p. 149.
[40] *Ibid.,* Art. 90, pp. 150–151. (Italics added.) Insofar as sexual desire may be part of this attraction, it also is excluded from love's compass.

If there is a tendential aspect to love as a passion, it is not acquisitive. Descartes's "desire" is what we have called acquisitive desire. In his view, acquisitive desire is only a secondary effect of love; benevolence is the primary effect. Having distinguished the essence of love from its effects, he adds:

> . . . for as soon as we have willed to join ourselves to some object . . . we have for it . . . benevolence, i.e., we also will to join to it the things we believe to be beneficial to it, which is one of the principal effects of love.

Then, "if we judge that it is good to possess it or to be associated with it in some way other than through the will, we desire it."[41] In other words, as soon as we love, benevolence follows directly.[42] "Desire" comes only after two more steps: the realization that the self actually or possibly lacks the object loved, and the realization that it would be good to possess. If, therefore, tendency is involved in love as a passion at all, it is benevolent.

Whether love is taken as a passion, as intellectual love, or as a combination of both of them, it is still essentially a cognitive conception that Descartes presents. Intellectual love is nothing but judgment, and Descartes observes that it and love as a passion ordinarily accompany each other when the soul is joined to the body.[43] Love among human beings, therefore, invariably involves love as a passion. But because love as a passion is primarily cognitive and also grounded upon intellectual love which is wholly cognitive, love, in Descartes's theory, is conceived as essentially judgmental.

David Hume

Of the three books of Hume's *Treatise of Human Nature*, "Of the Understanding," "Of the Passions," and "Of Morals," the principal source for his theory of love is Book II. But an adequate understanding of that theory presupposes familiarity with concepts and notions used in Book I, as well as in other works, such as *A Dissertation on the Passions* and *An Inquiry Concerning the Principles of Morals*.

Impression is the notion in Hume's systematic treatise most relevant to his conception of love. For him, impressions include "all our sensations, passions and emotions, as they make their first appearance in the soul."[44] Since love is a passion, it is also an impression. "By the term of impression," Hume says, "I would not be understood to express the manner, in

---

41 *Ibid.*, Art. 81, p. 146, *passim.*
42 Cf. pp. 435–436, *supra.*
43 See *Letter to Chanut*, pp. 655–656.
44 *A Treatise of Human Nature*, Book I, Part I, Sect. I, p. 1.

which our lively perceptions are produced in the soul, but merely the perceptions themselves; for which there is no particular name either in the *English* or any other language, that I know of."[45] All imprints on the soul, which derive from external objects,[46] are perceptions.

The two kinds of perceptions are: ideas and impressions. Impressions are those "perceptions, which enter with most force and violence," whereas ideas are "the faint images of these in thinking and reasoning."[47] The difference between them "consists in the degrees of force and liveliness with which they strike upon the mind."[48] Hume says that sometimes the difference is so small that it is difficult to make the distinction:

> Thus in sleep, in a fever, in madness, or in any very violent emotions of soul, our ideas may approach to our impressions: As on the other hand it sometimes happens, that our impressions are so faint and low, that we cannot distinguish them from our ideas.[49]

Hume adds another distinction to his analysis when he says that impressions are of two kinds: those of sensation, and those of reflection (what he also calls original and secondary impressions):

> Original impressions or impressions of sensation are such as without any antecedent perception arise in the soul, from the constitution of the body, from the animal spirits, or from the application of objects to the external organs. Secondary, or reflective impressions are such as proceed from some of these original ones, either immediately or by the interposition of its idea. Of the first kind are all the impressions of the senses, and all bodily pains and pleasures: Of the second are the passions, and other emotions resembling them.[50]

[45] *Ibid.*, p. 2, fn. 1.

[46] See *ibid.*, p. 4.

[47] *Ibid.*, p. 1. Hume's subsequent remark that the distinction between impressions and ideas is clear to anyone who perceives the difference between "feeling and thinking" does not mean that impressions are feelings, but only that they are caused by feelings. (See *ibid.*, p. 2.)

[48] *Ibid.*, p. 1.

[49] *Ibid.*, p. 2. See also Book II, Part III, Sect. III, p. 417.

[50] *Ibid.*, Part I, Sect. I, p. 275. In Book I, Hume explains how a reflective or secondary impression may arise: "An impression first strikes upon the senses, and makes us perceive heat or cold, thirst or hunger, pleasure or pain of some kind or other. Of this impression there is a copy taken by the mind, which remains after the impression ceases; and this we call an idea. This idea of pleasure or pain, when it returns upon the soul, produces the new impressions of desire and aversion, hope and fear, which may properly be called impressions of reflexion, because derived from it. These again are copied by the memory and imagination, and become ideas; which perhaps in their turn give rise to other impressions and ideas. So that the impressions of reflexion are only antecedent to their correspondent ideas; but posterior to those of sensation, and deriv'd from them." (*Ibid.*, Book I, Part I, Sect. II, pp. 7–8.)

The secondary impressions or those of reflection are divided further into two kinds: calm and violent. The calm have to do with our perception of beauty and deformity, whereas the violent, covering a much larger compass, are distinguished by their intensity, *e.g.*, love and hatred.[51] For Hume, only the violent impressions of reflection are properly called passions.

These impressions are divided again into the direct and the indirect. Direct passions are those that arise immediately from good or evil, from pain or pleasure. Among them Hume numbers "desire, aversion, grief, joy, hope, fear, despair, and security." The indirect are "such as proceed from the same principles, but by the conjunction of other qualities." Among these he numbers "pride, humility, ambition, vanity, *love*, hatred, envy, pity, malice, generosity, with their dependants."[52]

In Hume's terms, love may be described as an indirect, violent impression of reflection. Two considerations incline us to classify his conception of love as belonging to the cognitive or judgmental rather than the tendential sphere. First, all impressions, however qualified and sophisticated they may become, are species of perception; and when they reach the level of passion, they are perceptions of preference, *i.e.*, they involve good and evil. Passions, thus understood, are judgments. Second, Hume discusses perceptions (in their primitive forms especially) as the mental residue of physical stimuli, *i.e.*, the intellectual record, as it were, of physical and psychic changes originating in the body or outside of it. His basic conception of perception does not include these changes or tendencies themselves but only the immediate or lasting residue they imprint on the mind.

Hume understands love as a relational phenomenon, as always involving a judgment or perception by the self in regard to another. Accordingly, he denies that a reflexive evaluation of the self by the self can be called love.[53] Human love is always love between a person and someone or something else.

> As the immediate *object* of pride and humility is self or that identical person, of whose thoughts, actions, and sensations we are intimately conscious; so the *object* of love and hatred is some other person, of whose

---

[51] See *ibid.*, Book II, Part I, Sect. I, p. 276. Here, again, Hume remarks that this distinction can be blurred in certain instances. It is possible to reach an intense height of rapture in reacting to beautiful verse. It is also possible to experience love and hatred, joy and sorrow in such mild and tepid forms that they appear to be indistinguishable from the calm impressions. (See *ibid.*)

[52] *Ibid.*, pp. 276–277, *passim.* (Italics added.)

[53] Hume occasionally does use the phrase "self-love" in a colloquial sense to indicate concern with one's own interest or even selfishness. (See, for example, *ibid.*, Book III, Part II, Sect. I, p. 480.)

thoughts, actions, and sensations we are not conscious. . . . Our love and
hatred are always directed to some sensible being external to us; and when
we talk of *self-love,* 'tis not in a proper sense, nor has the sensation it
produces any thing in common with that tender emotion, which is excited
by a friend or mistress.[54]

The object of any passion is self or other and its sensation may be
pleasure or pain. Hume distinguishes between the object of a passion and
its cause. In the case of pride, whereas the object is always the self, the
cause may be mental, moral, and physical endowments, or the excellences
of one's associates, family, or property.[55] The cause of the passion, further,
must be distinguished as to quality and subject. The quality that excites
pride may be intellectual excellence. But the quality may reside in a
person's son rather than himself. The object of the passion is still the self.
The quality that excites it is intellectual excellence and the subject in
which that quality inheres is the son.[56]

Using these distinctions, Hume insists that none of the indirect passions
can arise unless there is "a double relation of impressions and ideas." In the
case of love, this double relation operates as follows: On the side of the
cause, one has an idea of the subject (another) as well as the sensation or
impression of pleasure produced by the quality inhering in the subject; on
the side of the object, one has the idea of that object (also another, though
not necessarily the same other as the subject) as well as the sensation or
impression of pleasure produced by the passion of love itself.[57] Hume's
insistence on this double relation removes any possibility of universal love,
since, though one can have an idea of mankind both as the subject (cause)
and object of the passion of love, one can have no impression or sensation
of mankind as a whole, but only those of its members with whom one is
directly or indirectly familiar.

> In general, it may be affirm'd, that there is no such passion in human minds,
> as the love of mankind, merely as such, independent of personal qualities, of
> services, or of relation to ourself. . . . We may affirm, that man in general,
> or human nature, is nothing but the object both of love and hatred, and
> requires some other cause, which by a double relation of impressions and
> ideas, may excite these passions.[58]

[54] *Ibid.,* Book II, Part II, Sect. I, p. 329.
[55] See *ibid.,* p. 330.
[56] See *ibid.,* Part I, Sect. II, pp. 277–279. See also Part II, Sect. I, pp. 329–330.
[57] See *ibid.,* Sects. I–II, pp. 329–347. See also Part I, Sect. II, p. 278.
[58] *Ibid.,* Book III, Part II, Sect. I, pp. 481–482. The impressions requisite for the
arousal of the passion of love need not be strong but they must be present. Whoever
is loved somehow must impress us, directly or vicariously, through *"relation, acquaintance,* and *resemblance."* (*Ibid.,* Book II, Part II, Sect. IV, pp. 354 ff.) The impres-

The impressions constituting the passion of love are not the actual stimuli or tendencies but their mental counterparts, which, because they are determinations of good and evil, or pleasure and pain, count as judgments.

Understanding pride and humility as approbative or disapprobative judgments applied to the self, Hume uses them to make clearer his notions of such judgments as applied to others: love and hatred.

> In running over all the causes which produce the passion of pride or that of humility, it would readily occur, that the same circumstance, if transferred from ourselves to another person, would render him the object of love or hatred, esteem or contempt.[59]

The correlation between the passion of love and the approving judgment of the qualities that inhere in, or are somehow related to, another person is made stronger when Hume says that "esteem and contempt are to be consider'd as species of love and hatred,"[60] and when he refers to "approbation or blame" as "a fainter and more imperceptible love or hatred."[61] Identifying love with judgment even more emphatically, he says: "*Love* or *Friendship* is a complacency in another, on account of his accomplishments or services: *Hatred*, the contrary."[62] Finally, Hume states that the only difference between the passions of love and esteem is intensity:

> Love and esteem are at the bottom the same passions, and arise from like causes. The qualities, that produce both, are agreeable, and give pleasure. But where this pleasure is severe and serious; or where its object is great, and makes a strong impression; or where it produces any degree of humility and awe: In all these cases, the passion, which arises from the pleasure, is more properly denominated esteem than love.[63]

---

sion may be very strong as in "the relation of blood." (*Ibid.*, p. 352.) It may be less strong as when it is caused by those who are the associates of someone we love strongly. (See *ibid.*, Sect. II, p. 341. See also Sect. V, p. 356.) And it may be weak as when we "love our country-men, our neighbours, those of the same trade, profession, and even name with ourselves." (*Ibid.*, Sect. IV, p. 352.) But, according to Hume, an impression sufficient to excite love invariably falls short of the whole human race.

[59] *A Dissertation on the Passions*, Sect. III, p. 218. See also *On the Immortality of the Soul*, p. 575; and *A Treatise of Human Nature*, Book II, Part II, Sect. I, p. 329. In addition to repeating the above point, Hume says: "I have suppos'd all along, that the passions of love and pride, and those of humility and hatred are similar in their sensations, and that the two former are always agreeable, and the two latter painful." He adds, however, that pride and love differ in effects. Pride "invigorates and exalts the mind," whereas love "is rather found to weaken and infeeble it." (*Ibid.*, Sect. X, p. 391, *passim.*)

[60] *A Treatise of Human Nature*, Book II, Part II, Sect. V, p. 357.

[61] *Ibid.*, Book III, Part III, Sect. V, p. 614. See also Book II, Part II, Sect. V, p. 364.

[62] *A Dissertation on the Passions*, Sect. II, p. 202.

[63] *A Treatise of Human Nature*, Book III, Part III, Sect. IV, p. 608, fn. 1.

At the end of this statement concerning love and esteem, Hume observes: "Benevolence attends both: But is connected with love in a more eminent degree."[64] As we have already noted, love is always concerned with another. The high estimation of another, which is love, always produces a tendency, whereas the high estimation of oneself, which is pride, does not.

> The passions of love and hatred are always followed by, or rather conjoined with benevolence and anger. It is this conjunction which chiefly distinguishes these affections from pride and humility. For pride and humility are pure emotions in the soul, unattended with any desire, and not immediately exciting us to action. But love and hatred are not complete within themselves, nor rest in that emotion which they produce, but carry the mind to something farther.[65]

Hume does not think that benevolence (or any tendency) is part of love but only an invariable consequence of it. For him "benevolence and anger are . . . different from love and hatred, and only conjoin'd with them, by the original constitution of the mind."[66] Benevolence is a consequence of love as it is of pity or sympathy.[67] In the case of the latter two, benevolence is preceded by valuation, *i.e.*, the decision to help this or that person. In the case of love, both valuation and esteem (which is the essence of love) *precede* the benevolent tendency. Love itself is not tendential.

Despite the fact that Hume's generic conception of love is exclusively judgmental, he mentions a love that does include tendency; the *"amourous passion,"* or love between the sexes. Hume understands it as one of the "compound passions," as consisting of two or more elements or "affections." Identified by our critical terms, these elements are: esteem (admiration for the beauty of another), benevolence, and sexual desire.

> 'Tis plain, that this affection, in its most natural state, is deriv'd from the conjunction of three different impressions or passions, *viz.* The pleasing

[64] *Ibid.* "Benevolence or the appetite, which attends love, is a desire of the happiness of the person belov'd, and an aversion to his misery." (*Ibid.*, Book II, Part II, Sect. IX, p. 382.) Hume observes that such a tendency is characteristic of pity also. Though love and pity are distinct in the cognitive order, their tendential aspect or consequence seems to be the same. (See *ibid.*, p. 381.)

[65] *A Dissertation on the Passions*, Sect. III, pp. 219–220. See also *An Inquiry Concerning the Principles of Morals*, Sect. VII, p. 335.

[66] *A Treatise of Human Nature*, Book II, Part II, Sect. VI, p. 368.

[67] See *Of Self-Love*, Appendix II, p. 381. Despite the fact that Hume denies freedom of the will and talks frequently in terms of determinants of pleasure and pain, he steadfastly maintains that benevolence is possible and that it cannot be reduced to self-interest. (See *ibid.*, pp. 378–386.)

sensation arising from beauty; the bodily appetite for generation; and a generous kindness or good-will.[68]

The three elements constituting love between the sexes do not arise in any necessary order. Hume says that it is possible that a man may begin with sexual desire and find that desire accompanied by a feeling of "momentary kindness" at least, and a belief that the object of his desire is beautiful. He says it is also possible to begin with benevolence, but observes that the most common sequence is one that begins with admiration for the beauty of another, to which kindness and, finally, bodily appetite are added.[69]

Hume's theory, then, contains two conceptions of love among human beings. In the generic conception, love and admiration are equated. In his conception of love between the sexes, the tendential elements of benevolence and sexual desire are added to admiration. Because the first conception of love is broader than the second and because the notion of admiration actually is contained in the second conception, we have classified Hume's theory as essentially a judgmental one.[70]

John Locke

Though from a somewhat different perspective, John Locke has a conception of the passion of love comparable to that of Descartes and Hume in the sense that it is judgmental. He says: "Pleasure and pain and that which causes them,—good and evil, are the hinges on which our passions turn."[71] The passions of love in relation to pleasure and to desire are understood as the judgments that what is loved will or can produce delight.[72] Locke defines love as valuation:

[68] *A Treatise of Human Nature*, Book II, Part II, Sect. XI, p. 394, *passim*. See also *A Dissertation on the Passions*, Sect. III, p. 221. Although Hume refers to all three of these elements as "impressions," he does not discuss sexual desire and benevolence as perceptions but rather as actual tendencies. To the extent that he does so, his use of the term "passion" in this context is broader than the original meaning he gave to it. (See *A Treatise of Human Nature*, Book II, Part II, Sect. XI, p. 396, where esteem—admiration of beauty—is the only element discussed in terms "of the double relation of impressions and ideas." See also Book III, Part II, Sect. I, p. 481.)

[69] See *ibid.*, Book II, Part II, Sect. XI, p. 395.

[70] We can do this despite the fact that Hume says "that love and hatred are common to the whole sensitive creation." (*Ibid.*, Sect. XII, p. 397.) This assertion is not inconsistent with his generic conception of love, since he says "no truth appears to me more evident, than that beasts are endow'd with thought and reason as well as men." (*Ibid.*, Book I, Part III, Sect. XVI, p. 176.) Animals "can judge of objects . . . by the sensible good or evil, which they produce, and from *that* must regulate their affections towards them." (*Ibid.*, Book II, Part II, Sect. XII, p. 397.)

[71] *An Essay Concerning Human Understanding*, Vol. I, Book II, Ch. XX, Sect. 3, p. 303.

[72] See *ibid.*, Sect. 15, p. 306.

. . . Thus any one reflecting upon the thought he has of the delight which any present or absent thing is apt to produce in him, has the idea we call *love*. For when a man declares in autumn when he is eating them, or in spring when there are none, that he loves grapes, it is no more but that the taste of grapes delights him: let an alteration of health or constitution destroy the delight of their taste, and he then can be said to love grapes no longer.[73]

The act of valuation which is love is distinguished sharply from the passion of desire which is a tendency:

. . . The uneasiness a man finds in himself upon the absence of anything whose present enjoyment carries the idea of delight with it, is that we call *desire;* which is greater or less, as that uneasiness is more or less vehement.[74]

Vladimir Solovyev

The most basic contrast in *The Meaning of Love* is between love and "egoism." Egoism "consists in the exclusive acknowledgement of absolute significance for oneself and in the denial of it for others." Egoism and selfishness often are used as synonyms. Solovyev does not mean by them simply a concern with one's own good. He means either an *exclusive* recognition of one's own worth, or a recognition of one's own worth that involves no *comparable* recognition of the worth of another. The egoistic or selfish person considers that he has "real" importance, but the falsehood of egoism does not consist in attributing such importance to oneself; it consists, rather, in not attributing it to others. The selfish person "relegates others to the circumference of his own being and leaves them only an external and relative value." Thus, he is cut off from others and is as incapable of appreciating their true "individuality" as he is of realizing his own.[75]

Though Solovyev regards egoism as "rooted in the deepest centre of our being" and as something that permeates all our activity, he nevertheless thinks of it as an evil which can be overcome by love.

There is only one force, which can from within sap egoism at the root, and effectively undermine it, namely love, and chiefly sex-love.[76]

Solovyev takes sexual love, or rather conjugal love, as the prototype of all love. It is the principal means for the achievement of true individuality

[73] *Ibid.*, Sect. 4, pp. 303–304.
[74] *Ibid.*, Sect. 6, p. 304.
[75] See *The Meaning of Love*, Ch. II, Sect. III, pp. 22–26.
[76] *Ibid.*, p. 25.

both for oneself and another. It is the most obvious way of overcoming exclusion of others and by others. It is the path to perfection.[77] "The foundation and type of . . . true existence remains and always will remain sexual or conjugal love."[78] Though all other loves mitigate egoism to some degree, they are less effective because they lack "either homogeneity, equality and reciprocity between the lover and the loved one, or the all-round diversity of those who are to complete the characters of each other."[79]

Sexual or conjugal love is neither exclusively nor primarily a matter of sexual desire.[80] "A mere external union, earthly, and in particular physiological, does not possess any definite relation to love. It exists without love, and love exists without it."[81] This does not mean that sexual desire is not some part of that complex Solovyev calls conjugal love, but only that sexual desire *alone* is not the essence of love. Solovyev understands conjugal love to involve both the physical and spiritual. In commenting on nonphysical love, he says that this "exclusively-spiritual love is quite obviously as much an anomaly as an exclusively-physical love and as an exclusively-earthly union."[82] True love is neither exclusively one nor the other.

The achievement of individuality is best accomplished through union with another person. In that union someone recognizes that at least one other person (and possibly more) has as much importance as he believes himself to have. That recognition or realization consists in respecting the other person as someone of equal intrinsic value. As soon as this happens, the lover is on his way to becoming an individual and overcoming his past egoism. An individual (*i.e.*, a lover) is distinguished from an egoist primarily in terms of his recognition of the worth and rights of another and secondarily in terms of the desires that follow from that realization. In other words, Solovyev advances an essentially cognitive conception in

[77] See *ibid.*, p. 26.

[78] *Ibid.*, Ch. V, Sect. IV, p. 77. See also Ch. II, Sect. I, p. 17, where Solovyev says that "sex-love is the highest flowering of the individual life."

[79] *Ibid.*, Sect. IV, p. 27. Solovyev regards parental love (and particularly mother love) as inferior to conjugal love because it is a one-sided relationship. (See *ibid.*, p. 28.)

[80] "I call sex-love, for want of a better term, the exclusive attachment (one-sided as well as mutual), between persons of different sexes, which renders possible the relation between them of husband and wife, but in no wise do I prejudge by this the question of the importance of the physical side of the matter." (*Ibid.*, Ch. III, Sect. I, p. 30, fn. 1.)

[81] *Ibid.*, Sect. IV, p. 40. He adds that sexual union "is necessary for love, not as its unalterable condition and independent goal, but only as the definitive realization of it. If this realization is set as the end in itself, prior to the ideal concern of love, it is the ruin of love." (*Ibid.*)

[82] *Ibid.*, Ch. IV, Sect. IV, p. 55.

which love is understood as a combination of respect and the tendencies following from that judgment.

That tendency in love that makes it the antidote for egoism is the desire for union. The way in which Solovyev understands this desire is very important for his theory of love, despite the fact that his conception of love is essentially nontendential. First and foremost, he maintains that the desire for union in love is, in all cases, the desire for the union of complementarity. Second, this desire has both an acquisitive and benevolent expression.

Solovyev emphasizes the complementary aspect of the desire for union when he says: "The feeling of love in itself is only an impulse, suggesting to us that we can and ought to restore the integrity of the human nature."[83] Ideally, that feeling of love is directed to another person who

> must in everything be distinguished from us, in order to be effectually other, i.e., possessing all that essential content, which we also possess, it must possess its different capacity or mode in another form. In this way every manifestation of our nature, every vital act would meet in this other with a corresponding, but not identical, manifestation, in such a way that the relation of the one to the other would be a complete and steadfast interchange, a full and continual affirmation of oneself in the other, with perfect reciprocity and communion.

He adds: "Such a fusion, or at least a close approximation to it, we find in sex-love, for which reason we attach to it exceptional importance."[84] In a shorter comment on the characteristic desire for complementary union in conjugal love, Solovyev says:

> Finally, man and his female *alter ego* mutually complete each other, not only in the real but also in the ideal sense, attaining perfection only through action upon one another.[85]

Or, as he says more generally:

> True union presupposes the genuine dissimilarity of those being united, i.e., a difference, in virtue of which they do not exclude, but mutually presuppose each other, finding each in the other the fulness of his own proper existence.[86]

The discovery of union with one other person opens the way for a discovery of union with all other persons.

[83] *Ibid.*, Ch. III, Sect. IV, p. 41.
[84] *Ibid.*, Ch. II, Sect. III, p. 26.
[85] *Ibid.*, Ch. IV, Sect. V, p. 57. See also Ch. III, Sect. I, p. 34.
[86] *Ibid.*, Ch. V, Sect. IV, p. 78.

As in the love of two individual creatures diverse, but enjoying equal rights and of equal worth, the one serves the other, not by negative limitations, but by positive completion, so in precisely the same way it must be also in all spheres of collective existence; every social organism ought to be for each member of it not an external limit of his activity, but a positive support and completion.[87]

Solovyev's remarks on the differing desires involved in the love relationship between a man and a woman (and, to some degree, in all others) imply that the central desire in love, the desire for the union of complementarity, takes both an acquisitive and a benevolent form. It is, of course, impossible for such a desire to take both an acquisitive and a benevolent expression simultaneously since these tendencies are mutually exclusive. On the other hand, because both are asserted to be part of the tendential aspect of love, we must assume that they occur sequentially.

The closest to a definition of love that we find is the following:

The meaning of human love, speaking generally, is *the justification and deliverance of individuality through the sacrifice of egoism.*[88]

That deliverance is, in part, the deliverance of oneself. The search for a personal good (though certainly never at the expense of another), *i.e.*, the triumph of individuality over egoism in oneself, is certainly one of the motives behind wanting to unite with another. One seeks to find, through union with another, "the positive and unconditional completion of one's own being."[89]

On the other hand, benevolence is also essential for real love. The lover must want not only to liberate himself from egoism but also to liberate his beloved. "Love is of importance; not only as one of our feelings, but as the transfer of all our interest in life from ourselves to another, as the shifting of the very centre of our personal life."[90] In conjugal love this benevolence (based upon the lover's attitude that the beloved is "a very end in itself"),[91] is at its most intense at the beginning. In time, that enthusiasm passes away to some extent. In the best cases, "the energy of altruistic feeling is not wasted and purposeless, but only having lost its concentration and spirit of high emprise, is transferred in a divided and weakened form to the children."[92]

[87] *Ibid.* Solovyev adds: "As for sexual love (in the sphere of personal existence), the single 'other' is at the same time all, so, on its side, the social *all.* . . ." (*Ibid.* See also Ch. II, Sect. III, p. 24.)
[88] *Ibid.*, pp. 22–23.
[89] *Ibid.*, Ch. V, Sect. IV, p. 77.
[90] *Ibid.*, Ch. III, Sect. I, p. 30. Here Solovyev says again: "This is characteristic of every kind of love, but *par excellence* of sex-love." (*Ibid.*)
[91] *Ibid.*, Ch. I, Sect. I, p. 7.
[92] *Ibid.*, Ch. III, Sect. I, p. 31.

Although the desire for union, in both its acquisitive and benevolent expressions, is important for Solovyev's theory, his conception of love is not primarily a tendential one. At its core is the notion of respect, *i.e.*, the recognition of another person as having an equal value with oneself simply in virtue of his humanity.

> The radical meaning of love, as has already been shewn, consists in the acknowledgement for another creature of unconditional significance.[93]

The problem of love not only "consists in *justifying in reality* that meaning of love which at first is given only in feeling";[94] it also involves raising love from the level of feeling to the level of judgment and knowledge. Passion or mere feeling alone "leads indeed only to a *twofold egoism*, and then to a threefold, and so on. Of course, this is anyhow better than the egoism of one living in isolation; but the dawn of love has revealed to us quite other horizons."[95] Respect is the essential element in the achievement of those horizons.

> Love is greater than intellectual knowledge, yet without the latter it could not take effect as an inward delivering force, enhancing, and not annulling the individuality.[96]

Blaise Pascal

Pascal's thoughts on love are to be found in his *Pensées* and the *Discours sur les Passions de l'Amour*. In neither (nor in both taken together) is there a systematically presented conception of love. Pascal's interest in love is more that of a moralist than an analyst.

The principal distinction he employs is between love of God and love of self. The love of God is man's only salvation; the love of self is his principal

[93] *Ibid.*, Ch. IV, Sect. VI, p. 59. See also Ch. II, Sect. III, p. 23. Solovyev denies that mother love does involve, "properly speaking," such an acknowledgement, since the mother's impulses are largely instinctive and "dependent on an external physiological bond." (*Ibid.*, Sect. IV, pp. 28–29.)

[94] *Ibid.*, Ch. III, Sect. I, p. 33.

[95] *Ibid.*, Ch. V, Sect. I, p. 66.

[96] *Ibid.*, Ch. II, Sect. II, p. 22. In conjugal love the approving judgment of the other goes beyond simple respect to admiration or *"idealization."* Solovyev questions the general assumption that the lover is necessarily deceived in his judgment: "It is well known to everyone, that in love there inevitably exists a special *idealization* of the beloved object, which presents itself to the lover in an entirely different light from that in which outsiders see it. I speak here of light not merely in a metaphorical sense, it is a matter here not only of a special moral and intellectual estimate, but moreover of a special sensuous reception: the lover actually *sees,* visually receives, what others do not. And if for him too this light of love quickly fades away, yet does it follow from this that it was false, that it was only a subjective illusion?" (*Ibid.*, Ch. III, Sect. III, pp. 36–37. See also Ch. IV, Sect. VII, pp. 62–63.)

downfall. "We must love God only and hate self only."[97] Love of God is true love because it is directed to a real and perfect object Who is worthy of it. Love of self is false love because it is directed to an imperfect and unworthy object.

It is in the area of judgment that the distinction between love of God and self-love is clearest. Self-love is bad because man attributes to himself the importance that belongs only to God; he replaces God by himself as that which is worthy of his admiration.[98] Pascal insists that man must love and can only give his love to whatever he sees as perfect. If he loves God, the perfection is real; if he loves himself, he must hate the truth about himself and blind himself to his own imperfections.[99]

The judgment, therefore, that God is perfect, or that one's own self is perfect, is the cardinal difference between love of God and love of self. The conception of love implied by that difference is one that, though it has tendential aspects, is a conception of love primarily as judgment, as esteem. When we love God, we properly esteem Him as perfect and worthy of our adoration. When we love ourselves as God or others as God, we improperly esteem ourselves or them as perfect and worthy of admiration. Since that esteem confronts the reality of a being not worthy of it, the misery of man without God consists essentially in the desperate effort to escape the truth through self-deception. For, without reference to God, one cannot esteem the real human self.[100] Natural love among human beings, then, is based on the illusion that the human self (either one's own or another's) is worthy of love, *i.e.*, of the admiration accorded to the good and the perfect. Man, says Pascal,

> wants to be the object of love and esteem among men, and he sees that his faults merit only their hatred and contempt. This embarrassment in which he finds himself produces in him the most unrighteous and criminal passion that can be imagined; for he conceives a mortal enmity against that truth which reproves him, and which convinces him of his faults. He would annihilate it, but, unable to destroy it in its essence, he destroys it as far as possible in his own knowledge and in that of others; that is to say, he devotes all his attention to hiding his faults both from others and from himself, and he cannot endure either that others should point them out to him, or that they should see them.[101]

The indications are that the tendential aspect of both loves is acquisitive desire. It is, therefore, in terms of object rather than mode that the two are

[97] *Pensées*, Sect. VII, No. 476, p. 132.
[98] See *ibid.*, No. 492, p. 136.
[99] See *ibid.*, Sect. II, No. 100, pp. 30–33.
[100] See *ibid.*, Sect. VII, No. 471, p. 131.
[101] *Ibid.*, Sect. II, No. 100, p. 31.

distinguished. Insofar as the love of God is tendential, it springs from man's need; he seeks through God to achieve the lasting happiness of salvation, without which he is miserable.[102] In self-love he seeks the same happiness through objects less worthy than God and through which he cannot achieve it. If all natural love among human beings is based on self-love, it must be totally acquisitive in tendency. "The nature of self-love and of this human Ego is to love self only and consider self only."[103]

Pascal's observations on human psychology reinforce the interpretation of his conception of love as one in which cognitive notions are joined with tendential ones. Though there is no sharp distinction between thoughts (*pensées*) and feelings (*sentiments*), Pascal emphasizes that both are functions of mind (*esprit*):

> The more highly developed the mind, the greater the passions, for the passions are but feelings and thoughts belonging solely to the mind.[104]

Or, as he says in another place:

> We have wrongly separated reason from love and have set them in opposition to each other without basis for doing so, because love and reason are actually one and the same thing. It is a precipitation of thoughts which leads to one side without well-examining everything, but it is nevertheless a reason, and one must not and cannot help but wish that it be so, for otherwise we would be rather poor [disagreeable] machines [creatures]. Let us therefore not exclude reason from love, because it is quite inseparable from it.[105]

---

[102] Pascal says that true religion "must give us an explanation of our opposition to God and to our own good." (*Ibid.*, Sect. VII, No. 430, p. 115.) He also says: "The God of the Christians is a God who makes the soul feel that He is her only good, that her only rest is in Him, that her only delight is in loving Him." (*Ibid.*, No. 543, pp. 145–146.)

[103] *Ibid.*, Sect. II, No. 100, p. 30. This interpretation is reinforced in light of Pascal's undisguised loathing for the corruption of human society which he says is built on mutual deceit. (See No. 100, pp. 30–33.) See also Sect. VII, No. 451, p. 127, where Pascal says: "All men naturally hate one another. They employ lust as far as possible in the service of the public weal. But this is only a [pretence] and a false image of love; for at bottom it is only hate."

[104] *Discours sur les Passions de l'Amour*, p. 121. (Our translation.)

[105] *Ibid.*, p. 136. See also *Pensées*, Sect. V, No. 323, p. 90, where Pascal argues that anyone who is loved is not loved for his self but loved, *i.e.*, admired, for the qualities that his self happens to exhibit.

B. JUDGMENTAL ASPECTS OF PRIMARILY TENDENTIAL CONCEPTIONS OF LOVE

(1) *From Chapter 6*

Søren Kierkegaard

Of the authors who hold binary theories of natural love, Kierkegaard is most explicit about including a judgmental aspect in his primarily tendential theory. One of the ways natural love is distinguished from supernatural love is through the presence of admiration in the former and its absence in the latter. Kierkegaard says that "there must be admiration in earthly love," but adds that "Christianity has never taught that one should admire the neighbor—but one must love him."[106] He connects the admiration that is part of natural love with the "passionate partiality" that is characteristic of a man's love for a woman, for another man, or for his own family or acquaintances. Such loves are invariably partial because they exclude those whom one does not, in some way, admire. Supernatural love is, by definition, a love for *all* men whether one admires them or not; it is directed to all men whether they are superior, equal, or inferior to the lover. The recognition that all men, whatever their character, are worthy of love, is respect rather than admiration. It consists in the awareness that all men not only share a common humanity but that all men "have human equality before God."[107]

In Kierkegaard's view, the admiration present in both the acquisitive and benevolent types of natural love among human beings is very often based upon illusion or "deception," particularly with "egoistically proud"[108] love. The love of Don Juan, the desire for the ideal woman, contains "the sensually idealizing power with which he at once embellishes and overcomes his prey. The reflex of this gigantic passion beautifies and develops its object."[109] Kierkegaard observes that, in general, an "egoistically proud love, because of its pride, regards a deception as impossible." The unwillingness to believe that one is deceived is also characteristic of natural benevolence. "Sympathetic love has the faith which can remove mountains; and the strongest defense is as nothing to it compared with the immovable certainty it possesses that there was no deception."[110]

---

[106] *Works of Love*, Vol. I, Ch. II, p. 45. See also p. 50.
[107] *Ibid.*, p. 50.
[108] *Either/Or*, Vol. I, p. 147.
[109] *Ibid.*, p. 81.
[110] *Ibid.*, p. 147.

Regarding supernatural love, Kierkegaard says, paradoxically, that *"Love believes everything—and is never deceived."* The paradox is resolved, however, when we understand that "to believe everything" means to love unconditionally. Unconditional love is not dependent on the qualities of the object loved and, in this sense, cannot be deceived, *i.e.*, betrayed.[111]

William James

William James understands most human actions as a blend of a variety of factors. Yet, there is a clear sense in which James applies the distinction between thinking and feeling in his discussion of the phenomena of love. Basically, he conceives of love as a tendency, most often as an emotion giving rise to, or resulting from, bodily change. But he also discusses certain expressions of love when a feeling is preceded by and joined with one or another form of judgment or perception. "Our *interest in things*," says James, "means the attention and emotion which the thought of them will excite, and the actions which their presence will evoke."[112] This interest may be either "connate" or "acquired." Even when an emotion or an action is instinctive, James observes that it is frequently occasioned by a fixing of attention, in itself something of a preferential act. "Something rivets my attention fatally, and fatally provokes the . . . response."[113] Particularly in strong emotions, that response has a bodily aspect. So much stress does James lay on this aspect of emotive tendency that he sees little left if it is removed:

> . . . *If we fancy some strong emotion, and then try to abstract from our consciousness of it all the feelings of its bodily symptoms, we find we have nothing left behind,* no "mind-stuff" out of which the emotion can be constituted, and that a cold and neutral state of intellectual perception is all that remains.[114]

These *"bodily changes follow directly the perception of the exciting fact, and that our feeling of the same changes as they occur IS the emotion."*[115] That "perception of the exciting fact" is often conscious, and, even though

111 See *Works of Love*, Vol. II, Ch. II, p. 190.

112 *The Principles of Psychology*, Vol. I. Ch. X, p. 320. He adds: "Thus every species is particularly interested in its own prey or food, its own enemies, its own sexual mates, and its own young. These things *fascinate* by their intrinsic power to do so; they are cared for for their own sakes." (*Ibid.* Italics added.)

113 *Ibid.* See also p. 319. That something is almost always, in James's view, a specific thing and not a general idea. Thus, a man eats not because he knows he must in order to stay alive, nor from any extended calculation of the pleasure of eating, but because the food in front of him attracts his attention and arouses his appetite. (See *ibid.*, Vol. II, Ch. XXIV, p. 386.)

114 *Ibid.*, Vol. II, Ch. XXV, p. 451.

115 *Ibid.*, p. 449.

James denies that it is solely intellectual, he does not deny that it contains something cognitive.[116] Since he always writes of love as tendential—as emotion or feeling and not merely "cold" approval—the judgmental aspect of love is, for him, valuation rather than admiration or respect. Whether the tendency be acquisitive or benevolent, the fixity of attention, the preference or the judgment is directly related to that tendency. "*Love* is the association of the agreeableness of certain sensible experiences with the idea of the object capable of affording them."[117] The association of the feeling with the idea implies some kind of judgment.[118]

(2) *From Chapter 7*

Among authors who affirm that love is primarily tendential and acquisitive, two, Stendhal and Spinoza, are explicit in their assertions that judgmental elements are part of love.

Marie-Henri Beyle (de Stendhal)

For Stendhal, love is a process consisting of a number of stages. Several involve judgmental elements, though the focus of the process (the fourth stage) is clearly a tendential one. This focus is both preceded and followed by varieties of judgment. In Stendhal's theory of love, admiration and valuation each appear twice, once before the arousal of desire and once subsequent to it. Both sets of judgments are part of the whole process Stendhal calls love. The primary difference between the admiration and valuation that precede and follow desire is that the former judgments are based upon *real* qualities in the beloved, whereas the latter are based on imagined qualities.

A man's love for a woman begins with simple admiration. Some quality about her—her charm, her beauty, her intelligence—solicits and receives his approbation. The next two stages ("loving admiration" and "hope") consist of judgments a man makes about the woman not only being good but good for him—what we have called valuation. These in turn produce the acquisitive desire that is the core of Stendhal's conception.

116 See *ibid.*, Vol. I, Ch. X, p. 323. See also Vol. II, Ch. XXIV, p. 410; and Vol. I, Ch. XIV, pp. 599–600.

117 *Ibid.*, Vol. I, Ch. XIV, p. 599. Such association need not be, and most often is not, one that we make with the whole object in all the ways in which it strikes us. Thus, though one aspect of the person loved may please us, others may not. James observes that love for someone can coexist with hatred for him. (See *ibid.*, Vol. II, Ch. XXVI, p. 543.)

118 The only other authors who present binary tendential theories of love with judgmental aspects are Sorokin and Scheler. Sorokin says little about the cognitive aspect of love, and Scheler's theory is an atypical one.

The process does not end there. Other things occur which can be understood either as independent though parallel acts of admiration and valuation, or as judgments which reinforce the original ones. Once beyond the fourth stage the man is driven to perfect his beloved, to embellish the image he has of her until he has rid it of all inadequacy. Prodded by his desire, his imagination continues to impose on the beloved fresh perfections on which his admiration feeds. Doubt is then born in the lover's mind, not about the beloved's beauty, intelligence, etc., but about her constancy. This is followed by his second act of valuation, in which he reaffirms, through self-delusion, that his beloved is constant, *i.e.*, is *still* good for him. Doubt continually reappears and is assuaged by this second judgment as long as the love lasts. In Stendhal's theory, a man's acquisitive desire for a woman (referred to occasionally as love proper) is complemented by the cognitive elements of admiration and valuation.

Benedict de Spinoza

For Spinoza, only one judgmental element—valuation—is present in love. Love is basically acquisitive desire aiming at pleasure and *"accompanied by the idea of an external cause."*[119] This idea of an external cause is an idea of something as good, *i.e.*, useful. It, therefore, is a judgment concerning the value of whatever is loved in relation to the lover's pleasure. Spinoza affirms that this judgment neither occurs before the desire nor is a cause of the desire. On the contrary, the judgment either occurs simultaneously with, or is immediately consequent upon, the emergence of the desire; it is the desire that fixes the judgment. Spinoza states "that in no case do we strive for, wish for, long for, or desire anything, because we deem it to be good, but on the other hand we deem a thing to be good, because we strive for it, wish for it, long for it, or desire it."[120]

(3) From Chapter 8

Among authors who affirm that benevolence is essential to love, three include judgmental aspects in their conception of love: Hartmann, Fromm, and C. S. Lewis.

Nicolai Hartmann

In Hartmann's theory, both "personal" love and "brotherly" love are benevolent in tendency. The conceptions of both loves also contain the

[119] *The Ethics*, Part III, Prop. XIII, Note, p. 140.
[120] *Ibid.*, Prop. IX, *Note*, p. 137.

cognitive notion of valuation. The two are distinguishable, not only by their respective ranges (personal love is extended to one or two others while brotherly love is, in principle, extended to all) but also by the different kind of esteem that each contains. Personal love presupposes and includes admiration; brotherly love presupposes and includes respect.

The esteem in personal love is more for the potential rather than the actual value of the other person. The lover, through love and only through love, discovers the ideal value of the beloved. Because the ideal value is discoverable only through love, only he can see it. The lover is not blind, therefore, but sees something admirable in the beloved which others do not and cannot see. Because what he sees is ideal rather than actual, the tendential consequence of the valuation that succeeds his admiration is his benevolent attempt to realize for the beloved the ideal value he has seen.

The esteem present in brotherly love is respect. It consists in the recognition of the worth of all men simply in virtue of their common humanity. The scope of brotherly love is not universal, however, because of the additional judgment added to respect: valuation. Valuation is the decision to help those with whom one has come into contact and whom one knows to be needy. Respect and such valuation constitute the preface to the tendential aspect of brotherly love, which, as in personal love, is benevolent.

Erich Fromm

Though the essence of Fromm's conception of love is benevolent desire, he also includes a judgmental aspect in it:

> Beyond the element of giving, the active character of love becomes evident in the fact that it always implies certain basic elements, common to all forms of love. These are *care, responsibility, respect,* and *knowledge.*[121]

Explaining the third of these, he says:

> Respect is not fear and awe; it denotes, in accordance with the root of the word (*respicere* = to look at), the ability to see a person as he is, to be aware of his unique individuality.[122]

Fromm speaks of love as an attitude or orientation of character,[123] but he does not understand this attitude to be static. He speaks of it rather as the "active penetration of the other person, in which my desire to know is stilled."[124]

[121] *The Art of Loving,* Ch. II, Sect. 1, p. 26.
[122] *Ibid.,* p. 28.
[123] See *ibid.,* Sect. 3, p. 46.
[124] *Ibid.,* Sect. 1, p. 30. Fromm adds: "If I penetrate to the core, I perceive our identity." (*Ibid.,* Sect. 3, p. 47.)

Fromm says: *"Love is the active concern for the life and the growth of that which we love."*[125] Such concern, however, must be accompanied by approval. "The basic affirmation contained in love is directed toward the beloved person as an incarnation of essentially human qualities."[126]

C. S. Lewis

Among the authors who hold that benevolence is indispensable to love, Lewis most explicitly includes a judgmental aspect in his conception of love. He affirms that the three natural loves among human beings are each made up, in varying proportions, of the three elements of love, which he calls "Appreciative love" (esteem), "Gift-love" (benevolent desire), and "Need-love" (acquisitive desire).[127]

Of friendship he says that "if it is not full of mutual admiration, of Appreciative love, it is not Friendship at all."[128] In the love between a man and a woman, Lewis affirms that "in Eros, a Need, at its most intense, sees the object most intensely as a thing admirable in herself, important far beyond her relation to the lover's need."[129] In the least distinctively human of the natural loves discussed by Lewis, simple affection, the presence of a cognitive element is not so explicitly affirmed. In affection, there is less of admiration or respect, strictly speaking, than of familiarity. But the preference for an acquaintance of long standing implies an almost imperceptible judgment that the familiar is better than the strange.

The presence of some kind of judgment in all loves, however, is affirmed by Lewis when he says that any natural love is made up of some combination of all three of the elements he uses to analyze love.[130] He most emphatically links esteem with natural benevolence when he says that "natural Gift-love is always directed to objects which the lover finds in some way intrinsically lovable."[131]

[125] *Ibid.*, Sect. 1, p. 26.
[126] *Ibid.*, Sect. 3, p. 59.
[127] See *The Four Loves*, Ch. II, p. 33.
[128] *Ibid.*, Ch. IV, p. 124.
[129] *Ibid.*, Ch. V, p. 136.
[130] Lewis does say that perhaps "Need-love" can momentarily exist apart from the others, but only for a short time. (See *ibid.*, Ch. II, p. 33.)
[131] *Ibid.*, Ch. VI, p. 177.

C. Judgmental Notions in Relation to Wholly Tendential Conceptions of Love

(1) *From Chapters 5 and 6*

A number of the authors who have binary and completely tendential theories of love relate their conception of love to one or another of our cognitive notions. Some understand judgment as preface to love (or to certain types of love), while others understand it as a consequence of love (or certain types of love). However important the cognitive notions may be for understanding their complete theories of love, all of the following authors think of judgment or perception of value as separate from love itself.

Plato

Plato's conception of love, though tendential, must be understood in terms of his theory of recollection or learning, a theory involving non-tendential notions. In the Platonic view, the most important love is the desire for knowledge or wisdom, a desire that, in some sense, is the paradigm of all others, since all desires are said to aim at the lasting. The desire to know, however, not only aims at knowledge but is preceded by knowledge. For Plato, cognition is recognition. The soul that is striving to learn is actually striving to recall the invisible realities or eternal ideas that it knew, to a greater or lesser extent, in its life before it was joined with the body. Joined with the body, its knowledge of the enduring realities is obscured, and it strives to recall them in the course of encountering, through the senses, their reflections and images—the things in the visible world.

> For the soul which has never seen the truth can never pass into human form. For a human being must understand a general conception formed by collecting into a unity by means of reason the many perceptions of the senses; and this is a recollection of those things which our soul once beheld.[132]

[132] *Phaedrus,* 249 B–C, p. 481. "For, as has been said, every soul of man has by the law of nature beheld the realities, otherwise it would not have entered into a human being, but it is not easy for all souls to gain from earthly things a recollection of those realities, either for those which had but a brief view of them at that earlier time, or for those which, after falling to earth, were so unfortunate as to be turned toward unrighteousness through some evil communications and to have forgotten the holy sights they once saw. Few then are left which retain an adequate recollection of them." (*Ibid.,* 250 A, p. 483.)

The eternal ideas inspire the love that draws the soul onward in its search for the truth. Their original perception or their reperception, however, is no part of love itself. When knowledge is achieved, love ceases: ". . . those who are already wise no longer love wisdom, whether they be gods or men."[133]

A human being is loved, in Plato's theory, because of the qualities he personifies, which remind the lover's soul of the real and permanent. Beauty is the idea most frequently involved, as it is the only one whose reflections can be perceived through the highest of the physical senses—sight.

> But beauty, as I said before, shone in brilliance among those visions; and since we came to earth we have found it shining most clearly through the clearest of our senses; for sight is the sharpest of the physical senses, though wisdom is not seen by it, for wisdom would arouse terrible love, if such a clear image of it were granted as would come through sight, and the same is true of the other lovely realities; but beauty alone has this privilege, and therefore it is most clearly seen and loveliest.[134]

Commenting on the growing intimacy between lover and beloved, Socrates says:

> And as this intimacy continues and the lover comes near and touches the beloved in the gymnasia and in their general intercourse, then the fountain of that stream which Zeus, when he was in love with Ganymede, called "desire" flows copiously upon the lover; and some of it flows into him, and some, when he is filled, overflows outside; and just as the wind or an echo rebounds from smooth, hard surfaces and returns whence it came, so the stream of beauty passes back into the beautiful one through the eyes, the natural inlet to the soul, where it reanimates the passages of the feathers, waters them and makes the feathers begin to grow, filling the soul of the loved one with love.[135]

These passages, together with the emphasis on love as tendency in the *Symposium*,[136] make it clear that Plato is numbered among those authors for whom the notions of judgment and perception, though essential to an understanding of their theories of love, are nevertheless no part of what they understand love to be.

[133] *Lysis*, 218 A, pp. 53–55.
[134] *Phaedrus*, 250 D–E, p. 485.
[135] *Ibid.*, 255 B–D, pp. 499–501. See also 250 E–252 E, pp. 487–491.
[136] See the *Symposium*, 184 A–185 B, pp. 117–121.

Aurelius Augustine

In dealing with knowledge in relation to love, Augustine says: "For it is possible something may be known and not loved: but I ask whether it is possible that what is not known can be loved."[137] Augustine's reply to his own question is: "Let no one say, I do not know what I love."[138] Even though Augustine repeatedly asserts that "we know most assuredly that nothing can be loved unless it be known,"[139] he is careful to indicate that complete knowledge of the beloved is not a prerequisite. Only total ignorance of the beloved precludes love "for that cannot be loved which is altogether unknown."[140]

The knowledge of the beloved that is the cause of love is not necessarily knowledge of that individual. It is more the knowledge of the good qualities or virtues that a given individual is believed by the lover to possess or personify. "The man therefore who is believed to be righteous, is loved through that form and truth which he who loves discerns and understands within himself."[141] Augustine uses this analysis, wherein love is always primarily of the qualities that are personified rather than of the person as such, to explain that

> love often arises from hearsay, when the reputation of anything for beauty inflames the mind to the seeing and enjoying it; since the mind knows generically wherein consists the beauties of corporeal things, from having seen them very frequently, and since there exists within a faculty of approving that which outwardly is longed for. And when this happens, the love that is called forth is not a thing wholly unknown, since its genus is thus known. But when we love a good man whose face we never saw, we love him from the knowledge of his virtues, which virtues we know in the truth itself.[142]

The knowledge the lover has of goodness and the belief that the beloved possesses good qualities are distinct. If the lover's belief is found to be false, then, although the love of the qualities remains unchanged, it is no longer extended to the beloved who was thought to possess them; or, if it is, it is extended for therapeutic reasons.

[137] *On The Trinity*, Book VIII, Ch. IV, p. 207.
[138] *Ibid.*, Ch. VIII, p. 218.
[139] *Ibid.*, Book X, Ch. I, p. 243. See also Book IX, Ch. III, p. 225.
[140] *Lectures or Tractates on the Gospel According to St. John*, Vol. II, Tractate XCVI, p. 369. See also *On The Trinity*, Book X, Ch. I, pp. 242, 244–245.
[141] *Ibid.*, Book VIII, Ch. VI, p. 215.
[142] *Ibid.*, Book X, Ch. I, p. 241.

I love therefore the faithful and courageous man with a pure and genuine love. But if he were to confess to me in the course of conversation, or were through unguardedness to reveal about himself in any way, that either he believes anything unseemly of God, and desires too somewhat carnal in Him, and that he bore these torments on behalf of such an error, or from the desire of money for which he hoped, or from empty greediness of human praise: *immediately it follows that the love with which I was borne towards him, displeased, and as it were repelled, and taken away from an unworthy man*, remains in that form, after which, believing him such as I did, I had loved him; unless perhaps I have come to love him to this end, that he may become such, while I have found him not to be such in fact.[143]

For Augustine, some knowledge of the good is the indispensable prelude to love. The belief that the beloved possesses good qualities determines either the existence of a certain love for the beloved, or at least the motive for which the love is extended. Whether the spur be belief or knowledge, love is a direct function of the judgment or perception of something as good.

Marcus Tullius Cicero

In Cicero's dialogue *De Amicitia*, Laelius, after noting that "it is love (*amor*), from which the word 'friendship' (*amicitia*) is derived,"[144] asserts that "he who takes reverence from friendship, takes away its brightest jewel."[145]

Though it is asserted that admiration is prerequisite to true friendship, it is not a part of that love, but rather the prelude or immediate cause of it.

. . . Virtue is complete harmony, in her is permanence, in her is fidelity; and when she has raised her head and shown her own light and has seen and recognized the same light in another, she moves towards it and in turn receives its beams; as a result love or friendship leaps into flame.[146]

And though admiration precedes true friendship, it is not a condition for all loves.

Therefore, I repeat the injunction, for it should be said again and again: you should love your friend after you have appraised him; you should not appraise him after you have begun to love him.[147]

143 *Ibid.*, Book IX, Ch. VI, p. 232. (Italics added.)
144 *De Amicitia*, VIII, 26, p. 139.
145 *Ibid.*, XXII, 82–83, p. 191.
146 *Ibid.*, XXVII, 100, p. 207. This admiration must be mutual, since "friendship cannot exist except among good men." (*Ibid.*, V, 18, p. 127.)
147 *Ibid.*, XXII, 85, pp. 191–193. See also XXI, 79, p. 187.

The notion of esteem, therefore, is relevant to Cicero's theory of love in the sense that it signifies a judgment that is an important prelude to at least one of the loves that theory encompasses.

Aristotle

In his theory of love, Aristotle mentions love (*eros*), friendly feeling (*filesis*), and friendship (*filia*).[148] His analysis of love is devoted, for the most part, to friendship. Of the three friendships he lists, that of utility, that of pleasure, and that of virtue, only the last is true friendship. And, as in Cicero's theory, mutual admiration is presupposed. In discussing the friendship of virtue, Aristotle says:

> . . . such friendship requires time and familiarity; as the proverb says, men cannot know each other till they have "eaten salt together"; nor, can they admit each other to friendship or be friends till each has been found lovable and been trusted by each. Those who quickly show the marks of friendship to each other wish to be friends, but are not friends unless they both are lovable and know the fact; for a wish for friendship may arise quickly, but friendship does not.[149]

Thomas Aquinas

Aquinas says that "good is not the object of the appetite [*love*], except as apprehended."[150] Even for human beings, this apprehension need not be strictly intellectual, but, whether its medium is the mind or the senses, it must involve awareness of something as good.

> For the movement of the appetite cannot tend to anything, either by hoping or loving, unless that thing be apprehended by the sense or by the intellect.[151]

Aquinas' answer to his own question, "Whether Knowledge Is a Cause of Love?" is clear and emphatic. For him, "knowledge is the cause of love for the same reason as good is, which can be loved only if known."[152]

[148] See *Nicomachean Ethics*, Book VIII, Chs. 2–5, 1155b–1157b, pp. 1059–64; and Book IX, Chs. 4–5, 1166b–1167a, pp. 1082–83.
[149] *Ibid.*, Book VIII, Ch. 3, 1156b, pp. 1061–62.
[150] *Summa Theologica*, Part I-II, Q. 27, Art. 2, Answer, Vol. I, p. 707.
[151] *Ibid.*, Q. 62, Art. 4, Answer, Vol. I, p. 853. Aquinas also says: "Love results from knowledge; for, nothing is loved except it be first known." (*Ibid.*, Part I, Q. 60, Art. 1, p. 297.)
[152] *Ibid.*, Part I-II, Q. 27, Art. 2, Answer, Vol. I, p. 707.

Dante Alighieri

For Dante, as for Aquinas, the prerequisite for human love is apprehension of the good. Dante, in his ascent through Purgatory, asks Virgil to say what love is. Virgil replies:

> "Direct the keen eyes of the intelligence
>   Toward me," he said, "and the error thou wilt prove
>   Of those, blind, who of leading make pretence.
> The mind which is created apt to love,
>   Soon as by pleasure it is stirred to act,
>   To every pleasing thing is quick to move.
> Your apprehension from a thing of fact
>   Draweth an image, shown to the inward view,
>   So that perforce it doth the mind attract.
> And if, being turned, it is inclined thereto,
>   The inclination is love: nature it is,
>   Which is through pleasure knit within ye anew.
> Then, just as fire to the upper region flies
>   By reason of its form which, where it best
>   Endureth in its matter, is born to rise,
> Even so the mind is with desire possessed,
>   Which is a motion of spirit, and cannot be,
>   Till the thing loved rejoiceth it, at rest."[153]

In Dante's view, the sequence for love is the apprehension of the good, inclination toward it, and then movement. Apprehension of the good, though presupposed by love, is not part of it. Love only begins with the mind's (or will's) inclination toward the beloved, an initial tendency that gives rise to or blends with desire. But, as for Aquinas, awareness of the attractiveness of the beloved is presupposed.[154]

One of the most celebrated of loves was Dante's own attachment for Beatrice. The veneration in which he held her was regarded by him as not only essential to his love but also to his salvation. His apprehension of her beauty and, through it, her goodness gave rise to a desire for perfection which draws him onward in his journey through Paradise.

The original vision that inspires love in Dante is more of Beatrice's beauty than her virtue. Dante describes his first encounter with the living Beatrice thus:

> And when I perceived her, all my senses were overpowered by the great lordship that Love obtained, finding himself so near unto that most gracious

[153] *The Divine Comedy*, "Purgatorio," Canto XVIII, Lines 16–33, p. 278.
[154] This is particularly clear in Dante's analysis of friendship. See *Convivio*, Tractate III, p. 167, where Dante refers to virtue as the efficient cause of friendship.

being, until nothing but the spirits of sight remained to me; and even these remained driven out of their own instruments because Love entered into that honoured place of theirs, that so he might the better behold her.[155]

In *La Vita Nuova*, which contains many of Dante's meditations on love and on his own love, a friend asks what love is. Dante answers with the following sonnet:

Love and the gentle heart are one same thing,
    Even as the wise man in his ditty saith.
    Each, of itself, would be such life in death
    As rational soul bereft of reasoning.
    'Tis Nature makes them when she loves: a king
Love is, whose palace where he sojourneth
Is call'd the Heart; there draws he quiet breath
At first, with brief or longer slumbering.
Then beauty seen in virtuous womankind
    Will make the eyes desire, and through the heart
    Send the desiring of the eyes again;
Where often it abides so long enshrined
    That Love at length out of his sleep will start.
    And women feel the same for worthy men.[156]

Writing of Beatrice in the *Convivio*, Dante uses the image of his perfect lady as the symbol of philosophy:

For her speech, by reason of her loftiness and sweetness, engenders in the mind of the listener a thought of love, which I call a heavenly spirit because its origin is from above, and its message comes from above as has been told already. From this thought we go on to a sure opinion that this is the marvellous Lady of virtue. And her acts on account of their sweetness and moderation cause love to be awakened and felt wherever the faculty of love is sown in the soil of a good nature.[157]

The spiritual dimension of Dante's love for Beatrice is more intense after her death than before. It is, in fact, what carries him through the last stages of Purgatory and through Paradise after taking his leave of Virgil. Beatrice first appears in *The Divine Comedy* as a veiled lady whom Dante sees "by no recognition of the eye." Of this recognition he says:

But virtue invisible that went out from her
Felt old love seize me in all its mastery.[158]

[155] *La Vita Nuova*, Ch. XIV, p. 566.
[156] *Ibid.*, Ch. XX, pp. 577–578.
[157] *Convivio*, Tractate III, pp. 150–151. See also pp. 124–127.
[158] *The Divine Comedy*, "Purgatorio," Canto XXX, Lines 37–39, p. 345.

The seizing he refers to here as elsewhere has the character of desire or tendency. But with Dante's intense love for Beatrice as with all other specifically human loves, a judgment or perception is presupposed.[159]

Baldesar Castiglione

Affirming that knowledge must precede the tendency of love, Castiglione, in *The Book of the Courtier*, has one of his principal speakers, Pietro Bembo, say:

> I say, then, that, according to the definition of ancient sages, love is nothing but a certain desire to enjoy beauty; and, as our desire is only for things that are known, knowledge must always precede desire, which by its nature turns to the good but in itself is blind and does not know the good. Therefore nature has ordained that to every cognitive power there shall be joined an appetitive power; and as in our soul there are three modes of cognition, namely, by sense, by reason, and by intellect: so, from sense comes appetite, which we have in common with animals; from reason comes choice, which is proper to man; from intellect, whereby man can communicate with the angels, comes will. Thus, even as sense knows only those things which the senses perceive, appetite desires these and no other; and even as intellect is turned solely to the contemplation of intelligible things, the will feeds only upon spiritual good.[160]

Applying this analysis to human love, specifically the love between a man and a woman, the Magnifico, the principal interlocutor in the third section of the book, comments that

> those men who are too precipitate and make advances so presumptuously, with a kind of fury and stubbornness, often lose these favors, and deservedly; for every noble lady deems herself to be little esteemed by one who fails to show her respect, seeking to gain her love before he has served her.[161]

Describing the ideal court lady, the Magnifico cites the dangers of succumbing to those who offer nothing but low love or indiscriminate desire:

> Hence, I would not have my Court Lady seem wantonly to offer herself to anyone who desires her, doing her best to captivate the eyes and affections of all who gaze upon her, but I would have her by her merits and virtuous behavior, by her charm and her grace, instill in the minds of all who look

[159] See *Convivio*, Tractate III, pp. 134–135.
[160] *The Book of the Courtier*, Book IV, 51, p. 336.
[161] *Ibid.*, Book III, 65, p. 270.

upon her the true love that lovable things deserve, and the respect that deprives anyone of hope who would think any dishonorable thing.[162]

Castiglione, as many other writers in the tradition of courtly love, is less concerned with an analysis of the nature of love than with what distinguishes high, true, or pure love from sheer carnal desire. Whether the love be high or low it is always tendential.[163] In the case of high love, the desire is inspired by veneration for the beloved, by esteem of a very high order. In the case of low love, the desire is inspired by an appreciation of the carnal qualities of the beloved and her easy availability. But whether it be admiration or valuation, the judgment is prior to and not part of love.

Sigmund Freud

Freud connects both esteem and valuation with his conception of love. Esteem in the form of admiration, or what he calls "idealization," is frequently concurrent with or consequent upon love; it never precedes love. Valuation, on the other hand, precedes love but does not, strictly speaking, give rise to it.

Idealization accompanies normal parental love. In Freud's view, the child often is seen in terms of the personal perfections the parents have sought for themselves. A high standard of "ego-ideal" is shifted by the parents onto the child and represents the revival of their own childish narcissism.[164] Idealization also can be present (through the same process of transfer) as a corollary of the love inclination between individuals of the same age, when it often takes a sensual form. Freud claims that, if the sensual tendencies are repressed, "the illusion is produced that the object has come to be sensually loved on account of its spiritual merits, whereas on the contrary these merits may really only have been lent to it by its sensual charm." Again Freud understands this phenomenon as a function of the transfer of the ego-ideal to the beloved; in fact what is being admired is the lover's glorified notion of himself. What happens is that "a considerable amount of narcissistic libido overflows on to the object." If the sensual

---

[162] *Ibid.*, 57, pp. 263–264.

[163] In the tradition of courtly literature, and in many other writings, the distinction between spiritual and carnal love, high and low love, or even love and lust is not parallel to the distinction between thinking and feeling. All the loves of which these authors speak are desires, while what we have called esteem is not. Loves are distinguished in various ways. Desire that is controlled or guided by reason is often called good love or spiritual love; that which is uncontrolled (and usually of the body) is often called low or vulgar love. The distinction many of these authors make between reasonable love and unreasonable love should not obscure the fact that all love, for them, is in the sphere of tendency.

[164] See *On Narcissism: an Introduction*, pp. 48–49. See also pp. 57–59.

inclination is intense and particularly if it is frustrated, the idealization of and devotion to the love object becomes correspondingly extreme. Freud summarizes this situation as follows: *"The object has taken the place of the ego ideal."*[165]

In either case the judgment is not one that concerns the real excellences of the beloved nor one that is uninfluenced by the libidinal or love tendencies that precede or accompany it. On the contrary, Freud maintains that idealization can only be understood as a direct result of libidinal urges and that, consequently, the admiration extended to the beloved is, more often than not, based upon a construct of the lover. Since the libidinal energy of the lover, in most cases, not only feeds, but feeds on, the illusion created, admiration is a judgment controlled by an appetite and behind which an appetite lurks.[166]

For Freud, valuation, or the "choice" of a loved object does not always occur on the conscious level and is invariably determined by factors in the unconscious. What is important to note about valuation, about the selection of one person or type of person rather than another as an object of love, is that this determination does not give rise to love but rather is merely the occasion for the outflow of previously and continuously existing love energy onto a specific object. Prior to the valuation, the love energy or libido exists but is unfocused and has no real object. Since Freud is a determinist, the selection of a love object in any given case must be understood in terms of current and past factors which have decisive influences on a person's psychological and emotional life. In Freudian terms, the demands of the id are repressed by taboos and decisive childhood experiences (mostly with the parents). These are stored in the super ego and further checked by the ego's weighing of these already altered demands against the difficulties posed by the external realities with which only the ego has contact. It is through this process that another person, through whom a person's libidinal energy is released in one or another form, is selected.[167] That selection, even though it is arrived at largely through unconscious

[165] *Group Psychology and the Analysis of the Ego*, Ch. VIII, p. 74–75, *passim*.

[166] Freud also discusses instances of abnormal love when admiration or idealization *cannot* be present if a certain type of (neurotic) individual is to love a particular person. In these cases the other person must be degraded before he can become the object of sensual desires. As soon as and not before the sensual object has been degraded in these cases, "sensual feeling can have free play, considerable sexual capacity and a high degree of pleasure can be developed." (*Contributions to the Psychology of Love. The Most Prevalent Form of Degradation in Erotic Life*, p. 208.)

[167] The valuation may differ depending on whether it is a prelude to acquisitive or benevolent desire.

processes, is some kind of judgment of valuation and is separate from the tendency Freud calls love.

(2) *From Chapter 7*

Plotinus

Of the authors whose conceptions of love include only acquisitive desire, several within the Platonic tradition echo the Platonic point that the arousal of love is occasioned by the glimpse of invisible reality through the perception of images in the visible world. Plotinus says:

> Take an example from love: so long as the attention is upon the visible form, love has not entered: when from that outward form the lover elaborates within himself, in his own partless soul, an immaterial image, then it is that love is born, then the lover longs for the sight of the beloved to make that fading image live again.[168]

Marsilio Ficino

Ficino, in his commentary on Plato's *Symposium*, places the emphasis on the perception of beauty when he discusses the "two Venuses" in the soul, each accompanied by its distinctive love:

> When the beauty of a human body first meets our eyes, the mind, which is the first Venus in us, worships and adores the human beauty as an image of the divine beauty, and through the first, it is frequently aroused to the second.[169]

Giovanni Pico della Mirandola

Pico, in his treatise *A Platonick Discourse upon Love*, reflects this view and continues to emphasize the importance of beauty in stimulating love:

> As Sight, so Beauty (its object) is twofold; (the two Venus's celebrated by Plato and our Poet): Sensible, called Vulgar Venus; Intellectual in Ideas (which are the object of the Intellect as colour of sight), nam'd Celestial Venus. Love also is twofold, Vulgar and Celestiall; for as Plato saith, "There must necessarily be as many Loves as Venus's."[170]

[168] *The Enneads,* Ennead VI, Tractate 7, p. 587.
[169] *Commentary on Plato's "Symposium,"* p. 143.
[170] *A Platonick Discourse upon Love,* Book II, p. 28.

Andreas Capellanus

The gentle love between a man and a woman of which Andreas writes, though not exclusively sexual, is acquisitive in tendency. Yet, even though Andreas thinks of love as completely tendential, the veneration in which the courtly lover holds the beloved is a part, not of what love is but of what gives the special love relationship that concerns him one of its most distinguishing characteristics. Obviously, the lover must choose a beloved; but the way in which he pursues his love is determined by the absence or presence of a certain idealizing reverence or awe. In Andreas' view, "low love" or "animal passion"—unrestrained sexuality—presupposes no such veneration. The object of such a desire is seen merely as a convenient means for the lover to slake his momentary impulse. Basing his analysis of love, in part, on class distinctions, Andreas even recommends such love as appropriate between gentlemen and peasant women.

The high or "true" love with which Andreas primarily is concerned, however (either in its "mixed" or "pure" form), must be preceded by admiration. He maintains that only three things can produce the esteem that is followed by courtly love: ". . . a beautiful figure, excellence of character, [and] extreme readiness of speech."[171] The lover can be struck by any one or any combination of these three traits. The awe thereby produced has no moderating effect on the desire that seizes the lover (indeed, it often intensifies it) but it does produce a wilful restraint on the lover's physical impulses. In the highest case it even inspires him to try to make himself estimable in the eyes of the beloved.[172] A lady in one of the dialogues Andreas constructs admits that the proper lover must have moral qualifications: "I admit that loving is a good thing and that we must give our love only to the good."[173]

The lover's aim is his lady, her body, her approval, her company. In another sense it is also the perpetuation of his love. The lover, accordingly, plays upon his desire, promotes the idea of the unattainability of his beloved, perpetuating his love as a kind of agonizing bliss. He believes that to live without desire is hardly to live at all. Love is his supreme happiness and the more frustrated the better. As the sexual reward often is desired for

[171] *The Art of Courtly Love*, Book I, Ch. VI, p. 33.
[172] In Andreas' dialogue between a man and a woman of the middle class, the man, at one point, says: "I give you all the thanks of which I am capable that you have so prudently promised that after much labor I may have your love, and I hope that neither I nor anyone else may enjoy the love of a woman as worthy as you are until I have acquired it with much labor." (*Ibid.*, Ch. VI, Dialogue 1, p. 44.)
[173] *Ibid.*, Dialogue 6, p. 88.

the sake of the fantasy of which it is, in some sense, the spur, it may be postponed indefinitely or dispensed with altogether. But the desire for it must remain, for this is the stuff out of which all love is made—low or high. The lover's idea of the blessedness of his lady, nourished by his intense yearning, is the lover's way of perpetuating his love indefinitely.[174]

Arthur Schopenhauer

For Schopenhauer, the tendency of love is not only acquisitive but completely sexual. His remarks about thinking or judging in relation to love are directed solely to the question of the "illusion" which he says often accompanies the pursuit of the sexual impulse. He accounts for this illusion primarily in terms of the competing interests of the species and of the individual in sexual matters. The interest of the species, *i.e.*, reproduction, impels a man toward a certain woman or a certain type of woman. That woman, according to Schopenhauer, is often the worst, or at least a bad choice, from the point of view of the man's personal happiness. Reinforced by the tremendous power of the sexual impulse, the man tries to cover that fact by bestowing on the woman all sorts of perfections which support the illusion that she is good for him.

> That which in the higher grades of love imparts such a tinge of poetry and sublimeness to his thoughts, which gives them even a transcendental and hyperphysical tendency, on account of which he seems to lose sight altogether of his real, very physical aim, is at bottom this, that he is now inspired by the spirit of the species whose affairs are infinitely more important than all those which concern mere individuals.[175]

However, the illusion is short-lived.

> Because the passion depended upon an illusion, which represented that which has only value for the species as valuable for the individual, the deception must vanish after the attainment of the end of the species.[176]

The admiration that accompanies a man's love for a woman endures, therefore, only as long as sexual desire lasts.

Schopenhauer also discusses the factors affecting a lover's preference for one woman over another, those that influence the judgment that gives rise to and focuses the sexual impulse. Schopenhauer claims that the lover's

---

[174] "Love gets its name (*amor*) from the word for hook (*amus*), which means 'to capture' or 'to be captured,' for he who is in love is captured in the chains of desire and wishes to capture someone else with his hook." (*Ibid.*, Ch. III, p. 31.)

[175] *The World as Will and Idea*, Vol. III, Ch. XLIV, p. 366.

[176] *Ibid.*, p. 370. See also pp. 339, 361–362.

valuation is, first and foremost, determined by age: "Youth without beauty has still always attraction; beauty without youth has none." The second consideration is health. The third is the skeletal shape of the woman (with emphasis on smallness of feet and good teeth). Then comes "fulness of flesh," etc.[177] All of these biological characteristics, which bear directly on the aim of the species, *i.e.*, the reproduction and improvement of the race, determine a man's preference for a partner.

Denis de Rougemont

De Rougemont sees the same phenomenon of unavoidable illusion in romantic love, as does Schopenhauer, but he explains it differently. In romance, the lover is seeking something natural love cannot provide. In an effort to find in natural love (*eros*) something that only a higher, super-natural love (*agape*) can give, the lover heaps upon the beloved a host of imaginary qualities. He does so in a vain effort to try, somehow, to fill the deficiency from which his passion springs. Since reality cannot satisfy the passion, it thrives on "absence, dream, and nostalgia." It can exist only on what is half seen and on the promise of the unexpected and ecstatic. As the relationship between the lover and the beloved "is essentially an imaginary one," both the admiration and valuation that sustain the lover's passion reflect only a projected image of another fashioned according to the lover's need.[178]

In sharp contrast is the perception of the beloved which accompanies "real," Christian love for the actual person. Such perception is based on reality and involves respect.[179] Women who are respected rather than idealized are seen as "persons instead of being reflections or means."[180] And what is respected "is what cannot be used by man as an instrument or thing."[181]

(3) *From Chapter 8*

Theodor Reik

Among the authors who affirm that benevolence is essential to love (or to a love relationship), Reik is the most explicit about the essential prior conditions:

[177] *Ibid.*, p. 352. See also p. 351.
[178] See *The Crisis of the Modern Couple*, pp. 109–110. See also *Love in the Western World*, Book IV, Ch. 17, pp. 224–227.
[179] See *The Crisis of the Modern Couple*, pp. 109–110.
[180] *Love in the Western World*, Book VII, Ch. 5, p. 313.
[181] *Ibid.*, p. 313, fn. 1.

In order to love someone we have to admire him or her. We need not always know what we admire in the object; we need not even know that we do admire, but only that we feel attracted or fascinated. It seems, however, that admiration is a necessary feeling of incipient love. I do not assert, of course, that admiration must lead to love, but only that it is a preliminary condition which is absolutely essential.

The admiration to which Reik refers has a special character. It cannot be the esteem someone may have for a person who possesses qualities that the admirer also possesses. "It is the kind of admiration that makes one feel small, inferior, unworthy by comparison with the object."[182] All love presupposes this kind of admiration since all "love is founded on a dissatisfaction with oneself. It is an attempt to escape from oneself in search of a better, an ideal self."[183]

Reik's assertion that envy "is one of the most important factors that necessarily precede the formation of love,"[184] is based on his understanding of love as that therapeutic measure most frequently employed by human beings to find their perfection. According to him, the "better self" that is sought is an "ego-ideal" that each human being builds up in the course of his development. Tacit admission of having fallen short of this ideal is given when one person envies another for possessing the qualities he lacks and would like to have, *i.e.*, are part of his ego-ideal. Admiration for another consists of a recognition of the possession of those qualities by another. And Reik adds that, *"the reverse or wrong side of this admiration for the love-object is envy."*[185] He also observes that this

> dissatisfaction with ourselves makes us especially sensitive and inclined to feel envious or jealous when we meet a person who has the qualities which we lack and who seems to be satisfied and self-contained. This object is not a substitute of the ego-ideal but can become one later on if love takes the place of envy and grudging admiration.[186]

Only those individuals who experience this special kind of admiration are capable of love. Such individuals are not destined to love, however, since this kind of admiration is only an essential preliminary condition, not a necessary cause. The admiration is "not a cool, dispassionate, impersonal kind of appreciation," and the valuation to which it can lead may be a preface to hatred as well as to love.[187] When it does lead to love, there is a mutual interchange.

---

182 *A Psychologist Looks at Love*, Ch. II, Sect. 3, p. 44.
183 *Ibid.*, Ch. III, Sect. 14, p. 190. "When people are entirely satisfied with their actual selves, love is impossible." (*Ibid.*, Ch. II, Sect. 2, p. 43.)
184 *Ibid.*, Sect. 3, p. 47.
185 *Ibid.*, p. 45.
186 *Ibid.*, p. 49.
187 See *ibid.*, p. 44.

Two people who love each other are interchanging their ego-ideals. That they love each other means they love the ideal of themselves in the other one.[188]

José Ortega y Gasset

Love is said by Ortega to be distinct from all intellectual functions, "perception, consideration, thought, recall, imagination."[189] However, he does claim that love must be preceded by an evaluation of sorts. For love to emerge it is essential for the lover *"to take notice"* of the beloved.

Such favor in attention knows nothing yet of love but is a preliminary condition to it. Without the first taking notice, the amorous phenomenon cannot take place, although the latter need not necessarily follow.[190]

For Ortega, such a judgment is not careful, cold, and premeditated. It is rather a state comparable to hypnosis or mystical concentration—a fixity of attention. In describing it he says that "what we do is to isolate one object to an abnormal degree and remain with it alone, fixed and paralyzed, like a rooster before a hypnotic white line."[191]

Such attention involves approval; for the beloved not only is perceived but her virtues are isolated and magnified. In discussing the love between a man and a woman, Ortega makes it particularly clear that the arousal of such love is contingent upon the perception of some excellence in the beloved:

Instead of existing prior to its object, it is always born in response to a being who appears before us, and who, by virtue of some eminent quality which he possesses, stimulates the erotic process.[192]

---

[188] *Ibid.*, p. 42. All of these remarks apply most strongly to that love relationship between a man and a woman that Reik calls "romance." Reik, however, also applies the same analysis to the other types of love that he mentions. He says, for example, that the "unconscious effect of envy and jealousy in friendship cannot be denied but it is not as concentrated as it is in love." (*Ibid.*, p. 172.)

[189] *On Love*, "Love in Stendhal," p. 46.

[190] *Ibid.*, "The Role of Choice in Love," p. 132. See also p. 97.

[191] *Ibid.*, "Love in Stendhal," p. 55. Ortega also says: "Attention is the supreme instrument of personality; it is the apparatus which regulates our mental lives. When paralyzed, it does not leave us any freedom of movement. In order to save ourselves, we would have to reopen the field of our consciousness, and to achieve that it would be necessary to introduce other objects into its focus to rupture the beloved's exclusiveness. If in the paroxysm of falling in love we could suddenly see the beloved in the normal perspective of our attention, her magic power would be destroyed. In order, however, to gain this perspective we would have to focus our attention upon other things, that is, we would have to emerge from our own consciousness, which is totally absorbed by the object that we love." (*Ibid.*, p. 56.)

[192] *Ibid.*, p. 40. Love "is only produced when we are confronted with something which we judge to be perfect. Let the reader try to imagine a state of love—of sexual love—in which the object is totally lacking in any trace of excellence in the eyes of the one in love, and he will see how impossible it is." (*Ibid.*, p. 38.)

Ortega adds, in commenting on Stendhal's theory of "crystallization," that the admiration and the valuation that precede love are based more on reality than unreality. He argues that "it is unlikely that any normal activity of man is based upon an essential error." Even if there is an illusion, he still insists that "some grounds of affinity" must exist between the real and the imaginary beloved.[193]

193 See *ibid.*, "The Role of Choice in Love," pp. 110–111.

Bibliography

Abraham, Karl. *Selected Papers of Karl Abraham*. Trans. by Douglas Bryan and Alix Strachey. London: Leonard & Virginia Woolf at the Hogarth Press, 1927.

Albert the Great. *Summa Theologica*, Vol. 32. Borgnet Edition. Paris: Paris Vives, 1895.

Alexander, Franz. *Fundamentals of Psychoanalysis*. New York: W. W. Norton & Company, 1948.

Andreas Capellanus. *The Art of Courtly Love*. Trans. by John Jay Parry. New York: Frederick Ungar Publishing Company, 1959.

Aquinas, Thomas. *On Aristotle's Love and Friendship*. Trans. by Pierre Conway. Providence, R.I.: Providence College Press, 1951.

————. *On Charity (De Caritate)*. Trans. by Lottie H. Kendzierski. Milwaukee, Wis.: Marquette University Press, 1960.

————. *On the Truth of the Catholic Faith (Summa Contra Gentiles)*, Book III. Trans. by Vernon J. Bourke. Garden City, N.Y.: Hanover House, 1956.

————. *Summa Theologica*. 3 vols. Trans. by Fathers of the English Dominican Province. New York: Benziger Brothers, 1947–48.

————. *Treatise on the Passions*. In *Summa Theologica. Ibid.*

————. *Truth*. Vol. II, trans. by James V. McGlynn, S.J.; Vol. III, trans. by Robert W. Schmidt, S.J. Chicago: Henry Regnery Company, 1953–54.

Aristotle. *Eudemian Ethics (Ethica Eudemia)*. Trans. by J. Solomon. In Vol. IX, *The Works of Aristotle*. Ed. by W. D. Ross. New York: Oxford University Press, 1940.

————. *Magna Moralia*. Trans. by St. George Stock. In Vol. IX, *The Works of Aristotle. Ibid.*

————. *Metaphysics (Metaphysica)*. Trans. by W. D. Ross. In *The Basic Works of Aristotle*. Ed. by Richard McKeon. New York: Random House, 1941.

————. *Nicomachean Ethics (Ethica Nicomachea)*. Trans. by W. D. Ross. In *The Basic Works of Aristotle. Ibid.*

————. *On the Soul (De Anima)*. Trans. by J. A. Smith. In *The Basic Works of Aristotle. Ibid.*

————. *Prior Analytics (Analytica Priora)*. Trans. by A. J. Jenkinson. In *The Basic Works of Aristotle. Ibid.*

————. *Rhetoric (Rhetorica)*. Trans. by W. Rhys Roberts. In Vol. XI, *The Works of Aristotle*. Ed. by W. D. Ross. New York: Oxford University Press, 1940.

————. *Topics (Topica)*. Trans. by W. A. Pickard-Cambridge. In Vol. I, *The Works of Aristotle. Ibid.*

Augustine, Aurelius. *Christian Instruction*. Trans. by John J. Gavigan. In Vol. 2, *The Fathers of the Church*, and Vol. 4, *Writings of St. Augustine*. New York: Fathers of the Church, Inc., 1947.

————. *The City of God*. 2 vols. Trans. by Marcus Dods. In Vol. II, *The Works of Aurelius Augustine*. Edinburgh: T. & T. Clark, 1871.

————. *The Confessions of St. Augustine*. Trans. by F. J. Sheed. New York: Sheed & Ward, 1943.

————. *Faith, Hope and Charity*. Trans. by Bernard M. Peebles. In Vol. 2, *The Fathers of the Church*, and Vol. 4, *Writings of St. Augustine*. New York: Fathers of the Church, Inc., 1947.

————. *Lectures or Tractates on the Gospel According to St. John*, Vol. II. Trans. by James Innes. In Vol. XI, *The Works of Aurelius Augustine*. Edinburgh: T. & T. Clark, 1871.

————. *On Christian Doctrine*. Trans. by J. F. Shaw. In Vol. IX, *The Works of Aurelius Augustine*. Edinburgh: T. & T. Clark, 1871.

————. *On the Trinity*. Trans. by Arthur West Haddan. In Vol. VII, *The Works of Aurelius Augustine. Ibid.*

Bembo, Pietro. *Gli Asolani*. Trans. by Rudolf B. Gottfried. Bloomington, Ind.: Indiana University Press, 1954.

Bernard of Clairvaux. *The Book of Saint Bernard on the Love of God*. Trans. by Terence L. Connolly, S.J. Westminster, Md.: The Newman Press, 1951.

————. *The Steps of Humility*. Trans. by George Bosworth Burch. Cambridge, Mass.: Harvard University Press, 1950.

Bossuet, Jacques Bénigne. *Oeuvres complètes de Bossuet*. 12 vols. Paris: Martin Beaupré, 1868.

Castiglione, Baldesar. *The Book of the Courtier*. Trans. by Charles S. Singleton. Garden City, N.Y.: Anchor Books, Doubleday & Company, 1959.

Cicero, Marcus Tullius. *De Amicitia (Laelius on Friendship)*. Trans. by William Armistead Falconer. In *De Senectute, De Amicitia, De Divinatione*. In the Loeb Classical Library. Cambridge, Mass.: Harvard University Press; London: William Heinemann, 1953.

Dante Alighieri. *Convivio*. Trans. by William Walrond Jackson, D.D. Oxford: Clarendon Press, 1909.

————. *The Divine Comedy*. Trans. by Laurence Binyon. In *The Portable Dante*. Ed. by Paolo Milano. New York: The Viking Press, 1947.

————. *La Vita Nuova*. Trans. by D. G. Rossetti. In *The Portable Dante. Ibid.*

D'Arcy, M. C. *The Mind and Heart of Love*. New York: Meridian Books, 1956.

Darwin, Charles. *The Origin of Species and The Descent of Man*. Modern Library Edition. New York: Random House, no date.

Denzinger, Heinrich. *Enchiridion Symbolorum (Enchiridion symbolorum definitionum et declarationum da rubus fidei et morum)*. Ed. by Clemente

Bannwart and Ioannes Umberg. 24–25 editions. Barcelona, Spain: Herder Publishing Co., 1948.

Descartes, René. *Discourse on the Passions of the Soul.* In *Essential Works of Descartes.* Trans. by Lowell Bair. New York: Bantam Books, 1961.

———. *Letter to Chanut (Lettre à Chanut).* In *Oeuvres Philosophiques et Morales.* Bibliotheque des Lettres. Vienna: Imprimerie Aubin, 1948.

Dublanchy, E., S.M. *Charité.* In *Dictionnaire de Théologie Catholique.* In Encyclopédie des Sciences Ecclésiastiques, II. Paris: Letouzey et Ané, 1910, cols. 2218–66.

Ebreo, Leone. *The Philosophy of Love (Dialoghi d'Amore).* Trans. by F. Friedeberg-Seeley and Jean H. Barnes. London: Soncino Press, 1937.

Ellis, Havelock. *Psychology of Sex.* Mentor Book Edition. New York: New American Library, 1960.

Epictetus. *Discourses.* In *The Stoic and Epicurean Philosophers.* Ed. by Whitney J. Oates. New York: Random House, 1940.

Fenelon, François de. *Explication des Maximes des Saints.* In *Oeuvres de Fenelon.* 2 vols. With a biography by Aimé Martin. Paris: Firmin Didot, 1865.

———. *Oeuvres de Fenelon. Ibid.*

Ficino, Marsilio. *Commentary on Plato's "Symposium."* Trans. by S. R. Jayne. Columbia, Mo.: University of Missouri Press, 1944.

Freud, Sigmund. *Beyond the Pleasure Principle.* Trans. by C. J. M. Hubback from the second German edition. New York: Boni and Liveright, no date.

———. *Civilization and Its Discontents.* Trans. by Joan Riviere. Garden City, N.Y.: Anchor Books, Doubleday & Company, no date.

———. *Collected Papers.* Vols. 2 and 4. Trans. by Joan Riviere *et al.* Ed. by Ernest Jones. New York: Basic Books, 1959.

———. *Contributions to the Psychology of Love. The Most Prevalent Form of Degradation in Erotic Life.* Trans. by Joan Riviere. In Vol. 4, *Collected Papers. Ibid.*

———. *The Dynamics of the Transference.* Trans. by Joan Riviere. In Vol. 2, *Collected Papers.* Ed. by Ernest Jones. New York: Basic Books, 1959.

———. *A General Introduction to Psychoanalysis.* Trans. by Joan Riviere. New York: Washington Square Press, 1960.

———. *Group Psychology and the Analysis of the Ego.* Trans. by James Strachey. New York: Boni and Liveright, no date.

———. *Instincts and Their Vicissitudes.* Trans. by Cecil M. Baines. In Vol. 4, *Collected Papers.* Ed. by Ernest Jones. New York: Basic Books, 1959.

———. *On Narcissism: An Introduction.* Trans. by Cecil M. Baines. In Vol. 4, *Collected Papers. Ibid.*

———. *An Outline of Psychoanalysis.* Trans. by James Strachey. New York: W. W. Norton & Company, 1949.

———. *Thoughts for the Times on War and Death.* Trans. by E. Colburn Mayne. In Vol. 4, *Collected Papers.* Ed. by Ernest Jones. New York: Basic Books, 1959.

Fromm, Erich. *The Art of Loving.* Ed. by Ruth Nanda Anshen. New York: Harper & Brothers, 1956.

Garrigou-Lagrange, Reginald. *Grace.* Trans. by Dominican nuns. St. Louis, Mo., and London: B. Herder Book Company, 1952.

————. *The Love of God and the Cross of Jesus*. London: B. Herder Book Company, 1947.

Geiger, Louis B. *Le Problème de l'Amour chez Saint Thomas d'Aquin*. Montreal: Institut d'Études Médiévales; Paris: Librairie Philosophique J. Vrin, 1952.

Gilson, Étienne. *The Christian Philosophy of Saint Augustine*. Trans. by L. E. M. Lynch. New York: Random House, 1960.

————. *The Spirit of Mediaeval Philosophy*. Trans. by A. H. C. Downes. New York: Charles Scribner's Sons, 1940.

Gourmont, Remy de. *The Natural Philosophy of Love*. Trans. by Ezra Pound. New York: Liveright, 1932.

Hartmann, Nicolai. *Ethics*. Vol. II. Trans. by Stanton Coit. London: George Allen & Unwin; New York: Macmillan, 1932.

Hazm, Ibn. *The Ring of the Dove*. Trans. by A. J. Arberry. London: Luzac, 1953.

Hegel, Georg Wilhelm Friedrich. *Early Theological Writings*. Trans. by T. M. Knox and Richard Kroner. Chicago: University of Chicago Press, 1948.

————. *Love*. Trans. by T. M. Knox. In *Early Theological Writings*. *Ibid*.

————. *The Phenomenology of Mind*. Second Edition. Trans. by J. B. Baillie. New York: Macmillan; London: George Allen & Unwin, 1949.

————. *The Philosophy of History*. Revised Edition. Trans. by J. Sibree. New York: John Wiley, 1944.

————. *Philosophy of Mind*. Trans. by William Wallace. Oxford: Clarendon Press, 1894.

————. *Philosophy of Right*. Trans. by T. M. Knox. Oxford: Clarendon Press, 1945.

————. *The Positivity of the Christian Religion*. Trans. by T. M. Knox. In *Early Theological Writings*. Chicago: University of Chicago Press, 1948.

————. *The Spirit of Christianity and Its Fate*. *Ibid*.

Hume, David. *A Dissertation on the Passions*. In *The Philosophical Works of David Hume*, Vol. IV. Edinburgh: Adam Black and William and Charles Tait, 1826.

————. *An Inquiry Concerning the Principles of Morals*. In *The Philosophical Works of David Hume*, Vol. IV. Edinburgh: Adam Black and William and Charles Tait, 1826.

————. *A Treatise of Human Nature*. Ed. by L. A. Selby-Bigge. Oxford: Clarendon Press, 1896.

————. *Of Self-Love*. In Appendix of *An Inquiry Concerning the Principles of Morals*. In *The Philosophical Works of David Hume*. *Ibid*.

————. *On the Immortality of the Soul*. In *The Philosophical Works of David Hume*. *Ibid*.

James, William. *The Principles of Psychology*. 2 vols. New York: Henry Holt and Company, 1902.

————. *The Varieties of Religious Experience*. New York: Longmans, Green & Company, 1908.

Johann, Robert O. *The Meaning of Love*. Wesminster, Md.: The Newman Press, 1959.

Jung, C. G. *Contributions to Analytical Psychology*. Trans. by H. G. and Cary F. Baynes. London: Routledge & Kegan Paul, 1928.

————. *Psychology of the Unconscious.* Authorized trans. by Beatrice M. Hinkle. New York: Dodd, Mead & Company, 1916.

————. *Two Essays on Analytical Psychology.* Trans. by R. F. C. Hull. New York: Pantheon Books (Bollingen Series XX), 1953.

Kant, Immanuel. *Critique of Practical Reason (Critical Examination of Practical Reason).* In *Kant's Critique of Practical Reason and Other Works on the Theory of Ethics.* Sixth Edition. Trans. by Thomas Kingsmill Abbott. London: Longmans, Green & Company, 1948.

————. *Fundamental Principles of the Metaphysic of Morals. Ibid.*

————. *Introduction to the Metaphysic of Morals. Ibid.*

————. *Lectures on Ethics.* Trans. by Louis Infield. New York and London: Century Company, no date.

————. *Of the Bad Principle in Human Nature.* In *First Part of the Philosophical Theory of Religion.* In *Kant's Critique of Practical Reason and Other Works on the Theory of Ethics.* Sixth Edition. Trans. by Thomas Kingsmill Abbott. London: Longmans, Green & Company, 1948.

————. *Preface to the Metaphysical Elements of Ethics.* In *Kant's Critique of Practical Reason and Other Works on the Theory of Ethics. Ibid.*

Kierkegaard, Søren. *Either/Or.* Vol. I, trans. by David F. Swenson and Lillian Marvin Swenson; Vol. II, trans. by Walter Lowrie. Princeton, N.J.: Princeton University Press, 1949.

————. *Works of Love.* Trans. by David F. Swenson and Lillian Marvin Swenson. Princeton, N.J.: Princeton University Press, 1949.

Leibniz, Gottfried Wilhelm. *New Essays Concerning Human Understanding.* Third Edition. Trans. by Alfred Gideon Langley. LaSalle, Ill.: The Open Court Publishing Company, 1949.

————. *Philosophical Papers and Letters.* 2 vols. Trans. by Leroy E. Loemker. Chicago: University of Chicago Press, 1956.

Lewis, C. S. *The Four Loves.* New York: Harcourt, Brace, 1960.

Locke, John. *An Essay Concerning Human Understanding,* Vol. I. Ed. by Alexander Campbell Fraser. Oxford: Clarendon Press, 1894.

Lucretius. *Of the Nature of Things.* Dutton Everyman Paperback Edition. Trans. by William Ellery Leonard. New York: E. P. Dutton, 1957.

Maritain, Jacques. *Moral Philosophy.* New York: Charles Scribner's Sons, 1964.

Matthews, E. R. *Sex, Love and Society.* London: Victor Gollancz, 1959.

Menninger, Karl (with Jeanetta Lyle Menninger). *Love Against Hate.* New York: Harcourt, Brace, 1942.

Nelson, John Charles. *Renaissance Theory of Love.* New York: Columbia University Press, 1958.

Niebuhr, Reinhold. *Christian Realism and Political Problems.* New York: Charles Scribner's Sons, 1953.

————. *Faith and History.* New York: Charles Scribner's Sons, 1949.

————. *An Interpretation of Christian Ethics.* New York and London: Harper & Brothers, 1935.

Nygren, Anders. *Agape and Eros.* Revised Edition. Authorized trans. by Philip S. Watson. London: S.P.C.K., 1953.

Ortega y Gasset, José. *On Love.* Greenwich Edition. Trans. by Toby Talbot. New York: Meridian Books, 1957.

Ovid. *The Art of Love*. Midland Books. Trans. by Rolfe Humphries. Bloomington, Ind.: Indiana University Press, 1957.

Pascal, Blaise. *Discours sur les Passions de l'Amour*. Intro. by Louis Lafuma. In Vol. III (1908), *Oeuvres*. 14 vols. Ed. by Leon Brunschvicg and Pierre Boutroux. Paris: Hachette et Cie, 1904–14.

————. *Pensées*. Dutton Everyman Paperback Edition. Trans. by W. F. Trotter. New York: E. P. Dutton, 1958.

Pfister, Oskar. *Love in Children and Its Aberrations*. Trans. by Eden and Cedar Paul. London: George Allen & Unwin; New York: Dodd, Mead & Company, 1924.

Pico della Mirandola, Giovanni. *A Platonic Discourse upon Love*. Ed. by Edmund G. Gardner. In Vol. VII in the Humanist's Library. Boston: Merrymount Press, 1914.

Plato. *The Apology*. Trans. by Harold North Fowler. In Vol. I, *Plato*, in the Loeb Classical Library. Cambridge, Mass.: Harvard University Press; London: William Heinemann, 1947.

————. *Laws*, Vol. II. Trans. by R. G. Bury. In Vol. IX, *Plato*, in the Loeb Classical Library. Cambridge, Mass.: Harvard University Press; London: William Heinemann, 1952.

————. *Lysis*. Trans. by W. R. M. Lamb. In Vol. V, *Plato*, in the Loeb Classical Library. Cambridge, Mass.: Harvard University Press; London: William Heinemann, 1946.

————. *Phaedrus*. Trans. by Harold North Fowler. In Vol. I, *Plato*, in the Loeb Classical Library. Cambridge, Mass.: Harvard University Press; London: William Heinemann, 1947.

————. *Symposium*. Trans. by W. R. M. Lamb. In Vol. V, *Plato*, in the Loeb Classical Library. Cambridge, Mass.: Harvard University Press; London: William Heinemann, 1946.

Plotinus. *The Enneads*. Second Edition Revised by B. S. Page. Trans. by Stephen MacKenna. New York: Pantheon Books, no date.

Quilliet, H. *Censures Doctrinales*. In *Dictionnaire de Théologie Catholique*. In Encyclopédie des Sciences Ecclésiastiques, II. Paris: Letouzey et Ané, 1910.

Reik, Theodor. *A Psychologist Looks at Love*. In *Of Love and Lust*. Evergreen Edition. New York: Grove Press, 1959.

————. *Psychology of Sex Relations*. Evergreen Edition. New York: Grove Press, 1961.

Rougemont, Denis de. *The Crisis of the Modern Couple*. In *The Anatomy of Love*. Laurel Edition. Ed. by A. M. Krich. New York: Dell Publishing Company, 1960.

————. *Love in the Western World*. Trans. by Montgomery Belgion. New York: Pantheon Books, 1956.

Rousseau, Jean Jacques. *A Discourse on the Origin of Inequality*. In *The Social Contract and Discourses*. Everyman's Library Edition. Trans. by G. D. H. Cole. New York: E. P. Dutton; London: J. M. Dent & Sons, 1950.

————. *A Discourse on Political Economy*. In *The Social Contract and Discourses*. *Ibid*.

Rousselot, Pierre. *Pour l'Histoire du Problème de l'Amour au Moyen Age*. Paris: Librairie Philosophique J. Vrin, 1933.

Sales, François de. *Traité de l'Amour de Dieu.* Tournai, Belgium: Desclée & Cie, 1958.

Santayana, George. *The Life of Reason,* Vol. II. New York: Charles Scribner's Sons, 1936.

Scheler, Max. *Der Formalismus in der Ethik und die materiale Wertethik: Neuer Versuch der Grundlegung Eines Ethischen Personlismum (Form).* Fourth Edition. Bern, Switzerland: Franke Verlag, 1954.

————. *The Nature of Sympathy.* Trans. by Peter Heath. London: Routledge & Kegan Paul, 1954.

————. *On the Eternal in Man.* Trans. by Bernard Noble. New York: Harper & Brothers, 1960.

————. *Ressentiment.* Trans. by William W. Holdheim. Glencoe, Ill.: The Free Press of Glencoe, 1961.

Schopenhauer, Arthur. *The Metaphysics of the Love of the Sexes.* In Vol. III, *The World as Will and Idea.* Trans. by R. B. Haldane and J. Kemp. New York: Charles Scribner's Sons; London: Routledge & Kegan Paul, 1948.

————. *The World as Will and Idea. Ibid.*

Simmel, Georg. *Fragment ueber die Liebe.* In *Brücke und Tür: Essays des Philosophen zur Geschicte, Religion Kunst und Gesellschaft.* Stuttgart, Germany: K. F. Koehler, 1957.

————. *The Secret and the Secret Society.* In *The Sociology of Georg Simmel.* Trans. and ed. by Kurt H. Wolff. Glencoe, Ill.: The Free Press of Glencoe, 1950.

————. *The Sociology of Georg Simmel. Ibid.*

Sina, Ibn. *A Treatise on Love.* Trans. by Emil L. Fackenheim. In Vol. VII, *Medieval Studies.* Toronto, Canada: Pontifical Institute of Medieval Studies, 1945.

Smith, Adam. *The Theory of Moral Sentiments.* London: George Bell & Sons, 1880.

Solovyev, Vladimir. *The Meaning of Love.* Trans. by Jane Marshall. New York: International Universities Press, 1947.

Sorokin, Pitrim A. *The Ways and Power of Love.* Boston: Beacon Press, 1954.

Spinoza, Benedict de. *The Ethics.* In Vol. II, *The Chief Works of Benedict de Spinoza.* Trans. by R. H. M. Elwes. New York: Dover Publications, 1951.

Stendhal, Marie-Henri Beyle de. *On Love.* Trans. by H. B. V. under the direction of C. K. Scott-Moncrieff. New York: Liveright Publishing Corporation, 1947.

Tillich, Paul. *Being and Love.* In Vol. VI, *Moral Principles of Action.* Ed. by Ruth Nanda Anshen. New York and London: Harper & Brothers, 1952.

————. *Love, Power, and Justice.* New York and London: Oxford University Press, 1954.

Valency, Maurice. *In Praise of Love.* Macmillan Paperbacks Edition. New York: Macmillan, 1961.

Index